# A·N·N·U·A·L  E·D·I·T·I·O·N·S

# Comparative Politics

## 03/04

*Twenty-First Edition*

## EDITOR

**Christian Søe**

*California State University, Long Beach*

Christian Søe was born in Denmark, studied at universities in Canada and the United States, and received his doctoral degree in political science at the Free University in Berlin. He is professor of political science at California State University, Long Beach, where he teaches courses in comparative politics. His research deals primarily with political developments in contemporary Germany. He visits that country annually to conduct research on political parties and elections. In these and other ways, he attempts to follow shifts in the balance of power and changes in political orientation within Germany as now represented by a new "red-green" coalition and a new generation of leaders in Berlin. The early phase of this transition in German politics is a main topic of the 1999 book, which he co-edited with Mary N. Hampton, *Between Bonn and Berlin: German Politics Adrift?* He is co-editor (with David Conradt and Gerald R. Kleinfeld) of another recent book, *Power Shift in Germany: The 1998 Bundestag Election and the End of the Kohl Era.* The same team is now completing a follow-up book that deals with the political record of the Schröder-Fischer government and its narrow victory in the Bundestag election of 2002. Three of his other fairly recent publications are a biographical essay on Hans-Dietrich Genscher, Germany's foreign minister from 1974 to 1992, in *Political Leaders of Contemporary Western Europe*; a chapter on the Free Democratic Party in *Germany's New Politics*; and another chapter on the Danish-German relationship in *The Germans and Their Neighbors.* Dr. Søe is also co-editor of the latter two books. He has been editor of the twenty-one volumes of *Annual Editions: Comparative Politics* since the beginning of this series in 1983.

*McGraw-Hill/Dushkin*

530 Old Whitfield Street, Guilford, Connecticut 06437

Visit us on the Internet
*http://www.dushkin.com*

# Credits

1. **Pluralist Democracies: Country Studies**
   Unit photo—© 2003 by PhotoDisc, Inc.
2. **Pluralist Democracies: Factors in the Political Process**
   Unit photo—Courtesy of Joan Martin.
3. **Europe—West, Center, and East: The Politics of Integration, Transformation, and Disintegration**
   Unit photo—© United Nations photo.
4. **Political Diversity in the Developing World**
   Unit photo—United Nations photo.
5. **Comparative Politics: Some Major Trends, Issues, and Prospects**
   Unit photo—United Nations photo.

# Copyright

Cataloging in Publication Data
Main entry under title: Annual Editions: Comparative Politics. 2003/2004.
1. Comparative Politics—Periodicals. I. Søe, Christian, *comp.* II. Title: Comparative Politics.
ISBN 0–07–283823–X    658'.05    ISSN 0741–7233

Twenty-First Edition

Cover image © 2004 PhotoDisc, Inc.
Printed in the United States of America    1234567890BAHBAH54    Printed on Recycled Paper

# Editors/Advisory Board

Members of the Advisory Board are instrumental in the final selection of articles for each edition of ANNUAL EDITIONS. Their review of articles for content, level, currentness, and appropriateness provides critical direction to the editor and staff. We think that you will find their careful consideration well reflected in this volume.

*JF*
*51*
*.C615*
*2004*

## EDITOR

**Christian Søe**
*California State University, Long Beach*

## ADVISORY BOARD

**Louis J. Cantori**
*University of Maryland, Baltimore County*

**Maureen A. Covell**
*Simon Fraser University*

**Jane Curry Palmer**
*Santa Clara University*

**John Echeverri-Gent**
*University of Virginia*

**Richard S. Flickinger**
*Wittenberg University*

**E. Gene Frankland**
*Ball State University*

**Ronald Inglehart**
*University of Michigan*

**Karl H. Kahrs**
*California State University - Fullerton*

**Aline M. Kuntz**
*University of New Hampshire*

**Anthony M. Messina**
*University of Notre Dame*

**Joyce Marie Mushaben**
*University of Missouri - St. Louis*

**Helen E. Purkitt**
*U.S. Naval Academy*

**Mark E. Rush**
*Washington and Lee University*

**Michael J. Sadaro**
*George Washington University*

**Wayne A. Selcher**
*Elizabethtown College*

**Martin W. Slann**
*Pennsylvania State University - Wilkes Barre*

**Judithe A. Thompson**
*University of Rio Grande*

**Timothy J. White**
*Xavier University*

**Joel D. Wolfe**
*University of Cincinnati*

**Rodger Yeager**
*West Virginia University*

**Eleanor E. Zeff**
*Drake University*

**Charles E. Ziegler**
*University of Louisville*

# Staff

**Jeffrey L. Hahn.** Vice President/Publishers

## EDITORIAL STAFF

**Theodore Knight, Ph.D.,** Managing Editor
**Roberta Monaco,** Managing Developmental Editor
**Dorothy Fink,** Associate Developmental Editor
**Addie Raucci,** Senior Administrative Editor
**Robin Zarnetske,** Permissions Editor
**Marie Lazauskas,** Permissions Assistant
**Lisa Holmes-Doebrick,** Senior Program Coordinator

## TECHNOLOGY STAFF

**Richard Tietjen,** Senior Publishing Technologist
**Jonathan Stowe,** Executive Director of eContent
**Marcuss Oslander,** Sponsoring Editor of eContent
**Christopher Santos,** Senior eContent Developer
**Janice Ward,** Software Support Analyst
**Angela Mule,** eContent Developer
**Michael McConnel,** eContent Developer
**Ciro Parente,** Editorial Assistant
**Joe Offredi,** Technology Developmental Editor

## PRODUCTION STAFF

**Brenda S. Filley,** Director of Production
**Charles Vitelli,** Designer
**Mike Campbell,** Production Coordinator
**Eldis Lima,** Graphics
**Juliana Arbo,** Typesetting Supervisor
**Julie Marsh,** Project Editor
**Jocelyn Proto,** Typesetter
**Cynthia Powers,** Typesetter

# To the Reader

In publishing ANNUAL EDITIONS we recognize the enormous role played by the magazines, newspapers, and journals of the public press in providing current, first-rate educational information in a broad spectrum of interest areas. Many of these articles are appropriate for students, researchers, and professionals seeking accurate, current material to help bridge the gap between principles and theories and the real world. These articles, however, become more useful for study when those of lasting value are carefully collected, organized, indexed, and reproduced in a low-cost format, which provides easy and permanent access when the material is needed. That is the role played by ANNUAL EDITIONS.

This collection of readings brings together current articles that will help you understand the politics of foreign countries from a comparative perspective. Such a study opens up a fascinating world beyond our borders. It will also lead to deeper insights into the American political process.

The articles in unit 1 cover Britain or the United Kingdom, France, Germany, and Japan in a serial manner. In terms of gross domestic product, these countries all belong among the top seven economies in the world. Each of these modern societies has an individual tradition of governance within a particular political framework. Nevertheless, as the readings of unit 2 show, it is possible to point to some shared patterns among these and many other representative democracies.

Unit 3 deals with the impact of two major changes that continue to transform the political map of Europe. One of them is the irregular, sometimes halting, but nevertheless impressive growth of the European Union (EU). It has grown to 15 member countries with nearly 300 million people. In the next few years, up to 10 more countries are slated to join. The other crucial change involves the outcome of the political and economic reconstruction of Central and Eastern Europe, including Russia, after the collapse of the Communist regimes in that region between 1989 and 1991. These developments underscore the continuing political importance of Europe.

Unit 4 looks first at the controversial topic of globalization and then turns to articles dealing with some of the developing countries and regions, including Mexico and Latin America as a whole, South Africa, Nigeria, India, China, and the Muslim world. The articles will give the careful reader a better understanding of the diversity of social and political conditions in these countries.

Unit 5 considers three major trends in contemporary politics from a comparative perspective. First, the past quarter of a century has seen a remarkable spread of democratic forms of government in the world. This recent "wave of democratization," sometimes described as the "third" of its kind in modern history seems likely to have a lasting effect on the political process in many countries that previously knew only authoritarian governments.

Second, beginning in the 1980s there has been a major shift in economic policy toward greater reliance on private enterprise and markets, and a corresponding reduction in state ownership and regulation in much of the world, including Communist-ruled China.

Third, many parts of the world have seen a surge of what has been called "identity politics." This trend has brought group identities more strongly into play when differences are being defined, played out and resolved in the political arena.

This is an unusually interesting and important time to study comparative politics. The past decade has seen a major restructuring of politics in many countries along with a generational shift in leadership. Even in a time of political transformation, however, there will be significant patterns of continuity as well as change.

This is the twenty-first edition of *Annual Editions: Comparative Politics*. Over the years, the successive editions have reflected the developments that eventually brought about the post–cold war world of today. This present volume tries to present information and analysis that are useful in understanding today's political world and its role in setting the parameters for tomorrow's developments.

A special word of thanks goes to my own past and present students at California State University, Long Beach. They are wonderfully inquisitive and help keep me posted on matters that this anthology must address. Several of my past students have helped me gather material. As always, I am particularly grateful to Susan B. Mason, who received her master's degree in political science over a decade ago. She has continued to volunteer as a superb research assistant. Once again I also wish to thank some other past and present students, Linda Wohlman, Erika Reinhardt, Erik Ibsen, Jon Nakagawa, Perry Oliver, Mike Petri, Richard Sherman, and Ali Taghavi. Like so many others, these individuals first encountered the anthology in my comparative politics courses. It is a great joy to have worked with such fine students. Their enthusiasm for the project has been contagious.

I am very grateful to members of the advisory board and McGraw-Hill/Dushkin as well as to the many readers who have made useful comments on past selections and suggested new ones. I ask you all to help improve future editions by keeping me informed of your reactions and suggestions for change. Please complete and return the article rating form in the back of the book.

Christian Søe
*Editor*

# Contents

## UNIT 1
## Pluralist Democracies: Country Studies

Twelve selections examine the current state of politics in the United Kingdom, Germany, France, and Japan.

**Unit Overview**    xx

The concepts in bold italics are developed in the article. For further expansion, please refer to the Topic Guide and the Index.

# UNIT 2
# Pluralist Democracies: Factors in the Political Process

Ten selections examine the functioning of Western European democracies with regard to political ideas and participation, money and politics, the role of women in politics, and the institutional framework of representative government.

The concepts in bold italics are developed in the article. For further expansion, please refer to the Topic Guide and the Index.

The concepts in bold italics are developed in the article. For further expansion, please refer to the Topic Guide and the Index.

# UNIT 3
## Europe—West, Center, and East: The Politics of Integration, Transformation, and Disintegration

Seven selections examine the European continent: the European Union, Western European society, post-communist Central and Eastern Europe, and Russia and the other post-Soviet Republics.

The concepts in bold italics are developed in the article. For further expansion, please refer to the Topic Guide and the Index.

# UNIT 4
# Political Diversity in the Developing World

Thirteen selections review the developing world's economic and political development in Latin America, Africa, China, India, and the Muslim world.

The concepts in bold italics are developed in the article. For further expansion, please refer to the Topic Guide and the Index.

# UNIT 5
# Comparative Politics: Some Major Trends, Issues, and Prospects

Five selections discuss the rise of democracy, how capitalism impacts on political development, and the political assertion of group identity in contemporary politics.

**Unit Overview**    **188**

The concepts in bold italics are developed in the article. For further expansion, please refer to the Topic Guide and the Index.

The concepts in bold italics are developed in the article. For further expansion, please refer to the Topic Guide and the Index.

# Topic Guide

This topic guide suggests how the selections in this book relate to the subjects covered in your course. You may want to use the topics listed on these pages to search the Web more easily.

On the following pages a number of Web sites have been gathered specifically for this book. They are arranged to reflect the units of this *Annual Edition.* You can link to these sites by going to the DUSHKIN ONLINE support site at *http://www.dushkin.com/online/.*

## ALL THE ARTICLES THAT RELATE TO EACH TOPIC ARE LISTED BELOW THE BOLD-FACED TERM.

## U.S. comparisons

## Women in politics

# World Wide Web Sites

The following World Wide Web sites have been carefully researched and selected to support the articles found in this reader. The easiest way to access these selected sites is to go to our DUSHKIN ONLINE support site at *http://www.dushkin.com/online/*.

# AE: Comparative Politics 03/04

The following sites were available at the time of publication. Visit our Web site—we update DUSHKIN ONLINE regularly to reflect any changes.

## General Sources

### Central Intelligence Agency
*http://www.odci.gov*

Use this official home page to get connections to *The CIA Factbook,* which provides extensive statistical and political information about every country in the world.

### National Geographic Society
*http://www.nationalgeographic.com*

This site provides links to National Geographic's archive of maps, articles, and documents. There is a great deal of material related to political cultures around the world.

### Penn Library: Resources by Subject
*http://www.library.upenn.edu/resources/subject/subject.html?general*

This vast site is rich in links to information about global politics and economic development. Its extensive population and demography resources address such concerns as migration, family planning, and health and nutrition in world regions.

### U.S. Agency for International Development
*http://www.info.usaid.gov*

This Web site covers such broad and overlapping issues as democracy, population and health, economic growth, and development about different regions and countries.

### U.S. Information Agency
*http://usinfo.state.gov/*

This USIA page provides definitions, related documentation, and discussion of topics on global issues. Many Web links are provided.

### World Bank
*http://www.worldbank.org*

News (press releases, summaries of new projects, speeches) and coverage of numerous topics regarding development, countries, and regions are provided at this site.

### World Wide Web Virtual Library: International Affairs Resources
*http://www.etown.edu/vl/*

Surf this site and its extensive links to learn about specific countries and regions, to research international organizations, and to study such vital topics as international law, development, the international economy, and human rights.

## UNIT 1: Pluralist Democracies: Country Studies

### British Information Service
*http://britain-info.org*

This site of the British Information Service leads to reams of material on Tony Blair and the Labour Party, the European Union, relations with Northern Ireland, and many other topics in the study of the British political system.

### France.com
*http://www.france.com*

The links at this site will lead to extensive information about the French government, politics, history, and culture.

### GermNews
*http://www.mathematik.uni-ulm.de/de-news/*

Search this site for German political and economic news covering the years 1995 to the present.

### Japan Ministry of Foreign Affairs
*http://www.mofa.go.jp*

Visit this official site for Japanese foreign policy statements and discussions of regional and global relations.

## UNIT 2: Pluralist Democracies: Factors in the Political Process

### American Foreign Service Association (AFSA)
*http://www.afsa.org/related.html*

The AFSA offers this page of related sites as part of its Web presence. Useful sites include DiploNet, Public Diplomacy, and InterAction. Also click on Diplomacy and Diplomats and other sites on the sidebar.

### Carnegie Endowment for International Peace
*http://www.ceip.org*

This organization's goal is to stimulate discussion and learning among both experts and the public at large on a wide range of international issues. The site provides links to the well-respected journal *Foreign Policy,* to the Moscow Center, to descriptions of various programs, and much more.

### Communications for a Sustainable Future
*http://csf.colorado.edu*

This site will lead you to information on topics in international environmental sustainability. It pays particular attention to the political economics of protecting the environment.

### Inter-American Dialogue (IAD)
*http://www.iadialog.org*

This is the Web site for IAD, a premier U.S. center for policy analysis, communication, and exchange in Western Hemisphere affairs. The 100-member organization has helped to shape the agenda of issues and choices in hemispheric relations.

### The North American Institute (NAMI)
*http://www.northamericaninstitute.org*

NAMI, a trinational public-affairs organization concerned with the emerging "regional space" of Canada, the United States, and Mexico, provides links for study of trade, the environment, and institutional developments.

## UNIT 3: Europe—West, Center, and East: The Politics of Integration, Transformation, and Disintegration

### Europa: European Union
*http://europa.eu.int*

This server site of the European Union will lead you to the history of the EU; descriptions of EU policies, institutions, and goals; discussion of monetary union; and documentation of treaties and other materials.

### NATO Integrated Data Service (NIDS)
*http://www.nato.int/structur/nids/nids.htm*

NIDS was created to bring information on security-related matters to the widest possible audience. Check out this Web site to review North Atlantic Treaty Organization documentation of all kinds, to read *NATO Review,* and to explore key issues in the field of European security.

### Research and Reference (Library of Congress)
*http://lcweb.loc.gov/rr/*

This massive research and reference site of the Library of Congress will lead you to invaluable information on the former Soviet Union and other countries attempting the transition to democracy. It provides links to numerous publications, bibliographies, and guides in area studies.

### Russian and East European Network Information Center, University of Texas at Austin
*http://reenic.utexas.edu/reenic.html*

This is *the* Web site for information on Russia and the former Soviet Union.

## UNIT 4: Political Diversity in the Developing World

### Africa News Online
*http://www.africanews.org*

Open this site for extensive, up-to-date information on all of Africa, with reports from Africa's leading newspapers, magazines, and news agencies. Coverage is country-by-country and regional. Background documents and Internet links are among the resource pages.

### ArabNet
*http://www.arab.net*

This home page of ArabNet, the online resource for the Arab world in the Middle East and North Africa, presents links to 22 Arab countries. Each country Web page classifies information using a standardized system of categories.

### ASEAN Web
*http://www.asean.or.id/*

This official site of the Association of Southeast Asian Nations provides an overview of Asian Web resources, Asian summits, economic and world affairs, political foundations, regional cooperation, and publications.

### Inside China Today
*http://www.insidechina.com*

Part of the European Internet Network, this site leads to information on China, including recent news, government, and related sites pertaining to mainland China, Hong Kong, Macao, and Taiwan.

### InterAction
*http://www.interaction.org*

InterAction encourages grassroots action and engages government bodies and policymakers on various advocacy issues. The organization's Advocacy Committee provides this site to inform people on its initiatives to expand international humanitarian relief, refugee, and development-assistance programs.

### Organization for Economic Cooperation and Development
*http://www.oecd.org*

Explore development, governance, and world trade and investment issues on this OECD site. It provides links to many related topics and addresses global economic issues on a country-by-country basis.

### Sun SITE Singapore
*http://sunsite.nus.edu.sg/noframe.html*

These South East Asia Information pages provide information and point to other online resources about the region's 10 countries, including Vietnam, Indonesia, and Brunei.

## UNIT 5: Comparative Politics: Some Major Trends, Issues, and Prospects

### Commission on Global Governance
*http://www.sovereignty.net/p/gov/gganalysis.htm*

This site provides access to *The Report of the Commission on Global Governance,* produced by an international group of leaders who want to find ways in which the global community can better manage its affairs.

### IISDnet
*http://www.iisd.org/default.asp*

This site of the International Institute for Sustainable Development, a Canadian organization, presents information through links on business and sustainable development, developing ideas, and Hot Topics. Linkages is its multimedia resource for environment and development policymakers.

### ISN International Relations and Security Network
*http://www.isn.ethz.ch*

This site, maintained by the Center for Security Studies and Conflict Research, is a clearinghouse for extensive information on international relations and security policy. Topics are listed by category (Traditional Dimensions of Security, New Dimensions of Security) and by major world regions.

### United Nations Environment Program
*http://www.unep.ch/*

Consult this home page of UNEP for links to critical topics about global issues, including desertification and the impact of trade on the environment. The site leads to useful databases and global resource information.

### Virtual Seminar in Global Political Economy/Global Cities & Social Movements
*http://csf.colorado.edu/gpe/gpe95b/resources.html*

This site of Internet resources is rich in links to subjects of interest in regional studies, covering topics such as sustainable cities, megacities, and urban planning. Links to many international nongovernmental organizations are included.

We highly recommend that you review our Web site for expanded information and our other product lines. We are continually updating and adding links to our Web site in order to offer you the most usable and useful information that will support and expand the value of your Annual Editions. You can reach us at: *http://www.dushkin.com/annualeditions/*.

# World Map

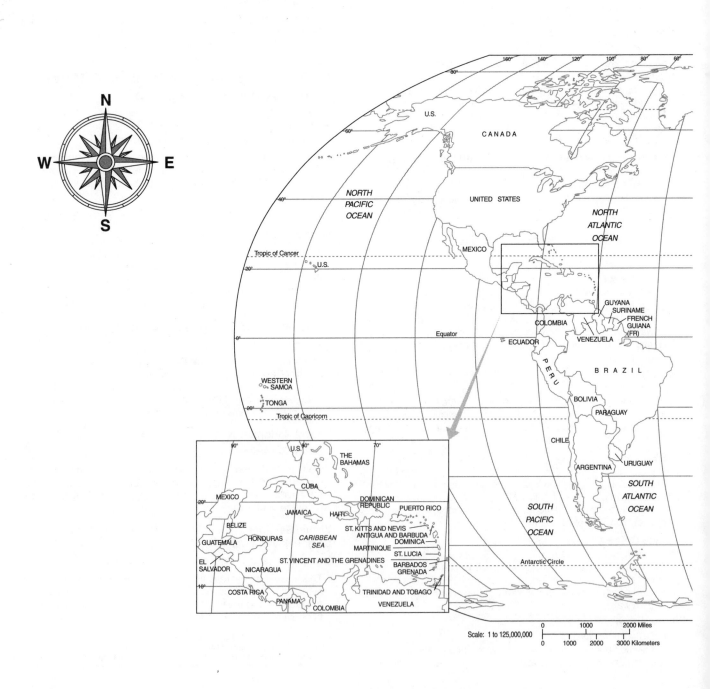

N
W    E
S

CANADA

U.S.

NORTH PACIFIC OCEAN

UNITED STATES

NORTH ATLANTIC OCEAN

MEXICO

Tropic of Cancer

U.S.

GUYANA
SURINAME
FRENCH GUIANA (FR)

COLOMBIA

VENEZUELA

Equator

ECUADOR

P E R U

B R A Z I L

WESTERN SAMOA

TONGA

BOLIVIA

PARAGUAY

Tropic of Capricorn

CHILE

ARGENTINA

URUGUAY

SOUTH ATLANTIC OCEAN

SOUTH PACIFIC OCEAN

Antarctic Circle

THE BAHAMAS

U.S.

MEXICO

CUBA

DOMINICAN REPUBLIC

PUERTO RICO

JAMAICA

HAITI

BELIZE

GUATEMALA

HONDURAS

CARIBBEAN SEA

ST. KITTS AND NEVIS
ANTIGUA AND BARBUDA
DOMINICA

MARTINIQUE

ST. LUCIA

EL SALVADOR

NICARAGUA

ST. VINCENT AND THE GRENADINES

BARBADOS
GRENADA

COSTA RICA

PANAMA

COLOMBIA

TRINIDAD AND TOBAGO

VENEZUELA

Scale: 1 to 125,000,000

0    1000    2000 Miles
0   1000   2000   3000 Kilometers

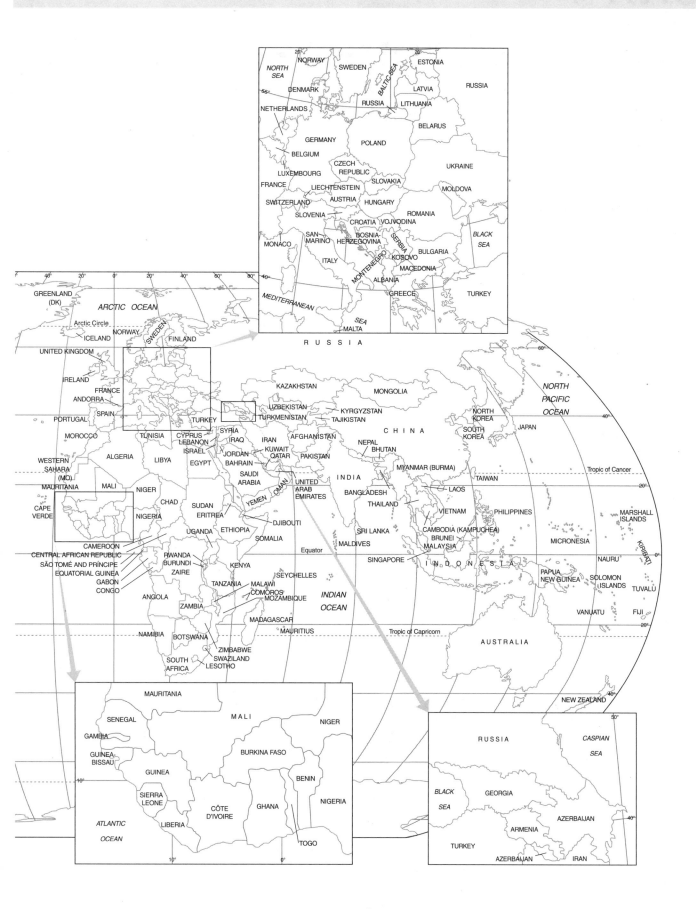

# UNIT 1

# Pluralist Democracies: Country Studies

## Unit Selections

## Key Points to Consider

- What were some major factors that helped Tony Blair and Labour win a second term in office in June 2001? What is "new" about Labour under Blair's leadership? What are the main items on the government's constitutional reform agenda, and how far have they become reality by now? How can his government's policy toward Iraq and public services create difficulties for Blair in his own party? What are the political prospects of the other two national parties in the House of Commons?

- Why did Jacques Chirac call an early parliamentary election in 1997, and how did the outcome produce a new form of "cohabitation" in the Fifth Republic? What are the signs that French politics have become more centrist or middle-of-the-road for the main political parties? How did Lionel Jospin and his government of the Left approach socioeconomic reform in France?

- Name three factors that helped the SPD in Germany find new supporters. How did some of the same factors revive the appeal of the Greens? How can the PDS still have two members sitting in the Bundestag? What happened to the liberal Free Democrats? What are some major difficulties that confront the "red-green" government after its victory?

- Explain why the LDP is jokingly said to be "neither liberal, nor democratic, nor a party." What has been the role of this party in postwar Japanese politics? How and why has a would-be reformer like Prime Minister Koizumi begun to resemble his predecessors? Why could a reform of the bureaucracy become a major political event in Japan?

 **Links: www.dushkin.com/online/**
These sites are annotated in the World Wide Web pages.

**British Information Service**
*http://britain-info.org*

**France.com**
*http://www.france.com*

**GermNews**
*http://www.mathematik.uni-ulm.de/de-news/*

**Japan Ministry of Foreign Affairs**
*http://www.mofa.go.jp*

The United Kingdom, France, and Germany rank among the most prominent industrial societies in Western Europe. Although their modern political histories vary considerably, they have all developed into pluralist democracies with diverse and active citizens, well-organized and competitive party systems and interest groups, and representative forms of governments. Japan appears to be less pluralist, but it occupies a similar position of primacy among the representative democracies in Asia. A study of comparative government can usefully begin by examining politics in these societies.

The articles in the first unit cover the political systems of the four countries consecutively. Each of them has developed its own set of governmental institutions, defined its own political agenda, and found its own dynamic balance of continuity and change. Nevertheless, as later readings will show more fully, it is possible to find some common denominators and make useful cross-national comparisons among these and other representative democracies. The common traits include a pattern of public disillusionment with established political institutions or, at least, politicians that is also shared with the United States.

Moreover, the West European countries all show the impact of three major developments, which are transforming the political map of the continent: (1) the growth of the European Union (EU), (2) the rise of new or intensified challenges to the established political order after the end of the cold war, often reflected in a reshuffling or weakening of the traditional party system, and (3) some spillover effects from the initial dislocations and the later reconstruction efforts in Central and East European countries as these emerged from a long period of communist rule. One obvious consequence has been a much greater migration of people from East to West in Europe. Another impact can be seen in the efforts to adjust the supranational framework of the European Union to the new post–cold war world. In addition, the European social and political order is trying to come to terms with a dual set of potentially revolutionary challenges brought about by the new information technologies and global market forces. Both are sources of tremendous dynamic change and wrenching dislocations that transcend the traditional political boundaries of region and nation.

These developments have underscored the continuing political importance of Europe. The integration of the European Community has been a process spanning half a century. However, it accelerated markedly in the last half of the 1980s as a result of the passage and stepwise implementation of the Single Europe Act (SEA), which set as a goal the completion of a free market among the EC–member countries by the end of 1992. The follow-up Maastricht Treaty, which was signed in 1991 and ratified by 1993, outlined a further advance toward supranational integration by setting up the goal of achieving a common European monetary system and foreign policy by the end of the twentieth century. Even if this process of integration has sometimes been more halting or irregular than had been hoped by some early European federalists, it is a remarkable example of long-term political coordination and cooperation in place of more traditional conflict.

By contrast, there was little advance notice or planning connected with the upheaval that ended many decades of communist rule in Central and Eastern Europe between 1989 and 1991. In the center of the continent, the unification of Germany in 1990 epitomizes the tremendous upheaval that swept away much of the political order created and maintained by the cold war. Each of the former communist-ruled countries has embarked on a cumbersome path of reconstruction, involving the transition from a repressive party-and-police state with a centrally planned economy to a pluralist democracy with the opportunities and uncertainties of a market-oriented economy. By now it is clear that this process was to take longer and involve more setbacks than anyone had imagined at the outset.

It is also evident that the established democracies in Western Europe have themselves been affected by this great transformation in the eastern part of the continent. In the older democracies of the West, the end of the cold war has been accompanied by political shifts of their own. A frequently heard word used to describe the political mood of Western Europe in recent years has been "malaise," which suggests a widespread mood of unease, anxiety, and disaffection that shows up in opinion polls and elections. Thus the "Europhoria," which a decade ago greeted the end of the cold war and a seemingly inexorable European integration, has to some degree given way to a new sobriety or even nostalgia in much of the continent. These mood swings can be important, but they do not seem to be permanent. It would be too early to claim that a new "Europtimism" is about to displace the recent "Europessimism" as long as the latter continues to be fed by a combination of economic disappointments, sociocultural tensions, political scandals, and the revival of right-wing populist parties and movements. While each country has been plagued by its own peculiar mix of such problems, the mood has been reflected in a fairly common pattern of voter distrust of the political establishment.

The events of September 11, 2001, have added a new element of organized violence and unpredictability to our political world. While the terrorist attacks on the World Trade Towers and the Pentagon were clearly directed at the United States, these acts were organized by a clandestine network that also reaches into European countries. Similar strikes could affect them at any time. This awareness has affected the politics of these countries and helped mobilize their early support for U.S.–led military counter-measures. It soon became clear that there is no trans-Atlantic consensus on the most effective strategy for dealing with the new terrorism or our own vulnerability to this type of attack. There is general agreement that a crucial assumption of the traditional policy of containment no longer holds, namely that the desire for self-preservation will restrain the actions of a potential opponent by making him reluctant to risk retaliation. The primary responsibility of the state, to provide security for its citizens in a dangerous world, has acquired a new dimension in light of the willingness to risk self-destruction (understood as self-sacrifice) among the new terrorists. It seems likely that the search for an appropriate and effective response will preoccupy our politics for a long time to come.

This is particularly evident in the controversy about the approach to be taken in dealing with Iraq under its leader Saddam Hussein. The U.S. government is determined to move decisively to disarm Iraq of weapons of mass destruction, which President George W. Bush believes are being gathered by the Baghdad government. The United States has openly spoken of seeking a "regime change" and it has clearly indicated its readiness to conduct a massive preemptive strike if Saddam does not comply with the UN–backed demands for disarmament. Gerhard Schröder and Jacques Chirac, the present leaders of Germany and France, have both shown themselves to be wary and even openly critical of the American position. Their preference for giving more time to UN weapons inspectors who are searching for hidden weapons in Iraq runs counter to the official American determination to use military pressure and intervention to force the issue. British Prime Minister Tony Blair has played a role that is markedly different, in the tradition of the "special relationship" with the United States. He has been largely supportive of President Bush's strategy. He has had to pay a heavy political cost for extending that support. Blair has run into an unprecedented barrage of criticism at home and from within his own party.

Not surprisingly, the divergence on policy toward Iraq has led to reflections on more fundamental differences between much of continental Europe and the United States. One of the most widely discussed theses has come from the American writer, Robert Kagan. He concludes that Europe and America are not just separated on this admittedly important issue, but that the "older" and weaker continent no longer shares the willingness or propensity of the more powerful United States to use military power as a means of foreign policy.

It is important to pay attention to such developments that carry with them major changes and new challenges. That is especially so for the new vulnerability discussed above. But we must not lose sight of some equally important if less dramatic aspects of politics. In the stable pluralist democracies of Western Europe, the political process is usually defined by a relatively mild blend of change and continuity. Here the political agendas are normally modified rather than discarded entirely, and shifts in the balance of power do not take the form of revolutionary displacements of a ruling group. Instead, there are occasional changes of government as a result of coalition disagreements or routine elections.

***Britain*** has long been regarded as a model of parliamentary government and majoritarian party politics. In the late 1960s and throughout the 1970s, however, the country became better known for its chronic governing problems. Serious observers spoke about Britain as "the sick man of Europe" and detected a special infirmity called "Englanditis," a condition characterized by such problems as economic stagnation, social malaise, political polarization, and a general incapacity of elected governments to deal effectively with such a situation of relative deterioration.

These developments were accompanied by several attempts to give a macro-explanation of Britain's problems. Some British political scientists, like Anthony King, defined their country's condition as one of "governmental overload." According to their diagnosis, British governments had become so entangled by socioeconomic entitlements that the country had reached the threshold of a condition of political paralysis or "ungovernability." In the United States, the political economist Mancur Olson developed a more general but in some ways similar explanation of political "sclerosis" in advanced pluralist democracies like Britain. He explained it in terms of the clotting effects of a highly developed interest group system that made excessive demands on governments, sapping them of energy, will, and resources.

A second explanation of the British governing crisis focused on the unusually sharp adversarial character of the country's party politics, symbolized by the parliamentary confrontation of government and opposition parties. This approach emphasized that Britain's famed "Westminster Model" of government by a single majority party had resulted in more polarizing and disruptive consequences than the broader power-sharing and more consensus-seeking forms of coalition government found in many other parliamentary systems in Western Europe. One problem with this explanation was that the adversarial aspects of British politics often seemed more symbolic than real. In retrospect, at least, observers are struck by the similarity of the main policy lines pursued by Labour and the Conservatives until the mid-1970s. There were only relatively minor policy changes whenever they replaced each other as governing party during the quarter of a century that followed the giant reform steps taken by Clement Atlee's government from 1945 to 1950. During those 5 years, Labour had taken charge of the rapid building of the welfare state, nationalized some of the "commanding heights" of industry, and made the first major moves toward decolonization. Apart from "denationalizing" some industries, the Conservatives did not really try to undo the basic reforms when they returned to power in 1951, so that until the mid-1970s Britain's two major parties largely acted in a reality shaped by what became known as "consensus politics," all their rhetorical fireworks notwithstanding.

Still other interpreters explained Britain's relative decline in terms of socioeconomic and institutional inertia that prevented the country from keeping pace with its European neighbors. Two of the most commonly cited problems were rooted in Britain's heritage as a class-divided society and a former imperial power. Compared to its more modern European neighbors, it was argued, the United Kingdom was hampered by a dysfunctional and outmoded social order at home, and an equally costly and unproductive legacy of overcommitment or "overstretch" in international affairs. The former thesis was invariably linked to reform proposals aimed at promoting greater equality of opportunity and a general societal "modernization." The thesis about the paralyzing costs of a global over-extension has later been given expression by the British-American historian, Paul Kennedy, in his widely discussed book on the rise and fall of the great powers.

As if to defy such pessimistic analyses of inexorable decline, Britain by the mid-1980s began to pull ahead of other West European countries in its annual rate of economic growth. This apparent turnabout could be linked in part to the expansionary policies of Prime Minister Margaret Thatcher, who headed a Conservative government after the election of May 1979. Her long period in office brought some sharp changes in economic and social direction for the country. She portrayed herself as a "conviction politician," determined to introduce a strong dose of economic discipline by encouraging private enterprise and reducing the interventionist role of government. This stood in marked contrast to what she dismissed as the centrist path of "consensus politicians," among whom she included both her Labour and Conservative predecessors. Her radical rhetoric and somewhat less drastic policy changes spawned yet another debate about what came to be called the Thatcher Revolution and its social and political consequences.

Fundamentally, the disagreement was not only about how to achieve economic growth but also about the kind of polity and society Britain ought to be. Even among the observers who were impressed by the economic revival of Britain in the mid-1980s, there were many who became disturbed by some of the apparent social and political trade-offs. By the late 1980s, moreover, the pragmatic argument in favor of Thatcher's approach seemed to have lost much of its force when the country appeared to slip back into stagflation, or sluggish economic performance coupled with fairly high inflation. Some critics were convinced that her policies contributed to an exacerbation of this new and severe recession that came to dog John Major, her successor in office after November 1990.

By the mid-1990s, however, the British economy seemed once again to have revived ahead of those on the mainland in Western Europe. Indeed, at the end of the century a growing number of observers were willing to conclude that Thatcher's "neoliberal" policies had at least made Britain more competitive. Ironically, these views were shared by the new Prime Minister, Tony Blair, who in 1997 finally had displaced John Major as Prime Minister, leading Labour back to power after 18 years in the opposition. Compared to most of its European neighbors, the U.K. today has a more flexible and dynamic economy with higher growth rates and lower unemployment—but also with greater income disparities and what often seems to be a dilapidated public service sector.

The British debate had in any case not been restricted to the economy only. Its concerns about an alleged "ungovernability" were now joined by questions about the dislocating consequences of Thatcher's and Major's economic and social policies. During the last decade of Conservative rule, until the power shift in 1997, there were also growing concerns about what some saw as emerging authoritarian tendencies in the governance of the country. These were perceived in all manner of high-handed efforts by the national government—such as its imposition of central direction over education at all levels, introduction of greater cost controls in the popular National Health Service, privatization of electricity and water industries, or drastic inroads upon what had long been considered established rights in such areas as local government powers and civil liberties.

In foreign affairs, Prime Minister Thatcher had combined an assertive role for Britain in Europe and close cooperation with the United States under the leadership of Presidents Ronald Reagan and George Bush. As a patriot and staunch defender of both market economics and national sovereignty, Thatcher distrusted the drive toward monetary and eventual political union in the European Community. She became known throughout the continent for her unusually sharp public attacks on what she pilloried as tendencies toward bureaucratic intervention or technocratic socialism in Brussels. There were critics in her own party who regarded her Eurocritical position as untenable, also because it isolated Britain and reduced its influence on questions of strategic planning for the EC's future.

For the mass electorate, however, nothing seems to have been so upsetting as Thatcher's introduction of the community charge or "poll tax." This was a tax on each adult resident that would replace the local property tax or "rates" as a means of financing local public services. Although the new tax was extremely unpopular from the start, the veteran prime minister resisted all pressure to abandon the project before its full national implementation in early 1990. Not only did such a poll tax appear inequitable or regressive, as compared to one based on property values, it also turned out to be set much higher by local governments than the national government originally had estimated.

The politically disastrous result was that, as a revenue measure, the poll tax was anything but neutral in its impact. It created an unexpectedly large proportion of immediate losers, that is, people who had to pay considerably more in local taxes than previously. The immediate winners were people who had previously paid high property taxes. Not surprisingly, the national and local governments disagreed about who was responsible for the high poll tax bills, but the voters seemed to have little difficulty in assigning blame to Margaret Thatcher and the Conservative Party as originators of the unpopular reform. Many voters were up in arms, and some observers correctly anticipated that the tax rebellion would undermine Thatcher's position in her own party and become her political Waterloo.

The feisty prime minister had weathered many political challenges, but she was now confronted with increasing speculation that the Tories might try to replace her with a more attractive leader before the next general election. The issue that finally triggered such a development was Thatcher's stepped-up attacks on closer European integration during 1990. It led her deputy prime minister and party colleague, Sir Geoffrey Howe, to resign on November 1, 1990, with an unusually sharp public rebuke of her attitude toward the EC. There followed a leadership challenge in the Conservative Party that ended with Thatcher's resignation, in advance of an expected defeat by her own parliamentary party.

The transition in power was remarkably smooth. John Major, who was chosen by his fellow Conservatives in Parliament to be Thatcher's successor as party leader and thus prime minister, had long been regarded as one of her closest cabinet supporters. He basically supported her tough economic strategy, which she had often described as "dry." He combined a market approach in economics with a somewhat more compassionate or "wet" social policy, without indulging in the Tory tradition of welfare paternalism, against which Margaret Thatcher had also railed. Not surprisingly, he abandoned the hated poll tax. Major's undramatic governing style was far less confrontational than that of his predecessor, and some nostalgic critics were quick to call him dull. In the Gulf War of 1991, he continued Thatcher's policy of giving strong British support for firm and ultimately military measures against the government of Iraq, whose troops had invaded and occupied oil-rich Kuwait.

By the time of Thatcher's resignation, Labour appeared to be in a relatively good position to capitalize on the growing disenchantment with the Conservative government. The big political question had become whether Prime Minister Major could recapture lost ground. Under its leader, Neil Kinnock, Labour had begun to move back toward its traditional center-left position, presenting itself as a politically moderate and socially caring reform party. Labour took a leading position in some opinion polls, and it won some impressive victories in various by-elections to the House of Commons. In the shadow of the Gulf War, Labour was overtaken by the Conservatives in the polls, but its position improved again a few months later.

As the main opposition party, however, Labour was now troubled by a new version of the Social Democratic and Liberal alternatives that had fragmented the non-Conservative camp in the elections of 1983 and 1987. The two smaller parties, which had operated as an electoral coalition or "Alliance" in those years, had concluded that their organizational separation was a hindrance to the political breakthrough they wanted. They seemed condemned to win at best a quarter of the popular vote, which was more than enough to keep Labour from winning a majority for itself, but not enough for the Alliance to win a balance of power in the House of Commons. After their defeat of 1987, the two small parties joined together as Liberal Democrats.

Under the leadership of Paddy Ashdown, the Liberal Democrats continued their attempt to overcome the electoral system's bias against third parties by promoting themselves as a reasonable centrist alternative to the Conservatives on the right and Labour on the left. Their strategic goal has been to win the parliamentary balance of power in a tightly fought election and then, as majority-makers, enter a government coalition with one of the two big parties. One of their main demands would then be that the existing winner-take-all system, based on plurality or "first-past-the-post" elections in single-member districts, be replaced by some form of proportional representation (PR) in multimember districts. Such a system, which is used widely in Western Europe, would almost surely guarantee the Liberal Democrats not only a much larger and more solid base in the House of Commons but also a pivotal role in a future process of what would henceforth become a form of government coalition politics in Britain. Given their considerable electoral support, the Liberal Democrats would then enjoy a strategic position at the fulcrum of party politics similar to but far more secure than that occupied for decades, until 1998, by their much smaller liberal counterpart in Germany, the Free Democrats (FDP).

The rise of this centrist "third force" in British electoral politics during the early 1980s had been made possible by a temporary leftward shift of Labour and a simultaneous but longer-lasting rightward movement of the Conservatives, beginning a few years earlier. The challenge from the middle had the predictable result that the two main parties eventually sought to "re-center" themselves, as became evident in the general election called by Prime Minister Major for April 9, 1992. The timing seemed terribly unattractive for the Conservatives as governing party, for Britain was still in the economic doldrums. Normally, a British government chooses not to stay in office for a full 5-year term, preferring to dissolve the House of Commons at an earlier and politically more convenient time. It will procrastinate, however, when the electoral outlook appears to be dismal. By the spring of 1992 there was hardly any time left for further delay, since an election had to come before the end of June under Britain's 5-year limit. At the time, many observers expected either a slim Labour victory or, what seemed more likely, a so-called "hung" Parliament, in which no single party would end up with a working majority. The latter result would have led either to a minority government, which could be expected to solve the political impasse by calling an early new election, or a coalition government, which would have included the Liberal Democrats as the majority-making junior partner.

Instead, the outcome of the 1992 general election gave the Conservatives an unprecedented fourth consecutive term of office and thus confounded all those who had expected a change in government. Despite the recession, the Tories garnered the same overall percentage of the vote (about 42 percent) as in 1987, while Labour increased its total share slightly, from 31 to 34 percent. Support for the Liberal Democrats declined to 18 percent, which amounted to about one quarter less than the impressive share the Alliance had won in its two unsuccessful attempts to "break the mold" of the party system in 1983 and 1987. In the House of Commons, the electoral system's bias in favor of the front-runners showed up once again. The Conservatives lost 39 seats but ended up with 336 of the 651 members—a slim but sufficient "working" majority, unless a major issue fragmented

the party or attrition eroded its parliamentary margin. Labour increased its number of seats from 229 to 271—a net gain of 42, but far short of an opportunity to threaten the majority party. The Liberal Democrats ended up with 20 seats, down from 22. A few remaining seats went to candidates of the small regional parties from Northern Ireland, Scotland, and Wales.

Soon after the 1992 election, John Major ran into considerable difficulties with a wing of his own party that followed Thatcher in opposing his own more pro-European policy. Only by threatening to dissolve Parliament and call an early new election did Major bring the dissidents into line during a crucial vote on the Maastricht Treaty in the summer of 1993. In by-elections over the next years, the Tories gradually saw their slim parliamentary majority dwindle.

In the years after the 1992 election, the Labour party came under the leadership first of John Smith and then, after the latter's sudden death, of Tony Blair. Labour soon took a commanding and continuous lead over the Conservative governing party in the public opinion polls. John Major therefore had good reason to delay the next election as long as possible, until May 1997. This time there were no surprises, except for the enormous parliamentary landslide that greeted the victor. With just over 44 percent of the British vote (or slightly more than the Conservatives had won in 1983, 1987, and again in 1992), the Labour Party won a commanding majority of 418 of 659 seats in the House of Commons. The Liberal Democrats saw their share of the vote drop by 1 percent, to 17 percent, but widespread tactical voting in swing districts more than doubled their number of parliamentary seats to 46, their best showing in about seven decades. They were not needed to form a majority government, however, and so they once again failed to reach their strategic goal of becoming pivotal partners in a coalition government. Thus the outcome of the 1997 general election in Britain gave yet another dramatic demonstration of the "disproportional" representation brought about by the country's "first-past-the-post" or winner-take-all electoral system.

Labour's victory has given prominence to the growing demand for constitutional change in Britain. In the late 1980s, an ad hoc reform coalition launched Charter 88, an interest group that called for a bill of rights, proportional representation, and a more general redefinition, modernization, and codification of constitutional "rules of the game" in British politics. The chartists chose the tricentennial of Britain's Glorious Revolution of 1688 to launch their effort, which triggered a broad discussion in the country and several different proposals for constitutional reform.

The Liberal Democrats had been in the vanguard of constitutional reform efforts from the beginning. But the growing importance of the issue was reflected in the fact that now even some Conservatives entered the fray. While the latter have so far not offered another draft constitution, they have sought to appropriate and redefine the debate about citizenship rights against state bureaucracy. Labour's position became crucial after it took office in May 1997. While he was still opposition leader, Tony Blair identified himself and his party with a constitutional reform agenda, with the notable exception of the electoral system that underpins the Westminster model of government by a single majority party.

One of the recurrent reform suggestions had been to create special regional assemblies for Scotland and Wales within the United Kingdom. Soon after Labour took power, regional referendums resulted in majority approval of such assemblies—a regional parliament (with very limited powers of taxation) for

Scotland, and a weaker assembly for Wales. The regional problem associated with the six counties that make up Northern Ireland or Ulster has long been recognized as far more intractable. It involves the coexistence of two peoples, who espouse rival identities and seem not to want to live together. Even if only relatively few have taken up arms, their paramilitary organizations have been responsible for considerable bloodshed and terrorization during the past three decades. Unionists make up a majority of some 60 percent of the population in Ulster. They feel British, are overwhelmingly Protestant, and wish to maintain Northern Ireland's ties to Britain. A very large minority of close to 40 percent are Republicans. They are overwhelmingly Catholics, feel Irish, and wish to unite the six counties with the Republic of Ireland that makes up the main part of the island.

The Blair government has worked assiduously to broker a deal for Ulster that would be acceptable to the two communities and their leaders. The negotiating process came to include outsiders, and important mediating roles came to be played by the Irish and U.S. governments as well as individually by former U.S. Senator George Mitchell and a retired Canadian general. An agreement was reached in April 1998. This so-called Good Friday Agreement was then approved in a regional referendum by 71 percent of the voters, on a turnout of 81 percent. It provides for the use of proportional representation in electing a regional assembly along with elaborate measures for power-sharing in the regional administration. The goal was to include representatives of the two communities and their several parties. By including the Republic of Ireland in the agreement, there is even an element of international consociationalism, as Donley Studlar explains in his article on British constitutional reform.

The settlement soon ran into disputes over its implementation, followed by political confrontations and a temporary suspension of the workings of the assembly or, in 2002, of the regional government. One of the most contentious and recurrent issues is tied to the halting progress in disarming the paramilitary Irish Republican Army (IRA). It is hardly surprising that persistent mutual fear and suspicion continue to hamper the relationship between people of the two communities.

In addition to creating these new regional levels of representative institutions, the Labour government has shown interest in another devolution of power to existing or newly created local governments, such as that of London. This is clearly a reversal of the shift in the opposite direction that took place under Prime Minister Thatcher. Yet another reform aims at a thorough revamping of the pre-democratic upper house of Parliament, the House of Lords, where most of the hereditary peers have now lost their right to vote. It is not yet clear how the partial "modernization" of the House of Lords, which remains an unelected second chamber, will affect the asymmetrical balance of power with the elected chamber, the House of Commons. Here and elsewhere, some critical observers invoke the "law of unanticipated consequences" when they point out that the institutional changes may bring with them some political trade-offs in terms of a reduced capacity to govern or even to keep Britain together.

In the first article on Britain, Donley Studlar takes stock of each of the major reforms as well as the reactions they have triggered until the end of the year 2002. Can one speak of a constitutional revolution taking place in a country we usually associate with evolutionary change? The author leaves no doubt that the series of institutional changes since 1997 are of great political significance. It is also clear that these matters would have been approached very differently, if at all, under a Conservative government.

What remains less certain is whether these important institutional reforms contributed to Labour's new electoral triumph in June 2001. This recent victory was not free of imperfections. Most serious was the very low voter turnout, which had consistently been over 70 percent since World War II but in 2001 sank below the 60 percent mark to only 59.4 percent. By attracting 42 percent of the popular vote in Britain (down from 44.4 percent in 1997), Labour won another strong parliamentary majority of 412 seats (down from 418) of the 659 seats in the House of Commons. The Conservatives won 32.7 percent (slightly up from 31.5 percent) and 166 seats (a gain of one). With 18.8 percent of the vote in Britain (up from 17.2 percent), the Liberal Democrats again failed to become a balancer, but they won six additional seats for a new high of 52. The disproportional result practically guarantees Labour its first ever full second term in office.

The second article covers various aspects of political change linked to Labour's current stay in power. It reviews the record of Tony Blair's first term in office as well as his agenda for the second. Here it predicts that his plans for a structural reform of the public sector will force him to make choices—and enemies.

There follows a cluster of three related articles, which all deal with the current state of the national political parties in Britain. One reports that after two successive election sweeps Labour is now confident that it can win a third election without Tony Blair as leader. He now faces considerable intraparty opposition both on his Iraq policy, where he is often criticized as a cheerleader for the U.S. president, and on his steps to restructure some public services. Another article deals with the dissolute state of the Conservatives after their second electoral debacle in a row. Their new "Euroskeptic" leader, Iain Duncan Smith, seems unable to bring unity to the Conservatives. His days may well be numbered in a party which has a history of dismissing leaders who do not deliver electoral success. Should the Conservatives fail to revive, the Liberal Democrats stand ready to take over second place under Charles Kennedy, as reported in the third of these articles. Their support is not needed by Labour, and their articulate leader has been moving the Liberal Democrats toward independent positions on a number of questions, even before the recent disagreement over policy toward Iraq. Ironically, it was the Liberal Democrats rather than Labour who in the 2002 campaign came out most clearly in favor of higher taxes to fund public services.

Although Blair's Labour government continues to have a formidable majority in Parliament, some observers wonder if he can keep his center-left party "on track" without engaging in more meaningful social reforms in addition to his agenda of institutional "modernization." There is at present no apparent danger from the weakened and divided Conservatives. But Labour is now divided over Blair's Iraq policy and continues to harbor some older factional disputes. The major ideological and strategic cleavage runs between traditional socialists, who favor more emphasis on public service programs, and the more pragmatic modernizers, who wish to continue the centrist policies identified with "New Labour." Tony Blair for a long time seemed impervious when party critics accused him of being lukewarm to traditional Labour concerns. But he is well aware that his government's record in the public service arena is a lackluster one. There are growing indications that he will turn his reform efforts in that direction.

Since the events of September 11, 2001, Tony Blair has taken a prominent role in strongly supporting the American-led military action in Afghanistan and other antiterrorist measures.

At the same time, but more subtly than other European leaders, he seems to prefer that the United States adopt a greater semblance of multilateral consultation in matters involving both military and political measures against the threat of international terrorism.

**France** must also cope with major political challenges within a rapidly changing Europe. The bicentennial of the French Revolution was duly celebrated in 1989. It served as an occasion for public ceremonies and a revival of historical-political debates about the costs and benefits of that great exercise in the radical transformation of a society. Ironically, however, by this time there was mounting evidence that the sharp ideological cleavages that had marked French politics for so much of the past two centuries were losing significance. Instead, there was emerging a more pragmatic, pluralist form of accommodation in French public life.

This deradicalization and depolarization of political discourse is by no means complete in France. The Communists have been significantly weakened and ideologically mellowed, even as they have joined a coalition government dominated by the Socialists. On the extreme Right, Le Pen's National Front seemed to have been weakened by internal splits and rivalries, but it continues to find some populist support for its xenophobic rhetoric directed primarily against the country's many residents of Arab origin. The apparent electoral appeal of such invective has tempted some leaders of the establishment parties of the more moderate Right to voice carefully formulated reservations about the presence of so many immigrants. An entirely new and different political phenomenon for France is the appearance of two small Green parties, one more conservative and the other more socialist in orientation.

Although it appears in the end to be increasingly centrist, French electoral politics can still be highly volatile. To gain a little perspective, it makes sense to go back to the parliamentary contest of 1993, when the Socialist suffered a major setback after 5 years of serving as the main government party. Together, the loosely organized center-right Giscardists (the Union for French Democracy, or UDF) and the more conservative neo-Gaullists (the Rally for the Republic, or RPR) won about 40 percent of the first-round popular vote. Beginning with that plurality these two coalition parties ended up with an overwhelming majority of nearly 80 percent of the seats in the 577-member National Assembly.

The Socialists and their close allies were clearly the big losers in this largest electoral landslide in French democratic history. Receiving less than 20 percent of the popular vote on the first round, the Socialists plummeted from their previous share of 274 seats to 61 seats or about one-quarter of their previous parliamentary strength. The Communists, with only 9 percent of the first-round vote, were able to win 24 seats because much of their electoral support was concentrated in a few urban districts. With a slightly higher share of the vote, the ultra-right National Front (FN) won no seats at all, having failed to be "first past the post" anywhere.

Socialist president François Mitterrand's second 7-year presidential term lasted until May 1995. After the parliamentary rout of the Socialists in March 1993, he had been faced with the question of whether to resign early from the presidency or, as under similar political circumstances in 1986, to begin a period of "cohabitation" with a conservative prime minister. Mitterrand opted once again for the latter solution, but he made sure to appoint a moderate Gaullist, Edouard Balladur, to this position.

For a time, the new prime minister enjoyed considerable popularity, and this encouraged him to enter the presidential race in 1995. By declaring his own candidacy, Balladur in effect snubbed Jacques Chirac, the assertive Gaullist leader who had himself served as prime minister in the first period of cohabitation (1986–1988). In 1995, Chirac had expected to be the only Gaullist candidate for the presidency, as he had been 7 years earlier, in 1988, when he lost against the incumbent Mitterrand.

The presidential race in France tends to become highly individualized. Eventually the tough and outspoken Chirac pulled ahead of his more consensual and lackluster party colleague. In the first round of the 1995 presidential election, however, a surprising plurality of the vote went to the main socialist candidate, Lionel Jospin, a former education minister and party leader. In the run-off election, 2 weeks later, Chirac defeated Jospin and thereby ended 14 years of Socialist control of the presidency. He appointed another Gaullist, Alain Juppé to replace the faithless Balladur as prime minister.

The new conservative dominance lasted only until 1997, when France entered into a new version of "cohabitation" as the result of another electoral upset. No parliamentary elections were necessary in France until the end of the National Assembly's 5 year term in 1998, but President Chirac sensed a leftward drift in the country and decided to renew the legislature 10 months early while the conservative coalition still appeared to be ahead of the Left. As it turned out, Chirac totally underestimated how far public confidence in Juppé's government had already deteriorated. The two-stage elections for the National Assembly took place in May and early June of 1997, and the result was a major setback for the neo-Gaullists (RPR) and their increasingly fragmented neo-liberal allies (mainly the loosely organized UDF). Their combined share of the popular vote dropped to 31 percent, and their parliamentary strength was reduced by 200 seats, to 249. The Socialists quadrupled their strength from 61 to 245 seats, while their non-Communist allies won another 13 seats in the 577-seat National Assembly. In order to form a majority coalition government, they included the small Communist Party, with its 37 seats.

The 1997 parliamentary election resembled all the elections to the National Assembly since 1981 in one respect. In each case, the French voters had thrown out the incumbent government. This time, ironically, President Chirac appointed the Socialist leader, Lionel Jospin, as prime minister—the very politician he had narrowly defeated in the presidential race barely 2 years earlier. Thus began France's third and so far longest experiment in cohabitation. It lasted a full parliamentary term of 5 years. The novelty was that this time the president was a conservative serving with a socialist prime minister rather than vice versa.

During periods of cohabitation, it appears that the Gaullist model of a strong presidential system has been diluted. So far, however, the end of cohabitation has always brought a return to the original dual executive of the Fifth Republic with its strong president dominating his prime minister—as from 1988 to 1993, from 1995 to 1997, and again since 2002.

In some ways, the new experiment in cohabitation can be seen as a test of how far the moderate Left and Right in France have really overcome their once very deep ideological differences. During the 1997 election campaign, the political distance between them seemed to have grown. The Socialists sharply criticized Juppé's austerity measures and the neoliberal measures of deregulation. Instead, they promised a more traditional program to attack unemployment by priming the economy, creating new public service jobs, and reducing the work week to 35 hours from 39 without lowering pay. Conservative political critics were quick to speak of the socialist platform as one of beguiling smoke and mirrors. Even they could not deny, however, that Jospin's government set off to an excellent start in restoring public confidence.

Meanwhile, the French parties of the Right seem to have been weakened by their internal disagreements on policy and strategy as well as personal rivalries at the leadership level. The UDF has always been a loose coalition of disparate political groups and tendencies that differed from the neo-Gaullists by showing a greater support for European integration, civil rights, and economic neoliberalism. The more conservative and nationally oriented RPR, founded by Jacques Chirac, has been weakened by its own internecine battles. Since 2002, when he successfully ran for another term as president, Chirac and some of his followers have attempted to revitalize the party as a more inclusive and less traditionalist party of the French center-right.

The two articles in this section provide many insights on a country that one author describes as a "divided self." Few who know the nation would refer without hesitation to "the new France." In fact, contemporary French politics and society combine some traits that reflect a strong sense of continuity with the past and others that suggest considerable innovation. One recurrent theme is the decline of the previously sharp ideological struggle between the Left and the Right. This may well result in a sense of loss among some French intellectuals who still prefer the political battle to have apocalyptic implications. They will find it hard to accept that the grand struggle between Left and Right has been replaced by a more moderate and seemingly more mundane party politics of competition among groups that cluster near the center of the political spectrum.

In the end, French intellectuals may discover that what they have long regarded as a tedious political competition between those promising a "little more" or a "little less" can have considerable practical consequences in terms of "who gets what, when, and how." Moreover, such incremental politics need not be without dramatic conflict, since new issues, events, or leaders often emerge to sharpen the differences and increase the stakes of politics. In the last months of 1995 and again in late 1996, for example, French politics took on a dramatic form and immediacy when workers and students resorted to massive strikes and street demonstrations against a new austerity program introduced by the then conservative government. The proposed cutbacks in social entitlements such as pension rights were perceived by many as unnecessary, drastic, and unfair. They were difficult to explain to the public at large, and many observers saw the political confrontation in France as a major test for the welfare state or "social market economy" that is now being squeezed in the name of international or global "competitiveness" throughout Western Europe.

The loss of the grand ideological alternatives may help account for the mood of political malaise that many observers have discovered in contemporary France. But the French search for political direction and identity in a changing Europe has another major origin as well. The sudden emergence of a larger and potentially more powerful Germany next door cannot but have a disquieting effect upon France. French elites now face the troubling question of redefining their country's role in a post–cold war world, in which Russia has lost in power and influence while Germany has gained in both. The French resistance to a large American role in Europe adds another source of friction. Together with Germany's Chancellor Schröder, President Chirac has recently gone out of his way to tout Franco-German friendship and cooperation. Both have publicly disagreed with what they regard as President Bush's unilateral and militaristic approach in the Iraq Question. They seem to be searching for a distinctive European position on such international problems. It will be hard to define or maintain such a common position in a continent that invented the idea of the sovereign nation state. On the other hand, Europe is also the continent which has gone furthest in dismantling some features of the nation state in its construction of the European Union.

In this new European setting, some observers have even suggested that we may expect a major new cleavage in French politics. It runs between those who favor a reassertion of the traditional French nation-state ideal—a kind of isolationist "neo-Gaullism" that can be found on both the Left and Right—and those who want the country to accept a new European order, in which the sovereignty of both the French and German nation-states would be further diluted or contained by a network of international obligations within the larger European framework.

A persistent question is whether the long-run structural problems of France—similar to those of some of her neighbors—can be handled without a resort to the very market-oriented "therapy" that the voters and political leaders seem so clearly to have rejected. French capitalism (like its German counterpart) is significantly different from its British and American counterparts, but careful observers point out that in his 5 years as prime minister, Jospin engaged in a skillful political sleight of hand by introducing some economic reforms like deregulation and privatization that have the effect of reducing the traditional interventionist role of the French state. Once again, the moderate Left appears to promote a kind of "new centrism" but with due respect to what is acceptable within a particular national and cultural setting.

The French faced an electoral marathon in 2002, when there were two-stage elections for both the presidency and the National Assembly. It was expected in advance that the focus of the relatively short presidential campaign would be on the two veteran warhorses, Chirac and Jospin. The big surprise was the elimination of Jospin in the first stage: He ran a close third behind Chirac, who came first, and the far right candidate, Le Pen, who came second. As in 1995, many people on the Left had apparently voted "with their hearts" in the first round. The result was that the Left vote was split among a multiplicity of candidates, none of whom had a chance of making it into the second round. This time, however, the result was the failure of the main candidate of the Left to make it into the second round, since Jospin gathered slightly fewer votes than Le Pen. In the run-off between Chirac and Le Pen, the incumbent president won an overwhelming victory by attracting moderate votes from both Right and Left. The electoral statistics will be found in the second article on France.

In the two-stage elections of the National Assembly in June of 2002, the parties of the moderate right-of-center, led by Chirac's RPR, won a major victory over the parties of the Left. Voter turnout was unusually low, and many observers detected a political alienation on the Left. As a result of the parliamentary election, President Chirac called on the relatively obscure Pierre Raffarin (DL) to form a new, moderately conservative government in place of the defeated left-of-center government that Jospin had headed for 5 years.

*Germany* was united in 1990, when the eastern German Democratic Republic, or GDR, was merged into the western Federal Republic of Germany. The two German states had been established in 1949, 4 years after the total defeat of the German Reich in World War II. During the next 40 years, their rival elites subscribed to the conflicting ideologies and interests of East and West in the cold war. East Germany comprised the territory of the former Soviet Occupation Zone of Germany, where the Communists exercised a power monopoly and established an economy based on Soviet-style central planning. In contrast, West Germany, which had emerged from the former American, British, and French zones of postwar occupation, developed a pluralist democracy and a flourishing market economy. When the two states were getting ready to celebrate their fortieth anniversaries in 1989, no leading politician was on record as having foreseen that the forced political division of Germany was about to come to an end.

Mass demonstrations in several East German cities and the westward flight of thousands of citizens brought the GDR government to make an increasing number of concessions in late 1989 and early 1990. The Berlin Wall ceased to be a hermetical seal after November 9, 1989, when East Germans began to stream over into West Berlin. Collectors and entrepreneurs soon broke pieces from the Wall to keep or sell as souvenirs, before public workers set about to remove the rest of this symbol of the cold war and Germany's division.

Under new leadership, the ruling Communists of East Germany made a last-ditch stand by introducing a form of power-sharing with noncommunist groups and parties. They agreed to seek democratic legitimation by holding a free East German election in March 1990, also in the hope of reducing the westward flight of thousands of people with its devastating consequences for the eastern economy.

Such popular demonstrations and the willingness of East Germans to "vote with their feet" had been made possible by two major preconditions. First, the Soviet leader, Mikhail Gorbachev, had abandoned the so-called Brezhnev Doctrine, under which the Soviets claimed the right of military intervention on behalf of the established communist regimes in Central and Eastern Europe. And second, the imposed communist regimes of these countries turned out to have lost their radical will and ability to hold on to power at any cost.

At first, the East German Communists only loosened their claim to an exclusive control of power and positions in the so-called German Democratic Republic. The results of the March 1990 election, however, made it clear even to them that the pressure for national unification could no longer be stemmed. An eastern alliance of Christian Democrats, largely identified with and supported by Chancellor Helmut Kohl's party in West Germany, won a surprisingly decisive victory, winning about one-half of the vote throughout East Germany. It advocated a short, quick route to unification, beginning with an early monetary union in the summer and a political union by the fall of 1990. Almost immediately a new noncommunist government was installed in East Germany. Headed by Lothar de Maizière (CDU), it followed a short-cut route to merge with the Federal Republic, under Article 23 of the West German Basic Law. The Social Democrats, or SPD, had won only 22 percent of the East German vote. That was widely interpreted as a defeat for their alternative strategy for unification that would have involved the protracted negotiation of a new German constitution, as envisaged in Article 146 of the Federal Republic's Basic Law.

During the summer and fall of 1990, the governments of the two German states and the four former occupying powers completed their so-called two-plus-four negotiations that resulted in a mutual agreement on the German unification process. The monetary union in July was quickly followed by a political merger in October 1990. In advance of unification, Bonn negotiated an agreement with Moscow in which the latter accepted the gradual withdrawal of Soviet troops from eastern Germany and the membership of the larger, united Germany in NATO, in return for considerable German economic support for the Soviet Union. The result was a major shift in both the domestic and international balance of power.

The moderately conservative Christian Democrats repeated their electoral success in the first Bundestag election in a reunited Germany, held in early December 1990. They captured almost 44 percent of the vote, against the long-time low of 33.5 percent for the rival Social Democrats. At the same time, Kohl's small coalition partner of liberal Free Democrats (FDP) did unusually well (11 percent of the vote). The environmentalist Greens, on the other hand, failed to get the required minimum of 5 percent of the vote in western Germany and dropped out of the Bundestag for the next 4 years. Under a special dispensation for the 1990 election only, the two parts of united Germany were regarded as separate electoral regions as far as the 5 percent threshold was concerned. That made it possible for two small eastern parties to get a foothold in the Bundestag. One was a coalition of political dissidents and environmentalists (Alliance 90/Greens), the other was the communist-descended Party of Democratic Socialism. The PDS was able to win about 11 percent of the vote in the East by appealing to those who felt displaced and alienated in the new order. Its voters included many former privileged party members but also some rural workers and young people. Ironically, the communist-descended party received only weak support among blue-collar workers.

The election results of December 1990 suggested that national unification could eventually modify the German party system significantly. By the time of the next national election, in October 1994, it became evident that a new east-west divide had emerged in German politics. This time, the far-left PDS was able to almost double its support and attract 20 percent of the vote in the East, where only one-fifth of Germany's total population lives. At the same time, the PDS won only about 1 percent of the vote in the far more populous West. Its total electoral support in Germany thus fell slightly below the famous "5 percent hurdle" established in Germany's electoral law as a minimum for a party to win proportional representation in the Bundestag. The PDS was nevertheless able to keep and expand its parliamentary foothold, because it met an almost forgotten alternative seating requirement of winning pluralities in at least three single-member districts under Germany's double-ballot electoral system. Thus the political descendants of the former ruling Communists were given proportional representation after all. They were now represented in the Bundestag by 30 deputies, who liked to present themselves as a democratically sensitive, far-left party of socialists and regionalists.

Despite a widespread unification malaise in Germany, the conservative-liberal government headed by Chancellor Helmut Kohl won reelection in 1994. His Christian Democrats, who benefited from a widely perceived if only temporary improvement in the German economy, won 41.4 percent of the vote. Their Free Democratic ally barely scraped through with 6.9 percent of the vote. Together, the two governing parties had a very slim majority of 10 seats more than the combined total of the three opposition parties, the SPD (36.4 percent), the revived and united Greens (7.3 percent), and the PDS (4.4 percent). In the federal upper house, or Bundesrat, the SPD continued to hold a comfortable majority of the seats, based on their control of many state governments. This situation gave a united SPD considerable leverage or blocking power in federal legislative politics. The Kohl government sometimes charged that it resulted in a German form of parliamentary gridlock that stalled some of its economic reform initiatives.

Between 1949 and 1999, the seat of government for the Federal Republic had been the small Rhineland town of Bonn. Reunification made possible the move of the government and parliament several hundred miles eastward to the old political center of Berlin. The transfer was controversial in Germany, because of both the costs and symbolism involved. Nevertheless, it had already been approved by the Bundestag in 1991, with a narrow parliamentary majority, and was then delayed until 1999. Observers generally agree that the "Berlin Republic" will continue the democratic tradition that has been firmly established in Germany. But they also point to the need for a revamping of the economic and social arrangements that worked so well during much of the Bonn period, if the country is to meet its new obligations within Europe and in the increasingly global market arena.

Unlike their British counterparts, German governments are regularly produced by the vagaries of coalition politics in a multiparty system, based on the country's modified form of proportional representation. It is remarkable that between 1949 and 1998 there had never been a complete replacement of a governing coalition in Bonn. Even when there was a change of government, at least one partner of the previous coalition had always managed to hang on as majority maker in the next cabinet. But this German pattern of incomplete power transfers came to an abrupt end with the clean sweep brought by the Bundestag election of September 1998.

In advance of the contest, it had been widely expected that the outcome once again would be only a partial shift in power, resulting from a "grand coalition" of Social Democrats (SPD) and Christian Democrats (CDU/CSU). In such a situation, the chancellorship would go to the leader of the front-running party—most likely the SPD. The result would have been a considerable continuity and, as interpreted by rival scenarios, either a disabling inertia or a newfound strength in dealing with Germany's backlog of social and economic reforms.

Instead, the 1998 election made possible a complete turnover in power. It brought what Germans like to call a "red-green" coalition by giving the Social Democrats, with 40.9 percent of the popular vote, a sufficient margin (almost 6 percent) over the Christian Democrats (35.1 percent) to form a majority coalition with the small party of Greens (6.7 percent). German voters in effect decided it was "time for a change" in their country, similar to the political turnabouts that had taken place in Britain and France in 1997. As in these neighboring countries, the main party of the Left was very careful to present itself as a moderate reform agent that would provide security along with both "continuity and change." The SPD borrowed freely from both British and American political imagery by proclaiming that it represented a decidedly non-radical "new middle" (neue Mitte). It was a successful, if rather vague, political formula.

The emergence of the Berlin Republic has coincided not only with a complete change in governing parties, but also with a generational turnover in the top levels of German government. In the federal chancellery, Social Democrat Gerhard Schröder, born in 1944, replaced Christian Democrat Helmut Kohl, born in 1930. Most of the other leading members of the new government spent their childhood years in postwar Germany. In many cases they had their initial political experiences in youthful opposition to the societal establishment of the late 1960s. By now the "68ers" are themselves well into middle age, but they have ascended to power as successors to Kohl's generation, whose politically formative years coincided with the founding period of the Federal Republic. Unlike the latter, the new German leaders do not have youthful memories of the Third Reich, World War II, or even, in many cases, the short era of military occupation. They are truly Germany's first postwar generation in power.

The larger political system was affected by the shifts in the power balance of the small political parties and their leaders after the milestone election of September 1998. On the far left, the post-communist PDS managed for the first time to pass the 5 percent threshold, if only barely, by winning 21.6 percent of the vote in eastern Germany, while advancing only slightly to 1.2 percent of the vote in the far more populous West, where approximately 80 percent of the German population lives. Clearly, the PDS is still very much a party rooted in the new federal states that emerged from the communist-ruled East Germany. The liberal Free Democrats ended up with another, even closer scrape (6.2 percent). In contrast to the PDS, the Liberals were now seen as a party of the West, where they received 7 percent of the vote as compared to 3.3 percent in the East. After 29 years as junior government party, their struggle for political survival now had to be conducted in the unfamiliar role as a marginal opposition party. The third small party, the Greens, also slid back (to 6.7 percent), but this was enough to replace the FDP as majority-maker in the federal government. The Greens were also marked by the east-west divide, receiving 4.1 percent in the East versus 7.3 percent in the West.

Germany now had a slightly more complex party system. It consisted of the two major parties of the moderate center-left (SPD) and the moderate center-right (CDU/CSU) along with three small parties that each had a regional concentration either in the West (Greens and FDP) or almost exclusively in the East (PDS). Some observers referred to a "two and three halves" party system. Each of the three "halves" had an impact on the overall balance of power and what the Germans call the system's "coalition arithmetic," but each was also tiny enough to be in danger of slipping below the 5 percent mark at any time. Another important result of the 1998 Bundestag election was the continued failure of the parties of the extreme right, with their authoritarian and xenophobic rhetoric, to mobilize a significant support in the German electorate.

For the Greens, the first-time role as junior coalition partner in the national government has not been easy. In fact, some close observers have spoken of an identity crisis of the German Left that includes parts of the Social Democratic Party. It was fed by controversies linked to domestic socioeconomic and environmental issues as well as the German military participation in Kosovo in early 1999. There followed a remarkable political recovery of the SPD in the latter half of that year. The abrupt resignation of the key Social Democrat Oskar Lafontaine, as both finance minister and party leader in March 1999, gave Schröder a welcome opportunity to gain more authority within the SPD and his own cabinet. In the second half of the year, the German business community welcomed some major tax reforms proposed by the new government.

Nevertheless, a string of serious setbacks for the Social Democrats in several state elections during 1999 led to their ouster from some state governments and a loss of their majority control of the federal upper house or Bundesrat. Beginning in late 1999, the adverse trend came to a halt, and the CDU for the following year could no longer register political gains from the problems of the red-green government. Instead, the Christian Democrats suddenly found themselves in shambles, resulting from the sensational revelations of a major party finance scandal that had taken place under the leadership of Helmut Kohl, the veteran chancellor. Basically the problem stemmed from transfers of huge political contributions to the party and its leader that were illegal because they were not reported as required by law.

The timing of what became known as "Kohlgate" resulted in setbacks for the CDU in several state elections. Some disaffected CDU supporters appear to have turned to the FDP as an acceptable center-right alternative. The small liberal party went through a significant leadership change, when it chose its former secretary general, the youthful Guido Westerwelle, to become its new head. With this single move, supported by a clever promotion campaign, the party seemed to experience a rejuvenation that boosted its poll standings somewhat and brought it well ahead of the Greens in advance of the September 2002 election. In what seemed a cocky mood, the FDP announced a year in advance that its election goal would be to attract 18 percent of the vote, at a time when its poll standings had improved to about 8 percent. Hardly anyone took the full double-digit figure seriously, but it supposedly reflected a party that exuded a new vigor and self-confidence. To say the least, the FDP could no longer be written off in its search to regain the strategic position of balancer in German electoral and coalition politics.

As the 2002 election approached, the CDU poll standings improved and even brought the party ahead of the SPD. The party hammered away at the persistent unemployment problem and other aspects of what was portrayed as a poor economic record. The conservative CDU also introduced law and order themes and sometimes played to anti-immigrant sentiments both before and after the September 11 events. At the beginning of 2002, the Christian Democrats decided against nominating as "chancellor candidate" their own leader, Angela Merkel. She is an East German woman who as a newcomer to politics rose rapidly in the party after unification and, untainted by political scandal, made it to the top when the CDU needed a face lift. As chancellor candidate, the Christian Democrats decided in favor of Edmund Stoiber, the governor of Bavaria and leader of the CSU, their more conservative sister party in that large state. Stoiber's main advantage was held to be a strong economic record in his home state, but it surely helped that he was an older male politician from the West with many personal supporters in the CDU/CSU. Some observers wondered whether he was not too right-leaning to attract many voters outside Bavaria. Stoiber trailed Schröder in his individual poll ratings, as did Angela Merkl. But a parliamentary election is also about party support, and here an electoral comeback of the CDU/CSU seemed to be in the making. By the mid-summer of 2002 it was widely believed that the revived Christian Democrats were likely to return to government office in coalition with the recharged FDP. The SPD's weak economic record, most vividly dramatized by a persistent unemployment problem, seemed likely to become its Achilles' heel in the September election.

Once again, the small parties were to play a key role in the electoral and parliamentary balance of power established by the 2002 Bundestag election. Until the summer of that year, the

Greens suffered a long string of electoral setbacks at the state level of politics. They had been damaged by their quarrels and also lost some of their traditional backing among younger voters, as the founder generation grew older and joined the establishment. Some critical voters now seemed to be attracted by the FDP's self-promotion as the real alternative. The FDP's constant focus on "Project 18" and a "fun" campaign helped maintain the illusion that the Free Democrats were likely to pass the Greens and again become the "third force" in German party politics. The PDS had most reason to tremble at its electoral prospects. It had passed the 5 percent hurdle in only one of the three Bundestag election since unification, and only barely at that (5.1 percent in 1998). Since then, it had lost some of its previous voters and largely failed to win many new ones. The alternative route to proportional representation in the Bundestag also looked bleak for the PDS, because the boundaries of the single-member districts in Berlin had recently been redrawn in a way that diluted the PDS strength and made its capture of at least three districts less likely.

Ironically, the national decline of the PDS came after some success in eastern state politics, where it had joined the SPD in two coalition governments, one of them in the city-state of Berlin. As a result, the PDS had gained greater visibility and, perhaps, "normality" in the eyes of some voters. Possibly the PDS lost some of its appeal as a regional protest party after joining the Berlin establishment, even if only at the city-state level. The PDS lost more of its aura when Gregor Gysi, by far its most popular politician, resigned from a top position in the Berlin government after he got caught up in a minor scandal that involved the personal use of officially gathered "frequent flyer" points.

In the end, the Bundestag election of 2002 did shut out the PDS from sharing in the proportional allocation of parliamentary seats. The post-Communists won two single-member districts in eastern Berlin, and is thus represented by two deputies. Had the PDS won a third district, its 4.0 percent of the party vote would have entitled it to about 24 of the 603 seats in the new Bundestag.

The near shut-out of the PDS enabled the red-green government to hold on to power in one of Germany's closest elections ever. The second of three articles on Germany analyzes the outcome in some detail. Both SPD and CDU/CSU won 38.5 percent of the vote, but a quirk in the two-vote electoral law gave the SPD three more seats than its major rival. The SPD had overcome its poor stand in the polls to come within 2.4 percent of its result in 1998. Most observers explain the electoral recovery by pointing to points earned by Chancellor Schröder by his performance in the televised debates with Edmund Stoiber, his critical remarks about President Bush's strategy toward Iraq, and his appearance as a decisive leader in dealing with the great floods that ravaged parts of eastern Germany in the month before the Bundestag election. The FDP had lost ground with a controversial campaign since mid-summer. It fell back to 7.4 percent of the vote—an improvement over its previous share of 6.2 percent but far less than its trumpeted goal of 18 percent. The Greens probably benefited from the revival of war fears in connection with Iraq as well as the popularity of their foreign minister, Joschka Fischer. While they continued to perform poorly in the eastern states, where the SPD picked up many former CDU and PDS voters, the Greens benefited from the renewal of ecological concerns in the wake of the August floods.

The third article on Germany discusses the controversy about the need for a basic economic reform. In its German version, this debate cannot ignore the special aspects that have come with the challenges and accomplishments of national unification. The task of post-communist reconstruction in eastern Germany goes far beyond the transfer of institutions and capital from the West. The transition to a pluralist democracy and a market economy also requires a measure of social and cultural transformation. Moreover, there are new problems facing the larger and more powerful Germany on the international scene, as it seeks to deal with an ambiguous mixture of expectations and anxieties that this European giant arouses abroad. Not least, there is a growing awareness that the generous social welfare model of Germany may have become unsustainable in the long run, as the country faces stiff economic competition from abroad. On the other hand, Germans have built a traditionally more social form of capitalism. They are unlikely to embrace the kind of shock therapy of massive deregulation and other market-oriented reforms that were introduced in the United States and Britain by conservative governments in the 1980s and largely accepted by their left-of-center successors in the following decade. Both the political culture and institutional framework of Germany (and much of mainland Europe) lean far more toward corporatist and communitarian solutions than their British and American counterparts.

*Japan,* the fourth country in this study of representative governments of industrial societies, has long fascinated comparative social scientists. After World War II, a representative democracy was installed in Japan under American supervision. This political system soon acquired indigenous Japanese characteristics that set it off from the other major democracies examined here.

For almost four decades the Japanese parliamentary system was dominated by the Liberal Democratic Party (LDP) which, as the saying goes, is "neither liberal, nor democratic, nor a party." It is essentially a conservative political force, comprising several rival and delicately balanced factions. The latter tend to be composed of the personal followers of political bosses who stake out factional claims to benefits of office. As David Ibison writes somewhat bluntly, the party's history has been "one of factionalism, backstabbing and corruption, mixed in with some genuine public service."

At periodic intervals the LDP's parliamentary hegemony has been threatened, but it was always able to recover and retain power until 1993. In that year, several of its important politicians defected in protest against the LDP's reluctance to introduce political reforms. As a result, the government lost its parliamentary majority. A vote of no confidence was followed by early elections in July 1993, in which the LDP failed to recover its parliamentary majority for the first time in almost four decades. Seven different parties, spanning the spectrum from conservative to socialist, thereupon formed what turned out to be a very fragile coalition government, incapable of producing coherent policy programs or agree on moves to energize an economy that by this time had begun its prolonged stay in the doldrums.

Two prime ministers and several cabinet reshuffles later, the rump LDP had managed by the summer of 1994 to return to the cabinet in coalition with its major former rival, the Socialists. The peculiar alliance was possible because of the basically pragmatic orientation adopted by the leadership of both major parties

at this juncture in the country's history. By December 1995, the LDP had recaptured the prime ministership as the result of winning a parliamentary majority for its candidate, Ryutaro Hashimoto. He became the country's eighth prime minister in 7 years and appointed a cabinet dominated by the old guard of Liberal Democrats. In 1998, Hashimoto took responsibility for an electoral setback for his party and resigned as head of government, but he remained one of the LDP's most powerful faction leaders. There were two more prime ministers in less than 3 years.

When Yoshiro Mori announced his intention to step down as prime minister in April 2001, there was a surprising number of willing successors. They included veteran leader Hashimoto with his conservative followers, who spoke somewhat unconvincingly about wanting to introduce some overdue reforms in fiscal and economic policy. To general surprise, the winner of the leadership contest in the LDP and new prime minister of Japan was Junichiro Koizumi, who seemed more credible but rather vague in his espousal of the need for structural change to revive the sluggish economy.

There was a surge of popular support for the new government leader, who seemed to personify a more unconventional approach than most veteran politicians in Japan. He immediately appointed five women to his cabinet, including the controversial Makiko Tanaka as head of the foreign ministry. As Ibison points out, Koizumi soon ran into resistance from the Hashimoto faction and other conservative elements in the political class and high civil service. By January 2002, he dismissed the assertive Tanaka, who had become a favorite target of those who opposed the new political style and possible major policy changes. The move triggered widespread public dissatisfaction, which Koizumi tried to temper by appointing another prominent women, Yoriko Kawaguchi, to head the foreign ministry. By this time, Koizumi's popularity rating was rapidly falling. It seemed unlikely that his remaining public support could be translated into sufficient political capital to offset the entrenched foes of a structural reform of the Japanese economy and fiscal policy. Moreover, there were independent critics who argued that Koizumi himself had little understanding of or commitment to the kind of change that Japan needed. For the time being, continuity seems more likely than basic change in Japan. The question remains as to whether the fragmented parliamentary opposition will one day be able take advantage of the situation and become a more coherent, alternative force for reform. Many observers find it remarkable that Japan's prolonged economic stagnation has not resulted in more political repercussions.

Observers themselves differ about the significance of recent political changes in Japan. There seems to be a growing belief, however, that the entrenched bureaucratic elites must lose some of their invincibility and themselves become the targets of reform geared at "opening up" a society and economy that seem in some ways to have become ossified. A setback for the entrenched bureaucrats could lead to a more significant long-term shift in Japan's balance of power than a new government leader or the end of one-party hegemony in the country. Some observers appear to have reached the conclusion that Japan is likely to remain a middle power, as Howard French reports.

# A Constitutional Revolution In Britain?*

## Donley T. Studlar

When the New Labor government led by Tony Blair took office in May 1997, one of its most distinctive policies was its program of constitutional reform. Indeed, few British parties have ever campaigned so consistently on constitutional issues. From its first days of power, Labor promoted its constitutional reform agenda: (1) devolution to Scotland and Wales, (2) an elected mayor and council for London and possibly other urban areas, (3) removal of the voting rights of hereditary peers in the House of Lords, (4) incorporation of the European Convention on Human Rights into British law, (5) a Freedom of Information Act, and (6) electoral reform at various levels of government, including a referendum on changing the electoral system for Members of Parliament. These reforms, plus a stable agreement for governing Northern Ireland, the constitutional implications of membership of the European Union, and the question of modernization of the monarchy will be considered here. This article analyzes the nature of Labor's constitutional proposals, including their inspiration, implementation, and potential impact.

## Traditional British Constitutional Principles

The United Kingdom as a state in international law is made up of four constituent parts—England, Scotland, Wales, and Northern Ireland—all under the authority of the Queen in Parliament in London. The constitution is the structure of fundamental laws and customary practices that define the authority of state institutions and regulate their interrelationships, including those to citizens of the state. Although in principle very flexible, in practice the "unwritten" British constitution (no single document) is difficult to change. The socialization of political elites in a small country leads to a political culture in which custom and convention make participants reluctant to change practices which brought them to power.

Even though Britain is under the rule of law, that law is subject to change through parliamentary sovereignty. Instead of a written constitution with a complicated amending process, a simple majority of the House of Commons can change any law, even over the objections of the House of Lords if necessary. Individual rights are protected by ordinary law and custom, not an entrenched Bill of Rights.

Officially Britain remains a unitary state, with all constitutional authority belonging to the central government, rather than a federal state with a formal, even if vague, division of powers between the center and a lower level. Some commentators argue that Britain should be considered a "union-state," since the relationship of the four parts to the central government varies rather than being on the same terms. Although limited devolution has been utilized in the past, especially in Northern Ireland, 1921–1972, central government retains the authority to intervene in lower-level affairs, including local government matters. The voters are asked once every four or five years to choose a team of politicians to rule the central authority through the parliament at Westminster. Under the single member district, simple plurality electoral system, the outcome usually has been a single-party government (prime minister and cabinet) chosen based on a cohesive majority in the House of Commons, a fusion of power between the legislature and the executive. Referendums have been few and are formally only advisory; parliament retains final authority. The judiciary seldom makes politically important decisions, and even then it can be overridden by a parliamentary majority. Thus, in the United Kingdom almost any alteration of the interrelationship of political institutions can be considered constitutional in nature.

Constitutional issues were one of the few on which there were major party differences during the 1997 General Election campaign. Labor and the third party, the Liberal Democrats, had an agreed agenda for constitutional change, developed in consultation over several years. The Conservatives upheld traditional British constitutional principles, including the unwritten constitution, no guarantees of civil liberties except through the laws of Parliament, maintenance of the unitary state, and a

House of Lords composed of hereditary peers and some life peers, the latter appointed by the prime minister.

Other features of the British constitution have also resisted change. British government has been one of the most secretive among Western democracies, with unauthorized communication of information punishable by law. Large cities did not elect their own mayors or even their own metropolitan governing councils. The House of Commons is one of the few remaining legislatures elected by the single member district, simple plurality electoral system, which rewards a disproportionate share of parliamentary seats to larger parties having geographically concentrated voting strength. Thus Britain has continued to have an overwhelmingly two-party House of Commons despite having a multiparty electorate.

Even though the elected Labor government proposed to change some of these procedures and to consider reform in others, there were good reasons to doubt its commitment. Traditionally, constitutional reform has evoked little sustained interest within the party. Like the Conservatives, it has embraced the almost untrammeled formal power that the "elective dictatorship" of British parliamentary government provides for a single-party majority in the House of Commons. Although Labor sometimes voiced decentralist and reformist concerns when in opposition, in government it usually proved to be as centralist as the Conservatives.

## Labor's Constitutional Promises

There was general agreement that the most radical aspect of Labor's 1997 election manifesto was constitutional reform. This program was designed to stimulate the normally passive, relatively deferential British public into becoming more active citizens. In addition to parliamentary elections, they would vote for other levels of government with enhanced authority and have enhanced individual rights. More electoral opportunities, for different levels and within the voting process itself, would provide a wider range of choice for citizens.

Tony Blair had for some years advocated an infusion of a more participatory citizenship into British constitutional practices. In *New Britain* (Westview Press, 1997), Blair criticized British government as too centralized, secretive, and containing unrepresentative hereditary peers in the House of Lords. Blair called Labor's constitutional program "democratic renewal," argued that there had been 80 years of erosion of consent, self-government, and respect for rights under governments of both Left and Right, and contended that the mission of a Left-of-center party involves the extension of political rights as well as economic and social equality.

## How and Why Labor Developed a Program for Constitutional Change

Several events and trends focused Labor's thinking on constitutional reform as never before. Labor suffered four consec-

utive general election losses (1979, 1983, 1987, 1992) even though the Conservatives never achieved above 43 percent of the popular vote. Eighteen consecutive years out of government made Labor fearful of ever returning as a single-party government, which made it more attentive to arguments for a more limited central authority.

Groups interested in constitutional reform were not difficult to find. The third party in Britain, the Liberal Democrats, have long been advocating changing the electoral system to have their voting strength better represented in parliament as well as decentralization and increased protection for civil liberties. Since 1988, a nonpartisan lobby group, Charter 88, has not only proposed most of the reforms that Labor eventually embraced but also others, such as a full-scale written constitution and a bill of rights. Other influential thinkers on the moderate left argued that a precondition for social and economic change in an increasingly middle-class Britain was to encourage citizen involvement by limiting central government authority. In Scotland, where the Conservatives had continuously declined as an electoral force, the cross-party Scottish Constitutional Convention encouraged devolution of power. Eventually Labor and the Liberal Democrats [worked together] to form a pre-election commission on constitutional matters, which continued after the election in the form of a special cabinet committee on constitutional reform.

Skeptics have argued that public support for constitutional change is a mile wide and an inch deep. Surveys indicate that the public usually supports constitutional reform proposals in principle without understanding very much about the specifics. Intense minorities, such as Charter 88 and the Electoral Reform Society, have fueled the discussion. During the 1997 election campaign constitutional issues featured prominently in elite discussions of party differences but did not emerge as a critical voting issue, except perhaps in Scotland.

New Labor had multiple incentives in developing an agenda for constitutional change. It provided a clear sense of Labor distinctiveness from the Conservatives, especially important when there were so few differences in social and economic policy between the two parties. It was designed to alleviate threats to Labor support by Scottish and Welsh nationalist parties arguing for more autonomy. There was also the longer-term prospect of possibly realigning the party system by co-opting the Liberal Democrats and their issues into a more permanent government of the center, thereby reducing both the Conservatives and die-hard socialists of the Labor party left wing to permanent minority status. Even with the large majority of parliamentary seats that Labor gained in the May, 1997 election, the government did not abandon constitutional reform.

## Constitutional Change after Five Years of Labor Rule

No British government since the early twentieth century has presided over such a large agenda of constitutional reform. There are now new legislatures with devolved powers in

Northern Ireland, Scotland, and Wales. All but 92 hereditary peers have been removed from the House of Lords, and further deliberations have taken place over the second stage of Lords reform. A report from the Independent Commission on the Voting System advocated a change in the electoral system for the House of Commons, but no further government action has been taken. The European Convention on Human Rights has been incorporated into British law through the Human Rights Act. A weak Freedom of Information Act was also passed. In 1998, Londoners approved a proposal for the city to be governed by a directly-elected Mayor and the Assembly, and in 2000 the first election was held. Other cities have now adopted this measure through referendums.

New Labor immediately instituted some elements of its constitutional reform agenda. The referendums held in 1997 showed support for devolution to be stronger in Scotland than in Wales. The Scottish Parliament has more authority over policy and limited taxation powers while the Welsh Assembly has less authority and no taxation powers. Elections for both were held in 1999 under a combination of the traditional single member district, simply plurality electoral system and party list proportional representation, which yielded no clear majority in either legislature. Initially a Labor-Liberal Democrat coalition government was formed in Scotland and a minority Labor government in Wales. The latter was eventually replaced by another Labor-Liberal Democrat coalition. Labor has experienced problems in maintaining its party leaders in both governments; otherwise both have functioned largely as anticipated. No major disagreements on the constitutional allocation of powers have occurred. The second elections for the devolved legislatures will occur in May, 2003. The Welsh Assembly is expected to petition the Westminster government for greater powers, similar to those of the Scottish Parliament.

Eighty percent of the population of the United Kingdom, however, lives in England, which has been treated as a residual consideration in the plans for devolution. Tony Blair has indicated that Labor would be willing to form devolved governments in "regions with strong identities of their own," but, aside from the Northeast, there has been no substantial demand. Finally, in the Queen's Speech in fall, 2002, devolution legislation for English regions, based on a demonstrated willingness for it through a referendum vote, was promised.

The Mayor of London is the first modern directly-elected executive in the United Kingdom. The introduction of party primary elections for mayoral candidates led to less central party control over candidates and a personalization of the contest. The eventual winner was a dissident Labor MP and former London official, Ken Livingstone, who, however, has been relatively conciliatory in office.

Northern Ireland is a perennial problem, a hangover of the separation of Ireland from the United Kingdom in 1922. Six counties in the northern part of the island of Ireland, with approximately two-thirds of the population consisting of Protestants favoring continued union with Great Britain, remained in the United Kingdom. Many Catholics north and south remain convinced that there should be one, united country of Ireland on the island. This fundamental division of opinion concerning to which country the territory belongs led to organized violence by proponents of both sides, especially since the late 1960s. The Irish Republican Army (IRA) was the principal organization fighting for a united Ireland.

The current peace accord in Northern Ireland, the Good Friday Agreement of 1998, has led to new institutions there as well. In December 1999, devolution of power from the Westminster parliament to the Belfast parliament ushered in a period of what the British call "power sharing," or "consensus democracy." This entailed not only joint authority over internal matters by both Protestants (Unionists) and Catholics (Nationalists) through the requirement of super-majorities in the Northern Ireland Assembly and executive, but also some sharing of sovereignty over the territory between the United Kingdom and Ireland. Both countries have pledged, however, that Northern Ireland will remain part of the United Kingdom as long as a majority of the population in the province wishes. According to the latest census, Protestants remain in the majority, by 53 to 44 percent.

Referendums on the Good Friday Agreement passed overwhelmingly in both Northern Ireland and the Irish Republic, which repealed its constitutional claim to the province. As expected, devolved government in Northern Ireland has been rocky. Groups representing formerly armed adversaries, including Sinn Fein, closely linked to the IRA, now share executive power; some dissident factions have refused to renounce violence. The major issues have been continued; IRA terrorist activity in light of its relationship to Sinn Fein, incorporation of Catholics into the police service, and divisions among Protestants about how far to cooperate in the new government. In October, 2002, the Northern Ireland Assembly and government were suspended for the fourth time in three years, and direct rule from London was reinstituted, at least temporarily. The May, 2003 elections for a new assembly remain in place. The Northern Ireland government will continue to have a difficult path in working for peaceful solutions to long-intractable problems.

Britain signed the European Convention on Human Rights in 1951. Since 1966 it has allowed appeals to the European Court of Human Rights at Strasbourg, where it has lost more cases than any other country. Under New Labor, a law was quickly passed incorporating the European Convention on Human Rights into domestic law, but it only went into effect in October 2000. British judges rather than European judges now make the decisions about whether Britain is conforming to the Convention. This enhances the ability of British citizens to raise issues of human rights in domestic courts. Nevertheless, parliamentary sovereignty is maintained because Westminster remains the final authority on whether judicial decisions will be followed.

The tougher questions of constitutional reform—the electoral system for the House of Commons, freedom of information, and the House of Lords—were delayed. Currently the United Kingdom remains one of the most secretive democracies in the world, under the doctrine of executive prerogatives of Ministers of the Crown. The Freedom of Information Act eventually enacted is generally viewed as one which still allows the government to withhold a large amount of information.

Superficially House of Lords reform appears simple since a government majority in the House of Commons eventually can override any objections. Because of the capacity of the Lords to delay legislation, however, reform is difficult to complete in a timely fashion. In fact, discussion of reform of the Lords has been ongoing for 90 years. New Labor pledged to abolish voting by hereditary peers, initially leaving only the prime-ministerially appointed life peers, often senior political figures, as constituting a second chamber. There is fear, however, that the power of the Commons would be enhanced even further if "Tony's Cronies," as critics have dubbed prime ministerial appointees, constituted an entirely patronage-based second chamber. In order to accomplish initial reform, Prime Minister Blair accepted a temporary arrangement in 1999 allowing 92 hereditary peers to remain in the 720-member House of Lords, while eliminating 600 others. He then appointed a Royal Commission on the House of Lords (Wakeham Commission) to consider the second stage of Lords reform.

After the Wakeham Commission reported, in 2001 the government proposed a 600-member chamber, with 60 percent appointed by the prime minister on the basis of party affiliations, 20 percent nonpartisan "cross-benchers" appointed by an independent commission, and 20 percent elected on a regional basis through party list proportional representation. This would occur over a transition period of ten years. The government's plans were greeted with widespread skepticism from all parties, especially because of the low proportion of elected representatives. In an attempt to generate a cross-party consensus, a joint committee of MPs and peers was established to reexamine the question. In December, 2002, the Committee initially reported a list of seven options for further discussion, ranging from a fully elected to a fully appointed second chamber. It is now hoped that agreement on the second stage of Lords reform can be reached by the end of Labor's second term in office.

Although the Prime Minister indicated that he was not "personally convinced" that a change in the electoral system was needed, he appointed an Independent Commission on the Voting System (Jenkins Commission) to recommend an alternative to the current electoral system for the House of Commons. In 1998, the Commission recommended what is called "Alternative Vote Plus." The single-member district system would be retained, but instead of casting a vote for one person only, the electorate would rank candidates in order of preference, thus assuring a majority rather than a plurality vote for the winner. There would also be a second vote for a "preferred party." These votes would be put into a regional pool, with 15–20 percent of the total seats being awarded to parties based on their proportional share of these second votes, a favorable development for smaller parties.

Even such a relatively mild reform, however, generated substantial political controversy, as expected when the very basis on which legislators hold their seats is challenged. The proposed change has been criticized not only by the opposition Conservatives, but also by Labor members because it might make it more difficult for Labor to obtain a single-party parliamentary majority. There are no prospects for enactment of Westminster electoral system reform in the near future.

Some analysts, however, argue that the most significant constitutional change in the United Kingdom has been brought about not by Labor but by three actions of Conservative governments—joining the European Community (now European Union) in 1972, approving the *Single European Act* (1986), and signing the *Maastricht Treaty* (1992). Within the ever-expanding areas of EU competence, EU law supersedes British law, including judicial review by the European Court of Justice. Already one-third of total legislation in the United Kingdom comes from the European Union. Famously, Lord Denning observed that the European Union is an incoming tide which cannot be held back. The current process of the European Constitutional Convention may lead to further government integration among the members.

Britain remains one of only three EU members not to join the new European currency, the euro. If Britain were to join the euro, then control over monetary policy as well would effectively pass into the hands of the European Union. Tony Blair had indicated that this step would only be taken with public support in a countrywide referendum. It is widely expected that the government will call for such a referendum before the end of its second full term of office in 2006.

Although not on the Labor party agenda of constitutional change, the role of the monarchy has also come under increased scrutiny in recent years. The Queen's Golden Jubilee Year, celebrating the first 50 years of her reign (2002), was not a happy one, with two deaths and more scandals in the royal family. A resolution of the Scottish Parliament, supported by some MPs and Lords at Westminster, petitions the government to allow the monarch either to be or to marry a Catholic. Currently this is forbidden by the *Act of Settlement* (1701), passed at the end of a period of religious wars. The heir to the throne, Prince Charles, has proposed removing the monarch's particular tie to the Church of England in favor of the title of a more general "defender of faith" in what is now, despite appearances, a secularized country.

More vaguely, the government has suggested moving toward a "people's monarchy"—a simpler, slimmer, and less ritualized institution, perhaps with a gender-neutral inheritance. This would be more like the low profile "bicycle monarchs" of some other European countries. For the first time since Queen Victoria, there is substantial, if muted, public expression of anti-monarchism (republicanism). Tampering with an established and still widely revered institution such as the monarchy, however, requires extremely careful consideration, as many traditionalists are opposed to all change.

## Conflicting Views on the Effects of Constitutional Change

Labor's program of constitutional renewal already has brought about some changes in Britain. Instead of near-uniform use of the single member district, simple plurality electoral system, now there are five different systems in operation: Single Transferable Vote (a form of proportional representation with candidate choice) in Northern Ireland, party list proportional representation for the June, 1999 European Parliament election, alternative member systems (a combination of single member district and party list proportional) for the devolved legislatures in Scotland and Wales and the London Assembly, and a popularly elected executive through the Supplementary Vote (voting for two candidates in order of preference) for London. Plurality elections remain the norm only for the House of Commons at Westminster and English local government elections.

Until 1997, there had been only four referendums in the history of the United Kingdom. Within nine months of taking power, Labor held four additional referendums (in Wales, Scotland, Northern Ireland, and London), with two others promised, on changing the Westminster electoral system and on joining the European single currency.

Broadly, five interpretations of these developments have been voiced by commentators, as outlined below. We might term these the (1) popular social liberalism, (2) lukewarm reform, (3) symbolic politics, (4) the doomsday scenario, and (5) constitutional incoherence. These contending explanations exist at least partially because Labor itself has never outlined a coherent theory behind its constitutional reforms beyond Blair's pre-election formulations. There has been no general constitutional convention; instead there have been a series of *ad hoc* measures.

The well-known American analyst of Britain, Samuel H. Beer, has compared Blair's reforms to the popular social liberalism of the early twentieth century Liberal governments, which included restricting the power of the House of Lords and devolving power to Ireland. After the First World War, however, electorally the Conservatives came to dominate a political Left divided between an insurgent Labor Party and the remaining Liberals. At least in the first term of office, social and constitutional reform served as a substitute for a more traditional Labor program of increased government spending. It is considered important as an element to help establish the long-term political dominance of a revitalized center-left.

Another constitutional scholar, Philip Norton, argues that New Labor's proposals are radical in concept but so far moderate in form and effects, e.g., lukewarm reform. Similarly, Anthony Barnett of Charter 88 claims that the government practices *constitutus interruptus*. Another British academic, Patrick Dunleavy, has suggested that constitutional reform for New Labor represents continuous but financially cheap activity at a time when the government is wary of alienating its middle-class supporters by appearing to be another Labor "tax and spend" administration. This amounts to little substantive change, however, until the two critical questions, electoral reform for the House of Commons and membership of the euro, are faced.

Although there has been grudging acceptance from constitutional conservatives who originally opposed change, they are still fearful of the implications of some reforms. The Conservative former editor of *The Times*, William Rees-Mogg, envisioned Labor's constitutional changes eroding democracy in the United Kingdom through a semi-permanent Labor-Liberal governing coalition in Westminster, Scotland, and Wales, a House

of Lords based on patronage, and a more centralized, bureaucratic European superstate. More sanguinely, *The Economist* foresaw a weakening of Westminster's authority through the combined forces of devolution and a more integrated European Union. But by the election of 2001, the Conservative party claimed that it could make devolved institutions work more efficiently as well as maintaining the integrity of an independent House of Lords. However, they continue to oppose a more centralized Europe and a changed electoral system.

Finally, the prominent British political scientist Anthony King has argued that Britain no longer has a coherent set of constitutional principles. Because of the piecemeal constitutional changes over the past quarter century by both Conservative and Labor governments, traditional interpretations of the British constitution no longer adequately describe contemporary practice, but there also is no set of alternative principles as a guide. Britain has moved away from majoritarian democracy without becoming a fully-fledged consensus democracy with proportional representation and coalition governments.

Despite its prominence in the election of 1997 and in New Labor's first term of government, constitutional reform was only a minor feature of the 2001 general election campaign. While the Liberal Democrats, as expected, gave it greater attention, all of the major parties deemphasized constitutional reform in their party manifestos. This was particularly surprising for Labor, which was content to claim that it had delivered on its 1997 commitments. Of Labor's "25 major goals for Britain," the only one touching on constitutional reform was a vague pledge for greater local democracy. Notably absent was any commitment to call a referendum on the Westminster electoral system. While some moves have been made to establish devolved regions in England and to complete Lords reform, as well to deal with the continuing problems in Northern Ireland, overall constitutional reform has been less prominent in Labor's second term of office.

## Unintended Consequences Over the Horizon?

Institutional rearrangements often have unanticipated consequences. Although New Labor legislation on constitutional matters claims not to disturb the principle of parliamentary sovereignty, the likelihood is that this constitutional convention will be compromised even more than it already has been under Britain's membership of the European Union. Congruent with the process of decentralization in other European countries, devolution is likely to be entrenched *de facto* if no *de jure*. Some journalists have begun calling British a "federal" political system. Although specific powers are granted to each devolved government, disputes over which level has authority over certain policies are likely to arise. Even without a comprehensive Bill of Rights, incorporation of the European Convention on Human Rights may mean a stronger, more politically active judiciary, a form of creeping judicial review. House of Lords reform, if it is not to be simply an appointed chamber reflecting the wishes of the government of the day, could also lead to a more symmetrical bicameralism.

Incorporation of the European Convention on Human Rights, as well as a limited form of joint authority with Ireland over Northern Ireland and possible membership of the European common currency and central bank, suggest that Britain may be moving into new patterns of international shared authority in areas heretofore considered exclusively within the domain of the sovereign state. Regional policies of the European Union even may be helping stimulate ethnonationalist demands. If the Scottish National Party, still committed to independence for Scotland, ever wins a majority in the Scottish Parliament, the United Kingdom could be faced with a "Quebec scenario," whereby control of a level of government enhances rather than retards its secessionist claims.

The "third way" ideas of Anthony Giddens, influential in the New Labor government, advocate a restructuring of government to promote "subsidiarity" (the taking of decisions at the lowest level possible) and correcting the "democratic deficit" through constitutional reform, greater transparency, and more local democracy. In such a process, Britain would become a more complex polity institutionally. This would demand cultivating habits of conciliation, cooperation, and consent rather than the usual reliance upon parliamentary laws and executive orders. Having additional levels of elected government already has created difficulties for central party organizations attempting to exert control over who becomes the party leader in these jurisdictions.

The electoral system, however, may be the lynchpin of the British parliamentary system as it currently exists. Even the relatively modest changes proposed by the Jenkins Commission might help realign the party system. Because of the fears this arouses within the Labor party, Prime Minister Blair has dealt with electoral reform at Westminster by indefinitely postponing it.

Whatever one's view of the desirability and impact of the changes, New Labor under Tony Blair has pursued and largely fulfilled its 1997 pledges on constitutional reform. Although delays and retreats have occurred on some issues, the implications of these changes will continue to be felt in British politics for some time to come.

---

**Donley T. Studlar is Eberly Family Distinguished Professor of Political Science at West Virginia University, Executive Secretary of the British Politics Group, and author of *Great Britain: Decline or Renewal?* (Westview Press). This article originated as the 1998 Taft Lecture, delivered to the undergraduate Honors recognition ceremony of the Political Science Department, University of Cincinnati.**

---

*This is a revised version of an article which first appeared in *Harvard International Review,* Spring 1999.

## The second term

# Tony's big ambitions

If Tony Blair is to achieve his ambitions for the second term,
he will have to make choices—and enemies

THIS time it really is "historic". No previous Labour prime minister has been re-elected with a majority big enough to carry him through a full second term. From the moment of his 1997 victory, Mr Blair was haunted by this history of failure and determined not to repeat it. This made him cautious; and the caution made him puzzling. He has admitted that the first phase of New Labour was designed to reassure voters that Labour would not again make its old mistakes: trade unions could expect no special favours; there would be no old-style tax and spend; business would be welcomed as a partner. The precious second term allows him at last to show his true colours. But what are they?

To some, Mr Blair is Bill Clinton minus the complications (and minus the charisma, too). But David Marquand, a former Labour MP and now an Oxford don, draws a parallel with Margaret Thatcher. Like Lady Thatcher, Mr Blair's political genius lies in having reached across familiar ideological boundaries to the core constituency of his opponents. Both have a rootless quality. She was cut off by sex and he is cut off by upbringing from the cultures of their respective parties. Mr Blair calls this a strength: he is proud not to fit into the conventional political categories. It may also be his weakness: according to Mr Marquand, Mr Blair differs from Lady Thatcher in that he has not yet found a distinctive ideology of his own.

### The things he did

You do not need an ideology in order to be busy. After 18 years out of office, Labour burst back in 1997 like a cork popping from a champagne bottle. Mr Blair freed the Bank of England and rewrote much of the British constitution. He half-repaired relations with the European Union by signing the "social chapter", promoting a more independent European defence policy and promising—pending a referendum—to join the euro. He pushed Britain to the forefront of NATO's Kosovo war and negotiated a half-peace in Northern Ireland. He launched a "New Deal" for the young unemployed and imposed a minimum wage.

He also made mistakes—and showed a rare ability to recover from them. The Millennium Dome became a symbol of incompetence. A protest against fuel taxes brought Britain to a standstill. Mr Blair was forced—twice—to sack his friend Peter Mandelson from the cabinet. But none of this damaged the government for long. On balance, and especially given Gordon Brown's successful management of the economy, it was a successful first term.

This does not make it a reliable pointer to the second. Now that he has reassured Britain, Mr Blair wants to transform it, not just run it competently the way it is. This puts him squarely in the Labour tradition—except for one complication. Winning power entailed creating New Labour, which in turn meant throwing away the tools—state ownership and planning, crude redistribution—that previous Labour prime ministers relied on. What can he do without them?

Through the cloud of speeches, three ambitions stand out. Mr Blair wants to change Britain's position in the world, to "modernise" its politics and to re-engineer the welfare state. With a renewed mandate, plus all the political capital he hoarded during the first term, he can be forgiven for fancying his chances. But he might still fail.

### Britain in the world

Mr Blair is no "declinist". He believes that Britain can lead in Europe, not just take its place as a loyal member of the Union. Nor does he accept that leading in Europe implies weakening Britain's bond with America. He argues that Britain has a "pivotal" role in world politics by virtue of its seat on the Security Council, closeness to the United States, membership of the European Union and the G7, the credibility of its armed forces and the power of the English language. Mr Blair has relished cutting a dash on the world scene as an evangelist for his "third way", saviour of Kosovo and the first western leader to befriend Russia's President Putin.

The second term could bring this world-bestriding statesman down to earth with a bump. In some foreign eyes, traffic jams, stalled trains and pyres of burning cows have turned Cool Britannia back into the sick man of Europe. Mr Blair is not going to be able to re-create with George Bush, his ideological opposite, the affinity he had with Bill Clinton. Gerhard Schröder, the German chancellor who seemed for a while to defer to the more experienced British prime minister, shows declining interest in Britain's third way. Lionel Jospin was never a fan. When Mr Blair told the French parliament that "what matters is what works", the French prime minister was unimpressed. A market economy was all very well, he said later, but not the "market society" which French Socialists suspect Mr Blair of trying to foist on Europe.

Besides, to change Britain's position in the world, Mr Blair has to change Britain's attitude to Europe. This a harder job than it may sound in the immediate afterglow of re-election. He says that he wants to re-solve British ambivalence towards the mainland "once and for all", but the opposite has happened on his watch so far. Since 1997, the British have become more suspicious of the EU, not less. More than seven out of ten oppose joining the euro, almost half favour leaving the EU itself and most of those who would like to stay would also like to trim the EU's powers.

This is a fragile base from which to win the euro referendum he has promised to call when the five economic tests for entry laid down by Mr Brown have been met. Mr Blair promises to pronounce on these tests within two years, which gives him precious little time to turn opinion in favour of the euro even if he could be confident that developments on the mainland would buttress his arguments for joining. The chances are that they will not.

Lady Thatcher said in Bruges 13 years ago that she had not rolled back the frontiers of the state in Britain only in order to see them re-imposed from Brussels by a European super-state. Mr Blair offers two answers to this. First, he dismisses as "theology" the possibility of the EU becoming a super-state. At last December's Nice summit, Mr Blair infuriated some of his European partners by blocking some of their steps towards "ever closer union". Second, he claims that Britain is winning the economic argument inside Europe. His prize exhibit here is the Lisbon summit of March 2000, after which he boasted that the EU had moved decisively from the mainland's "old social model" towards a less regulated and more open economy.

Really? The "theology" of the superstate still has believers on the mainland. The German chancellor and foreign minister are more (in the case of Joschka Fischer, the foreign minister) or less (in the case of Mr Schröder) frank advocates of turning the EU into something akin to such a state. Mr Jospin talked a fortnight ago about the need for a European "economic government". As for winning Europe's economic argument, this claim is premature. After Lisbon, a summit this year in Stockholm was a flop. Plenty of mainland politicians continue to say that the EU's job is, precisely, to protect Europe's social model from the cold winds of globalisation.

Mr Blair claims that Britain has no need to choose between America and Europe. The closer Britain is to each, he says, the greater its value to both. But here, too, the matter is not quite settled. During the Kosovo war Britain was a bridge, if a wobbly one, between the two halves of the Atlantic alliance. It may be harder in the second term for Mr Blair to bridge the gap between the EU and an American administration with uncongenial views on climate change, missile defence, China and the Middle East. Mr Blair insists that the EU's defence initiative poses no threat to the primacy of NATO. Some in the French government hope it will do just that.

## A new politics

"Are you a pluralist or a control freak?", Paddy Ashdown, the former leader of the Liberal Democrats, asked Mr Blair. The answer is still pending. Mr Blair protests that no control freak would have complicated his own life by devolving power to new parliaments and assemblies in Scotland, Wales, Northern Ireland and London. But far from proving that Mr Blair is a pluralist at heart, his reforms have persuaded many people of the opposite. The disappointed constitutional reformers of Charter 88, a pressure group that was thrilled by Labour's election in 1997, ran an advertising campaign during this one depicting the prime minister as a Pinocchio, with a fibber's nose to match.

It is possible that Mr Blair is genuine when he says that one of his ambitions is to "reconnect" people with politics. But he does not appear to see constitutional change as the instrument. His first-term reforms, inherited in the main from John Smith, the former party leader, were not conceived with pluralism in mind. Scottish devolution was a way to head off the Scot-

tish Nationalists' demand for independence, and the Welsh assembly was offered because Wales would otherwise have resented Scotland's Parliament. The Northern Ireland Assembly was part of an attempt to end the province's civil war—a virtuous aim in itself but not evidence of a general preference for spreading power from the centre.

If Mr Blair had really believed in that, he would not have tried in both Wales and London to override local preferences by putting his own lieutenants in charge of the new power centres; nor neutered his own government's Freedom of Information Act; nor ruled out, as Labour's manifesto seems to, turning the House of Lords into an all-elected chamber. He could have pushed devolution further in England, and called the referendum on voting reform which he promised both to Mr Ashdown and to the voters of 1997. But on the eve of this week's poll he mused about the disproportionate power proportional representation tends to give small parties. In retrospect, the lofty talk of using voting reform to herald a "progressive" realignment in British politics seems to have been so much flannel intended to keep the third party sweet in case he needed it.

Will Mr Blair use the second term to make amends? Further reform of the Lords, devolution in England and another look at proportional representation make cautious appearances in Labour's manifesto. If, as some argue, Mr Blair is the true heir of Gladstone, valuing diversity for its own sake, he will seize these opportunities to weaken the power of the over-mighty centre. But as Vernon Bogdanor, a professor of government at Oxford University, points out, this would mark a break with Labour's past. A party intent on engineering equal social outcomes, across regions as well as classes, is bound to think that doing so requires a centralised state. Mr Blair is no socialist, and not much of an egalitarian either (he believes in "equal worth", not equality). But he is no less keen than his Labour predecessors were on using the state to engineer desired outcomes. This is the idea at the heart of his third way.

## A new welfare state

Mr Blair talks of imposing a third post-war "settlement" on Britain, one that will combine and transcend Attlee's creation of the welfare state after 1945 and Lady Thatcher's pro-market reforms after 1979. The linking of opposites is to be achieved by the third way, the main idea of which is

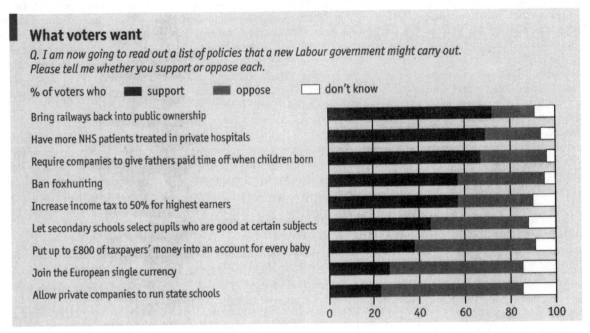

## What voters want

Q. I am now going to read out a list of policies that a new Labour government might carry out.
Please tell me whether you support or oppose each.

% of voters who ■ support ■ oppose □ don't know

Bring railways back into public ownership

Have more NHS patients treated in private hospitals

Require companies to give fathers paid time off when children born

Ban foxhunting

Increase income tax to 50% for highest earners

Let secondary schools select pupils who are good at certain subjects

Put up to £800 of taxpayers' money into an account for every baby

Join the European single currency

Allow private companies to run state schools

0    20    40    60    80    100

Source: MORI, sample of 1,010 adults (June 4th–5th 2001), interviewed by telephone

to make the state cleverer and more entrepreneurial, helping citizens to help themselves rather than spooning out "bog-standard" (as Mr Blair's spokesman called comprehensive schools) services through unimaginative bureaucracies.

This vision does not entail shrinking the state, as Thatcherism tried to. Mr Blair resents nothing more than being labelled a softer sort of Tory. He continues to believe in the power of government to make the lives of people better, even to make them better people. He sees the need for a "post-Thatcherite revitalisation and renewal of collective provision". Whereas Lady Thatcher deliberately lowered citizens' expectations of what the state could do for them, Mr Blair spent his first term—and this election—raising expectations.

He will not be able to meet them just by spending more on public services, though there will be a lot more cash for a while. Having built up big surpluses for its first two years, the government is to increase spending over the next three years by almost 4% a year, with rises of 6% for health and education, and 11% for transport. But the relief will be temporary. Since this is faster than the growth rate of the economy, it cannot go on indefinitely without raising taxes. The Institute for Fiscal Studies reckons that Mr Blair would need to increase taxation by £5 billion ($7 billion) a year if he wanted to extend his spending spree beyond three years.

Mr Blair's hope is that the extra money will strip public-service providers of their excuse to resist his big reforms. Labour promises in the second term to "hit the ground running". Immediate ideas include streamlining the machinery of government, for example by bringing employment and social security under one roof in a new ministry of work and the family, and creating a "policy-delivery unit" in Downing Street.

Tinkering with the machinery of government will be easier than finding a formula to rejuvenate Britain's public services. So far, the nearest thing to a big idea is a proposal to make greater use of the private sector and sweep away outdated demarcations. What does it matter, asks Mr Blair, whether a particular hospital is private, so long as the service is free at the point of use? But public-service unions from Unison to the British Medical Association have already voiced dismay at what they call this "back-door privatisation". Polls suggest that wider opinion is hostile to running public services at a profit. If this is his big idea for the second term, Mr Blair will have to overcome widespread prejudices as well as vested interests.

That would be a fight worth having, if the prize were indeed the transformation of public services. But Mr Blair's thinking on this is still a study in vagueness. There is no great merit in using private money to finance public services: quite often, this merely raises the cost to taxpayers with no offsetting benefit, apart from hiding that long-term consequence for a decade or two if the money is borrowed. Nor is there much point in Mr Blair turning to private providers if he will not embrace the heresy that users of public services have a better understanding of their requirements than Whitehall does. If he grasped this, Mr Blair would introduce real competition into public services so that schools and hospitals could fight it out for publicly funded clients, with the government concentrating on ensuring that everyone, regardless of income, has the means to get better services and make his preferences count.

## Time to make choices, and enemies

Behind Mr Blair's blokeish manner is a compulsive competitor. His tennis partners say that he cannot bear to lose. But he also hates confrontation. He showed in Kosovo that he can be daring, but his watchword is caution. He would sooner bring a convert inside his big tent than make an unnecessary enemy. His biographer, John Rentoul, says he likes to string people along and keep options open, while waiting to see what falls into his lap.

The second term will provide fewer opportunities for prevarication and more for making enemies. A MORI poll this week for *The Economist* (see chart) suggests that he will face pressure to do things he has ruled out (such as renationalising the railways and increasing income-tax rates) and opposition to the things he wants to do (joining the euro, letting private companies run state schools, increasing school selection).

What of his three big ambitions? If Mr Blair's destiny is to settle Britain in Europe "once and for all", he cannot use Mr Brown's five tests to keep his euro-options open indefinitely, even if closing them means conflict with his chancellor. If he is really to modernise British politics, the pluralist in him will have to drive out the control freak, even if this makes his other aims harder to achieve. If he is to transform the public services, he will have to be bolder about competition, even if this means war with the unions. The danger otherwise is of stepping on to the familiar treadmill of higher spending and taxes, followed by disappointed expectations, followed by higher spending and taxes.

Like Lady Thatcher, Mr Blair does not want for self-belief: this is what they admire in one another. She had her "wets"; he is hemmed in by the Labour movement's own forces of conservatism. The difference is that she was fortified by a clear ideology which everybody in her administration could understand, and which gave them a sense of direction. If Mr Blair has an ideology, it is to run with the hare and hunt with the hounds. Only he knows exactly which way he is heading.

# Laborites Meet and Blair Takes a Beating

By WARREN HOGE

BLACKPOOL, England, Sept. 30—This working-class resort on the Irish Sea is the busiest vacation spot in Britain, but delegates to the Labor Party annual conference here were in no holiday mood today as they greeted their leader, Prime Minister Tony Blair.

Their anger at him boiled over on two issues: his unflagging support for President Bush in the campaign against Iraq and his government's determination to raise funds for Britain's crippled public services by tapping private money.

Mr. Blair has been Labor's most successful leader and the party holds a 165-seat majority in Parliament. But the debate in the cavernous beachfront convention hall was as boisterous as in the days before he refined the party organization, rid it of its socialist orthodoxy, calmed the customary feuding and made it a unified and commanding political force in Britain.

Mr. Blair suffered a rare defeat this afternoon when 68 percent of the delegates voted for a trade union motion calling on the government to reconsider its so-called private finance initiative, allowing the use of private contractors for public services.

On Iraq, a motion was defeated that would have barred British support for military action against Iraq under any circumstances, but only by 60 percent to 40 percent. Another that would permit such action if it were sanctioned by the United Nations was approved.

Tony Benn, a retired member of Parliament and veteran left-winger, said waging war in Iraq would amount to "tearing up" the United Nations Charter. "The problem for the prime minister," he said, "is not the Labor conference. It is the people of Britain, and half the people of the U.S., who regard war as a total and absolute denial of the principles of the U.N."

Mr. Blair speaks to the conference himself on Tuesday, and he has already declared that while he will listen to his critics, he will not be dissuaded from sticking to his plans. Digging in ahead of today's debates, he said he would continue to insist on forcing Saddam Hussein to disarm and would not call any halt to involving private contractors to build schools and hospitals. The party votes are not binding on the government.

Blackpool was the traditional place for Labor conferences until four years ago, when the party abandoned the town for more polished English Channel resorts like Brighton and Bournemouth that were felt to be more in keeping with the modern party that Mr. Blair calls New Labor.

In returning today, the party found that the tradition of bruising debate in the gaudy Winter Garden Center seemed to be just as much a permanent fixture of Blackpool as the candy floss stands, rows of rooming houses with geranium pots on the windowsills and the shorefront knockoff of the Eiffel Tower for which the town is known.

Restoring public services is the principal demand of British voters, and that has focused the government on the need to move quickly. But while ministers have signaled that they will not be deterred from using private companies for public projects, they have been alarmed at the strength of the unions in fighting back.

Bill Morris, a senior union leader, made a passionate speech declaring that the plan was a betrayal of the postwar project cherished by Labor that led to the creation of the National Health Service and the British welfare state. "I for one have no wish to move on from the founding principle," he said, describing that fundamental standard as "publicly funded, publicly delivered and publicly accountable."

But with Mr. Blair looking on and applauding his encouragement, Gordon Brown, the powerful chancellor of the exchequer, defended the program as the only way to keep Labor's promise to build much-needed modern schools and hospitals without unsustainable borrowing. "We must keep our promise to the people," he said.

In a throwback to old Labor conference behavior, Mr. Brown's senior minister, Paul Boateng, was heckled with shouts of "rubbish" and "sit down" and drowned out by protesting hand clapping. Britain's labor movement has been emboldened by the election of former Communists and other militants to the leadership of major unions. They have made the government's program to use private contractors their main target.

A succession of union leaders took the podium to take on what they called "creeping privatization." They charged that the government was taking away worker protections, wasting taxpayer money and giving business a chance to make windfall profits.

"The taxpayer is being ripped off," said Mick Rix, leader of the train drivers' union. "The public can see that we are mortgaging our kids' future basically to make the fat cats fatter."

# Scandals and Squabbles Weigh Down Britain's Sinking Tories

## By WARREN HOGE

BOURNEMOUTH, England, Oct. 7— Britain's Conservative party opened its annual conference in this English Channel resort today against a backdrop of plummeting poll ratings, fresh news of a sex scandal and speculation over efforts to oust its leader, Iain Duncan Smith.

Beleaguered officials said they hoped to point to the future, but in their speeches and remarks, they appeared more agitated by the past.

"In recent years, a number of politicians have behaved disgracefully and then compounded their offenses by trying to evade responsibility," said Theresa May, the party chairwoman. "We all know who they are. Let's face it, some of them have stood on this platform."

She did not mention names, and she did not have to. The press has been dominated by stories about former Prime Minister John Major's newly revealed affair in the 1980's with former Health Minister Edwina Currie; by the syndicated prison diaries of the party's disgraced former deputy leader, Jeffrey Archer, the millionaire novelist and a member of the House of Lords; and by the diary of Alan Clark, a Tory minister and roguish bon vivant who died in 1999 and was famous for seducing a mother and her two daughters and then writing a best-selling book about it and other conquests.

In addition, a number of Conservative officials this weekend questioned the effectiveness of Mr. Duncan Smith, a little-known former military man. He was the surprise choice as leader of the party a year ago, when William Hague stepped down the day after the party suffered its second successive electoral loss to the Labor Party.

Malcolm Rifkind, a former foreign secretary and defense secretary, criticized Mr. Duncan Smith for not challenging the government over its policy on Iraq. Former Deputy Prime Minister Michael Heseltine faulted the party's leader's lack of charisma and was reported to be discussing his removal with party colleagues. A former transportation minister, Steven Norris, described Mr. Duncan Smith's reform agenda as "intellectually incoherent"; John Gummer, a former party chairman, accused Mr. Duncan Smith of surrounding himself with assistants who were weak and out of touch; and Kenneth Clarke, a former chancellor of the exchequer, said that Mr. Duncan Smith had yet to have any effect as the party leader.

"It isn't so much about it's going badly," Mr. Clarke told The Sunday Telegraph. "It's just not going."

Commenting on this outburst of internal fractiousness, Ms. May told the delegates, "Some Tories have indulged themselves in petty feuding or personal sniping instead of getting behind a leader who is doing an enormous amount to change a party which has suffered two massive landslide defeats."

On arriving here Sunday night, Mr. Duncan Smith dismissed talk of unease in the ranks and compared himself to Margaret Thatcher, who faced dissent after her first year in leadership in 1976 and stayed on to become a dominant figure in British political history. He conceded that "there will always be some who disagree" but added, "I am going to show this week that we have broken free of the public perception of us."

He said he would be proposing 25 new policies to the conference that would focus on "quality of life" issues rather than the traditional Tory territory of taxes, family values and independence from overbearing European bureaucracy. They are to be published in a pamphlet which party officials said would give fresh direction to the party the way a similar publication, "The Right Approach," prompted a Conservative rebound under Lady Thatcher.

Once commonly referred to as the natural party of government, the Conservatives are battling to remain even second in popularity to Labor.

In a series of preconference polls, Mr. Duncan Smith came in third as the most suitable person to be prime minister, behind Mr. Blair and the leader of the Liberal Democrats, Charles Kennedy. The liberals had been the distant third force in British politics for more than 80 years.

The Conservatives have foundered since losing office to Mr. Blair's recast "New Labor," which has adopted some traditionally Tory stances. Labor has left the Tories struggling to appear fresh and original.

Gentlemanly to the point of priggishness, Mr. Duncan Smith has so far been no match for the glamorous, telegenic Mr. Blair.

Mr. Duncan Smith's potentially most formidable opponent in the party, Mr. Clarke, put out word this weekend that he might be available for a challenge. He lost convincingly to Mr. Duncan Smith in the leadership runoff a year ago, largely because of his pro-Europe stance, but he remains the more experienced politician with a bruising debating style and the kind of glad-handing, pub-counter personality that may be necessary to win back disaffected Tory voters from middle England.

A year's acquaintance with the colorless style of Mr. Duncan Smith may have made Mr. Clarke a more competitive alternative.

# Second place up for grabs, Kennedy believes

## Opposition Party ready to displace Tories, leader will say

**Patrick Wintour,**
**chief political correspondent**

**Thursday September 26, 2002**
*The Guardian*

Charles Kennedy will claim today that politics is in a state of flux unknown for a century and assert that his party has the capacity to overtake the Conservatives as the chief opposition party of Britain.

In his set piece conference speech in Brighton, the Liberal Democrat leader, buoyed by a strong performance on Iraq in the Commons, will make his boldest claim yet that his party can end its status as the perennial third party of postwar Britain.

His speech will, however, stop short of the bloated and ultimately absurd claim by a previous party leader, David Steel, in 1985 that the Liberals should go home and prepare for government.

His aides believe it is a realistic ambition to increase the party's crop of 53 MPs and overtake the Tories in two general elections. The bulk of the Liberal Democrat gains will have to be made in Tory seats.

Mr Kennedy will tell his audience: "British politics is up for grabs in a way that it has not been for 100 years. The prize is very great. There is no law that suggests that when the Conservative party is down, it must come up again. And there is no law that suggests that the Liberal Democrats must remain third among British parties."

He will claim that the Conservative party is "going backwards" and the "trouble with the Tory party is not just individual personalities or policies. It is the party itself. They look faded, they sound jaded."

He will also say: "The Conservatives are the party of yesteryear and the Liberal Democrats the party of tomorrow."

He will base this assertion on the growing number of surveys showing Liberal Democrat support among young people rising.

His campaign team recognises that he needs at least a 5% swing to start challenging the Tories in their heartlands, and probably needs a high profile byelection in a Tory marginal to test the party's credibility.

The latest *Guardian* poll shows Labour support starting to erode, but with little sign that the bulk of disenchanted Labour voters are going towards Mr Kennedy.

However, Mr Kennedy believes the party is on strong intellectual and strategic ground after the conference this week adopted a set of policies on public services that shifts the emphasis from demanding extra spending and instead proposes new systems of service delivery, including decentralisation to the regions and a variety of service providers, including the private sector.

The ditching of the party's tax and spend image is seen by Mr Kennedy as the single biggest achievement of this conference. The change was achieved by skilful political management which avoided the threatened public rows with the party's frontbench education and health spokesmen. But it has left some of the younger Liberal Democrat MPs restless that the review did not go further.

Mr Kennedy believes that the Tory party will be unable, with any credibility, to follow the Liberal Democrats down the road of decentralisation, given the previous Tory government's record of reining back local council power.

The Liberal Democrats are also pleased they have shifted to a slightly tougher policy on crime, an area in which the party's libertarian instincts have been seen to put it on the side of the culprit, rather than the victim.

Mr Kennedy's camp believes the party also holds an advantage by adopting its new policy positions early in the parliament, well ahead of the Tories, giving Mr Kennedy time to get his new messages across to the electorate.

Mr Kennedy himself, after a low key year, has also been given a boost by mapping out a distinctive and quizzical position on Iraq. Foreign policy was always a field in which his predecessor Paddy Ashdown thrived, but Mr Kennedy, with little relevant experience, had until now failed to convey any authority.

# France?
# It's like 1970s America

## Joe Klein

**Tuesday May 28, 2002**
*The Guardian*

An act of nostalgia: I approach Europe by sea, on the Dover-Calais ferry. This is how I first encountered the continent in the summer of 1966. The ferry has changed. It is a floating duty-free commerce and gambling parlour now; open-air access is limited to a scruffy patch of deck aft on the topmost level. There are no signs pointing the way, perhaps because nothing is being sold out there.

But it is glorious in the fresh air, a calm sunny day on the channel. A group of British schoolkids in maroon uniforms chase each other about the deck and feed seagulls, which appear to be set on hover. From halfway across the water, the Dover cliffs remain formidable and proud; ahead, France is misty, not nearly so well defined. But it is France, none the less: I remember the anticipation of 1966—I approached Europe then with Hemingwayesque intent. I would run with the bulls in Pamplona; lounge in the cafes of Paris and say things like, "The wine, it is very good." I would endure a few museums and chase after dark-eyed lovelies with narrow waists, sharp features and difficult personalities.

In other words, I approached Europe then as most Americans have for the past half-century: anticipating an adult theme park. One went there to find history, culture, sophistication and, of course, naughtiness. One was daunted by the sophistication, but there was condescension as well: Europe wasn't nearly so serious or businesslike a place as America—or Britain, for that matter. The Soviet threat seemed remote, sequestered behind barbed wire; in the American imagination, the real threat was Rossano Brazzi, who wooed a repressed Katharine Hepburn in the dreadfully romantic film Summertime without telling her that he was married. (Hepburn succumbed for a time, then fled to Ohio—what a perfect Yank she's always been.)

Things have changed, apparently. Europe is in crisis, and in a fairly pissy mood besides. There is a growing "rift" with America. We are seen as naive, arrogant, unilateral barbarians. (But wasn't that always the case: "Monsewer, van rooge see voo play?") And Europe itself is becoming less fun: there is

crime, there is a tide of immigrants, there are rightwing demagogues, there are rightwing demagogues being assassinated, there are lunatic children firing weapons in schools. Indeed, the news from Europe sounds… rather American, don't you think? Could this possibly be true? Where are the accordion players of yesteryear? The Guardian has put me on the case: a six-country Arrogant Yank tour, starting in France, anti-Americanism's most fragrant vineyard. My trip begins at the very same moment that a rather more arrogant Yank, my president, George Bush, is beginning his own truncated tour—a six-day flash across the continent. Mine will last six weeks, unless I'm detained in a villa somewhere. I have refused the Guardian's offer of a pink Cadillac convertible as a means of conveyance. I have purchased a Eurailpass. I mean to be inconspicuous. My first words in Calais: "Pardonnay mwa, ooo ehhh le… uh… train station?"

The train from Calais to Lille is a disgrace. I had hoped for the Orient Express. What I get is double-deckered, graffiti-smeared (the artist "Eczema '97" has claimed this for his own) and vinyl-seated. On my seat, someone has written, "A spliff a day keeps the doctor away." We haven't seen trains as anarchic as this in the States for years—and I experience an epiphany: is it possible that Europe really has become just like America, but an America of the recent past: the 1970s, to be precise, a period for which I harbour zero nostalgia.

Think about it: In the 70s American politicians were still caught in the turbulence of the George Wallace phenomenon—Wallace, the American Le Pen, who had stood in the schoolhouse door to block integration, who had coined the greatest of all political slogans, "Send them a message!" and who had actually won primary elections in reasonably proper states like Michigan and Maryland. In the 70s, too, Americans were reacting against an exploding crime rate (it had quadrupled in the 60s) and a rush of new immigrants from such un-American places as Mexico, Korea, Vietnam, Africa and South Asia. Young people were alienated. The economy was sluggish; American products weren't nearly so nifty as those from Germany and Japan. Jimmy Carter was worried about a national "malaise", which was reflected in the polls: for the first time in the history of the country, a majority of Americans didn't think next year would be better. Much of this was handled over time:

crime abated, industry reorganised itself, the immigrants proved themselves brilliant Americans, "Eczema '74" stowed the spray paint and learned computer programming, Donny and Marie Osmond retired. We vanquished the Evil Empire, and made the world safe for Disney. We've even made some progress on race. But it was rather painful there for a while. One wonders if Europe can make a similar recovery (one wonders if America can sustain its triumphs, but that's another story).

# Lille and Lens

Why start here, in these grungy northern burghs? Because in 1973, the place to go in America was Michigan—home to disgruntled auto workers moving from the left to Wallace to—we didn't quite know it yet—Reagan. Le Pen was very strong in Lille and Lens. There are also a great many Arab immigrants. Hence the question: have the socialists yet comprehended the threat they face? (In America, it took the Democrats 25 years to get their act together.)

Interpreter Kate and I attend a meeting of the Socialist party in Lens, a coal-mining town that is historically a leftwing bastion; now, a city divided between socialists and Le Pen supporters. The socialists remind me very much of the post-McGovern, pre-Clinton Democrats. They have no idea how irrelevant they've become. We are greeted by the mayor, a fabulous, brushy-haired, pipe-smoking Gallic sort called Guy Delcourt. He is, in turn, greeting new recruits to the Socialist party with a champagne reception (this would not happen in America; beer, at best). There are 60 new recruits, a Le Pen-inspired doubling of the usual rate. And Delcourt is happier than any Frenchman is supposed to be: just unremittingly cheery about his party's prospects. Yes, Lionel Jospin, the Socialist candidate for president of France was humiliated; yes, the local socialist vote was down four points to 25%; yes, Le Pen was up a bit (to 21% in Lens). But prospects for the parliamentary voting in June are much better and the problems really aren't that horrible. Crime is not a problem. Crime is a television show that scares old people. Immigrants, well: "I remind people that they have worked for years in the mines with the Moroccans," Delcourt says, not realising that Algerians and Tunisians hate being called Moroccans. If a label is necessary, they would rather be called Arabs or beur (the latter a slang reverse play on the word Arab).

Jean-Claude Bois, the local socialist candidate for the national assembly, appears—wavy grey hair, glasses, weak chin, a kind man but not nearly so powerful a presence as the mayor. We discuss Jospin. "He scared a lot of people by talking too much about modernity," Bois says. "He had too idealistic a vision of the future."

Translation: "modernity" is the French euphemism for the European Union. I ask Delcourt and Bois what they think about the plans to enlarge the EU to include Poland, the Czech Republic and eight other eastern European countries in 2004. "That will probably not happen," Delcourt says, although I've been told that it probably will. "It would result in a levelling of all the economies. We can't take responsibility for everyone else's problems. We need to fortify Europe first."

Translation: "Europe" is the French euphemism for France, Germany, Italy, Scandinavia, the Benelux countries and perhaps, grudgingly, the Iberian peninsula (and—they hope against hope—the United Kingdom). Poland, the Czechs and all the rest, however, are perceived to be a hellhole of porous borders, rutted byways, smoky industrial dinosaurs and antique farmers (and lots of them: 40 million Poles alone!). It will cost a gazillion euros to bring these places up to western standards.

We move on to an assembly hall—much more pleasant than its American analogue, flags and flowers abound—where several hundred local leftists are gathered for a Socialist party struggle session, a post-election hashing out of the party's problems. The audience is mostly Gallic, a few black and beur faces sprinkled about. The Jospin defeat was a failure of communication, says one. Chirac manipulated Jospin, says another. The party hasn't done enough for local businessmen, says a local businessman. The former mayor, an elderly man, stands and delivers a rambling jeremiad about the failure of the party to adhere to its socialist past, the failure to distinguish itself from the centre-right—this is perhaps the most popular Parisian assessment of the Socialist crumple; it is assumed to be the reason why so many leftists indulged themselves with silly votes for three different Trotskyite parties, the Greens and other Marxist cats and dogs. Mayor Delcourt, fidgeting through all this, leans over and whispers, "He wants more socialism, but he doesn't realise the state pays for it."

The crime issue rears its ugly head. Maybe it isn't just a television programme, after all. A middle-aged beur says he is tired of being patted down by the police every day because they think he's a drug dealer. I look over at Mayor Delcourt, who shrugs: "Well yes, Lens unfortunately is along the route that drug dealers coming from the Netherlands use on their way to Paris." And yes, most of these drug dealers are, erm, "Moroccans." And yes, "It is a very serious problem." Yes.

The next day, interpreter Kate and I wander about the industrial city of Lille, mostly talking to Arabs. Across from a disastrous, dilapidated public-housing bloc, with women in hijabs leaning out the windows and a massive graffito—"Nique La Police" [F--- the police]—scrawled above the entrance, we enter the modern offices of Archimed, a purveyor of multimedia softwear systems. The president of Archimed is Mongi Zidi, a prosperous 37-year-old Tunisian who is, we are told, making quite a name for himself in French hi-tech circles. "I put our offices in this neighbourhood as a social statement," he says, "to provide some hope for the young people across the street."

Unfortunately, he admits, the young people across the street are mostly interested in tossing rocks through his windows. Zidi has curly black hair, quick dark eyes and a wrestler's build. He is an information-age optimist, an entirely contemporary man. He worries about business, mostly. Raising money isn't easy for a small company in France. The mandated 35-hour working week is a disaster. And then there are the culture-content laws: Among other things, Archimed specialises in multimedia information retrieval systems for libraries—but the systems are built with Microsoft components, so French libraries won't buy them. "We just sold a system to a library in Cerritos, California," he says. "Mrs Bush presided at the opening."

He insists, at first, that being a first-generation Arab immigrant hasn't been much of a problem for him. He came to France for an education, decided to stay, and found French backers for his company. Later, though, he admits the Le Pen vote has unsettled him. "You stand in line at the supermarket and hear snickering behind you. You see people whispering to each other and you wonder—one out of five are Le Pen voters—are they laughing at you?"

I ask him about America. He loves America (except for its policy toward Israel). He loves the business atmosphere. And there is one American politician he absolutely adores. "Al Gore," he says. "He is a very seductive politician, a strong man for the future. I am inspired by his global approach. He is the granpére of the information superhighway."

Zidi admits that he hasn't had much contact with the poor, angry young people who throw rocks at his building, but he passes me along to a friend, a journalist named Abdel Kirim Saifi, who offers a tour of the other side of town. But first he offers some sociology: "It is the second generation who are the problem," Saifi says. "The first generation was recruited to work in the mines and mills; they were treated badly, but they had no expectations. They did have hopes for their children—and the children have been treated no better by society. The second generation is very angry. Many of them see no hope. They drop out of school, get involved with crime and drugs."

Saifi is thin, quiet, studious—a second generation Algerian whose sister has made a remarkable leap: she has been named agriculture minister in the new Chirac government, the first Arab to become a cabinet minister since the colonial era. She had been a leftist for 15 years, he says, but made no progress in the Socialist party. When she switched, the right greeted her with open arms. Saifi remains a man of the left, but now he must concede that his sister has a point: if the Arab vote is not a wholly owned subsidiary of the left, perhaps the Arabs will gain more influence. There are some other unexpected developments in his community. "There has been a revival of religion," he says. "It is not only a comfort, but it is also a means of self-affirmation, of communal protest, a reaction against the problems of immigrants."

That night, Saifi takes us to the mosque in Lille Sud, which indeed seems the neighbourhood centre. Clutches of old men chatting outside; and young people as well, dressed in American athletic gear, the universal costume of the young and the restless. Saifi introduces us to a young man named Farid Sellani, who is immediately and obviously a politician. He speaks quickly, angrily. "I was born in this neighbourhood," he says. "I have been committed to this cause since I was 20." He is now 28—another second-generation Algerian and a former socialist. "I was elected to the town council on the socialist list, but I was just a token Arab. I tried to get a six-year project to improve this neighbourhood, but they would never listen to me, so now I am running for the national assembly as an independent."

We crowd into Saifi's car and take a drive around the neighbourhood, which is a monument to the sterility of socialist dreams past: we'll build these nice, modern high-rise buildings

for the poor. They'll be so nice, the middle class will be envious. In truth, these aren't as awful as some of the places I've seen in America: there is graffiti and garbage, but an absence of weaponry and menace. The harsh yellow crime lights throw fuzzy glares through a film of dirt.

Sellani the politician begins a rant about integration. He hates the idea; it is demeaning. Either his people are French or they're not. "We're only French in the eyes of the politicians during election time. They exploited our parents, worked them to death," he is screaming now. "And we are supposed to go to them like beggars. Please can we have a house. Please can we have an education. Please can we be part of society. Integration! I want to see that word banished from the dictionary."

The 1970s indeed.

# Paris

There is an accordion player on the Metro. France, at last! I suddenly remember that a part of my job is to confront the allegedly reflexive Gallic anti-Americanism. But I haven't found any anti-Americans in Lens or Lille. Surely, in Paris there must be a few. My first stop is with students at the Institut d'Études Politiques (popularly known as Sciences-Po), which is the training ground for the French political and diplomatic elite and, no doubt, a hotbed of raving Yank-bashers.

"So," I say, confronting five incipient political elitists, "what do you think of America these days?" As my daughter would respond: well, duh! Bush is an idiot cowboy. Unilateralism is outrageous. The axis of evil is a ridiculous formulation. Americans are hypocrites about free trade. The Jewish lobby runs the show. You've heard these things before? Me too. (What's more, I only disagree with two of the five: Bush is neither an idiot nor a cowboy; the Jewish lobby is influential, but not nearly so powerful as the dairy farmers; the other propositions are viable.) Interesting thing, though: not much heat to any of this. The students are reciting. They've done this before. They're not even bothered by American cultural imperialism. That was five years ago. They're drinking Cokes. And so, bored, I ask them about Europe.

A young woman named Nadia, who may well turn out to be the French Margaret Thatcher, takes centre stage. She has a face that is simultaneously round and severe—a church-lady look—and rimless glasses, and an air of superiority. She is a doctoral candidate and an employee—already!—of the European commission. Her job is to go around France giving speeches about enlargement of the European Union. And guess what? "It is shocking. No one knows it is going to happen!" she says. "And when I tell them, they don't want it. It is an economic burden they don't need. Remarkably, this wasn't an issue in the presidential election."

Why not? I ask. Suddenly the table is alive. There is real emotion. The students are infuriated with an elite that will not countenance a discussion, much less a vote, on this question. To an American, this seems preposterous, impossible, an open invitation to the worst sort of know-nothing, populist reaction. "Wasn't it Jacques Delors who said, 'Europe is too serious to be left to the people?'" offers a small, puckish fellow who is a specialist in social policy. "Perhaps we are going to see what the people think of that." (I don't know if Delors actually said this, but most of the people I spoke to seemed to think so—which may be all that matters.)

The talk turns back to immigration—enlargement could add a tsunami of immigrants from the east—and then it turns to the difficulties France has had assimilating Islamic immigrants. "Religion should be left in the home," Madame Thatcherre avers, regaining control of the table. "We believe in a secular society. For a Frenchman to see a woman wearing a veil, that is perceived as a failure of society. We seem to have difficulty succeeding with the Muslims. We made Frenchmen out of the Italians, the Poles, the Spanish immigrants…"

Ryan, an American student from Seattle, begins to laugh. "How can the French coexist in the European Union if they want to make everyone into Frenchmen?" he asks Thatcherre, the EU employee, who is nonplussed. "This is something I've learned here," he explains to me. "Egalité has a special meaning. It means everyone is welcome to become an equal Frenchman."

Having failed miserably in my effort to manage a proper row over America with the students—and then, later, with several other Paris intellectuals—I ask a friend, Patrick Weil, a professor at the University of Paris, to find me a really smart, really extreme anti-globalist. He recommends Serge Halimi of Le Monde Diplomatique.

"Bush is a godsend," says Halimi—who is, indeed, very smart—over coffee in a cafe across the street from his office. "Clinton was almost as bad as Bush, a globalist through and through, but he was much tougher to make an argument against because he made it appear the things he wanted were good for everyone, not just America. Bush, the rich man who pretends he's a cowboy, is so patently ridiculous. He makes our argument easy."

We descend the inevitable stairway into the murky depths of globaloney. Neither of us says anything surprising. You've had such conversations, no doubt. Yawn. Finally, I tell him about my surprising afternoon at Sciences-Po and ask about EU enlargement. "The Socialist party was a movement of the people until the 1980s. It had a programme that was very popular with the people: socialism," Halimi says, beginning a lecture. "When socialism fell out of fashion, they tried to replace it with the idea of Europe. That was not so popular. It was an elite, technocratic notion. They can't even use the proper word for it: they call it modernity. And now they give us these incredibly foolish bank-notes."

He pulls several euros from his appropriately thin wallet. "Look at them! Bridges—over what? Doors—leading where? What empty, ugly symbols! Symbols of nothing! On a European continent famous for its artistic and intellectual geniuses, there are no people on them. As if the French would not tolerate a banknote with Da Vinci on it. As if the Italians would not tolerate Victor Hugo!"

I mention that he is shouting. I add that he wasn't nearly so passionate when the topic was America. He looks at me and smiles, tacitly conceding that what he is about to say is a matter of personal pride rather than of complete conviction. "Well," he says, "of course, this European federation is only a part of the American project of globalisation."

# A divided self:
# A Survey of France

France has an identity problem. It needs to find the courage
to redefine itself, says John Andrews

"I HAVE heard and understood your call: that the republic should live, that the nation should reunite, that politics should change." On a cold evening in early May, Jacques Chirac found the right words for the moment. He had just been re-elected president of the French republic, with 82% of the vote, in a run-off with Jean-Marie Le Pen, the leader of the extreme-right National Front. Two weeks earlier, in the first round of the election, Mr Le Pen had eliminated the Socialist candidate (and incumbent prime minister), Lionel Jospin, from the contest. For left-leaning voters, Mr Chirac was clearly the lesser evil, so in the run-off they joined forces with Mr Chirac's centre-right to humble Mr Le Pen. Hence Mr Chirac's carefully chosen words: his victory may have been sweet, but it was hardly unqualified.

Doubtless that is why as prime minister of his "government of mission", Mr Chirac appointed Jean-Pierre Raffarin, a pudgy and amiable former senator from the Poitou-Charentes region. Mr Raffarin's motto is *la France d'en bas*, grassroots France, which is supposed to mean not only a government closer to the people but a government that comes from the people.

So six months later, is the nation "reunited"; has politics changed; is the republic "alive"? The answers are horribly muddled, mainly because the French themselves are muddled: over France's place in Europe, over the impact of globalisation and, at root, over what it means to be French. In their hearts they want precious little to change; in their heads they suspect change is inevitable.

If it is, their worry is not just what the change will be, but how and when it will come. On June 17th, the day after a parliamentary election in which Mr Chirac's supporters (most of them members of the newly assembled and aptly named Union for the Presidential Majority) won 399 of the National Assembly's 577 seats, the headline of the conservative *Le Figaro* proclaimed: "Five years to change France". Given that there will be no significant elections before the next presidential and parliamentary polls, due in 2007, the opportunity is there. But if change does come, many will not like it: the leftist *Libération*'s headline sarcastically predicted "A five-year sentence".

Whatever the headlines say, for most of France's 59m people not much has changed since the bout of elections in the spring. Around 9% of the workforce is still without a job; the rest troop off to their offices and factories just as before, cosseted by laws that protect them from quick lay-offs, provide them with one of the world's shortest working weeks—just 35 hours—and give them holiday entitlements Americans can only dream of. Meanwhile, their country remains as beautiful and seductive as ever, and the two-hour lunch is alive and well. Add trains that run fast and on time, modern motorways in good repair, and a med-

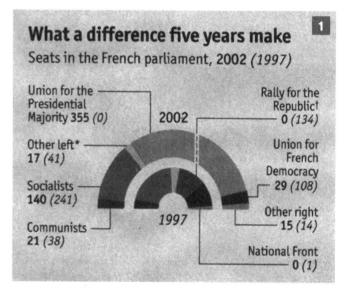

## What a difference five years make

Seats in the French parliament, 2002 *(1997)*

Union for the Presidential Majority 355 *(0)*

2002

Rally for the Republic† 0 *(134)*

Other left* 17 *(41)*

Union for French Democracy 29 *(108)*

Socialists 140 *(241)*

1997

Other right 15 *(14)*

Communists 21 *(38)*

National Front 0 *(1)*

*Includes Radical Party of the Left, 7 *(12)*; Greens, 3 *(7)*
†In 2002 it was absorbed into the Union for the Presidential Majority
Sources: French interior ministry; *The Economist*

ical system at the top of the World Health Organisation's international rankings. Surely the French have a right to feel pleased with themselves?

## Not altogether superior

So why do they feel so insecure? Why do politicians, pundits and philosophers (a breed revered on French television) feel a need to bolster the country's collective morale by pointing out the deficiencies of the "Anglo-Saxon" way, be they fraudulent accountancy practices in America or decrepit private railways in Britain?

One reason is doubtless a dash of *Schadenfreude*. Within the lifetime of its senior citizens, France has been occupied by Germany, rescued by America and Britain, and then divested—bloodily in the case of Algeria and Indochina—of almost all its colonies. Since then English has become the world's common language (so much so that France's own politicians will now

# Same bed, different dreams

## Better to cohabit than be out in the cold

IS IT sensible for France to have a president from one side of the political divide and a government from the other? Olivier Schrameck, chief of staff to Mr Jospin from 1997 until May this year, devoted much of a recent book, "Matignon Rive Gauche, 1997–2001", to denouncing such "cohabitation" as a waste of energy and a recipe for immobility. Under cohabitation, the government would run the country, but the president, who retains traditional authority over defence and foreign policy (the constitutional authority is rather vague), would be tempted to snipe from the sidelines.

Yet French voters have forced such liaisons on their country three times since the birth of the Fifth Republic in 1958. The first time was when the left was defeated in the parliamentary elections of 1986. The Socialist François Mitterrand, who had been elected president in 1981, had to put up with a centre-right government led by Jacques Chirac as prime minister. In 1988 Mitterrand was re-elected president and dissolved parliament. In the ensuing elections the Socialists returned to power. In 1993, however, the left-wing government was voted out and Mitterrand had to cohabit with the centre-right once again, this time with Edouard Balladur as prime minister. Two years later this cohabitation ended with the election of Mr Chirac as president. But in 1997 Mr

Chirac provoked the third cohabitation—much tenser than the first two—by calling early parliamentary elections that the left, led by Mr Jospin, won handsomely.

Such cohabitations could happen because the presidential term was for seven years and that of the lower house of parliament, the National Assembly, for five. But in future there will be less opportunity for these oddball relationships. In September 2000, after an arcane debate between constitutional experts and self-interested politicians, a bemused electorate decided in a referendum (in which only 30% cast a vote) that, beginning with the elections of 2002, the president would have the same five-year term as the parliament.

Since a president might die in office, or might dissolve parliament early, there could still be cohabitations in the future. But as long as President Chirac remains in the post, he is unlikely to call early elections again. For the record, he used to be a fierce opponent of reducing the seven-year presidential term, but changed his mind. His critics say he feared that voters in 2002 might think him too old for another seven-year term but young enough for five years (he will be 70 later this month). He himself claims he supported the change in order to modernise France.

speak it in public), America has turned into the world's only superpower and Hollywood has come to dominate the world's entertainment industry. For France, a country which believes that its revolution, just as much as America's, bears a universal message, these changes have not been easy to accept. Seeing someone else having a hard time provides some light relief.

But there are also more troubling reasons for this lack of confidence. One is the feeling, especially among industrialists and businessmen, that France's economic formula, involving higher taxes and social charges than in most of the countries its firms compete with, will not work forever. Indeed, it is already fraying at the edges. At the start of the 1990s, France ranked eighth in the world in terms of economic output per person, but by the end of the decade it had slipped to 18th.

The most important reason, however, is a lurking suspicion that French society itself is not working. Go back to the first round of the presidential election on April 21st, with its 16 can-

didates, and ask a few simple questions. Why did Mr Jospin, arguably France's most effective prime minister in the 44 years of the Fifth Republic, get only 16.2% of the vote? Why, in that round, did Mr Chirac get only 19.9%, the lowest ever for an incumbent president? Why did 13 no-hoper candidates gather up 47% of the vote between them? And why did a record 28.4% of the electorate abstain? Most bothersome of all, why did Mr Le Pen, ostracised throughout his 40-odd years in politics, win 16.9% of the vote and so pass through to the second round?

There are plenty of superficial answers: Mr Jospin lacked charm; Mr Chirac was stained by alleged corruption; the electorate felt free to indulge its whims because it assumed that a run-off between Messrs Jospin and Chirac was pre-ordained; and Mr Le Pen is a brilliant orator. But there is a more fundamental explanation. As one French journalist, Philippe Manière, puts it in a recent book, the first-round result was "the vengeance of the people".

# A question of colour, a matter of faith

## France must face up to its immigrant problems

JEAN-MARIE LE PEN, at ease in his drawing room, waves an arm as if to state the obvious: "The greatest challenge is demographic. The countries of the north—the world of the white man, or let's say the non-black world—have an ageing population. They are rich, and they are facing a third world of 5 billion people, maybe more tomorrow, who are very young and dynamic. This dynamism will be translated into immigration."

Outside the room, the guard-dogs are asleep. In the urban plain below the Le Pen mansion (inherited from a political admirer) in Saint-Cloud, the Paris evening rush-hour is under way. The National Front leader goes on: "The rise of Islam is more the result of its youth and dynamism than its religious values. It's a demographic problem which will lead to immigration, whose consequences could lead, if nothing is done, to the submersion of our country, our people, our civilisation… No government, whether by ideology or by blindness, has realised the danger."

France's far-right bogeyman gained second place in the presidential election by saying what few other politicians would either want to or dare to: that the French republic has too many immigrants, who in turn have too many children. But that is putting it politely. What the National Front and the National Republican Movement, its rival on the extreme right, really mean is that France has too many inhabitants who are black, brown and Muslim. And lots of them are not immigrants at all, but were born in France and are French citizens.

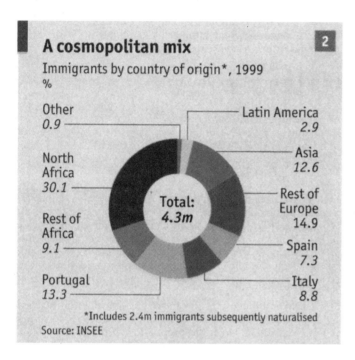

**A cosmopolitan mix** [2]

Immigrants by country of origin*, 1999
%

Other 0.9

Latin America 2.9

North Africa 30.1

Asia 12.6

Total: 4.3m

Rest of Europe 14.9

Rest of Africa 9.1

Spain 7.3

Portugal 13.3

Italy 8.8

*Includes 2.4m immigrants subsequently naturalised

Source: INSEE

There are plenty of other politicians who have dabbled in the politics of race. Governments of the right have over the years enacted increasingly strong laws to restrict immigration, and governments of the left have for the most part accepted them. Mr Chirac, definitely not a racist himself, found it useful in the 1988 presidential election campaign to refer to the "odours" of immigrant cooking.

What makes Mr Le Pen different is that he has consistently preached the same xenophobic message ever since he entered politics. He became France's youngest member of parliament in 1956, at the age of 27, and first stood for the presidency in 1974. France's ills, he has said all along, are the fault of foreigners, including fellow members of the European Union. The remedy is to keep out foreigners, produce more French children, build more prisons, cut taxes and leave the EU.

The question is why that message suddenly found more resonance with the voters in last spring's presidential election than ever before in Mr Le Pen's political career. Mr Le Pen's previous best score was 14.4% in the first round in 1988, and the only time his party has ever gained more than one seat in the National Assembly was in 1986, when the elections, exceptionally, were held by proportional representation.

The answer is surely not that nearly a fifth of the voters suddenly decided that Mr Le Pen's programme made practical sense, nor that all those who cast their ballot for him are anti-Semitic fascists (Mr Le Pen has described the gas chambers as a "detail" of the second world war, and thinks that Maurice Pa-

pon, the Vichy official who in the late 1990s was eventually convicted for crimes against humanity, was innocent). More likely, the voters wanted to jog the governing elite into action. As a former Socialist prime minister, Laurent Fabius, once said, "Le Pen poses good questions and offers bad solutions."

So what might a good solution look like? A useful start would be, literally, to enumerate France's problems. Malek Boutih, the French-born son of Algerian immigrants and now the president of SOS-Racisme, an anti-racism organisation, argued in a recent book that "France is wrong not to publish, as other countries like America do, statistics of criminality by social category, age, place, type of city development and so on. It is even more wrong not to establish a public debate on the question, as though the French are so irrational that they cannot calmly consider the reality of their problems."

## Crime matters

But should that mean a debate on crime as well? Polls before the election showed that the subject topped the list of their concerns, ahead of the state of the economy or pensions or even unemployment. Whether crime in France is worse than in other countries is a moot point: criminal statistics are hard to compare, and although one study showed that France in 2000 had proportionately more crimes than America, other studies suggest that it did a little better than, say, Germany or Belgium. However, what matters to French people is what happens in France.

Or more precisely, what they think is happening. Nicolas Sarkozy, the interior minister, has won plaudits for not only identifying crime as a serious problem but being seen to be doing something about it. Barely a week goes by without him being photographed with a smiling collection of police or gendarmes. Mr Sarkozy has secured the money to add another 6,500 police to the 146,000 he took over from his predecessor. And Mr Raffarin has appointed a junior minister in the justice ministry specifically to supervise a building programme that will add 11,000 prison places to the 47,000 already occupied.

In terms of public perception, such measures will help. One poll in September found that the proportion of those questioned who felt they were "often" at risk of crime was 49%—shockingly high in absolute terms but actually slightly less than in the autumn of last year. Mr Sarkozy has been able to trumpet a reduction in reported crime, by 4.5% in August compared with a year earlier, the first such fall for five years. In Paris, where the tourist industry has long complained about the plague of pickpockets, the fall was 11%.

Whether the momentum can be sustained is another matter. In the country that produced the Declaration of Human Rights (in 1789, a satisfying two years before America's Bill of Rights), the new enthusiasm for "zero tolerance" becomes hard to swallow when it means giving the authorities greater powers of arrest and punishment.

According to critics, many of them well placed in the judiciary and the media, the government is eroding the presumption of innocence (never particularly robust in France, which has no Anglo-Saxon protection of *habeas corpus*); it casually treats many young offenders as though they were adults; and it is callously cracking down on France's most marginal residents, from Romanian beggars to African prostitutes. In other words, the critics allege that the Raffarin government—and Mr Sarkozy in particular—is doing the work of Mr Le Pen for him.

Press Mr Boutih on whether criminal statistics should include a breakdown by race or religion, and he immediately says no: "I remain convinced that ethnic origin is less relevant than the level of education and social status." He has a point: a well-educated Arab or black Frenchman with a decent job is unlikely to turn to petty drug-dealing or car-stealing. The trouble, according to Tahar Ben Jelloun, a Moroccan who is one of France's finest writers, is that only 4% of the children of immigrants get to university, compared with 25% of their native contemporaries.

## Our ancestors the Gauls

But the main reason for Mr Boutih's resistance is that to collect information by race or religion would offend the very French concept of "republican values", because it would discriminate between citizens rather than treat them as equal. France makes no allowance for cultural differences: "our ancestors the Gauls" applies to schoolchildren of every hue. In this secular republic, the idea of collecting racial and religious statistics is a virtual taboo across the whole of the political spectrum. Such statistics, it is feared, will lead France along the Anglo-Saxon road of "communautarisme" (in which the idea of separate communities within the country as a whole is acceptable). In the words of the constitution, the French republic is indivisible, and having separate communities is seen as automatically leading to divisions.

Yet the sad reality is that France's race relations are no better than anyone else's. Arab and black minorities are as much as ever excluded from the mainstream. In opinion polls in the late 1990s, two-fifths of the respondents admitted to being at least "a little bit" racist (more than in any other European Union country except Belgium), and just over half thought there were "too many Arabs" in France.

The lack of solid figures leads to the sort of guesswork that plays into the far-right's hands. The state statistics office, INSEE, reckons that in 1999 (the year of the most recent census) the total number of foreign-born residents in metropolitan France, including 2.4m who have acquired French nationality, was 4.3m, or 7.4% of the metropolitan population of 58.5m. Of these, 1.3m had come from Algeria, Morocco and Tunisia. But the official figures end with that breakdown by country of origin.

The best estimate for the religious breakdown that INSEE is not allowed to publish comes from a scholarly report presented to the prime minister two years ago by the High Council for Integration, a committee of academics and experts. The report reckoned that France is home to 4m–5m Muslims—defined by culture rather than religious observance—of whom up to half have French nationality. Of the Muslim total, almost 3m are of North African origin or ancestry, with 1.5m from Algeria, 1m from Morocco and the rest from Tunisia. Of the other Muslims, Turks probably number 350,000, sub-Saharan Africans about 250,000, and assorted Middle Easterners (Iranians and Kurds, as well as Arabs) the remainder. So France's Muslims make up at most one in 12 of the population—and its Arabs one in 20.

Yet the media keep repeating that there are at least 6m Arabs in France, and quite possibly as many as 8m, who are regularly accused of crime, vandalism, the abuse of social services and other wrongdoings. It is easy for the elite and the comfortable middle classes to dismiss Mr Le Pen's view of the world, but less so for those—especially *les petits blancs* (poor whites)—who live in crime-ridden working-class neighbourhoods. According to the analysts, in the first round of the presidential election Mr Le Pen won the support of only 8% of those with a college education, but 30% of blue-collar voters and 38% of the unemployed.

## Chronic or curable?

Pessimists argue that the situation will get worse before it gets better. France's high rate of unemployment is not about to tumble overnight. Nor are the high-rise public housing blocks built from the 1950s to the 1970s in the *banlieue*, or suburbs, of most French towns. At the time, they were intended to provide affordable housing to the influx of workers from the countryside and from the colonies or ex-colonies. Now they have all too often become virtual ghettoes, each storey dotted with satellite dishes pointed towards the television stations of the Maghreb. But the problem extends far beyond the *banlieue*. The same combination of poverty, race and social exclusion can be found in the medieval villages of Provence, or in some down-at-heel parts of Paris such as the 10th or 19th *arrondissements*.

The passage of time, say the pessimists, is not healing cultural rifts but making them worse. The generation of immigrants from the Maghreb were often illiterate peasants, keen to work hard in a country whose language they could barely understand. By contrast, their children, and now their children's children, are French-born and French-educated, and have lost respect for their immigrant parents or grandparents. That has caused a loss of parental authority, and often a multitude of behavioural problems in the disciplined world of French schools.

## How French can you get?

Moreover, being French-born and French-educated does not mean that an Abdel-Karim or a Samira will be treated the same as a Jean-Pierre or a Marianne. To be white and born in France of French parents and grandparents means you are a *Français de souche*—of "French stock". But to be born in France of Arab ancestry makes you a *beur*, a word which for most Arab Frenchmen has no pejorative undertone (there is, for example, the Beur-FM radio station). The word is a kind of inversion of the word *Arabe*, part of an argot of inversion called *verlan* (*l'envers*, or back-to-front), which turns *français* into *cefran* and *café* into *féca*. This is undoubtedly of linguistic interest, but the language is also a sign of exclusion, sometimes self-imposed. *Beur* is now so universal that the new word among the *beurs* is *rebeu*, a *verlan* of a *verlan*.

How to end that exclusion? In America the answer might be affirmative action or positive discrimination, but in France such notions are seen as a threat to a republic which presumes its citizens to be free, equal and brotherly to begin with. When Sciences-Po, an elite university, last year began a special entry programme for a handful of bright students from the "zones of priority education" in the *banlieue* around the cities of Paris and Nancy, current and former students reacted with horror: their beloved meritocratic institution was slipping down the Anglo-Saxon slope.

Mr Boutih understands the gap between republican theory and everyday practice all too well: "The republican model is not a natural one. It exists through political will. Communautarisme is the natural model." So why not adopt the natural one instead? "Because society will explode from within. Each community will define itself against another, as in the United States."

Arguably, that process is already under way. In October last year, at a soccer match in Paris between France and Algeria, young *beurs* greeted the French national anthem with a storm of whistles and later invaded the pitch, brandishing Algerian flags. Young *beurs* are increasingly turning to Islam, not so much as a faith but as a symbol of identity: they fast during the month of Ramadan, insist on religiously correct food in their school canteens and stay at home to mark religious holidays.

A small minority go a lot further, falling under the influence of extremist imams from the Gulf or North Africa. In their fight to dismantle al-Qaeda, Europe's and America's intelligence services have uncovered a disturbing number of French suspects, not least Zacarias Moussaoui, currently on trial in America for his alleged role in the September 11th attacks on America last year. And a number of young *beur* layabouts have used the excuse of the Arab-Israeli conflict to indulge in anti-Jewish violence and vandalism (at over 600,000, France's Jewish minority is Europe's largest).

The *Français de souche* are accomplices in this process, not just in the April 21st vote for Mr Le Pen or in their reluctance to offer Arabs (and blacks) the same job prospects as whites, but also in the open antagonism some of them display towards the Arabs in their midst. To justify their stance, they quote the inferior status of Muslim women, or the dreadful gang-rapes of "easy" Muslim girls that some Muslim boys regard as a rite of passage. It is no accident that Oriana Fallaci's book "The Rage and the Pride", an extremist tirade against Muslims in general and Arabs in particular, spent so many weeks on this year's French bestseller list.

Could the pessimists be wrong? Back in 1998, France rejoiced in the World Cup victory of a French soccer team starring plenty of blacks and *beurs* (including the incomparable Zinedine Zidane, born of Algerian parents in the Marseilles *banlieue*). Sami Naïr, an Algerian-born member of the European Parlia-ment and formerly an adviser on immigration to the Jospin gov-ernment, points out that in an earlier wave of immigration into France, in the early part of the 20th century, Roman Catholics from Italy and Poland were accused of "trying to impose reli-gion on our secular state". Yet in the end, he says, the discrimi-nation fades and the newcomers' descendants end up as *Français de souche*: "I think it will be solved in a generation."

Yet there is an obvious difference between the present wave of migrants and previous waves: the *beurs* and their parents are the first minority that can be physically distinguished from the *Français de souche*. Their assimilation cannot be achieved by fad-ing into the background. Instead, Mr Naïr proposes a pact: the government must live up to the values of the republic when dealing with its Arabs—and the *beurs* must accept the duties that go with them, including equality of the sexes. That might be easier if the economy could deliver more jobs.

# A new kind of solidarity

### France needs more jobs and less state. The two are not unconnected

N OW is not a good time to be prime minister of France, and Jean-Pierre Raffarin knows it only too well. The world economy is in the doldrums, and the French economy is becalmed with it; investor confidence is low; and the trade unions are restive. Last month, for example, thousands of public-sector workers (80,000 according to the unions; 40,000 according to the police) marched through the centre of Paris to defend their privileges as public servants or agents of the state, and to denounce modest plans for privatisation. On the same day, INSEE, the government statistical office, announced that economic growth for this year was now likely to be only 1%, compared with its forecast in June of 1.4% (and the previous government's self-serving prediction of 2.5% before the elections).

If INSEE is right, then the budget for next year presented in October by the finance minister, Francis Mer, becomes an exer-cise in fiction. It assumes growth of 1.2% this year and 2.5% next, and a budget deficit of 2.6% of GDP. Instead, the deficit could well break through the 3% limit set by the European Union in its collective quest for economic stability. In other words, crisis looms: the EU will want French belts to be tightened, whereas the voters, worried about their jobs and mortgages, want them loosened.

Engraved in the country's political consciousness is the memory of 1995, the last time a centre-right president was elected with a centre-right majority in parliament. The prime minister of the day was the intellectually brilliant but aloof Alain Juppé; he was determined that France should qualify for membership of the euro zone, which meant keeping the franc closely in line with the D-mark while simultaneously cutting the budget deficit (then running at 5% of GDP). This he hoped to do by reforming the public sector, which would restrain public spending. Instead, he saw hundreds of thousands of public-sec-tor workers taking to the streets in a wave of protests and strikes, with the sympathy of most of the population. Two years later, when President Chirac rashly called an early general elec-tion to obtain a popular mandate for the EU's single currency, the right was swept from power.

Not surprisingly, Mr Raffarin and his colleagues are keen to prevent history repeating itself. Their strategy is to tread softly, even to speak softly. In opposition, the right accused Lionel Jospin of "immobility". Now the bosses' association, Medef (Mouvement des Entreprises de France), lays the same charge

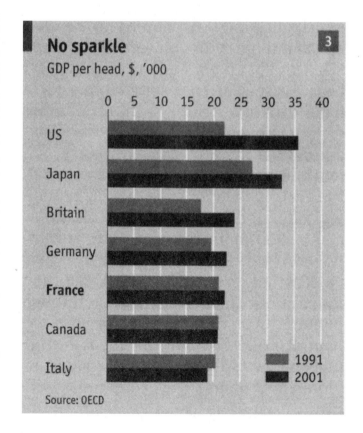

**No sparkle**

GDP per head, $, '000

Source: OECD

(legend: 1991 / 2001)

against Mr Raffarin: it accuses him of being too timid in dealing with the consequences of the 35-hour working week, introduced by Mr Jospin (who cut it from 39 hours with no loss of pay), or with the previous government's "Law on Social Modernisation" (which makes it harder than ever for employers to fire people, thus discouraging them from hiring in the first place). The bosses fear that if Mr Raffarin shows the same timidity in other areas, notably slimming down the civil service and reforming pensions, the country will continue its slide down the international scale of GDP per person.

Just as this is a bad time for Mr Raffarin to be prime minister, the previous period was a good time for Mr Jospin. The world economy, powered by America and its dotcom infatuation, was growing strongly, and France, the world's fifth-biggest exporter, reaped the benefits. A series of partial privatisations (or "openings of capital", in the words of Mr Jospin, an ex-Trotskyist well aware of the need to placate the Communists in his coalition) helped to keep the country's finances in excellent shape. Inflation, the public debt and the budget deficit were all low, and economic growth in 1998–2000 averaged 3.3% a year. Successive finance ministers basked in the plaudits of the International Monetary Fund and the OECD.

## Growing jobs

All this may have encouraged Mr Jospin to believe that full employment had become a realistic target for France. Certainly a report in December 2000 by Jean Pisani-Ferry, of the Council of Economic Analysis, a body of experts set up by Mr Jospin to give him independent advice, seemed to be suggesting as much. The report noted that in the four years from the start of 1997 France had created 1.6m jobs, "twice as many as during the 1960s and ten times the number created between 1974 and 1996". The drop in the jobless, it said, was "unprecedented".

The government was keen to take the credit. In the run-up to this year's elections, it claimed that the 35-hour week, which came into effect in February 2000 for firms with more than 20 employees (it has yet to be fully applied to small firms), had already created 400,000 jobs. The idea was that to compensate for the shorter week, bosses would have to take on more employees, and could be encouraged to do so through temporary relief on their payroll taxes. The government noted, too, that 320,000 young people had found work since 1997 through the youth employment scheme, under which young people were given five-year contracts in the public sector, for example as school playground assistants or as guards at railway stations and other public buildings. At the beginning of 2001 the government had also taken steps to lessen the poverty trap, in which recipients of state benefits lose out if they take a low-paid job.

## A success of sorts

But how much of the credit for all these extra jobs did the Jospin government really deserve? On closer scrutiny, the Pisani-Ferry report reads less like a congratulatory pat on the government's back and more like a warning that things must change. For a start, much of the job creation was simply the result of economic growth. Further, full employment was defined as a jobless rate of 5% or less of the workforce, a rate that in happier days for the world economy would have been considered fairly disastrous in, say, Japan or Singapore. The report also argued that to achieve this target by 2010, the country would have to create at least 300,000 new jobs a year, perhaps as many as 400,000.

That, however, would require large-scale liberalisation, of the sort introduced by Margaret Thatcher, Britain's radical prime minister of the 1980s—and French vested interests are most unlikely to allow that to happen. Besides, there is little sign of a French Lady Thatcher emerging. Only Alain Madelin, of the Liberal Democrats, currently speaks a Thatcherite language of free markets and a minimalist state, and he won a mere 3.9% of the vote on April 21st.

All this puts a different perspective on the labour-market "success" of the Jospin term. True, unemployment fell from the 12.2% of the workforce inherited from the right in 1997, but only

to 9%, getting on for twice as much as in Britain or America—at a time when the economy was booming and employers had jobs they could not fill. The economists concluded that 9%, or a smidgen less, was—and is—France's "structural" rate of unemployment, which can be reduced only by changing the make-up of the economy.

Go to the lovely Place du Capitole in Toulouse, or ride the subway system in Lyons, or watch a game of street-soccer in a Marseilles housing estate, and the economic jargon translates into bored young men whiling away their days doing nothing in particular: no wonder many of them trade drugs to supplement their meagre state benefits. People over 25 receive the RMI (*revenu minimum d'insertion*), created in 1988 to provide a "minimum income for inclusion in society". For a single man with no dependants, this amounts to €406 ($405) a month. In a land of plenty, some 1m of France's 24m households rely on the income of the country's 2.2m *eremistes*.

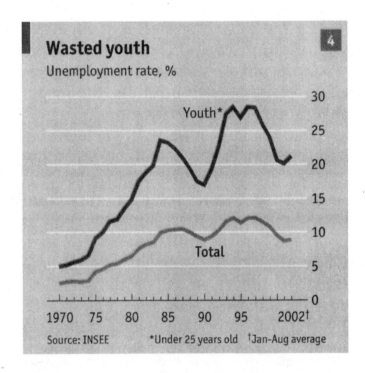

**Wasted youth**
Unemployment rate, %

Youth*

Total

1970   75   80   85   90   95   2002†

Source: INSEE    *Under 25 years old   †Jan-Aug average

That is a waste of young energy and talent; but a similar waste goes on at the other end of the age range too. In Antibes, a town on the Côte d'Azur sandwiched between Cannes and Nice, men in their 50s and 60s go down to the seafront each afternoon to play *boules*, as do thousands of other perfectly healthy contemporaries throughout the country (albeit perhaps in less pleasant surroundings). In most other industrialised countries, they would still be toiling at the office desk or on the factory floor; in France, they are enjoying a comfortable retirement.

In other words, France's unemployment rate, already bad enough by international standards, is even worse than it looks. In Switzerland, more than 70% of the 55–64 age group are in the labour market; in Japan two-thirds; and in Britain just over half. The average for the OECD group of rich countries is 51%. But in France the share is a mere 37%.

So what, you might say with a Gallic shrug. One of France's many attractive features is that its people work to live, not the other way round (which is what critics say is wrong with the Anglo-Saxon model). Patrick Artus, the chief economist of the Caisse de Dépôts et Consignations, a venerable state-owned bank, makes a joke of it: "No one wants to increase the [labour-market] participation rate except economists over the age of 55.

As the Pisani-Ferry report notes: "Inactivity was viewed in France for many years as an alternative to unemployment." In other words, the government encouraged mothers to stay at home and workers over 50 to retire. This was particularly true for the Mitterrand era of the 1980s and early 90s: legislation to protect workers' rights and the proliferation of payroll charges created an exceptionally illiquid labour market. As a result, *les trentes glorieuses* (the 30 years from 1945 to 1975 when the economy boomed and jobs were there for the taking) were followed by a quarter-century in which high unemployment, especially among the young, became part of the economic landscape.

## Embracing business

Could the Raffarin government begin to turn things round? Not in the short term, but at least Mr Raffarin and his team have understood a vital precondition: it is business that must create the jobs of the future, not government. The daily *Le Figaro* went to the trouble of analysing the words used by Mr Raffarin in a recent television programme about his future plans, and found that the second most frequent subject on his lips was *"entreprise"* (business)—surpassed only by the word "France". Compared with Mr Jospin, who spent little time with business bosses during his five-year tenure, Mr Raffarin's interest in *entreprise* seems promising. On the other hand, words are not the same as deeds. For all its alleged antipathy to business, the Jospin government privatised far more of French industry than its centre-right predecessors had done. Mr Raffarin will have to show that he can do better than Mr Jospin.

In part, this will involve more privatisation. Amazingly, there are still around 1,500 companies—compared with 3,500 in 1986—in which the state has a controlling share. In theory, most of the icons of French industry are up for grabs—France Telecom, Air France and even the hitherto sacrosanct Electricité de France (EDF) and Gaz de France (GDF). But at least three things could get in the way.

One is a disinclination on the part of the government to let key industries such as electricity escape from its control, which means that in practice only minority stakes will be sold; a second is union opposition to any loss of pension and other privileges if control goes to the private sector; and the third is the abysmal state of the stockmarket. Air France, 54% owned by the state, may—when market conditions eventually suit the government—be a safe enough bet to fly further into private ownership; France Telecom, 55.5% owned by the state, risks a flop thanks to its debt of around €70 billion.

But the main challenge for Mr Raffarin goes far beyond selling the family silver: it involves lightening the government's hold on the economy in general and the private sector in particular. Government spending accounts for over 53% of GDP, way above the OECD average of 38%. A steeply progressive system of income tax, for example, can claim as much as 60% of an individual's pay-packet, and even the moderately rich have to pay a wealth tax. Virtually every French citizen gripes about taxes or social charges. Admittedly, because of various exemptions, only half of all wage-earners have to pay income tax; the trouble is that the non-paying half are still subject to a variety of payroll charges that make no allowances for income differentials. Value-added tax, levied at 19.6%, also has to be paid by rich and poor alike.

Taxes on business were reduced by the Jospin government, but employers complain that heavy payroll charges still make it hard for them to compete internationally. Medef has calculated that the Jospin government's measures, if they had been fully implemented by their 2003 deadline (in fact some changes will be made), would still have left France bottom out of 14 EU countries. For example, for every €100 an employee takes home, a French employer would still have had to shell out €288, compared with €227 for a German boss and €166 for a British one. Only a Belgian employer would pay more.

Individual taxpayers who are rich and mobile enough vote with their feet. For instance, Laetitia Casta, a model whose face now graces the country's stamps as the national figurehead, Marianne, lives for the most part outside the country; so do virtually all of the French soccer team who won the World Cup for France in 1998 (and lost it so ingloriously in 2002). It is said that up to 300,000 French people now live in south-east England, where the taxes are lower. There is clear evidence that fewer foreigners want to set up business in France, and more French people want to shift their investment abroad.

The government seems to have accepted the need to act. During his election campaign, President Chirac promised to cut income tax by 5% this year and by 30% over his five-year term; to reduce bureaucracy; and to create a million new businesses. Last month Mr Raffarin and his minister for small and medium-sized businesses, Renaud Dutreil, announced that from next autumn the charge for setting up a limited-liability company will be cut from €7,500 to just €1; the company will be able to operate from the entrepreneur's home for up to five years, instead of two (which still raises the question why this kind of restriction should be imposed at all); the tax-exemption limit for capital gains will rise by a third or more; and payment of the first year's social charges can be spread over five years.

French entrepreneurs will be grateful for any lightening of their load. Two years ago the OECD found that France had more business red tape than any other member, and more barriers to entrepreneurs than all but Italy. For example, simply to register a company could take four months.

## Let 1m flowers bloom

Will Mr Dutreil's measures meet Mr Chirac's target for 1m new businesses by the next election? At present more than 170,000 companies are created each year, so another 30,000 a year does not look out of the question. It is not as though the country lacked talent and initiative: the Côte d'Azur science park of Sophia-Antipolis is full of high-technology start-ups and foreign investment.

The question is whether France wants that business badly enough. Back in 1925, an American president, Calvin Coolidge, famously declared: "The chief business of the American people is business." It is hard to imagine a French politician ever embracing that sentiment on behalf of his countrymen. In an opinion poll last year, 56% of the respondents said their idea of France was "a country of solidarity and social justice".

They are deluding themselves. According to Timothy Smith, a Canadian historian who specialises in French social policy, "a truly solidaristic society is one which pays the price for its solidarity in the here and now, instead of leaving the bill for future generations, instead of taking raises and an extra month of paid vacation (which is the consequence of the shift from the 39-hour to the 35-hour week) or an expensive pension at 55 years of age, on the backs of 2m-3m unemployed people—most of them under the age of 40." But in France that sort of solidarity still seems a long way off.

# The French exception

## From agriculture to Europe, France gets away with doing its own thing

THE vineyards bake in the sun of Provence; vast cornfields stretch golden across the plains of Picardy; in Brittany the cattle slowly munch their way from one deep green field to another; in the Dordogne the geese are having their livers fattened for the world's best foie gras. All this is *la France profonde*, that entrancing country of picturesque villages and revered cuisine. No wonder France is by far the world's most popular tourist destination for foreigners. And no wonder the French themselves, not least President Chirac, are determined to preserve it.

Yet the pastoral idyll is in part a myth. The country towns are surrounded by hypermarkets and car-lots; the villages have garish kiosks dispensing videos; and, all too often, the fields and rivers are polluted with pesticides. Meanwhile, the true *paysans* (the word translates better as "country folk" rather than "peasants") are dwindling in number: down to 627,000 in the 1999 census, a drop of 38% on ten years earlier. Their place has been taken by the modern barons of industrialised agriculture (the average farm now is half as large again as in 1988); or the workers who commute to the nearest town; or the Parisians and foreigners who have bought second homes in the country.

## Rus in urbe

So why is the myth so important? The answer is a mix of nostalgia, culture and economic self-interest. Only two generations ago, agriculture accounted for one-third of the nation's workforce, which explains why even the most confirmed city types usually still have some rural connection. Mr Chirac once said: "The farmers are the gardeners of our country and the guardians of our memory." But there is rather more to it than gardening: helped by an EU Common Agricultural Policy designed with French farmers in mind, France has become the world's fourth-biggest producer of cereals and meat and pockets a quarter of the CAP's funds.

That does not please José Bové, the pipe-smoking, moustachioed leader of the Confédération Paysanne. Mr Bové, a former student activist turned occasional goat-cheese maker, is demanding a more literal interpretation of the myth. He has become a popular hero by attacking globalisation and the CAP for industrialising agriculture at the expense of the small farmer. Two years ago, when he appeared in court for trashing the site for a new McDonalds restaurant, 30,000 demonstrators gathered in his support. He was briefly imprisoned earlier this year.

By contrast, the politicians think the myth is best served by holding on to the status quo. When the European Commission earlier this year proposed replacing production subsidies for farmers with direct payments geared to their care for the environment, Hervé Gaymard, France's agriculture minister, led the counter-attack. Gathering the signatures of six other EU agriculture ministers, Mr Gaymard sent a letter to several European newspapers, noting: "For us, agricultural products are more than marketable goods; they are the fruit of a love of an occupation and of the land, which has been developed over many generations... For us, farmers must not become the 'variable adjustment' of a dehumanised and standardised world."

Cri de coeur or hypocritical power politics? Perhaps a bit of both. Mr Gaymard's argument is that the CAP has served Europe well, and that its reform should not be rushed, but should involve a debate going back to first principles. Then again, the letter was published on September 24th, to coincide with a meeting of agriculture ministers in Brussels. Moreover, it guaranteed a French victory: the signatories represented a minority big enough to defeat not just the commission's plans but also the wish of several northern countries, particularly Britain, to renegotiate the CAP before the present agreement on the EU's finances expires at the end of 2006.

## What kind of Europe?

All this, say the critics, is proof that France, a founder member of the EU, sees it only as a vehicle for its own national interests. But that hardly seems a damning verdict. After all, why join a club if it does not serve your interests? For France, the European club has always served two purposes: to ensure peace with Germany after three wars within a century; and to provide a counterweight to America's power.

Still, the French seem to have a way of bending the club rules to their advantage. For example, back in 1965, when the France of President De Gaulle boycotted Europe's institutions for six months, its "empty chair" policy successfully checked Europe's supranational course, guaranteeing each nation the right to a veto if its vital interests were at stake. And in the early 1990s France held the Uruguay Round of trade negotiations hostage until it won the right to a "cultural exception", allowing it, in effect, to subsidise French films and discriminate against American ones.

In the same vein, Mr Raffarin's finance minister, Francis Mer, blithely told his EU colleagues last June that their "Stability and Growth Pact", a 1997 accord under which all countries had pledged to balance their public-sector budgets by 2004, was "not set in stone." The commission and the other EU members agreed, giving France until 2006 to meet the deadline. But the medium-term budget plans which Mr Mer announced in September show that France will still have a 1% deficit in 2006, prompting open criticism by the commission. Mr Mer seemed unfazed. After a meeting with his EU counterparts last month, he declared: "We decided there were other priorities for France—for instance, increased military spending. Other countries have not taken this kind of decision, but we are still in a Europe where budgetary policy and political decisions are under national control."

It sounds rather like a Europe in which France remains an independent nation-state, choosing for itself when and how to co-operate with the rest of the club. That is one reason why the tie with Gerhard Schröder's federalist-minded Germany has come under strain. However, the tie still holds: last month in Brussels, Mr Chirac, outmanoeuvring—and enraging—Britain's prime minister, Tony Blair, persuaded Mr Schröder that the CAP should remain unchanged until 2006.

Back home, François Bayrou, leader of the Union for French Democracy and a member of the European Parliament, is one of very few French politicians to share the Belgian, Italian or German vision of a powerfully supranational EU. Other visions for the future of the EU, from a confederation of nation-states to a "hard core" of "the willing and the able", all have one thing in common: in essence, France will retain its freedom of action and Europe will serve France's purpose. How else could De Gaulle and his political descendants, including Mr Chirac, have accepted the notion of a communal Europe? Nor are such attitudes confined to Gaullists: the Socialists' François Mitterrand may

# High and mighty

## France's elite is too clever by half

**A**LL nations—even those who once believed in Marx—have their elites, so why should France be any different? Philippe Méchet, a well-known opinion pollster, jokes: "We're a very royalist country, and we killed the king. So now we've monarchised the republic."

You can see his point. The American president lives in the White House, but the French president lives in the Elysée Palace, a choice of noun that conjures up a whole retinue of courtiers and uniformed flunkies. Indeed, when the Socialist François Mitterrand inhabited the Elysée, he lavished so much public money on grand schemes for the capital and its monuments that he was often compared to Louis XIV, the "Sun King".

Take the analogy a touch further and you have a modern nobility, products of the *grandes écoles*, a handful of universities—such as Sciences-Po in Paris or the Polytechnique just south of the capital—that are acknowledged to be centres of excellence. In particular, you have the *énarques*, graduates of the Ecole Nationale d'administration (ENA), a postgraduate school established by De Gaulle in 1945 to train a civil service untarnished by the Vichy regime's collaboration with the Nazis.

It has long been fashionable, even among *énarques*, to criticise ENA as being too elitist for the national good. Recruiting through fiercely competitive written and oral exams, the school has an intake of just 120 students a year for its 27-month-long curriculum. Multiply that by the number of years since ENA was established, allow for some natural wastage, and you get a total figure for living *énarques* of perhaps 5,000.

## Monarchs of all they survey

That elite, minuscule compared with the massed alumni of Britain's Oxbridge or America's Ivy League, commands most of what matters in France. Mr Chirac is an *énarque*, as is Mr Jospin (but not Mr Raffarin); so too the head of the employers' association, Ernest-Antoine Seillière, and many of the bosses of leading banks and businesses, from Jean Peyrelevade of Crédit Lyonnais to Jean-Cyril Spinetta of Air France.

Is this a good or a bad thing? It depends how you look at it. As one *énarque* at the finance ministry says scathingly, "*Énarques* are pretty smart individually, and pretty dumb collectively." ENA's graduates can hardly help being clever: the meritocratic recruitment process is designed to draw bright children from humble backgrounds into the elite (one example is Hervé Geymard, the agricultural minister). They are also competant: having been groomed for the task of administering the state, by and large they make a good job of it.

The reason that they can be "collectively dumb" is that they all come from the same educational mould, which makes their responses somewhat predictable. Their civil-service instinct is to mistrust the private sector and private initiative. Given their predominance in so many key posts, they have been criticised for holding back France's energy and creativity. But perhaps the dumbest thing they do is to ignore the views of lesser mortals, and assume that they always know best.

---

have talked of "the European project" and "the European construction", but in his alliance with Germany's Chancellor Kohl he preserved France's role as the architect.

## Quite contrary

The same streak of Gaullist independence is evident in the way France so often disagrees in public with the United States, in particular over the Middle East. The most obvious example is the squabbling over what kind of UN resolution to use against Iraq, but there are plenty of others. When President Bush linked Iraq, Iran and North Korea in an "axis of evil", the Socialist foreign minister of the day described the American approach as

"simplistic"—the same adjective Mr Raffarin now uses for America's policy.

All this is fine for France's *classe politique*, trained to deal with the intellectual contortions of being an insider in the rich world's councils yet an outside critic at the same time. Earlier this year, for example, both the Jospin government and the opposition sent representatives to the World Economic Forum in New York—but also sent twice as many to the rival, anti-globalisation summit in Porto Alegre, Brazil.

But what of those lesser mortals who make up the electorate? For them it smacks of double-talk. No wonder so many, either by abstaining or by casting a protest vote, took their revenge in the presidential election last spring. They felt lost, and the elite had not bothered to show them the way.

---

# A magic moment

## President Chirac has five years in which to reform France

**T**HE French body politic has had quite a momentous year, but the sense of shock is now fading. The new obsession of the chattering classes is Iraq and American foreign policy (which has catapulted two thoughtful books on French anti-Americanism into the bestseller list). For the political right, the obsession is unity: let the rival parties that coalesced into the Union for the Presidential Majority become a single vehicle to elect the next president in 2007 (Mr Juppé, or Mr

Sarkozy, or—some now whisper—Mr Chirac again?). For the opposition, so much in retreat that the Communist Party, once the largest party of the left, is now struggling to survive with just 21 supporters in the National Assembly, the task is not so much to bind its wounds, but to fight it out until the would-be modernisers of the Socialist Party, such as Dominique Strauss-Kahn and Laurent Fabius, either win or lose.

The government, for its part, talks of "decentralisation". Patrick Devedjian, the "minister of local freedoms", argues that it is time to give power to local officials and to get away from the Napoleonic military logic of a "chain of command" that always leads to Paris. In that way, perhaps a solution could at last be found for Corsica, whose bomb-planting extremists are bent on secession.

But does any of this indicate that the country is facing up to its problems? Sadly, not enough. The *fracture sociale*—a campaign slogan of Jacques Chirac's in his first bid for the presidency, in 1995—still divides the nation; the elites still pontificate at an arrogant distance from *la France d'en bas*; necessary economic reforms still remain a matter of talk rather than achievement; and policy is all to often a consequence of confrontation rather than negotiation. Worst of all, perhaps, is the temptation to seek refuge in a false comfort zone: France as an independent nuclear power, as a permanent member of the UN Security Council, as a member of the G8 club of economic powers—and, of course, as a country that takes culture seriously. France may not match the Anglo-Saxons for Nobel laureates in economics, but in literature it comes top.

Yet there is no need for such a comfort zone. France's engineers are among the best in the world—witness not just high-technology triumphs such as the Ariane rocket programme or the TGV railway system, but also lower-technology successes such as Michelin tyres or the cars of Citroën and Renault (a good enough company to take over Japan's Nissan and return it to profit). The same is true of some of its bankers, insurers and retailers, who successfully compete on the world stage. AXA, for example, will insure your life in America; Carrefour will sell you groceries whether you live in China or Chile.

The disappointment is that such assets are undervalued in the public mind, especially since the fall from grace of Jean-Marie Messier (a graduate both of ENA and the Polytechnique), with his improbable dream of turning a sewage and water company into the Vivendi Universal media giant. Denis Ranque, the boss of Thalès, a French defence and electronics group operating in more than 30 countries, has an explanation: "Popular knowledge of the economy is weak in France. We have important industries, but the French don't like them. They associate them with pollution, not jobs."

Elie Cohen, the economist at Sciences-Po, argues that France has been an ordinary market economy since the mid-1980s, when the folly of Mitterrand's nationalisation programme of 1981–82 became obvious even to the president, but: "The spirit of Gallo-capitalism remains. Each time there's a problem, you appeal to the state." Yet surely an "ordinary" market economy would not go to the lengths France does to resist the liberalising demands of the EU, in particular in the energy market, where EDF is protected at home even as it creates an empire abroad.

## Face up to reality

No matter, you might say: France has prospered regardless. Indeed, there is a certain pragmatism behind the rhetoric: criticise globalisation but profit from it too; criticise America but support it at the same time. The problem is that sooner or later this form of self-deception could turn into self-destruction. In 1995, it prevented France's government from getting the popular backing to carry out reforms that have now become all the more necessary.

During his first presidential term, Jacques Chirac's critics had a common taunt: he was a man who knew how to win power, but now how to wield it. But there was a reason: from 1995 he was locked by the voters into cohabitation with his political opponents. For the next five years, he has no such excuse: having promised to reform France, he now has the power to do so. May he use it wisely.

# How Germany was suffocated

For 57 years Germany has been struggling to make amends for its Nazi past and be accepted by its neighbours. But has its desire to avoid discord stifled the nation's public life and prevented much needed reform? On the fourth leg of his European tour, **Joe Klein** finds a society addled by 'ferocious blandness'

Wednesday June 19, 2002
*The Guardian*

A few weeks ago, Sir Charles Powell told me a story, which he has probably told a thousand times, about visiting Germany with his old boss, Margaret Thatcher. Their host was Helmut Kohl, who took them to his home town of Oggersheim, and to lunch at his favourite bistro and to the cathedral at Speyer, where the first holy Roman emperors—the first pan-Europeans—were buried. At the cathedral, Kohl took Powell aside and said: "It is absolutely crucial that Mrs Thatcher knows that I consider myself a European first and a German second."

Powell and Thatcher returned to their plane. Thatcher kicked off her shoes, leaned back in her chair and said: "Kohl is such a German."

The story says a bit more about Thatcher, perhaps, than it does about Kohl—but it says something about Germany, too. For 57 years, this has been the most admirable of nations. It responded with care, humility and responsibility after the Nazi disgrace (it reserved its martial fervour for the football pitch, and even there was gracious enough to yield the World Cup to England in 1966, a reparation, perhaps, for the blitz). West Germany stood on the front lines of the cold war, steadfast

when the Soviets blockaded and then walled Berlin. It reunited graciously, generously with the east (indeed, at an estimated cost of €600bn, a sacrifice that still is having an effect on the domestic economy).

And it has been the most quietly persistent force in the formation of the European Union. Since the second world war, Germany has worked patiently not just to be accepted by its neighbours, but more—to subsume itself in them. It is as if the Germans don't quite trust themselves to be left to their own devices. "I don't know what will become of Germany," Konrad Adenauer once said, "unless we manage to create Europe in time."

Hence Kohl at the cathedral. Indeed, there is something crashingly Teutonic about the mania to become the precise opposite of Hitler's Reich: thoughtful and peaceful and fair and cooperative and just another country. The effort has been extraordinary, it permeates every corner of post-war German culture; it is as if a quiet decision was made, after 1945, to insert Prozac into the water supply. Political correctness rules; political contentiousness exists, but it is frowned upon; consensus is the holy grail. "There is the assumption that if we keep our heads down we're likely to have success," said Dr Christoph Bertram, a national security expert. "And we have had a lot of success

doing things that way. I wonder, though, if the time hasn't come for us to take a more active role, especially in Europe. Of course, if you use words like 'leadership', you get pushed out of the room. Joschka Fischer [the German foreign minister] still talks about how fragile our basis of acceptance is."

Consensus is, of course, a natural consequence of a multi-party system, where alliances must be formed; all European countries have powerful elites who quietly organise the social arrangements. But there have been recent upheavals in the political cultures of Italy, France and even the Netherlands; there are great debates about the future taking place all over Europe. In Germany, however, a ferocious blandness has set in. Public life has the congealed quality of a Bavarian Kartoffelsuppe left cooling on the stove overnight. Which leads to this week's questions: has Germany become too nice for its own good? Has it consensualised itself into a coma?

"I think that sensibility is fading," a leading newspaper editor told me. "Look at the recent incidents of anti-semitism." Indeed, there are two contretemps simmering—but either could easily be seen as an example of the enduring power of German political correctness. One concerns a novel called *The Death of a Critic* by Martin Walser, a roman à clef about a novelist's revenge on a powerful Jewish critic who has assaulted his work. (Walser's own work has been ravaged by Marcel Reich-Ranicki, an aged and celebrated Jewish critic.) The Frankfurter Allgemeine, which was to publish an excerpt, decided the book was too raw and reneged. Needless to say, the book would be a minor scandal in most other countries; in Germany, it has caused grave soul-searching about the revival of certain national "tendencies".

Then there is the Möllemann dispute. Jürgen Möllemann, deputy chairman of the right-of-centre Free Democratic party, a former paratrooper who has been known to skydive into political rallies, recently said that Ariel Sharon's government in Israel and certain members of the German Jewish establishment—he named one, in particular, a journalist named Michael Friedman—were bringing anti-semitism upon themselves by their extreme behaviour. There was an immediate uproar, of course. There were calls for Möllemann's head. The Free Democrats, who have been rising in the polls on a Thatcherite agenda, dithered a bit and then chivvied an apology from Möllemann. Two hours after he apologised, though, Möllemann issued a clarification: the apology didn't apply to Friedman. The notion that Jews bring anti-semitism upon themselves is repulsive, of course—and the possibility that Möllemann is trolling for the votes of German Arabs and native anti-semites is even more so—but the comments themselves are mild compared to the opinions routinely found in European newspapers: the cartoon in La Stampa, for example, of the baby Jesus in a manger surrounded by Israeli tanks.

The German sensitivity to anti-semitic nuance can't be gainsaid… or can it? In both cases, there is an unhealthy edge of panic—the assumption that if the genie gets out of the bottle there will be jackboots on the Rhine before you can sieg heil. But there are consequences to such skittishness, to a public debate where only the alleged victims are allowed to speak freely. Paul Spiegel, the chairman of the Central Council of Jews in Germany, called the Möllemann affair "the biggest insult uttered by a party in the federal republic since the Holocaust". Yet no one was able to say, "Paul, put a lid on it," for fear of being accused of anti-Jewish sentiments themselves. I suspect the role of national conscience is not a long-term winner for Germany's Jews, any more than the role of national scourge was.

There is another consequence: this frantic German thoughtfulness has led to a society so well padded that no one is willing to take a risk, a society where no one feels comfortable asserting herself. The muffled public debate bores most people silly… and the risk-free economy is sinking under its own weight.

There is, yes, consensus on the latter point. The words "Everyone knows what has to be done" were uttered to me no fewer than 10 times during the course of the week, by leading politicians of all four parties, newspaper editors, economists, and the inevitable taxi driver. "Everyone knows" the economy has to be reformed. The huge manufacturing combines that produce high-quality cars and other products remain brilliantly productive. But almost every other sector is suffering. The strict labour arrangements agreed to by, say, Volkswagen, have become the national norm, but they tend to cripple entrepreneurs trying to start new businesses (the rate of new business formation is among the worst in Europe). The unemployment rate stands at 8.5%—but there are at least another 8.5% who have given up trying to work and are receiving a relatively comfortable level of state support.

The cost of hiring new employees is prohibitive, especially for small employers. "There are about 10 million people working in the shadow economy, many of whom also receive social assistance," said Roland Berger, a management consultant in Munich. "The black market is grow-

ing at about 5% per year—it's the only sector of the Germany economy that actually is growing. So the number of people paying for the welfare state keeps diminishing compared to the number of people getting paid. And then there's the demographic problem every country has—low birth rates, longer lives. The system as it stands can't be sustained."

Of course, not everyone agrees to the medicine that "everyone knows" will work: a thinner welfare state, a less restrictive labour market, a more competitive economy. "I can not move until we get everyone in the boat," Chancellor Gerhard Schröder has told friends. But the unions will probably never get in the boat. His main opponent in the September 22 election, Edmund Stoiber, takes great pains to reassure people that he has no intention of moving toward "American-style" capitalism, either.

The inertia is stultifying, but not impermeable. Twenty years ago, my contemporaries, the greens, made a valiant run at the establishment; eventually they joined it (Joschka Fischer, a green leader, is the most popular politician in the country). Recently there have been signs that the children of the greens are growing impatient, too, but moving in a different direction from their parents—toward the neo-libertarian politics of the Free Democrat party (or yellows). These two groups, green and yellow, are far more interesting than the mummified middle. I'll talk to them this week.

## Berlin

Youth first. Dinner with three young entrepreneurs, aged 31, 32 and 36, at a lovely Italian cafe in Charlottenburg. Each is wearing a suit and tie. Alex, handsome and voluble, is taking over the family office-furniture and interior-design business. He cuts to the chase. "The labour laws are impossible. We have 18 employees; this month, we'll add two more. But I just fired a woman who's been with us for six years. She made several big mistakes, but that wasn't really the problem. She just wasn't committed to the company. She does what she is told to do and nothing more. Look, we're on our way, we're ready to grow—ready to rock and roll—and we just can't afford to have anyone on the team who isn't totally committed. So now I have to go to court in four weeks to defend my right to fire her." (Ask any businessperson and you will be told that small but difficult decisions such as this are often the difference between success and failure; ask any European social democrat and you will be told that honouring the employee's "right" to a job is a price that business must pay to operate in a just society.)

Trosten, 36, runs a company that manages commercial office buildings. He is the rarest of entrepreneurs, a native of East Germany, and he has the most employees of anyone at the table: 60, 30 in Berlin and 30 in Frankfurt. He has a story about regulations. Every company in the real-estate business has to get a letter from the state certifying that it pays taxes and hires no illegal immigrants. This is reasonable enough, but there is more: every time Trosten's company does business with an outside contractor, it has to receive a copy of that company's certification letter. If it doesn't receive the copy, it is required to pay 15% of the bill to the state. "I have 200 suppliers," he said. "My accountant has to spend 10% of her time on this one law. Every transaction has to have copies of the appropriate certification."

There is much talk of silly regulations. Roland Berger had told me a regulatory joke: "Do you know why so few German companies start in garages like Hewlett-Packard did? Because it's illegal. There's a law that says every office must have a window—and another law that says garages are not allowed to have windows."

I've also heard businessmen say that if Bill Gates had been born German, he'd be middle-management at Siemens. "That's not true! That's not

true!" said Frank, a self-employed management consultant. "You have to have a university degree to be middle-management at Siemens. Gates is a college dropout. They wouldn't allow him to be middle-management at Siemens."

When I ask them about politics, the entrepreneurs sigh and say that they'll vote for the nominally conservative Christian Democratic Union. "I wanted to vote yellow [for the Free Democrats]," Alex said, "but I can't now because of Möllemann."

"We can't encourage even the appearance of anti-semitism," said Frank.

Two days later, I had a cup of coffee with a high-ranking Free Democrat who asked to remain nameless. "What a nightmare!" he said, after I told him about the entrepreneurs. The Free Democrats, he explained, had the reputation of being the older, stingier partners of the Christian Democrats during the 16-year reign of Helmut Kohl; the party was dying of senility—it remains the oldest of the four main parties. But a decision was made in 1998 to recharge the batteries. The new party leader, Guido Westerwelle, is only 40; a glitzy advertising campaign has begun. (Example: a group of Indian men in turbans, working at computers, and the words: "They Think Germany is a Developing Country.") The style, as much as the neo-libertarian content—economic and personal freedom—appealed to young people. The Free Democrats doubled their strength in the polls from 6% to 12%. "We're hoping for 18%," said he who would be nameless. "That way we have the power. We are part of any coalition. We are headed that way, at least I hope we still are."

This talk of "power" was very un-German, and the FDP's very use of language is probably part of its appeal. "The culture is very strict about humility," said Frank, the young management consultant. "In school, if you said anything so mild as, 'This is my aim in life, this is what I want to achieve,' people would have

thought that you were crazy and unsuitable."

Alex, the office furniture salesman, laughed and said: "That's right." He took a deep breath, puffed himself up and let fly, "But I want to have a really big company!"

If the most recklessly self-promotional of Germans can get only guilty pleasure from stating his life's goals, one wonders how Germany as a nation will ever be able to freely express its point of view on the international stage, in fact foreign policy and security issues were raised so infrequently as to be virtually absent in any of my conversations with German officials.

"We learned in school that we were responsible for the past," said Frank. Literally responsible. If you ever said, 'Hey, I'm just 15, I'm not responsible for anything,' you'd have some serious trouble on your hands. I think that's part of why we're so nervous about asserting ourselves."

## Hanover

"I want to have power. I like being in power," said Claudia Roth, co-chair of the Green party, as we sat in her bright, militantly informal Berlin office. "I got into a lot of trouble when I said that a few weeks ago. 'How dare she! Power is bad, power is dangerous!' But you need power to change the world."

Roth had begun our conversation with a tribute to the Prince of Wales, who had recently visited Germany. "He's so green. He spoke about nature and biodiversity, genetic agriculture and nuclear power, and he was so clear, so intelligent. I was so impressed I want to propose him for honorary membership in the German Green party." She noticed that I was laughing. "No, really," she insisted.

If ever there was going to be an antidote to the stifling consensuality of Germany, it promised to be the greens—and look at them now: Prince Charles is their idea of a radical. The greens are the only significant party to have been formed since Germany became the federal republic, my baby-boomer generation's contribution to political discourse, and they did change things a bit. They popularised the notion of women's and human rights, and, of course, they brought the environment to centre stage. They were fanatic peaceniks at first, but that only served to reinforce the prevailing German unease with all things military.

Over time the party's establishment drift has caused an endless, garrulous marital spat between two factions: the fundis and the realos (names that recall the 60s split between realies and feelies). The realos have won. They became part of the government in 1998, when Gerhard Schröder formed his red-green coalition. They supported military action in Kosovo and Afghanistan (the fact that German troops are currently operating in Afghanistan, the first time the country's soldiers have been deployed outside Europe since the war, doesn't seem to be much of an issue to anyone in Germany) and they are making noises—safe, consensual noises—in favour of the sort of economic reforms "everyone knows" are needed. But, the fundis would argue, the realos lost, too: They lost their ideological purity—and the party is losing altitude in the polls, down from 12% to about 7%.

In Hanover last week, the greens celebrated the 20th anniversary of their arrival in the Lower Saxony Landtag (legislature). It was a wildly nostalgic evening. Jürgen Trittin, Germany's minister of the environment and a member of the greens'

first legislative delegation in 1982, told the crowd gathered in a courtyard of the Landtag complex: "My first speech in the Landtag was to demand the expulsion of the leader of the parliament. It didn't pass."

The Hanover greens had been at the epicentre of the fight to prevent the storage of nuclear waste at Gorleben. I was introduced to an unprepossessing man with short white hair and a moustache, whose name was Rolf Grösch. "I was in the streets with Joschka Fischer in Frankfurt in 68," Grösch said. Fischer's streetfighting past is now famous in Germany. Grösch was also a leader of the Gorleben protests and another member of the greens' first Landtag delegation. "We all rotated out of the parliament after two years. That used to be party policy: one term and then out. I'm sorry we've abandoned it. My son, who is 20, thinks we're just another establishment party now."

Next, I was introduced to a realo-fundi mixed marriage: Doctor Thea Dückers (R) and Johannes Kempmann (F). Actually, Kempmann was formerly a fundi, a leader of the Gorleben anti-nuke protests. He is now a board member of an energy company. "I wanted to see," he said sheepishly, "if I could make a difference from the inside."

We sat on the back steps of the Lower Saxony parliament building, drinking beer, the setting sun in our eyes, talking about the strange lessons that experience teaches. "We were part of the local red-green parliamentary alliance," said Dückers, who is now a member of the Bunde-

stag and a leading green economic expert. "But after we were turned out in 1994, my husband and I started a humanitarian agency and were working with the Kurds in northern Iraq. Every day, we saw the American jets fly over and we'd be so happy. Their presence allowed us to do our work. It was an important moment for us, a big change. We both began to understand the importance of military power. I voted for the military actions in Kosovo and Afghanistan in the Bundestag."

I asked Johannes about the young people going yellow. "We call them the spass generation," he said. "The fun generation. They like having new cars and big houses and fun drinks and clothes. They don't like to talk about politics, they like to talk about fun. The FDU is all about fun. That's not the green way. We can argue about politics all night."

"Are they rebelling against you?" I asked.

"What do you think? We had long hair and they have no hair. We were going to change the world and they—well, with the internet and the global economy and all these other things, they think the world is too complicated to change. So why not have fun?"

I suggested that our generation had been a burden on our children, "and it's only going to get worse as we retire and they have to pay for us".

Kempmann laughed. "A terrible burden, yes," he said, and then grew quiet. "Yet another burden."

---

# Germany's general election:

# Gerhard Schröder clings on

**The incumbent German chancellor has won a cliff-hanging election but with no real mandate for reform**

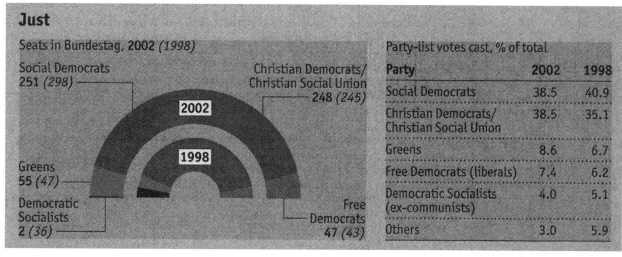

**Just**

Seats in Bundestag, 2002 *(1998)*

Social Democrats
251 *(298)*

Christian Democrats/
Christian Social Union
248 *(245)*

Greens
55 *(47)*

Democratic
Socialists
2 *(36)*

Free
Democrats
47 *(43)*

| Party-list votes cast, % of total | | |
|---|---|---|
| **Party** | **2002** | **1998** |
| Social Democrats | 38.5 | 40.9 |
| Christian Democrats/ Christian Social Union | 38.5 | 35.1 |
| Greens | 8.6 | 6.7 |
| Free Democrats (liberals) | 7.4 | 6.2 |
| Democratic Socialists (ex-communists) | 4.0 | 5.1 |
| Others | 3.0 | 5.9 |

Source: Bundeswahlleiter

BERLIN

**I**N ONE of the tightest German elections for half a century, Chancellor Gerhard Schröder's coalition of Social Democrats and Greens managed to cling on to power by its fingertips. Together the pair have 306 seats, a majority of nine in the Bundestag, the lower house of parliament. In the outgoing one, they had a majority of 21, and could usually count on at least the abstention of the 36 ex-communist Democratic Socialists who this time failed to clear the hurdle to obtain any seats by proportional representation and got only two directly elected seats.

Mr Schröder's slim majority will not only make it harder for his government to push through painful reforms but also puts a question-mark over its longevity. Previous governments, notably Helmut Kohl's after 1994, have had equally thin majorities yet have survived; a sitting chancellor can be displaced in mid-term only by a "constructive vote of no confidence", meaning that parliament has to vote for an alternative administration and not just ditch a beleaguered one.

Still, Mr Schröder will find the going tough. Discipline within the left-wing parties is often loose, particularly among the idiosyncratic Greens. The conservative opposition has gained ground. It already controls the Bundesrat, Germany's upper house, where about half of federal legislation has to be passed. And the economy is continuing to stagnate. Edmund Stoiber, the defeated conservative challenger, says he expects the new government's life to be "very, very short".

# Charlemagne: **Europe marching left, right, left**

## Why political taboos are being broken in Europe

The Germans invented the word *Zeitgeist,* but anyone hoping that their latest election would confirm a new "spirit of the age" in Europe will have been disappointed. In the past year or so, a clear trend seemed visible. Left-wing governments were ousted by the right in Italy, France, the Netherlands, Denmark, Portugal and Norway. Germany looked like the next and biggest domino to fall. But though Gerhard Schröder's "red-Green" coalition wobbled, it refused to topple. Just the week before Mr Schröder's victory, Sweden's Social Democrats also bucked the trend, easily winning another stint in office. Now Austria's Social Democrats have a chance of regaining power later this year. So much for Europe's inexorable move to the right.

The broader truth, however, is that on the big economic and social issues facing Europe the differences between centre-right and centre-left—between Christian democracy and social democracy— are pretty paltry. Certainly the right is still closer to business, the left to the trade unions. But the resulting differences in policy have more to do with nuance than deep philosophy. In Germany, for example, Edmund Stoiber on the right proposed a top rate of income tax of 40%, while Mr Schröder wants to bring it down to 42%. Mr Stoiber said the state should consume no more than 40% of GDP, Mr Schröder stuck to his own favourite number, 42%. Economists and businessmen may clamour for a drastic revamp of Germany's generous welfare state and for decisive moves to tackle public pensions, but neither candidate was prepared to risk suggesting anything daring. As Mr Stoiber drily remarked, he had not noticed anyone demonstrating for a radical overhaul of social security.

What is true of Germany is true of the rest of Europe. Italy's Silvio Berlusconi admires Margaret Thatcher but has done nothing to tackle Italy's pensions problem and little to free up the labour market. France's new centre-right government has moved cautiously to mitigate the worst effects of its Socialist predecessor's introduction of a 35-hour week but is committed to an extensive welfare state and shows no desire to take on the unions.

Faced with such tiny differences between left and right on the big issues of social and economic management, voters tend to plump for the most appealing personalities. One big reason why Mr Schröder and Sweden's Goran Persson won while Lionel Jospin, a French socialist, lost is that the winning pair are highly effective politicians while Mr Jospin came across as dull and stiff. Tony Blair's mastery of British politics relies at least as much on his personality—and his Schröder-like sense of what people want to hear—as on any particular policies.

It was Mr Blair who made the last real attempt to define a new pan-European (and indeed transatlantic) political *Zeitgeist.* When the centre-left held sway on both sides of the ocean, he earnestly pushed forward his big idea—"the third way". Mr Schröder tried briefly to echo him with cosy talk of a "new middle". But the whole Blairite

philosophy was too vague to catch on and much of the European left disliked what little it understood of it, assuming it was code for a kind of soft-edged Thatcherism. Mr Blair has now almost given up talking about the third way. In a recent interview in *Prospect,* a British magazine, he was reduced to claiming that "in parts of Latin America [the third way] is seen as a ground-breaking moment." (They speak of little else in the queues outside Argentina's banks.)

But while a welfarist consensus may still hold sway across the European Union, consensus politics are fraying around the edges in other ways. The most striking recent trend has been the rise of populist parties openly hostile to immigration. When Austria's People's Party became the first such party to join a governing coalition, there was outrage across the EU. But the rise of politicians making similar appeals elsewhere in other EU countries has muted the outcry. The Pim Fortuyn list in the Netherlands and Umberto Bossi's Northern League in Italy have both joined governing coalitions after campaigns that highlighted the supposedly bad effects of immigration. The new centre-right Danish government relies on the votes of an anti-immigration party. As Bertel Haarder, Denmark's immigration minister, points out, there may be a connection between addiction to welfarism and hostility to immigrants. Partly because of high minimum wages and welfare benefits, there are very few jobs for unskilled immigrants: around 60% of them in Denmark have no job. So they are easily stigmatised as free-loading parasites.

Mainstream politicians have reacted in different ways to the rise of anti-immigration parties. In France the National Front's Jean-Marie Le Pen won close to 20% of the votes in the presidential election but remains firmly beyond the pale. The new French government has nonetheless begun to toughen both rhetoric and actions against illegal immigrants. All across the EU, asylum-seekers are getting a frostier welcome.

## Vox populi, a pox on civility?

The rise of anti-immigration populists has demonstrated the political potential of voicing sentiments often heard in the street but rarely in parliamentary chambers. Mr Schröder's campaign was a variation on this theme. Struggling in the polls, he decided to express the anti-Americanism that is a strong current of public opinion in Germany and the rest of the EU. Warning against "adventures" in Iraq and carping at the American economic model was just a mild version of commonplace feelings. Mr Schröder's supporters took the hint—and helped him cling on to power. However, as with the immigration debate elsewhere in Europe, once a political taboo is broken it is hard to control the consequences. German relations with America have nose-dived. And new and queasy-making sentiments are popping out of the closet at home, such as the ill-fated comparison between George Bush and Hitler allegedly made by Mr Schröder's justice minister. Sometimes taboos are there for a reason.

On a night of nerves, with both leaders at different moments claiming victory, the two main formations—the Social Democrats and the combined Christian Democrats and their Bavarian sister party, the Christian Social Union—each got 38.5% of the vote. In the end, the Social Democrats pipped the conservatives, by almost 9,000 votes and three seats. The new Bundestag is expected to have its first sitting in the week that starts on October 14th, with the formal re-election of Mr Schröder as chancellor on the same day or soon after.

With the Social Democrats losing ground since the previous election, in 1998, it was the Greens who kept the ruling coalition afloat. They emerged as the election's only real winners, with 8.6% of the vote, their highest score since they first won seats in parliament in 1983. They are now clearly the country's third force.

Barely a year ago, after a string of electoral setbacks, they seemed tired, bland and on the way out. Mr Schröder had even begun eyeing the Free Democrats, Germany's liberals, as alternative coalition partners. But the combined effect of recent floods in the east (which revived many voters' environmental concerns), of the chancellor's stand against a war in Iraq, and of a strong campaign by Joschka Fischer, the Greens' foreign minister and Germany's most popular politician, helped them bounce back. Mr Schröder can thank the Greens for letting him keep his crown. In turn, they will now expect more influence, and say they will press the chancellor to raise the tempo of reform.

The liberals, despite doing a little better than last time, were the election's losers. Their expectations had been high. Pollsters throughout the campaign had put them ahead of the Greens. Only last month, one poll gave them 13%, double the Greens' projected score. They had begun to assume that no government could be formed without them. But they ended up with a modest 7.4%, a point behind the Greens and a far cry from the 18% they had set themselves. A renewed rumpus over anti-Israeli comments by Jürgen Möllemann was partly to blame. He has now resigned as the liberals' deputy leader. But the "fun party" image projected by their leader, Guido Westerwelle, though attracting young voters, may well have put off many of the party's older, more earnest supporters. Many Germans think Mr Westerwelle lacks gravitas.

Despite failing to hit all three of his proclaimed targets—to have the biggest group in parliament, to win more than 40% of the vote, and to topple the government—Mr Stoiber has emerged beaten but unbowed. His conservatives upped their 1998 vote by more than three percentage points, while the Social Democrats dipped by a couple. In Mr Stoiber's Bavarian homeland, his party's share shot up by 10.9 points to 58.6%, its best score in nearly two decades. Indeed, with 9% of the total national vote, Mr Stoiber's Christian Social Union can claim to be Germany's third biggest party, ahead of the Greens. He says he has no intention of retiring quietly back to his home state but stands ready to take the chancellor's job should the government collapse.

Were it not for last month's floods in the east and the threat of an American-led war in Iraq, Mr Schröder would probably have failed to win a second term. Neither event was of his making, of course. But he exploited them both to his benefit. As a result, says Donald Rumsfeld, the American defence secretary, relations between Germany and the United States have been "poisoned". He refused even to talk to his German counterpart at this week's meeting of NATO defence ministers in Warsaw, and President George Bush failed to send Mr Schröder the customary congratulations. The chancellor is eager for reconciliation and has even asked Britain's Tony Blair to help. But he insists that there will be "no change" in his opposition to Germany's participation in an attack on Iraq, even under a United Nations mandate.

This, says Mr Schröder, is "a difference of opinion" that should be accepted among friends; the relationship, he insists, is "intact". That is not the view in Washington. Matters were not helped last week by the German justice minister, who was accused of lumping Mr Bush with Hitler by saying that the American president has sought to distract voters from problems at home by talk of war—tactics, she is said to have added, that were once used by "Adolf Nazi". She has denied making the remarks, but says she will resign anyway. Relations between the countries, and between Mr Schröder and Mr Bush, who have not talked since June, remain strained.

It is on the home front, however, that Mr Schröder faces his hardest task. Speeding up Germany's dismal growth rate, creating jobs and loosening the country's labour rigidities should be his top priorities. But the election does not suggest that the German people have an appetite for radical reform. Mr Schröder has no mandate for it. Nor would Mr Stoiber, if he had won. That is the election's gloomiest lesson.

From *The Economist*, September 28, 2002, pp. 45, 46, 53. © 2002 by The Economist, Ltd. Distributed by the New York Times Special Features. Reprinted by permission.

# GERMANY ADRIFT:
## The New Germany

Germans went to the polls in September at a strange time in their nation's history. The sudden reunification that caused so much joy only a few years ago now seems a costly burden. The prosperity that once made Germany the envy of its neighbors has given way to talk that the country is "the sick man of Europe." **Martin Walker** reflects on Germany's prospects, and on the past it seems unable to escape.

On September 22, in Germany's closest election in more than 50 years, a divided and uncertain electorate gave a narrow victory to the governing coalition of Chancellor Gerhard Schröder's Social Democrats and their Green Party allies. But the voters declined to give the new government a clear mandate, and the prospect of four years of weak government and political deadlock now looms. Schröder's coalition held just enough seats in parliament to avoid dismissal and must now try to govern with a majority of only nine seats in the Bundestag. The conservatives won a three percent greater share of the national vote than they did in the previous election four years ago, but they and the Free Democrats, their likely partners in a coalition, fell short of a governing majority. The ex-Communists of the former East Germany, running as the Party of Democratic Socialism, won only four percent of the vote and two seats. Various extreme right-wing parties fared even worse, winning barely three percent of the vote in all—and no seats.

It's some consolation that Germany chose between moderates of the center-Left and center-Right, and that extremist parties of the Right and Left did poorly. But the closeness of the election result has left the new German government looking fragile. The conservative leader, Bavarian premier Edmund Stoiber, has predicted that the majority is too small to work and too unstable to last: "Should the result not allow us to form a government, I predict that this Schröder government will rule for only a very short time." And he returned to a campaign theme: "This coalition will not heal our country's economy, and there will be no release from the isolation from Europe and the United States."

The new government faces two immediate challenges: a damaging rift with its American allies over Iraq, and an economic and political crisis with its European partners. Despite the efforts of the conservatives to focus on the stagnant economy and Germany's four million unemployed, the main drama of the election campaign stemmed from foreign policy. Schröder's blunt refusal to support an American-led assault on Iraq, even if it were to have a United Nations mandate, helped him claw back from an eight-point deficit in the opinion polls. The task of repairing relations with Washington has been made no easier by the heatedly anti-American campaign rhetoric, including an episode that outraged the White House: a bizarre comparison of George W. Bush to Adolf Hitler by Schröder's justice minister, Herta Däubler-Gmelin.

The international focus of the campaign was all the more surprising in view of the grave domestic conditions in Germany. For the past seven years, German has recorded the worst economic performance in Europe. Further, the main political parties all agree that the constitution needs amending: The powers of the second chamber in parliament, the Bundesrat, must be weakened so that the elected government can govern without being blocked. But that change requires the agreement of the Bundesrat, and of a majority of the powerful *Länder*, the 16 individual states that make up the Federal Republic of Germany. No wonder Josef Joffe, editor of *Die Zeit*, calls Germany "a blocked society, incapable of reform." And yet the election hinged on foreign policy. Germans found to their surprise that the celebrated mantra of Bill Clinton's 1992 campaign—"It's the economy, stupid!"—did not work. The headlines and the public imagination were caught by the country's aversion to war with Iraq, by its suspicion of the United States, and by controversy over Germany's attitudes toward Israel, still strongly colored by guilt and bitter memories of World War II and the Holocaust.

The composition of the new German government was decided not by the two main political parties, which finished almost neck and neck, but by the smaller parties, which were able to furnish the votes needed for a majority coalition. The Greens, scoring their best-ever result, campaigned as pacifists, deeply opposed to war and wary of military operations, even peacekeeping missions with a UN mandate. The Free Democrats, liberal centrists who now advocate far-reaching economic reform, have traditionally held the balance of power. But this time they faltered and, after highly critical remarks about Israel by their deputy leader, Jürgen Möllemann, won only 7.4 percent of the vote. The prominent coverage given Möllemann's outbursts and Däubler-Gmelin's clumsy references to Bush and Hitler was a reflection of how the campaign skirted the serious issues of economic and social stagnation. Neither the voters nor the politicians seemed to know what to do about those issues, so they chose to talk about other things, and held an election that decided little—except that Germany is a country in denial.

In what she described as the one "unambiguous failure" of her foreign policy, British prime minister Margaret Thatcher tried without success to block the unification of Germany after the fall of the Berlin Wall. "A reunited Germany is simply too big and too powerful to be just another player within Europe," she concluded in her memoirs. Germany, she said, is "by its very nature a destabilizing rather than a stabilizing force in Europe." The perception that a united Germany would be uncomfortably powerful for its European neighbors was widespread at the time. Lady Thatcher even claimed subsequently that French president François Mitterrand and Dutch premier Ruud Lubbers agreed with her in private but believed that German unification could not be stopped and should therefore be tamed within an ever closer European Union (EU), with the mighty deutsche mark absorbed into a single European currency.

The defining fact about post-Cold War Germany is that successive governments, political parties, and the broad public were all happy to make the accommodation to Europe. Indeed, since the 1950s a national consensus had developed behind a phrase coined by the novelist Thomas Mann: "a Europeanized Germany, rather than a Germanized Europe." One of the central issues now, for Germany and Europe both, is how far the process of accommodation will go. And like so much else that will affect Germany's future, from the global economy to prospects for the Atlantic Alliance, the matter is not entirely in German hands. The British and French—and other partners in the European Union—stand firmly against German proposals for a federal Europe, in part because they still fear that Germany could dominate it.

Before unification, West Germany had the strongest economy in Europe. Its population of just over 60 million was roughly equal to that of France, Britain, or Italy, but its gross domestic product (GDP) was half again as large as Britain's. Unification brought an additional 18 million new citizens from the former East Germany, which was perceived to be the most advanced and efficient of the Warsaw Pact economies. With both the largest population in Europe (and thus the largest voting block in the European Parliament) and the largest economy, Germany in the 1990s seemed destined to achieve by peaceful means what two world wars had failed to secure for it by force of arms.

It is one of the major surprises of the post-Cold War era that the united Germany has lived up neither to its own hopes nor to the fears and expectations of its neighbors. In 1999, Otmar Issing, chief economist of the European Central Bank, warned that Germany could become "the sick man of Europe unless it drastically reformed its costly welfare state." In July 2002, the research group of Deutsche Bank issued a thoughtful report, "Is Germany Heading the Same Way as Japan?" that was intended to set the tone for the German general election in September. The report stressed that Germany's growth had lagged behind that of its EU partners for almost a decade: "Gloomy prospects and chronically weak growth in the 1990s... have raised the question, now being asked publicly, whether Germany is following Japan to become a second potential trouble spot among the large industrial nations—an area with weak economic momentum, reliant on other countries for most of its growth impetus."

The nation's plight is worrying its partners in the EU, who are accustomed to Germany's paying $10–12 billion more annually into the EU budget (which falls just short of $100 billion) than it receives. An EU without this German contribution would be a far more cantankerous body. Daniel Gros, director of the Center for European Policy Studies in Brussels, calls the situation "the new German problem." "Until recently," he has said, "the 'German problem' in European affairs was how to deal with a country that was stronger than its neighbors and thus a menace to equilibrium on the continent. It now seems that the problem is the opposite—how to deal with a country that constantly underperforms."

In addition to economic disappointments, other factors have contributed to the German mood of malaise. The German education system, once a source of pride, is faltering badly. The media sounded a note of panic this spring when German high school students per-

formed poorly in an international comparative test of 15-year-olds. Of the 32 participating countries, Germany ranked 25th in overall reading, mathematics, and science literacy. The outcome compounded an already present concern about recurrent spasms of skinhead violence and isolated neo-Nazism among the young, particularly in the former East Germany, where youth unemployment in some regions is as high as 30 percent. The sense of crisis in Germany's crowded and underfunded universities is best caught by the titles of two recent best-selling books, *Im Kern verrottet?* (Rotten to the core?) and *Ist die Uni noch zu retten?* (Can the university still be saved?).

So Germans are feeling a deep concern about the future. Sobering demographic trends suggest that a low birth rate and ever-longer life expectancy are making the current German social system unsustainable; there are too few Germans of working age to finance the pensions of the increasing numbers of old people. In 1990 German women had an average of 1.45 children each, a figure already well below the replacement rate of 2.1. (American women in 2001 had, on average, 2.1 children.) By 2000, according to Eurostat, the European Union's official statistics body, the average number of children had dropped to 1.34 for each woman.

But there's a paradox here. Despite the economic statistics, modern Germany is not just a rich and prosperous democracy but one of the most agreeable societies on earth, with a high quality of life. It has less crime than France, Britain, or the United States, recycles more of its waste, and enjoys cleaner and safer streets. There are salmon again in the cleansed Rhone and Elbe rivers, once two of the most polluted waterways in Europe. The cities of Berlin and Hamburg alone spend more on culture than the whole of Britain does. Germans spend more on books than the British, French, and Dutch combined, and more on tourism than the British, French, and Swedish combined. Wages are high. It takes a German autoworker 35 hours to earn enough to buy a color TV, as against 51 hours for a French autoworker and 78 hours for a Belgian.

There's a further paradox. Germany has become, as Chancellor Gerhard Schröder promised in the 1998 election campaign, "a normal nation." By this he meant a country that could, at last, play a full role on the world stage. The traditional self-constraints on German foreign policy have almost disappeared. German warplanes took part in the 1999 Kosovo campaign, which also saw German troops sent to combat outside their own borders for the first time since 1945. Since Kosovo, German special forces have fought alongside their British and American counterparts in the Afghanistan campaigns against Al Qaeda. And yet there is not the slightest sign of militarism in the country. Indeed, Germany's allies in the North Atlantic Treaty Organization, in particular the United States, complain that the country spends only 1.5 percent of its GDP on defense, roughly half the proportion of America, Britain, or France. But veteran officials such as Horst Teltschik, national security adviser to former chancellor Helmut Kohl, warn that Germany's small defense budget, along with Chancellor Schröder's outspoken attacks on the Bush administration's pledge of "regime change" in Iraq, "seriously undermine our alliance with America, the bedrock of our foreign policy for 50 years."

Which leads to the cruelest paradox of all. So long as it was divided, and in a fundamental way subordinate to the grand strategies of the Cold War, Germany boomed. As noted above, West Germany became the most powerful economy in Europe, and East Germany was, by a considerable margin, the most prosperous of the Warsaw Pact states. Once the division ended, Germany languished under high unemployment, economic sluggishness, and social unease. Having lost the excuse of the Cold War to explain its problems, it appeared to lose its way and to become less than the sum of its reunited parts.

Any analysis of modern Germany must begin with the unfinished business of unification. Thirteen years after the fall of the Berlin Wall, the absorption of the former East Germany has been immensely expensive and far from successful. With 20 percent of the country's population, the former German Democratic Republic produces just 10 percent of the new Germany's GDP. Unemployment is twice as high as in the West, and productivity barely 70 percent of Western levels, despite almost a trillion dollars in state subsidies since 1990. (That's 10 times more money, allowing for inflation, than the Marshall Plan pumped into West Germany after 1949.) The government has resignedly announced that federal aid to the East will have to be extended for another 20 years, along with the income tax surcharges to pay for it.

The problem, it seems widely accepted, stems from the decision of then-chancellor Kohl to speed up unification by exchanging West German and East German marks at near parity. In real purchasing power, a more appropriate exchange rate would have been three or four East marks to one West mark. This strain on the federal budget forced up interest rates in Germany and across Europe. Though the measure brought most East Germans appreciably closer to West German living standards, it also left East German industry massively overpriced and unable to use its one structural asset, cheap skilled labor, at the very time the East Germans were losing their traditional markets in Eastern Europe and the Soviet Union. Thus, the East Germans had the worst of both worlds: Their goods were too crude and ill packaged for Western markets and too costly for Eastern ones.

There are, of course, a few bright spots. Volkswagen built a $187 million plant in Dresden to assemble its new Phaeton car, creating more than 500 new jobs earlier this year. BMW announced this year that it would build a new plant in Leipzig instead of shifting production abroad; it was persuaded to remain in Germany by tax breaks and subsidies that will pay more than a third of the plant's construction costs. There have even been some local successes—erstwhile East German industrial concerns that have restructured and prospered. The most commonly cited example is JenaOptik, an optical engineering group that employed more than 20,000 people when it made the cameras, binoculars, and gun sights for many of the Warsaw Pact armies. It was turned into a thriving company by Lothar Späth, a popular, hard-driving former chief minister of his native Baden-Württemburg state. As a result, Späth is something of a hero in the East and was recruited for this year's election campaign to be the economics czar of a future conservative government. But Späth's success at JenaOptik came at high cost: $2 billion in state subsidies and the elimination of some 16,000 jobs. The firm, which suffered a small loss this year after a period of impressive growth, now employs some 7,000 people worldwide, but only 1,100 of them are in the former East Germany.

Politicians, desperate to proclaim light at the end of the unification tunnel, hail these occasional successes. The Social Democratic Party's position paper insists that the overall picture is "not as dire as is portrayed in public." Actually, it may be even worse. The tax base of the old East is declining, as young people continue to leave. Between the fall of the Berlin Wall in 1989 and the formal declaration of unification the following year, some 800,000 East Germans—mainly the young—moved to the West. Since then, more than a million others have followed, while fewer than 100,000 Westerners have made the journey the other way. The region has lost a quarter-million jobs in the past four years, mainly because the construction industry has shrunk now that the state's main infrastructure investments in roads, rail, and telecommunications have been completed. And the $2.6 billion a year that the

East receives from EU Structural Funds, which are meant to help lower-income regions, is about to be shifted to the even more deserving cases of Poland, Hungary, the Baltic states, and other new EU members. (Some EU aid to the East will continue because its more rural regions are so poor.) To the anger of Germans living in the East, German corporations have beaten the EU to investment in those other countries. Volkswagen, for example, has pumped more money into the old Czech Skoda car works than it has put into East Germany. Indeed, Germans are by far the leading foreign investors in Eastern Europe.

Eastern Germans also complain of being patronized by their compatriots in the West, and they've indulged in a nostalgia boom for the old communist-era brands of East German beer, biscuits, confectionery, and washing powder. A similar kind of nostalgia helps explain the importance in the East of the Party of Democratic Socialism, the reformed Communists of the past, who have shared power in Berlin with the Social Democrats. But the success of the reformed Communists undermines the power of the Eastern bloc voting to help the main political parties win or lose national elections. In 1990, in response to Chancellor Kohl's unification drive, Easterners gave most of their votes to the Christian Democrats, securing Kohl's landslide. In 1998, feeling disillusioned with Kohl, they switched to give the bulk of their votes to the Social Democrats, and thereby delivered the chancellorship to Gerhard Schröder. Their recent disappointment with Schröder, because of his unfulfilled promise to cut unemployment, and their enthusiasm for Lothar Späth as the Christian Democrats' new economics chief, were a real concern for the Social Democrats during the 2002 campaign.

The difficulties of absorbing the East would have been less worrisome had the traditional vigor of German industry been maintained, but the German economic miracle of the 1950s and 1960s has faltered. In the seven years since 1995, Germany has shared with Italy the bottom rung on the European growth ladder. To an American observer, the wonder is that the German economy works as well as it does, given the extraordinary constraints upon it. First, labor costs are high, and labor unions are so strong that it's difficult to fire workers. Second, the generous welfare system imposes a huge cost on employer and employee alike. Norbert Walter, chief economist of Deutsche Bank, argues that the focus of Germany's leaders on unification derailed prospects of social reform: "I thought unification would have provided a turning point. For those who had looked into the German welfare system and its instability before the Wall came down, it was obvious it could no longer be sustained. The need for a complete overhaul of the German socioeconomic system is even more urgent now."

The German skilled worker is the third highest paid in the world, after the Swiss and the Danish. But of a gross income of $34,400 a year, the average German takes home just $20,100. Moreover, that worker costs an employer almost exactly $50,000, when social security and insurance provisions are factored in. It's cheaper, complain officials from the state of Hesse, for a German bank to post executives to London and fly them back twice a week for meetings than to keep them in their native Frankfurt. "We are risk-averse as a society. Germans do not want to give up the social safety nets," says Walter. "The problem is not the politicians, but the electorate itself, which fears change. And there's another problem, the dominant mindset of the generation of 1968, who are just not gifted with the entrepreneurial and fighting spirit."

The software giant SAP remains a relatively rare "new economy" success. Germany's best-known companies are still rooted in the traditional technologies of engineering, automobiles, and chemicals, industries where labor unions are particularly strong. The three sectors account for two-thirds of German exports. A breakthrough seemed to have occurred in 1996, when the massive Deutsche Telekom monopoly began selling its shares to the public as the first step in the country's most ambitious privatization drive. Although fewer than one German in 10 owned stocks at the time, millions flocked to buy the Deutsche Telekom shares at an initial-offer price of $25. The price swiftly soared to $100—and then fell to $18. The hesitant German conversion to the Anglo-Saxon entrepreneurial model has been further battered by the collapse of the Neuer Markt, the German equivalent of NASDAQ, which has lost 90 percent of its value in the past two years—a period in which the main Frankfurt stock exchange has lost 52 percent of its value.

The fall in stock prices undermined Schröder's attempt to tackle the looming demographic threat to pensions by putting a modest two percent of the work force's national insurance payments into individual savings accounts. The idea was attractive while stock prices were rising, but it became far more controversial when prices plunged. Schröder's promised tax cuts ran into two additional problems: the estimated $20 billion cost of this year's catastrophic floods in central Europe, and what is known as the Stability Pact of the new euro currency. Inspired by a former German government that feared fiscal profligacy in Italy and other EU members, the Stability Pact requires EU states to keep their budget deficits below three percent of their GDP—and imposes fines of one-half percent of GDP if the target is breached. Because recession drove Germany dangerously close to the three percent limit, the pact threatened an annual fine of $10 billion just as the country faced the flood emergency.

In 2002 the German commitment to Europe began to appear, for the first time, a problem rather than a solution. The fiscal straitjacket of the Stability Pact limited the government's options in dealing with the floods. At the same time, EU rules against state aid to industry, in the name of fair competition, constrained Germany's strategic determination to lift the East to the West's economic standards. The EU's competition watchdogs also challenged the privileges long granted to Germany's powerful regional banks, which have benefited from state-backed financial guarantees. The Stability Pact posed a subtle threat to Germany's admirably decentralized constitutional system, which grants unusually wide powers to the *Länder*, or state governments. The *Länder* account for roughly half of government spending, and they've helped swell the deficit.

These difficulties with the EU are throwing into sharper relief the costs, as well as the advantages, of the international structure into which Germany has chosen to fit. The issue first emerged publicly in the 1998 campaign, when candidate Schröder warned that the EU should "not rely forever on the German wallet." They emerged again in the 2002 campaign, with Christian Democratic candidate Edmund Stoiber warning, in a blunt speech this past May, that EU enlargement must have its limits—and should not include Turkey. "I believe there must be geographical borders for the EU," he said. "Europe cannot end on the Iraqi-Turkish border. Whoever wants that endangers the cohesion of Europe."

Stoiber also raised the delicate issue of German nationalism during the 2002 campaign, in a way that jolted the EU enlargement process. He demanded that the Czech Republic retract the Benes Decrees of 1945, under which some three million Czechs of German descent were deported from their homes in the border region of the Sudetenland on the grounds that they were Hitler's fifth column in the 1930s. Stoiber, married to a former Sudeten German, outraged the Czech government and alarmed other Eastern Europeans, particularly the Poles, who wondered whether the issue would put at risk the whole 1945 settlement of Europe's borders.

Because of Germany's history, such issues are intensely sensitive. Margaret Thatcher is not the only European who continued to see

modern Germany through the perspective of World War II and the Holocaust. Her prejudices were reinforced by an unusual seminar she conducted at her country residence, Chequers, in March 1990, when she was fighting her doomed delaying action against unification. Six academic experts on Germany and Europe were summoned to join her. A memorandum on the session, subsequently leaked to the British press, listed what were seen as the negative aspects of the German character: "angst, aggressiveness, assertiveness, bullying, egotism, inferiority complex, and sentimentality."

The list is a caricature. Nearly 60 years after the end of World War II, it should be possible to consider modern Germany apart from Hitler's shadow. But Germans themselves make it difficult to do so, because an official anti-Nazism practically defines the identity of modern Germany. In this election year, which saw the banning of a small but unpleasant neo-Nazi group, the issue of Germany's Nazi past arose repeatedly. The first such occasion was when Stoiber demanded the retraction of the Benes Decrees. The second was when outspoken criticism of Israel greeted its response to the Palestinian suicide bombings. The deputy leader of the Free Democratic Party was driven to stand down for suggesting that, in the Palestinians' place, he too would be provoked into fighting back. It was left to Foreign Minister Joschka Fischer, of the Green Party, to say in an op-ed piece that Germany would have to consider whether it would ever be legitimate to criticize Israeli policies without plunging into the troubled waters of anti-Semitism.

And then there was the cultural drama over a novel that topped the German bestseller lists throughout the summer, *Death of a Critic*, by the acclaimed writer Martin Walser. The novel, which seems to blur the line between fictional and real characters, deals with the murder by an outraged writer of a well-known Jewish literary critic. The book was condemned by the country's leading newspaper—in whose pages Germany's leading critic, who is Jewish, had made his reputation—as a kind of intellectual Nazism. Walser is perhaps best known outside Germany for a forthright speech, in the context of Schröder's ambition that Germany become "a normal nation," in which he said that it was time to stop battering Germany with "the bludgeon of Auschwitz."

And yet, the recurrent echoes of the past and the reminders of the old Germany no longer seem to fit. The face of modern Germany is to be found less in the dwindling numbers of its beer halls than in its stylish new restaurants, a thriving art scene, the splendid new modern art museum in Munich, and events such as this July's 14th annual Love Parade in Berlin, which saw half a million young people dance to a deafening techno beat from monumental loudspeakers as 45 floats snaked toward the Tiergarten's Victory Column. The new Germany is a country of immigrants and refugees and not, as in the past, of nationality based purely on German blood. More than 480,000 immigrants have become naturalized citizens since the reform in 1999 of the law restricting citizenship to those of German blood.

The new Germany can be seen as well in a host of experiments that, like Schröder's economic reforms, may seem tentative to non-Germans but are actually changing the habits of the country. Private universities are springing up to cope with the overcrowded mess of the free public institutions. Rather than start early and close at lunchtime, some experimental schools are staying open all day (a change that might increase the relatively modest numbers of women in the work force). Shops are open a little longer, increasing numbers of Germans are working part-time, and the country is catching up with the Scandinavia and America in Internet connections. Thanks to mortgages, a nation of apartment dwellers is becoming a nation of homeowners, and the traditionally thrifty Germans now have a higher level of debt than free-spending Americans. With political and media consultants serving all parties, and the novelty of TV debates between the candidates, this year's election felt less German (about sober party platforms) than British or American (about personalities).

In education, the media, and the service sector, and in Germany's image abroad, a cultural revolution is struggling to be born, even as the political system appears deeply resistant to change or reform. The leading contenders in this year's election made clear that neither of the main parties wanted drastic change. In a long interview, Stoiber stressed that "discontinuity is best avoided in a society that faces far-reaching changes like globalization, September 11, enlargement of the EU, and the population trend. If we fail to safeguard prosperity and the welfare network, there will be serious protests." His was a strikingly modest agenda for a candidate campaigning on the dire plight of the German economy and taking as his central issue "that Germany must move up from last place in Europe."

The aftermath of this year's devastating floods in the Eastern city of Dresden suggests that unification is indeed working. Rudi Völler, coach of Germany's national soccer team, was stunned when he asked the players for donations to flood relief and the World Cup finalists raised $500,000 in three minutes. Public appeals have raised more than $100 million. "The wave of donations has been overpowering—there's never been anything on this scale before," said Lübbe Roewer of the Red Cross. Tens of thousands of volunteers trekked to Dresden. At the city's famed opera house, reported Volker Butzmann, the opera's technical director, "everyone from cloakroom ladies to singers came to help with the clean-up."

The heartwarming response to the floods of Dresden may say more about the new united Germany than do the giant building projects of Berlin, the presence of German troops on international missions, and complaints about the Benes Decrees. Germany may think it's the sick man of Europe, in dire need of reforms it shrinks from making. But Germany feels like one nation again. And that, friends and critics alike might agree, is a genuine transformation.

---

MARTIN WALKER, *a former Wilson Center public policy scholar, is a journalist and author. His books include* America Reborn: A Twentieth-Century Narrative in Twenty-Six Lives *(2000) and the recently published novel* The Caves of Périgord.

From *The Wilson Quarterly,* Autumn 2002, pp. 31-34, 50-51. © 2002 by Martin Walker.

# Radical reverts to the old pattern

## The hard edges of planned reforms by Junichiro Koizumi have given way to the more soothing language of consensus

by David Ibison

On numerous street corners around Tokyo there are posters of Junichiro Koizumi, prime minister, that were pasted up ahead of his election in April last year. He is un-smiling, his sleeves are rolled up and he is staring icily ahead of him.

Tokyo's humid summer, bitter winter and windy spring having weathered the posters, and here and there an arm has been torn away, and grime splashed on to his shirt and face.

The transformation from dazzling propaganda to weatherbeaten reminders of a short-lived era of confidence sums up the prime minister's first 18 months in office, during which the hard edges of his reforms have been eroded away.

During visits to small towns around Japan, it is almost possible to see the high tide line left behind by Mr Koizumi's popularity before the wave rolled away, leaving behind it the familiar debris of Liberal Democratic party rule.

A bold legislative agenda has been gradually ground into a more modest format and the stormy language that promised to "change the LDP and change Japan" has given way to a more soothing whisper of consensus.

Mr Koizumi has sought to portray this shift as a victory on his part. He is claiming that as a result of his political skills he had seduced the members of his own party he termed "forces of resistance" into becoming forces for co-operation.

But behind these opportunistic claims the shrill departing words of Makiko Tanaka, the popular politician sacked by Mr Koizumi as foreign minister, can still be heard. "Koizumi has become one of the forces of resistance," she spat.

The evidence indicates strongly that in the battle for the balance of power between the forces of resistance and Mr Koizumi's reforms, the resistance forces have their heels dug in and are slowly but steadily pulling the reformers towards them.

But a straight battle for control would be too obvious for the quixotic world of Japanese politics. Instead, this is a game that is being won in a way that allows the loser to claim that he is the winner.

Take, for example, post office reform. Mr Koizumi's proposed legislation was diluted significantly by the forces of resistance before it was finally passed in parliament, but as soon as it was passed Mr Koizumi and the resisters joined to praise the achievement.

"Backward steps are presented as forward steps and retrograde moves are sold as proof of reform," says one economist.

When it was announced that a number of banks had agreed to forgive debts to Daiei, a barely alive retailer, Mr Koizumi, his cabinet and noted members of the forces of resistance issued statements saying the move "demonstrated Mr Koizumi's commitment to reform."

## 'Bankrupt banks continuing to lend to bankrupt companies does not sound very reformist'

"Bankrupt banks continuing to lend to bankrupt companies does not sound very reformist," the economist says.

On highway corporation reform, a radical "reformist" novelist has been placed in charge of the committee overseeing reform even though he can be out-voted numerically by anti-reformers at any time.

Even the decision to sack Mrs Tanaka has been linked to a deal whereby the forces of resistance would agree to pass Mr Koizumi's watered-down legislation if he agreed to sacrifice her. The list goes on until a pattern emerges.

The Koizumi administration has entered a second phase. Phase one was characterised by a clarity of vision and brimming confidence. In phase two, the impression of reform remains while the substance of reform dissipates.

"For those familiar with Japanese political conundrums, this falls pleasantly into the pattern. For those who believed Mr Koizumi presented a chance for genuine change, this reverts unhappily to type," says one diplomat.

This subjective split also applies to attitudes towards Mr Koizumi. For those who expected the worst, he has been cowed into submission by the forces of resistance. For those who expected the best, he has woken up to political reality and decided to deal with the devil in order to get something done.

The extremist view that Mr Koizumi is achieving nothing is incorrect. Reforms are being implemented. The opposing extremist view, that he is going too far towards reform, is equally incorrect.

"What we are seeing is compromise," said one political analyst. "And this is not a new concept in Japanese politics. Despite his image, Mr Koizumi falls very firmly into a 50-year tradition of LDP politicians."

## *Setting Sun?*
# Japan Anxiously Looks Ahead

### By HOWARD W. FRENCH

TOKYO

**Y**EAR in and year out since Japan's financial bubble burst in 1990, American presidents have needled and cajoled the country's leaders to fix their economy and restore Japan to its rightful place in the world.

Gradually, though, as this country has continued its drift, a more skeptical view has begun to gain ground: Japan *is* returning to its rightful place in the world, that of a middling country of vastly diminished and still declining importance in world affairs.

From the ashes of World War II, Japan enjoyed one of the fastest economic rises ever seen. Its successes made it widely envied by developing nations everywhere, as an example of how much a democratic, capitalistic country could achieve in a short period of time. Now, if its decline continues, it could have profound implications for American diplomatic and military policy in Asia.

Twelve years after its stock market collapsed, along with its dreams of superpower status, Japan is still frozen in denial about a dysfunctional political system built on institutionalized cronyism. By contrast, the United States is already seeing strong stirrings of reform just weeks into a crisis over business ethics.

Not everyone is ready to turn out the lights on Japan. The Hudson Institute, for example, has just published a book titled "The Re-Emergence of Japan as a Super State." In a recent opinion column in The Wall Street Journal, the institute's president, Herbert London, cited Japan's "100 percent literacy rate, stable leadership, products valued in world markets, mastery of Western management techniques and a belief in purposeful communal action," and

concluded "it is not hard to be confident in Japan's future."

But recent signals from Washington suggest much greater skepticism, as diplomats say the Bush administration has increasing doubts that Japan will ever again become a global mover and shaker.

It is not just that Japan is not what it used to be. Some analysts say even its decline matters far less than it might once have, because it failed, when times were still good, to convert some of the immense wealth it had accumulated into more lasting power and influence.

"Looked at objectively, Japan is a rather insignificant power in terms of its contributions to the rest of the world," said Ronald A. Morse, a professor of Japanese studies at the University of California at Los Angeles who is also an executive with a telecommunications firm here. "If the country keeps receding, or even disappeared, there is hardly anything that would have a major negative impact abroad. The reason this sounds shocking is because everybody still remembers the Godzilla image of a Japan not so long ago that was going to swallow up America."

For other observers, however, Japan's long slide has huge implications for the future of Asia and beyond. Japan is a model for few in Asia these days, and with the country's diplomacy in disarray, those who take their cues from Tokyo are a fast dwindling number, leaving a vacuum that may be filled by less closely allied friends of the United States, or by outright rivals.

Indeed, from Central Asia to the Korean peninsula, many analysts believe the coming decades are shaping up to be a competition for diplomatic and economic sway between Russia and China. And if Moscow and Washington draw closer, that would only accelerate Japan's declining influence in Asia, and make Japan less able to serve as a counterweight to China.

"IF the Japanese really lost hope, they might start thinking more about acquiescing in Chinese power," said Robyn Lim, an expert in international relations at Nanzan University in Nagoya, "so Japan's return to some semblance of economic health is a vital interest of the U.S. for both security and economic reasons.

"How to influence Japanese policy is the big problem, since the leadership is now completely paralyzed."

Japan's stalemate is especially striking when compared to the energetic diplomacy of Russia, another diminished Asian power, and one with virtually no economic hand to play. Still, by virtue of its nuclear prowess and proximity to central Asia, the Caucasus and eastern Europe, Russia has gone in the blink of an eye from nuclear enemy of the United States to strategic partner, even contemplating cooperation on missile shield development. Over that same stretch, Japan, which was disarmed by the United States in 1945 and remains pacifist, has never overcome its ambivalence about American missile shields, despite its longstanding alliance with Washington.

The rise of China presents Japan with its greatest challenge since the Second World War, but has left Tokyo seeming both intimidated and confused, shifting nervously between appeasement with generous development assistance, and provocations. These include visits by Prime Minister Junichiro Koizumi to a controversial shrine, Japan's imperial army veterans and trade spats.

Japan's discomfort reflects what experts say are the painful choices that loom as its population shrinks and ages dramatically.

Some Japanese may be tempted to rearm and go it alone behind a leader like Tokyo's popular governor Shintaro Ishihara. Mr. Ishihara is a sort of East Asian Jean-Marie Le Pen, who demonizes ethnic minorities and taunts China as well as the West, as in his famous 1989 book, "The Japan That Can Say No." But with low economic growth its best-case outcome, realism will oblige Japan to cling ever more tightly to the United States for its security.

Japan's recent failure of dynamism is of a piece with a pattern seen at least since 1868, when the Meiji Restoration threw off feudalism and two centuries of isolationism to meet the challenge from the West. The country has veered between catastrophes, marshaling its energies fantastically well toward recovery, as after World War II, and then blindly holding on until the next crash.

What's changed is that the world moves far faster now, and squandered moments, even Japan's lost decade, may be irretrievable. The country's moment of truth may have been in the Persian Gulf war in 1991, when, as Yoichi Funabashi, the international affairs commentator of the Asahi Shimbun newspaper, wrote, "Japan found itself merely an automatic teller machine, one that needed a kick before dispensing the cash."

As inadequate as mere checkbook diplomacy is, the Japan that is being written off today is increasingly unable even to play that game the way it once did because of its huge debt and pension woes. But even when Japan had wealth to spare, it was unable to overcome the deep historic wounds left over from its imperial conquests of the 1930's, or to systematically strengthen its political and economic ties with Asian neighbors.

"If you look beyond the United States, the countries that have been able to play a significant role in the world of ideas are all rather second-rate European countries: the British, the French, even the Swedish," said Sheldon M. Garon, a historian of Japan at Princeton University. "Japan has contributed very little to the discussion. They don't really have the vision to become world citizens, and have done a really horrible job of promoting alternatives to American dominance."

Perhaps the most essential element in Japan's relative decline is its insularity. Although familiar, this feature of the country reflects a great irony. With its mastery of the production and marketing of consumer electronics, Japan was an early mover in globalization. And yet here again it has failed to adjust, placing alongside isolated North Korea in international rankings of English-speaking ability. Meanwhile, even Japan's coming population crunch has failed to open the country to immigrants.

As the country's bureaucrats cook up one costly high tech plan after another in hopes of putting Japan back into the driver's seat, few here seem to have realized that money alone doesn't build Silicon Valleys. No, that is a task for open societies that draw on the world's best brains.

"I see only two things Japan can do, and they are inseparable: opening up the country and its institutions," said Jean-Pierre Lehmann, a longtime Japan specialist at I.M.D., a graduate management school in Lausanne, Switzerland. "But I don't see this happening, because Japan just doesn't want foreigners. Meanwhile, you can't rebel in Japan, so the most talented young people are leaving the country or are simply resigned."

Originally from the *Los Angeles Times*, August 11, 2002. © 2002 by The New York Times Company. Reprinted by permission.

# UNIT 2

# Pluralist Democracies: Factors in the Political Process

## Unit Selections

## Key Points to Consider

- How do you explain the apparent shifts toward the political center made by parties of the moderate Left and moderate Right in recent years? Discuss the recent trend toward governments of the moderate Left in Western Europe. How do Social Democrats present themselves as reformers of capitalism? What are the main sources of electoral support for the far-right political parties?

- Why are women so poorly represented in Parliament and other positions of political leadership? In what way has this begun to change, and why? What came of France's interesting experiment with legislating gender parity for party nominations of political candidates? How do institutional arrangements, such as election systems, help or hinder an improvement in this situation?

- Would you agree with the inventory of democratic essentials as discussed by Philippe Schmitter and Terry Lynn Karl? What do you regard as most and least important in their inventory? What are some of the major arguments made in favor of the parliamentary system of government? How does the use of judicial review in some other countries compare with our own?

 **Links: www.dushkin.com/online/**
These sites are annotated in the World Wide Web pages.

**American Foreign Service Association (AFSA)**
*http://www.afsa.org/related.html*

**Carnegie Endowment for International Peace**
*http://www.ceip.org*

**Communications for a Sustainable Future**
*http://csf.colorado.edu*

**Inter-American Dialogue (IAD)**
*http://www.iadialog.org*

**The North American Institute (NAMI)**
*http://www.northamericaninstitute.org*

Observers of contemporary Western societies frequently refer to the emergence of a new politics in these countries. They are not always very clear or in agreement about what is supposedly novel in the political process or why it is significant. Although no one would dispute that some major changes have taken place in these societies during the past three decades, affecting both political attitudes and behavior, it is very difficult to establish clear and comparable patterns of transformation or to gauge their endurance and impact. Yet making sense of continuities and changes in political values and behavior must be one of the central tasks of a comparative study of government.

In two of the most important lines of comparative inquiry, political comparativists have examined the rise and spread of a new set of "postmaterial" values and, more recently, the growing signs of political disaffection in both "older" and "newer" democracies. The articles in this reader also explore some other trends with major impacts on contemporary politics. Very high on the list is the recent wave of democratization—that is, the uneven, incomplete, and unstable but nevertheless remarkable spread of democratic forms of governance to many countries during the last quarter of a century. An important place must also go to the highly controversial "paradigm shift" toward a greater reliance on some kind of market economics in much of the world. This move, which has created its own problems and conflicts, also comes in different forms that span the gamut from partial measures of deregulation and privatization in some countries to the practical abandonment of central planning in others. Finally, political scientists recognize the important rise or revival of various forms of "identity politics." This shift has intensified the political role of ethnicity, race, gender, religion, language, and other elements of group identification that go beyond more traditional social, economic, and ideological lines of political division.

Since the early 1970s, political scientists have followed Ronald Inglehart and other careful observers who first noted a marked increase in what they called postmaterial values, especially among younger and more highly educated people in the skilled service and administrative occupations in Western Europe.

Such voters showed less interest in the traditional material values of economic well-being and security, and instead stressed participatory and environmental concerns in politics as a way of improving democracy and the general "quality of life." Studies of postmaterialism form a very important addition to our ongoing attempt to interpret and explain not only the so-called youth revolt but also some more lasting shifts in lifestyles and political priorities. It makes intuitive sense that such changes appear to be especially marked among those who grew up in the relative prosperity of Western Europe, after the austere period of reconstruction that followed World War II. In more recent years, however, there appears to have been a revival of material concerns among younger people, as economic prosperity and security seem to have become less certain. There are also some indications that political reform activities evoke considerably less interest and commitment than they did earlier.

None of this should be mistaken for a return to the political patterns of the past. Instead, we may be witnessing the emergence of a still somewhat incongruent new mix of material and post-material orientations, along with "old" and "new" forms of political self-expression by the citizenry. Established political parties appear to be in somewhat of a quandary in redefining their positions, at a time when the traditional bonding of many voters to one or another party seems to have become weaker, a phenomenon also known as dealignment. Many observers speak about a widespread condition of political malaise in advanced industrial countries, suggesting that it shows up not only in opinion polls but also in a marked decline in voter participation and, on occasion, a propensity for voter revolt against the establishment parties and candidates.

The readings in this unit begin with three political briefs that present a comparative perspective on public disillusionment and the decline in voter turnout, the partial weakening of the political parties, and the apparent growth of special interest lobbying. These briefs contain a rich assortment of comparative data and interpretation.

Without suggesting a simple cause-effect relationship, the British observer Martin Jacques has pointed to possible connections between electoral malaise or dealignment and the vague rhetoric offered by many political activists and opinion leaders. He believes that the end of the cold war and the collapse of communism in Europe have created a situation that demands a reformulation of political and ideological alternatives. In light of the sharpened differences between much of Europe and the United States over how to approach the Middle East and some other topics such as the Kyoto Accords, some observers wonder whether the end of the cold war will also mean the permanent weakening of the familiar trans-Atlantic relationship. At this point, events are still in flux.

Most established parties seem to have developed an ability to adjust to change, even as the balance of power within each party system shifts over time and occasional newcomers are admitted to the club. Each country's party system remains uniquely shaped by its political history, but it is possible to delineate some very general patterns of development. One frequently observed trend is toward a narrowing of the ideological distance between the moderate Left and Right in many European countries. It now often makes more sense to speak of the Center-Left and Center-Right respectively.

Despite such convergence, there are still some important ideological and practical differences between the two orientations. Thus the Right is usually far more ready to accept as "inevitable" the existence of social or economic inequalities along with the hierarchies they reflect and reinforce. The Right normally favors lower taxes and the promotion of market forces—with some very important exceptions intended to protect the nation as a whole (national defense and internal security) as well as certain favorite groups and values within it. In general, the Right sees the state as an instrument that should provide security, order, and protection for an established way of life. The Left, by contrast, traditionally emphasizes that government has an important task in promoting opportunities, delivering services, and reducing social inequalities. On issues such as higher and more progressive taxation, or their respective concern for high rates of unemployment and inflation, there continue to be considerable differences between moderates of the Left and Right.

Even as the ideological distance between Left and Right narrows but remains important, there are also signs of some political differentiation within each camp. On the center-right side of the party spectrum in European politics, economic neoliberals (who speak for business and industry) must be clearly distinguished from the social conservatives (who are more likely to advocate traditional values and authority). European liberalism has its roots in a tradition that favors civil liberties and tolerance but that also emphasizes the importance of individual achievement and laissez-faire economics.

For such European neoliberals, the state has an important but very limited role to play in providing an institutional framework within which individuals and social groups pursue their interests. Traditional conservatives, by contrast, emphasize the importance of social stability and continuity, and point to the social danger of disruptive change. They often value the strong state as an instrument of order, but many of them also show a paternalist appreciation for welfare state programs that will help keep "the social net" from tearing apart. For them, there is a conservative case for a limited welfare state that is not rooted in social liberal or socialist convictions. Instead, it is supported by traditional sentiments of "noblesse oblige" (roughly translated as "privilege has its obligations") and a practical concern for maintaining social harmony.

In British politics, Margaret Thatcher promoted elements from each of these traditions in what could be called her own mix of "business conservatism." The result was a peculiar tension between "drys" and "wets" within her own Conservative Party, even after she ceased to be its leader. In France, on the other hand, the division between neoliberals and conservatives has run more clearly between the two major center-right parties, the very loosely united Giscardist UDF, and the seemingly more stable neo-Gaullist RPR, who have been coalition partners in several recent governments. In Germany, the Free Democrats (FDP) would most clearly represent the traditional liberal position, while some conservative elements can be found among the country's Christian Democrats (CDU/CSU).

On the Left, democratic socialists and ecologists stress that the sorry political, economic, and environmental record of communist-ruled states in no way diminishes the validity of their own commitment to social justice and environmental protection in modern industrial society. For them, capitalism will continue to produce its own social problems and dissatisfactions. No matter how efficient capitalism may be, they argue, it will continue to result in inequities that require politically directed redress. Many on the Left, however, show a pragmatic acceptance of the modified market economy as an arena within which to promote their reformist goals. Social Democrats in Scandinavia and Germany have long been known for taking such positions. In recent years their colleagues in Britain and, to a lesser degree, France have followed suit by abandoning some traditional symbols and goals, such as major programs of nationalization. The Socialists in Spain, who governed that new democracy after 1982, went furthest of all in adopting some very business-friendly policies before their loss of power in early 1996.

Some other West European parties further to the left have also moved in the centrist direction in recent years. Two striking examples of this shift can be found among the Greens in Germany and in what used to be the Communist Party of Italy. The Greens are by no means an establishment party, but they have served as a pragmatic coalition partner with the Social Democrats in several state governments and have gained respect for their mixture of practical competence and idealism. Their so-called realist faction (Realos) appears to have outmaneuvered its more radical rivals in the party's so-called fundamentalist (or Fundi) wing. Despite some loss in voter support, which can be explained by a revival of the party's internal divisions over strategy and goals, the Greens were finally able to enter government at the national level in 1998. In Gerhard Schröder's government of Social Democrats and Greens, the leading "realo" Joschka Fischer is foreign minister and two other cabinet posts are held by fellow environmentalists. Many German Greens have had a difficult time accepting their country's military involvement in the Kosovo conflict in 1999 and, more recently, in Afghanistan. There is a longer list of moves by the new government that are difficult to square with their idealistic and pacifistic origins.

Both center-left and center-right moderates in Europe face a challenge from the populists on the Far Right, who often seek lower taxes and drastic cuts in the social budget as well as a sharp curtailment of immigration. On the Ultra Right, there is sometimes a neo-fascist or fascist-descended challenge as well. These two orientations on the Far Right can often be distinguished, as in Italy, where the populist Northern League and the fascist-descended National Alliance represent positions that seem to be polar opposites on such key issues as government devolution (favored by the former, opposed by the latter). Sometimes a charismatic leader can speak to both orientations, by appealing to their shared fears and resentments. That seems to be the case of Jürg Haider, whose Freedom Party managed to attract over one-quarter of the vote in Austria in the late 1990s. The electoral revival of the right-wing parties can be linked in considerable part to the anxieties and tensions that affect some socially and economically insecure groups in the lower middle class and some sectors of the working class.

Ultra-right nationalist politicians and their parties typically eschew a complex explanation of the structural and cyclical problems that beset the European economies. Instead, their simple answer blames external scapegoats, namely the many immigrants and refugees from Eastern Europe as well as developing countries in northern Africa and elsewhere. These far-right parties can be found in many countries, including some that have an earned reputation for tolerance like the Netherlands and Denmark. Almost everywhere some of the established parties and politicians have been making symbolic concessions on the refugee issue, in order to prevent it from becoming monopolized by extremists.

***Women in politics*** is the concern of the second section in this unit. There continues to be a strong pattern of underrepresentation of women in positions of political and economic leadership practically everywhere. Yet there are some notable differences from country to country, as well as from party to party. Generally speaking, the parties of the Left have been readier to place women in positions of authority, although there are some remarkable exceptions, as the center-right cases of Margaret Thatcher in Britain, Angela Merkl in Germany, and Simone Weil in France illustrate. Far-right parties tend to draw markedly less support from female voters, but at least one of them is led by a women: Pia Kjaersgaard founded and still heads the People's Party of Denmark.

On the whole, the system of proportional representation gives parties both a tool and an added incentive to place female candidates in positions where they will be elected. But here too, there can be exceptions, as in the case of France in 1986 when women did not benefit from the one-time use of proportional representation in the parliamentary elections. Clearly it is not enough to have a relatively simple means, such as proportional representation, for promoting women in politics: There must also be an organized will and a strategy among decision makers to use the available tool for the purpose of such a clearly defined reform.

This is where a policy of affirmative action can become a decisive strategy. The Scandinavian countries illustrate better than any other example how the breakthrough may occur. There is a markedly higher representation of women in the parliaments of Denmark, Finland, Iceland, Norway, and Sweden, where the political center of gravity is somewhat to the Left and where proportional representation makes it possible to set up party lists that are more representative of the population as a whole. It is of some interest that Iceland has a special women's party with parliamentary representation, but it is far more important that women are found in leading positions within most of the parties of this and the other Scandinavian countries. It usually does not take long for the more centrist or moderately conservative parties to adopt the new concern of gender equality, and these may even move toward the forefront. Thus women have recently held the leadership of three of the main parties in Norway (the Social Democrats, the Center Party, and the Conservatives), which together normally receive roughly two-thirds of the total popular vote. Ane the present Swedish government of Social Democrats has an equal number of women and men in the cabinet.

In another widely reported sign of change, the relatively conservative Republic of Ireland several years ago chose Mary Robinson as its first female president. It is a largely ceremonial post, but it has a symbolic potential that Mary Robinson, an outspoken advocate of liberal reform in her country, was willing to use on behalf of social change. In 1998, a second woman president was elected in Ireland. Perhaps most remarkable of all, the advancement of women into high political ranks has now also touched Switzerland, where they did not get the right to vote until 1971. It is equally noteworthy that Prime Minister Koizumi of Japan appointed five women to his cabinet when he assumed office in 2001, an absolute first in that male-dominated society.

Altogether, there is a growing awareness of the pattern of gender discrimination in most Western countries, along with a greater will to do something to rectify the situation. It seems likely that there will be a significant improvement over the course of the next decade if the pressure for reform is maintained. Several countries have now passed the 30 percent level in their national parliaments, regarded by some observers as a "critical mass." For lack of political will, one of the most remarkable recent steps was a failure, at least on the first try. It consisted of a statute, promoted by the recent socialist-led government of France, which required the country's political parties to field an equal number of male and female candidates for office in most elections. The first major test of this new parity measure came in the French parliamentary elections of 2002, where it was widely flouted, as Megan Rowling reports in her article. Ironically, the egalitarian measure had provoked some feminist criticism in advance. It is possible to see the new parity law as being in a sense regressive, since it incorporates an essentialist vision of women as females first, citizens second.

Changes that erode gender inequality have already occurred in other areas, where there used to be significant political differences between men and women. At one time, for example, there

used to be a considerably lower voter turnout among women, but this gender gap has been practically eliminated in recent decades. Similarly the tendency for women to be somewhat more conservative in their party and candidate preferences has given way to a more liberal disposition among younger women in their foreign and social policy preferences than among their male counterparts. These are aggregate differences, of course, and it is important to remember that women, like men, do not represent a monolithic bloc in political attitudes and behavior but are divided by other interests and priorities. One generalization seems to hold: namely, that there is much less inclination among women to support parties or candidates that have a decidedly "radical" image. Thus the vote for extreme right-wing parties in contemporary Europe tends to be considerably higher among males.

In any case, there are some very important policy questions that affect women more directly than men. Any careful statistical study of women in the paid labor force of Europe would supply evidence to support three widely shared impressions: (1) There has been a considerable increase in the number and relative proportion of women who take up paid jobs; (2) These jobs are more often unskilled and/or part-time than in the case of men's employment; and (3) Women generally receive less pay and less social protection than men in similar positions. Such a study would also show that there are considerable differences among Western European countries in the relative position of their female workers, thereby offering support for the argument that political intervention in the form of appropriate legislation can do something to improve the employment status of women—not only by training them better for advancement in the labor market, but also by changing the conditions of the workplace to eliminate some obvious or hidden disadvantages for women.

The socioeconomic status of women in other parts of the world is often far worse. According to reports of the UN Development Program, there have been some rapid advances for women in the field of education and health opportunities, but the doors to economic opportunities are barely ajar. In the field of political leadership, the picture is more varied, as the UN reports indicate, but women generally hold few positions of importance in national politics. To be sure, there have been some remarkable breakthroughs, for example in South Africa, where women won 100 of the 400 seats in the first post-apartheid parliament in 1994, and 120 seats (34 percent) in 1999.

*The institutional framework of representative government* is the subject of the third section of this unit. Here the authors examine and compare a number of institutional arrangements: (1) essential characteristics and elements of a pluralist democracy, (2) two major forms of representative government, (3) different forms of regulation of campaign and party finance, (4) the varying use of judicial review, and (5) the use of national and regional referendums as well as other forms of direct democracy.

The topic of pluralist democracy is a complex one, but Philippe Schmitter and Terry Lynn Karl manage to present a very comprehensive discussion of the subject in a short space. Gregory Mahler focuses on legislative-executive relations, drawing primarily on the Canadian and American examples. He avoids the trap of idealizing one or the other way of organizing the functions of representative government. The next two political briefs examine the remarkable growth and variety of judicial review in recent years as well as the arguments for and against the use of the referendum as a way of increasing the electoral involvement with policymaking.

# Public Opinion: Is there a crisis?

After the collapse of communism, the world saw a surge in the number of new democracies. But why are the citizens of the mature democracies meanwhile losing confidence in their political institutions? This is the first in a series of articles on democracy in transition.

Everyone remembers that Winston Churchill once called democracy the worst form of government—except for all the others. The end of the cold war seemed to prove him right. All but a handful of countries now claim to embrace democratic ide-als. Insofar as there is a debate about democracy, much of it now centers on how to help the "emerging" democracies of Asia, Africa, Latin America and Eastern Europe catch up with the established dem-ocratic countries of the West and Japan.

The new democracies are used to having well-meaning observers from the mature democracies descend on them at election time to ensure that the voting is free and fair. But is political life in these mature de-mocracies as healthy as it should be?

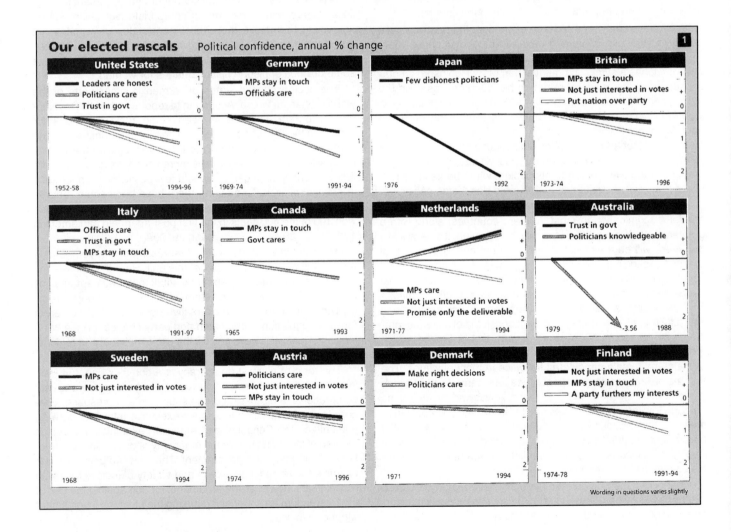

**Our elected rascals** — Political confidence, annual % change

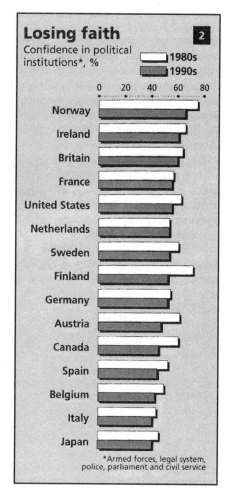

**Losing faith** ☐2
Confidence in political institutions*, %
☐ 1980s
▨ 1990s

0  20  40  60  80

Norway
Ireland
Britain
France
United States
Netherlands
Sweden
Finland
Germany
Austria
Canada
Spain
Belgium
Italy
Japan

*Armed forces, legal system, police, parliament and civil service

Sources: R. Dalton; World Values Surveys

If opinion research is any guide, the mature democracies have troubles of their own. In the United States in particular, the high opinion which people had of their government has declined steadily over the past four decades. Regular opinion surveys carried out as part of a series of national election studies in America show that the slump set in during the 1960s. The civil-rights conflict and the Vietnam war made this an especially turbulent decade for the United States. But public confidence in politicians and government continued to decline over the next quarter-century. Nor (remember the student unrest in Paris and elsewhere in 1968) was this confined to the United States.

It is hard to compare attitudes toward democracy over time, and across many different countries. Most opinion surveys are carried out nation-by-nation: they are conducted at different times and researchers often ask different sorts of questions. But some generalizations can be made. In their introduction to a forthcoming book "What is Troubling the Trilateral Democracies?", Princeton University Press, 2000) three ac-

ademics—Robert Putnam, Susan Pharr, and Russell Dalton—have done their best to analyze the results of surveys conducted in most of the rich countries.

Chart 1 summarises some of these findings. The downward slopes show how public confidence in politicians seems to be falling, measured by changes in the answers voters give to questions such as "Do you think that politicians are trustworthy?"; "Do members of parliament (MPS) care about voters like you?"; and "How much do you trust governments of any party to place the needs of the nation above their own political party?" In most of the mature democracies, the results show a pattern of disillusionment with politicians. Only in the Netherlands is there clear evidence of rising confidence.

Nor is it only politicians who are losing the public's trust. Surveys suggest that confidence in political institutions is in decline as well. In 11 out of 14 countries, for example, confidence in parliament has declined, with especially sharp falls in Canada, Germany, Britain, Sweden and the United States. World-wide polls conducted in 1981 and 1990 measured confidence in five institutions: parliament, the armed services, the judiciary, the police and the civil service. Some institutions gained public trust, but on average confidence in them decreased by 6% over the decade (see chart 2). The only countries to score small increases in confidence were Iceland and Denmark.

Other findings summarised by Mr Putnam and his colleagues make uncomfortable reading:

• In the late 1950s and early 1960s **Americans** had a touching faith in government. When asked "How many times can you trust the government in Washington to do what is right?", three out of four answered "most of the time" or "just about always". By 1998, fewer than four out of ten trusted the government to do what was right. In 1964 only 29% of the American electorate agreed that "the government is pretty much run by a few big interests looking after themselves". By 1984, that figure had risen to 55%, and by 1998 to 63%. In the 1960s, two-thirds of Americans rejected the statement "most elected officials don't care what people like me think". In 1998, nearly two-thirds agreed with it. The proportion of Americans who expressed "a great deal of" confidence in the executive branch fell from 42% in 1966 to 12% in 1997; and trust in Congress fell from 42% to 11%.

• **Canadians** have also been losing faith in their politicians. The proportion of Canadians who felt that "the government doesn't care what people like me think" rose from 45% in 1968 to 67% in 1993. The proportion expressing "a great deal of" confidence in political parties fell from 30% in 1979 to 11% in 1999. Confidence in the House of Commons fell from 49% in 1974 to 21% in 1996. By 1992 only 34% of Canadians were satisfied with their system of government, down from 51% in 1986.

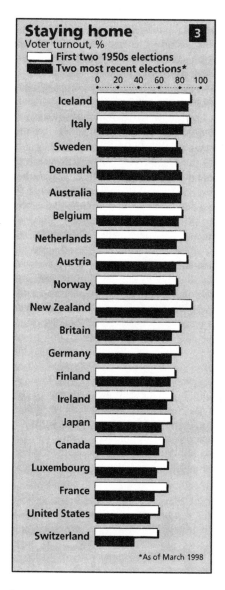

**Staying home** ☐3
Voter turnout, %
☐ First two 1950s elections
■ Two most recent elections*

0  20  40  60  80  100

Iceland
Italy
Sweden
Denmark
Australia
Belgium
Netherlands
Austria
Norway
New Zealand
Britain
Germany
Finland
Ireland
Japan
Canada
Luxembourg
France
United States
Switzerland

*As of March 1998

Source: Martin P. Wattenberg, University of California, Irvine

• Less information is available about attitudes in **Japan**. But the findings of the few surveys that have been carried out there match the global pattern. Confidence in political institutions rose in the decades following the smashing of the country's old politics in the second world war. Happily for democracy, the proportion of Japanese voters who agree that "in order to make Japan better, it is best to rely on talented politicians, rather than to let the citizens argue among themselves" has been falling for 40 years. However, the proportion who feel that they exert at least "some influence" on national politics through elections or demonstrations also fell steadily between 1973 and 1993.

• Although it is harder to generalize about **Western Europe**, confidence in political institutions is in decline in most countries. In 1985 48% of Britons expressed quite a lot of confidence in the House of Commons. This number had halved by 1995. The proportion of Swedes disagreeing with the statement that "parties are only interested in people's votes, not in their opinions" slumped from 51% in 1968 to 28% in 1994. In 1985 51% expressed confidence in the Rikstad (parliament); by 1996 only 19% did. In Germany, the percentage of people who said they trusted their Bundestag deputy to represent their interests rose from 25% in 1951 to 55% in 1978, but had fallen again to 34% by 1992. The percentage of Italians who say that politicians "don't care what people like me think" increased from 68% in 1968 to 84% in 1997.

Such findings are alarming if you take them at face value. But they should be interpreted with care. Democracy may just be a victim of its own success. It could just be that people nowadays expect more from governments, impose new demands on the state, and are therefore more likely to be disappointed. After all, the idea that governments ought to do such things as protect or improve the environment, maintain high employment, arbitrate between moral issues, or ensure the equal treatment of women or minorities, is a relatively modern and still controversial one. Or perhaps

the disillusionment is a healthy product of rising educational standards and the scepticism that goes with it. Or maybe it is caused by the media's search-light highlighting failures of government that were previously kept in the dark. Whatever the causes, the popularity of governments or politicians ought not to be the only test of democracy's health.

Moreover, there is encouraging evidence to put beside the discouraging findings. However much confidence in government may be declining, this does not seem to have diminished popular support for democratic principles. On average, surveys show, more than three out of four people in rich countries believe that democracy is the best form of government. Even in countries where the performance of particular governments has been so disappointing as to break up the party system itself (such as Japan and Italy in 1993–95), this has brought no serious threat to fundamental democratic principle. It may seem paradoxical for people to express strong support for democracy even while their confidence in politicians and political institutions crumbles. But it hardly amounts to the "crisis of democracy" which political scientists tend to proclaim from time to time.

Nor, though, is it a ringing endorsement, especially given that the evidence of opinion surveys is reinforced by other trends. These include a decline both in the membership of political parties and in the proportion of people who turn out to vote. Numbers compiled by Martin Wattenberg, also at the University of California, show that in 18 out of 20 of the rich established democracies the proportion of the electorate voting has been lower than it was in the early 1950s (see chart 3), with the median change being a decline of 10%. More controversially, some political scientists see the growth of protest movements since the

1960s as a sign of declining faith in the traditional institutions of representative democracy, and an attempt to bypass them. Others reckon that the most serious threat comes from the increasingly professional pressure groups and lobbying organisations that work behind the scenes to influence government policy and defend special interests, often at the expense of the electorate as a whole.

What is to be done? Those who believe that government has over-reached itself call on governments to become smaller and to promise less. Thus, it is hoped, people will come to do more for themselves. But whatever the appropriate size and reach of governments, there is also scope for making the machinery of democracy work better.

Indeed, some commentators see the public's declining confidence in political institutions as an opportunity for democratic renewal. Pippa Norris, at Harvard University's Kennedy School of Government, hails the advent of a new breed of "critical citizens" (in a book of that name, Oxford University Press, 1999) who see that existing channels of participation fall short of democratic ideals and want to reform them.

There are some signs of this. Countries as different as Italy, Japan, Britain and New Zealand have lately considered or introduced changes in their electoral systems. Countries around the world are making growing use of referendums and other forms of direct democracy. Many are reducing the power of parliaments by giving judges new powers to review the decisions that elected politicians make. And governments everywhere are introducing new rules on the financing of politicians and political parties. The rest of the articles in this series will look at some of these changes and the forces shaping them.

# Political Parties: Empty vessels?

**Alexis de Tocqueville called political parties an evil inherent in free governments. The second of our briefs on the mature democracies in transition asks whether parties are in decline**

W HAT would democracy look like if there were no political parties? It is almost impossible to imagine. In every democracy worth the name, the contest to win the allegiance of the electorate and form a government takes place through political parties. Without them, voters would be hard put to work out what individual candidates stood for or intended to do once elected. If parties did not "aggregate" people's interests, politics might degenerate into a fight between tiny factions, each promoting its narrow self-interest. But for the past 30 years, political scientists have been asking whether parties are "in decline". Are they? And if so, does it matter?

Generalising about political parties is difficult. Their shape depends on a country's history, constitution and much else. For example, America's federal structure and separation of powers make Republicans and Democrats amorphous groupings whose main purpose is to put their man in the White House. British parties behave quite differently because members of Parliament must toe the party line to keep their man in Downing Street. An American president is safe once elected, so congressmen behave like local representatives rather than members of a national organisation bearing collective responsibility for government. Countries which, unlike Britain and America, hold elections under proportional representation are different again: they tend to produce multi-party systems and coalition governments.

Despite these differences, some trends common to almost all advanced democracies appear to be changing the nature of parties and, on one view, making them less

influential. Those who buy this thesis of decline point to the following changes:

People's behaviour is becoming more **private**. Why join a political party when you can go fly fishing or surf the web? Back in the 1950s, clubs affiliated to the Labour Party were places for Britain's working people to meet, play and study. The Conservative Party was, among other things, a marriage bureau for the better-off. Today, belonging to a British political party is more like being a supporter of some charity: you may pay a membership fee, but will not necessarily attend meetings or help to turn out the vote at election time.

## Running out of ideas

Politics is becoming more **secular**. Before the 1960s, political struggles had an almost religious intensity: in much of Western Europe this took the form of communists versus Catholics, or workers versus bosses. But ideological differences were narrowing by the 1960s and became smaller still after the collapse of Soviet communism. Nowadays, politics seems to be more often about policies than values, about the competence of leaders rather than the beliefs of the led. As education grows and class distinctions blur, voters discard old loyalties. In America in 1960, two out of five voters saw themselves as "strong" Democrats or "strong" Republicans. By 1996 less than one in three saw themselves that way. The proportion of British voters expressing a "very strong" affinity with one party slumped from 44% to 16% between 1964 and 1997. This process of **"partisan de-**

**alignment"** has been witnessed in most mature democracies.

The erosion of loyalty is said to have pushed parties towards the **ideological centre**. The political extremes have not gone away. But mainstream parties which used to offer a straight choice between socialists and conservatives are no longer so easy to label. In the late 1950s Germany's Social Democrats (SPD) snipped off their Marxist roots in order to recast themselves is a *Volkspartei* appealing to all the people. "New" Labour no longer portrays itself as the political arm of the British working class or trade-union movement. Bill Clinton, before he became president, helped to shift the Democratic Party towards an appreciation of business and free trade. Neat ideological labels have become harder to pin on parties since they have had to contend with the emergence of what some commentators call **post-material issues** (such as the environment, personal morality and consumer rights) which do not slot elegantly into the old left-right framework

The **mass media** have taken over many of the information functions that parties once performed for themselves. "Just as radio and television have largely killed off the door-to-door salesman," says Anthony King, of Britain's Essex University, "so they have largely killed off the old-fashioned party worker." In 1878 the German SPD had nearly 50 of its own newspapers. Today the mass media enable politicians to communicate directly with voters without owning printing presses or needing party workers to knock on doors. In many other ways, the business of winning elections has become more capital-intensive and less labour-intensive, making political donors matter more and political activists less.

Another apparent threat to the parties is the growth of **interest and pressure groups**. Why should voters care about the broad sweep of policy promoted during elections by a party when other organisations will lobby all year round for their special interest, whether this is protection of the environment, opposition to abortion, or the defence of some subsidy? Some academics also claim that parties are playing a smaller role, and **think tanks** a bigger one, in making policy. Although parties continue to draw up election manifestos, they are wary of being too specific. Some hate leaving policymaking to party activists, who may be more extreme than voters at large and so put them off. Better to keep the message vague. Or why not let the tough choices be taken by **referendums**, as so often in Switzerland?

Academics have found these trends easier to describe than to evaluate. Most agree that the age of the "mass party" has passed and that its place is being taken by the "electoral-professional" or "catch-all" party. Although still staffed by politicians holding genuine beliefs and values, these modern parties are inclined to see their main objective as winning elections rather than forming large membership organisations or social movements, as was once the case.

Is this a bad thing? Perhaps, if it reduces participation in politics. One of the traditional roles of political parties has been to get out the vote, and in 18 out of 20 rich countries, recent turnout figures have been lower than they were in the 1950s. Although it is hard to pin down the reasons, Martin Wattenberg, of the University of California at Irvine, points out that turnout has fallen most sharply in countries where parties are weak: Switzerland (thanks to those referendums), America and France (where presidential elections have become increasingly candidate- rather than party-centred), and Japan (where political loyalties revolve around ties to internal factions rather than the party itself). In Scandinavia, by contrast, where class-based parties are still relatively strong, turnout has held up much better since the 1950s.

## Running out of members

It is not only voters who are turned off. Party membership is falling too, and even the most strenuous attempts to reverse the decline have faltered. Germany is a case in point. The Social Democrats there increased membership rapidly in the 1960s

and 1970s, and the Christian Democrats responded by doubling their own membership numbers. But since the end of the 1980s membership has been falling, especially among the young. In 1964 Britain's Labour Party had about 830,000 members and the Conservatives about 2m. By 1997 they had 420,000 and 400,000 respectively. The fall is sharper in some countries than others, but research by Susan Scarrow of the University of Houston suggests that the trend is common to most democracies (see chart). With their membership falling, ideological differences blurring, and fewer people turning out to vote, the decline thesis looks hard to refute.

Or does it? The case for party decline has some big holes in it. For a start, some academics question whether political parties ever really enjoyed the golden age which other academics hark back to. Essex University's Mr King points out that a lot of the evidence for decline is drawn from a handful of parties—Britain's two main ones, the German SPD, the French and Italian Communists—which did indeed once promote clear ideologies, enjoy mass memberships, and organise local branches and social activities. But neither of America's parties, nor Canada's, nor many of the bourgeois parties of Western Europe, were ever mass parties of that sort. Moreover, in spite of their supposed decline, parties continue to keep an iron grip on many aspects of politics.

In most places, for example, parties still control **nomination for public office**. In almost all of the mature democracies, it is rare for independent candidates to be elected to federal or state legislatures, and even in local government the proportion of independents has declined sharply since the early 1970s. When state and local parties select candidates, they usually favour people who have worked hard within the party. German parties, for example, are often conduits to jobs in the public sector, with a say over appointments to top jobs in the civil service and to the boards of publicly owned utilities or media organisations. Even in America, where independent candidates are more common in local elections, the parties still run city, county and state "machines" in which most politicians start their careers.

Naturally, there are some exceptions. In 1994 Silvio Berlusconi, a media tycoon, was able to make himself prime minister at the head of Forza Italia, a right-wing movement drawing heavily on his personal fortune and the resources of his television empire. Ross Perot, a wealthy third-party

candidate, won a respectable 19% vote in his 1992 bid for the American presidency. The party declinists claim these examples as evidence for their case. But it is notable that in the end Mr Perot could not compete against the two formidable campaigning and money-raising machines ranged against him.

This suggests that a decline in the membership of parties need not make them weaker in **money and organisation**. In fact, many have enriched themselves simply by passing laws that give them public money. In Germany, campaign subsidies to the federal parties more than trebled between 1970 and 1990, and parties now receive between 20% and 40% of their income from public funds. In America, the paid professionals who have taken over from party activists tend to do their job more efficiently. Moreover, other kinds of political activity—such as donating money to a party or interest group, or attending meetings and rallies—have become more common in America. Groups campaigning for particular causes or candidates (the pro-Republican Christian Coalition, say, or the pro-Democrat National Education Association) may not be formally affiliated with the major party organisations, but are frequently allied with them.

The role of the mass media deserves a closer look as well. It is true that they have weakened the parties' traditional methods of communicating with members. But parties have invested heavily in managing relations with journalists, and making use of new media to reach both members and wider audiences. In Britain, the dwindling of local activists has gone hand-in-hand with a more professional approach to communications. Margaret Thatcher caused a stir by using an advertising firm, Saatchi & Saatchi, to push the Tory cause in the 1979 election. By the time of Britain's 1997 election, the New Labour media operation run from Millbank Tower in London was even slicker.

Another way to gauge the influence of parties is by their **reach**—that is, their power, once in office, to take control of the governmental apparatus. This is a power they have retained. Most governments tend to be unambiguously under the control of people who represent a party, and who would not be in government if they did not belong to such organisations. The French presidential system may appear ideal for independent candidates, but except—arguably—for Charles de Gaulle, who claimed to rise above party, none has ever been elected without party support.

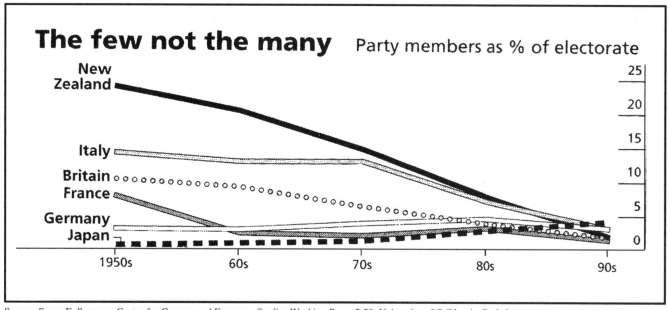

Source: Susan E. Scarrow, Centre for German and European Studies Working Paper 2.59, University of California, Berkeley

## The fire next time

Given the cautions that must be applied to other parts of the case for party decline, what can be said about one of the declinists' key exhibits, the erosion of ideological differences? At first sight, this is borne out by the recent movement to the centre of left-leaning parties such as America's Democrats, New Labour in Britain, and the SPD under Gerhard Schröder. In America, Newt Gingrich stoked up some fire amongst Republicans in 1994, but it has flickered out. The most popular Republican presidential hopefuls, and especially George W. Bush, the front-runner, are once again stressing the gentler side of their conservatism.

Still, the claim of ideological convergence can be exaggerated. It is not much more than a decade since Ronald Reagan and Mrs Thatcher ran successful parties with strong ideologies. And the anecdotal assumption that parties are growing less distinct is challenged by longer-term academic studies. A look at the experience of ten western democracies since 1945 ("Parties, Policies and Democracy", Westview Press, 1994) concluded that the leading left and right parties continued to keep their distance and maintain their identity, rather

than clustering around the median voter in the centre. Paul Webb of Britain's Brunel University concludes in a forthcoming book ("Political Parties in Advanced Industrial Democracies", Oxford University Press) that although partisan sentiment is weaker than it was, and voters more cynical, parties have in general adapted well to changing circumstances.

Besides, even if party differences are narrowing at present, why expect that trend to continue? In Western Europe, the ending of the cold war has snuffed out one source of ideological conflict, but new sparks might catch fire. Battered right-wing parties may try to revive their fortunes by pushing the nationalist cause against the encroachments of the European Union. In some places where ideas are dividing parties less, geography is dividing them more. Politics in Germany and Britain has acquired an increasingly regional flavour: Labour and the Social Democrats respectively dominate the north, Conservatives and Christian Democrats the south. Disaffected *Ossis* are flocking to the Party of Democratic Socialism in eastern Germany. Britain, Italy, Canada and Spain have strong separatist parties.

So there is life in the party system yet. But the declinists are on to something. The

Germans have a word for it. One reason given for the rise of Germany's Greens in the 1980s and America's Mr Perot in 1992 was *Parteienverdrossenheit*—disillusionment with mainstream parties that seemed to have abandoned their core beliefs and no longer offered meaningful choices. A "new politics" of citizens' protests appeared to be displacing conventional politics.

In the end, far from undermining the domination of the parties, the German Greens ended up by turning themselves into one and joining the government in an uneasy coalition with the SPD. The balance of evidence from around the world is that despite all the things that are changing them, parties continue to dominate democratic politics.

Indeed, there are grounds for wondering whether their continuing survival is more of a worry than their supposed decline. Is it so very comforting that parties can lose members, worry less about ideas, become detached from broader social movements, attract fewer voters and still retain an iron grip on politics? If they are so unanchored, will they not fall prey to special-interest groups? If they rely on state funding instead of member contributions, will they not turn into creatures of the state? The role of money in politics will be the subject of another brief.

# Interest Groups:
# Ex uno, plures

**The last article in our series on the mature democracies asks whether they are
in danger of being strangled by lobbyists and single-issue pressure groups**

PREVIOUS briefs in this series have looked at the imperfections in democracy as it is currently practised in the rich countries, and at some of the efforts that different countries are making to overcome them. Evidence that all is not well includes declining public confidence in politicians, falling membership of political parties and smaller turnouts for elections. Ideas for improvement range from making greater use of referendums and other forms of direct democracy, to giving more power to courts to check the power of politicians. This article asks a different question: far from being too powerful, are elected politicians in modern democracies too weak?

When Alexis de Tocqueville visited the United States in the 19th century, he was impressed by the enthusiasm of Americans for joining associations. This, he felt, spread power away from the centre and fostered the emergence of democratic habits and a civil society. Until quite recently, most political scientists shared De Tocqueville's view. Lately, however, and especially in America, doubts have set in. At a certain point, say the doubters, the cumulative power of pressure groups, each promoting its own special interests, can grow so strong that it prevents elected politicians from adopting policies that are in the interest of the electorate as a whole.

## A hitch-hiker's guide

A key text for such critics was a short book published in 1965 by Mancur Olson, an American economist. Called "The Logic of Collective Action", this took issue with the traditional idea that the health of democracy was served by vigorous competition between pressure groups, with governments acting as a sort of referee, able to choose the best policy once the debate between the contending groups was over. The traditional view, Olson argued, wrongly assumed that pressure groups were more or less equal. In fact, for a reason known to economists as the free-rider problem, they weren't.

Why? Take the example of five car firms, which form a lobbying group in the hope of raising the price of cars. If they succeed, each stands to reap a fifth of the gains. This makes forming the group and working for its success well worth each firm's investment of time and money. If the car makers succeed, of course, motorists will suffer. But organising millions of individual motorists to fight their corner is a great deal harder because it involves co-ordinating millions of people and because the potential gain for each motorist will be relatively small. Individual motorists will be tempted to reason that, with millions of other people involved, they do not need to do anything themselves, but can instead hitch a "free ride" on the efforts of everyone else.

This simple insight has powerful implications. Indeed, in a later book Olson went on to argue that his theory helped to explain why some nations flourish and others decline. As pressure groups multiply over

time, they tend to choke a nation's vitality by impairing the government's ability to act in the wider interest. That, he argued, is why countries such as Germany and Japan—whose interest groups had been cleared away by a traumatic defeat—had fared better after the second world war than Britain, whose institutions had survived intact. With its long record of stability, said Olson, "British society has acquired so many strong organisations and collusions that it suffers from an institutional sclerosis that slows its adaptation to changing circumstances and changing technologies."

Olson's ideas have not gone unchallenged. But they have had a big impact on contemporary thinking about what ails American democracy. In "Demosclerosis" (Times Books, 1994), Jonathan Rauch, a populariser of Olson's work, says that America is afflicted by "hyperpluralism". With at least seven out of ten Americans belonging to at least one such association, the whole society, not just "special" parts of it, is now involved in influence peddling.

The result is that elected politicians find it almost impossible to act solely in the wider public interest. Bill Clinton wants to reform the health system? The health-insurance industry blocks him. China's membership in the World Trade Organisation would benefit America's consumers? America's producers of textiles and steel stand in the way. Jimmy Carter complained when he left the presidency that

Americans were increasingly drawn to single-issue groups to ensure that, whatever else happened, their own private interest would be protected. The trouble is, "the national interest is not always the sum of all our single or special interests".

Pressure groups are especially visible in the United States. As Oxford University's Jeremy Richardson puts it ("Pressure Groups", Oxford University Press, 1993), "pressure groups take account of (and exploit) the multiplicity of access points which is so characteristic of the American system of government—the presidency, the bureaucracy, both houses of Congress, the powerful congressional committees, the judiciary and state and local government."

Nevertheless pressure groups often wield just as much influence in other countries. In those where parliaments exercise tighter control of the executive—Canada, Britain or Germany, say—the government controls the parliamentary timetable and the powers of committees are much weaker. This means that pressure groups adopt different tactics. They have more chance of influencing policy behind closed doors, by bargaining with the executive branch and its civil servants before legislation comes before parliament. In this way pressure groups can sometimes exert more influence than their counterparts in America.

## Political tribes

Many European countries have also buttressed the influence of pressure groups by giving them a semi-official status. In Germany, for example, the executive branch is obliged by law to consult the various big "interest organisations" before drafting legislation. In some German states, leading interest groups (along with political parties) have seats on the supervisory boards of broadcasting firms.

French pressure groups are also powerful, despite the conventional image of a strong French state dominating a relatively weak civil society. It is true that a lot of France's interest groups depend on the state for both money and membership of a network of formal consultative bodies. But a tradition of direct protest compensates for some of this institutional weakness. In France, mass demonstrations, strikes, the blocking of roads and the disruption of public services are seen as a part of normal democratic politics.

In Japan, powerful pressure groups such as the Zenchu (Central Union of Agricultural Co-operatives) have turned large

areas of public policy into virtual no-go areas. With more than 9m members (and an electoral system that gives farming communities up to three times the voting weight of urban voters), farmers can usually obstruct any policy that damages their interests. The teachers' union has similarly blocked all attempts at education reform. And almost every sector of Japanese society has its *zoku giin* (political tribes), consisting of Diet members who have made themselves knowledgeable about one industry or another, which pays for their secretaries and provides campaign funds. A Diet member belonging to the transport tribe will work hand-in-glove with senior bureaucrats in the transport ministry and the trucking industry to form what the Japanese call an "iron triangle" consisting of politicians, bureaucrats and big business.

Pressure groups are also increasingly active at a transnational level. Like any bureaucracy, the European Union has spawned a rich network of interest groups. In 1992 the European Commission reckoned that at least 3,000 special-interest groups in Brussels employing some 10,000 people acted as lobbyists. These range from big operations, such as the EU committee of the American Chamber of Commerce, to small firms and individual lobbyists-for-hire. Businesses were the first to spot the advantages of influencing the EU's law making. But trade unions swiftly followed, often achieving in Brussels breakthroughs (such as regulations on working conditions) that they could not achieve at home.

## The case for the defense

So pressure groups are ubiquitous. But are they so bad? Although it has been influential, the Olson thesis has not swept all before it. Many political scientists argue that the traditional view that pressure groups create a healthy democratic pluralism is nearer the mark than Olson's thesis.

The case in favour of pressure groups begins with some of the flaws of representative democracy. Elections are infrequent and, as a previous brief in this series noted, political parties can be vague about their governing intentions. Pressure groups help people to take part in politics between elections, and to influence a government's policy in areas that they care and know about. Pressure groups also check excessive central power and give governments expert advice. Although some groups may flourish at the expense of the common weal, this danger can be guarded against if there are

many groups and if all have the same freedom to organise and to put their case to government

Critics of Olson's ideas also point out that, contrary to his prediction, many broad-based groups have in fact managed to flourish in circumstances where individual members stand to make little personal gain and should therefore fall foul of his "free-rider" problem. Clearly, some people join pressure groups for apparently altruistic reasons—perhaps simply to express their values or to be part of an organisation in which they meet like-minded people. Some consumer and environmental movements have flourished in rich countries, even though Olson's theory suggests that firms and polluters should have a strong organisational advantage over consumers and inhalers of dirty air.

Moreover, despite "demosclerosis", well-organised pressure groups can sometimes ease the task of government, not just throw sand into its wheels. The common European practice of giving pressure groups a formal status, and often a legal right to be consulted, minimises conflict by ensuring that powerful groups put their case to governments before laws are introduced. Mr Richardson argues in a forthcoming book ("Developments in the European Union", Macmillan, 1999) that even the pressure groups clustering around the institutions of the EU perform a valuable function. The European Commission, concerned with the detail of regulation, is an eager consumer of their specialist knowledge. As the powers of the European Parliament have grown, it too has attracted a growing band of lobbyists. The parliament has created scores of "intergroups" whose members gain expertise in specific sectors, such as pharmaceuticals, from industry and consumer lobbies.

Governments can learn from pressure groups, and can work through them to gain consent for their policies. At some point, however, the relationship becomes excessively cosy. If pressure groups grow too strong, they can deter governments from pursuing policies which are in the wider public interest. The temptation of governments to support protectionist trade policies at the behest of producer lobbies and at the expense of consumers is a classic example supporting Olson's theories. But problems also arise when it is governments that are relatively strong, and so able to confer special status on some pressure groups and withhold it from others. This puts less-favoured groups at a disadvantage, which they often seek to redress by finding new and sometimes less democratic ways of making their voices heard.

In Germany, for example, disenchantment with what had come to be seen as an excessively cosy system of bargaining between elite groups helped to spark an explosion of protest movements in the 1980s. In many other countries, too, there is a sense that politics has mutated since the 1960s from an activity organised largely around parties to one organised around specialised interest groups on the one hand (such as America's gun lobby) and broader protest and social movements on the other (such as the women's movement, environmentalism and consumerism). One reason for the change is clearly the growth in the size and scope of government. Now that it touches virtually every aspect of people's lives, a bewildering array of groups has sprung up around it.

Many of Olson's disciples blame pressure groups for making government grow. As each special group wins new favours from the state, it makes the state bigger and clumsier, undermining the authority of elected parties, loading excessive demands on government in general, and preventing any particular government from acting in the interest of the relatively disorganised majority of people. By encouraging governments to do too much, say critics on the right, pressure groups prevent governments from doing anything well. Their solution is for governments to do less. Critics on the left are more inclined to complain that pressure groups exaggerate inequalities by giving those better-organised (ie, the rich and powerful) an influence out of all proportion to their actual numbers.

So what is to be done? A lot could be, but little is likely to be. There is precious little evidence from recent elections to suggest that the citizens of the rich countries want to see a radical cut in the size or scope of the state. As for political inequality, even this has its defenders. John Mueller, of America's University of Rochester, argues that democracy has had a good, if imperfect, record of dealing with minority issues, particularly when compared with other forms of government But he claims that this is less because democratic majorities are tolerant of minorities and more because democracy gives minorities the opportunity

to increase their effective political weight—to become more equal, more important, than their arithmetical size would imply—on issues that concern them. This holds even for groups held in contempt by the majority, like homosexuals. Moreover, the fact that most people most of the time pay little attention to politics—the phenomenon of political apathy—helps interested minorities to protect their rights and to assert their interests.

## Adaptability

This series of briefs has highlighted some of the defects in the practice of democracy, and some of the changes that the mature democracies are making in order to improve matters. But the defects need to be kept in perspective.

One famous critic of democracy claimed that for most people it did nothing more than allow them "once every few years, to decide which particular representatives of the oppressing class should be in parliament to represent and oppress them". When Marx wrote those words in the 19th century, they contained an element of truth. Tragically, Lenin treated this view as an eternal verity, with calamitous results for millions of people. What they both ignored was democracy's ability to evolve, which is perhaps its key virtue. Every mature democracy continues to evolve today. As a result, violent revolution in those countries where democracy has taken deepest root looks less attractive, and more remote, than ever.

# Women
# in National Parliaments

*Situation as of 25 November 2002*

The data in the table below has been compiled by the Inter-Parliamentary Union on the basis of information provided by National Parliaments by 25 November 2002. **181 countries** are classified by **descending order of the percentage of women in the lower or single House.** Comparative data on the world and regional averages as well as data concerning the two regional parliamentary assemblies elected by direct suffrage can [also] be found on this Web site. You can use the PARLINE database [www.ipu.org/parline-e/parlinesearch.asp] to view detailed results of parliamentary elections by country.

*New: you can now consult an archive of statistical data on women in National Parliaments.*

| | | WORLD CLASSIFICATION | | | | | | | |
|---|---|---|---|---|---|---|---|---|---|
| **Rank** | **Country** | **Lower or single House** | | | | **Upper House or Senate** | | | |
| | | **Elections** | **Seats*** | **Women** | **% W** | **Elections** | **Seats*** | **Women** | **% W** |
| 1 | Sweden | 09 2002 | 349 | 157 | 45.0 | — | — | — | — |
| 2 | Denmark | 11 2001 | 179 | 68 | 38.0 | — | — | — | — |
| 3 | Finland | 03 1999 | 200 | 73 | 36.5 | — | — | — | — |
| 4 | Norway | 09 2001 | 165 | 60 | 36.4 | — | — | — | — |
| 5 | Costa Rica | 02 2002 | 57 | 20 | 35.1 | — | — | — | — |
| 6 | Iceland | 05 1999 | 63 | 22 | 34.9 | — | — | — | — |
| 7 | Netherlands | 05 2002 | 150 | 51 | 34.0 | 05 1999 | 75 | 20 | 26.7 |
| 8 | Germany | 09 2002 | 603 | 194 | 32.2 | N.A. | 69 | 17 | 24.6 |
| 9 | Argentina | 10 2001 | 257 | 79 | 30.7 | 10 2001 | 72 | 24 | 33.3 |
| 10 | Mozambique | 12 1999 | 250 | 75 | 30.0 | — | — | — | — |
| 11 | South Africa** | 06 1999 | 399 | 119 | 29.8 | 06 1999 | 89 | 17 | 31.5 |
| 12 | New Zealand | 07 2002 | 120 | 35 | 29.2 | — | — | — | — |
| 13 | Spain | 03 2000 | 350 | 99 | 28.3 | 03 2000 | 259 | 63 | 24.3 |
| 14 | Cuba | 01 1998 | 601 | 166 | 27.6 | — | — | — | — |
| 15 | Viet Nam | 05 2002 | 498 | 136 | 27.3 | — | — | — | — |
| 16 | Grenada | 01 1999 | 15 | 4 | 26.7 | 01 1999 | 13 | 1 | 7.7 |
| 17 | Bulgaria | 06 2001 | 240 | 63 | 26.2 | — | — | — | — |
| 18 | Dem. Rep. of East Timor*** | 08 2001 | 88 | 23 | 26.1 | — | — | — | — |
| 19 | Turkmenistan | 12 1999 | 50 | 13 | 26.0 | — | — | — | — |
| 20 | Rwanda | 11 1994 | 74 | 19 | 25.7 | — | — | — | — |
| 21 | Australia | 11 2001 | 150 | 38 | 25.3 | 10 1998 | 76 | 22 | 28.9 |
| 22 | Namibia | 11 1999 | 72 | 18 | 25.0 | 11 1998 | 26 | 2 | 7.7 |
| 23 | Uganda | 06 2001 | 304 | 75 | 24.7 | — | — | — | — |
| 24 | Seychelles | 03 1998 | 34 | 8 | 23.5 | — | — | — | — |

| Rank | Country | Lower or single House | | | | Upper House or Senate | | | |
|------|---------|-----------|--------|-------|------|-----------|--------|-------|------|
| | | Elections | Seats* | Women | % W | Elections | Seats* | Women | % W |
| 25 | Belgium | 06 1999 | 150 | 35 | 23.3 | 06 1999 | 71 | 20 | 28.2 |
| 26 | Switzerland | 10 1999 | 200 | 46 | 23.0 | 10 1999 | 46 | 9 | 19.6 |
| 27 | Lao People's Democratic Rep. | 02 2002 | 109 | 25 | 22.9 | — | — | — | — |
| 28 | Saint Vincent & the Grenadines | 03 2001 | 22 | 5 | 22.7 | — | — | — | — |
| 29 | United Rep. of Tanzania | 10 2000 | 274 | 61 | 22.3 | — | — | — | — |
| 30 | Monaco | 02 1998 | 18 | 4 | 22.2 | — | — | — | — |
| 31 | Eritrea | 02 1994 | 150 | 33 | 22.0 | — | — | — | — |
| 32 | China | 1997-98 | 2984 | 650 | 21.8 | — | — | — | — |
| 33 | Nicaragua | 11 2001 | 92 | 19 | 20.7 | — | — | — | — |
| 34 | Canada | 11 2000 | 301 | 62 | 20.6 | N.A. | 105 | 34 | 32.4 |
| 35 | Croatia | 01 2000 | 151 | 31 | 20.5 | 04 1997 | 65 | 4 | 6.2 |
| 36 | Poland | 09 2001 | 460 | 93 | 20.2 | 09 2001 | 100 | 23 | 23.0 |
| 37 | Dem. People's Rep. of Korea | 07 1998 | 687 | 138 | 20.1 | — | — | — | — |
| 38 | Guyana | 03 2001 | 65 | 13 | 20.0 | — | — | — | — |
| 39 | Trinidad and Tobago | 10 2002 | 36 | 7 | 19.4 | 12 2001 | 31 | 10 | 32.3 |
| 40 | Senegal | 04 2001 | 120 | 23 | 19.2 | — | — | — | — |
| 41 | Portugal | 03 2002 | 230 | 44 | 19.1 | — | — | — | — |
| 42 | Dominica | 01 2000 | 32 | 6 | 18.8 | — | — | — | — |
| 43 | Bolivia | 06 2002 | 130 | 24 | 18.5 | 06 2002 | 27 | 4 | 14.8 |
| 44 | Burundi | 06 1993 | 179 | 33 | 18.4 | 01 2002 | 54 | ? | ? |
| 45 | Peru | 04 2001 | 120 | 22 | 18.3 | — | — | — | — |
| 46 | Latvia | 10 2002 | 100 | 18 | 18.0 | — | — | — | — |
| 47 | United Kingdom | 06 2001 | 659 | 118 | 17.9 | N.A. | 713 | 117 | 16.4 |
| 48 | Estonia | 03 1999 | 101 | 18 | 17.8 | — | — | — | — |
| " | Philippines | 05 2001 | 214 | 38 | 17.8 | 05 2001 | 24 | 3 | 12.5 |
| 49 | Suriname | 05 2000 | 51 | 9 | 17.6 | — | — | — | — |
| 50 | The f.Y.R. of Macedonia | 09 2002 | 120 | 21 | 17.5 | — | — | — | — |
| 51 | Dominican Republic | 05 2002 | 150 | 26 | 17.3 | 05 2002 | 32 | 2 | 6.3 |
| 52 | Botswana | 10 1999 | 47 | 8 | 17.0 | — | — | — | — |
| " | Czech Republic | 06 2002 | 200 | 34 | 17.0 | 11 2000 | 81 | 10 | 12.3 |
| 53 | Luxembourg | 06 1999 | 60 | 10 | 16.7 | — | — | — | — |
| " | San Marino | 06 2001 | 60 | 10 | 16.7 | — | — | — | — |
| 54 | Mexico | 07 2000 | 500 | 80 | 16.0 | 07 2000 | 128 | 20 | 15.6 |
| 55 | Angola | 09 1992 | 220 | 34 | 15.5 | — | — | — | — |
| 56 | Andorra | 03 2001 | 28 | 4 | 14.3 | — | — | — | — |
| 57 | Israel | 05 1999 | 120 | 17 | 14.2 | — | — | — | — |
| 58 | United States of America | 11 2002 | 435 | 60 | 13.8 | 11 2002 | 100 | 13 | 13 |
| 59 | Ireland | 05 2002 | 166 | 22 | 13.3 | 07 2002 | 60 | 10 | 16.7 |
| " | Saint Kitts and Nevis | 03 2000 | 15 | 2 | 13.3 | — | — | — | — |
| 60 | Republic of Moldova | 02 2001 | 101 | 13 | 12.9 | — | — | — | — |
| 61 | Tajikistan | 02 2000 | 63 | 8 | 12.7 | 03 2000 | 34 | 4 | 11.8 |
| 62 | Chile | 12 2001 | 120 | 15 | 12.5 | 12 2001 | 49 | 2 | 4.1 |
| 63 | Slovenia | 10 2000 | 90 | 11 | 12.2 | — | — | — | — |

| Rank | Country | Lower or single House | | | | Upper House or Senate | | | |
|---|---|---|---|---|---|---|---|---|---|
| | | Elections | Seats* | Women | %W | Elections | Seats* | Women | %W |
| 64 | France | 06 2002 | 577 | 70 | 12.1 | 09 2001 | 321 | 35 | 10.9 |
| " | Uruguay | 10 1999 | 99 | 12 | 12.1 | 10 1999 | 31 | 3 | 9.7 |
| 65 | Colombia | 03 2002 | 166 | 20 | 12.0 | 03 2002 | 102 | 9 | 8.8 |
| " | Liechtenstein | 02 2001 | 25 | 3 | 12.0 | — | — | — | — |
| " | Zambia | 12 2001 | 158 | 19 | 12.0 | — | — | — | — |
| 66 | Singapore | 11 2001 | 85 | 10 | 11.8 | — | — | — | — |
| 67 | Burkina Faso | 05 2002 | 111 | 13 | 11.7 | — | — | — | — |
| 68 | Tunisia | 10 1999 | 182 | 21 | 11.5 | — | — | — | — |
| 69 | Cape Verde | 01 2001 | 72 | 8 | 11.1 | — | — | — | — |
| " | Saint Lucia | 12 2001 | 18 | 2 | 11.1 | 05 1997 | 11 | 2 | 18.2 |
| 70 | Morocco | 09 2002 | 325 | 35 | 10.8 | 09 2001 | 270 | 1 | 0.4 |
| 71 | Barbados | 01 1999 | 28 | 3 | 10.7 | 01 1999 | 21 | 7 | 33.3 |
| " | Cyprus | 05 2001 | 56 | 6 | 10.7 | — | — | — | — |
| " | Romania | 11 2000 | 345 | 37 | 10.7 | 11 2000 | 140 | 8 | 5.7 |
| 72 | Lithuania | 10 2000 | 141 | 15 | 10.6 | — | — | — | — |
| 73 | Azerbaijan | 11 2000 | 124 | 13 | 10.5 | — | — | — | — |
| " | Mongolia | 07 2000 | 76 | 8 | 10.5 | — | — | — | — |
| 74 | Kazakhstan | 10 1999 | 77 | 8 | 10.4 | 09 1999 | 39 | 5 | 12.8 |
| " | Malaysia | 11 1999 | 193 | 20 | 10.4 | 03 1998 | 69 | 18 | 26.1 |
| " | Syrian Arab Republic | 11 1998 | 250 | 26 | 10.4 | — | — | — | — |
| 75 | Belarus | 10 2000 | 97 | 10 | 10.3 | 12 2000 | 61 | 19 | 31.1 |
| 76 | Mali | 07 2002 | 147 | 15 | 10.2 | — | — | — | — |
| 77 | Kyrgyzstan | 02 2000 | 60 | 6 | 10.0 | 02 2000 | 45 | 1 | 2.2 |
| " | Zimbabwe | 06 2000 | 150 | 15 | 10.0 | — | — | — | — |
| 78 | Panama | 05 1999 | 71 | 7 | 9.9 | — | — | — | — |
| 79 | Italy | 05 2001 | 630 | 62 | 9.8 | 05 2001 | 321 | 25 | 7.8 |
| 80 | Sudan | 12 2000 | 360 | 35 | 9.7 | — | — | — | — |
| " | Venezuela | 07 2000 | 165 | 16 | 9.7 | — | — | — | — |
| 81 | El Salvador | 03 2000 | 84 | 8 | 9.5 | — | — | — | — |
| 82 | Bhutan | N.A. | 150 | 14 | 9.3 | — | — | — | — |
| " | Malawi | 06 1999 | 193 | 18 | 9.3 | — | — | — | — |
| 83 | Gabon | 12 2001 | 119 | 11 | 9.2 | 01 1997 | 91 | 12 | 13.2 |
| " | Malta | 09 1998 | 65 | 6 | 9.2 | — | — | — | — |
| " | Thailand | 01 2001 | 500 | 46 | 9.2 | 03 2000 | 200 | 21 | 10.5 |
| 84 | Hungary | 04 2002 | 386 | 35 | 9.1 | — | — | — | — |
| 85 | Ghana | 12 2000 | 200 | 18 | 9.0 | — | — | — | — |
| 86 | Cameroon | 06 2002 | 180 | 16 | 8.9 | — | — | — | — |
| 87 | Guatemala | 11 1999 | 113 | 10 | 8.8 | — | — | — | — |
| " | India | 09 1999 | 543 | 48 | 8.8 | 03 2000 | 242 | 22 | 9.1 |
| 88 | Greece | 04 2000 | 300 | 26 | 8.7 | — | — | — | — |
| 89 | Cote d'Ivoire | 12 2000 | 223 | 19 | 8.5 | — | — | — | — |
| 90 | Indonesia | 06 1999 | 500 | 40 | 8.0 | — | — | — | — |
| 91 | Guinea-Bissau | 11 1999 | 102 | 8 | 7.8 | — | — | — | — |

| Rank | Country | Lower or single House | | | | Upper House or Senate | | | |
|------|---------|-----------|--------|-------|------|-----------|--------|-------|------|
| | | Elections | Seats* | Women | % W | Elections | Seats* | Women | % W |
| " | Liberia | 07 1997 | 64 | 5 | 7.8 | 07 1997 | 26 | 5 | 19.2 |
| 92 | Ethiopia | 05 2000 | 547 | 42 | 7.7 | 05 2000 | 120 | 10 | 8.3 |
| 93 | Iraq | 03 2000 | 250 | 19 | 7.6 | — | — | — | — |
| " | Russian Federation | 12 1999 | 449 | 34 | 7.6 | N.A. | 178 | 6 | 3.4 |
| 94 | Madagascar | 05 1998 | 160 | 12 | 7.5 | 03 2001 | 90 | ? | ? |
| 95 | Cambodia | 07 1998 | 122 | 9 | 7.4 | 03 1999 | 61 | 8 | 13.1 |
| 96 | Central African Republic | 11 1998 | 109 | 8 | 7.3 | — | — | — | — |
| " | Japan | 06 2000 | 480 | 35 | 7.3 | 07 2001 | 247 | 38 | 15.4 |
| 97 | Georgia | 10 1999 | 235 | 17 | 7.2 | — | — | — | — |
| " | Uzbekistan | 12 1999 | 250 | 18 | 7.2 | — | — | — | — |
| " | Yugoslavia | 09 2000 | 138 | 10 | 7.2 | 09 2000 | 40 | 1 | 2.5 |
| 98 | Belize | 08 1998 | 29 | 2 | 6.9 | 06 1993 | 8 | 3 | 37.5 |
| 99 | Algeria | 05 2002 | 389 | 24 | 6.2 | 12 1997 | 144 | 8 | 5.6 |
| 100 | Samoa | 03 2001 | 49 | 3 | 6.1 | — | — | — | — |
| 101 | Benin | 03 1999 | 83 | 5 | 6.0 | — | — | — | — |
| " | Maldives | 11 1999 | 50 | 3 | 6.0 | — | — | — | — |
| 102 | Nepal | 05 1999 | 205 | 12 | 5.9 | 06 2001 | 60 | ? | ? |
| " | Republic of Korea | 04 2000 | 273 | 16 | 5.9 | — | — | — | — |
| 103 | Albania | 06 2001 | 140 | 8 | 5.7 | — | — | — | — |
| " | Fiji Islands | 08 2001 | 70 | 4 | 5.7 | 08 2001 | 32 | ? | ? |
| " | Gambia | 01 2002 | 53 | 3 | 5.7 | — | — | — | — |
| " | Mauritius | 09 2000 | 70 | 4 | 5.7 | — | — | — | — |
| 104 | Honduras | 11 2001 | 128 | 7 | 5.5 | — | — | — | — |
| 105 | Antigua and Barbuda | 03 1999 | 19 | 1 | 5.3 | 03 1999 | 17 | 2 | 11.8 |
| 106 | Equatorial Guinea | 03 1999 | 80 | 4 | 5.0 | — | — | — | — |
| 107 | Togo | 10 2002 | 81 | 4 | 4.9 | — | — | — | — |
| 108 | Kiribati | 09 1998 | 42 | 2 | 4.8 | — | — | — | — |
| 109 | Sri Lanka | 12 2001 | 225 | 10 | 4.4 | — | — | — | — |
| 110 | Iran (Islamic Rep. of) | 02 2000 | 290 | 12 | 4.1 | — | — | — | — |
| 111 | Haiti | 05 2000 | 83 | 3 | 3.6 | 05 2000 | 27 | 7 | 25.9 |
| " | Kenya | 12 1997 | 224 | 8 | 3.6 | — | — | — | — |
| 112 | Nigeria | 02 1999 | 351 | 12 | 3.4 | 02 1999 | 108 | 3 | 2.8 |
| 113 | Armenia | 05 1999 | 131 | 4 | 3.1 | — | — | — | — |
| " | Swaziland | 10 1998 | 65 | 2 | 3.1 | 10 1998 | 30 | 4 | 13.3 |
| 114 | Marshall Islands | 11 1999 | 33 | 1 | 3.0 | — | — | — | — |
| 115 | Paraguay | 05 1998 | 80 | 2 | 2.5 | 05 1998 | 45 | 8 | 17.8 |
| 116 | Egypt | 11 2000 | 454 | 11 | 2.4 | — | — | — | — |
| 117 | Lebanon | 08 2000 | 128 | 3 | 2.3 | — | — | — | — |
| 118 | Bangladesh | 10 2001 | 300 | 6 | 2.0 | — | — | — | — |
| 119 | Vanuatu | 05 2002 | 52 | 1 | 1.9 | — | — | — | — |
| 120 | Jordan | 11 1997 | 80 | 1 | 1.3 | 11 1997 | 40 | 3 | 7.5 |
| 121 | Niger | 11 1999 | 83 | 1 | 1.2 | — | — | — | — |
| 122 | Yemen | 04 1997 | 299 | 2 | 0.7 | — | — | — | — |

| Rank | Country | Lower or single House | | | | Upper House or Senate | | | |
|---|---|---|---|---|---|---|---|---|---|
| | | Elections | Seats* | Women | % W | Elections | Seats* | Women | % W |
| 123 | Djibouti | 12 1997 | 65 | 0 | 0.0 | — | — | — | — |
| " | Kuwait | 07 1999 | 65 | 0 | 0.0 | — | — | — | — |
| " | Micronesia (Fed. States of) | 03 1999 | 14 | 0 | 0.0 | — | — | — | — |
| " | Nauru | 04 2000 | 18 | 0 | 0.0 | — | — | — | — |
| " | Palau | 11 2000 | 16 | 0 | 0.0 | 11 2000 | 9 | 0 | 0.0 |
| " | Solomon Islands | 12 2001 | 50 | 0 | 0.0 | — | — | — | — |
| " | United Arab Emirates | 12 1997 | 40 | 0 | 0.0 | — | — | — | — |
| ? | Austria | 11 2002 | 183 | ? | ? | N.A. | 64 | 13 | 20.3 |
| ? | Bahamas | 05 2002 | 40 | ? | ? | 05 2002 | 16 | ? | ? |
| ? | Bosnia and Herzegovina | 10 2002 | 42 | ? | ? | 11 2000 | 15 | 0 | 0.0 |
| ? | Brazil | 10 2002 | 513 | ? | ? | 10 2002 | 80 | ? | ? |
| ? | Chad | 04 2002 | 155 | ? | ? | — | — | — | — |
| ? | Congo | 05 2002 | 137 | ? | ? | 07 2002 | 60 | ? | ? |
| ? | Ecuador | 10 2002 | 123 | ? | ? | — | — | — | — |
| ? | Guinea | 06 2002 | 114 | ? | ? | — | — | — | — |
| ? | Jamaica | 10 2002 | 60 | ? | ? | 10 2002 | 21 | ? | ? |
| ? | Lesotho | 05 2002 | 120 | ? | ? | 05 1998 | 33 | 9 | 27.3 |
| ? | Libyan Arab Jamahiriya | 03 1997 | 760 | ? | ? | — | — | — | — |
| ? | Mauritania | 10 2001 | 81 | ? | ? | 04 2000 | 56 | 1 | 1.8 |
| ? | Pakistan | 10 2002 | 342 | ? | ? | 10 2002 | 92 | ? | ? |
| ? | Papua New Guinea | 06 2002 | 109 | ? | ? | — | — | — | — |
| ? | Sao Tome and Principe | 03 2002 | 55 | ? | ? | — | — | — | — |
| ? | Sierra Leone | 05 2002 | 80 | ? | ? | — | — | — | — |
| ? | Slovakia | 09 2002 | 150 | ? | ? | — | — | — | — |
| ? | Tonga | 03 2002 | 30 | ? | ? | — | — | — | — |
| ? | Turkey | 11 2002 | 550 | ? | ? | — | — | — | — |
| ? | Tuvalu | 07 2002 | 15 | ? | ? | — | — | — | — |
| ? | Ukraine | 03 2002 | 450 | ? | ? | — | — | — | — |

*Figures correspond to the number of seats currently filled in Parliament

**South Africa: the figures on the distribution of seats do not include the 36 special rotating delegates appointed on an ad hoc basis, and the percentages given are therefore calculated on the basis of the 54 permanent seats

***Democratic Republic of East Timor: The purpose of elections held on 30 August 2001 was to elect members of the Constituent Assembly of East Timor. This body became the National Parliament on 20 May 2002, the date on which the country became independent, without any new elections.

From *Inter-Parliamentary Union*, November 2002. © 2002 by Inter-Parliamentary Union (IPU), www.ipu.org.

# EUROPE CRAWLS AHEAD...

## By Megan Rowling

As Speaker of the Riksdagen, the Swedish parliament, Birgitta Dahl holds Sweden's second-highest political office. But when she was first elected back in 1969, as a 30-year-old single mother, she was regarded as "very odd."

"To be accepted and respected, you had to act like a bad copy of a man," Dahl recalls of her early years in politics. "But we tried to change that, and we never gave up our identity. Now women have competence in Parliament, and they have changed its performance and priorities."

Back then, women of her generation were eager for change. From the beginning, they based their demands on the right of the individual—whether male or female—to have equal access to education, work and social security. And as politicians, they fought hard to build a legal framework for good childcare and parental leave, for fathers as well as mothers. "We got this kind of legislation through," Dahl says, "even though it took 15 years of serious conflict, debate and struggle."

And their efforts paid off. Sweden now has the highest proportion of women parliamentarians in the world, at 42.7 percent—up from just 12 percent in 1969. Two of its three deputy speakers are also women. Other Nordic countries too have high levels of female representation: In rankings compiled by the Inter-Parliamentary Union (IPU), Denmark takes second place behind Sweden, with women accounting for 38 percent of parliament members, followed by Finland and Norway with around 36.5 percent. (Finland also has one of the world's 11 women heads of state.) These nations' Social Democratic and far-left governing coalitions have made impressive progress toward equality in all areas of society in the past 40 years. But the nature of their electoral systems is also very important.

Julie Ballington, gender project officer at the Stockholm-based International Institute for Democracy and Electoral Assistance (IDEA), points out that the top 10 countries in the IPU ranking all use some form of proportional representation. This kind of voting system, in which parties are allocated seats in multi-member districts according to the percentage of votes they win, Ballington says, "offers a way to address gender imbalance in parliaments." With single-member districts, parties are often under pressure to choose a male candidate. But where they can contest and win more than one seat per constituency, they tend to be more willing to field female candidates. And by improving the gender balance on their slates, they widen their appeal among women voters.

Most European countries now use proportional representation or a combination of proportional representation and majoritarian voting, the system in use in the United States and the United Kingdom. In Europe, the widespread use of proportional representation has boosted the number of women politicians—particularly in the past three decades. And in the Nordic countries, where left-wing parties have enjoyed long periods in power and feminism has received strong support, the combination of these factors has led to significant progress toward gender parity in politics.

But even within Europe, some countries continue to lag behind. In Britain, which uses a single-member district plurality system, women members of parliament make up just 17.9 percent of the House of Commons. In the general elections of 2001, the ruling Labour Party stipulated that half those on its candidate shortlists be women. But research conducted by the Fawcett Society, a British organization that campaigns for gender equity, showed that some female hopefuls experienced overt discrimination and even sexual harassment when interviewed by local party members during the selection process.

"You are told things like 'your children are better off with you at home'... 'you are the best candidate but we are not ready for a woman.' They would select the donkey rather than the woman," said one candidate. Another complained: "They are absolutely adamant they will not consider a woman.... It was said to me... 'we do enjoy watching you speak—we always imagine what your knickers are like.' It is that basic." In light of such attitudes, it is not surprising that women candidates were selected for only four out of 38 vacant seats.

Thanks to new governmental legislation, however, the party is set to reintroduce the controversial method of all-women shortlists it used in the general election of 1997. The use of these shortlists saw the number of British women MPs double to 120 in that election, which swept

Labour to power with a landslide victory. The technique was later ruled illegal because it was judged to discriminate against men. But in early 2002, the government returned to the idea, passing a bill that will allow political parties to take measures in favor of women when choosing parliamentary candidates—what's often referred to as "positive discrimination."

# "Critical mass," or the level of representation above which women make a real difference to the political agenda, is widely judged to be around 30 percent.

Judith Squires, a political researcher at Bristol University, believes that the new legislation got such an easy ride partly because it does not stipulate that parties must take action: "We had expected it to be a hard battle. But there has been a change of mood in the Conservative Party, and the fact that it is permissive, and there is a sunset clause [the legislation expires in 2015], all helped to push it through."

In France, where until the recent election women accounted for only 10.9 percent of National Assembly members, the government opted for a more extreme method: a law aimed at securing political parity between men and women. Now half of all contesting parties' candidates in National Assembly elections and most local ballots must be women. In National Assembly elections, which do not use proportional representation, parties that deviate from the 50 percent target by more than two percent are fined a proportion of their public financing.

The law's first test in the municipal elections of March 2001 saw the percentage of elected women councilors in towns of more than 3,500 almost double, to 47.5 percent. But in June's National Assembly elections, the proportion of women deputies increased by less than 1.5 points, to just 12.3 percent—way below expectations. The main factor behind this disappointing result was the success of right-wing parties that ignored the new law, says Mariette Sineau, research director at the Center for the Study of French Political Life. "The big parties decided it was better to incur the financial penalty than to sacrifice their 'favored sons.' And this was particularly so with parties on the right."

Another problem with the law, Sineau explains, is that it does not apply to regional assemblies, "which is a shame, because most National Assembly deputies are recruited there." And the recent victory of the right suggests that France's ruling—and predominantly male—elite are in no hurry to change the system that has allowed them to hold on to power up until now, law or no law. As Chantal Cauquil, a French deputy at the European Parliament and member of the Workers' Struggle Party, argues, other aspects of French society must change before real

parity can be achieved. "There's no doubt that economic and social conditions—which weigh on women earning the lowest salaries, in the most precarious situations, and with the biggest problems caused by a notable lack of childcare infrastructure—have a negative impact on women's political participation," she says. Moreover, governing parties of both the right and left are influenced by social prejudices and are not inclined to regard women as full citizens. It requires real political will to go against such prejudices and allow women to take on the same responsibilities as men."

Such deep-rooted but hidden obstacles, faced by women everywhere, are precisely why proponents of the use of gender quotas on lists for both party and national elections believe positive discrimination is essential. "Everybody hates quotas, and everyone wishes they weren't necessary," says Drude Dahlerup, professor of politics at the University of Stockholm. "But we have to start from the point that there are structural barriers. Then quotas can be seen as compensation." Currently, political parties in some 40 countries appear to agree, with quota systems in operation from Argentina and India to Uganda.

The use of quotas in Europe varies significantly from country to country and from party to party, but where a quota system is applied, it tends to lead to a rise in women's representation. In 1988, for example, Germany's Social Democrats adopted a system of flexible quotas, under which at least one-third of all candidates for internal party election must be female—and between 1987 and 1990, the number of Social Democratic women in the German parliament, the Bundestag, doubled. In Sweden, parties didn't introduce quotas until the '90s, but the principle of "Varannan Damernas" ("Every Other Seat A Woman's Seat") has been widespread since the '80s. Dahl, the Swedish speaker, argues that "it is not only legislation that changes the world, but convincing people that change is necessary."

Yet, as Dahlerup notes, women in some Scandinavian countries have worked to improve gender equality since the end of World War I, and "other countries are not going to wait that long—they are showing impatience." "Critical mass," or the level of representation above which women make a real difference to the political agenda, is widely judged to be around 30 percent. And in countries such as France and the United Kingdom, where that is still a long way off, measures such as parity laws and all-women shortlists are a way to speed up progress.

Even in countries that are close to achieving political parity, however, women are quick to warn against complacency. Dahlerup emphasizes the case of Denmark, where quotas have been abandoned. "Young women say they don't want and don't need quotas. The discourse is that equality has already been achieved. But I think Denmark could go backward again, and that is dangerous."

Squires of Bristol University also talks about a backlash in Britain's Liberal Democratic Party against what younger women regard as "old-fashioned feminist policies." At the party conference last year, she says, many women in their twenties and early thirties lobbied against any form of positive discrimination, wearing pink T-shirts emblazoned with the words "I'm not a token woman." But Squires suggests that this attitude is somewhat misguided: "All parties [in the United Kingdom] have set criteria that discriminate against women. It is not a supply-side problem, it is a demand-side problem."

## "People are waking up and saying that it's not right that there are so few women in politics."

In an attempt to address this "demand-side problem," activists are targeting not only national political institutions, but also those of the European Union. The number of women members of the European Parliament increased from 25.7 percent in 1994 to 29.9 percent in the 1999 elections—not very impressive considering that some countries introduced proportional representation voting, and some parties alternated women and men on their lists to boost women's chances. More worrying perhaps is the gender imbalance in the convention on the Future of Europe, a body charged with the important task of drafting a new treaty for the European Union. Its presidium includes only two women among its 12 members, and the convention itself only 19 out of 118 members.

"The establishment of the convention is a response to the need for transparency and democracy. How can we explain the fact that women are not included?" asks Denise Fuchs, president of the European Women's Lobby. "It is simply not coherent." The EWL has launched a campaign to rectify the problem and is lobbying to achieve parity democracy across all other European institutions as well.

Yvonne Galligan, director of the Belfast-based Center for Advancement of Women in Politics, points out that "there has been a groundswell of support for women in political life across Western Europe, but this has not yet translated into numbers in the United Kingdom, Ireland and the European Union." In May's elections in the Irish Republic, for example, women parliamentarians in Ireland's Dail gained just one seat, and are now at 12.7 percent, according to the IPU.

Galligan is now working with political parties to set targets for Ireland's local elections in a couple of years' time—a tough job, because most parties oppose any form of positive discrimination. Parity in Ireland isn't likely to happen for a long while yet, but Galligan believes the social backdrop is improving. She cites a controversial referendum in March, in which the Irish electorate narrowly voted against a proposal to tighten the country's strict abortion laws even further. "That raised the status of women," she explains. "The underlying question was, how do we perceive the role of women? Now that is carrying over into elections. People are waking up and saying that it's not right that there are so few women in politics."

But where a sea-change in attitudes has not already occurred, it is almost certainly emerging. Naturally, there are fears that the apparent resurgence of the right in Europe could reverse the trend. But most of those interviewed for this article say women have already progressed far enough to prevent a significant decline in representation.

As Linda McAvan, deputy leader of Britain's Labour MEPs, argues: "If we look at how things were 20 years ago, they have changed enormously. Young women are different now. They see what has been done by women politicians before them, and they want to do it too."

From *In These Times*, July 22, 2002. © 2002 by In These Times.

# Campaign and Party Finance: What Americans Might Learn From Abroad

**Arthur B. Gunlicks**
*University of Richmond*

When the Clinton Administration took office in January 1993 with a Democratic-controlled Congress, many Americans were hoping that the long-standing "gridlock" between the Congress and President would finally be broken on a wide variety of issues, not the least of which was a reform of campaign finance laws and practices. Ross Perot had raised the issue during the presidential campaign, and Democratic-passed reform legislation which had been vetoed by President Bush now seemed to have a good chance of being revived, perhaps modified, passed, and signed by the new President.

It was not to be. Democratic House leaders gave President Clinton's campaign reform proposals of May 7, 1993, a lukewarm reaction, and Senator Robert Dole threatened to use the filibuster to block congressional action. Reform is a risky business for both parties, and what looks good from the perspective of political scientists or even the White House may not be very appealing to politicians in the trenches who worry that would-be challengers might actually have a fighting chance. In any case, the Democrats in the Senate and House could not agree on a compromise bill, and by the time they finally did in the fall of 1994 their efforts were defeated by the inability to end a Republican filibuster in the Senate. In the summer 1995, President Clinton and House Speaker Newt Gingrich agreed informally to work together to promote campaign finance reform, but again nothing happened.

For the second year in a row, on September 15, 1999, 54 Republicans joined 197 Democrats in the House of Representatives to pass the Shays-Meehan campaign finance bill, which would have banned unrestricted "soft money." But, for the fourth year in a row, Senate Republicans blocked a vote on the McCain-Feingold Senate version of the legislation via a filibuster, which the 45 Democrats and their 8 Republican allies could not break with less than the 60 required votes. Campaign finance was dead for 1999 and probably until after the 2000 election.

During the presidential primaries of 2000, Senator John McCain of Arizona focused his campaign for the Re-

publican nomination on issues of reform, including campaign finance reform. Governor Bush, who proceeded to win both the Republican nomination and the presidency, generally opposed Senator McCain's ideas on campaign reform, because he feared they would result in being disadvantageous to the Republican Party. Vice-President Gore, the Democratic nominee, was generally supportive. Following the assumption of office by President Bush in January 2001, Senator McCain introduced his proposals in the Senate in spite of a lack of support from the new Administration, and the Senate approved the Bipartisan Campaign Reform Act of 2001 (McCain-Feingold Bill) by a vote of 59–41. However, in the House of Representatives the Shays-Meehan bill, the counterpart of the Senate bill, became hostage to the House speaker, Dennis Hastert, who said he would not bring the bill out of committee until a majority of the House members had signed a discharge petition. By the end of December 2001, this had not happened, in spite of the fact that several Congressmen from both parties who had supported the legislation in past years had not signed.

Finally, however, in February 2002 the House of Representatives passed the Shays-Meehan bill with the support of 41 Republicans. The Senate's McCain-Feingold version had been passed in April [2001]. In March a single bill was presented to President Bush, who signed it reluctantly and over the objections of Republican congressional leaders. However, the bill did not take effect until after the November 2002 elections.

The McCain-Feingold and Shays-Meehan bills were concerned above all with "soft money." "Soft money" refers to often large amounts of money donated to political parties that use the funds for "party building" purposes rather than specific campaigns and to PACs that focus on general expenditures such as travel and fund raising events. Money used for individual election contests is called "hard money"; it was limited to $1,000 (changed to $2,000 in the new law) per contributor per race and to a total of $20,000 for all donations to various candidates and parties. Soft money contributions have become a particular focus of attention not only because of the large amounts raised from individual contributors and corporations but also because of the abuses associated with them. For example, the Clinton campaign was required to return large amounts of soft money collected illegally from foreign donors during the 1996 presidential race.

Those advocating reform pointed to the perception that many Americans have that politicians can be "bought" by large contributors and that special interests, rather than the general interest, are served by the system of financing in the United States. They also note the inordinate amount of time and effort that politicians must devote to fund-raising in order to be able to scare off potential opponents or to campaign against real opposition, whether serious or not (most incumbents do not face serious opposition). The result is that many would-be candidates are discouraged from running for office, and American elections are then less competitive. Those opposing reform cite the 1976 Supreme Court decision in *Buckley v. Valeo* that upheld the $1,000 limits on individual campaign contributions but also ruled that under the free speech provision of the First Amendment candidates had the right to spend unlimited amounts of their own money. They also ruled that groups could make "independent expenditures," which take a strong stand on an issue that in fact helps one candidate over another but that does not suggest specifically how the viewer should vote. These opponents of reform argue that a ban or limitations on soft money contributions would violate free speech, and they advocate a dramatic increase in the contribution limits for "hard money," since inflation has reduced the value of the dollar by more than 60 percent since 1974 (when the limitations were first imposed by federal law).

From 1999 to 2001 the Federal courts heard a number of cases dealing with soft money and reform efforts in certain states. After its decision in *FEC v. Colorado* in June 2001 which permitted political parties to be treated legally like individuals, whose behavior can be regulated, the Supreme Court instructed the Eighth Circuit Court of Appeals to reconsider its decision in 2000 which overturned a District Court decision in 1999 approving a Missouri law limiting the amount of money that could be donated to political parties. In November 2001 the Court of Appeals affirmed the District Court's decision (*Missouri Republican Party v. Lamb*), which means that states can now pass reform measures concerning soft money in spite of the opponents' arguments about free speech. The Court of Appeals suggested that the limitations on donations for candidates via the parties would not prevent the parties from helping candidates through other means, such as issue advertising. In August 2002 a Federal Appeals Court panel decided on a two-to-one vote that a Vermont law imposing spending limits of $300,000 on candidates for governor and $100,000 on candidates for lieutenant governor was constitutional. This ruling was seen by opponents as contradicting the *Buckley v. Valeo*

decision mentioned above, and it added fuel to those who had already decided to challenge the new campaign finance law in the Federal courts. In December a special three-judge panel met in Washington, D.C., to hear arguments. Whatever its decision in 2003, the case will be heard by the Supreme Court.

In this debate it might be easy and very tempting to argue that we should look at what other Western democracies do and adopt some of their practices. One of the difficulties we face, however, lies in the uniqueness of our political system, which raises questions about the relevance of foreign experiences. First, we have to focus on the party system. Our politics are candidate-oriented. In most democracies, they are more party-oriented. Many of us may regret this fact and even devote some energy and effort toward strengthening American parties, but the probability of a major change seems slight. The party orientation found elsewhere has an effect on political financing. Indeed, the concept of "political finance" is likely to mean candidate and campaign financing in the United States and party financing in other democracies. Therefore, it is not surprising that in its early legislative proposals, the Clinton Administration backed away from the idea of public funds to the parties.

Second, our institutions are different. Virtually all countries that we might look to for comparison are parliamentary democracies. France may have a semi-presidential system, but its parliamentary features still distinguish it from the United States. Most democracies are unitary states. Canada, Australia, Germany, Switzerland and Austria are federal states, but they differ in significant respects from the United States in their division of powers as well as in population and/or size of territory. They are also parliamentary democracies.

Third, we have a political culture which is not very conducive to government assistance to political parties. Anti-party and anti-government sentiments in the United States have deep roots, and reform proposals that might cost taxpayers money and bring about more government involvement must overcome serious obstacles. It may be that public financing is not very popular in other countries, either, but the fact remains that it is widespread abroad and not here.

It is clear that the kind of massive public funding of parties found, for example, in Germany, Austria, and Sweden has little prospect of being implemented in the United States. The generously funded party foundations which perform a number of useful tasks in Germany and Austria also are unlikely ever to gain majority support in Congress. Public funding on this scale would be unacceptable for very practical budgetary reasons, let alone the different American party system and political culture.

What, then, are some foreign practices that might be deserving of some careful consideration in spite of the odds against their passage? It should be possible to convince the public—and then Congress—that television and radio stations must provide a certain amount of free media time, a common practice in almost every other democracy. The Clinton Administration's proposal to provide congressional candidates vouchers to pay for television, printing and postage if they agree to adhere to spending limits was a step in the right direction, but it differs significantly from other democracies where free time is provided to the parties rather than individual candidates. Free billboard and poster space for political advertisements might also be offered by local governments, as is common in Europe. There can be no question, however, that the focus on individual candidates in this country makes free television time and billboard space more complicated to administer. It would probably be very difficult to convince Americans to ban altogether the purchase of media time by individual candidates, as is done in Canada, Britain and the European Continent.

In order to reduce the influence of the widely disliked PACs, which are not found abroad, one can make a strong case for limiting the amounts they may give individual candidates. Thus it is not surprising that the Clinton Administration moved at least modestly in this direction. But placing limits on PACs raises the question of where the necessary campaign money is to come from besides wealthy candidates, their supporters, and other private interests. Some European countries, e.g., Germany, provide generous tax deductions for donations to political parties. The very modest deductions that were available in the United States were eliminated in the 1986 tax reforms. Surely small donations of up to at least $250 should be encouraged through tax deductions and/or public matching funds for candidates who have demonstrated that they enjoy minimal political support. Contributions to political parties should be promoted, and parties should be encouraged to assume more responsibility for financing the campaigns of their candidates. Perhaps "soft money" *to the parties* could be better regulated or limited rather than banned.

We do, of course, have a $3 federal tax check-off to pay for presidential campaigns and national political conventions, but only a small percentage (less than 10 percent in 2000, but 28 percent in 1980!) of taxpayers actually check the appropriate boxes even though it costs them nothing. A few states also have tax check-offs for helping to finance certain candidates or parties, while another handful of states have tax add-ons, where the taxpayer actually increases his or her tax liability by giving up a small portion of the refund due. As a result only about one percent of state taxpayers participate in tax add-on schemes. In other words, the amount of public political financing that exists in the United States, except for presidential races, is minimal.

To level the playing field even more, Congress could again try to impose limits on individual spending by candidates in the hope that the Supreme Court might reconsider its decision in *Buckley v. Valeo*. The British and Canadians have limited expenditures by individual candidates without, at last check, weakening freedom of speech in any notable way. The British also require candidate approval of what we call "independent expenditures," which has hardly led to a serious undermining of free speech.

Some reformers have argued that tightening the regulation of parties and candidates, such as improved disclosure and reporting procedures, would "clean up" problems of political finance. Aside from the suspicion that such proposals reflect the "puritan" streak in American political culture, it is difficult to see how these measures would deal effectively with the funding problems we face.

If large amounts of money are being spent by individual candidates, PACs and special interests in general, and there is understandable public dissatisfaction with this state of affairs, it seems apparent that alternate sources of financing must be found. Placing ceilings on expenditures is probably not a very effective solution. Tightening regulations will not produce more private donations. The dilemmas—and there are several—are that alternatives seem to be very expensive, and there is the problem of increasing dependency on the state. This dependency may lead to a separation of the party from the grassroots, as appears to be happening in Germany and several other countries, especially Italy, which voted by referendum in the early 1990s to end public subsidies for the parties.

American parties are a very long way from becoming dependent on the state for their finances. Indeed, by international comparison we rank low on the dependency scale, especially if one excludes the presidential campaigns. Were we to adopt free media time, free billboard space, tax deductions for small donations to parties and candidates, or modest public subsidies for legislative candidates, all of which are practices common in numerous other democracies, we would not solve all of our current problems. But it seems difficult to believe that the conditions of political financing in the United States would not benefit from the adoption of some of these measures.

Arthur B. Gunlicks is the editor of *Comparative Party and Campaign Finance in Europe and North America*, published by Westview Press and now available at iuniverse.com/bookstore.

---

# WHAT DEMOCRACY IS... AND IS NOT

Philippe C. Schmitter & Terry Lynn Karl

For some time, the word democracy has been circulating as a debased currency in the political marketplace. Politicians with a wide range of convictions and practices strove to appropriate the label and attach it to their actions. Scholars, conversely, hesitated to use it—without adding qualifying adjectives—because of the ambiguity that surrounds it. The distinguished American political theorist Robert Dahl even tried to introduce a new term, "polyarchy," in its stead in the (vain) hope of gaining a greater measure of conceptual precision. But for better or worse, we are "stuck" with democracy as the catchword of contemporary political discourse. It is the word that resonates in people's minds and springs from their lips as they struggle for freedom and a better way of life; it is the word whose meaning we must discern if it is to be of any use in guiding political analysis and practice.

The wave of transitions away from autocratic rule that began with Portugal's "Revolution of the Carnations" in 1974 and seems to have crested with the collapse of communist regimes across Eastern Europe in 1989 has produced a welcome convergence toward [a] common definition of democracy.[1] Everywhere there has been a silent abandonment of dubious adjectives like "popular," "guided," "bourgeois," and "formal" to modify "democracy." At the same time, a remarkable consensus has emerged concerning the minimal conditions that polities must meet in order to merit the prestigious appellation of "democratic." Moreover, a number of international organizations now monitor how well these standards are met; indeed, some countries even consider them when formulating foreign policy.[2]

## WHAT DEMOCRACY IS

Let us begin by broadly defining democracy and the generic *concepts* that distinguish it as a unique system for organizing relations between rulers and the ruled. We will then briefly review *procedures*, the rules and arrangements that are needed if democracy is to endure. Finally, we will discuss two operative *principles* that make democracy work. They are not expressly included among the generic concepts or formal procedures, but the prospect for democracy is grim if their underlying conditioning effects are not present.

One of the major themes of this essay is that democracy does not consist of a single unique set of institutions. There are many types of democracy, and their diverse practices produce a similarly varied set of effects. The specific form democracy takes is contingent upon a country's socioeconomic conditions as well as its entrenched state structures and policy practices.

*Modern political democracy is a system of governance in which rulers are held accountable for their actions in the public realm by citizens, acting indirectly through the competition and cooperation of their elected representatives.*[3]

A *regime or system of governance* is an ensemble of patterns that determines the methods of access to the principal public offices; the characteristics of the actors admitted to or excluded from such access; the strategies that actors may use to gain access; and the rules that are followed in the making of publicly binding decisions. To work properly, the ensemble must be institutionalized—that is to say, the various patterns must be habitually known, practiced, and accepted by most, if not all, actors. Increasingly, the preferred mechanism of institutionalization is a written body of laws undergirded by a written constitution, though many enduring political norms can have an informal, prudential, or traditional basis.[4]

For the sake of economy and comparison, these forms, characteristics, and rules are usually bundled together and given a generic label. Democratic is one; others are autocratic, authoritarian, despotic, dictatorial, tyrannical, totalitarian, absolutist, traditional, monarchic, obligarchic, plutocratic, aristocratic, and sultanistic.[5] Each of these regime forms may in turn be broken down into subtypes.

Like all regimes, democracies depend upon the presence of *rulers*, persons who occupy specialized authority roles and can give legitimate commands to others. What distinguishes democratic rulers from nondemocratic ones are the norms that condition how the former come to power and the practices that hold them accountable for their actions.

## "However central to democracy, elections occur intermittently and only allow citizens to choose between the highly aggregated alternatives offered by political parties..."

The *public realm* encompasses the making of collective norms and choices that are binding on the society and backed by state coercion. Its content can vary a great deal across democracies, depending upon preexisting distinctions between the public and the private, state and society, legitimate coercion and voluntary exchange, and collective needs and individual preferences. The liberal conception of democracy advocates circumscribing the public realm as narrowly as possible, while the socialist or social-democratic approach would extend that realm through regulation, subsidization, and, in some cases, collective ownership of property. Neither is intrinsically more democratic than the other—just *differently* democratic. This implies that measures aimed at "developing the private sector" are no more democratic than those aimed at "developing the public sector." Both, if carried to extremes, could undermine the practice of democracy, the former by destroying the basis for satisfying collective needs and exercising legitimate authority; the latter by destroying the basis for satisfying individual preferences and controlling illegitimate government actions. Differences of opinion over the optimal mix of the two provide much of the substantive content of political conflict within established democracies.

*Citizens* are the most distinctive element in democracies. All regimes have rulers and a public realm, but only to the extent that they are democratic do they have citizens. Historically, severe restrictions on citizenship were imposed in most emerging or partial democracies according to criteria of age, gender, class, race, literacy, property ownership, tax-paying status, and so on. Only a small part of the total population was eligible to vote or run for office. Only restricted social categories were allowed to form, join, or support political associations. After protracted struggle—in some cases involving violent domestic upheaval or international war—most of these restrictions were lifted. Today, the criteria for inclusion are fairly standard. All native-born adults are eligible, although somewhat higher age limits may still be imposed upon candidates for certain offices. Unlike the early American and European democracies of the nineteenth century, none of the recent democracies in southern Europe, Latin America, Asia, or Eastern Europe has even attempted to impose formal restrictions on the franchise or

eligibility to office. When it comes to informal restrictions on the effective exercise of citizenship rights, however, the story can be quite different. This explains the central importance (discussed below) of procedures.

*Competition* has not always been considered an essential defining condition of democracy. "Classic" democracies presumed decision making based on direct participation leading to consensus. The assembled citizenry was expected to agree on a common course of action after listening to the alternatives and weighing their respective merits and demerits. A tradition of hostility to "faction," and "particular interests" persists in democratic thought, but at least since *The Federalist Papers* it has become widely accepted that competition among factions is a necessary evil in democracies that operate on a more-than-local scale. Since, as James Madison argued, "the latent causes of faction are sown into the nature of man," and the possible remedies for "the mischief of faction" are worse than the disease, the best course is to recognize them and to attempt to control their effects.[6] Yet while democrats may agree on the inevitability of factions, they tend to disagree about the best forms and rules for governing factional competition. Indeed, differences over the preferred modes and boundaries of competition contribute most to distinguishing one subtype of democracy from another.

The most popular definition of democracy equates it with regular *elections*, fairly conducted and honestly counted. Some even consider the mere fact of elections—even ones from which specific parties or candidates are excluded, or in which substantial portions of the population cannot freely participate—as a sufficient condition for the existence of democracy. This fallacy has been called "electoralism" or "the faith that merely holding elections will channel political action into peaceful contests among elites and accord public legitimacy to the winners"—no matter how they are conducted or what else constrains those who win them.[7] However central to democracy, elections occur intermittently and only allow citizens to choose between the highly aggregated alternatives offered by political parties, which can, especially in the early stages of a democratic transition, proliferate in a bewildering variety. During the intervals between elections, citizens can seek to influence public policy through a wide variety of other intermediaries: interest associations, social movements, locality groupings, clientelistic arrangements, and so forth. *Modern democracy, in other words, offers a variety of competitive processes and channels for the expression of interests and values—associational as well as partisan, functional as well as territorial, collective as well as individual. All are integral to its practice.*

Another commonly accepted image of democracy identifies it with *majority rule*. Any governing body that makes decisions by combining the votes of more than half of those eligible and present is said to be democratic, whether that majority emerges within an electorate, a parliament, a committee, a city council, or a party caucus.

For exceptional purposes (e.g., amending the constitution or expelling a member), "qualified majorities" of more than 50 percent may be required, but few would deny that democracy must involve some means of aggregating the equal preferences of individuals.

A problem arises, however, when *numbers* meet *intensities*. What happens when a properly assembled majority (especially a stable, self-perpetuating one) regularly makes decisions that harm some minority (especially a threatened cultural or ethnic group)? In these circumstances, successful democracies tend to qualify the central principle of majority rule in order to protect minority rights. Such qualifications can take the form of constitutional provisions that place certain matters beyond the reach of majorities (bills of rights); requirements for concurrent majorities in several different constituencies (confederalism); guarantees securing the autonomy of local or regional governments against the demands of the central authority (federalism); grand coalition governments that incorporate all parties (consociationalism); or the negotiation of social pacts between major social groups like business and labor (neocorporatism). The most common and effective way of protecting minorities, however, lies in the everyday operation of interest associations and social movements. These reflect (some would say, amplify) the different intensities of preference that exist in the population and bring them to bear on democratically elected decision makers. Another way of putting this intrinsic tension between numbers and intensities would be to say that "in modern democracies, votes may be counted, but influences alone are weighted."

*Cooperation* has always been a central feature of democracy. Actors must voluntarily make collective decisions binding on the polity as a whole. They must cooperate in order to compete. They must be capable of acting collectively through parties, associations, and movements in order to select candidates, articulate preferences, petition authorities, and influence policies.

But democracy's freedoms should also encourage citizens to deliberate among themselves, to discover their common needs, and to resolve their differences without relying on some supreme central authority. Classical democracy emphasized these qualities, and they are by no means extinct, despite repeated efforts by contemporary theorists to stress the analogy with behavior in the economic marketplace and to reduce all of democracy's operations to competitive interest maximization. Alexis de Tocqueville best described the importance of independent groups for democracy in his *Democracy in America*, a work which remains a major source of inspiration for all those who persist in viewing democracy as something more than a struggle for election and re-election among competing candidates.[8]

In contemporary political discourse, this phenomenon of cooperation and deliberation via autonomous group activity goes under the rubric of "civil society." The diverse units of social identity and interest, by remaining independent of the state (and perhaps even of parties), not only can restrain the arbitrary actions of rulers, but can also contribute to forming better citizens who are more aware of the preferences of others, more self-confident in their actions, and more civic-minded in their willingness to sacrifice for the common good. At its best, civil society provides an intermediate layer of governance between the individual and the state that is capable of resolving conflicts and controlling the behavior of members without public coercion. Rather than overloading decision makers with increased demands and making the system ungovernable,[9] a viable civil society can mitigate conflicts and improve the quality of citizenship—without relying exclusively on the privatism of the marketplace.

*Representatives*—whether directly or indirectly elected—do most of the real work in modern democracies. Most are professional politicians who orient their careers around the desire to fill key offices. It is doubtful that any democracy could survive without such people. The central question, therefore, is not whether or not there will be a political elite or even a professional political class, but how these representatives are chosen and then held accountable for their actions.

As noted above, there are many channels of representation in modern democracy. The electoral one, based on territorial constituencies, is the most visible and public. It culminates in a parliament or a presidency that is periodically accountable to the citizenry as a whole. Yet the sheer growth of government (in large part as a byproduct of popular demand) has increased the number, variety, and power of agencies charged with making public decisions and not subject to elections. Around these agencies there has developed a vast apparatus of specialized representation based largely on functional interests, not territorial constituencies. These interest associations, and not political parties, have become the primary expression of civil society in most stable democracies, supplemented by the more sporadic interventions of social movements.

The new and fragile democracies that have sprung up since 1974 must live in "compressed time." They will not resemble the European democracies of the nineteenth and early twentieth centuries, and they cannot expect to acquire the multiple channels of representation in gradual historical progression as did most of their predecessors. A bewildering array of parties, interests, and movements will all simultaneously seek political influence in them, creating challenges to the polity that did not exist in earlier processes of democratization.

## PROCEDURES THAT MAKE DEMOCRACY POSSIBLE

The defining components of democracy are necessarily abstract, and may give rise to a considerable variety of institutions and subtypes of democracy. For democracy to thrive, however, specific procedural norms must be followed and civic rights must be respected. Any polity that fails to impose such restrictions upon itself, that fails to follow the "rule of law" with regard to its own procedures, should not be considered democratic. These procedures alone do not define democracy, but their presence is indispensable to its persistence. In essence, they are necessary but not sufficient conditions for its existence.

Robert Dahl has offered the most generally accepted listing of what he terms the "procedural minimal" conditions that must be present for modern political democracy (or as he puts it, "polyarchy") to exist:

1. Control over government decisions about policy is constitutionally vested in elected officials.
2. Elected officials are chosen in frequent and fairly conducted elections in which coercion is comparatively uncommon.
3. Practically all adults have the right to vote in the election of officials.
4. Practically all adults have the right to run for elective offices
5. Citizens have a right to express themselves without the danger of severe punishment on political matters broadly defined....
6. Citizens have a right to seek out alternative sources of information. Moreover, alternative sources of information exist and are protected by law.
7. ... Citizens also have the right to form relatively independent associations or organizations, including independent political parties and interest groups.[10]

These seven conditions seem to capture the essence of procedural democracy for many theorists, but we propose to add two others. The first might be thought of as a further refinement of item (1), while the second might be called an implicit prior condition to all seven of the above.

1. Popularly elected officials must be able to exercise their constitutional powers without being subjected to overriding (albeit informal) opposition from unelected officials. Democracy is in jeopardy if military officers, entrenched civil servants, or state managers retain the capacity to act independently of elected civilians or even veto decisions made by the people's representatives. Without this additional caveat, the militarized polities of contemporary Central America, where civilian control over the military does not exist, might be classified by many scholars as democracies, just as they have been (with the exception of Sandinista Nicaragua) by U.S. policy makers. The caveat thus guards against what we earlier called "electoralism"—the tendency to focus on the holding of elections while ignoring other political realities.
2. The polity must be self-governing; it must be able to act independently of constraints imposed by some other overarching political system. Dahl and other contemporary democratic theorists probably took this condition for granted since they referred to formally sovereign nation-states. However, with the development of blocs, alliances, spheres of influence, and a variety of "neocolonial" arrangements, the question of autonomy has been a salient one. Is a system really democratic if its elected officials are unable to make binding decisions without the approval of actors outside their territorial domain? This is significant even if the outsiders are relatively free to alter or even end the encompassing arrangement (as in Puerto Rico), but it becomes especially critical if neither condition obtains (as in the Baltic states).

## PRINCIPLES THAT MAKE DEMOCRACY FEASIBLE

Lists of component processes and procedural norms help us to specify what democracy is, but they do not tell us much about how it actually functions. The simplest answer is "by the consent of the people"; the more complex one is "by the contingent consent of politicians acting under conditions of bounded uncertainty."

In a democracy, representatives must at least informally agree that those who win greater electoral support or influence over policy will not use their temporary superiority to bar the losers from taking office or exerting influence in the future, and that in exchange for this opportunity to keep competing for power and place, momentary losers will respect the winners' right to make binding decisions. Citizens are expected to obey the decisions ensuing from such a process of competition, provided its outcome remains contingent upon their collective preferences as expressed through fair and regular elections or open and repeated negotiations.

The challenge is not so much to find a set of goals that command widespread consensus as to find a set of rules that embody contingent consent. The precise shape of this "democratic bargain," to use Dahl's expression,[11] can vary a good deal from society to society. It depends on social cleavages and such subjective factors as mutual trust, the standard of fairness, and the willingness to compromise. It may even be compatible with a great deal of dissensus on substantive policy issues.

All democracies involve a degree of uncertainty about who will be elected and what policies they will pursue. Even in those polities where one party persists in winning elections or one policy is consistently implemented, the possibility of change through independent collective action still exists, as in Italy, Japan, and the Scandinavian social democracies. If it does not, the system is not democratic, as in Mexico, Senegal, or Indonesia.

But the uncertainty embedded in the core of all democracies is bounded. Not just any actor can get into the competition and raise any issue he or she pleases—there are previously established rules that must be respected. Not just any policy can be adopted—there are conditions that must be met. Democracy institutionalizes "normal," limited political uncertainty. These boundaries vary from country to country. Constitutional guarantees of property, privacy, expression, and other rights are a part of this, but the most effective boundaries are generated by competition among interest groups and cooperation within civil society. Whatever the rhetoric (and some polities appear to offer their citizens more dramatic alternatives than others), once the rules of contingent consent have been agreed upon, the actual variation is likely to stay within a predictable and generally accepted range.

This emphasis on operative guidelines contrasts with a highly persistent, but misleading theme in recent literature on democracy—namely, the emphasis upon "civic culture." The principles we have suggested here rest on rules of prudence, not on deeply ingrained habits of tolerance, moderation, mutual respect, fair play, readiness to compromise, or trust in public authorities. Waiting for such habits to sink deep and lasting roots implies a very slow process of regime consolidation—one that takes generations—and it would probably condemn most contemporary experiences *ex hypothesi* to failure. Our assertion is that contingent consent and bounded uncertainty can emerge from the interaction between antagonistic and mutually suspicious actors and that the far more benevolent and ingrained norms of a civic culture are better thought of as a *product* and not a producer of democracy.

## HOW DEMOCRACIES DIFFER

Several concepts have been deliberately excluded from our generic definition of democracy, despite the fact that they have been frequently associated with it in both everyday practice and scholarly work. They are, nevertheless, especially important when it comes to distinguishing subtypes of democracy. Since no single set of actual institutions, practices, or values embodies democracy, polities moving away from authoritarian rule can mix different components to produce different democracies. It is important to recognize that these do not define points along a single continuum of improving performance, but a matrix of potential combinations that are *differently* democratic.

1. *Consensus*: All citizens may not agree on the substantive goals of political action or on the role of the state (although if they did, it would certainly make governing democracies much easier).

2. *Participation*: All citizens may not take an active and equal part in politics, although it must be legally possible for them to do so.

3. *Access*: Rulers may not weigh equally the preferences of all who come before them, although citizenship implies that individuals and groups should have an equal opportunity to express their preferences if they choose to do so.

4. *Responsiveness*: Rulers may not always follow the course of action preferred by the citizenry. But when they deviate from such a policy, say on grounds of "reason of state" or "overriding national interest," they must ultimately be held accountable for their actions through regular and fair processes.

5. *Majority rule*: Positions may not be allocated or rules may not be decided solely on the basis of assembling the most votes, although deviations from this principle usually must be explicitly defended and previously approved.

6. *Parliamentary sovereignty*: The legislature may not be the only body that can make rules or even the one with final authority in deciding which laws are binding, although where executive, judicial, or other public bodies make that ultimate choice, they too must be accountable for their actions.

7. *Party government*: Rulers may not be nominated, promoted, and disciplined in their activities by well-organized and programmatically coherent political parties, although where they are not, it may prove more difficult to form an effective government.

8. *Pluralism*: The political process may not be based on a multiplicity of overlapping, voluntaristic, and autonomous private groups. However, where there are monopolies of representation, hierarchies of association, and obligatory memberships, it is likely that the interests involved will be more closely linked to the state and the separation between the public and private spheres of action will be much less distinct.

9. *Federalism*: The territorial division of authority may not involve multiple levels and local autonomies, least of all ones enshrined in a constitutional document, although some dispersal of power across territorial and/or functional units is characteristic of all democracies.

10. *Presidentialism*: The chief executive officer may not be a single person and he or she may not be directly elected by the citizenry as a whole, although some concentration of authority is present in all democracies, even if it is exercised collectively and only held indirectly accountable to the electorate.

11. *Checks and Balances*: It is not necessary that the different branches of government be systematically pitted against one another, although governments by assembly, by executive concentrations, by judicial command, or even by dictatorial fiat (as in time of war) must be ultimately accountable to the citizenry as a whole.

While each of the above has been named as an essential component of democracy, they should instead be seen either as indicators of this or that type of democracy, or else as useful standards for evaluating the performance of particular regimes. To include them as part of the generic definition of democracy itself would be to mistake the American polity for the universal model of democratic governance. Indeed, the parliamentary, consociational, unitary, corporatist, and concentrated arrangements of continental Europe may have some unique virtues for guiding polities through the uncertain transition from autocratic to democratic rule.[12]

## WHAT DEMOCRACY IS NOT

We have attempted to convey the general meaning of modern democracy without identifying it with some particular set of rules and institutions or restricting it to some specific culture or level of development. We have also argued that it cannot be reduced to the regular holding of elections or equated with a particular notion of the role of the state, but we have not said much more about what democracy is not or about what democracy may not be capable of producing.

There is an understandable temptation to load too many expectations on this concept and to imagine that by attaining democracy, a society will have resolved all of its political, social, economic, administrative, and cultural problems. Unfortunately, "all good things do not necessarily go together."

First, democracies are not necessarily more efficient economically than other forms of government. Their rates of aggregate growth, savings, and investment may be no better than those of nondemocracies. This is especially likely during the transition, when propertied groups and administrative elites may respond to real or imagined threats to the "rights" they enjoyed under authoritarian rule by initiating capital flight, disinvestment, or sabotage. In time, depending upon the type of democracy, benevolent long-term effects upon income distribution, aggregate demand, education, productivity, and creativity may eventually combine to improve economic and social performance, but it is certainly too much to expect that these improvements will occur immediately—much less that they will be defining characteristics of democratization.

Second, democracies are not necessarily more efficient administratively. Their capacity to make decisions may even be slower than that of the regimes they replace, if only because more actors must be consulted. The costs of getting things done may be higher, if only because "payoffs" have to be made to a wider and more resourceful set of clients (although one should never underestimate the degree of corruption to be found within autocracies). Popular satisfaction with the new democratic government's performance may not even seem greater, if only because necessary compromises often please no one completely, and because the losers are free to complain.

Third, democracies are not likely to appear more orderly, consensual, stable, or governable than the autocracies they replace. This is partly a byproduct of democratic freedom of expression, but it is also a reflection of the likelihood of continuing disagreement over new rules and institutions. These products of imposition or compromise are often initially quite ambiguous in nature and uncertain in effect until actors have learned how to use them. What is more, they come in the aftermath of serious struggles motivated by high ideals. Groups and individuals with recently acquired autonomy will test certain rules, protest against the actions of certain institutions, and insist on renegotiating their part of the bargain. Thus the presence of antisystem parties should be neither surprising nor seen as a failure of democratic consolidation. What counts is whether such parties are willing, however reluctantly, to play by the general rules of bounded uncertainty and contingent consent.

Governability is a challenge for all regimes, not just democratic ones. Given the political exhaustion and loss of legitimacy that have befallen autocracies from sultanistic Paraguay to totalitarian Albania, it may seem that only democracies can now be expected to govern effectively and legitimately. Experience has shown, however, that democracies too can lose the ability to govern. Mass publics can become disenchanted with their performance. Even more threatening is the temptation for leaders to fiddle with procedures and ultimately undermine the principles of contingent consent and bounded uncertainty. Perhaps the most critical moment comes once the politicians begin to settle into the more predictable roles and relations of a consolidated democracy. Many will find their expectations frustrated; some will discover that the new rules of competition put them at a disadvantage; a few may even feel that their vital interests are threatened by popular majorities.

Finally, democracies will have more open societies and polities than the autocracies they replace, but not necessarily more open economies. Many of today's most successful and well-established democracies have historically resorted to protectionism and closed borders, and have relied extensively upon public institutions to promote economic development. While the long-term compatibility between democracy and capitalism does not seem to be in doubt, despite their continuous tension, it is not clear whether the promotion of such liberal economic goals as the right of individuals to own property and retain profits, the clearing function of markets, the private settlement of disputes, the freedom to produce without government regulation, or the privatization of state-owned enterprises necessarily furthers the consolidation of democracy. After all, democracies do need to levy taxes and regulate certain transactions, especially where private monopolies and oligopolies exist. Citizens or their representatives may decide that it is desirable to protect the rights of collectivities from encroachment by individuals, especially propertied ones, and they may choose to set aside certain forms of property for public or cooperative ownership. In short, notions of economic liberty that are currently put forward in neoliberal economic models are not synonymous with political freedom—and may even impede it.

Democratization will not necessarily bring in its wake economic growth, social peace, administrative efficiency, political harmony, free markets, or "the end of ideology." Least of all will it bring about "the end of history." No doubt some of these qualities could make the consolidation of democracy easier, but they are neither prerequisites for it nor immediate products of it. Instead, what we should be hoping for is the emergence of political institutions that can peacefully compete to form governments and influence public policy, that can channel social and economic conflicts through regular procedures, and that have sufficient linkages to civil society to represent their constituencies and commit them to collective courses of action. Some types of democracies, especially in developing countries, have been unable to fulfill this promise, perhaps due to the circumstances of their transition from authoritarian rule.[13] The democratic wager is that such a regime, once established, will not only persist by reproducing itself within its initial confining conditions, but will eventually expand beyond them.[14] Unlike authoritarian regimes, democracies have the capacity to modify their rules and institutions consensually in response to changing circumstances. They may not immediately produce all the goods mentioned above, but they stand a better chance of eventually doing so than do autocracies.

## Notes

1. For a comparative analysis of the recent regime changes in southern Europe and Latin America, see Guillermo O'Donnell, Philippe C. Schmitter, and Laurence Whitehead, eds., *Transitions from Authoritarian Rule*, 4 vols. (Baltimore: Johns Hopkins University Press, 1986). For another compilation that adopts a more structural approach see Larry Diamond, Juan Linz, and Seymour Martin Lipset, eds., *Democracy in Developing Countries*, vols. 2, 3, and 4 (Boulder, Colo.: Lynne Rienner, 1989).

2. Numerous attempts have been made to codify and quantify the existence of democracy across political systems. The best known is probably Freedom House's *Freedom in the World: Political Rights and Civil Liberties*, published since 1973 by Greenwood Press and since 1988 by University Press of America. Also see Charles Humana, *World Human Rights Guide* (New York: Facts on File, 1986).

3. The definition most commonly used by American social scientists is that of Joseph Schumpeter: "that institutional arrangement for arriving at political decisions in which individuals acquire the power to decide by means of a competitive struggle for the people's vote." *Capitalism, Socialism, and Democracy* (London: George Allen and Unwin, 1943), 269. We accept certain aspects of the classical procedural approach to modern democracy, but differ prima-

rily in our emphasis on the accountability of rulers to citizens and the relevance of mechanisms of competition other than elections.

4. Not only do some countries practice a stable form of democracy without a formal constitution (e.g., Great Britain and Israel), but even more countries have constitutions and legal codes that offer no guarantee of reliable practice. On paper, Stalin's 1936 constitution for the USSR was a virtual model of democratic rights and entitlements.

5. For the most valiant attempt to make some sense out of this thicket of distinctions, see Juan Linz, "Totalitarian and Authoritarian Regimes" in *Handbook of Political Science*, eds. Fred I. Greenstein and Nelson W. Polsby (Reading Mass.: Addison Wesley, 1975), 175–411.

6. "Publius" (Alexander Hamilton, John Jay, and James Madison), *The Federalist Papers* (New York: Anchor Books, 1961). The quote is from Number 10.

7. See Terry Karl, "Imposing Consent? Electoralism versus Democratization in El Salvador," in *Elections and Democratization in Latin America, 1980–1985*, eds. Paul Drake and Eduardo Silva (San Diego: Center for Iberian and Latin American Studies, Center for US/Mexican Studies, University of California, San Diego, 1986), 9–36.

8. Alexis de Tocqueville, *Democracy in America*, 2 vols. (New York: Vintage Books, 1945).

9. This fear of overloaded government and the imminent collapse of democracy is well reflected in the work of Samuel P. Huntington during the 1970s. See especially Michel Crozier, Samuel P. Huntington, and Joji Watanuki, *The Crisis of Democracy* (New York: New York University Press, 1975). For Huntington's (revised) thoughts about the prospects for democracy, see his "Will More Countries Become Democratic?," *Political Science Quarterly* 99 (Summer 1984): 193–218.

10. Robert Dahl, *Dilemmas of Pluralist Democracy* (New Haven: Yale University Press, 1982), 11.

11. Robert Dahl, *After the Revolution: Authority in a Good Society* (New Haven: Yale University Press, 1970).

12. See Juan Linz, "The Perils of Presidentialism," *Journal of Democracy* 1 (Winter 1990): 51–69, and the ensuing discussion by Donald Horowitz, Seymour Martin Lipset, and Juan Linz in *Journal of Democracy* 1 (Fall 1990): 73–91.

13. Terry Lynn Karl, "Dilemmas of Democratization in Latin America" *Comparative Politics* 23 (October 1990): 1–23.

14. Otto Kirchheimer, "Confining Conditions and Revolutionary Breakthroughs," *American Political Science Review* 59 (1965): 964–974.

**Philippe C. Schmitter** *is professor of political science and director of the Center for European Studies at Stanford University.* **Terry Lynn Karl** *is associate professor of political science and director of the Center for Latin American Studies at the same institution. The original, longer version of this essay was written at the request of the United States Agency for International Development, which is not responsible for its content.*

# Congress and the House of Commons: Legislative Behavior and Legislative Roles in Two Democracies

**Gregory Mahler**
Kalamazoo College

Aristotle long ago observed that man is a "political animal." He could have added that men—and women—by their very nature note the political status of their neighbors and, very often, perceive their neighbors' lot as being superior to his own. The old saying that "the grass is greener on the other side of the fence" can be applied to politics and political structures as well as to other, more material, dimensions of the contemporary world: people often find their neighbors' situation to be preferable to their own. In this day and age in which the world is constantly observed as becoming "smaller" and "smaller," in which technology permits individuals to be more aware of how others live and behave, it should come as no surprise that legislatures are included in the subjects about which people are increasingly well informed.

Legislators are not immune from the very human tendency to want to know how their neighbors are doing, how members of other legislatures exist in their respective settings, and, sometimes, to look longingly at these other settings. When legislators do observe the conditions under which their peers operate in other countries, it is not at all uncommon for them to be sensitive to the ways in which their peers operate in *better* circumstances, and legislators may, occasionally, think that they prefer the alternative legislative settings to their own. Features that legislators admire or envy in the settings of their colleagues include such things as: the characteristics of political parties (their numbers, or degrees of party discipline), legislative committee systems, staff and services available to help legislators in their tasks, office facilities, libraries, and salaries.

This essay suggests that it is not uncommon for legislators in one type of legislative setting to see the advantages of other settings as being very attractive; this is especially true in relation to a dimension of the legislative world that is regularly a topic of conversation when legislators from a number of different jurisdictions meet: the ability or inability of legislatures to check and control the executive. Here we shall briefly comment on the role of the legislature in both the Canadian (parliamentary) and American (congressional) political settings, and then try to draw conclusions about the validity of the observations that are often made about the strengths and weaknesses of their particular legislative systems.

## The Decline of Parliament

The theme of the "decline of parliament" has a long and well-studied history.[1] It generally refers to the gradual flow of true legislative power away from the legislative body in the direction of the executive. By "true legislative power" is meant here not only the technical passage of statutory laws, but also the more amorphous characteristic of the *genesis* of the laws, the *ideas* for the laws, the *motivation* and *perceived need* of the laws. The "decline of parliament" argument suggests that the executive does the *real* law-making—by actually conceptualizing and drafting most legislation—and the legislature takes a more "passive" role by simply approving executive proposals.

Legislators are very concerned about their duties and powers, and over the years have jealously guarded their prerogatives when these prerogatives have appeared to be threatened. In most parliamentary democracies in the world today, the majority of challenges to legislative power that develop no longer come from the ceremonial executive, the Crown, but from the political executive, the government of the day.

It can be argued that the ability to direct and influence public policy is a "zero sum game," that is, that there is only room for a limited amount of power and influence to be exercised in the political world, and a growth in the relative power of the political chief executive must come at the expense of the power of the legislature. It follows from this idea that if the legislature is concerned about maintaining its prerogatives, concerned about protecting its powers from being diminished, it must be concerned about every attempt by the political executive to expand its powers.

Some contend that real "legislative power" cannot, and probably never did, reside in the legislature. There was no "Golden Age" of Parliament. The true legislative role of parliament today is not (and in the past was not) to create legislation, but rather was to scrutinize and ratify legislation introduced by the Government of the day. Although an occasional exception to this pattern of behavior may exist (with private members' bills, for example), the general pattern of behavior is clear: the legislature today does not actively initiate legislation as its primary *raison d'être*.

Although parliamentarians may not be major initiators of legislation, studies have indicated a wide range of other functions.[2] Certainly one major role of the legislature is the "oversight" role, criticizing and checking the powers of the executive. The ultimate extension of this power is the ability of the legislature to terminate the term of office of the executive through a "no confidence" vote. Another role of the legislature involves communication and representation of constituency concerns. Yet another function involves the debating function, articulating the concerns of the public of the day.

Many years ago Professor James Mallory indicated the need to "be realistic about the role of Parliament in the Westminster system."[3] He cited Bernard Crick's classic work, *The Reform of Parliament*: "… the phrase 'Parliamentary control,' and talk about the 'decline of parliamentary control', should not mislead anyone into asking for a situation in which governments can have their legislation changed or defeated, or their life terminated… Control means influence, not direct power; advice, not command; criticism, not obstruction; scrutiny, not initiation; and publicity, not secrecy."[4]

In fact, in the Canadian case efforts were made in the recent past to give the House of Commons a more effective role in the legislative process. Under Prime Minister Brian Mulroney legislation was passed in the 1980's[5] to guarantee that a certain minimal number of legislative proposals coming out of the legislature (as distinct from legislative proposals coming from the executive branch of

government) would be debated and voted upon each year. This was a significant departure from the direction in which Canadian parliamentary government was evolving, and received the support of an overwhelming majority of Canadian legislators. While it did result in a modest increase in legislative activity in the House of Commons, it did not result in an overall shift in the balance of power between the House and the Prime Minister, however. The fact that parliament may not be paramount in the creation and processing of legislation is certainly not a reason to condemn all aspects of parliamentary institutions, however. Nor should legislators in parliamentary systems be convinced that legislative life is perfect in the presidential-congressional system. In fact, some American legislators look to their parliamentary brethren and sigh with envy at the attractiveness of certain aspects of parliamentary institutions.

## Desirability of a Congressional Model for Canada?

Many Canadian parliamentarians and students of parliament look upon presidential-congressional institutions of the United States as possessing the answers to most of their problems. The proverbial "grass" is often seen as being "greener" on the southern side of the border. The concepts of fixed legislative terms, less party discipline, and a greater general emphasis on the role and importance of individual legislators (that implies more office space and staff for individual legislators, among other things) are seen as standards to which Canadian legislators should aspire. A perceived strength of the American congressional system is that legislators do not automatically "rubber stamp" approve executive proposals. They consider the president's suggestion, but feel free to make substitutions or modifications to the proposal in question, or even to reject it completely. Party discipline is relatively weak; there are regularly Republican legislators opposing a Republican president (and Democratic legislators supporting him), and vice versa. Against the need for party discipline congressmen argue that their first duty is to either (a) their constituency or (b) what is "right," rather than simply to party leaders telling them how to behave in the legislature. To take an example from several years back, in 1976 Jimmy Carter was elected President with large majorities of Democrats in both houses of Congress. One of Carter's major concerns was energy policy. He introduced legislative proposals (that is, he had congressional supporters introduce legislation, since the American president cannot introduce legislation on his own) dealing with energy policy, calling his proposals "the moral equivalent of war." In his speeches and public appearances he did everything he could to muster support for "his" legislation. Two years later when "his" legislation finally emerged from the legislative process, it could hardly be recognized as the proposals submitted in such emotional terms two years earlier.

The experience of President Carter was certainly not unique. Any number of examples of such incidents of legislative-executive non-cooperation can be cited in recent American political history, ranging from President Wilson's unsuccessful efforts to get the United States to join the League of Nations, through Ronald Reagan's battles with Congress over the size of the federal budget, through President Clinton's failed efforts at significant health care reform early in his term of office in 1992 and 1993. The Carter experience was somewhat unusual by virtue of the fact that the same political party controlled both the executive and legislative branches of government, and cooperation *still* was not forthcoming. There have been many more examples of non-cooperation when one party has controlled the White House and another party has controlled one or both houses of Congress.

This lack of party discipline ostensibly enables the individual legislators to be concerned about the special concerns of their constituencies. This, they say, is more important than simply having to follow the orders of the party whip in the legislature. It was not any more unusual to find Republican legislators voting against specific proposals of (Republican) President Bush on the grounds that the legislation in question was not good for their constituencies, than to find Democratic legislators voting against President Clinton's policy proposals on the grounds that the proposals were not good for their constituencies.

Congressional legislators know that they have fixed terms in office—the President is Constitutionally unable to bring about early elections—and they know that as long as they can keep their constituencies happy there is no need to be concerned about opposing the President, even if he is the leader of their party. It may be nice to have the President on your side, but if you have a strong base of support "back home" you can survive without his help. Conversely, even if the President does support you, if the voters in your constituency don't like what you (and, by extension, the President) are doing, you simply will not be reelected.

In fact, one of the major characteristics of the congressional-presidential system is the absence of *party discipline*. By party discipline here we mean the behavioral pattern of having members of the political party in the legislature vote together. When the president, as leader of his party, can count on having all party members support his position simply because they are members of his party—whether or not they personally agree with the policy position in question—we say that the principle of party discipline is active and strong. This almost never happens in the American Congress.

Are there any benefits to the public interest in the absence of party discipline? The most commonly cited argument is that the legislature will independently and actively consider the executive's proposals, rather than simply accepting the executive's ideas passively. This, it is claimed, allows for a multiplicity of interests, concerns, and perspectives to be represented in the legislature, and ostensibly results in "better" legislation.

In summary, American legislative institutions promote the role of the individual legislator. The fixed term gives legislators the security necessary for the performance of the functions they feel are important. The (relative) lack of party discipline enables legislators to act on the issues about which they are concerned. In terms of the various legislative functions frequently cited in the literature about legislatures,[6] congressmen appear to spend a great deal of their time in what has been termed the legislative aspect of the job: drafting legislation, debating, proposing amendments, and voting (on a more or less independent basis).

While many parliamentarians are impressed by the ability of individual American legislators to act on their own volition, it is ironic that many congressional legislators look longingly at the legislative power relationships of their parliamentary brethren. The "grass," apparently, is "greener" on the *northern* side of the border, too.

## Desirability of a Parliamentary Model for America?

The "decline of congressional power" is as popular a topic of conversation in Washington as is "the decline of parliamentary power" in Ottawa or London. Over the last several decades American legislators have sensed that a great deal of legislative power has slipped from their collective grasp.[7] Many have decried this tendency and tried to stop, or reverse, this flow of power away from the legislative branch and toward the executive.

One of the major themes in the writings of these congressional activists is an admiration for the parliamentary model's (perceived) power over the executive. Many American legislators see the president's veto power, combined with his fixed term in office, as a real flaw in the "balance of powers" of the system, leading to an inexorable increase in executive power at the expense of the legislature. They look at a number of parliamentary structures that they see as promoting democratic political behavior and increased executive responsibility to the legislature, including the ability to force the resignation of the executive through a non-confidence vote. The regular "question period" format that insures some degree of public executive accountability is also perceived as being very attractive.

Americans saw in 1999 that the impeachment power of Congress is not an effective instrument of legislative oversight. While the impeachment power might work in instances of major criminal offenses—and we do not have a historical basis for saying that this is necessarily the case since the impeachment of Richard Nixon in 1973 in a case involving far more significant political and criminal offenses than those of President Clinton in 1999 was averted by Nixon's resigning the presidency—we now can say that for political and criminal offenses of less significance the impeachment power is almost *too* powerful, and therefore perhaps incapable of responding to the needs of the time.

Critics of the congressional system do not confine their criticism only to the growth of executive power. There are many who feel there is too much freedom in the congressional arena. To paraphrase the words of Bernard Crick cited earlier, advising has sometimes turned into issuing commands; and criticism has sometimes turned into obstruction. This is not to suggest that congressional legislators would support giving up their ability to initiate legislation, to amend executive proposals, or to vote in a manner that they (individually) deem proper. This does suggest, however, that even congressional legislators see that independence is a two-sided coin: one side involves individual legislative autonomy and input into the legislative process; the other side involves the incompatibility of complete independence with a British style of "Responsible Government."

In 1948 Hubert Humphrey, then mayor of Minneapolis, delivered an address at the nomination convention of the Democratic Party. In his comments he appealed for a "more responsible" two party system in the United States, a system with sufficient party discipline to have meaningful party labels, and to allow party platforms to become public policy if the parties won control of government in an election.[8] Little progress has been made over the last half-century in this regard. In the abstract, the concept of a *meaningful* two party system may be attractive; American legislators have not been as attracted to the necessary corollary of the concept: decreased legislative independence and increased party discipline.

While American Senators and Representatives are very jealous of executive encroachments upon their powers, there is some recognition that on occasion—usually depending upon individual legislators' views about the desirability of specific pieces of legislation—executive leadership, and perhaps party discipline, can serve a valuable function. Congressional legislators are, at times that correspond to their policy preferences, envious of parliamentary governments' abilities to carry their programs into law because MPs elected under their party labels will act consistent with party whips' directions. They would be loath to give up their perceived high degrees of legislative freedom, but many realize the cost of this freedom in this era of pressing social problems and complex legislation. Parliamentary style government is simply not possible without party discipline.

A Democratic Congressman supporting President Clinton's health policy proposals might have longed for an effective three-line whip to help to pass the proposals in question. An opponent of those policy proposals would have argued, to the contrary, that the frustration of the president's proposals was a good illustration of the wisdom of the legislature tempering the error-ridden policy proposals of the president. Similarly, many conserva-

tive Republican supporters of President Reagan condemned the ability of the Democratic House of Representatives to frustrate his economic policies. Opponents of those policies argued, again, that the House of Representatives was doing an important job of representing public opinion and was exercising a valuable and important check on the misguided policies of the executive.

## Some Concluding Observations

The parliamentary model has its strengths as well as its weaknesses. The individual legislator in a parliamentary system does not have as active a role in the actual legislative process as do his American counterparts, but it is not at all hard to imagine instances in which the emphasis on individual autonomy in the congressional system can be counterproductive because it delays much-needed legislative programs.

The problem, ultimately, is one of balance. Is it possible to have a responsible party system in the context of parliamentary democracy that can deliver on its promises to the public, and also to have a high degree of individual legislative autonomy in the legislative arena?

It is hard to imagine how those two concepts could coexist. The congressional and parliamentary models of legislative behavior have placed their respective emphases on two different priorities. The parliamentary model, with its responsible party system and its corresponding party discipline in the legislature, emphasizes efficient policy delivery, and the ability of an elected government to *deliver on its promises*. The congressional model, with its lack of party discipline and its emphasis on individual legislative autonomy, places more emphasis on what can be called "*consensual politics*": it may take much more time for executive proposals to find their way into law, but (the argument goes) there is greater likelihood that what does, ultimately, emerge as law will be acceptable to a greater number of people than if government proposals were "automatically" approved by a pre-existing majority in the legislature acting "under the whip."

We cannot say that one type of legislature is "more effective" than the other. Each maximizes effectiveness in different aspects of the legislative function. Legislators in the congressional system, because of their greater legislative autonomy and weaker party discipline, are more effective at actually legislating than they are at exercising ultimate control over the executive. Legislators in the parliamentary system, although they may play more of a "ratifying" role in regard to legislation, do get legislation passed promptly; they also have an ultimate power over the life of the government of the day.

The appropriateness of both models must also be evaluated in light of the different history, political culture, and objectives of the societies in which they operate. Perhaps the "grass" is just as "green" on both sides of the fence.

## Notes

1. There is substantial literature devoted to the general topic of "the decline of legislatures." Among the many sources that could be referred to in this area would be classics such as the work of Gerhard Loewenberg, *Modern Parliaments: Change or Decline?* Chicago: Atherton, 1971; Gerhard Loewenberg and Samuel Patterson, *Comparing Legislatures*, Boston: Little, Brown, 1979; or Samuel Patterson and John Wahlke, eds., *Comparative Legislative Behavior: Frontiers of Research*, New York: John Wiley, 1972.

2. A very common topic in studies of legislative behavior has to do with the various functions legislatures may be said to perform for the societies of which they are a part. For a discussion of the many functions attributed to legislatures in political science literature, see Gregory Mahler, *Comparative Politics: An Institutional and Cross-National Approach*, Prentice-Hall, 2000, pp. 86–88.

3. This is a classic work in the literature. See James R. Mallory, "Can Parliament Control the Regulatory Process?" *Canadian Parliamentary Review* Vol. 6 No. 3, 1983, p. 6.

4. Bernard Crick, *The Reform of Parliament*, London, 1968, p. 80.

5. See the essay by James McGrath, "Reflections on Reform," *The Parliamentarian* 67:1(1986): 5–8.

6. See Note 2 above.

7. One very well written discussion of the decline of American congressional power in relation to the power of the president can be found in Ronald Moe, ed., *Congress and the President*, Pacific Palisades, Ca.: Goodyear Publishing Col, 1971.

8. Subsequently a special report was published by the Committee on Political Parties of the American Political Science Association dealing with this topic. See "Toward a More Responsible Two-Party System," *American Political Science Review* 44:3 (1950), special supplement.

"Congress and the House of Commons: Legislative Behavior and Legislative Roles in Two Democracies" by Gregory Mahler for *Annual Editions: Comparative Politics 00/01*. © 2000 by Gregory S. Mahler. Reprinted by permission.

# The gavel and the robe

**Established and emerging democracies display a puzzling taste in common: both have handed increasing amounts of power to unelected judges. Th[is] article examines the remarkable growth and many different forms of judicial review.**

To SOME they are unaccountable elitists, old men (and the rare women) in robes who meddle in politics where they do not belong, thwarting the will of the people. To others they are bulwarks of liberty, champions of the individual against abuses of power by scheming politicians, arrogant bureaucrats and the emotional excesses of transient majorities.

Judges who sit on supreme courts must get used to the vilification as well as the praise. They often deal with the most contentious cases, involving issues which divide the electorate or concern the very rules by which their countries are governed. With so much at stake, losers are bound to question not only judges' particular decisions, but their right to decide at all. This is especially true when judges knock down as unconstitutional a law passed by a democratically elected legislature. How dare they?

Despite continued attacks on the legitimacy of judicial review, it has flourished in the past 50 years. All established democracies now have it in some form, and the standing of constitutional courts has grown almost everywhere. In an age when all political authority is supposed to derive from voters, and every passing mood of the electorate is measured by pollsters, the growing power of judges is a startling development.

The trend in western democracies has been followed by the new democracies of Eastern Europe with enthusiasm. Hungary's constitutional court may be the most active and powerful in the world. There have been failures. After a promising start, Russia's constitutional court was crushed in the conflict between Boris

Yeltsin and his parliament. But in some countries where governments have long been riven by ideological divisions or crippled by corruption, such as Israel and India, constitutional courts have filled a political vacuum, coming to embody the legitimacy of the state.

In western democracies the growing role of constitutional review, in which judges rule on the constitutionality of laws and regulations, has been accompanied by a similar growth in what is known as administrative review, in which judges rule on the legality of government actions, usually those of the executive branch. This second type of review has also dragged judges into the political arena, frequently pitting them against elected politicians in controversial cases. But it is less problematic for democratic theorists than constitutional review for a number of reasons.

## Democracy's referees

The expansion of the modern state has seemed to make administrative review inevitable. The reach of government, for good or ill, now extends into every nook and cranny of life. As a result, individuals, groups and businesses all have more reason than ever before to challenge the legality of government decisions or the interpretation of laws. Such challenges naturally end up before the courts.

In France, Germany, Italy and most other European countries, special administrative tribunals, with their own hierarchies of appeal courts, have been established to handle such cases. In the

United States, Britain, Canada and Australia, the ordinary courts, which handle criminal cases and private lawsuits, also deal with administrative law cases.

The growth of administrative review can be explained as a reaction to the growth of state power. But the parallel expansion of constitutional review is all the more remarkable in a democratic age because it was resisted for so long in the very name of democracy.

The idea was pioneered by the United States, the first modern democracy with a written constitution. In fact, the American constitution nowhere explicitly gives the Supreme Court the power to rule laws invalid because of their unconstitutionality. The court's right to do this was first asserted in *Marbury v Madison*, an 1803 case, and then quickly became accepted as proper. One reason for such ready acceptance may have been that a Supreme Court veto fitted so well with the whole design and spirit of the constitution itself, whose purpose was as much to control the excesses of popular majorities as to give the people a voice in government decision-making.

In Europe this was the reason why the American precedent was not followed. As the voting franchise was expanded, the will of the voting majority became ever more sacrosanct, at least in theory. Parliamentary sovereignty reigned supreme. European democrats viewed the American experiment with constitutionalism as an unwarranted restraint on the popular will.

Even in the United States, judicial review was of little importance until the late 19th century, when the Supreme Court became more active, first nullifying laws passed after the civil war to give former slaves equal rights and then overturning laws regulating economic activity in the name of contractual and property rights.

After a showdown with Franklin Roosevelt over the New Deal, which the court lost, it abandoned its defence of laissez-faire economics. In the 1950s under Chief Justice Earl Warren it embarked on the active protection and expansion of civil rights. Controversially, this plunged the court into the mainstream of American politics, a position it retains today despite a retreat from Warren-style activism over the past two decades.

Attitudes towards judicial review also changed in Europe. The rise of fascism in the 1920s and 1930s, and then the destruction wrought by the second world war, made many European democrats reconsider the usefulness of judges. Elections alone no longer seemed a reliable obstacle to the rise of dangerously authoritarian governments. Fascist dictators had seized power by manipulating representative institutions.

The violence and oppression of the pre-war and war years also convinced many that individual rights and civil liberties needed special protection. The tyranny of the executive branch of government, acting in the name of the majority, became a real concern. (Britain remained an exception to this trend, sticking exclusively to the doctrine of parliamentary sovereignty. It is only now taking its first tentative steps towards establishing a constitutional court.)

While the goals of constitutional judicial review are similar almost everywhere, its form varies from country to country, reflecting national traditions. Some of the key differences:
• **Appointments.** The most famous method of appointment is that of the United States, largely because of a handful of televised and acrimonious confirmation hearings. The president appoints a Supreme Court judge, subject to Senate approval, whenever one of the court's nine seats falls vacant. Political horse-trading, and conflict, are part of the system. Judges are appointed for life, though very few cling to office to the end.

Other countries may appoint their constitutional judges with more decorum, but politics always plays some part in the process. France is the most explicitly political. The directly elected president and the heads of the Senate and the National

Assembly each appoint three of the judges of the Constitutional Council, who serve non-renewable nine-year terms, one-third of them retiring every three years. Former presidents are awarded life membership on the council, although none has yet chosen to take his seat.

Half of the 16 members of Germany's Federal Constitutional Tribunal are chosen by the Bundestag, the lower house of parliament, and half by the Bundesrat, the upper house. Appointments are usually brokered between the two major parties. The procedure is similar in Italy, where one-third of the 15-strong Constitutional Court is chosen by the head of state, one-third by the two houses of parliament and one-third by the professional judiciary.

Senior politicians—both before and after serving in other government posts—have sat on all three constitutional courts, sometimes with unhappy results. In March Roland Dumas, the president of France's Constitutional Council, was forced to step down temporarily because of allegations of corruption during his earlier tenure as foreign minister. The trend in all three countries is towards the appointment of professional judges and legal scholars rather than politicians.
• **Powers.** Most constitutional courts have the power to nullify laws as unconstitutional, but how they do this, and receive cases, varies. Once again, the most anomalous is France's Constitutional Council which rules on the constitutionality of laws only before they go into effect and not, like all other courts, after.

The 1958 constitution of France's Fifth Republic allowed only four authorities to refer cases to the council: the president, the prime minister, and the heads of the two houses of parliament. In 1974, a constitutional amendment authorised 60 deputies or senators to lodge appeals with the council as well. Since then, the council has become more active, and most appeals now come from groups of legislators. Individuals have no right to appeal to the council.

French jurists argue that judicial review before a law goes into effect is simpler and faster than review after a law's promulgation. But it is also more explicitly political, and leaves no room for making a judgment in the light of a law's sometimes unanticipated effect.

No other major country has adopted prior review exclusively, but it is an option in Germany and Italy as well, usually at the request of the national or one of the

regional governments. However, most of the work of the constitutional courts in both countries comes from genuine legal disputes, which are referred to them by other courts when a constitutional question is raised.

The Supreme Courts of the United States, Canada and Australia, by contrast, are the final courts of appeal for all cases, not just those dealing with constitutional issues. The United States Supreme Court does not give advisory or abstract opinions about the constitutionality of laws, but only deals with cases involving specific disputes. Moreover, lower courts in the United States can also rule on constitutional issues, although most important cases are appealed eventually to the Supreme Court.

Canada's Supreme Court can be barred from ruling a law unconstitutional if either the national or a provincial legislature has passed it with a special clause declaring that it should survive judicial review "notwithstanding" any breach of the country's Charter of Rights. If passed in this way, the law must be renewed every five years. In practice, this device has rarely been used.
• **Judgments.** The French and Italian constitutional courts deliver their judgments unanimously, without dissents. Germany abandoned this method in 1971, adopting the more transparent approach of the common-law supreme courts, which allow a tally of votes cast and dissenting opinions to be published alongside the court's judgment. Advocates of unanimity argue that it reinforces the court's authority and gives finality to the law. Opponents deride it as artificial, and claim that publishing dissents improves the technical quality of judgments, keeps the public better informed, and makes it easier for the law to evolve in the light of changing circumstances.

Also noteworthy is the growth in Europe of supra-national judicial review. The European Court of Justice in Luxembourg is the ultimate legal authority for the European Union. The court's primary task is to interpret the treaties upon which the EU is founded. Because EU law now takes precedence over national law in the 15 member states, the court's influence has grown considerably in recent years. The European Court of Human Rights in Strasbourg, the judicial arm of the 41-member Council of Europe, has, in effect, become the final court of appeal on human-rights issues for most of Europe. The judgments of both European courts carry great weight and have forced many countries to change their laws.

Despite the rapid growth of judicial review in recent decades, it still has plenty of critics. Like all institutions, supreme courts make mistakes, and their decisions are a proper topic of political debate. But some criticisms aimed at them are misconceived.

## Unelected legislators?

To criticise constitutional courts as political meddlers is to misunderstand their role, which is both judicial and political. If constitutions are to play any part in limiting government, then someone must decide when they have been breached and how they should be applied, especially when the relative powers of various branches or levels of government—a frequent issue in federal systems—are in question. When a court interprets a constitution, its decisions are political by definition—though they should not be party political.

Supreme courts also are not unaccountable, as some of their critics claim.

Judges can be overruled by constitutional amendment, although this is rare. They must also justify their rulings to the public in written opinions. These are pored over by the media, lawyers, legal scholars and other judges. If unpersuasive, judgments are sometimes evaded by lower courts or legislatures, and the issue eventually returns to the constitutional court to be considered again.

Moreover, the appointment of judges is a political process, and the complexions of courts change as their membership changes, although appointees are sometimes unpredictable once on the bench. Nevertheless, new appointments can result in the reversal of earlier decisions which failed to win public support.

Constitutional courts have no direct power of their own. This is why Alexander Hamilton, who helped write America's constitution, called the judiciary "the least dangerous branch of government." Courts have no vast bureaucracy, revenue-raising ability, army or police force at their command—no way, in fact, to enforce their rulings. If other branches of government ignore them, they can do nothing. Their power and legitimacy, especially when they oppose the executive

or legislature, depend largely on their moral authority and credibility.

Senior judges are acutely aware of their courts' limitations. Most tread warily, preferring to mould the law through interpretation of statutes rather than employing the crude instrument of complete nullification. Even the American Supreme Court, among the world's most activist, has ruled only sections of some 135 federal laws unconstitutional in 210 years, although it has struck down many more state laws.

Finally, it is worth remembering that judges are not the only public officials who exercise large amounts of power but do not answer directly to voters. Full-time officials and appointees actually perform most government business, and many of them have enormous discretion about how they do this. Even elected legislators and prime ministers are not perfect transmitters of the popular will, but enjoy great latitude when making decisions on any particular issue. Constitutional courts exist to ensure that everyone stays within the rules. Judges have the delicate, sometimes impossible, task of checking others' power without seeming to claim too much for themselves.

# The people's voice

Is the growing use of referendums a threat to democracy or its salvation? The fifth article in our series on changes in mature democracies examines the experience so far, and the arguments for and against letting voters decide political questions directly.

**W**HEN Winston Churchill proposed a referendum to Clement Attlee in 1945 on whether Britain's wartime coalition should be extended, Attlee growled that the idea was an "instrument of Nazism and fascism". The use by Hitler and Mussolini of bogus referendums to consolidate their power had confirmed the worst fears of sceptics. The most democratic of devices seemed also to be the most dangerous to democracy itself.

Dictators of all stripes have continued to use phony referendums to justify their hold on power. And yet this fact has not stopped a steady growth in the use of genuine referendums, held under free and fair conditions, by both established and aspiring democracies. Referendums have been instrumental in the dismantling of communism and the transition to democracy in countries throughout the former soviet empire. They have also successfully eased democratic transitions in Spain, Greece, South Africa, Brazil and Chile, among other countries.

In most established democracies, direct appeals to voters are now part of the machinery for constitutional change. Their use to resolve the most intractable or divisive public issues has also grown. In the 17 major democracies of Western Europe, only three—Belgium, the Netherlands and Norway—make no provision for referendums in their constitution. Only six major democracies—the Netherlands, the United States, Japan, India, Israel and the Federal Republic of Germany—have never held a nationwide referendum.

## The volatile voter

Frustrated voters in Italy and New Zealand have in recent years used referendums to force radical changes to voting systems and other political institutions on a reluctant political elite. Referendums have also been used regularly in Australia, where voters go to the polls this November to decide whether to cut their country's formal link with the British crown. In Switzerland and several American states, referendums are a central feature of the political system, rivalling legislatures in significance.

Outside the United States and Switzerland, referendums are most often called by governments only when they are certain of victory, and to win endorsement of a policy they intend to implement in any case. This is how they are currently being used in Britain by Tony Blair's government.

But voters do not always behave as predicted, and they have delivered some notable rebuffs. Charles de Gaulle skilfully used referendums to establish the legitimacy of France's Fifth Republic and to expand his own powers as president, but then felt compelled to resign in 1969 after an unexpected referendum defeat.

Francois Mitterrand's decision to call a referendum on the Maastricht treaty in 1992 brought the European Union to the brink of breakdown when only 51% of those voting backed the treaty. Denmark's voters rejected the same treaty, despite the fact that it was supported by four out of five members of the Danish parliament. The Danish government was able to sign the treaty only after renegotiating its terms and narrowly winning a second referendum. That same year, Canada's government was not so lucky. Canadian voters unexpectedly rejected a painstakingly negotiated constitutional accord designed to placate Quebec.

Referendums come in many different forms. **Advisory referendums** test public opinion on an important issue. Governments or legislators then translate their results into new laws or policies as they see fit. Although advisory referendums can carry great weight in the right circumstances, they are sometimes ignored by politicians. In a 1955 Swedish referendum, 85% of those voting said they wanted to continue driving on the left side of the road. Only 12 years later the government went ahead and made the switch to driving on the right without a second referendum, or much protest.

By contrast, **mandatory referendums** are part of a law-making process or, more commonly, one of the procedures for constitutional amendment.

Both advisory and mandatory referendums can usually be called only by those in office—sometimes by the president, sometimes by parliamentarians, most often by the government of the day. But in a few countries, petitions by voters themselves can put a referendum on the ballot. These are known as **initiatives**. Sometimes these can only repeal an already existing law—so-called "abrogative" initiatives such as those in Italy. Elsewhere, initiatives can also be used to propose and pass new legislation, as in Switzerland and many American states. In this form they can be powerful and unpredictable political tools.

The rules for conducting and winning referendums also vary greatly from country to country. Regulations on the drafting of ballot papers and the financing of Yes and No campaigns are different everywhere, and these exert a great influence over how referendums are used, and how often.

The hurdle required for victory can be a critical feature. A simple majority of those voting is the usual rule. But a low turnout can make such victories seem illegitimate. So a percentage of eligible voters, as well as a majority of those voting, is sometimes required to approve a proposal.

Such hurdles, of course, also make failure more likely. In 1978 Britain's government was forced to abandon plans to set up a Scottish parliament when a referendum victory in Scotland failed to clear a 40% hurdle of eligible voters. Referendums have also failed in Denmark and Italy (most recently in April) because of similar voter-turnout requirements. To ensure a wide geographic consensus, Switzerland and Australia require a "double majority", of individual voters and of cantons or states, for constitutional amendments.

The use of referendums reflects the history and traditions of individual countries. Thus generalising about them is difficult. In some countries referendums have played a central, though peripatetic, role. In others they have been marginal or even irrelevant, despite provisions for their use.

## Hot potatoes

Although referendums (outside Switzerland and the United States) have been most often used to legitimise constitutional change or the redrawing of boundaries, elected politicians have also found them useful for referring to voters those issues they find too hot to handle or which cut across party lines. Often these concern moral or lifestyle choices, such as alcohol prohibition, divorce or abor-

tion. The outcome on such emotive topics can be difficult to predict. In divorce and abortion referendums, for example, Italians have shown themselves more liberal, and the Irish more conservative, than expected.

One of the best single books on referendums—"Referendums Around the World" edited by David Butler and Austin Ranney, published by Macmillan—argues that many assumptions about them are mistaken. They are not usually habit-forming, as those opposed to them claim. Many countries have used them to settle a specific issue, or even engaged in a series of them, and then turned away from referendums for long periods. But this is mostly because politicians decide whether referendums will be held. Where groups of voters can also put initiatives on the ballot, as in Switzerland and the United States, they have become addictive and their use has grown in recent years.

Messrs Butler and Ranney also point out that referendums are not usually vehicles for radical change, as is widely believed. Although they were used in this way in Italy and New Zealand, referendums have more often been used to support the status quo or to endorse changes already agreed by political parties. Most referendums, even those initiated by voters, fail. In Australia, 34 of 42 proposals to amend the constitution have been rejected by voters. According to an analysis by David Magleby, a professor at Brigham Young University in Utah, 62% of the 1,732 initiatives which reached the ballot in American states between 1898 and 1992 were rejected.

Arguments for and against referendums go to the heart of what is meant by democracy. Proponents of referendums maintain that consulting citizens directly is the only truly democratic way to determine policy. If popular sovereignty is really to mean anything, voters must have the right to set the agenda, discuss the issues and then themselves directly make the final decisions. Delegating these tasks to elected politicians, who have interests of their own, inevitably distorts the wishes of voters.

Referendums, their advocates say, can discipline representatives, and put the stamp of legitimacy on the most important political questions of the day. They also encourage participation by citizens in the governing of their own societies, and political participation is the source of most other civic virtues.

## The case against

Those sceptical of referendums agree that popular sovereignty, majority rule and consulting voters are the basic building blocks of democracy, but believe that representative democracy achieves these goals much better than referendums. Genuine direct democracy, they say, is feasible only for political groups so small that all citizens can meet face-to-face—a small town perhaps. In large, modern societies, the full participation of every citizen is impossible.

Referendum opponents maintain that representatives, as full-time decision-makers, can weigh conflicting priorities, negotiate compromises among different groups and make well-informed decisions. Citizens voting in single-issue referendums have difficulty in doing any of these things. And as the bluntest of majoritarian devices, referendums encourage voters to brush aside the concerns of minority groups. Finally, the frequent use of referendums can actually undermine democracy by encouraging elected legislators to sidestep difficult issues, thus damaging the prestige and authority of representative institutions, which must continue to perform most of the business of government even if referendums are used frequently.

Testing any of these claims or counter-claims is difficult. Most countries do not, in fact, use referendums regularly enough to bear out either the hopes of proponents or the fears of opponents. The two exceptions are Switzerland and some American states, where citizen initiatives are frequent enough to draw tentative conclusions on some of these points, although both examples fall far short of full-fledged direct democracy.

Voters in both countries seem to believe that referendums do, in fact, lend legitimacy to important decisions. The Swiss are unlikely now to make a big national decision without a referendum. Swiss voters have rejected both UN membership and links with the EU in referendums, against the advice of their political leaders. Similarly, American polls show healthy majorities favouring referendums and believing that they are more likely to produce policies that most people want. Polls also show support for the introduction of referendums on the national level.

The claim that referendums increase citizen participation is more problematic. Some referendum campaigns ignite enormous public interest and media attention. Initiatives also give political outsiders a way to influence the public agenda. But in the United States, much of the activity involved in getting initiatives on the ballot, such as collecting signatures, has been taken over by professional firms, and many referendum campaigns have become slick, expensive affairs far removed from the grassroots (so far, this is much less true in Switzerland). Even more surprising, voter participation in American referendums is well below that of candidate elections, even when these are held at the same time. The average turnout for Swiss referendums has fallen by a third in the past 50 years to about 40%. On big issues, however, turnout can still soar.

Many of the fears of those opposed to referendums have not been realised in either country. Initiatives have not usually been used to oppress minorities. A proposal to limit the number of foreigners allowed to live in Switzerland was rejected by two-thirds of voters in 1988. In 1992 Colorado's voters did approve an initiative overturning local ordinances protecting gays from discrimination, but more extreme anti-gay initiatives in Colorado and California have been defeated by large majorities. Since 1990 voters have consistently upheld certain abortion rights in initiative ballots. Minorities and immigrants have been the targets of initiatives in some states, but voters have generally rejected extreme measures and have often proven themselves no more illiberal than legislators. Most initia-

tives are, in fact, about tax and economic questions, not civil liberties or social issues, although the latter often gain more attention.

While the frequent use of initiatives has not destroyed representative government, as some feared, it has changed it. Party loyalty among Swiss voters is strong at general elections, but evaporates when it comes to referendum voting. Initiatives, and the threat of mounting one, have become an integral part of the legislative process in Switzerland, as they have in California, Oregon and the other American states where they are most used. Referendums now often set the political agenda in both countries. In the United States they are frequently seen, rightly or wrongly, as a barometer of the national mood. And they can occasionally spark a political revolution. California's Proposition 13, for example, a 1978 initiative lowering local property taxes, set off a tax revolt across America. Elected officials themselves are often active in launching initiatives, and relatively successful in getting their proposals approved, which hardly indicates that voters have lost all faith in their politicians. Initiatives have made legislating more complicated, but also more responsive to the public's concerns.

There is some evidence that American voters, at least, are sometimes overwhelmed by the volume of information coming their way, and cast their vote in ignorance, as critics contend. Mr Magleby cites studies showing that on several ballots, 10–20% of the electorate

mistakenly cast their vote the wrong way. Ballot material dropping through the letterboxes of residents in California is now often more than 200 pages long. According to one poll, only one in five Californians believes that the average voter understands most of the propositions put before him. Quite rationally, this has also bred caution. Californians approve only one-third of initiatives.

## Hybrid democracy?

The Swiss and American experience suggests that in the future there is unlikely to be a headlong rush away from representative to direct democracy anywhere, but that, even so, the use of referendums is likely to grow. The Internet and other technological advances have not yet had much impact on referendums, but they should eventually make it easier to hold them, and to inform voters of the issues they are being asked to decide upon.

Representative institutions are likely to survive because of the sheer volume of legislation in modern societies, and the need for full-time officials to run the extensive machinery of government. Nevertheless in an age of mass communication and information, confining the powers of citizens to voting in elections every few years seems a crude approach, a throwback to an earlier era. In a political system based on popular sovereignty, it will become increasingly difficult to justify a failure to consult the voters directly on a wider range of issues.

Reprinted with permission from *The Economist*, August 14, 1999, pp. 45-46. © 1999 by The Economist, Ltd. Distributed by The New York Times Special Features.

# UNIT 3

# Europe—West, Center, and East: The Politics of Integration, Transformation, and Disintegration

## Unit Selections

## Key Points to Consider

- What are the major obstacles to the emergence of a more unified Europe? What differentiates the optimists and the skeptics as they assess the outlook for greater integration? What are the major institutional characteristics of the European Union?

- What is the evidence that the economic problems of Western Europe are not just cyclical but also structural in origin?

- What are the main problems facing the newly elected governments in Eastern and Central Europe?

- How do you assess Yeltsin's legacy, and how well is Putin equipped to lead his country to a better future?

 **Links: www.dushkin.com/online/**
These sites are annotated in the World Wide Web pages.

**Europa: European Union**
*http://europa.eu.int*

**NATO Integrated Data Service (NIDS)**
*http://www.nato.int/structur/nids/nids.htm*

**Research and Reference (Library of Congress)**
*http://lcweb.loc.gov/rr/*

**Russian and East European Network Information Center, University of Texas at Austin**
*http://reenic.utexas.edu/reenic.html*

Most of the articles in this unit are in some way linked to one or the other of two major developments that have fundamentally altered the political map of Europe in recent years. The first of these major changes is the long-term movement toward supranational integration of many Western European countries within the institutional framework of the European Community, or EC, which officially became the European Union, or EU, on November 1, 1993. Here the development has primarily been one by which sovereign states piecemeal give up some of their traditional independence, especially in matters dealing with economic and monetary policy. Many important economic decisions that used to be taken by national governments in Paris, Rome, Bonn, Dublin, or Copenhagen have become the province of EU policymakers in Brussels. Theoretically, the trend toward integration is neither automatic nor irreversible. In practice, the process has developed a momentum that would be difficult to stop and a supportive interest group structure that would seem impossible to unravel.

It is an important indication of the EU's continuing attractiveness that other countries seek to join the club. Austria and two of the Scandinavian nations (Sweden and Finland) became the newest EU members in 1995, after the entry had been approved in national referendums in each country. In the case of another Scandinavian holdout, Norway, the voters decided against membership for a second time in recent history. In Norway, there is a deep split between supporters and opponents, with a considerable resistance to membership coming from farmers and fishers as well as many women. A similar but weaker gender split is noticeable in the other Scandinavian countries, including Denmark, which has been a member since 1973. It appears that many Scandinavian women fear losing some of their social rights inside a European Union in which gender equality has not yet reached the level of their own countries.

The second major challenge to the established European state system is of a more disruptive nature. It consists of the disintegration brought about by the sudden collapse of Communist rule in Central and Eastern Europe at the end of the 1980s. Here states, nations, and nationalities have broken away from an imposed system of central control, asserting their independence from the previous ruling group and its ideology. In their attempts to construct a new order for themselves, the post-communist countries have encountered enormous difficulties. Their transition from one-party rule to pluralist democracy and from centrally planned state socialism to a market-based economy turned out to be much rockier than had been anticipated. The resulting destabilization has had consequences for the whole continent.

In some areas of the former Soviet bloc, one encounters some nostalgia for the basic material security and "orderliness" provided by the communist welfare states of the past. This should rarely be understood as a wish to turn back the wheel of history. Instead, it seems to represent a desire to build buffers and safety nets into the new market-oriented systems. Communist-descended parties have responded by abandoning most or all of their Leninist baggage. They now engage in the competitive bidding for votes with promises of social fairness and security. In Poland and elsewhere, such parties have recently gained

political leverage. By contrast with the recent past, they must now operate in a pluralist political setting. They have adapted by adopting new strategies and goals. As David Ost reports from Poland, the democratic Left plays a key role in criticizing a neoliberal market model that has brought instability and sharp inequality with it.

It will be interesting to follow how the EU will deal with the up to 10 new members, mostly from eastern Europe and including Poland, who are slated to join in the next few years. Some commentators believe that the relative poverty of most of the newcomers will seriously challenge the EU's ability to contain and resolve the many potential conflicts of interest with the more affluent Western members of the Community.

A closer look at the countries of Western Europe reveals that they have their own internal problems, even if in a far less acute form than their counterparts to the East. Their relative prosperity rests on a base that was built up during the prolonged postwar economic boom of the 1950s and 1960s. By political choice, a considerable portion of their affluence was channeled toward the public sector and used to develop a relatively generous system of social services and social insurance. Between the early 1970s and the mid-1980s, however, Western industrial societies were beset by economic disruptions that brought a slowdown to the long period of rapidly growing prosperity. The last half of the 1980s marked some improvement in the economic situation throughout most of Western Europe, partly as a result of some favorably timed positive trade balances with the United States. In the early 1990s, however, economic recession gripped these countries once again. Even if the business cycle may be turning in a positive direction once again, it is becoming clear that there are more fundamental reasons why European countries no longer can take increasing affluence for granted in a more competitive global economy.

Almost every one of these countries is beset by economic problems that appear to be structural in origin, rather than merely cyclical and passing. In other words, it will take much more than an upturn in the business cycle to galvanize these economies.

The economic shock that first interrupted the prolonged postwar boom came in the wake of sharp rises in the cost of energy, linked to successive hikes in the price of oil imposed by the Organization of Petroleum Exporting Countries (OPEC) after 1973. In the 1980s, OPEC lost its organizational bite, as its members began to compete against each other by raising production and lowering prices rather than abiding by the opposite practices in the manner of a well-functioning cartel agreement. The exploitation of new oil and gas fields in the North Sea and elsewhere also helped alleviate the energy situation, at least for the present. The resulting improvement for the consumers of oil and gas helped the Western European economies recover, but they did not as a whole rebound to their earlier high growth rates.

The short Gulf War did not seriously hamper the flow of Middle East oil in 1991, but it once again underscored the vulnerability of Europe to external interruptions in its energy supply. During the year 2000, there were again signs of a petroleum shortage, partly as a result of increased demand, but partly, also, as a result of supply limitations imposed by some of the oil producers. In the fall months of that year, irate citizens demonstrated in several countries, including France, Germany, and Britain, in protest against sharp price hikes in oil and gasoline.

Because of their heavy dependence on international trade, Western European economies are especially vulnerable to global cyclical tendencies. Another important challenge to these affluent countries is found in the stiff competition they face from the new industrial countries (NICs) of East and South Asia, where productivity is sometimes fairly high and labor costs remain much lower. The emerging Asian factor probably contributed to the increased tempo of the European drive for economic integration in the late 1980s. Some observers have warned of a protectionist reaction, in which major trading blocs in Europe, North America, and Eastern Asia could replace the relatively free system of international trade established in recent decades.

A related issue is how the increase in international trade within and outside the European Union will affect the established "social market economies" of continental Europe. The economic gains derived from international competition could have a positive consequence, by providing a better base for supporting, consolidating and invigorating the social welfare systems. However, a different scenario could be enacted, which results in a pruning and reduction in social services, carried out in the name of efficiency and international competitiveness. Some writers allude to the social problems that have resulted in Europe's growing "underclass." It also seems evident that the corporatist and welfare state arrangements, which appear to have served these countries well for so long, now face other demographic and economic challenges as well. The debate about the best policy response to such problems will probably continue to agitate West Europeans for years to come. It seems likely, however, that the famous "Swedish Model," like its German counterpart, will in some ways be revamped in the name of affordability.

In the mid-1980s, there was widespread talk of a malaise or "Europessimism" that had beset these countries. Thereafter, the mood appeared to become more upbeat, and for a while some observers even detected a swing toward what they labeled "Europhoria." The optimism in turn gave way to a more sober spirit in Western Europe. Observers plausibly linked this recent shift in mood to the economic and social problems associated with the prolonged recessionary developments described above as well as to the impact of the dislocations that have accompanied the end of the cold war. By the beginning of the new century, however, another turn toward cautious optimism seemed to be affecting several EU states, notably including Germany. It seems to have been cut short by the events of September 11, 2001, and the subsequent counter-measures in domestic and foreign policy. By now, the rift between the United States and some Western European countries over how to deal with Iraq's ruler has generated a skepticism about America's leadership role among Europeans that may affect the public mood and the political process in these countries for a long time.

The demise of the Soviet bloc removed one major external challenge but replaced it with a set of others. The countries of Western Europe were simply unprepared for the chaotic conditions left behind by the former Communist regimes to the East. They are now affected by the fierce competition for scarce capital, as the countries in Eastern Europe seek to attract investments that will build a new and modern economic infrastructure. At the same time, the grinding poverty and disorder of life in Eastern Europe have encouraged a migration to the relatively affluent societies of the West.

Those who attempt the big move to the "Golden West" resemble in many ways the immigrants who have been attracted to the United States in the past and present. Many Western Europeans are unwilling to accept, however, what they regard as a flood of unwanted strangers. The newcomers are widely portrayed as outsiders whose presence will further drain their generous welfare systems and threaten their economic security and established way of life. Such anxieties are the stuff of sociocultural mistrust, tensions, and conflicts. One serious political consequence has been the emergence of an anti-immigrant populist politics on the Far Right. In response, the governments in several countries have changed their laws on citizenship, asylum, and immigration.

As Seyla Benhabib points out in his essay, there can be little doubt that the issues of immigration and cultural tensions in Western Europe will occupy a central place on the political agenda in the coming years. Some of the established parties have already made symbolic and substantive accommodations to appease protesting voters, for fear of otherwise losing them to extremist ultra-right movements. But it is important to remember that there are also groups that resist such compromises and instead oppose the xenophobic elements in their own societies. Some enlightened political leaders and commentators seek to promote the reasonable perspective that migrants could turn out to be an important asset rather than a liability. This argument may concede that the foreign influx also involves some social costs in the short run, at least during a recessionary period, but it emphasizes that the newcomers can be a very important human resource that will contribute to mid- and long-term economic prosperity. Quite apart from any such economic considerations, of course, the migrants and asylum-seekers have become an important test of liberal democratic tolerance on the continent.

Prudent observers had long warned about a premature celebration of "Europe 1992," which really referred to the abolition on restrictions in the flow of goods, capital, services, and labor by January 1, 1993, under the EC's Single Europe Act (SEA), adopted and ratified a few years earlier. They suggested that the slogan served to cover up some remaining problems and some newly emerging obstacles to the full integration of the European Community. The skeptics seemed at least partly vindicated by some setbacks that followed the new and supposedly decisive "leap" forward, which was taken in the summit meeting of EC leaders at the Dutch town of Maastricht in December of 1991. The Maastricht Treaty envisaged a common European monetary system and a European Reserve Bank as well as common policies on immigration, environmental protection, external security, and foreign affairs.

In 3 of the then–12 member countries—Denmark, Ireland, and France—ratification of the Maastricht Treaty was tied to the outcome of national referendums. In the first of these expressions of the popular will, Danish voters in June 1992 decided by a very slim majority of less than 2 percent to reject the treaty. A huge Irish majority in favor of the treaty was followed by a very slim French approval as well. The negative Danish vote seemed to have had the effect of legitimating and releasing many pent-up reservations and second thoughts in other member countries, not least Germany. But in May 1993, Danish voters approved a modified version of the agreement, pruned down with special "opt-out" provisions that met Denmark's particular reservations.

Some weeks later British prime minister John Major was able to hammer together a fragile parliamentary majority for the treaty in the House of Commons. The last formal hurdle to the Maastricht Treaty was passed in Germany, where the Constitutional Court turned down a legal challenge based on an alleged violation of national sovereignty. But the difficult ratification process has revealed widespread political resistance that continues to hamper the course toward a federal union.

The first article in this section asks "Can These Bones Live?" referring to the future of the European Union. It has been clear for some time that the European Union has effectively reached a crossroads, even with the adoption of a common currency, the euro, by 12 of the 15 member nations. The European nation-state has turned out to have more holding power than some federalists had expected, especially in a time of economic setbacks and perceived threats to the social order. The absence of a quick and coherent West European response to the violent ethnic conflict in Bosnia and other parts of former Yugoslavia added a further reason for doubt concerning the EU's imminent progression toward an elementary form of political federation. For these and other reasons, the present seems to be a time for new thought and debate about the EU's further goals and its route for reaching them. Two of the articles in this unit deal with the major attempt by Europe's Convention to work out a constitutional framework or "architecture" for Europe.

While much academic and political ink has been spilled on the problems of a transition from a market economy to state socialism, we turn out to have little theory or practice to guide Central and Eastern European countries that have tried to make a paradigm shift in the opposite direction. The question of what would be the best strategy for restructuring the economies of the former Communist countries is far more than an interesting theoretical issue, for its answer has important policy consequences. Some academics believe that a quick transition to a market economy is a preferable course, indeed the only responsible one, even though such an approach would be very disruptive and painful in the short run. They argue that such a "shock therapy" would release human energies and bring economic growth more quickly and efficiently. At the same time, these supporters of a "tough love" approach warn that compassionate halfway measures could end up worsening the economic plight of these countries. Yet, as David Ost reports from Poland, tough love may turn out to be rejected as having failed to deliver the promised goods.

Other strategists have come out in favor of a more gradual approach to economic reconstruction in these countries. They warn that the neoclassical economists, who would introduce a full-scale market economy by fiat, not only ignore the market system's cultural and historic preconditions but also underestimate the turmoil that is likely to accompany the big transition. As a more prudent course of action, these gradualists recommend the adoption of pragmatic strategies of incremental change, accompanied by a rhetoric of lower expectations.

Experience and the passage of a few more years would give us better insights into the relative merits of each argument. A pluralist society, however, rarely permits itself to become a social laboratory for controlled experiments of this kind. Instead, it seems likely that political factors will promote a "mix" of the two approaches as the most acceptable and practical policy outcome. Moreover, decision makers must often learn on the job. They cannot afford to become inflexible and dogmatic in these matters, where the human stakes are so high. Meanwhile, the prospect of membership in the EU is a major incentive for continuing to promote market economics and pluralist democracy in many Central and Eastern European countries.

A similar debate about the best strategy for economic reconstruction has been carried out in the former Soviet Union during the past few years. In some ways, it could be argued that Mikhail Gorbachev, the last Soviet head of government (1985 to 1991), failed to opt clearly for one or the other approach to economic reform. He seems not only to have been ambivalent about the means but about the ends of his perestroika, or restructuring, of the centrally planned economy. In the eyes of some born-again Soviet marketers, he remained far too socialist, while Communist hard-liners never forgave him for dismantling a system in which they had enjoyed a modicum of security and privilege.

Gorbachev appears to have regarded his own policies of glasnost, or openness, and democratization as essential accompaniments of perestroika in his modernization program. He seems to have understood (or become convinced) that a highly developed industrial economy needs a freer flow of information along with a more decentralized system of decision making if its component parts are to be efficient, flexible, and capable of self-correction. In that sense, a market economy has some integral feedback traits that make it incompatible with the traditional Soviet model of a centrally directed, authoritarian economy.

But glasnost and democratization were clearly incompatible with a repressive political system of one-party rule as well. They served Gorbachev as instruments to weaken the grip of the Communist hard-liners and at the same time to rally behind him some reform groups, including many intellectuals and journalists. Within a remarkably short time after he came to power in 1985, a vigorous new press emerged in the Soviet Union headed by journalists who were eager to ferret out misdeeds and report on political reality as they observed it. A similar development took place in the history profession, where scholars used the new spirit of openness to report in grim detail about past Communist atrocities that had previously been covered up or dismissed as bourgeois lies. There was an inevitable irony to the new truthfulness. Even as it served to discredit much of the past along with any reactionary attempts to restore "the good old days," it also brought into question the foundations of the Soviet system under the leadership of the Communist Party. Yet Gorbachev had clearly set out to modernize and reform the Soviet system, not to bring it down.

Most important of all, democratization gave those ethnic minorities in the Soviet Union, which had a territorial identity, an opportunity to demand autonomy or independence. The first national assertions came from the Baltic peoples in Estonia, Latvia, and Lithuania, who had been forced back under Soviet rule in 1940, after some two decades of national independence. Very soon other nationalities, including the Georgians and Armenians, expressed similar demands through the political channels that had been opened to them. The death knell for the Soviet Union sounded in 1991, when the Ukrainians, who constituted the second largest national group in the Soviet Union after the Russians, made similar demands for independence.

In a very real sense, then, Gorbachev's political reforms ended up as a mortal threat not only to the continued leadership role by the Communist Party but also to the continued existence of the Soviet Union itself. Gorbachev seems to have understood neither of these ultimately fatal consequences of his reform attempts until quite late in the day. This explains why he could set in motion forces that would ultimately destroy what he had hoped to make more attractive and productive. In August 1991, Communist hard-liners attempted a coup against the reformer and his reforms, but they acted far too late and were too poorly organized to succeed. In fact, the would-be coup d'etat became instead a coup de grace for the Soviet Communists and, in the end, the Soviet Union as well. Somewhat reluctantly, Gorbachev declared the party illegal soon after he returned to office. The coup was defeated by a popular resistance, led by Russian President Boris Yeltsin, who had broken with Communism earlier and, as it seemed, far more decisively.

After his formal restoration to power following the abortive coup, Gorbachev became politically dependent on Yeltsin and was increasingly seen as a transitional figure. His days as Soviet president were numbered, when the Soviet Union ceased to exist a week before the end of 1991.

More than anything else, the Achilles' heel of the Soviet Union turned out to have been its multiethnic character. Gorbachev was not alone in having underestimated the potential centrifugal tendencies of a Union of Soviet Socialist Republics (USSR) that had been implanted on the territory of the old, overland Empire that the Russian tsars had conquered and governed before 1917. Many of the non-Russian minorities retained a territorial identification with their ancestral lands, where they were often lived as ethnic majorities. This made it easier for them to demand greater autonomy or national independence, when the Soviet regime became weakened. The dissolution of the Soviet state took place quickly and essentially without armed conflict. It was formally replaced by the Commonwealth of Independent States (CIS), a very loose union that lacked both a sufficient institutional framework and enough political will to keep it together. Almost from the outset, the CIS seemed destined to be little more than a loosely structured transitional device.

There is an undeniable gloom or hangover atmosphere in many of the accounts of post-Communist and post-Soviet Europe. One of the most shocking developments is the drastic decline in male life expectancy, but there are many other serious social problems as well. It seems clear that much will become even worse before improvements can be expected in the life of some of the former Soviet republics, including Russia. The political consequences could be very important, for social frustrations can now be freely articulated and represented in the political process. Here the transition from one-party rule to pluralist democratic forms resembles the economic passage to a market economy in being neither easy nor automatic. A turn to some form of authoritarian nationalist populism cannot be ruled out in several countries, including Russia. Former Communists with leadership skills are likely to play a major role in the process in countries like Poland, Belarus, and the Ukraine. They sometimes cooperate with ultra-right nationalists, with whom they share the passion for a much stronger societal control by the state.

Specialists on the former Soviet Union disagree considerably in their assessments of the current situation or what brought it about. One of the hotly debated issues concerns the then-President Yeltsin's decision in September 1993 to use a preemptive strike to break a deadlock between his government and a majority in the Russian Parliament. When a majority of the legislators, who had been elected more than 2 years earlier, persisted in blocking some of his major economic reforms, Yeltsin simply dissolved Parliament and called new elections for December 1993.

The electoral result was a political boomerang for Yeltsin. It resulted in a major setback for the forces that backed rapid and thoroughgoing market reforms. The new Parliament, based on a two-ballot system of elections, was highly fragmented, but Nationalists and former Communists occupied key positions in the Duma. Henceforth Yeltsin played a more subdued role, and the new government pursued far more cautious reform policies. In 1994, the military intervention in Chechnya, a breakaway Caucasian republic located within the Russian Federation, failed to give Yeltsin a quick and easy victory that might have reversed his slide into political unpopularity among Russians. Nor could it stem the surge of authoritarian and nationalist political expression, which also thrived as a reflex to crime and social disorder.

New parliamentary elections in December 1995 provided a further setback for the democratic and economic reformers in Russia. However, it was far less their rivals' strength than their own disunity and rivalry both before and after the election that weakened their parliamentary position. Together, the reformers received close to a quarter of the vote. That was slightly more than the Communists, led by Gennady Zyuganov, and it was twice as much as the far-right nationalists in Vladimir Zhirinovsky's Liberal Democratic Party. Under the Russian electoral law, however, the Communists received 35 percent of the seats in the new Duma. Observers of Russian politics differed in their assessments of this development, but all agreed that it left the cause of political and economic reform in disarray.

During the spring of 1996, Russian political leaders had their eyes fixed on the presidential elections of June, in which the incumbent Boris Yeltsin faced the toughest political challenge of his career. As expected, he did not win a clear majority in the first vote, but he defeated Zyuganov with relative ease in a run-off election. By this time, ill health added seriously to Yeltsin's governing problems. His successive and seemingly erratic replacements of prime ministers did not improve the situation.

In the latter half of 1999, however, Yeltsin selected a stronger figure for what turned out to be his last prime minister. Vladimir V. Putin, 47 years old, quickly turned his attention to the tough conduct of a new military intervention in Chechnya. Within Russia, his strong determination to suppress the breakaway province was widely popular, based on its perception as a counterterrorist move. The new prime minister's aura of tough leadership in turn helped check a further parliamentary advance of the communist-led opposition in the new Duma elections of December 1999. Then suddenly, just as the century and millennium came to an end, Yeltsin surprised the world by announcing his own immediate retirement from the presidency. Putin became the new acting president and easily won the presidential election a few months later. He inherited some very difficult problems, but optimists point to some hopeful signs of improvements in the Russian economy, that has partly resulted from an inflow of hard currencies earned from the export of oil. On the international scene, Putin has managed to improve Russia's image and role in the international efforts to combat terrorism. In the wake of the events of September 11, 2001, it seems that many outside observers are less ready than before to condemn the brutal measures taken by the Russian military in the combat with violent separatists in Chechnya.

Some worried observers still do not rule out the possibility of a "Bonapartist" solution, in the form of a coup, or the danger that a Russian form of fascism could come to power. An antidote to doomsday speculation about Russia can be found in David Foglesong and Gordon M. Hahn's spirited dismissal, "Ten Myths About Russia."

The future of the European Union

# Can these bones live?

So far, it's just the skeleton of an outline of a draft of a may-yet-be EU constitution. But it may come to life

Brussels

H E'S a bit of a cadaverous figure himself, Valéry Giscard d'Estaing, the former French president dug out to head the group of Euro-notables charged with producing the first outline of a constitution for the new, soon-to-be-enlarged European Union. This week he offered its first results: "the skeleton", not much more than a few general headings, of what he hopes for. Some strange anatomical features it has.

Mr Giscard d'Estaing wants the skeleton now to be fleshed out by the EU's more-or-less constitutional convention, over which he presides. Less, rather than more, in fact: modestly styled the "convention on the future of Europe", its mandate from the EU's leaders is not itself to pass a constitution, but to offer ideas, both to overhaul the EU treaties and to bring the EU "closer to the people", on which the EU governments can build.

Most of the 105 members of the convention are representatives from national governments and parliaments, from the 15 present EU countries and from countries that are currently negotiating to join the club. There are also two from the European Commission and 16 from the European Parliament. But this week's outline is, inevitably, the work of the inner 12-member praesidium of the convention. And, as inevitably, not all members of the convention are happy with it.

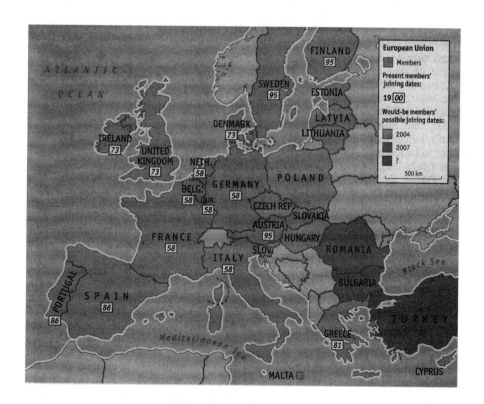

For a seemingly trivial start, should the EU change its name? The present treaties linking the 15 member states refer at times to the European Community (its former name), at times to the European Union. If the treaties are replaced, only one name will be necessary. The draft—while leaving it open whether to change at all—floats "United Europe" or "United States of Europe". Ha, cry the Eurosceptics, proof of schemes for a super-state; the British government has already expressed its dislike of any change.

The draft also proposes that every citizen of a member state would enjoy "dual citizenship, national citizenship and European citizenship, and is free to use either, as he or she chooses". In practice, it seems, the two would be inseparable. The rights of an EU citizen depend on being a citizen of an EU country. Were a country to leave the EU—the draft suggests a clause permitting this—its citizens would lose their EU citizenship, willy-nilly. Eurosceptics think that this talk of dual citizenship yet again betrays an ambition to create a European super-state. But it may simply be evidence of woolly thinking.

These skirmishes over details are an indication of more serious battles to come, between those who want a strong centre at the heart of the Union and those who want to limit the power ceded by national governments. The latter are not united, however. To some sceptics, any constitution is anathema; others believe that one could halt the aspiration of the original 1957 Rome treaty towards "ever closer union". One French member of the European Parliament calls the draft "the skeleton of a diplodocus, with an extremely small federalist brain and a huge intergovernmental body". The question would be which part of the beast was really in charge.

For the moment, Mr Giscard d'Estaing has left open the question whether the European Council, where the member states are represented, should elect a long-term president, so strengthening the hands of the (larger) states, at the expense of the European Commission. Nor does the draft make clear what powers the EU, as distinct from its constituent members, would have in foreign policy, nor how those powers would be allocated between the commission and the council. The draft rather clumsily bundles EU competence for foreign and external security together with internal security.

The convention has to thrash these issues out before making recommendations next summer. And despite a passing reference in the draft to "liberty, security and justice", Mr Giscard d'Estaing may also need to find some poetry to breathe life into the constitution's bones. Constitution-making by committee in 11 languages is not conducive to that. And yet the bones do hang together. Future generations of Europeans may look at the skeleton and see in it, not the relics of some extinct creature, but a crude, early, yet recognisable version of their days' *homo europaeus*.

Europe

## A constitution for Europe

# The latest battle for the continent's new shape

**At a summit in Belgium next weekend, European leaders will start framing a constitution for the European Union. It will be fiercely argued over**

BRUSSELS

"**A**LL references to founding fathers and 1787 should be banned," grumbles a British politician closely involved in the "future of Europe" debate. Too late. Germany and France have already agreed that the haggle that will get under way in the Brussels suburb of Laeken on December 14th should culminate by 2004 in a "European constitution". Efforts to narrow the discussion down to technical and institutional matters are bound to give way to much grander themes. The EU's future is indeed at stake.

Given the range of opinions within the EU, no one can foretell the final version. But the ambitions of those keenest to bring European countries ever more tightly together are apparent in a "draft declaration" circulated by Guy Verhofstadt, Belgium's prime minister and the summit's host. His letter poses a series of questions. But a disgruntled Scandinavian diplomat says it is "clearly written by someone with a blueprint for a full-fledged federal state in mind". It floats ideas for creating a "European political area", such as directly electing the European Commission's president and giving more powers to the European Parliament and to the commission.

Mr Verhofstadt's draft is sure to be revised at Laeken and will in any event be only the first shot in a long campaign. But it shows how widely the future-of-Europe

debate will range. When Europe's leaders first agreed to the idea of a constitutional convention, just four issues were mooted: the division of powers between the EU and its countries and regions; the relationship between national parliaments and the EU; the legal status of the EU's recently drafted charter of rights; and the simplification of Europe's many overlapping treaties. Restricting the debate to just four topics was seen as the work of people hostile to tighter integration, in particular Britons and Scandinavians. But, as a senior EU official points out, "Those questions are open to very broad interpretation—and anyway, once the convention gets going in March, it will basically talk about what it likes."

Still, the big issues at stake have already become plain. The Germans were first to ask for a clearer division of powers to be laid down in a **charter of competences**, partly because the governments of their 16 *Länder* (states) feared that Brussels was eroding their powers (to bail out local industry, for instance). So Germany's ruling Social Democrats suggested that Brussels should gain some powers while Europe's nation-states should retain or win back others. The Germans want the EU to play a bigger part in foreign policy, defence and policing. But the Social Democrats' paper also floated the idea of "renationalising" agricultural and regional aid, which accounts for 80% of the EU's budget—for which Germany pays a disproportionate amount. Not surprisingly,

the main beneficiaries of EU money, including Spain and France, strongly oppose such a change. The British keenly endorse the idea that powers can be repatriated from the Union.

The **role of national parliaments** is another big topic for debate. Britain's Tony Blair has proposed a second chamber for the European Parliament that would consist of national MPs to strengthen links between national democracies and European institutions. This idea, however, has gained little favour elsewhere. Officials at the European Commission say that it would just confuse an already complex European administration and that national views are already reflected in the Council of Ministers, which brings together ministers from the 15 national governments. Mr Verhofstadt and the German government have suggested that the council itself should become a "second chamber", implying that its legislative discussions should be held in public.

A **charter of rights** has already been drafted, but at the EU's summit a year ago in Nice, Britain stopped it having legal force. The British dislike the charter for going beyond the European Convention on Human Rights, which already has legal force in all EU countries, by adding new "social" rights. Expect the British, now in a minority of one, eventually to give way.

**Simplifying the treaties** is another item on the menu. European law has been made by a series of treaties signed by each of the countries in the EU. Minimalists say there should be a single, consolidated text. Maximalists want a whole new European constitution to be written.

Several other issues, beyond the original big four, will also be discussed:

**Majority voting**. Many people argue that a bigger EU will be unable to function if countries can keep their veto in a wide range of issues. Romano Prodi, the commission's president, thinks any new constitutional arrangements that fail to endorse a big increase in majority voting will be inadequate.

**A European president**. Mr Verhofstadt wants the commission's president to be directly elected, to strengthen its democratic legitimacy—and its power. Germany and the Benelux countries probably agree. France and Britain are against. Mr Prodi, who wants more integration in most areas, thinks the proposal premature. Others think the commission's president should be elected by the European Parliament.

**Foreign policy and judicial affairs**. At present, it is mainly governments that run the EU's fledgling foreign policy; the commission has little say. Integrationists want to end this distinction and make the EU's high representative for foreign policy (at present, Javier Solana) the commission's vice-president. And foreign-policy decisions, they say, should be taken by majority vote. Germany would probably favour this idea; Britain and France would oppose it. But the British agree with the Germans that the commission should have more of a say in Europe-wide justice and home affairs, including asylum and immigration.

**Direct taxation**. Integrationists want to move away from the present system under which individual countries pay for most of the EU's budget. They argue that a direct EU tax, probably a share of sales taxes, would make the Union's finances more open; *sotto voce*, they note that in the long run that might increase its revenues.

In any event, the convention will not produce a single blueprint for the 15 governments to "take or leave" but a batch of "options". Moreover, a "firebreak" of a few months will allow time for reflection between the end of the convention and a summit conference where governments will be expected to nail down a final EU constitution.

---

**Europe's constitutional convention**

# Who will run it—and how and when?

**BRUSSELS**
**A contest has begun over how and by whom the convention should be run**

**A**S WELL as setting the agenda, the EU's sumiteers must decide on procedure for the constitutional convention—and on who will preside over it. It will start in March. The integrationists want it to finish about a year later and all governments to have signed a new constitutional treaty by the end of 2003. This timetable would have the advantage, from their point of view, of wrapping up the new constitution's final draft while the EU presidency is held by Italy, which by tradition favours integration. It would also prevent negotiations spilling over into the ensuing Irish presidency, which might be bad in the eyes of integrationists, who now suspect the Irish of Euroscepticism. And it would mean that the 15 countries already in the EU would stitch up a deal before newcomers arrive. But an actual timetable is unlikely to be agreed on at Laeken.

The convention's shape is clearer. Just one representative from the European Commission will attend. Another 100-odd delegates will represent national governments and parliaments, the European Parliament and countries trying to join the EU. Turkey, though it has not even begun negotiations to join, is likely to have a voice. A five-strong presidium will oversee the convention's work.

Finding the right person for the job of chairing the show may prompt a hearty row at Laeken. The front-runner, despite his 75 years, is Valéry Giscard d'Estaing, a former French president. The Germans, it is muttered, have accepted France's request for a French chairman. This might rattle the British and make others edgy too, since the commission's representative in the presidium will be Michel Barnier, another Frenchman, giving France two out of the convention's five-strong steering committee.

Martti Ahtisaari, a former Finnish president, is also in the running. In his favour is the possibility that the not-so-wildly enthusiastic might think him, as a Nordic, to be less zealous for integration. But his chances may shrink because—bizarre as this may seem—it may be decided at Laeken that the European Food Agency should be housed in Finland. The Finns, a commission man explains, "mustn't have too many presents".

Another runner is Giuliano Amato, a former Italian prime minister and keen federalist. But his candidacy may be blocked on the ground that the commission's president, Romano Prodi, is also Italian. Too many presents for Italians.

A dark horse? Maybe Wim Kok, the Dutch prime minister, whom the British would probably back. But he might find it hard to stand down as prime minister until next summer—after the convention is meant to have started.

---

## THE FUTURE OF EUROPE

# From talking shop to crucible of high politics: Europe's convention is evolving into a historic undertaking

Political leaders are starting to take seriously discussions on a new constitution for an enlarged Union. With the debate hotting up, the first draft will soon be ready, writes **George Parker**

Picture the scene, a year from now. At a grand ceremony in Rome, under the auspices of the Italian presidency of the European Union, 25 countries assemble to sign a historic new constitution for Europe.

That such an occasion is even being talked of is testament to the remarkable—even surprising—progress achieved this year in the convention on the future of Europe.

When, early on, Valéry Giscard d'Estaing, the imperious former French president who chairs the meetings, compared its work to the Philadelphia convention of 1787 you could hear the guffaws resounding around Europe's chancelleries. "Most people thought it would be a talking shop, a harmless public relations stunt," admits one EU diplomat. "We would let him produce his draft treaty and then we would rewrite the whole thing behind closed doors as usual."

But since getting down to business in February the convention has evolved into something far more substantial. Some 46 years after the treaty of Rome created the EU, the future shape of an enlarged Union is being hammered out in public debate and in private negotiations. Mr Giscard d'Estaing has good reason to believe that the substance of his draft, due to be produced within four months, will closely resemble the treaty that will be agreed by European leaders. When he declares that the treaty will endure for "50 years," far fewer people now snigger in disbelief.

The convention was initiated at the EU's summit in Laeken, Belgium, in late 2001, a time when far-right nationalist sentiment was on the rise and populist politicians were gaining ground by campaigning against "Brussels." Europe's leaders worried about a "democratic deficit." The edifice they were

constructing had, they came to recognise, made ordinary voters feel left out.

The prospect of an enlarged union of 25 members, from Lisbon to Lithuania, also made a redesign necessary, to prevent the political machinery from grinding to a halt.

Even so, for a time it seemed as if the doubters might be right. During the initial "listening phase" of the convention, assorted groups representing civil society and "Europe's young people" would make presentations to sparsely attended sessions. Nobody paid much attention.

The notable exception was Britain. Tony Blair took the convention seriously from the beginning. Peter Hain, the UK's minister for Europe, was dispatched to Brussels and became ever-present at the debates and in the informal gatherings, lobbying fellow delegates.

With France and Germany distracted by domestic elections, Mr Hain managed to plant one idea firmly on the convention's agenda: the creation of a powerful new EU president, representing member states, who would lead political debate at home and be a figurehead on the world stage.

The idea epitomised a view, held by Britain, France and Spain, that the new Europe should largely develop through cooperation among member states rather than through the so-called *communautaire* model of deeper integration, with more power for the European Commission and European parliament.

"Britain is leading the dance on the convention," lamented Pascal Lamy, the EU's trade commissioner and a leading proponent of deeper integration. And in a moment of self-congratulation, perhaps hubris, Mr Hain boasted in October: "Britain is winning the battle of ideas in Europe."

# Giscard: ageing, haughty yet effective

At first sight, Valéry Giscard d'Estaing looks like a figure from another era. Forty years ago he was Charles de Gaulle's finance minister. Twenty years ago, he had already lost his job as France's president. More recently, he sent a letter to his old foe Jacques Chirac begging for the job of president of the European Central Bank—a post for which he was never in contention.

But since taking charge of the convention on the future of Europe in February, the former French president has performed much better than many expected. Under him, the unwieldy 105-member convention has moved towards a consensus that has eluded the European Union for the past decade.

That is all the more surprising, since two of Mr Giscard d'Estaing's own pet proposals—to change the EU's name to "United Europe" and convoke a Grand Congress of national and European parliaments—look all but doomed. By contrast, the idea that the convention should write a new constitution for the EU, which Mr. Giscard d'Estaing himself opposed only last year, has gained broad acceptance.

The 76-year-old stands a reasonable chance of going down in history as the man who did the most to shape Europe's future balance of power.

His central role stems from one crucial fact about the convention's procedure, as well as his own personal standing and a sense of urgency the EU has rarely felt. Conceived as an exercise in consensus-building, rather than party politics, the convention takes no votes.

To an extent, Mr Giscard d'Estaing can shape the conclusions of debates, which are "reflected" in documents drawn up by the convention's bureaucracy, rather than in roll-calls and binding resolutions.

He can also take the initiative through his chairmanship of the convention's governing "praesidium," which will present the convention floor with its latest draft constitution and its thoughts on the EU's division of power over the next few months.

But Mr Giscard d'Estaing's authority does not come from procedure alone. As a former member of the exclusive club of European leaders, he is perhaps the man who can best sell the convention's results to the governments that will need to approve them. This was one of the main reasons he was chosen by an EU summit for his current job.

He has the necessary *hauteur* to "invent" consensus where it sometimes barely exists and brush aside a few voices of dissent that could otherwise lead to a revolt.

Though his presidential style seems unlikely to win through on proposals that have excited the hostility of a broad range of convention representatives—such as the Congress and the name change—he has been able to pull off the trick in many others where consensus is building.

"The convention is made up of different components: the MEPs, the national parliamentarians, the government representatives and so on," says one observer. "What Giscard has to do is to command some sort of majority in each group."

What is more, he has won support from several big countries for perhaps his most deeply held idea: a president of the European Council. This is a subject in which he has been interested since the 1970s. However, the Commission and some of the more *communautaire* member states remain furiously opposed.

The convention chairman also benefits from the sense of urgency. The convention was instituted after the last old-fashioned treaty conference, in Nice in 2000, was deemed to have failed and to have been unduly divisive. The EU's impending enlargement has also focused minds on the challenge of fixing Europe's flaws.

This is one of the supreme ironies of the latter-day prominence of Mr Giscard d'Estaing. Although enlargement may allow him to make the mark he so wants to leave, he is one of the least enthusiastic of all mainstream politicians about the process.

"The Balkans, the Scandinavian countries [and] Mediterranean countries are all very different. That is why the idea that we can have a uniform constitution for all these countries is not realistic," he said in an interview last year.

His intemperate comments last month opposing Turkey's entry to the EU may cost him some of this goodwill, while his proposals for the council have already led one commissioner to refer to him as a "menace."

"Giscard should be aware that if he's going to use his political capital up on issues outside the convention's remit, his ability to carry through a consensus could be diminished," warns one member of the praesidium.

Nevertheless, this aristocratic figure may well be the man to call a truce on the EU's 50-year long dispute on where power should lie. Whether he is quite so well placed to succeed in the convention's other task of bringing Europe closer to its citizens is quite another matter.

**Daniel Dombey**

It did not last. A few days after Mr Hain's comment, Gerhard Schröder, German chancellor, sent Joschka Fischer, his foreign minister, to represent Berlin at the court of Mr Giscard d'Estaing. "I've come here because I gather you're running the show," the staunchly federalist Mr Fischer reputedly told Mr Hain on their first encounter in Brussels.

Shortly afterwards Jacques Chirac, French president, followed suit. Out went Pierre Moscovici, the marginalised former socialist Europe minister; in came Dominique de Villepin, the new foreign minister. Ana de Palacio, Spain's foreign minister, and Gianfranco Fini, Italian deputy prime minister, are also there.

# A work in progress

## Five areas of agreement

**1    A constitution for Europe**
**Purpose:** a simple text, defining the European Union's role and values. Giscard d'Estaing will try to come up with a lyrical preamble to match the 'We the people' introduction to the US constitution

**2    Charter of fundamental rights**
**Purpose:** to set out the common rights of all EU citizens; could form the preamble to the constitution. The UK has now relaxed its initial opposition in return for assurances that the charter may be legally enforceable only for EU institutions, not member states

**3    Immigration and migration**
**Purpose:** member states, including the UK, increasingly believe that national vetoes need to be discarded in such areas, to stop deadlock in crucial border issues. But related proposals to give EU institutions more power in criminal and judicial areas are much more controversial

**4    Simplifying Europe**
**Purpose:** to cut through the confusion by giving the EU a single legal personality and eliminating its complex 'three pillar' structure. EU jargon would be discarded in favour of terms such as 'EU laws'

**5    Role of national parliaments**
**Purpose:** to ensure that the EU does not become remote from its citizens, national parliaments could monitor the Commission's legislative proposals to ensure that the EU is not gaining powers best exercised by member states

## Ten areas of controversy

**1    Does the EU need a new name?**
**The debate:** Giscard wants to rebrand the new-look EU 'United Europe.' Not much enthusiasm in other quarters.
**Likely outcome:** name stays the same

**2    Europe's foreign policy**
**The debate:** federalists want to see power over foreign policy gradually shifting away from member states towards the European Commission, with majority voting. Britain and France strongly resist.
**Likely outcome:** the same person could exercise the roles of Javier Solana, EU foreign policy chief, and Christopher Patten, the Commission's external relations chief. Member states likely to retain control over most aspects of foreign policy

**3    A new EU President**
**The debate:** Britain, France and Spain want to strengthen the European Council (forum for national leaders) by giving it a powerful full-time president, directing EU business and some foreign policy. Most smaller countries firmly opposed.
**Likely outcome:** EU presidency could be created, but probably with a fairly short mandate and limited powers. An outside chance that the European Council and the Commission could end up sharing a president

**4    Strengthening the Commission**
**The debate:** most smaller countries look to the Commission for protection and believe its president should be elected by MEPs. Many inside the Commission fear the politicisation of the president's role would reduce his impartiality.
**Likely outcome:** some sort of election for Commission president. New powers for the Commission, especially in the field of justice and home affairs

**5    Congress**
**The debate:** Giscard d'Estaing wants to create a 'Congress of the Peoples of Europe,' a body comprising national MPs and MEPs, to meet occasionally for grand debates on important European issues. But many think the last thing the EU needs is another institution
**Likely outcome:** no congress

**6    Exit clause**
**The debate:** many believe the EU needs a mechanism for a country voluntarily to leave the union in an orderly fashion. Others fear that a clearly marked route to the exit door would spark a series of secession crises
**Likely outcome:** in the balance

**7    Europe's defence policy**
**The debate:** Europe woefully underperforms on the military front. Strong consensus for greater cooperation on procurement but Britain and France determined to maintain national identity of their armed forces
**Likely outcome:** more procurement cooperation, through a new agency, but national veto remaining over EU defence policy. Possibly a mutual defence pact against terrorism

**8    Tax harmonisation**
**The debate:** a majority, including Germany and France, want tax harmonisation in areas affecting the single market, such as VAT and corporation tax. Rates would be settled by majority voting. Britain, Ireland and Estonia are among those wanting to keep the national veto in all tax matters.
**Likely outcome:** depends on whether Tony Blair is prepared to give way. One compromise would allow tax decisions to be taken if almost all member states agree

**9    Reforming the euro**
**The debate:** an enlarged EU of 25 will mean that fewer than half of all members—12 in total—will be using the euro. Should the informal 'eurogroup' meeting of 12 finance ministers have formal powers to decide policy on the euro? Some believe this would alienate the new EU members, some of which could be using the euro within five years.
**Likely outcome:** in the balance. Some kind of informal grouping likely to stay; but there could also be a new, formal gathering of eurozone ministers

**10   What happens if a country refuses to ratify the new treaty?**
**The debate:** many in the praesidium think there is no alternative to ripping up the present treaties and starting with a new one, so that those countries that do not ratify the treaty become mere associate members of the EU. But there are huge legal and political issues—few governments want to be strong-armed into signing Giscard d'Estaing's constitution.
**Likely outcome:** this could be the biggest fight of all

There was by now a realisation that the convention was building up so much momentum that, after 18 months of debate, it would be hard for EU leaders to ignore its conclusions. "Those who f'rst scoffed at the convention—what they called a 'talking shop' for Brussels insiders—are now silent and rightly so," said Romano Prodi, European Commission president.

Although the arrival of the big guns may have given the convention clout, some of its original members fear that its nature may change. Instead of being a democratic forum for its 105 members—who include national MPs and MEPs—some believe it will turn into an intergovernmental conference, where national ministers agree the main deals.

However, the close involvement of the likes of Mr Fischer and Mr de Villepin makes it less likely that the convention's final draft treaty will be unpicked by EU leaders.

---

## The search is on for a lasting settlement between those who favour more intergovernmental co-operation and those who seek a more federal model of deeper integration. Germany is the pivotal player

---

As the convention moves into its last stages, the search is on for a lasting settlement between those who favour more intergovernmental co-operation and those who seek a more federal model of deeper integration. Germany is pivotal. Under Mr Schröder, Germany has become more assertive: less inhibited by the guilt of its past, it is willing to throw its weight around, like the other "big" member states. But because of its attachment to a federal model of government, it also instinctively favours a federal solution for Europe with a strong centre.

Many smaller countries, which see strengthened EU institutions as the best way to preserve equality in Europe, look to Germany as an ally. France, staunch defender of national sovereignty in areas such as defence and foreign policy, is trying to pull Germany in the other direction.

The decisive moment may come in January when Mr Chirac and Mr Schröder are expected to produce a joint Franco-German paper on Europe's future institutional arrangements, as part of events to mark the 40th anniversary of the Elysée treaty that began the post-war reconciliation of the two countries. "Franco-German initiatives are welcome but they should never be the main business," says John Bruton, praesidium member

and former Irish prime minister, airing concerns that the two governments might hijack the proceedings.

Many people see a compromise emerging, in which all of the EU's institutions are strengthened: the council (representing the member states), the Commission and the parliament.

Britain, France and Spain will probably get a watered-down version of a new EU president but the Commission will also have more powers and its president's authority will be strengthened by election by the European parliament. One suggestion the Germans are considering would see the Commission president also chair the council.

The EU's foreign policy will probably be represented by one person; currently the job is split between Javier Solana, who represents member states, and Christopher Patten, the external affairs commissioner—but only if Britain and France are assured of their primacy on all matters of significant foreign policy.

Other issues, often those that cut across traditional EU dividing lines, remain to be resolved. Most observers agree that an enlarged EU needs to decide more policies by majority voting, given the danger of gridlock when 25 or more countries can wield their national veto.

There is consensus that policies on tackling international crime or migration flows should be decided by majority vote—but should some tax rates be harmonised to facilitate the working of the EU's single market? Britain, Ireland and Estonia are among those that say No; Germany and France say Yes.

There is a fierce debate about whether countries should be given an "exit clause" to leave the Union. But would that prompt a series of secession crises, with member states threatening to leave unless they got their way on a certain issue? And what happens if members refuse to agree the new treaty? Should they be forced to leave? This could turn out to be the most sensitive issue of all.

Mr Giscard d'Estaing and his inner "praesidium" will start producing answers to these questions over the next few months and aim at producing a complete text for the convention to deliberate on in April. They are determined that their work will be largely acceptable to the EU leaders, who will be presented with a final document at a summit at Thessaloniki in June. "The old man is not writing this for the library shelf," says one aide.

Some in Mr Giscard d'Estaing's inner circle observe that any treaty they produce will never be wholly acceptable both to defenders of the sovereign state such as Mr Blair and Mr Chirac and to the more federalist-minded members of the convention. "We'll put the treaty on the table and run for the fire escape," jokes one.

Whatever treaty Mr Giscard d'Estaing produces over the next few months, it is set fair to become the core of the constitution for a Europe that could one day incorporate Turkey and even Ukraine. If it really does endure for 50 years or more, some of the Jeffersonian rhetoric may seem just that bit less overblown.

---

# In Search of Europe's Borders

## *The Politics of Migration in the European Union*

### Seyla Benhabib

On March 11, 1882, the great French scholar Ernest Renan gave a lecture with the provocative title, "What is a Nation?"* Still recovering from the shock of the defeat of France by Prussia in the Franco-Prussian War of 1871, Renan, like many liberal nationalists before and after him, walked a thin line between the affirmation of the individual nation, which he described as "a soul, a spiritual principle," and the celebration of the peaceful plurality of nations. For Renan, nations were not eternal: they emerged through suffering and struggle in the past; they were sustained by the will to live together in the future. Nations had their beginning and their end. One day, he prophesied, "A European confederation will probably replace them. But such is not the law of the century in which we are living."

Twice in the twentieth century nationalist wars convulsed Europe and led to worldwide carnage; the dream of a European confederation that would end such wars has inspired European intellectuals at least since the Napoleonic conquests in the aftermath of the French Revolution. Recent developments within the European Union—the adoption of a common currency by twelve of the fifteen member countries and the launching in February 2002 of a year-long European constitutional convention—have given "Euro-federalists" new hope and energy. Starting from a coal and steel consortium among Germany, France, the Benelux countries, and Italy in 1951, the EU currently encompasses 370 million residents in fifteen member countries. Despite occasional setbacks (Denmark's veto of the Maastricht Treaty, for example) and despite the more serious discord caused by the election of right-wing governments in Austria, Italy, Denmark, and the Netherlands, most Euroskeptics have to admit that the EU is moving inexorably forward. The question no longer is "whether the EU?" but "whither the EU?"

By 2003, the EU intends to expand its current membership to twenty-one countries, including the Czech Republic, Cyprus, Poland, Hungary, Slovenia, and Estonia. An ambitious second expansion by 2007 is intended to bring in Romania, Bulgaria, Lithuania, Latvia, the Slovak Republic, and Malta. Since the Copenhagen accords of 1993, conditions for admission to full membership have been defined very broadly to include (1) a demonstration of a country's commitment to functioning democratic institutions, human rights, the rule of law, and respect for and protection of minorities; (2) a competitive market economy as well as the capacity to cope with competitive pressure; and (3) evidence that the country is able to take on the obligations of membership, including adherence to the aims of political, economic, and monetary union. By focusing on such broad institutional criteria, the EU avoids the much more controversial issues concerning cultural, linguistic, religious, and ethnic identities. The EU supposedly rests on a proven capacity to sustain a set of institutions, which, although originating in the West, are in principle capable of functioning on other soils and in other cultures as well. European identity is not given a thick cultural or historical coating; no exclusionary appeals are made to commonalities of history or faith, language or customs. In Renan's terms, it is the will to live together in the future, and not the fractious past, that defines the new European federation.

Despite these noble wishes to build the EU on "thin" liberal-democratic institutional criteria rather than "thick" cultural identities, a deep conflict between institutional principle and identity is unfolding, both within member states and at their borders. Intense debates range throughout the EU regarding the integration of sizable guest-worker populations and their descendants into their host countries, and many countries are passing new and more restrictive immigration and naturalization bills. These topics have been exploited by right-wing parties and politicians in Austria, Italy, Denmark, the Netherlands, France, and Spain. Social democratic governments in Britain and Germany are also feeling the pressure to cater to more xenophobic sentiments. While the British Labour Party is pushing a restrictive Immigration and Asylum Bill through Parliament, the German coalition government of Social Democrats and Greens has voted for an immigration bill that permits legalized immigration into the country but restricts the rights of asylum and refuge seekers. Despite the signing of the bill into law by President Johannes Rau, the German Christian Democrats, who are favored to win this fall, are threatening to raise objections against the bill in the German Supreme Court.

As has often been the case in European history, xenophobic politics is an easy politics, but the social factors and institutional trends behind European immigration are much more complicated and intractable. Europe's "others," be they guest workers or refugees, asylum seekers or migrants, have become an obvious focus for the anxieties and uncertainties generated by Europe's own "othering," its transformation from a continent of nation-states into a transnational political entity, whose precise constitutional and political form is still uncertain. Will the future EU be a federation of nation-states? A transnational European state in which nation-states are dissolved? Or a post-democratic administrative and bureaucratic conglomerate, bearing more affinities with medieval Europe than with republican traditions of popular sovereignty? These are daunting questions, to which there are no clear answers. As the journalist Joachim Fritz-Vannahme wrote in *Die Zeit*, the only common immigration policy that EU states have is fear itself: "The Europeans are building a fortress against refugees. Each wants to be the architect."

Shortly after the Second World War, as Europe entered a period of economic and civil reconstruction, its foreign population stood at 1.3 percent. By 1992-1993 this number had increased to 4.9 percent; the growth stopped in the 1990s, when the countries of the EU began to monitor and control the influx of guest workers, refugees, and asylum seekers into their territories; the current figure is around 5 percent. But these aggregate numbers do not tell the whole story. In many countries the percentage of foreigners in the population is much higher: 9.0 percent in Austria and Belgium; around 8.9 percent in Germany; about 6.3 percent in France. In other EU countries, such as Spain, Denmark, Sweden, and Great Britain, the percentage hovers between 3 percent and 5 percent (note that this figure is well below the 9.7 percent that the U.S. census of 2000 revealed).

Germany and France have been intake countries for longer periods of time than Austria, whose foreign population more than doubled in the 1990s from 4.1 percent to 9 percent. The first *Gastarbeiter* arrived in Germany in the 1950s, and the largest influx of Algerian-born immigrants came to France in 1956–1957. Primary immigration to both Germany and France has slowed down more recently and has been restricted largely to family unification; by contrast over a million and a half "ethnic Germans" from the former Soviet Union and other East European territories were permitted to enter Germany during this period. Great Britain, with its large number of citizens from former colonies as well as ex-colonial British subjects, presents an even more complex picture: according to the *Times* of London "there has been a net loss of British citizens and a net gain of foreign citizens in the past decade." Interestingly, the *Times* reports that immigration of those born in the EU and the old members of the Commonwealth—Canada, Australia, and New Zealand—declined, while net immigration from newer countries of the Commonwealth in Africa and the Asian subcontinent increased. In other words, the face of the 183,000 new Britons is mainly black and brown—an unmentioned fact that is the subtle subtext of the intense debate about immigration in Great Britain.

European societies that once, despite their imperialist history, considered themselves homogeneous nation-states are now experiencing changes in the make-up of their population that they did not foresee and about which they feel deeply ambivalent. Caught among the exigencies of a global economy in which the free movement of cheap labor across national borders is essential to capital expansion, urged by their liberal-democratic consciences to help asylees and refugees from the breakup wars of former Yugoslavia and the third world in general, and preoccupied with their own national histories and cultural legacies, EU countries are struggling with radically new collective self-definitions. Even Greece, Italy, Spain, and Portugal, which had traditionally been sender rather than receiver countries, now have to deal with large numbers of legal and illegal immigrants.

Reflecting these contradictory trends, EU countries have made sure that every step of the European integration process is accompanied by a redefinition of Europe's relation to its "others." Thus the Schengen accord of 1985, which abolished internal border controls between Belgium, the Netherlands, Luxembourg, the former German Federal Republic, and France, was accompanied by some of the harshest restrictions on refugee and asylum policies. The Dublin Convention of June 1990, which followed upon Schengen, stipulated further restrictions upon the movements within the EU of foreigners or third country nationals; that is, foreigners who are not citizens of EU member countries. The Dublin Convention set up an EU-wide data base of asylees and refugees and clarified responsibility for processing asylum seekers who had applied to several EU countries.

Schengen and Dublin had marked consequences. In the mid-1990s, entry into Belgium, Denmark, Finland, and Luxembourg leveled off, and there were sharp falls in entry figures in Germany, France, and Sweden. But the "fortress Europe" that Schengen and Dublin intended to create was a fantasy, and another wave of liberalized entry into the EU—driven primarily by labor markets and the realities of Europe's aging labor force—is now on the European agenda. Even as right-wing parties denounce migrants and foreigners for "invading" their cities and cultures, demographic trends in many of Europe's social democracies as well as the demands of certain industries for specifically qualified workers make it likely that tides of migrant labor will continue to rise.

Throughout the nineteenth century, Europe was a continent of emigration as well as immigration. What accounts for the explosive potential of these issues at the present? The answer lies partly in the great ferment generated by processes of European unification and the difficulties of bringing rapid institutional change and the evolution of collective identities into some kind of compatible pace.

Since the Maastricht Treaty of 1993, citizens of the fifteen European states have acquired EU citizenship. Article 8 of the treaty states, "Citizenship of the Union is hereby established. Every Person holding the *nationality* of a member state shall be a citizen of the Union" [emphasis added]. This article has been the subject of intense debate from the start. Is European citizenship analogous to ancient Roman citizenship, something like membership in an empire, with attendant privileges but with little room for democratic participation? Should European citizenship be conceived principally as social citizenship, eventually entitling everyone who shares this status to an equivalent package of health, retirement, and old age benefits across the union states? Certainly, these problems are not unique to Europe and reflect dilemmas affecting citizenship in liberal democracies everywhere. There is a general concern that contemporary citizenship is defined less by political responsibilities and participation than by the entitlement to social benefits and privileges. Against the background of falling electoral participation rates and the ossification of established party mechanisms, political citizenship appears obsolete. Within the European context, however, the linkage between citizenship and "national" membership expresses a deeper ambivalence about the future of European identity.

EU CITIZENSHIP grants its holders the right to free movement, residence, and employment throughout the EU. Although EU citizens do not have the right to vote in the national elections of their respective host countries, they can vote and run for office in local as well as EU-wide elections. Thus a Dutch resident of London or Dublin can be a candidate for city and county government seats, hold office if elected, and still vote for the Dutch members of the EU Parliament. Although there is skepticism about how rigorously these rights are being claimed and exercised by the EU citizens entitled to them, the Maastricht Treaty delivered a blow to nationalist conceptions of sovereignty and citizenship.

These conceptions are exemplified in a German Supreme Court ruling in 1987 on attempts by Bremen and Hamburg to grant municipal voting rights to foreign residents who had fulfilled certain residency requirements (following the example of Denmark, which gives all foreign residents such rights). The Court barred the grant, claiming that "the people's sovereignty is indivisible." The right of election could only rest upon the sovereignty of a united people, who shared a common past and fate (*"die Nation als Schicksalsgemeinschaft"*). This decision has since been revised to conform to the requirements of the Maastricht Treaty. In a 1997 decision, the Court argued that the possession by non-German citizens of electoral rights did not prejudice the rights of German citizens to political representation through "general, direct, free, equal, and secret" elections. In the case of municipal and district elections, the concept of the sovereign people could be interpreted to include persons "who possess the citizenship of a member-state of the European Union," as well as those who became German citizens in accordance with Article 116 of the German Constitution.

The Court did not explain, as it had done previously, what concept of the people it was now invoking and how it was interpreting popular sovereignty. What political, moral, and juridical principles give certain kinds of people the right of democratic voice while excluding others? Is it only by virtue of its treaty obligations that the democratic franchise can and should be extended to EU citizens? And if the local franchise, why not extend the national one as well? And if to EU citizens, why not to Turks, Moroccans, and Serbians who may have lived and worked in Hamburg or Bremen longer than their Dutch or British neighbors? What is the link between national membership and the democratic franchise?

The EU upholds this link in that access to EU citizenship is based upon national citizenship. But insofar as the active exercise of political rights at local levels no longer requires shared linguistic, ethnic, or religious belonging, but rather is based on interests, affiliations, and associations emerging from a common life in a certain locality, a different conception of democratic citizenship is also becoming visible. The exercise of political citizenship at the subnational level means that the interests of all long-term residents of an electoral district are worthy of equal consideration and respect; therefore democratic participation rights should be extended to all those whose long-term interests would be affected by them. The laws should bind those who can see their own will reflected in them.

Many countries such as Denmark, Netherlands, Sweden, Ireland, and Great Britain, which are EU members, and others such as Norway and Switzerland, which are not, actually extend local and—in some cases—regional political rights to non-EU foreigners resident in their territories. So what is emerging in contemporary Europe is a mixed bag of rights, entitlements, and privileges, distributed quite unevenly across resident populations, in accordance with varying principles.

At the same time, throughout the EU, a great rift has opened between the status of its citizens and that of those foreign residents who are third country nationals. The latter include Turks as well as U.S. citizens, Moroccans as well as Bosnians, Argentinians as well as Chinese. Of course, in every democratic country the rights of citizens are distinct from those of tourists, and those of permanent residents are distinct from both. What is unique about the situation of third country nationals in contemporary Europe is that this category includes large numbers of people who have been guest workers in residence for ten to twenty-five years. It also includes people who are asylees and who will most likely never return to the countries from which they fled, and still others who are refugees, whose fate depends upon changing political conditions in their host countries as well as their countries of origin. The social and political rights and entitlements of these groups differ across the EU; they are dependent upon the national and local legislatures of their countries of residence. Furthermore, the rules governing "naturalization" procedures that would give access to citizenship are distinct for each EU member country. Although the European Convention of Human Rights applies to all residents of the union and not just to EU citizens, third country nationals have limited civil rights in that their freedom of movement, domicile, and employment is strictly regulated by each host country and across the Schengen and Dublin borders. Add to this complex tapestry of identities, entitlements, and rights the urgent need for young migrant laborers, in order to stave off the disastrous effects of low birth-rates upon social security and old age pensions, and the magnitude of Europe's problems in articulating fair and democratic principles of membership becomes evident.

A more precise breakdown of third country nationals shows that their differential juridical status corresponds to significant ethnocultural and religious cleavages. Turks and ethnic Kurds (who are in most cases Turkish citizens) are the largest group of foreigners, not only in Germany but in Western Europe in general. In 1993, they numbered 2.7 million. Of that number, 2.1 million live in Germany and as of 1999 made up 2.8 percent of the population. The second largest group of foreigners is the members of former Yugoslav states, many of whom enjoy either full or temporary refugee status: 1.8 million Croats, Serbians, Bosnian Muslims, and Albanians. Among the EU countries most affected by the breakup wars of former Yugoslavia are the Netherlands, where as of 1998, citizens of former Yugoslavia numbered 47,500; Sweden, where the corresponding figure is 70,900; and Italy, in which 40,800 former citizens of Yugoslavia, as well as 91,500 Albanians, have settled. This picture is complicated by the presence in countries such as France of former colonials. As of the 1990 census, France counted 614,200 Algerian-born individuals among its population and 572, 200 Moroccans.

After the fall of communism in Eastern and Central Europe, a slow but increasing tide of immigration from the former Eastern bloc countries to the EU began. In 1998, 66,300 Poles entered Germany, about 10,400 entered France, and about 14,000 the Netherlands. In 1998, there were 20,500 members of the Russian Federation resident in Finland; Greece is host to about 5,000 Russians, 3,000 Bulgarians, and approximately 2,700 Albanians.

It is obvious that EU expansion, if and when it comes, will do little to alter the legal status of most third country nationals, since neither Turkey nor the former Yugoslav states—with the exception of Slovenia—nor Algeria, Morocco, or Albania will join the EU in the foreseeable future. To the contrary, given that the largest number of third country nationals within the EU are from Muslim countries, it is to be expected that after the attacks of September 11, 2001, there will be less sympathy for their plight and less readiness to bring their juridical status into line with that of other residents. The shift from employing laborers from such predominantly Muslim countries as Morocco, Algeria, Tunisia, and Albania to those from Eastern European countries has already started. In Spain, which is dependent upon large numbers of migrant laborers in its agricultural sector, this displacement has not been missed by the migrants themselves. Rachid Benyaia, a forty-year-old Algerian who has been in Spain for eight years, for example, told the *International Herald Tribune* that the East Europeans "have the same culture as Spain—that's what they tell us."

The EU reproduces at the supranational level some of the internal tensions of modern nation-states, while showing tendencies toward evolution along a different path. Common identity and the democratic understandings of the citizenry were fused together in the modern nation-state, where the citizen was socialized, schooled, and disciplined to embody a specific national identity. Of course, cultural homogeneity was more an ideal than an actual historical fact. Modern nation-states incorporated through annexation and oppression large cultural groups who were not given democratic voice. Yet contemporary developments are splitting apart aspects of citizenship that modern nation-states usually bundled together.

Citizenship in the modern nation-state has three aspects: shared collective cultural identity; political rights and privileges; and social entitlements such as unemployment compensation, old age pensions, health care, educational subsidies, and so on. For EU citizens, both political rights and privileges (except those at the national level) and social entitlements, which in most cases accrue as a consequence of the wage-labor contract, are no longer dependent upon sharing a common national identity. Some commentators therefore view EU citizenship as a case of "postnational membership" heralding developments that will not remain confined to the EU. Postnational membership brings with it the dissociation of national identity from democratic rights, as well as the allocation of social entitlements on criteria other than those of national origin. But for the millions of third country residents of the EU, the classical model of national belonging is retained as a precondition for the exercise of political rights. Even so, insofar as the entitlement to social rights and benefits is dependent upon one's status as a wage laborer and not upon one's ethnic origin, the significance of nationality is waning.

Whether these developments presage the general decline of democratic citizenship and the emergence of a model of postdemocratic governance or whether they can lead to a new form of citizenship, dissociated from nationality and closely tied to the local, regional, and transnational networks of a global civil society, is not easy to say. The disaggregation of citizenship carries danger as well as promise. For the EU's third country nationals, the danger is all too clear: despite the considerable social benefits enjoyed by those who have secured jobs and long-term residency in Europe's wealthy democracies, they remain culturally as well as politically "mere auxiliaries to the commonwealth," as Kant once called women, children, and servants. Their voices are not heard at the level of the newly emerging union. Many decisions—on family unification, for example—that deeply affect them are taken without their effective participation. As long as political participation rights are linked with nationality, many foreign residents of the EU will, in effect, trade political voice for social benefits.

These juridical discrepancies and political confusions can be seen in part as the growing pains of a new union. After September 11, however, they assume greater significance. As I have already pointed out, the majority of third country nationals who do not enjoy representation at the EU or local levels are Muslim (Turks, Kurds, Algerians, Moroccans, Albanians, Bosnians); a smaller number are Orthodox Slav in origin (Serbians, Bosnians, and Albanians); and so the institutional fault lines concerning rights and privileges perilously track ethnic and religious ones. Easing the naturalization process is certainly one way of dealing with this problem. Granting the right to participate in elections to the EU Parliament, as well as in local elections, according to some shared criteria across the EU, would be another. This political harmonization ought to be accompanied by the right to EU-wide mobility and employment for legal permanent residents.

A further question that needs to be addressed by the EU, the United States, and many other states and international organizations concerns the status of long-term refugees and asylees. At what point does the receiving state incur an obligation to incorporate these people? When and how can they assume immigrant status in legal fashion? There are no clear answers to these questions in either the theory or the practice of international law. The will of the national legislatures remains sovereign, despite continued lip service to human rights agreements.

As representatives of the fifteen member countries convene in an EU-wide constitutional convention this year, and as they negotiate the dialectic of identities and institutions, they will redraw the boundaries of their union. Whether the dream of the Euro-federalists to establish a multifaith, multinational, and multicultural Europe becomes a reality depends in large measure on the treatment of the foreigners in their midst. Given how closely the dividing line between those who enjoy full and complete citizenship status and those who do not corresponds to religious, ethnic, and class cleavages, it is important that a new European federation not perpetrate the historical divisions between Europe and its "others."

But political indicators since September 11 provide a different signal. In Hamburg during city-wide elections the Social Democratic Party was replaced by the conservative Christian Democratic Union; in Portugal a neoliberal has taken over from the socialists; in Denmark, the socialists have lost their hold on the government for the first time in eighty years. In the Netherlands, after the assassination of its leader, Pym Fortyn's anti-Muslim, anti-immigrant party picked up seats in the Parliament. The French Socialists lost the June 2002 elections; after scaring themselves and the world by giving Jean-Marie Le Pen a symbolic political victory, French voters provided President Jacques Chirac's rightists with an impressive majority in the National Assembly. With national elections pending in Germany this fall, which the Social Democrats seem likely to lose, Tony Blair's Labour Party may remain the only social democratic party in power in a major European country. At this juncture, the EU is turning sharply to the right, and in this continental shift, Europe's migrants are the first to lose.

---

* Ernest Renan, "What is a Nation?" in *Nation and Narration*, ed. by Homi Bhabha (Routledge, 1990), pp. 8–23.

---

**SEYLA BENHABIB** is the Eugene Meyer Professor of Political Science and Philosophy at Yale University and author of *The Claims of Culture, Equality and Diversity in the Global Era*.

From *Dissent*, Fall 2002, pp. 33-39. © 2002 by Dissent Magazine.

# Letter from Poland

## by David Ost

You know things have changed when you go to the historic Gdansk shipyard, where Solidarity was born, and find unemployed shipworkers hired out as ushers for a theater company renting part of the famed site. The company's doing a run of Brecht's *Happy End*, and these workers escort theatergoers from the factory gate to the theater, telling stories about the glory days. You thank them when you get there and wish them better luck, but then the curtain comes up and there they are, on stage, holding signs reading "UNEMPLOYED! WE WANT WORK!"

In other words: unemployed workers temping as former workers doubling as part-time actors playing unemployed workers. Right by the monument erected in 1980 to those "who died so that we might live in dignity."

Taken together, the pieces of the decline of the neoliberal model in Poland are all right here. The dire economic situation has created critics where once there were only boosters. The humbling of a powerful labor movement has led to the specter of an authoritarian populist backlash. And then there's Brecht. This Old Left master was purged from the repertoire after 1989. His revival here is a sign too, of the willingness of a new generation to think left alternatives again.

The success story so often told about Poland is not what you find when you get there. "When I go abroad," the leader of the Solidarity trade union in the Krakow region told me, "and everyone starts congratulating me on how well Poland is doing, all I'm thinking is, Are they talking about the place where unemployment is 18 percent, youth unemployment near 50 percent and hundreds of firms, both old and new, are this close to collapse?" It's not that the country has not had successes. It has a number of modernized plants, a sizable, if recently declining, middle and professional class, and exciting world-class cities in Warsaw and Krakow. But it has hit a wall, both economically and politically, that has people more frightened than they've been in quite some time. Unemployment is now higher than at any time since the fall of Communism, and hundreds of thousands of young people, a product of the baby boom following the imposition of martial law in 1981, are entering the labor market with no prospects whatsoever.

The country had a severe crisis after 1989 too, but while that was a crisis of the transition to capitalism, this is a crisis of the real thing. Whereas that one was expected to happen, this one was not. That it has happened seems to throw everything into disarray. Where once the TINA shibboleth—"There is no alternative"—was on everyone's lips, now it seems all anyone can talk of is precisely that: alternatives.

Because this is post-Communism, however, the interest in alternatives first of all strengthens the radical right, which has been the chief opponent of capitalist transformation all along. While the former left-liberal oppositionists of Solidarity (Adam Michnik, Jacek Kuron, Bronislaw Geremek, Tadeusz Mazowiecki) saw marketization as the chance to "join Europe" and create an enlightened civil society, and the former Communists cheered them on in order to demonstrate their democratic bona fides, the religious-nationalist right denounced the post-1989 transformation as a betrayal of the nation, an assault on Christianity and a sellout to (a new set of) foreigners. One of the most dismaying things is to see the extremist right-wing newspaper *Nasz Dziennik* filled not only with authoritarian and anti-Semitic diatribes but with sympathetic coverage of the plight of the poor and powerful criticism of the ravages wrought by the new elite. Liberals have so focused on the positive sides of the transition that they have left the field of criticism wide open to the right. When things go so wrong, as they have now, it's no surprise the right is the first to benefit.

For now, that means "Self-Defense," the right-wing party that polled more than 10 percent of the vote in last year's parliamentary elections and has since emerged as the second-largest party in opinion polls. Its pugnacious leader, Andrzej Lepper, cultivates himself as a cross between Mussolini and Robin Hood, combining the former's bullying swagger with the latter's espousal of banditry for the people. Particularly strong among the impoverished rural population, still about a third of the total, Lepper looks increasingly like a Polish Le Pen, replete with tirades against liberals, bankers and foreigners (though the foreigners he opposes are the rich rather than the poor). He organizes road blockades, flouts the law with impunity and harbors private goon squads. When the governing party tried to "domesticate" Self-Defense by giving it some parliamentary authority, Lepper responded with a McCarthyite speech charging corruption throughout the political class, earning him sanction by Parliament and accolades from the dispossessed—exactly, of course, what he hoped to achieve.

All Self-Defense needs now, it would seem, is to piggyback onto a mass popular protest movement. And this past July such a movement emerged in Szczecin, following the bankruptcy of the city's Solidarity Shipyard, which left thousands without work. Named to evoke comparisons with the famous precursor of Solidarity, the Interfactory Protest Committee brought together labor representatives from more than 100 factories throughout the country that were facing bankruptcy. Besides protesting the government, however, the IPC attacked the main trade unions too, seeing them as part of the same cabal that brought about the mess.

The IPC is an embodiment of that peculiar post-Communist phenomenon, the right-wing labor movement. For while this was undoubtedly a workers' protest, a cry of the dispossessed, its rhetoric portrayed foreigners as the enemy and a strong state ready to punish the wrong-doers as the solution. It called for aid to "Polish banks, Polish culture and the Polish army," and for rejection of the European Union. It is less critical of official policy on unemployment than of the policy toward domestic capital (it says the government favors Western business interests over domestic ones). And its pugnacious style of politics, like Lepper's, can be seen in the team it sent to a nearby textile firm whose women workers had not been paid in months. With television cameras following along (or egging them on, though they were happy to oblige), about a dozen workers stormed the offices and roughed up the firm's director. While press headlines read "Lynch Mob!" Lepper volunteered to pay their bail.

**D**espite its growth, this nationalist right is not likely to come to power anytime soon. The reason is as simple as what one farmer told me: "Are we supposed to sell our goods to Russia instead?" While many Poles today, in contrast to a few years ago, are indeed aware that entering the EU has its costs, they just don't see an alternative. Russia hasn't paid its bills in years. And so, "even though I might not do so well in 'Europe,'" the farmer continued, "at least it might be better for my kids."

It is this gut antinationalism, along with the new distrust of capitalism, that has led to the growth of a democratic left for the first time since 1989. This goes far beyond the Democratic Left Alliance (heir to the Communist Party), now in power. Despite the party's name, its left-wing credentials are actually quite scanty. Apart from a recent bill forgiving the debts of large enterprises if they undergo restructuring, DLA representatives are usually overeager to support neoliberal politics. Indeed, business circles make up one of their core constituencies, along with critics of clericalism, voters fed up with the incompetence of other parties and those attracted by its slogans of social justice. Once in power, however, they seem to make sure not to offer any alternatives. My conversation with Tadeusz Iwinski, a party leader and secretary of state for international affairs, found him unable to articulate just what the leftness of the DLA entails, aside from a "sensitivity" to social injustice. In essence, the DLA is a pure vote-getting machine, refusing to confront the right over any serious issues. (It recently withdrew its commit-ment to abortion rights in return for the church's agreement not to oppose EU accession.)

**A**nd so it is chiefly outside the DLA that new left voices are emerging in Poland. The signs are everywhere, such as in the increased prominence of feminist discourse, or in the first real organizing effort of trade unions since 1989. Because of Solidarity, Poland has a reputation as a place of militant unionism. In fact, the Solidarity leadership has been so firmly on the side of market reform that not only has membership withered but workplace rights and opportunities for employee input have deteriorated dramatically. The situation is particularly severe in the large and growing private sector, which now makes up most of the economy. Because of an early post-Communist belief, repeated to me by Solidarity unionists with numbing regularity in the early 1990s, that private ownership means that "people who work hard get paid well," unions made no attempt to organize in new private firms and scaled back their involvement in privatized ones. The result, as the industrial sociologist Juliusz Gardawski explains, is that "labor has been marginalized while owners do whatever they want, without concern for rules." Hours are dictated, forced overtime common, safety concerns hushed up and, even though the law requires each firm to have a "social fund" for workplace improvement or employee assistance, employers regularly squander this on Christmas parties or managerial retreats. A popular way for employers to evade labor law entirely is to demand that employees register themselves as independent entrepreneurs, leading to a veritable boom in single-person firms of saleswomen, welders, food preparers and bus drivers. Besides boosting official statistics on the growth of private enterprise, this means that if, say, "self-employed" X-ray technicians (they have these too) "choose" to expose themselves to more radiation than the law allows, well, that's their free choice.

Not surprisingly, all this has led to a hemorrhaging of union membership (down to about 2.5 million total and 17 percent density, with Solidarity under 1 million, down nearly two-thirds from its 1989 level) and a widespread perception among workers that unions are simply irrelevant. Recently, however, things have begun to change. In direct response to experiences with "actually existing capitalism," Solidarity has set up a Union Development Office (UDO) targeting the private sector. Even the normally timid old official union federation is doing the same, via its new Confederation of Labor (created by former Solidarity activists disappointed with its pro-management and religious bent).

As it happens, retail has been at the cutting edge of this new organizing drive; in particular, the Western European-owned "hypermarkets" (think supermarket plus mini-mall, all in one store). Originally greeted as a symbol of the alluring, garish opulence of capitalism, with thousands lining up hopefully with job applications, they quickly became known as places of breakneck work pace, constantly changing job criteria, draconian supervision, mandatory unpaid overtime and immediate firing at the first sign of discontent. With workers themselves coming to the unions looking for help, the latter finally responded with an organizing drive filled with pickets, leaflets and press conferences—all hitherto unknown elements of Polish trade unionism.

If this sounds like something out of an American SEIU organizing campaign, it's because the latter conducted the training workshops that got it started. And this points to another promising development in Poland: the emergence of close international trade-union cooperation. Solidarity's UDO emerged out of a workshop organized by John Sweeney's SEIU, with more aid coming when Sweeney took over the AFL-CIO. (Unfortunately, US unions have not aided the Confederation of Labor, perhaps wrongly identifying it as a holdover from the old regime.) In private manufacturing plants, meanwhile, cooperation with European trade unions has been crucial. Stanislaw Ciepiera, Solidarity leader at General Motors' Opel plant in the depressed mining city of Gliwice, formed the local union there, thanks to contacts with a Polish Jesuit monk who had once worked at a German Opel plant and knew the head of its European Works Council. The monk arranged for his visit to Germany, where Ciepiera met with IG Metall unionists from Opel—"and we then felt we had someone behind us." This strategy soon spread to other companies. Ciepiera has contacts throughout Europe now, and even though he holds on to his conservative Catholic beliefs and considers himself antisocialist, he talks like a class-conscious social democrat when he says, "To have a united Europe, with a single, centralized, united union—this is my dream. When there's globalized capital, labor has no other way forward."

Liberal intellectuals are also starting to think about internationalism in a new way. Earlier this year the first sympathetic account of the "antiglobalization" movement appeared. *A World Not for Sale*, by Artur Domoslawski, a young journalist for Adam Michnik's liberal daily *Gazeta Wyborcza*, is a pathbreaking account that succeeds where many Western books do not, in that it begins with an understanding of how previous radical movements have degenerated into apologies for dictatorship, and then seeks to bring that awareness into this new movement. Domoslawski peppers activists he meets in Porto Alegre with questions about whether they understand the brutalities anticapitalism is capable of, and warns them not to ignore Eastern Europe's lessons (and thus lose Eastern European supporters). He admonishes Polish readers to stop thinking of Western leftists as crypto-Communists, and to recognize that their struggles against capitalist globalization constitute a large part of the hope for a better world in Poland too. It's hard to think of a better way to make "antiglobalization"—or, as Domoslawski

calls it, "alterglobalization"—a truly global movement. Moreover, by legitimizing a left critique, Domoslawski undercuts the appeal of the extreme right, which has hinged on its being the main critic of globalization.

Unlike in 1980, few in the West—or, for that matter, in Poland—seem to think the country has much to offer the rest of the world. Yet its experiences since 1989 do deserve to be mined more fully. With "privatization" still a globalization buzzword, Poland's experience with different types of employee-owned firms can be relevant not only to the search for effective alternatives but, with the bogus nature of some of them, as cautionary tales. And the budding "alterglobalization" awareness there needs to be cultivated as well. Ironically, Poland's traditional pro-Americanism is rather helpful here, for it means that the current search for alternatives need not pass through the facile anti-Americanism now in vogue in Western Europe. This search is already allowing thoughtful criticism of American policy toward Iraq, such as that of conservative theorist Aleksander Hall, who recently spoke out against "an international order in which the world superpower punishes and rewards sovereign states according to its own whims, even if that power represents our values and rendered great service in the defeat of Communism."

But all this needs to be nurtured. For if there's one thing not only Poland but all Eastern Europe has lacked since 1989, it's concerned engagement by Western progressives. Disappointed by the mad rush to capitalism (as if their own societies had not done that long before), and perhaps even by the fierce rejection of bankrupt "socialism," many progressives turned away, leaving concern for the region to the IMF-sanctioned privatizers and neoliberals, who made sure no alternatives would be recommended. As the labor sociologist Wlodzimierz Pankow once complained to me, "We don't have enough left anti-Communists discussing with us the real history of capitalism, so of course people believe in the imaginary kind instead." Recent Polish interest in alterglobalization and union internationalism lays the basis for changing all this, provided the Western left pays more attention.

A few years ago Boeing workers went on strike against outsourcing. Among the objects of their wrath was the contract given to a dying aircraft manufacturing plant in southeastern Poland to build doors for 767s, providing sixty jobs in a plant where about 10,000 were threatened. I still remember the words of the local union leader at the time: "Don't they know in Seattle that we're not their enemy?" They didn't know, of course, but more international cooperation along the lines of what has been happening lately could make a difference.

---

*David Ost (ost@hws.edu), who teaches politics at Hobart and William Smith Colleges in Geneva, New York, has written widely on labor and democratization in Eastern Europe.*

# Ten Myths About Russia

## Understanding and Dealing with Russia's Complexity and Ambiguity

Many characterizations of Russia don't get it right.

### David Foglesong and Gordon M. Hahn

Since the collapse of the Soviet Union in 1991, American thinking about Russia has been distorted by at least ten major myths. Both conservatives and liberals, Russophobes and Russophiles, have clouded understanding of Russia by promoting unrealistic expectations about a rapid transformation, oversimplifications of Russia's history, essentialist ideas about its political culture, and exaggerated notions of a threat to American interests. The illusions that have clouded U.S.-Russian relations during the last decade must be dispelled if the present shaky cooperation against terrorism is to lead to a more stable partnership.

## Myth 1
### A Popular Revolution, Led by Liberal Democrats, Overthrew the Communist System and Launched Russia on a Speedy Journey to Democracy and a Free Market Economy

Early accounts of the demise of the Soviet Union depicted a miraculous transfiguration of the Russian people, who had suddenly cast off the fearful habits of the past, courageously resisted hard-line communist efforts to re-impose totalitarian oppression, and enthusiastically embraced the Western model of democracy and free enterprise.[1] Along with many politicians and journalists, political scientists were caught up in the early

euphoria about the supposed victory of Russian civil society against an oppressive state. Many espoused the transitology approach, presuming that Russia had made a radical break with Soviet institutions and embarked on an inexorable "transition" to democracy. This "democratic teleology" became dogma for those who interpreted the dissolution of the Soviet communist regime as a struggle between state and society.[2] Even some critics of the transition paradigm joined in the widespread tendency to interpret the *perestroika* era as a long "struggle with state institutions" waged by an "insurgent political society" and "the organized, independent, revolutionary opposition."[3]

Although there are elements of truth in such portrayals, they greatly exaggerate the level of popular participation in the demise of the Soviet regime. In fact, prior to the August coup attempt, Mikhail Gorbachev and Boris Yeltsin had led efforts to dismantle the Soviet regime. Gorbachev's reforms and nascent transitional policies, combined with the powers Yeltsin gained as leader of the Russian Soviet Federated Socialist Republic (RSFSR), eroded the authority of the Communist Party of the Soviet Union (CPSU). From 1985 to 1991 the party-state was increasingly incapacitated as the regime split three ways: regime soft-liners like Gorbachev, opposition moderates like Yeltsin, and hard-line conservatives with considerable influence in the organs of coercion and the Party apparat.[4]

In 1990, Yeltsin and his allies took control of the Russian republic's Party machinery and used it to undermine the dominance of the CPSU. They expanded Gorbachev's efforts to partially separate the Party from the state and to decentralize the Union's relations with its republics, ultimately breaking the Soviet party-state's control over the Russian republic's bureaucracy, finances, and natural resources. These revolutionaries-from-above mobilized society for additional support, but the mobilization was minimal and society's resources were limited. Thus, society opposition played only a limited role in destroying the old order and building the new. Demonstrators in Moscow, St. Petersburg, and several other large cities, in relatively small numbers, actively resisted the attempted coup of August 1991, but across the country most Russians remained on the sidelines.[5] The coup's failure resulted from the three-way regime split, which by 1991 had extended to the party-state, the power ministries,[6] and the Party *apparat.* After the coup collapsed, the final destruction of the Soviet state and the construction of a new Russian regime were actually led by former Communist Party officials (including Yeltsin), opportunistic state bureaucrats, and younger members of the privileged *nomenklatura* class.[7] In sum, the revolution was a bureaucrat-led, state-based "revolution from above" far more than a popular revolution from below.[8]

Moreover, Yeltsin and his cohort were quick to demobilize societal opposition, restraining the development of civil society and a multi-party system in Russia. They soon cut a deal with the Soviet-era economic elite to co-opt the opposition emerging from the more partocratic element in the new ruling alliance against the domestic "neo-liberalism" and "pro-American" foreign policy of the young radicals.[9] Old apparatchiks and young members of the former *nomenklatura* divvied up Party and state property, excluding society from the great Soviet going-out-of-business sale.[10] In addition to the oligarchic-bureaucratic economy, the federal and political systems were constructed on the basis of intra-elite agreements. For example, the Russian Federation was built on the basis of bilateral treaties and agreements between the federal and regional executive branches that divided state property and finances among groups of bureaucrats. The political system was constructed in large part by incorporating Soviet state institutions (and apparatchiks) into the Russian state.[11]

The mistaken view of the revolution as one generated from below, and merely another case in a "third wave"[12] of global democratization, led to a cascade of unrealistic and false expectations, East and West, about the fate of Russia's third revolution in the twentieth century. The fall of the *ancien régime,* it was presumed, would lead almost inevitably to the consolidation of democracy and the market. This democratic teleology reinforced and sustained the view among decisionmakers that Russia could integrate into the West and the global economy with limited political and economic assistance. Like Estonia or Hungary, Russia, too, would find its way without anything akin to a Marshall Plan. The West could expand NATO without fear of provoking Moscow, because Russia was already on its way westward. If Moscow turned back, Russia and its culture were entirely to blame. The West would bear no responsibility for failure, which was unlikely anyway because a strong democrat was leading the transition.

# Myth 2
## *Yeltsin Was a Democrat*

Yeltsin has been lionized as the bold, white-haired leader who mobilized the Russian people from atop a tank.[13] In reality, he was a semi-democratic, semi-authoritarian personalistic ruler, schooled in the ways of bureaucratic intrigue by years of working in the Party machinery. Aside from those memorable three days in August 1991, Yeltsin fought the Soviet party-state more with presidential decrees, government instructions, and Russian state institutions than with demonstrations or general strikes. To be sure, he skillfully used the growing popular opposition to win concessions from Gorbachev's increasingly divided party-state. Deploying a tactical populism, Yeltsin appealed to the people when he needed to exert greater pressure on the regime to advance his revolutionary takeover of state institutions and Party resources.

However, after defeating the bumbling coup plotters, Yeltsin and his aides stifled the development of a multi-party system and civil society. Yeltsin refused to lead or even join a political party. He postponed promised regional elections and instead appointed regional governors until 1996. He co-opted any and all willing party-state apparatchiks into the state bureaucracy, regardless of their past records or attitudes toward developing democracy and a market economy. Few members of Yeltsin's administration—including Yeltsin himself—had more than a limited understanding of how a market economy functions. He made deals with former Soviet economic elites to reduce their opposition to the pro-American economic and foreign policies advocated by his more liberal advisers. This approach reached its logical conclusion in December 1992, when Prime Minister Egor Gaidar, the architect of market reforms, was replaced by the communist soft-liner Viktor Chernomyrdin, who had served Gorbachev as fuel and energy minister and a Central Committee member. Then, in 1993, Yeltsin forced the Russian legislature into a corner, abolished it, and ordered tanks to bombard the parliament building. After crushing the October 1993 rebellion, he closed down all the regional soviets. Although he finally held elections to a new federal parliament, the results of the simultaneous referendum on the new constitution may well have been falsified. When public approval of his government's painful and failing policies fell below 10 percent in 1996, Yeltsin came exceedingly close to canceling the scheduled presidential elections. He was able to secure victory only by buying votes with state funds and handing over the state's most valuable enterprises to oligarchs like Boris Berezovskii.[14]

While it is inaccurate to portray Yeltsin as a principled democratic leader, it is equally misleading to paint him as the embodiment of oppressive Russian authoritarianism. Despite his declining popularity, he refused to curb freedom of association, and he accepted the revived Communist Party of the Russian Federation. Although he sometimes manipulated and tried to intimidate the mass media, he tolerated substantial criticism of his policies from journalists. In short, Yeltsin was a hybrid figure—personalist and populist, authoritarian and democratic all at once. In terms of this internal contradiction, he was not unlike the country he ruled.

# Myth 3
## *Russia Is Subject to Universal Laws of Development*

Over the last decade, many policy advisers and scholars posited that Russia's inevitable destiny is to conform—or succumb—to the universal process of modernization. According to these arguments, Russia has no choice but to belatedly follow the paths to democracy and capitalism blazed decades or centuries ago by more advanced Western countries.[15]

In fact, Russia is not just another country to be plugged into preconceived formulas. It has a number of peculiarities that must be taken into account both to understand its "non-conformity" and to help transform it where possible. The main peculiarities include Russia's vast size, its geostrategic location, and the residual Soviet impression on its economic geography.

Russia's size has significant implications for both domestic and foreign policy that no other state can claim. By far the largest country in the world, Russia counts ten countries as neighbors. Its border with Kazakhstan alone is the same length as the boundaries of the continental United States. Russia's extensive borders and seacoasts require a large standing army and navy, which burden the budget and deplete economic manpower. These costs and the reality of a territorial expanse spanning eleven time zones would make it difficult for the federal government to build and maintain infrastructure (roads, railroads, bridges, power lines, etc.) even without the challenges of economic transformation. Russian officials and scholars now speak of a coming national techno-infrastructural catastrophe and of Russia's need to restore its "familiarization" with, and "possession" of, distant Siberia and the Far East.[16] The resources required to stave off the collapse of the country's infrastructure and develop Siberia and the Far East sufficiently to ensure their orientation toward Moscow would stretch the capacity of any economy, let alone Russia's weak post-communist one.

Geostrategically, Russia is the only country in the world that borders the European, Asian, and Muslim worlds. This places special burdens on its foreign and security policies. Russian national security strategists argue (sometimes with hyperbole) that the threat from each of these worlds is arguably growing.[17] In the east, the sleeping dragon is awake. In the south, the Muslim world is in turmoil, leading to terrorist jihads against the West and Russia, assistance for Chechen militants, and a threat to the stability of reasonably friendly secular regimes in Central Asia. In the west, NATO is expanding ever eastward, apparently to Russia's borders with the Baltic states, and eventually perhaps to Ukraine and Georgia. Any exacerbation of Russian security concerns in the three regions could set back progress on reforming the economy and post-Soviet institutions.

Russia's economic geography also hinders the conversion and modernization of its once heavily militarized industries. Russia has the only post-communist economy that consists of hundreds of one-company towns that, in many cases, dominate half the budgets of regions several times larger than medium-sized European countries. Closing, privatizing, or selling the company to foreigners will affect an entire region that is likely to be located hundreds of miles from any other population center. This constrains Russian willingness to engage in uncontrolled large-scale privatization, especially in the outlying regions. With the privatization of large enterprises, oligarchs came to dominate regional economies. Many are now parlaying their economic power into political power, becoming governors and senators. They seek office not to lobby for development aid for their regions, but to gain favors for their firms and immunity from prosecution.

These factors make it inadvisable to force a one-size-fits-all Western model on Russia. Transitology envisaged a rapid, almost automatic, transformation from hostile, autarchic Soviet totalitarianism to a Western-style Russian democracy and market. This mindset led to the belief that overhauling Russia's inefficient economy would not require massive Western financial assistance or new approaches tailored to Russian conditions.

# Myth 4
## *Russia's Unique Culture Dooms It to Eternal Backwardness*

When the illusions of sweeping overnight reforms failed to pan out, they gave way to disappointment, disenchantment, and disdain for Russia's alleged inability to change for the better. Bruce Clark, a British correspondent who stressed "Russia's sheer incomprehensibility," was one of the first to argue that the "Eastern Church" was a major obstacle to the Westernization. A little later, the political scientist Samuel Huntington defined Russia as the core of an inscrutable Orthodox civilization that was almost impossible to change. More recently, Matthew Brzezinski, another journalist, attributed the "loss" of the country to Russians' congenital corruption, their peculiar "Slavic soul," and their scheming, non-Western leaders.[18]

Such gloomy views were the opposite of the earlier euphoric universalism. While the zealous optimists had been overconfident about rapidly converting Russia, the pessimists wrongly disparaged Russians as irredeemably averse to Western values. As some pessimists exaggerated the influence of the Orthodox Church (despite seventy years of atheist persecution), others vented a racially tinged scorn for supposedly innate Russian traits (e.g., superstition, laziness, dishonesty). Overreacting to specific setbacks, especially the financial collapse of August 1998, the doomsayers prematurely wrote off Russia's ability to develop a prosperous economy.[19]

# Myth 5
## *Russia Lacks the Cultural Requisites for Democracy and a Market Economy*

After Russian voters elected an alarming number of communists and xenophobic nationalists to parliament in 1993 and 1995, many Western journalists and scholars began to voice gloomy appraisals of the incorrigible authoritarianism of "eternal Russia."[20] In 1993, they exaggerated the election outcome as a victory for the quirky quasi-fascist Vladimir Zhirinovskii's Liberal Democratic Party (63 deputies) and the communists.[21] In fact, the party of liberal pro-Western Egor Gaidar took a plurality of seats (76 deputies) in the Duma, and democratic and centrist parties took a majority of the Duma seats (51.7) after deputies elected in majoritarian single-member districts were factored in.[22] Such Russophobic pessimism faded in some circles when Yeltsin triumphed over his communist opponent in the 1996 presidential election and when the Russian stock market became bullish the following year. However, after Yeltsin handed over the presidency to former KGB officer Vladimir Putin at the end of 1999, there was a resurgence of scornful views of Russia as an impenetrable, irredeemable land of cruel masters and servile subjects. In the first days of Putin's presidency, for example, one relatively sophisticated correspondent declared: "Russians have been crushed for so long that they have learned to respond only to an iron fist."[23]

---

> *There have been numerous revolts against despotism and brief periods of quasi-democratic government that might have been more lasting had circumstances been more favorable.*

---

In fact, there has been a recessive but nonetheless rich liberal-democratic sub-strain in Russian political culture that is too often ignored.[24] While Russian political history has indeed been dominated by authoritarianism and totalitarianism, there have been numerous revolts against despotism and brief periods of quasi-democratic government that might have been more lasting had circumstances been more favorable. The liberal Provisional Government of February–October 1917, in particular, might have been able to establish the foundations for democracy if Russia had not been entangled in World War I. Even in the darker periods of tsarist and Soviet rule, Russians formed revolutionary or dissident organizations, secretively circulated banned publications, and gained knowledge about the outside world from smuggled books or partially jammed radio broadcasts. Members of the "eternal Russia" school are fond of citing the Marquis de Custine's nineteenth-century indictment of Russians as obsequious Orientals, but like Custine, they miss the dynamic development of Russian society.[25]

Even as Russophobes in the West reproduce the myth that Russians are genetically antagonistic to democratic values, public opinion polls and in-depth interviews show that Russians have grown deeply attached to democratic processes and principles, despite their frequently acute disappointment with post-Soviet leaders and institutions.[26] Although the word *demokratiia* has acquired pejorative associations with corruption and foreign imposition, a recent in-depth survey conducted by the Carnegie Endowment for International Peace shows that the overwhelming majority of Russians treasure free elections (87 percent), freedom of expression (87 percent), freedom of the mass media (81 percent), freedom to choose place of residence (75 percent), and freedom of religion (70 percent).[27] Other recent polls show also a growing sense of economic well-being among Russians, an important prerequisite of middle-class democratic attitudes. According to one survey, over the last three years the number of survey respondents who regard the situation in Russia as catastrophic has fallen from 51 percent to 14 percent. Between 1995 and 2000, more than 50 percent of respondents felt that "life like this cannot go on any longer." By the end of 2001, only 27 percent claimed that life was intolerable. Although almost 42 percent believe they have suffered from the reforms, almost two-thirds view their current social status as "satisfactory," and 41 percent consider themselves to be middle-class.[28]

Contrary to the tendency of cultural essentialists to view Russians as passive, Russia now possesses a civil society that is a reasonably active, autonomous force. There are tens of thousands of non-governmental labor, business, environmental, anti-war, and other organizations that employ hundreds of thousands of citizens and represent the interests of around 20 million people. Some can already point to victories. Russia's trade unions recently forced the Duma to amend a draft Labor Code before passage. To be sure, Russian society could be more highly mobilized and better organized. But the enormous size of the country makes building nationwide organizations a difficult, expensive task, and with 80 percent of the capital concentrated in the city of Moscow, the overwhelming majority of Russians are too resource-starved for optimally effective self-organization. However, this is an argument not for dismissing the capacity of Russians for democratic activity, but for increasing Western aid to non-governmental organizations.

Even under current conditions, Russians manage to express their grievances and demand changes. On February 9, 2002, for example, 500 residents of Krasnoiarsk braved the Siberian winter to block a railroad used to import nuclear waste for processing in their region. At the same time, small business organizations protested tax hikes and other governmental decisions in regions across Russia.[29] In response, the federal government modified its tax policy to ease the burden on small businesses. There is also a strong social movement to institute alternatives to military service, and several regions began experimenting with such a system. Although the administration halted these illegal experiments, and stubborn military opposition forced the Putin administration to back, and the Duma to pass, an alternative service bill that requires a three and a half year commitment, the first step has been taken.[30] Moreover, the mayor of Nizhnii Novgorod recently reinstated his city's experiment after the Duma vote and vowed to support an NGO court challenge to the federal ban on regional versions of alternative service.

# Myth 6
## *Putin Is a Dictator*

Since the end of 1999, when he assumed the Russian presidency, Western commentators have asserted that the wellspring of Vladimir Putin's politics is his background as a KGB officer from the 1970s to 1980s and as head of the Federal Security Service (FSB) in the late 1990s. Simplistically labeled a "former KGB operative," Putin is accused of seeking to return Russia to a "police state" and "dictatorship" by centralizing political control, suppressing the independent media, and cracking down on dissent. In July 2000, for example, only months after his inauguration, two American national security analysts asserted that "Putin is now building a police state using primarily the police organs of the Federal Security Service, known as the FSB, and the army to seize all key power positions in Russia, eliminate dissent and attack both internal and external enemies."[31] Similarly, *New York Times* columnist William Safire alleged that Putin planned to follow China's model and crush all democratic tendencies, and he implied that Putin would make himself "president for life."[32]

Such nightmarish predictions are one-sided and ill-informed. An accurate portrait of Putin, like that of Yeltsin or of Russia as a whole, must see him in all his complexity. The simplistic assumption that anyone formerly associated with the KGB must possess the very worst totalitarian impulses of the old regime and be incapable of countenancing democratic reforms reflects an ignorance of history. For example, Gorbachev ascended to the Soviet leadership with support from a former KGB chief, Iurii Andropov, and key KGB leaders played critical roles in the defeat of the August 1991 putsch by refusing orders to assault democratic forces.[33]

In fact, there is some evidence that Putin himself showed mildly semi-nonconformist and democratic inclinations during his KGB career. As Putin has told Russian journalists, in the early 1980s agents in the intelligence service "were permitted to think differently. And we could say things that few ordinary citizens could allow themselves to say."[34] Putin seems to have thought and spoke quite freely during his tenure as a KGB operative in East Germany. According to one relatively unknown biography, he told German friends as early as 1987 that he thought Soviet leaders should be chosen by secret ballot in popular elections.[35]

More important, the cynical view of Putin as first and last a KGB man ignores his tenure in the democratic government of St. Petersburg, an experience that exerts considerable influence on his political makeup. Like many *apparatchiki* in the Gorbachev era, Putin soon shifted from being a supporter of the sinking Soviet regime to a moderate revolutionary. In 1990, he effectively left the KGB and returned to St. Petersburg State University, where he had earned a law degree. There he became an assistant to rector in charge of international liaison at St. Petersburg State University, where USSR People's Deputy Anatolii Sobchak was still a law professor a leading moderate democrat, was elected mayor of St. Petersburg later that year. During the attempted hard-line coup of August 1991, Putin reportedly played a key role by negotiating with the commander of the Baltic Military District to prevent troops from entering the city. After the Soviet collapse, the St. Petersburg administration, with Putin as Sobchak's top deputy, followed Yeltsin's lead in banning the CPSU, abolishing the Soviet Union, and privatizing state property. (This also meant that Putin became involved with the corruption that was part-and-parcel of the economic revolution from above.)

After Sobchak lost his re-election bid in 1996, Putin jumped to Yeltsin's presidential administration, where he eventually became intimately familiar with one of the leading alleged state inside traders of the Yeltsin era. As deputy to Kremlin property manager Pavel Borodin, Putin probably was privy to at least some of Borodin's financial and property machinations and the Kremlin's dirty dealings with oligarchs. Later, as chief of the administration's State Control Directorate, he monitored implementation of laws and presidential decrees. Putin saw first-hand the regions' disdain for federal law as well as the institutional chaos at the federal level created by the flood of presidential decrees, governmental orders, and other normative documents that were often self-contradictory and ignored by competing bodies. This is a source of Putin's efforts to re-centralize power in Moscow, harmonize regional law with federal law, and make federation institutions more efficient.

Putin and his cohort of pragmatic former Soviet officials are neither solely authoritarian nor purely democratic. Although Putin has condemned violations of the law by KGB officers in the Soviet era, he has also stated his opposition to declassifying files and his abhorrence at having a democrat, Vadim Bakatin, head the post-Soviet FSK after the 1991 coup.[36] While Putin and his associates respect the democratic processes (mainly free elections) established in the 1990s that serve to legitimate their power, they were disturbed by the drastic decline of federal authority in the Yeltsin era and the degeneration of Russia to near lawlessness.

Since his election as president in March 2000 with 53.44 percent of the vote, Putin has centralized federal power at the expense of the formerly wayward regions, consolidated several centrist parties into one large party, "United Russia," united factions in the Duma, and sought to co-opt into state-organized corporatist structures members and groups previously organized in autonomous associations. His authoritarian measures have been undertaken with a soft sleight of hand rather than an iron fist, as in the effort to remove the NTV and TV-6 television stations, respectively, from the control of the oligarchs Vladimir Gusinskii and Berezovskii. Putin has tolerated oligarchs as long as they limit their clandestine political activities, forgo building independent media empires, and perform economic tasks for the state. Here, he seems to be caught between two of his formative political experiences: his rise to power with the help of oligarchs like Borodin and Berezovskii, and his disdain for the oligarchs' corrupting effect on the state.

The more liberal Petersburg experience in Putin's political biography also informs his presidency. Putin has taken some quasi-democratic political positions, such as ignoring numerous calls, many from governors themselves, for regional governors and republic presidents to be appointed rather than elected. He has also twice quashed efforts to lengthen presidential terms from four to seven years. In economics, Putin has taken important steps to cut taxes and business regulations, encourage foreign investment, and begin reforms of the judiciary, procuracy, and military. In sum, neither Putin's pre-presidential background nor his policies as president match the caricature of him as an untrustworthy KGB spook turned would-be dictator.

Depictions of Yeltsin as a bold, heroic democrat and Putin as a sneaky, sinister autocrat are therefore seriously misleading and mask the important continuities between the Yeltsin and Putin eras. Both manipulated democratic processes and showed some authoritarian tendencies while blocking a totalitarian restoration. The worst-case outcome of Putin's likely eight years in power is probably a very soft authoritarian regime still plagued by high rates of crime, corruption, and rights violations—a situation not much worse than that left behind by Yeltsin. The best-case scenario is a somewhat better institutionalized democracy and market economy, with a slightly stronger civil society, considerable structural reform in the economy, less penetration of the state by business interests, somewhat greater horizontal accountability, and fewer violations of civil and political rights in the regions—a situation slightly better than that bequeathed by Yeltsin to Putin.

## Myth 7
### Russians Are Inherently Anti-Western and Anti-American

Outbursts of anger and bitterness by nationalist and communist demagogues because of harsh economic policies and Russia's declining global prestige have led many in the West to conclude that xenophobia is implanted in the bones of Russians like some long-lived radioactive isotope. However, most increases in Russian anti-Western sentiment have been provoked by Western policies and actions.

To some extent, the rise of anti-American feeling in the mid-1990s was a predictable counterpart to the naive idealization of the United States between 1989 and 1992. With the downfall of the Soviet Union, many urban Russians vaguely hoped that their country would magically become as prosperous as the United States, and they expected massive financial aid as a reward for overthrowing the "evil empire." When no Marshall Plan for Russia materialized and the economic reforms pushed by American advisers brought widespread hardship, many became disillusioned and embittered.[37]

While anti-American attitudes were held by roughly 30–40 percent of Russians in 1993, the figure doubled later in the decade in reaction to the expansion of NATO into Eastern Europe, the NATO bombing of Bosnian Serbs in 1994, and the NATO bombing of Serbia in 1999.[38] When 60–70 percent of Russian respondents say that the United States or NATO poses a threat to Russia, it should be understood as a reflection of the history of military invasions of Russia from the West and the emotional tribulations Russians have undergone over the last decade more than an inherited cultural paranoia. It is also not a completely irrational response to such Western policies as the expansion of NATO up to Russia's borders, the increase in the number of

Russian cities listed as potential targets of U.S. nuclear missiles, and the challenges to Russia's right to a sphere of influence in the Commonwealth of Independent States.

Unlike the rabidly anti-American extremists who have drawn disproportionate media coverage, an overwhelming majority of Russians have either a friendly or an ambivalent attitude toward the United States and the West. Among those who are ambivalent, opinion is subject to abrupt changes of attitude in response to specific events. For example, the terrorist attacks of 9/11 induced a wave of sympathy for America from Russians who believe their own country has been the victim of terrorist raids and bombings by Chechen rebels. Russians generally supported the U.S. effort to bring to justice al Qaeda and its Taliban supporters. An October 2001 public opinion survey conducted by the Russian Center for the Study of Public Opinion, for example, showed that 56 percent of Russians wished the United States success in its war against terrorism in Afghanistan.[39] In early 2002, anti-Americanism became more pronounced, partly because many believed that Russian competitors had been victimized by unfair judging and scapegoating at the Salt Lake City Olympic Games. However, the anger over Salt Lake soon faded, and anti-American sentiment again centered on the sizeable minority who are suspicious of NATO expansion and believe the United States is seeking to subordinate Russia to American interests rather than pursuing a respectful partnership.[40]

Like President Putin, who emphatically declares "we are Europeans," many Russians, especially in the younger generations, believe that Russia is or should be a part of Europe.[41] But if Russians feel humiliated, insulted, and excluded by the West, they will be more likely to look for allies in the East and to define themselves as Eurasian.[42]

## Myth 8
### Russia Is an Expansionist, Neo-Imperialist Menace

Despite the drastic decline of Russian power since 1991, Russophobes like the New York Times columnist William Safire have repeatedly charged Russia with harboring its "old imperialist urge." Even as Russia provided much valuable intelligence to assist the U.S. war in Afghanistan, one American think tank deployed its experts to denounce the Northern Alliance's occupation of Kabul as part of a grand Russian "military strategy" and an "ominous gambit" to expand Russian influence in South Asia.[43] Stratfor director George Friedman went a step further, warning that Russia's cooperation with the West in Afghanistan was paving the way for Russia's resurgence and the next war, which would pit Russia against the West.[44] Such views perpetuate reflexive cold war suspicions and wrongly draw a straight line from the nineteenth-century "Great Game" through the alleged Soviet quest for a warm-water port on the Indian Ocean to the new Russia's supposed expansionist aims in Central and South Asia. Proponents seem to have forgotten that Russia was but one of several players in the Great Game, as it was in the much older European game of partitioning Poland.

> *A long-range view of American-Russian relations thus suggests that collisions are more likely to stem from the expansion of U.S. commercial interests and security commitments than from rampant Russian imperialism.*

The projection of cold war antagonism into the post–cold war era rests, in part, on a shallow historical perspective. In more than 200 years of Russian-American relations, the two countries' vital interests rarely clashed before the cold war. When the United States expanded across the North American continent in the nineteenth century, Russia withdrew from settlements in the Pacific Northwest and then sold Alaska for pennies an acre. As American commerce expanded in Northeast Asia around 1900, Theodore Roosevelt and others briefly feared that Russia's prolonged occupation of Manchuria jeopardized the Open Door policy, but between the Japanese thrashing of Russia in 1904–5 and VJ Day in 1945, most U.S. leaders realized that Russia was actually a potential ally against the most formidable threat to U.S. interests across the Pacific. A long-range view of American-Russian relations thus suggests that collisions are more likely to stem from the expansion of U.S. commercial interests and security commitments than from rampant Russian imperialism.

In more recent years, the specters raised by Russophobic analysts have repeatedly failed to materialize. Putin's turn to the West after September 2001 was a ruse, they warned—Russia would use the "alliance" against terror to bolster its oil and gas pipeline dreams, and then exploit its resulting enhanced international status to challenge American hegemony. Despite the alarms raised by Russophobes, the deployment of Russian Emergency Ministry forces to build a high-tech field hospital and re-establish a Russian embassy in Kabul generated no challenge to U.S. policy in Afghanistan. Indeed, Putin later revealed that the Russian descent on Kabul was carried out with the aid of U.S. forces.

Beyond Afghanistan, there have been few major Russian challenges to U.S. initiatives. Although the two governments squabbled in the spring of 2002 over U.S. duties on Russian steel and a Russian ban on imports of American chicken, Putin calmly accepted the U.S. abandonment of the Antiballistic Missile Treaty, supported U.S. military aid to the Republic of Georgia against terrorists in the Pankisi Gorge, and bowed to Pentagon demands for flexibility to secure a nuclear weapons reduction treaty. Moscow's top priority has clearly been not to defy Washington, but to speed Russia's economic integration into the West.

Even if the Russian government wanted to pursue a sustained imperialist foreign policy, it lacks sufficient military and economic power to do so. An economy no larger than that of the Netherlands is barely capable of supporting imperialist aspira-

tions in Eurasia, much less beyond. Russia has been unable to invigorate the Commonwealth of Independent States (CIS) as a viable international organization, much less as a precursor to a renewed economic union. Only Belarus, Tajikistan, Kyrgyzstan, and Kazakhstan have joined the CIS Customs Union, and these are the states that are least viable and most dependent on Russia to begin with.

All of Russia's seeming neo-imperialist gambits in the post-Soviet era have been either exaggerated by Western analysts or episodic in implementation, intended to manipulate weak bordering states rather than re-incorporate them into a revived Soviet Union. Russia has played a clearly positive role by stationing the 201st Division in Tajikistan, thereby deterring Islamic incursions from Afghanistan and stabilizing the weak and corrupt—but secular—regime of Imomali Rokhmonov in Dushanbe. Western critics of the involvement of Russian forces in Georgia and Transdniestr have ignored the financial costs Russia will incur by withdrawing its troops and equipment, as well as the instability that might result. In Central Asia, where Russian national security really is threatened, weak regimes like Tajikistan, Kazakhstan, and Kyrgyzstan have not been pressured to join a political union with Russia. The so-called Russia-Belarus Union is largely a fiction, even as an economic union. The two sides cannot agree on a common currency, and even the customs agreement has been the subject of repeated disputes between the parties. Any prospects of a real Belarus-Russia Union are minimal until President Aleksandr Lukashenka leaves the scene, since the economies of the two states are vastly different, with Russia having implemented economic liberalization far beyond the virtually unreformed Soviet-style Belarusian economy.

## Myth 9
### *Russia Is No Longer an Important International Player*

Many so-called realists believe that Russia is so weakened that it is no longer a serious international player whose interests need to be taken into account when planning American foreign policy.[45] For example, Eugene B. Rumer of the National Defense University's Institute for National Strategic Studies advised the Bush administration that Russia "will not bounce back from its troubles anytime soon" and suggested "Its current decline may well continue indefinitely."[46] More colorfully, journalist Jeffrey Tayler called Russia "Zaire with Permafrost" and argued that its history doomed the country to shrink, decay, and disintegrate.[47]

Although Russia has experienced a breathtaking decline in its fortunes since the cold war, when the Soviet superpower confronted the United States around the world, it is not so weak that it no longer counts as a great power, and its problems are not necessarily permanent or irremediable. Russia's possession of thousands of nuclear weapons is not the only factor that explodes the myth of its insignificance. Besides the United States, Russia is the only country that is a major player in Europe, the Pacific, South and Central Asia, and the Middle East simultaneously. Because of its geostrategic position and relatively high level of technological development, Russia is a major player in the global energy market as well as in several other natural resource exports. It maintains a faltering but still major space program that is matched only by NASA.

To be sure, Russia's economy is small compared not only with other major powers in the Group of Seven (G-7), but also with many smaller states. However, Russia's vast natural resources, strong human capital, and potential for investment growth represented by the hundreds of billions of dollars secreted in foreign bank accounts suggest, taken together, that a fairly rapid revitalization is possible. With the right policies in these areas, including investors' rights, banking reform, and money-laundering, anti-corruption, and anti-crime laws, a Russian economic revival is quite conceivable. In the last three years, Russia's economy has experienced steady, substantial growth, and Moscow has taken important steps to reverse capital flight, encourage foreign investment, and overhaul its financial system. Russia recovered from its earlier "times of troubles" (in the seventeenth century, during the Crimean War, and during the civil war of 1917–21). It may now be on the way to recovery again.

## Myth 10
### Russia and the United States Are Strategic Allies

The newest myth is that the United States and Russia became strategic partners, even allies, after the events of September 11, 2001. To be sure, 9/11 reshuffled international affairs in general, and Russian-American relations in particular—at least temporarily. The terrorist attacks highlighted the previously ignored mutual interest in combating militant Islam and international terrorism that Washington and Moscow have shared since the end of the cold war. But there is no guarantee that this common interest will remain clear or paramount to Russian and American policymakers.

Some leaders on each side read developments in Afghanistan as justifying a suspicion that the other country is pursuing selfish gains at the expense of their own country. Thus, certain American actions reinforced the suspicions of some Russians that the United States is seeking to parlay the war against terror into a war for control of oil, gas, and pipeline routes. American special operations forces and marines were first deployed mainly in the south among the Pashtun, who make up the majority of the population of Pakistan, and the United States has had good relations with Pakistan since the cold war. The Pashtun also make up the bulk of the Taliban, who, Russian analysts have long suspected, were backed by Washington to counter Russian interests in Central Asia. The United States inserted Afghan Pashtun leader Abdul Haq into southern Afghanistan in order to entice local Pashtun leaders and Taliban commanders to defect from Osama bin Laden. This was viewed by Russian commentators as an effort to rally Pashtuns around a charismatic leader against the Afghan minorities of Uzbeks, Tajiks, and Khazaris that make up the Northern Alliance,

backed for years by Russia, Iran, and India. In addition, American bombing sorties around the town of Mazar i Sharif and the Baghram airport in the initial stage of the campaign in the north were regarded by many observers both East and West, including the Northern Alliance, as surprisingly tame. This fact, and later warnings by President Bush that the alliance should refrain from immediately entering Kabul, led some Russian officials to fear that Washington wanted to delay Kabul's capture so its southern allies could enter before the Northern Alliance.

Back in Washington, some experts claimed that Moscow's outward show of cooperation masked an effort to utilize American power for its own ulterior purposes. For example, Toby Gati, a State Department official in the Clinton Administration, declared that Putin "had the Americans doing his business in Afghanistan and he was fighting to the last American."[48] In a similar vein, Russia's dispatch of Emergency Ministry personnel to Kabul to set up a hospital was variously interpreted as a second Pristina,[49] the beginning of Russian troop deployments, and an intelligence operation.

As of the summer of 2002, potential ruptures have been averted or smoothed over by a division of labor. The Russians are working closely with the largely Tajik and Uzbek Northern Alliance, providing assistance for infrastructure and military development, while the United States maintains close ties to the Pashtuns and leads the military struggle against the terrorists in the south. However, there is no guarantee that there will be no friction in the future.

There is also a potential for conflict in the Republic of Georgia, where the U.S. military is training Georgian units for an operation against Taliban and al Qaeda forces holed up in Georgia's Pankisi Gorge. Despite Putin's tempered response, statements by foreign Minister Igor Ivanov, Defense Minister Sergei Ivanov, and others clearly indicate that many Russian leaders are dissatisfied with this American incursion into the post-Soviet space. The tension will only be exacerbated if the American-Georgian operation does not eliminate Chechen militants in the gorge.

> ### Russian and American interests that coincided relatively well in destroying the Taliban will be less harmonious if and when the campaign shifts to Iraq.

Moreover, Russian and American interests that coincided relatively well in destroying the Taliban will be less harmonious if and when the campaign shifts to Iraq. Saddam Hussein's regime owes $7 billion to Russia and offers the potential for billions of dollars more in future oil and other contracts once sanctions are lifted. Russia also has economic interests in Iran, which is a major purchaser of Russian arms and a recipient of Russian nuclear technology. Moscow has already warned that it does not agree with Bush's categorization of Iraq, Iran, and North Korea as a new "axis of evil." When push comes to shove, Russia is likely to exercise its veto in the UN Security Council, forcing the Bush administration to act alone or at least with fewer allies. Tension over Iraq and Iran could complicate over pivotal issues in Russian-American relations, including Russian human rights violations in Chechnya, U.S. plans for a national missile defense system, and a second round of NATO expansion likely to reach Russia's western border.

Putin has brought Russia along so far, but expanding the anti-terrorism campaign to include Russian trading partners and debtors like Iran and Iraq could exhaust his political skills. Facing strong criticism of his cooperation with the United States from the Russian military, security forces, military-industrial complex, communists, and Muslims, Putin could buckle and revert to a Eurasian strategy of seeking much closer ties with China and Arab and Islamic states. Similarly, the Bush administration, split between militant unilateralists and moderate multilateralists, could tilt away from consultation and conciliation with Russia in order to pursue priority objectives unilaterally, some of which are believed to offer domestic political payoffs. In short, it is premature to be celebrating a Russian-American strategic partnership.

## Beyond the Myths: Understanding and Dealing with Russia

To have a stable and positive relationship with Putin's Russia, the United States must move beyond the myths and polarized perspectives of the past decade. It is dangerous for both U.S.-Russian relations and international security for Washington to see Russia through monochromatic glasses, either dark or bright. Like the overly optimistic assessments of Russia's progress toward democracy and capitalism in the 1990s, the rosy views of a strategic partnership with the United States may produce a new round of disappointment and disdain. On the other hand, excessively pessimistic or alarmist views of Russia's supposedly failed democratization, innate authoritarians, and imperialism can undermine Russian-American cooperation and close off opportunities to influence Russia's political and social evolution.[50] To avoid falling into the overreaction trap once more, we must have a clear, nuanced, and balanced view of Russia.

Russia is a kaleidoscope of interacting positive and negative trends. These must be detected and sorted out by way of objective analysis free of political science preconceptions, historical simplifications, and Russophobic prejudices. The contradictory trends in this sprawling country cannot be captured by crude stereotypes or rigid transition paradigms. Russia, like many other states, is stuck somewhere between a predominantly authoritarian and predominantly democratic order. It can be moving in two directions at once in different spheres, creating a hodge-podge of trends that is difficult to understand, much less model. Thus, Moscow's economic strategy involves greater openness to Western investment and deeper integration into the global economy, but the government's prosecution of critics and scientists for selling classified documents has discouraged open discussion and contacts with foreign colleagues. Russia

has adopted a new legal code with many amendments modeled on practices in the United States and Western Europe, yet Putin's vision of a "dictatorship of law" simultaneously entails moving away from Western conceptions of liberty and justice. Important electoral reforms have been implemented, but political parties have been stagnating or losing adherents. Russian judges have gained greater independence, but that independence has not dramatically improved the criminal justice system.[51] Not only have Putin's federal reforms re-centralized power in Moscow, they are also forcing the regions to rescind many of their undemocratic laws.[52] Given such complicated and surprising developments, Western analysts must consciously refrain from extrapolating disappointment over negative trends in one area onto the Russian government or people as a whole.

The pessimists and the optimists share a presumption that Russia's historically determined fate or natural evolutionary endpoint can be seen in advance. The first step in escaping the bipolar swings in American views of Russia is to abandon prophetic pretensions and jettison teleological hubris. Instead of focusing on forecasting the future and constructing (or tinkering with) abstract paradigms, students of post-communist Russia should concentrate on careful empirical study of developments and dynamics in its politics, business, culture, and society. Scholars should spend more time investigating what is really happening and less time judging how the transition measures up according to some predetermined finish line.

While Russophobic essentialists write as if cultural prerequisites were the key, if not sole, determinant for the development of democracy and markets, transitologists tend to eschew culture as an explanatory factor. Both are wrong. Cultural values are one of several important elements facilitating or obstructing democratic and market development. Contrary to the assumptions of Russophobes in the West and Slavophile nationalists in Russia, cultures are not monolithic. They are malleable under the influence of external forces, especially in the era of globalization. This does not mean that Americans can easily complete the cultural transformation and democratization of Russia by launching cold war–style propaganda programs to exploit the presumed gap between the supposedly pro-American Russian people and the obdurate Russian government. It does mean that Western (especially American) culture has strongly affected post-Soviet Russia, though often not in the ways or to the extent Westerners might wish.

Although propaganda campaigns based on an adversarial relationship to the Russian government are unlikely to be very successful (and may actually backfire), there are many ways that Westerners might exert a modest positive influence on Russia's development. This is not the place for a full set of proposals, but a few examples of practical initiatives can be mentioned. While being humbly cognizant of financial misconduct in Western businesses and governments, Western advisers (as Larry Diamond has suggested) can encourage and support the establishment and strengthening of corruption watchdog bodies in Russia, such as an Independent Counter-Corruption Commission and the Audit Chamber.[53] Western non-governmental organizations can promote the establishment of human rights ombudsmen in each of Russia's regions (at present they are set up in perhaps one-third of the regions) and the expansion of their powers so that they can more effectively investigate complaints regarding violations of press freedom and national minority rights.

Finally, the United States and American corporations can expand their cooperation in the development of energy resources and economic infrastructure in Siberia and the Far East, eventually including a trans-Bering rail tunnel for passenger and oil transport. This would simultaneously boost Russia's economic growth, earn the revenue its government needs for projects such as the modernization of schools and hospitals, and reduce Western dependence on energy resources from Arab and Muslim states.[54] To reinforce this strategy, Russia can be brought into the International Energy Association, and the IEA can be reformed to function as a counter to the OPEC cartel, as Ira Strauss has proposed.[55]

These prescriptions do not presume that Russia is already an ally because of Putin's demonstrated support for the United States in the war against Islamic terrorists. They do suggest some ways to assist the evolution of Russia's domestic institutions and to facilitate a closer international partnership. They should be complemented by other measures, such as gradually deepening Russia's relationship with NATO and its integration into the World Trade Organization, the Asia-Pacific Economic Community, and the Group of Eight (the Group of Seven since Russia's inclusion) to take advantage of the new opening for Russian-Western relations. Russian involvement in these international institutions will ease changes in its political culture, economy, and strategic thinking that will in turn alleviate Western fears and undermine Western stereotypes. Thus, a more stable basis for a Russian-American partnership can be established.

# Notes

1. See, for example, James Billington, *Russia Transformed—Breakthrough to Hope: Moscow, August 1991* (New York: Free Press, 1992).

2. For an insightful critique of transitology's democratic teleology, see Thomas Carothers, "The End of the Transition Paradigm," *Journal of Democracy* 13, no. 1 (winter 2002): 3–21.

3. M. Steven Fish, *Democracy from Scratch: Opposition and Regime in the New Russian Revolution* (Princeton, NJ: Princeton University Press, 1995), p. 3. For Fish's critique of transitology, see idem, "Postcommunist Subversion: Social Science and Democratization in East Europe and Russia," *Slavic Review* 58, no. 4 (winter 1999): 798.

4. The *apparat* comprises the bureaucratic institutions and personnel of the Communist Party, as opposed to state institutions. Its personnel were known as *apparatchiki.*

5. On the relatively small proportion of the population that participated in the urban resistance, see, for example, Victoria Bonnell, Ann Cooper, and Gregory Freidin, eds., *Russia at the Barricades: Eyewitness Accounts of the August 1991 Coup* (Armonk, NY: M. E. Sharpe, 1994), pp. 13–14, 19.

6. The "power ministries" include the Ministry of Defense, the Ministry of Internal Affairs, and the KGB.

7. The *nomenklatura* were the elite members of the Communist Party, individuals who received privileges and promotions based on their rank.

8. See Gordon M. Hahn, *Russia's Revolution from Above, 1985–2000: Reform, Transition, and Revolution in the Fall of the Soviet Communist Regime* (New Brunswick, NJ: Transaction, 2002). For an illustration of the younger elites' approach to a revolution from above, see Egor Gaidar, *Dni porazhenii i pobed* (Days of Defeat and Victory) (Moscow: Vagrius, 1996).

9. On the politics of this grand compromise, see Gordon M. Hahn, "Opposition Politics in Russia," *Europe-Asia Studies* 46, no. 2 (1994): 305–35.

10. On the privatization scams, see Chrystia Freeland, *Sale of the Century: Russia's Wild Ride from Communism to Capitalism* (New York: Crown, 2000) and Janine Wedel, *Collision and Collusion: The Strange Case of Western Aid to Eastern Europe, 1989–1998* (New York: St. Martin's Press, 1998).

11. See Hahn, *Russia's Revolution from Above,* chaps. 10 and 11.

12. Larry Diamond and Marc Plattner, eds., *Consolidating the Third Wave of Democracies* (Baltimore: Johns Hopkins University Press, 1997).

13. Leon Aron, *Yeltsin: A Revolutionary Life* (New York: St. Martin's Press, 2000).

14. See Freeland, *Sale of the Century;* Paul Klebnikov, *Godfather of the Kremlin: Boris Berezovsky and the Looting of Russia* (New York: Harcourt, 2000).

15. Anders Åslund, *Building Capitalism: The Transformation of the Soviet Bloc* (New York: Cambridge University Press, 2001); Martin Malia, *Russia Under Western Eyes: From the Bronze Horseman to the Lenin Mausoleum* (Cambridge, MA: Belknap Press, 1999). On the imperative of modernization, see Jerry Hough, *Democratization and Revolution in the USSR, 1985–1991* (Washington, DC: Brookings Institution Press, 1997).

16. See *Novoe Osvoenie Sibiri i Dal'nego Vostoka* (Reclaiming Siberia and the Far East) (Moscow: Sovet po vneshnei i oboronnoi politike, 2002).

17. Soveta Voennoi i oboronnoi politike, *Rossiskaia vneshniaia politika perede vyzovami XXI veka* (Russian Foreign Policy Challenges for the 21st Century), esp. chap. 1, "Mir Vokrug Rossii" (The World Around Russia) (www.svop.tu/yuka/832.shtml); Aleksandr Dugin, *Osovy geopolitiki* (The Fundamentals of Geopolitics) (Moscow, 1997); A. S. Panarin, *History's Revenge* (Revansh istorii) (Moscow: Logos, 1998).

18. Bruce Clark, *An Empire's New Clothes: The End of Russia's Liberal Dream* (London: Vintage, 1995), esp. pp. 1, 93–94; Samuel Huntington, *The Clash of Civilizations and the Remaking of World Order* (New York: Simon & Schuster, 1996), esp. pp. 29, 142; Matthew Brzezinski, *Ca-*

*sino Moscow: A Tale of Greed and Adventure on Capitalism's Wildest Frontier* (New York: Free Press, 2001), esp. pp. 311, 268, 186. Matthew is a nephew of former U.S. national security advisor Zbigniew Brzezinski.

19. See, for example, Freeland, *Sale of the Century,* pp. 8, 22, 171. Ironically, the 1998 devaluation of the ruble that led many to give up on the dream of Russian capitalism actually helped to pave the way for a return to economic growth by the end of the century.

20. See Richard Pipes, "Russia's Past, Russia's Future," *Commentary* 101, no. 6 (June 1996): 30–38, esp. p. 32; Jonathan Steele, *Eternal Russia: Yeltsin, Gorbachev, and the Mirage of Democracy* (Cambridge: Harvard University Press, 1995); Clark, *Empire's New Clothes.*

21. Astrid S. Tuminez, "Russian Nationalism and the National Interest in Russian Foreign Policy," in *The Sources of Russian Foreign Policy After the Cold War,* ed. Celeste A. Wallander (Boulder, CO: Westview, 1996), p. 53.

22. Gordon M. Hahn, "Russia's Polarized Political Spectrum," *Problems of Post-Communism* 43, no. 3 (May/June 1996): 19.

23. Alessandra Stanley, "A Man Who Rode a Tank Became the Man on Horseback," *New York Times* (January 2, 2000): A3; see also Alison Smale, "Russia's Leaders Are Different. It's the People Who Are the Same," *New York Times* (January 6, 2002): A5.

24. See Nicolai Petro, *The Rebirth of Russian Democracy: An Interpretation of Political Culture* (Cambridge: Harvard University Press, 1995); V. V. Leontovich, *Istoriia Liberalizma v Rossii, 1762–1914* (A History of Liberalism in Russia, 1762–1914) (Moscow: Russkii Put, 1995).

25. For George F. Kennan's similar critique of Custine, see David S. Foglesong, "Roots of 'Liberation': American Images of the Future of Russia During the Early Cold War, 1948–1953," *International History Review* 21, no. 1 (March 1999): 63.

26. Ellen Carnaghan, "Thinking About Democracy: Interviews with Russian Citizens," *Slavic Review* 60, no. 2 (summer 2001): 336–67.

27. Timothy J. Colton and Michael McFaul, "Are Russians Undemocratic?" Carnegie Endowment for International Peace, Russian and Eurasian Program: Russian Domestic Politics Project, Working Paper No. 20, June 2001.

28. See the summary of the results of surveys conducted by the Russian Institute for Comprehensive Social Research, the Russian Independent Institute for Social and National problems, and Germany's Ebert Foundation, in Mikhail Gorshkov, Natalia Tikhonova, and Vladimir Petukhov, "Tak dal'she zhit' mozhno" (To Live This Way Anymore Is Impossible) *Obschaia gazeta,* no. 10 (March 7, 2002).

29. Gordon M. Hahn, "Growing Middle Class Reinforces Civil Society," *Russia Journal* 5, no. 5. (April 26–May 2, 2002): 10.

30. *New York Times* (June 29, 2002).

31. Mortimer B. Zuckerman, "A Great Step Backward," *U.S. News & World Report* (October 9, 2000); Stephen Blank and Theodore Karasik, "'Reforms' That Hark Back to Stalinist Times," *Los Angeles Times* (July 20, 2000).

32. William Safire, "Reading Putin's Mind," *New York Times* (July 23, 2001): A27 and (December 10, 2001): A29.

33. Their refusal was a consequence of the tripartite regime split noted earlier. On the KGB's behavior during the coup, see, for example, Bonnell, Cooper, and Freidin, *Russia at the Barricades,* pp. 18–19; Hahn, *Russia's Revolution from Above,* pp. 429–31.

34. Natalia Govorkian, Natalia Timakova, and Andrei Kolesnikov, *Ot pervogo litsa: razgovory s Vladimirom Putinym* (In the First Person: Conversations with Vladimir Putin) (Moscow: Vagrius, 2000), p. 61.

35. Iu. S. Bortsov, *Vladimir Putin* (Rostov: Feniks, 2001), p. 83.

36. Govorkian, Timakova, and Kolesnikov, *Ot pervogo litsa,* pp. 128–29.

37. Eric Shiraev and Vladislav Zubok, *Anti-Americanism in Russia: From Stalin to Putin* (New York: Palgrave, 2000), pp. 1, 18, 38, 43.

38. Ibid., pp. 145–47.

39. *Vremia MN* (October 26, 2001). See the VTsIOM survey showing an ambivalent attitude toward the United States in *Izvestiia* (September 28, 2001).

40. A survey conducted in May 2002 by the ROMIR agency found that 29 percent of Russians considered the United States "friendly," 28 percent thought it was "neutral," and 40 percent characterized it as "hostile." *San Jose Mercury News* (May 24, 2002): 10.

41. Govorkian, Timakova, and Kolesnikov, *Ot pervogo litsa,* pp. 156, 160.

42. For a classic reflection of this dynamic among Russia's Eurasianists, see Panarin, *History's Revenge.*

43. S. Frederick Starr, "Russia's Ominous Afghan Gambit," *Wall Street Journal* (December 11, 2001): 8; Glen Howard, "Moscow's Bid for Influence in Afghanistan: The Kiss of Death of a Broad-Based Government," *Central Asia–Caucasus Analyst* (November 21, 2001) (www.cacianalyst.org).

44. George Friedman, "The Geopolitical Price of War," (October 2, 2001) (www.Stratfor.com).

45. William E. Odom, "Realism About Russia," *National Interest,* no. 65 (fall 2001): 56–67.

46. Quoted in Michael Wines, "In Czar Peter's Capital, Putin Is Not a Great," *New York Times* (May 20, 2002): A7.

47. Jeffrey Tayler, "Russia Is Finished," *Atlantic Monthly* 287, no. 5 (May 2001): 35–52.

48. *New York Times* (December 16, 2001): A4.

49. At the end of the 1999 NATO campaign in Kosovo, Russian troops rushed to occupy the Pristina airport ahead of NATO forces, briefly triggering an international incident.

50. See, for example, Tayler, "Russia Is Finished."

51. See Todd Foglesong, "Lost in Translation: The Lessons of Russian Judicial Reform," (Carnegie Endowment for International Peace January 12, 2002); Peter H. Solomon and Todd S. Foglesong, *Courts and Transition in Russia: The Challenge of Judicial Reform* (Boulder, CO: Westview, 2000).

52. See Gordon M. Hahn, "Putin's Federal Reforms and De-mocratization in the Regions," *Russia Journal* 5, no. 22 (June 14–20, 2002); idem, "The Past, Present, and Future of Russia's Federal State," *Demokratizatsiya* (fall 2002): forthcoming.

53. Larry Diamond, "Winning the New Cold War on Terror-ism: The Democratic-Governance Imperative," Institute for Global Democracy, Policy Paper No. 1 (March 2002), p. 11.

54. For some specifics, see Gordon M. Hahn, "Russia's Far East and U.S. National Security," *Russia Journal* 5, no. 24 (June 29–July 4, 2002): 11; Ronald R. Kotas, "The Linking of Two Great Continents By Rail Connections under the Bering Straits," *New Electric Railway Journal,* Free Con-gress Foundation Online (www.trolleycar.org/observations/kotas010905.htm).

55. Ira Strauss, "How to Secure Russia's Place as an Oil Ally," *Russia Journal* 4, no. 47 (November 30–December 6, 2001): 12.

DAVID FOGLESONG, an associate professor of history at Rutgers University, is completing a book on American dreams of remaking Russia. GORDON M. HAHN, a visiting scholar at Stanford Universi-ty's Hoover Institution and political analyst for the *Russia Journal,* is the author of *Russia's Revolution from Above, 1985–2000* (2002).

From *Problems of Post-Communism,* Vol. 49, No. 6, November/December 2002, pp. 3-15. © 2002 by M.E. Sharpe, Inc. Reprinted by permission.

# Deepening Russian Democracy

## *Progress and Pitfalls in Putin's Government*

### GRAHAM ALLISON

In December 1991, the Soviet Union ceased to exist. In its place, a newly independent Russian democracy was born, alongside 14 other republics. The 10th anniversary of that momentous event provides a fitting occasion to pause and take stock, to consider how much has been accomplished and how much remains to be done. It is also an opportunity for advocates and students of democratization to reflect on the Russian case, as well as other cases across the former Soviet Union and Eastern Europe. It is an opportunity to reassess our conceptualization of Western-assisted democratization. This essay provides a sketch of a new conceptual framework for analyzing democratization in terms of institutional developments. Against that backdrop, I offer a brief assessment of Russia's democratic development over the past decade.

> **The path of democratization resembles stairs; each step forward provides a foundation from which a state can move forward or slide back. Once some steps toward democracy are taken, it becomes much harder to reverse the process.**

Although the last decades of the 20th century witnessed a fast march to democracy in Eastern and Central Europe, they also revealed powerful tendencies toward greater central authority in the countries of the former Soviet Union, including Russia. This dynamic is apparent in leaders who believe they are undertaking great tasks in rebuilding and modernizing their countries and who seek to mobilize cooperation and support, not criticism and dissent. Public demands for both order and a higher standard of living create an environment that allows for backsliding toward centralized authority and even authoritarianism. It is no accident that such ideas resonate with leaders whose formative political experiences occurred in communist party structures.

Despite romantic enthusiasm and expectations to the contrary, democratization is neither linear nor quick. Consolidation of democracy occurs across several dimensions both in the economy and in the society. The process advances in fits and starts. The path of democratization resembles stairs; each step forward provides a foundation from which a state can move forward or slide back. Once some steps toward democracy are taken, it becomes much harder to reverse the process. Therefore, in striving to deepen democracy in transitional states, the primary challenge is to think strategically about the types of institutions, sources of power, and forms of behavior that can work to encourage early democratic steps and secure them against countervailing pressure. These institutional and behavioral pillars constitute, in effect, barriers against backsliding into authoritarianism.

## *Barriers to Backsliding*

We need a working definition of democracy. While Robert Dahl and others have taught us how complex a concept democracy is, for this article's purpose we will take Joseph Schumpeter's definition of democracy as our starting point. Democracy is a political system that provides for (1) meaningful and extensive competition among individuals and organized groups (especially political parties) for all effective positions of government power at regular intervals, excluding the use of force; (2) a "highly inclusive" level of political participation in the selection of leaders and policies, at least through regular and fair elections, so that no major social group is excluded; and (3) a level of civil and political liberties—freedom of expression, freedom of the press, freedom of association—sufficient to ensure the integrity of political competition and participation. Democracies survive because of social

# ONE DECADE LATER

## Civil Development

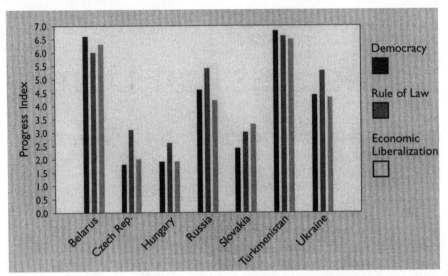

This figure measures the progress of seven former members of the Soviet bloc using three indicators of democratic progress as of October 2000. Measured on a seven-point scale determined by Freedom House, countries that exhibit greater progress are assigned lower scores: a score of one indicates the highest level of progress and a score of seven indicates the lowest level of progress.

Freedom House *Nations in Transit Report 2001* www.freedomhouse.org

## Democracy and Freedom

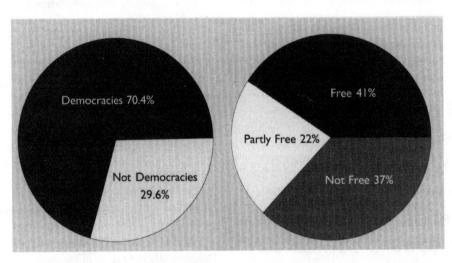

These two figures represent the pervasiveness of democracy (left) and the level of freedom (right) as percentages of the 27 countries studied in Central and Eastern Europe and the former Soviet Union. Ten years after the dissolution of the Soviet Union, democracy dominates the region with more than 70 percent prevalence, but the pervasiveness of freedom remains tenuous, with 10 out of 27 nations deemed not free, and 11 out of 27 nations reported free.

Freedom House *Nations in Transit Report 2001* www.freedomhouse.org

forces that can withstand inevitable pressures toward back-sliding.

One of the most significant institutional pillars of democracy is the pluralization of economic power, meaning that centers of economic power are independent of the state. The more pluralistic the ownership of sources of finance and what Karl Marx called the "means of production" in a country, the more widely power is dispersed. Economic pluralization provides "substruc-

ture" for political democratization. The middle class operates in much the same way. As Dahl has noted, the middle class typically seeks education, autonomy, personal freedom, property rights, the rule of law, and participation in government. Democratization also relies significantly on a nation's integration into the global economy. Trade depends on compliance with international standards, including World Trade Organization requirements for openness and transparency, which bolster democracy. At the private level, adopting internationally accepted standards for corporate governance, accounting, transparency, and ownership normalizes economic life and reinforces democratic proclivities.

The freedom of press, one of the hallmarks of democracy, provides another check on the tendency to centralize power. To the extent that mass media is independent of state influence (legally, financially, and professionally), citizens have access to better information about their society. Politicians of all stripes, including opposition figures, are more able to find outlets for their political views. A strong independent press also has a vested interest in resisting state attempts to control the mass media, making it a stalwart barrier to backsliding. As Thomas Jefferson once observed, "Were it left to me to decide whether we should have a government without newspapers or newspapers without a government, I should not hesitate a moment to prefer the latter."

The media should also be pluralistic. If the media is not only independent but plural, competition is assured. The more real competition there is among media outlets, the more consumers will be able to choose those sources of information that provide them with the best, most accurate information. For the media to function optimally, a professional journalistic community guided by principles of professional ethics is also required. Strong traditions of journalistic ethics can constrain, or at least help identify and isolate, those in the media who would use their power to undermine democratic norms.

An independent and accessible judiciary is another tried-and-true check on authoritarian power. The judicial branch must be capable of enforcing (and have incentive to fairly interpret) laws guaranteeing the rights and freedoms that undergird democracy. Supremacy of law over the will of individual authorities is among the most powerful protections of pluralism. Sustainable democracy must also include a well developed and independent legal profession. When lawyers actually see law as the basis of their activity and are held accountable to an independent body (like the American Bar Association), that ensures some degree of adherence to ethical standards, rights are then more likely to be protected, and laws are more likely to be observed.

Democracy thrives best when its processes are stimulated by agents for political activism and accountability. One can conceive of democracy without political parties, as the crafters of the US Constitution did. But in practice, parties play an essential role. They organize choice, thereby providing an important element of stability, and they play a large role in helping candidates communicate their views to voters and gain the political experience necessary to compete effectively. While many in the United States see them as obstacles to effective democracy, "special interests" nonetheless have a vested interest in resisting authoritarian encroachments on their autonomy. Special interests also generally have a basis in power—including the potential to mobilize people (trade unions) or resources (industry lobbies) as part of this resistance. Nongovernmental organizations (NGOs) represent an increasingly important form of activism and come in many forms. Some are directly involved in supporting democracy or protecting the environment. Others

bring citizens together to solve problems that affect their daily lives. The stronger these organizations are in a society, the more difficult it is to roll back democratic processes.

At the foundational level, a constitutional framework incorporating institutionalized checks and balances is essential for democracy. In theory, constitutions establish agreed-upon, fundamental ground rules, preventing any one branch from usurping the authority of other basic institutions. Russia's Constitution of 1993 created a semi-presidential system with separate branches of power but with overwhelming authority concentrated in the hands of the president. A federal-regional distinction in government also checks backsliding. To the extent that the federal government does not have direct control over who occupies local government posts, these local organs will have a direct interest in resisting the federal government's attempts to take away their autonomy. Democracies are strongest, therefore, when officials at all levels are elected and are not overly dependent on central governments for financing their activity. An important related threat comes from the central military command, which is a ready-made nondemocratic source of power that would-be authoritarians can wield to roll back democracy. Civilian institutions that restrain the autonomous activity of the military make an anti-democratic coup or other forms of coercion less likely.

# Russian President Vladimir Putin's actions show signs of authoritarian restoration, but those looking for evidence of democratic state-building in Russia find ample support for their thesis as well.

Even forces external to the country can prevent backsliding. The internalization of democratic values and human rights is a good example. Citizens' beliefs about their basic rights—freedom of speech, freedom of assembly, freedom of religion, freedom from arbitrary arrest, freedom of movement, and other basic liberties—are enshrined in the Russian Constitution. More importantly, these values have taken root in Russians' hearts and minds. To the extent that citizens believe they actually possess these rights and freedoms, they will resist infringements upon them.

Former observers of the Soviet Union continue to be amazed by the extent to which Russian citizens have embraced the "democratic presumption," the idea that the best way to determine who should govern is to hold an open, competitive election. Over the past decade, thousands of leaders from the district and city council level to the president have been chosen through direct, competitive elections. The more widespread and deeply rooted the idea of being free in a democratic society, the more difficult it becomes to deny people such rights.

## *Russian Democratization*

With these barriers to backsliding as our framework, how can we assess the state of democracy in Russia today? Should we consider Russia's progress since the days of the Soviet Union, or should we evaluate Russia's failure to meet the standards of established democracies? Perceptions and misperceptions about the status of Russia's political development have varied widely over time. Russian President Vladimir Putin's actions show signs of authoritarian restoration, but those looking for evidence of democratic state-building in Russia find ample support for their thesis as well.

Russia continues to be what I have called "a kaleidoscope of contradictions." There have been extraordinary—indeed, almost inconceivable—changes in Russia since the Soviet period. In the communist system, citizens had no alternatives to the Communist Party, no free press, no free speech, no freedom of religion, and no freedom of movement. Buying and selling without government permission was a crime; opening a business was impossible. Today, Russians can think, speak, worship, teach, buy, sell, and travel more freely than was imaginable during the Soviet period.

In assessing Russia's success at democratization and gaining a deeper understanding of its contradictions, we are confronted with the challenge of not only choosing the appropriate measure, but also of weighing each properly. As Jorgen Elklit rightly pointed out in his comparative analysis of electoral democracy, "Is the Degree of Electoral Democracy Measurable?" comparative studies of political development and democratization are often too quantitative in focus, omitting a thorough analysis of the influence of political institutions on democratization.

The Freedom House survey "Nations in Transit" rates 27 post-communist states on a comparative basis in three categories: democratization, rule of law, and economic liberalization. Each of these categories has sub-areas that include more concrete factors for rating, such as civil society; independent media; constitutional, legislative, and judicial frameworks; and macroeconomic policy. Based on its scores, a state is classified as a consolidated democracy, a transitional government, or a consolidated autocracy. According to the 2001 survey results, a tendency toward authoritarianism is developing in the former Soviet Union, with particularly negative developments in Russia's democratization indicators. Russia falls into the Freedom House category of "transitional government," with a democratization score of 4.63, compared to an autocratic low of 7. Compared with other former Soviet states, Russia ranked above only Azerbaijan and the Central Asian countries.

Other studies of democratizing practices and institutions continue to express similar concern over Putin's consolidation of vertical power in Russia, the persistence of human rights violations (particularly abuses during Russia's campaign in Chechnya), the stifling of independent media, electoral irregularities, and the lack of adherence to internationally accepted economic and political norms. Russia under Putin is consistently coming up short according to these benchmarks.

Fewer studies have been conducted evaluating the adoption of democratic ideas by leaders and citizens, which, as noted above, acts as a barrier to authoritarian backsliding and as a measure of democratization. The most noteworthy study, "Are Russians Undemocratic?" was conducted by Timothy Colton and Michael McFaul. They argue that although the current political system in Russia is an illiberal democracy and that its limitations are not caused or reinforced by popular attitudes toward democracy. According to their data, many Russian citizens recognize the difference between the democracy practiced in Russia and the ideal of democracy that Russia has not yet achieved. Furthermore, Colton and McFaul conclude that the Russian case exhibits a dynamic deviation from the norm of top-down democratization, noting that the people have assimilated democratic values faster than the elite have built democratic institutions.

Although concerns about Russia's current stage in the democratization process and the role played by Putin are valid, it is necessary to maintain a balanced perspective on the complex and multifaceted developments that have taken place in Russia in the two years since Putin took office. The fundamental dilemma is how to distinguish between, on the one hand, actions of the Putin government that legitimately strengthen the state in ways that are necessary for a successful democracy and market economy and, on the other hand, actions that may be precursors to a new authoritarianism. The crackdowns against influential media oligarchs like Vladimir Gusinsky and Boris Berezovsky for tax evasion and fraud have, ironically, served simultaneously to enforce laws equally without deference to established oligarchs and to undermine powerful and vocal critics of Putin's government. The latter interpretation finds particular resonance in a society with a long history of forbidding criticism against authority.

## *Putin's Performance*

Since he took office, Putin has undoubtedly improved the effectiveness of the Russian government in ways that are both necessary and beneficial. A government that cannot fulfill its essential functions—protecting citizens, enforcing laws, and collecting taxes—has no legitimacy to rule. Moreover, the collapse of the Russian state would have dire consequences for Russians' lives and liberties, as well as for the safety of the rest of the world. But strengthening the state (and particularly state security and law enforcement structures) at the expense of other equally important institutions in society can have dangerous consequences. Invigorating organizations such as the FSB (the domestic successor to the KGB) and the General Prosecutor threatens democracy and weakens organizations that derive their authority directly from citizen members, such as NGOs and political parties. The underlying dilemma is reflected in political theory: a government strong enough to perform its essential functions, such as ensuring citizens' freedom, is also strong enough to abuse those same rights.

Consider the actions of the Putin government during the past two years. Upon taking office, Putin announced that the central task of his government would be to strengthen the Russian state. To that end, he has undertaken measures both to "reinvent government" and to recentralize power. Shortly after he became acting president, Putin announced a campaign against corruption and his determination to separate the financial oligarchs from the political decision-making process. While skeptics argued that enforcement of the law would not extend to friends of the Kremlin, Berezovsky, Abramovich, and others have found themselves subject to investigations and have lost a substantial part of their former political clout. Putin ended 2001 with investigation into corruption among his own ranks, firing one of Russia's most notorious officials, Railways Minister Nikolai Aksenenko.

The Putin government is composed of the most consistently pro-reform cabinet of ministers Russia has had since the early 1990s. It has begun to implement a plan to revive and reconstruct the Russian economy that includes simplifying and slashing taxes; balancing the budget by cutting expenditures and subsidies; sustaining low inflation through prudent monetary policy; reversing capital flight; attracting international investment by creating a stable, predictable rule of law (especially enforceable contracts and protection for shareholders); renegotiating, reducing, and repaying external debt; and guaranteeing property rights. These measures, combined with the effects of the 1998 devaluation and the increases in oil prices in 2000, make Russia the fastest-growing economy in the world in the past two years with a gross domestic product growth rate of 8.4 percent in 2000 and 5 percent in 2001. Personal income has risen at almost twice these rates, moving hundreds of thousands of citizens into an emerging middle class.

While recentralizing power in the Russian Federation, Putin has insisted that Russia's 89 regions must have a "single constitutional, legal, and economic framework." In contrast to former President Boris Yeltsin, who invited Russia's 89 governors to "take all the sovereignty you can swallow," Putin has created a superstructure of seven administrative districts—each with a newly empowered presidential representative—in order to reimpose the vertical chain of power. He has also passed legislation to reduce the governors' influence, eliminating their seats in the upper house of the legislature and allowing for their dismissal by the president. The pro-Putin Duma has made significant strides in strengthening the rule of law as well, passing comprehensive judicial reforms in 2001 that aim to strengthen the judiciary and bolster its independence.

However, some of the most liberal Russian reformers, such as Duma member and Yabloko political party head Grigory Yavlinsky, assess recent Russian democratization less positively. According to Yavlinsky, the current system in Russia is becoming a "managed" or "controlled" democracy, in which democratic institutions exist but are adjusted as necessary by those in power in order to achieve desired needs and goals.

We thus return to the proverbial question: is the glass half full or half empty? Encroachments on the free press under Putin's administration are a genuine cause for concern. Since Putin came to power, the federal government has managed to take control over all national television stations, with the elimination of TV-6, the last independent national network, as the most recent example. Institutionalized checks and balances have not received due attention under Putin's plans to "strengthen the state," nor have transparency and accountability. Local and regional governments, though less powerful than before, have not become more democratic. And though the democratic presumption has become more widespread, civic culture remains underdeveloped. Human rights in Chechnya, meanwhile, continue to deteriorate. It remains to be seen whether sufficient democratic infrastructure exists to avoid backsliding into authoritarianism.

---

GRAHAM ALLISON is Douglas Dillon Professor of Government and Director of the Belfer Center for Science and International Affairs at the John F. Kennedy School of Government, Harvard University.

# UNIT 4
# Political Diversity in the Developing World

## Unit Selections

## Key Points to Consider

- What have developing countries in common, and how are they diverse? How do explanations of Third World poverty and slow development differ in assigning responsibility for these conditions to external (foreign) and internal (domestic) factors?

- What is dependency theory, and why has it had so much appeal, especially in Latin America? How do you explain the current wave of market-oriented reforms? How could Mexico's PRI hold on to office so long, and why did it finally fall from power?

- Why do economic development and representative government run into such difficulties in most of Latin America and much of Africa? What are some of the major political, economic, and social problems that South Africa still has to face?

- How do you explain China's relative success in turning toward market reforms, as compared to the Soviet Union?

 **Links: www.dushkin.com/online/**
These sites are annotated in the World Wide Web pages.

**Africa News Online**
*http://www.africanews.org*
**ArabNet**
*http://www.arab.net*
**ASEAN Web**
*http://www.asean.or.id/*
**Inside China Today**
*http://www.insidechina.com*
**InterAction**
*http://www.interaction.org*
**Organization for Economic Cooperation and Development**
*http://www.oecd.org*
**Sun SITE Singapore**
*http://sunsite.nus.edu.sg/noframe.html*

Until recently, the Third World was a widely used umbrella term for a disparate group of states that are now more frequently called the developing countries. Their most important shared characteristic may well be that these countries have *not* become relatively modern industrial societies.

Most of these developing nations also share the problems of poverty and, now less frequently, rapid population growth. It is very important to keep in mind that the developing countries vary tremendously in their sociocultural and political characteristics. Some of them have representative systems of government, and a few of these, such as India, even have an impressive record of political stability. Closer examination will reveal that the avowed determination of leaders to improve their societies is frequently less significant than their determination to maintain and expand their own power and privilege.

In recent years, market-oriented development has gained in favor in many countries that previously subscribed to some version of heavy state regulation or socialist planning of the economy. The renewed interest in markets resembles a strategic policy shift that has also occurred in former Communist-ruled nations or the more advanced industrial countries. It usually represents a pragmatic acceptance of a "mixed economy" rather than a doctrinaire espousal of laissez-faire capitalism.

In studying the attempts by developing countries to create institutions and policies that will promote their socioeconomic development, it is important not to leave out the international context. In the recent past, the political and intellectual leaders of these countries have often drawn upon some version of what is called *dependency theory* to explain their plight, sometimes combining it with demands for special treatment or compensation from the industrial world. In some of its forms, dependency theory is itself an outgrowth of the Marxist or Leninist theory of imperialism, according to which advanced capitalist countries have established exploitative relationships with the weaker economic systems of the less developed world. The focus of such theories has often been on alleged external reasons for a country's failure to generate self-sustained growth. They differ strikingly from explanations that give greater emphasis to a country's internal obstacles to development (whether sociocultural, political, environmental, or a combination of these). The theories themselves are likely to provide the intellectual basis for strikingly different policy conclusions and development strategies.

The debate has had some tangible consequences in recent years. It now appears that dependency theory, at least in its simplest and most direct form, has lost intellectual and political support. Instead of serving as an explanatory paradigm, it is now more frequently encountered as part of more pluralist explanations of lagging development that recognize the tangled complexity of both internal and external factors likely to affect economic growth and change. There is much to be said for middle-range theory that pays greater attention to the contextual or situational aspects of each case of development, for multivariable explanations seem preferable to single-cause ones.

Sometimes called the Group of 77, but eventually consisting of some 120 countries, the developing states used to link themselves together in the United Nations to promote the interests they seemed to have in common. They focused on promoting changes designed to improve their relative commercial position vis-a-vis the affluent industrialized nations of the North. It would be a mistake to assume that there must necessarily be an essential identity of interest among these countries or that they tend to pursue complementary foreign policies.

Outside the United Nations, some of these same countries have occasionally tried to increase and control the price of industrially important primary exports through the building of cartel agreements among themselves. The result has sometimes been detrimental to other developing nations. The most successful of these cartels, the Organization of Petroleum Exporting Countries (OPEC), was established in 1973 and held sway for almost a decade. Its cohesion eventually eroded, resulting in drastic reductions in oil prices. While this latter development was welcomed in the oil-importing industrial world as well as in many developing countries, it left some oil-producing nations, such as Mexico, in economic disarray for a while. Moreover, the need to find outlets for the petrodollars, which had been deposited by some oil producers in Western banks during the period of cartel-induced high prices, led some financial institutions to make huge, often ill-considered loans to many developing nations.

Some of the poorer oil-producing nations recaptured a degree of economic leverage at the turn of the new century. In a reduced form, the situation resembled a déja vu, as global energy consumption increased and the OPEC countries proved willing and able, at least for a while, to return to a coordinated policy of limiting the production and hence the supply of petroleum. As a result, energy prices rose rapidly, and the advanced industrial nations were once again made aware of their economic vulnerability, stemming from a dependence on a regular flow of relatively low-priced oil.

The problems of poverty, hunger, and malnutrition in much of the developing world are socially and politically explosive. In their fear of revolution and their opposition to meaningful reform, the privileged classes have often resorted to brutal repression as a means of preserving a status quo favorable to themselves. In Latin America, this led to a politicalization during the 1970s of many lay persons and clergy of the Roman Catholic Church, who demanded social reform in the name of what was called *liberation theology*. For them, this variant of dependency theory filled a very practical ideological function by providing a relatively simple analytical and moral explanation of a complex reality. It also gave some strategic guidance for political activists who were determined to change this state of affairs. Like dependency theory, liberation theology today appears to have been effectively absorbed into more pluralist outlooks and pragmatic strategies for socioeconomic development.

The collapse of Communist rule in Europe has had a profound impact on the ideological explanation of the developing world's poverty and on the resulting strategies to overcome it. The Soviet model of modernization now appears to offer very little of practical value. The fact that even the Communists who remain in power in China have been willing to experiment widely with market reforms, including the private profit motive, has added to the general discredit of the centrally planned economy.

Perhaps even more important, there seemed for a while to be a positive demonstration effect in some countries in Africa and Latin America that pursued more market-oriented strategies of development. On the whole, they appeared, at least until recently, to perform much better than some of their more statist neighbors tied to highly regulated and protected economies. This realization may help explain the intellectual journey of someone like the now-deceased Michael Manley, the former prime minister of Jamaica, who broke away from the combination of dependency theory and socialist strategies that he had once defended vigorously. During the 1980s, Manley made an intellectual U-turn as he gained a new respect for market-oriented economic approaches, without abandoning his interest in using reform politics to promote the interests of the poor. A similar political shift was taken by Fernando Henrique Cardoso, who came to embrace market economics before he became president of Brazil until the end of 2002. Another recent example is the political scientist and activist Jorge G. Castameda, who ended up calling on the Left in Latin America to abandon utopian goals and seek social reforms within "mixed" market economies. Until his resignation in 2003, he served as foreign minister of Mexico in President Fox's relatively market-friendly government.

***Latin America*** illustrates the difficulty of establishing stable pluralist democracies in many parts of the developing world. Some authors have argued that its dominant political tradition is basically authoritarian and corporatist rather than competitively pluralist. They see the region's long tradition of centralized oligarchic governments or strong man rule, whether of the Left or Right, as the result of an authoritarian "unitary" bias in the political culture. From this perspective, there would seem to be little hope for a lasting pluralist development, and the recent trend toward democratization in much of Latin America would also appear unlikely to last. Yet it is no mean accomplishment that one after the other dictatorship in the region has been replaced by an elected government. The demonstration effect of successful democratic governments in Spain and Portugal may also have been important for the Latin American countries. Finally, the negative social, economic, and political experience with authoritarian rulers would appear to be one of the strongest cards held by their democratic successors. But unless they also meet the pragmatic test ("Does it work?"), by providing evidence of social and economic progress, the new democracies in Latin America could also be in trouble shortly. They may yet turn out to have been short interludes between authoritarian regimes. Strife-torn Venezuela is a case in point. The even grimmer example of Argentina, which was one of the world's most prosperous countries at the beginning of the twentieth century, serves as a warning that both authoritarian-populist and neoliberal policy directions can end in social and political disaster. On the other hand, the new president of Brazil appears to have had a promising start. Right after winning office as a politician with left-wing credentials, he sought to calm the financial markets by announcing a policy orientation that will seek to strike a reasonable balance between equity and efficiency.

In much of Latin America there seems to be a new questioning of the turn toward a greater emphasis on market economics that replaced the traditional commitment to strategies of statist interventions. The two articles in this section deal with some dilemmas that have encouraged this shift. A basic problem is that when there has been economic growth, the benefits have not "trickled down" much. Instead, there are many real victims of the economic dislocation brought on by free market reforms.

There can be other serious problems as well, as shown in the attempt by former president Carlos Salinas of Mexico to move his country toward a more competitive form of market enterprise. His modernization strategy included Mexico's entry into the North American Free Trade Agreement (NAFTA) with the United States and Canada. In a time of enormous socioeconomic dislocations, however, Salinas showed considerable reluctance to move from an economic to a thorough political reform. Such a shift would have undermined the long-time hegemony of his own *Institutional Revolutionary Party* (PRI) and given new outlets for protest by self-perceived losers in the process. On the other hand, some observers criticized the market-oriented approach as too technocratic in its implicit assumption that economic modernization could be accomplished without a basic change of the political system. During his last year in office, Salinas was confronted by an armed peasant rebellion in the southern province of Chiapas, which gave voice to the demand for land reform and economic redistribution. Mexican criticism of Salinas intensified after he left office in December 1994 and 3 months later sought political exile abroad. Soon after, some top Mexican officials and their associates were accused of having links to drug traffickers with a sordid record of corruption and political assassination.

The successor to Salinas was elected in August 1994, in a competitive contest that was reported as not seriously distorted by fraud. The ruling party won with 51 percent of the vote. The PRI's first presidential candidate, Luis Donaldo Colosio, had been assassinated in the early part of the campaign. His place was taken by Ernesto Zedillo, an economist and former banker who fit the technocratic mold of recent Mexican leaders. As president, he continued the basic economic policies of Salinas, but Zedillo appeared far more willing to listen to demands for meaningful political reform as well. In other ways too, his governmental performance was remarkable. Shortly after he took office at the beginning of December 1994, the Mexican peso collapsed and brought the economy into disarray. A major factor was the country's huge trade deficit and the resultant loss of confidence in the peso. This setback could have paralyzed the new president. Instead, he dealt energetically and skillfully with the problem. By early 1997, the Mexican government was able to announce that it had paid back a huge relief loan provided by the United States. The overall economic prospect for the struggling country appeared to improve considerably.

The Mexican elections of July 1997 represented something of a political milestone in the country's recent history. In retrospect, they were an omen of things to come. The basic result was a major setback for the Institutional Revolutionary Party—an outcome that would have been unthinkable in earlier years. In the lower house of Congress, the two main opposition parties deprived the ruling PRI of its habitual controlling majority. They began to transform what had been regarded as a rubber stamp chamber into a political check on the president.

Some months before the new presidential elections in the summer of 2000, the PRI appeared to have recovered electoral support. Many observers thought it could once again win the country's highest political office, which the party had occupied for 72 years. This time, however, the election process appeared to be more democratic than in the past, beginning with a much-touted, first-ever selection of the PRI candidate in a contested "primary" race that differed from the traditional "handpicking" used in the past. Looked at more closely, the political reality was not so very different, for the party apparatus was geared to promote Francisco Labastida, who eventually won the nomination.

In the end, the PRI lost its grip on power when Labastida was defeated decisively by the charismatic businessman, Vicente Fox. The latter's center-right National Action Party (PAN) also became the leading force in both houses of Congress. As a result, Mexico has now experienced a major political turnover.

**South Africa** faces the monumental task of making democracy work in a multiracial society with a long record of repressive rule by a white minority that had for many years enforced an official policy of racial of inequality and segregation, known as apartheid. A new transitional constitution was adopted in late 1993, followed by the first multiracial national elections in April 1994. Former president F. W. de Klerk may go into history as a late reformer, but his political work was bound to displease many members of South African society. If the reforms were judged to have gone much too far and too fast by many members of the privileged white minority, they clearly did not go sufficiently far or come quickly enough for many more people who demanded measures that went much beyond formal racial equality.

Nelson Mandela, who succeeded de Klerk in the presidency, faced an even more difficult historical task. On the other hand, he possessed some strong political cards in addition to his undisputed leadership qualities. He represented the aspirations of a long-repressed majority, yet he was able to retain the respect of a large number of the white minority. It will be important that his successor continues to bridge the racial cleavages that otherwise threaten to ravage South African society. In an early and interim constitution for post-apartheid South Africa, the reformers had sought political accommodation through an institutional form of power sharing. A new constitution, adopted in 1996, lays the foundation for creating simple majority-based governments that are bound to be dominated for now by the African National Congress (ANC), Mandela's political party. The new charter contains many guarantees of individual and group rights, but political prudence would seem to recommend some form of meaningful interracial coalition-building as a kind of power sharing in South Africa's policy-making process.

The continued task of finding workable forms of power sharing is only one of many problems. In order for the democratic changes to have much meaning for the long-suppressed majority, it will be necessary to find policies that reduce the social and economic chasm separating the races. The politics of redistribution will be no simple or short-term task, and one may expect many conflicts in the future. Nevertheless, for the first time since the beginning of colonization, South Africa now offers some hope for a major improvement in interracial relations. There is a plethora of social problems and conflicts in this country, but optimists believe that a firm foundation has been laid that should ensure political stability also in the post-Mandela era.

In December 1997, Mandela stepped down from the leadership of the ANC as a first step in his eventual retirement from politics. His place was taken by Thabo Mbeki, the country's deputy president, who became president in June 1999, soon after the parliamentary elections in which the ANC won 266 of the 400 seats, or one short of a two-thirds majority. The new leaders appear to have done their best to provide for political continuity instead of a divisive power struggle after Mandela's departure. Mbeki (and everyone else) lacks Mandela's great moral authority. He is widely described as "businesslike" and competent, but Mbeki's dismissive and poorly informed views on the country's serious AIDS problem have caused international alarm. Recently Mandela has stepped back into the public limelight by announcing his intention to play a leading role in promoting policies that will seriously identify and confront this serious health problem.

**Nigeria** will be another focus of attention. It covers a large area and has more than 100 million inhabitants, making it the most populous country in Africa. The former British colony has returned to electoral politics after 15 years of oppressive military rule that brought economic havoc to the potentially rich nation. The path toward democratic governance in this culturally diverse country will be long and difficult. Ethnic and religious conflicts threaten the emergence of both a well-functioning civil society and a stable form of representative government. Nigeria bears close watching by students of comparative politics.

**China** is the homeland of nearly 1.3 billion people, or about one-fifth of the world's population. Here the reform Communists, who took power after Mao Zedong's death in 1976, began much earlier than their Soviet counterparts to steer the country toward a relatively decontrolled market economy. They also introduced some political relaxation, by ending Mao's recurrent ideological campaigns to mobilize the masses. In their place came a domestic tranquillity such as China had not known for over half a century. But the regime encountered a basic dilemma: it wished to maintain tight controls over politics and society while freeing the economy. When a new openness began to emerge in Chinese society, comparable in some ways to the pluralism encouraged more actively by Gorbachev's glasnost policy of openness in the Soviet Union, it ran into determined opposition among hard-line Communist leaders. The aging reform leader, Deng Xiaoping, presided over a bloody crackdown on student demonstrations in Beijing's Tiananmen Square in May 1989. The regime has refused to let up on its tight political controls of society, but it continues to loosen the economic controls in the areas or zones designated for such reforms. In recent years, China has experienced a remarkable economic surge with growth rates that appear unmatched elsewhere in the world. A still unanswered question is whether the emerging market-oriented society can long coexist with a tightly controlled political system. In February 1997 Beijing announced the death of Deng Xiaoping.

Jiang Zemin, chosen by Deng as his successor in 1989, had been the country's president since 1993. He appeared determined to continue the relatively pragmatic course adopted by Deng. It needs to be added that the regime has revived a hard line in dealing with real, imagined, or potential political dissidence, which includes some forms of religious expression. Moreover, there are familiar signs of social tension, as China's mixed economy leaves both "winners" and "losers" in its wake. With the country's undeniable problems and shortcomings, however, China's leaders have steered clear of the chaos that has plagued post–Soviet Russia. They seem determined to continue with their tight political controls, even as their economy becomes freer and more market-oriented. Some observers believe that the basic economic and political norms will eventually begin to converge, but that remains to be seen. A test case is the movement known as Falun Gong, which the ruling Communists see as a threat because of its effective organization and solidarity—qualities that no longer characterize the Communist Party to the same degree as earlier. It remains to be seen whether Hu Jintao, who as expected was chosen as "fourth generation" party leader in late 2002, will turn out to move the country further in a technocratic direction, as many observers expect.

# Globalization's Double Edge

*Growing Market Offers Huge Potential—but Also Peril*

## By Robert J. Samuelson

*Special to the International Herald Tribune*

At the edge of a new century, globalization is a double-edged sword: a powerful vehicle that raises economic growth, spreads new technology and increases living standards in rich and poor countries alike, but also an immensely controversial process that assaults national sovereignty, erodes local culture and tradition and threatens economic and social instability.

A daunting question of the 21st century is whether nations will control this great upheaval or whether it will come to control them.

In some respects globalization is merely a trendy word for an old process. What we call the market is simply the joining of buyers and sellers, producers and consumers and savers and investors. Economic history consists largely of the story of the market's expansion: from farm to town, from region to nation and from nation to nation. In the 20th century, the Depression and two world wars retarded the market's growth. But after World War II ended, it reaccelerated, driven by political pressures and better technology.

The Cold War, from the late 1940s through the 1980s, caused the United States to champion trade liberalization and economic growth as a way of combating communism. A succession of major trade negotiations reduced average tariffs in industrialized countries to about 5 percent in 1990 from about 40 percent in 1946.

After two world wars, Europeans saw economic unification as an antidote to deadly nationalism. Technology complemented politics. Even before the Internet, declining costs for communication and transportation—from jet planes, better un-

dersea telephone cables and satellites—favored more global commerce. By the early 1990s, world exports (after adjusting for inflation) were nearly 10 times higher than they had been four decades earlier.

Globalization continues this process but also departs from it in at least one critical respect. Until recently, countries were viewed as distinct economic entities, connected mainly by trade. Now, this is becoming less true. Companies and financial markets increasingly disregard national borders when making production, marketing and investment decisions.

As recently as 1990, governments either individually or through such multilateral institutions as the World Bank provided half the loans and credits to 29 major developing countries (including Brazil, China, India, South Korea and Mexico), according to the Institute for International Finance, a banking industry research group in Washington.

A decade later, even after Asia's 1997–98 financial crisis, private capital flows dwarf governmental flows. In 1999, private flows (bank loans, bond financing, equity investment in local stock markets and direct investment by multinational companies) totaled an estimated $136 billion to these 29 countries, compared with government capital flows of $22 billion, according to the institute.

Meanwhile, multinational companies have gone on an international acquisition binge. In the first half of 1999 alone, the value of new cross-border mergers and acquisitions passed $500 billion in both advanced and developing countries.

The total roughly matched the amount for all 1998 ($544 billion) and was almost

seven times larger than the 1991 levels ($85 billion), according to the World Investment Report by the United Nations. The recent takeover struggle between British and German wireless giants—Vodafone AirTouch PLC and Mannesmann AG—is exceptional only for its size and bitterness.

Behind the merger boom lies the growing corporate conviction that many markets have become truly global. By trying to maximize their presence in as many nations as possible, companies seek to achieve economies of scale—that is, to lower costs through higher sales and production volumes—and to stay abreast of technological changes that can now occur almost anywhere.

In addition, companies increasingly organize production globally, dividing product design, component manufacturing and final assembly among many countries.

But it is not just multinational companies, seeking bigger sales and profits, that drive globalization. Governments do, too. In Europe, the relentless pursuit of the "single market" is one indicator. This reflects a widespread recognition that European companies will be hard-pressed to compete in global markets if their local operations are hamstrung by fragmented national markets.

Among poorer countries, the best sign of support is the clamor to get into the World Trade Organization. Since 1995, seven countries—Bulgaria, Ecuador, Estonia, Kyrgyzstan, Latvia, Mongolia and Panama—have joined. And 32 (the largest being China) are seeking membership. There is a belief that global trade and investment can aid economic development by providing new products, technologies and management skills.

It's no myth. Countries succeed or fail mainly based on their own workers, investment and government policies. But engaging the wider world economy can help.

Consider Asia. Despite its financial crisis, rapid trade expansion and economic growth sharply cut the number of the desperately poor. From 1987 to 1998, those in the region, including China, with incomes of $1 or less a day dropped to 15 percent from 27 percent of the population, the World Bank estimates.

Meanwhile, Latin America and sub-Saharan Africa—whose embrace of the world economy has been late or limited—fared much less well. In Africa, for example, the World Bank reckons that 46 percent of the population lived on less than $1 a day in 1998, exactly what the percentage was in 1987.

Well, if globalization is so good, why is it also so risky? The answer is that two problems could neutralize its potential benefits.

The first is economic instability. The global economy may be prone to harsher boom-bust cycles than national economies individually. The theory that international trade and investment raise living standards works only if investment funds are well used and if trade flows do not become too lopsided.

The Asian financial crisis raised questions on both counts. In the early 1990s, most of Asia thrived because it received vast flows of foreign capital as bank loans, direct investment in factories or stock-market investment in local companies.

The ensuing spending boom in turn aided Europe, Japan and the United States by increasing imports from them. Then the boom abruptly halted in mid-1997 when it became apparent that as a result of "crony capitalism," inept government investment policies and excess optimism, much of the investment had been wasted on unneeded factories, office buildings and apartments.

What prevented the Asian crisis from becoming a full-scale global economic downturn has been the astonishing U.S. economy.

Its relentless growth helped the rest of the world by purchasing more and more of their exports. Since 1996, the U.S. current-account deficit in its balance of payments, the broadest measure of the country's international trade, has more than doubled, from $129 billion to an estimated total of $330 billion in 1999.

The world economy, as Treasury Secretary Lawrence Summers has repeatedly said, has been flying on one engine. The trouble is, as Mr. Summers has also warned, this cannot go on forever.

The great danger is that the world has become too dependent on American prosperity and that a slowdown or recession reflecting a decline in the stock market, a loss of consumer confidence or higher interest rates might snowball into a international slump.

By economic forecasts, Europe and Japan are going to do better. In 2000, the European Union's gross domestic product will grow 2.8 percent, up from 2.1 percent in 1999, according to projections by the Organization for Economic Cooperation and Development in Paris.

Japan is projected to grow 1.4 percent, the same as the OECD is predicting for 1999 but a big improvement from the 2.8 percent drop in 1998. If the forecasts materialize—and the OECD's growth estimates for Japan exceed most private forecasts—they will restore some balance to the world economy and relieve fears of a global recession.

Asia and Latin America can continue to recover without relying solely on exports to the United States. But until that happens, no one can be certain that Asia's financial crisis has truly ended. It remains possible that abrupt surges of global capital, first moving into Asia and then out, will have caused, with some delay, a larger instability.

Globalization's other problem is political, cultural and social. People feel threatened by any kind of economic change—and change from abroad naturally seems especially alien and menacing.

The street protesters at the Seattle meeting of the World Trade Organization in early December may have lacked a common agenda or even a coherent case against trade. But they accurately reflected the anxiety and anger that globalization often inspires. So do European fears of genetically modified food or nationalistic opposition to cross-border mergers.

What is local and familiar is suddenly being replaced or assaulted by something that is foreign and unfamiliar. And even if trade helps most people, it will usually create some losers. In the United States, workers in some high-cost industries—steel and autos, most conspicuously—suffered from intensified import competition.

Just because globalization is largely spontaneous—propelled by better communications and transportation—does not mean that it is inevitable or completely irreversible. Governments can, in subtle and not-so-subtle ways, shield local industries and workers against imports or discriminate against foreign investors. If only a few countries do, their actions will not matter much.

Global capital and trade will go where they are most welcome and productive. Indeed, it is precisely this logic that has persuaded so many countries to accept globalization. If they don't, someone else will. Judged by their behavior, most governments believe they have more to gain than to lose.

But this does not mean that a powerful popular backlash, with unpredictable consequences, is not possible. In a global recession, too many sellers will be chasing too few buyers. A plausible presumption is that practical politicians would try to protect their constituents from global gluts. If too many countries did, globalization could implode.

It's a scary prospect. Economic interdependence cuts both ways. Under favorable conditions, it helps everyone; under unfavorable conditions, it hurts everyone. Globalization's promise may exceed its peril but the peril is still real. Both await the new century. One of the great dramas will be to see which prevails.

From the *International Herald Tribune*, January 4, 2000, pp. 1, 3. © 2000 by Robert J. Samuelson. Reprinted by permission.

# Why Outsiders Are In in Latin America

**Voters have set aside ideology in their desire for a higher standard of living. But populist campaign promises may be hard to keep.**

By T. Christian Miller and Hector Tobar
*Times Staff Writers*

QUITO, Ecuador—Across Latin America, people are trading in the old for the new. In country after country, voters are rejecting political parties and powerful party bosses who have long dominated the economic and social landscape in favor of outsiders.

It's a trend rooted less in ideology than in a desire for change. Voters do not seem to care whether candidates are of the left or right, but whether they are likely to deliver a better standard of living.

As a result, they are turning to anti-establishment leftists such as Ecuador's newly elected president, Col. Lucio Gutierrez, who has never before held political office, or Luiz Inacio Lula da Silva of Brazil, who spent a lifetime outside mainstream politics as a committed leftist.

At the same time, they have supported conservatives such as Colombia's new president Alvaro Uribe, a hard-liner who ran as an independent, and Mexico's President Vicente Fox, who shattered the decades-long dominance of the entrenched Institutional Revolutionary Party.

"There's a discontent that has manifested itself as a desire for people outside the system," said Pablo Franky, a political analyst at Javeriana University in Bogota, the Colombian capital. "The traditional parties have not been able to solve the problems of poverty, corruption and inequality."

Many of the traditional parties had embraced the so-called Washington consensus, pursuing open markets and free trade. Few of the new generation of anti-establishment leaders have rejected outright the drive toward globalization. But many of them have expressed the desire to soften its effects on the poor and middle class.

Politicians of both types have made extravagant populist promises to put a chicken in every pot. Gutierrez's opponent pledged to build 200,000 homes that could be purchased for $48 a month. Gutierrez responded by promising 200,000 homes for $37 apiece.

Neither man explained exactly how he would pay for such a program. Ecuador faces $2 billion in payments on its $13-billion foreign debt next year, an amount equal to nearly half the country's budget.

It is also unclear whether there is a genuine surge in anti-American feeling, or whether voters are simply rejecting discredited U.S.-backed elites and the U.S. prescription for their economies.

None of the outsiders seems particularly ideological. Uribe, perhaps the most conservative president in the region, won partly on his promises to crack down on leftist rebels, but also pledged to vastly increase the number of schools in the country.

South America's most leftist leader, Venezuelan President Hugo Chavez, has been careful to maintain close economic ties with the U.S., his country's largest market. And Lula has promised to honor Brazil's payments to the International Monetary Fund.

"This turn toward the left in Latin America is very peculiar," said Fausto Maso, a radio talk show host in Caracas, the Venezuelan capital, and columnist for the El Nacional daily. The left "doesn't have Russia anymore and… this limits them. During the campaign they say one thing, but when they get elected they end up talking to Washington, and later end as failures."

Not all Latin American governments are distracting themselves from Washington. In Central America, memories of failed ideological experiments in countries such as Nicaragua have left the region firmly committed to deeper economic and social integration with the U.S. Leaders are rushing to take advantage of a possible free trade agreement with the Bush administration. Recent elections in Honduras and Nicaragua saw the return of conservative politicians.

In South America, most countries remain committed to the hemisphere-wide free trade agreement scheduled to be completed by 2004, though Ecuador and Brazil have expressed reservations.

"There is still an enormous push to achieve some kind of more productive economic relationship with the United States," said Peter Hakim, president of Inter-American Dialogue, a left-center think tank in Washington, D.C.

More than anything, the region's continued poverty explains the rise of unorthodox, outsider and messianic leaders. A recent U.N. report indicated that after a decade of decline, poverty rates have begun increasing in some Latin American countries, especially Argentina.

The region's growing number of poor still face shortages in health care, education and pensions. Many have seen the success of Asian competitors, some of which are taking jobs away from South America, and wonder why they have not benefited from the globalization boom. Continuing problems with corruption also have left voters disillusioned.

"What we are seeing is the result of the failure of all the models that have been tried up to now. All of them—left and right, populist and neoliberal—have failed to deliver the goods," said Anibal Romero, a political analyst in Caracas. "People in Latin America are looking for some kind of hope in the future. They want freedom, prosperity, a better life. If that can be delivered by the left, very well. If it can be delivered by the right, just as good."

The new leaders are men and women of widely varying ideological stripe, but most of whom share one characteristic: charisma.

In troubled Paraguay, one of the poorest countries in South America, politics is dominated by the shadow of a leader who shares much in common with Venezuela's Chavez and Ecuador's Gutierrez. Like both those men, Lino Oviedo is a military leader who led a coup against his country's elected government.

Oviedo now lives in exile in Brazil, where he rails against the endemic corruption in Paraguay, ruled for decades by the dictator Alfredo Stroessner and then later by the Colorado Party.

President Luis Gonzalez Macchi declared a state of siege in September when Oviedo supporters marched in Asuncion, the capital, demanding the president's resignation. Recent polls have shown that a third of Paraguayan voters would back an Oviedo presidency, even though he is barred from running.

"People want a strongman, someone who can provide security and jobs in the middle of this chaos," said Carlos Martini, a sociologist and journalist at the Catholic University in Asuncion. "His support points to a longing for the Stroessner era. For me, Oviedo is just the symptom of a failed political model."

In Argentina, one of the front-runners in polls leading up to elections scheduled for early next year is a figure who just months ago would have been considered a long shot at best.

Adolfo Rodriquez Saa, a Peronist governor, was president for a week last December following the fall of Fernando de la Rua in a wave of protests against poverty, budget cuts and the crash of the nation's banking system.

Elected by Congress as an interim preinsert, Rodriquez Saa delivered an inauguration speech that was a model of Peronist populism. Even though Argentina was—and still is—nearly bankrupt, he promised an ambitious government jobs program.

Rodriquez Saa was driven from office by his fellow Peronists who would not support his radical prescription for the Argentine economy. Now he's back, promising to break Argentina's dependency on the International Monetary Fund.

"These victories ware clearly the consequence of an economic model that isn't working anymore for the people of Latin America," said Gustavo Valenzuela, a spokesman for Rodriquez Saa, reflecting on the recent elections in Brazil and Ecuador. "People talk about globalization and neoliberalism. Whatever you want to call it, it isn't working."

Venezuela is perhaps the oldest example of the Latin Americans' experiment with anti-establishment figures—and the most disastrous.

Chavez triumphed over corrupt political parties when he ran for office in 1998 and enjoyed the support of more than 90% of the population in a poll taken at the beginning of his term.

He moved quickly to realize his ill-defined "Bolivarian" revolution, an attempt to improve the lives of the country's poor by rejecting free trade policies. He pushed through laws to require greater state ownership in oil ventures and to permit the seizure of privately owned land. Four years later, the economy of the world's fifth-largest oil producer is worse than ever, with unemployment on the rise and the national currency falling.

Politically, the outlook is also grim. Chavez was briefly felled by a coup in April. His return to power has been marked by increasing bitterness that has left society deeply divided.

Just last week, Chavez seized control of Caracas' police force, which had been under the control of a political opponent. The move led to violent protests and a call for the country's fourth nationwide strike in 12 months.

Opposition leaders are pushing for early elections, perhaps the clearest sign that Venezuelans care more about results than about ideology.

"The people will inevitably vote against Chavez. They will vote for the person who has the best chance of beating Chavez, it's that simple," said Maso, the radio talk show host. "It doesn't matter what political tendency the person has."

*Miller reported from Quito and Tobar from Buenos Aires. Special correspondents Christopher Toothaker in Caracas and Paula Gobbi in Rio de Janeiro contributed to this report.*

# Fox's Mexico: Same as It Ever Was?

**"Since the arrival of Vicente Fox to the presidency, Mexico has been stuck in neutral. The executive has been characterized by confusion, indecision, and repeated policy mistakes. Mexican political parties have shown a striking inability to adjust their behavior to the new democratic political environment. And Mexicans of all stripes remain steeped in an authoritarian culture that has prevented them from embracing the political opportunities offered by Mexico's new democratic setting."**

PAMELA K. STARR

Vicente Fox's inauguration as president on December 1, 2000 brought with it great expectations for Mexico's future. Fox's electoral victory over the Institutional Revolutionary Party (PRI) the previous July had broken over 70 years of continuous PRI control of an authoritarian presidency and hence of the country. It thus promised to usher in a new era of expanded democracy, increased individual rights, and a significant positive change in the country's political and economic course.

> *During its first year in office, the Fox administration has shown a striking inability to get things done.*

Fox's victory undoubtedly has deepened democracy in Mexico, created a new image for the country in the world, and established a new style of governance. And no one honestly expected significant policy advances would come quickly and easily. The new government lacked experience and faced enormous challenges. Errors in strategy and tactics were virtually inevitable as the first opposition administration in living memory took the reins of power, and efforts to change a highly institutionalized and deeply ingrained political order would inevitably be painfully slow. Further, the enormously high expectations produced by the first post-PRI government guaranteed that Fox's advances would be seen as insufficient by a country desperate for change. Yet even considering these caveats, the performance of the Fox administration during its first year in office has been disappointing.

Since the arrival of Vicente Fox to the presidency, Mexico has been stuck in neutral. The executive has been characterized by confusion, indecision, and repeated policy mistakes. Mexican political parties have shown a striking inability to adjust their behavior to the new democratic political environment. And Mexicans of all stripes remain steeped in an authoritarian culture that has prevented them from embracing the political opportunities offered by Mexico's new democratic setting. The consequence has been a year dominated by political bickering and legislative inaction on reforms essential to the long-term health of the Mexican economy and of Mexico's democratic experiment.

If nothing changes in Mexico during 2002, the country can look forward to a future characterized by a lack of robust economic growth and increased vulnerability to international economic shocks, and a growing likelihood that an only moderately reformed PRI will retake full control of the national legislature in 2003 and of the presidency in 2006.

## CONFUSION AND INCONSISTENCIES REIGN

During its first year in office, the Fox administration has shown a striking inability to get things done. It did manage to get two austere budget laws through Congress and win the approval of important elements of a much-needed financial reform. But there is little else legislatively to crow about. The Fox administration managed to ensure the approval of a new law on indigenous people, its top legislative priority. But after extensive revisions imposed by Congress, the law was unable to achieve its true objective of convincing the Zapatista rebels in Chiapas to initiate peace negotiations with the federal government. Meanwhile, fiscal, energy, and labor reform, improved security, reforms designed to increase democracy and efficiency in the Mexican state, and increased investment in human capital and infrastructure development all made little headway during 2001, and a desperately needed judicial reform never found its way onto the agenda. Behind this failure to deliver is the administration's inability to pursue an established policy course and send a clear policy message to the nation, and its failure to work effectively with the legislature. Although blame for this circumstance does not lie entirely with the Fox administration, much of it reflects a marked lack of consistency and coordination within the executive branch.

One of the most striking features of the Fox government's first year in office has been its tendency to contradict itself, creating the perception that the government does not know what it is doing or where it is going. For example, throughout the presidential campaign Fox insisted that he would transform the national oil company, PEMEX, into an autonomous firm managed on the basis of market principles. In this vein, soon after taking office he announced the appointment of four prominent businessmen to the administrative board of PEMEX. Not surprisingly, this move produced a great deal of consternation within the political opposition. The opposition's deep mistrust of Fox's ultimate aims for PEMEX led it to conclude that the inclusion of private-sector interests on the board was a first step toward the privatization of the firm. The president of the PRI, Dulce Maria Sauri, referred to this move as the "silent privatization" of the firm and vowed to block it. Also unsurprising was the opposition of PEMEX's union, which feared the move signaled future job cuts. What was surprising was Fox's decision to back down. Within weeks Fox caved into opposition pressure, apparently fearing that the issue could obstruct other, more important administration objectives.

In much the same way, after insisting for months that a new 15 percent value-added tax on food, medicines, and books was completely nonnegotiable, Fox suddenly changed his mind. At an event with Carlos Fuentes during August in which the most famous of Mexican novelists criticized the tax on books, Fox unexpectedly reversed course and announced the elimination of the tax from his proposal. Backtracking from an established position is an obvious and commonly used negotiating tactic. But in these two instances the Fox administration gave without receiving anything in return from its opponents. This produced a growing perception on the part of the opposition that the administration was weak and could be bullied into abandoning its policies. The result was a more aggressive and obstructionist opposition.

Inconsistencies and contradictions have also emerged regularly from within the Fox cabinet. The debate on fiscal reform was punctuated throughout the spring and early summer by conflicting statements from seemingly every corner of the president's cabinet. And following the September 11 attacks on the World Trade Center and the Pentagon, Mexican foreign policy was a perfect muddle. Foreign Minister Jorge Castañeda immediately announced Mexico's full backing for the United States and any response it might deem appropriate. This statement of unconditional support for the United States produced a nationalist backlash in the Mexican political class and unease throughout the country. Sensing a political opportunity, Interior Minister Santiago Creel took over the leadership of this opposition. An open dispute between the two ministers persisted for over two weeks before President Fox finally ended it by coming down on the side of Castañeda. In the meantime, confusion reigned. What was the government's policy? Why didn't Fox end the debate sooner? Was he incapable of making a decision or was he incapable of controlling his own cabinet? Whatever the answers to these questions, the incident raised doubts about Fox's ability to lead the nation.

## THE MONTESSORI CABINET

The continuing cacophony of disparate policy opinions emerging from within Fox's cabinet has earned it an unwanted nickname: the Montessori cabinet. Each minister seems to be following his or her own script with little or no policy coordination and without anyone willing or able to impose order. This dynamic has three drivers: the institutional structure of the administration, the political inexperience of the cabinet, and Fox's governing style.

The institutional structure of the executive branch under Vicente Fox is more complex than that of his predecessors. In addition to 19 cabinet secretaries it includes a new innovation: 7 coordinators with the responsibility of easing communication and increasing policy management within the cabinet. To this end the executive branch has been organized into three groups—quality growth, order and respect, and social development—with a coordinator to oversee each group. These chiefs of staff for the ministries under their purview were expected to increase the operational efficiency of the executive branch. Quite the opposite occurred. Rather than increasing cooperation and communication, they have deepened confusion and inconsistency within the administration.

Created out of nothing, the coordinators lacked the funds and institutional base that would have given them the legitimacy and power needed to coordinate the activities of cabinet ministries jealous of their autonomy. Nor did the cabinet secretaries adapt easily to someone other than the president giving them policy direction. They thus often limited communication and cooperation with their coordinator and thereby directly and intentionally undermined the capacity of the coordinators to do their job. The coordinators thus became another layer of government designing their own policy proposals independent of the offices they were supposed to coordinate. Since these proposals often differed from those of the ministries, increased policy conflict and confusion rather than greater coordination and efficiency ensued.

Policy confusion and inefficiency also have reflected the inexperience of most of the Fox cabinet. Although Fox made a point of choosing people highly qualified to head each ministry, in most cases he neglected to include political experience in the mix of qualifications. The result has been a cabinet with strong personalities and extensive experience in the private sector but with very little understanding of the subtleties of politics. Fox's cabinet secretaries have thus regularly ruffled congressional feathers and publicly aired contradictory and often polemical points of view.

The costs of a cabinet lacking government experience have been deepened by Fox's governing style. Fox runs Mexico much as one would manage a firm: he sets out policy goals and allows his cabinet to design and implement the means to achieve them. Although a delegative managerial style can be a very efficient strategy of governing under appropriate conditions, it does not work well under a flawed organizational structure and with ministers who are very self-assured yet politically inexperienced.

## AN UNSUPPORTIVE GOVERNING PARTY...

The inability of the Fox administration to make legislative advances during its first year in government is not solely the consequence of policy confusion and inconsistencies in the executive branch. It also reflects the limited ability of Mexican political parties to adjust their operations to the demands of Mexico's new democratic political environment. The National Action Party (PAN) has not yet figured out what it means to be the party in government. The Democratic Revolutionary Party (PRD) continues to believe that the opposition's only job is to oppose. And the PRI has been politically paralyzed by an internal leadership struggle and the search for an identity as the opposition. The result has been a legislature both unwilling and unable to take the political risks associated with the passage of essential but controversial legislation.

The relationship between Vicente Fox and the party under whose emblem he was elected to the presidency, the PAN, has never been an easy one. Fox has not gotten along with the leader of the PAN's dominant traditionalist faction, Diego Fernandez de Cevallos, since 1991, when Fernandez de Cevallos sacrificed Fox on the altar of political expediency. (As candidate for governor of Guanajuato state, Fox was declared the loser in a clearly fraudulent election. Fernandez de Cevallos negotiated a compromise with then-President Carlos Salinas under which both Fox and his PRI opponent would step aside in favor of another PAN politician.)

When Fox decided to make a run for the presidency, he correctly recognized that a party structure controlled by Fernandez de Cevallos would not be overly friendly to his candidacy. So Fox made an end run around the party hierarchy. He established a campaign structure independent of the party, appealed directly to the voters, and forced the party to accept his candidacy as a fait accompli. He succeeded, but at the price of further angering the traditionalist wing of the party. Given this history, it was not surprising when President Fox named a cabinet virtually devoid of traditional PAN politicians and when he made little effort to involve the party in the process of governing. It was equally unsurprising when this sort of treatment generated resentment within the party even among Fox's supporters.

While Vicente Fox was doing little to make the PAN feel like the party in government, the party itself was suffering an identify crisis that undermined its ability to support President Fox. The PAN feared that Fox's election would transform it into what it had criticized for over 60 years. It was petrified of becoming a new PRI—a party controlled from the presidency, indistinguishable from the government, and devoid of an independent identity. In its zeal not to become the new party of state, the PAN has been hesitant to give its full support to President Fox and his legislative proposals.

This combination of factors—a traditionalist wing of the party led by Fernandez de Cevallos, who also controls the party leadership and its legislative leadership, Fox's disdainful treatment of the PAN, and the PAN's fear of becoming a new PRI—culminated in a party that operated as if it were the opposition during the first months of the Fox presidency. The most visible example of this relationship was the PAN's opposition to the new Indigenous Law, the first legislative initiative sent to Congress by President Fox.

The PAN had long opposed the proposal to increase the autonomy of indigenous communities on which Fox based his legislative measure. This opposition and the party's lukewarm support for President Fox led the PAN to work actively in Congress to modify this proposal. The real showdown between the PAN and Vicente Fox, however, came over the Zapatista rebels' request that their representative be permitted to speak before Congress in favor of the Fox proposal. Fox strongly supported this request while the PAN delegation in both houses of Congress unanimously opposed it. The leader of the PAN in the Chamber of Deputies insisted that neither Subcommander Marcos (the leader of the Zapatistas) nor Fox would dictate to the legislature. The PAN leader in the Senate, Fernandez de Cevallos, received an ovation at a party assembly when he argued that Fox "is the promoter, he is the representative and the publicist of Marcos." The lower house of Congress ultimately authorized a Zapatista appearance, but not a single PAN deputy voted in favor. In late April the Indigenous Law passed the legislature, but it was the PAN's highly modified version of the Fox proposal. Given that the Zapatistas had demanded the measure's approval without any modifications, the legislation was insufficient to convince the rebels to initiate peace talks. The PAN thus delivered a clear defeat to Vicente Fox on his very first legislative initiative as president, and it did so in a manner highly critical of the president.

This political disaster chastened both sides in the dispute. In the ensuing weeks, Fernandez de Cevallos lowered his tone significantly, the party leadership made a concerted effort to develop a working relationship with its president, and Fox and his cabinet ministers began to communicate more effectively with PAN legislators. But this entente came only after a great deal of political damage had been done. Further, even after its change of heart, the PAN remained hesitant to support Fox unconditionally.

## ...AN IMPOTENT OPPOSITION...

The opposition of the PRD to Fox's legislative agenda has been unrelenting throughout the president's first year in office, and it seems unlikely that this posture will change. For the PRD, the transition from the PRI to the PAN has brought few real changes in the policy direction of the nation, and the party remains a minority in the legislature and thus has limited incentives to collaborate with the government.

The PRD strongly opposes the market-based economic strategy former President Ernesto Zedillo initiated and Fox continued. From the party's perspective, the market is not sufficiently efficient to provide economic well-being for the majority of Mexicans. Given this bias in economic policy, the party finds very little of value in the administration's economic strategy. On questions such as the reform of the state—changing the structure of the Mexican state to make it more democratic and more efficient—there is more room for cooperation. But even here a deep-seated mistrust of the ultimate objectives of the Fox administration will obstruct cooperation.

The PRD also lacks institutional incentives to modify its behavior in Congress. As a minority party whose votes are not sufficient to build a majority even when combined with those of the PAN, the PRD is a minor player whose legislative cooperation is not essential. The PRD can therefore oppose the government without actually obstructing the legislative process—not unlike its position during the era of PRI governments. This institutional reality will not likely change any time soon. The PRD lacks national appeal and shows no sign of reversing this trend. To the contrary, the nourishment the party had traditionally received from defecting PRI politicians fell off sharply in 2001 as the revival of the PRI got under way.

The appeal of the party at the ballot box is also not improving. Even the party's great victory of 2001, the election of Lázaro Cárdenas Batel (the son of former Mexico City Mayor Cuauhtémoc Cárdenas and grandson of the legendary former President Lázaro Cárdenas) as governor of Michoacán state was actually a near defeat. Even with the historical name of Cárdenas in the family's home state, a charismatic personality, a divided PRI, and a 20-point lead at the start of the campaign, Cárdenas Batel edged the PRI by only 5 points. This does not bode well for the PRD's future electoral prospects.

## ...AND A HYDRA-HEADED BEHEMOTH

With a majority in the Senate, the largest plurality of seats in the Chamber of Deputies, and holding more than half the nation's governorships, the PRI is undoubtedly the dominant opposition force in Mexico. Little legislatively can be achieved without its support. But the PRI has not been highly cooperative during the first year of the Fox administration. In part, this stems from honest policy differences, but, more important, it reflects the party's extreme difficulty in adapting to its new role as the opposition.

From its inception the PRI has existed to serve the interests of the national president, was led by that president, and hence never developed any autonomous identity. When the PRI lost the presidency in July 2000, it lost more than the leadership of the country. It lost its bearings. Who would lead the party? What would the party stand for? How would the party proceed? The first year of the Fox presidency was, therefore, blighted by an essential opposition force trying to find its way in a totally new political world.

In the absence of a national president, the PRI developed three competing centers of power: the PRI governors, the party leadership, and the legislative leadership. Each attempted to lead the party in a somewhat different policy direction. Despite efforts to coordinate their positions, the result was a confused compilation of competing positions emanating from within a single party. With which element of this hydra-headed behemoth should the government negotiate?

Worse still, while each PRI power center made demands of the government, internal party politics prevented them from making any significant sacrifices in return. Throughout 2001 the party leadership was dominated by supporters of the vanquished presidential candidate, Francisco Labastida, yet it faced a continuing challenge from the supporters of Roberto Madrazo, a former governor of Tabasco state and determined adversary of Ernesto Zedillo and his heir apparent, Labastida. As the PRI struggled to find a means to resolve this leadership battle without dividing the party, there was no room for the party leadership or its allies in the congressional leadership to stick out their necks and support any controversial policy positions.

The PRI's eighteenth national assembly held in late November took important strides toward establishing a legitimate and powerful party leadership. It called for the direct election of the new party president and effectively concentrated political power in the hands of the party president and his/her National Executive Council. But it left the resolution of the factional battle for control of the party to the February election for party president. Until the new party president takes power on March 4, 2002, PRI internal politics will continue to prevent the party from taking any controversial positions.

## THE CASE OF FISCAL REFORM

Vicente Fox's proposal to reform Mexico's fiscal policy failed to win legislative approval during 2001, the victim of a misguided legislative strategy combined with confusion in the executive branch and maladjusted political parties. For the first six months of his presidency, Vicente Fox followed a legislative strategy built on the logic of presidentialism even though the political setting in which he operated was characterized by a tangible separation of powers. The executive thus did not countenance any negotiations with the opposition on the content of its reform proposal for months. When the government finally reversed course, Fox's honeymoon was over and the PRI had become increasingly distracted by the demands of internal party politics. Negotiations continued in earnest throughout the remainder of the year but to little effect. Rather than the thoroughgoing fiscal reform Mexico very much needs, the outcome was a compilation of isolated tax increases incorporated into the 2002 budget.

From the moment word began to leak out in early December 2000 that the new fiscal reform would include a value-added tax of 15 percent on food, medicine, books, and school fees, objections were strong. The PRD immediately announced its total opposition, the PRI expressed opposition but couched in terms that suggested that there might be room for negotiation, and the PAN raised strong concerns about the political costs of such a measure. Despite this evident discomfort in the legislature with its proposed tax changes (opposition to a reduction in the income tax was also quite strong), the executive made no effort to negotiate either with the opposition or with its own party. It did not attempt to work out a consensus proposal prior to presenting the legislation to Congress in the first days of April. Instead it designed the proposal in splendid isolation from the political process in the best tradition of the old PRI system.

The government apparently believed it could convince the PAN to support the project and would be able to win the support of a sufficient number of PRI members of Congress by wooing the governors who were believed to control their votes (the initial proposal included a carrot directed specifically at the governors—40 billion pesos [$4.2 billion] of the increased tax collection would be directed to states and municipalities). The problem with this strategy was threefold. First, the PAN was not willing to support the president unconditionally on the issue. To the contrary, half the PAN deputies either openly opposed the initiative or were undecided. And in the midst of the party's revolt against its president on the issue of the Indigenous Law, there was no guarantee that the PAN would back the president on fiscal reform. In fact, PAN legislators preempted the president by presenting their own fiscal reform proposal in early March.

The second problem with the initial Fox legislative strategy is that the governors were not the only center of power within the PRI making their hold over party legislators much less than absolute. The legislative leadership and the party leadership also mattered, and their support for the fiscal reform was undermined by three other factors: the lack of PAN support for the initiative, the absence of public support, and history. It should not be surprising that the PRI was unwilling to go out on a limb for President Fox if he was not even able to guarantee the support of his own party. This sentiment was deepened by polls showing that the vast majority of the Mexican populace opposed the centerpiece of the Fox fiscal reform proposal. The weight of history also came into play. In 1995 the PRI supported the initiative of President Ernesto Zedillo to increase the value-added tax from 10 percent to 15 percent. To this day the PRI is convinced that this decision was a determining factor in its electoral losses of 1997 and 2000. The PRI thus withheld its support.

The third shortcoming of the government's legislative strategy was its assumption that the Indigenous Law and hence the start of peace negotiations would be quick and easy. With this victory in hand, it was believed that Fox would enjoy the increased political capital needed to push the fiscal reform through Congress. This supposition was patently wrong, yet even after this became evident the government failed to modify its legislative strategy. Instead, the fiscal reform was introduced in the midst of the debate on the Indigenous Law. Given that 44 percent of legislators gave greater priority to passing the Indigenous Law in the spring congressional session while only 29 percent prioritized the fiscal reform, the fiscal reform took a back seat. On April 17 Congress decided to postpone consideration of the fiscal reform until a special session of Congress could be arranged, or until the next regular congressional session began in September.

Following this congressional decision, the executive modified its legislative strategy on the margins. Still unwilling to negotiate the contents of the proposal, it began to apply pressure on the legislature to approve the president's proposal as soon as possible. Fox's coordinator for public policy, Eduardo Sojo, referred to the congressional decision to postpone consideration of the reform as "irresponsible" and the president himself called on all political forces to put aside their differences and to come together in the national interest to approve the fiscal reform. In late May a newly cooperative PAN aired a series of television spots that took a more hard-line approach. They argued that in the past, tax increases were absorbed by corrupt politicians rather than applied to productive investments. In the new post-PRI democratic reality, however, this would no longer occur.

Not surprisingly, the PRI reacted badly to this new strategy. More troubling was the strategy's total failure to generate pressure on the PRI and thereby force it to cooperate. The strategy was based on the belief that a popular president could go over the heads of the politicians and appeal directly to the people. Popular support for the president would pressure legislators to cooperate out of fear of the electoral consequences associated with defying public opinion. This strategy failed for two reasons. It incorrectly assumed that Mexican legislators are susceptible to public pressure. In a political system that prohibits reelection, the political future of politicians is determined by the party rather than by voters. As such, politicians are not accountable to the electorate and hence largely immune to public opinion. Further, the Mexican public never supported Vicente Fox's proposal to tax food and medicines. The likelihood that they would pressure legislators to approve this measure, even if they had the power to do so, was far-fetched at best.

Only following the failure of this "revised" legislative strategy did the Fox administration begin to negotiate with the legislature in search of a consensus proposal. Unfortunately, the negotiations quickly stalled over the value-added tax. Without progress through June and July, President Fox began to lobby personally for his initiative in meetings with business leaders, union leaders, and the national governors, but still without success.

Throughout the fall the fiscal reform remained hostage to PRI party politics, a total lack of public support for the initiative, and more strategic errors. As the November date of the PRI's national assembly approached, there was little hope that any competing power bases within the PRI would be willing to risk approving a massively unpopular tax reform. Driving this point home was the decision by the party leadership to prohibit PRI legislators from voting for any fiscal reform that included a value-added tax on food and medicine. Meanwhile, the failure of the Fox government to convince the public of the wisdom of its proposed reform guaranteed that the electoral costs during the 2003 legislative and the 2006 presidential elections associated with this obstinacy would be few.

Elements of the government's political strategy also did little to advance the fiscal reform. With the fiscal reform stalled in Congress, the executive began to blame the legislature for the lack of progress on the initiative. Not only was this argument disingenuous, it backfired. In a political order where the legislature recently won its independence after decades of subjection to the executive, any attack on the legislature by the executive will inevitably be seen as an effort to reduce Congress's newfound autonomy. The unsurprising reaction of the Mexican Congress in this circumstance was a jealous protection of its autonomy against "unwarranted attacks" and an associated reduction in its willingness to cooperate with the government.

---

*The Fox administration has found governing much more difficult than campaigning for the presidency.*

---

As the end of the legislative session approached and with no significant progress on the tax issue being made, the government's strategy seemed to shift once more. The government now seemed willing to consider any and all recommendations to modify its value-added tax proposal. The flurry of proposals that emerged from government circles in early December created the impression of an administration desperate for reform. This image of desperation only deepened the PRI's conviction that it could block all the core elements of the government's reform proposal and benefit from it politically. In the end Mexico was left with some tax increases incorporated in the 2002 budget instead of a comprehensive fiscal reform.

## WHAT LIES AHEAD FOR MEXICO?

The first year of the Fox administration produced much less legislatively than even the worst prognostications anticipated. This poor legislative performance owes much to the difficulties encountered by all Mexican political actors in their effort to adapt to Mexico's post-PRI political environment. The Fox administration has found governing much more difficult than campaigning for the presidency. As the candidate capable of successfully challenging the PRI, popular opinion tended to discount Fox's inconsistencies. In the presidency this characteristic has made the administration appear weak and rudderless. As president of Coca-Cola, a delegative managerial strategy worked very well but in a presidency populated by powerful personalities with overlapping responsibilities and very limited experience in government, it has proved problematic at best. Emerging from a sociopolitical culture shaped by over 70 years of authoritarian rule, the Fox government initially adopted a legislative strategy steeped in presidentialism but without the presidentialist structures to make it operate. And in its effort to fine-tune its legislative strategy, the Fox administration drew heavily on tactics designed in the advanced democracies but ineffective in a fledgling democratic order.

Mexican political parties have also shown a limited aptitude for adjustment during 2001. The process within the PAN of adapting its behavior to the reality of being the party in government has been difficult and remains incomplete. The PAN's resulting early opposition to the Fox government followed by somewhat tepid support created a strong disincentive for opposition cooperation with the administration and thereby helped torpedo Fox's legislative initiatives during 2001. For the PRD, the small size of its legislative faction continues to create a powerful disincentive to adapt its legislative strategy to Mexico's more democratic political environment. Obstructionism remains the rule of the day. And the internal PRI struggle throughout 2001 to determine how the party would be governed in the absence of presidential leadership prevented it from working constructively with the Fox government.

There is great hope in Mexico that the country's political actors will learn from their mistakes in 2001, adapt tolerably to democratic politics, and finally begin to get things done in 2002. Some positive signs point in this direction. The PAN ceased to operate as an opposition force and by the end of the year the party's legislative leadership was leading the charge for the administration in the search for a consensus on fiscal reform. The PRI will have a strong and legitimate president as of March 4, 2002, which should finally give the party a unified leadership structure with the capacity to take political risks. And the executive has clearly learned that it must negotiate with Congress and that it must establish a much more unified and coherent image as government.

But many signs also suggest that Mexico is likely to remain in neutral during 2002. Although the PAN is cooperating more with the government, it is still extremely jealous of its autonomy and continues to search for a means to avoid damaging party interests while supporting its president. The PRI may have an effective leadership beginning in March, but it remains a party dedicated almost exclusively to the mission of retaking political power. If working with Fox will further this aim, the PRI will cooperate. But if the party perceives weakness on the part of the executive or sees political opportunity to be had by opposing its initiatives (especially in the run-up to the 2003 legislative elections), the PRI will be obstructionist. And there is much to suggest that the Fox administration will not perform significantly better in 2002 than in 2001. Although there were rumors in late 2001 of a significant restructuring of the executive branch, it seems likely that whatever changes are implemented will not be sufficient to alter the essential structural characteristics of the Fox government. The administration will remain one composed of strong personalities with limited political sensibilities, overlapping missions, and without strong guidance from the top.

Mexico during 2002 is therefore likely to continue muddling along. It will make few positive advances toward the implementation of essential structural reforms, but neither will it descend into ungovernability and economic crisis. Mexico is on a trajectory toward economic growth constrained significantly by unresolved structural problems such as rising fiscal liabilities, insufficient energy production, and an inefficient judicial system. Slow growth and the resultant increase in the country's economic vulnerability will inevitably undermine the popularity of the Fox government and generate opportunities for the opposition. Although the PRI is still seen by most Mexicans in a negative light, this image could easily change should public disappointment with the Fox government deepen. Mexico thus faces the real prospect of a return to power by a largely unreconstructed PRI in the near future.

---

PAMELA K. STARR *is a professor of international relations at the Instituto Technológico Autónomo de México (ITAM) in Mexico City. She has written extensively on the Mexican political economy.*

From *Current History*, February 2002, pp. 58-65. © 2002 by Current History, Inc. Reprinted by permission.

# SOUTH AFRICA: DEMOCRACY WITHOUT THE PEOPLE?

*Robert Mattes*

**P**erhaps more than any other democratizing country, South Africa generates widely differing assessments of the present state and likely future prospects of its democracy. If one takes the long view—comparing South Africa today to where it was just 12 years ago—it is difficult not to be enthusiastic about its accomplishments and its future. South Africa successfully emerged from the shadow of apparently irreconcilable conflict and unavoidable racial civil war to create a common nation. It has negotiated two democratic constitutions and has held four successful nationwide elections for national and local government. On the economic front, it has avoided the triple-digit inflation that many feared would accompany a populist economic strategy of redistribution and government intervention. It has stabilized the expanding debt and reversed the double-digit inflation inherited from the apartheid-era government. There have been impressive gains in employment opportunities and income for the growing black middle class, and poor blacks have seen unprecedented improvements in access to basic necessities.

Yet if one looks at South Africa's new democracy in a comparative perspective, one's enthusiasm is greatly tempered, if not altogether removed. Crossnational analysis has highlighted three broad sets of factors crucial to democratic consolidation: a growing economy that steadily reduces inequality; stable and predictable political institutions; and a supportive political culture. In terms of these factors, an analysis of South Africa yields, at best, some reasons for guarded optimism and, at worst, many grounds for serious concern.

In each area, today's South Africa presents a paradox. In terms of political culture, South African society played a key role in achieving democracy through its widespread opposition to the apartheid regime. The country's numerous and diverse civil society organizations range from community grassroots groups to national trade unions and nongovernmental organizations. Yet citizens are not particularly supportive of democratic rule and now display low levels of community and political participation. Economically, macroeconomic stability, fiscal discipline, and low inflation sit alongside weak business confidence, low growth, massive unemployment, and ris-

ing intraracial inequality. Politically, an internationally praised constitution designed to promote multiparty competition and individual rights is overshadowed by one-party dominance and limited governmental accountability. Thus, seven years into its new dispensation, South Africa's democracy in form appears to be relatively healthy, but in substance shows signs of early decay.

## Economic Development

South Africa's economic policy makers should be proud of a number of accomplishments. The national budget deficit has shrunk from 8 percent to around 2 percent of GDP. Public and private affirmative-action initiatives in education, business ownership, and hiring have created a sizeable black middle class.[1] Since 1995, more than a million low-cost houses have been built, and the poor now have access to free medicine and more than 700 additional healthcare clinics. More than 5 million needy children now get a fifth to a quarter of their daily nutritional needs through school-based programs. More than 2 million people have received access to electricity and 7 million to water.[2] Relatively low inflation, around 6 percent, means that working South Africans are able to keep up with the cost of living.

Yet the sluggish economy has actually shed 500,000 formal jobs over this period and deprived hundreds of thousands of households of the income needed to make ends meet. Broadly defined, unemployment now stands at 36 percent.[3] A lack of business confidence has stifled both domestic and foreign investment, thereby hampering growth. While growth has been running at approximately 3 percent annually since 1995, the government sees growth of 6 to 7 percent as a prerequisite to cutting unemployment and reducing inequality.

Interracial inequalities have been reduced as a result of increasing black incomes and the redistributive effects of government spending, but inequality within all race groups has increased. Among blacks the top one-fifth of all households have made impressive strides while the bottom two-fifths have moved backwards.[4]

Recently, a new specter has appeared on the economic horizon. In its September 1999 decision to move forward with a R29.9 billion package of arms purchases, the government appears to have ignored internal feasibility studies warning that any depreciation of the currency could increase cost significantly. This has in fact happened, and the full costs of the deal are now estimated to be at least R50 billion. Indeed, the costs of this deal threaten to spiral out of control and consume any future funds the government had intended for increased poverty alleviation.

## Disappointing Institutions

South Africa's 1996 Constitution is the darling of both liberals and social democrats around the world. Widely seen as a "state of the art" document, it contains a wide array of classic political and socioeconomic rights, institutional innovations such as the National Council of Provinces, a range of independent watchdog agencies and commissions, and an activist Constitutional Court. The electoral system (pure proportional representation with no thresholds) has induced virtually all parts of political society to play the electoral game and has allowed the representation of a wide range of organized tendencies. Yet the constitutional framework is significantly flawed in several respects, particularly with regard to the interaction among party politics, voter representation, and legislative-executive relations.

First of all, various features of the Constitution limit voters' control over their elected representatives. While the electoral system provides for high degrees of "collective representation" (the overall balance among parties mirrors aggregate election results) and "descriptive representation" (the legislature tends to look like the electorate in terms of ideology, race, and ethnicity), it has created no direct link between legislators and voters. Constitutional provisions also eject from Parliament any member who leaves or is forced out of a political party, further reducing any incentive for MPs to represent public opinions running counter to the party line.

In addition, the Constitution does little to effect the separation of powers between the legislature and the executive; other than a formal vote of no confidence, few mechanisms exist with which the legislature may check executive action. Any rigorous parliamentary oversight by majority-party MPs places them in the difficult position of criticizing senior party leaders, who could eject them from the party and hence from Parliament. This ability to substitute loyal MPs for disloyal ones also potentially enables the governing party to preclude any vote of no confidence.

A minimalist theory of democracy would argue that, even with this constitutional framework, sufficient public influence over government can still be secured simply by holding regular free and fair elections. The threat of the next election forces the ruling party to "anticipate the voters' reactions" to current policy decisions and thus brings

about an acceptable level of popular control and accountability. In South Africa, however, what is in theory a multiparty system is in fact completely dominated by one party. The ruling African National Congress (ANC) won 66 percent of the vote in 2000, up 4 percent from 1994, and is just one seat shy of the two-thirds majority necessary to amend the Constitution unilaterally. It also is the majority party in seven of the nine provincial governments—enjoying overwhelming dominance in at least five—and has decisive control in five of the country's six largest city governments. Part of this dominance is due to positive voter evaluations of its performance, but part of it is also thanks to the substantial number of dissatisfied black voters who do not identify with the ANC yet have thoroughly negative views of virtually all other parties.[5] For all intents and purposes, the ANC has few reasons to worry about future voter reactions to its current decisions.

Over the past five years, this constitutional and electoral landscape has resulted in several worrisome tendencies. First of all, there has been a trend toward centralism within the ANC. National party structures have increasingly extended their powers at the provincial and local levels; candidates for provincial premierships and local mayoralties are now nominated by a central committee rather than by provincial or local branches. Several provincial party structures have simply been dissolved and reformed by the national party, ostensibly because of "disunity" or "ill discipline," but critics have viewed these actions as attempts to head off grassroots movements critical of the president. The national party machinery has also deposed several provincial premiers, some of whom have been popular leaders widely seen as future challengers for party leadership.

The ANC's ability to eject people from Parliament by expelling them from the party was underscored in 1997 when it jettisoned one of its most popular figures, Bantu Holomisa, because he had publicly accused a sitting cabinet minister and former Bantustan ruler of apartheid-era corruption. Indeed, imposing party discipline has been an increasing preoccupation. At a 2000 national party meeting, Secretary-General Kgalema Motlanthe reminded members that "the principles of democratic centralism still guided party structures." New ANC members must promise to combat "any tendency toward disruption or factionalism."[6] Moreover, the interval between party conferences has been extended from three years to five, thereby limiting opportunities for the rank and file to elect senior party organs.

Very recently, the ANC suddenly dropped its steadfast opposition to legislators crossing the floor. This shift was prompted by a conflict that emerged between the key partners of the main opposition coalition, the Democratic Alliance (DA). As a result, the New National Party (the NNP is the direct heir of the architects of apartheid) decided to exit the coalition and enter into talks with the ANC. The ANC changed its position principally to enable NNP Cape Town city councilors to leave the DA and cross into an alliance with the ANC, thus giving it control of the only city government it did not already dominate. As this article went to press, it has tabled legislation that would allow the president to declare specific windows of time in which legislators at national, provincial, and municipal levels could cross the floor to new or existing parties and still keep their seats.[7] Apart from the naked political opportunism exhibited by these events, the ANC has yet to explain how it can allow members to switch parties and still observe the constitutional requirement that election results must result in proportional representation.

The increasing tendency of ANC central party bosses to stifle open debate and dissent perhaps explains how the government was able to impose one of its most important policies—the neoliberal "Growth, Employment and Reconstruction" (GEAR) program—over the strong objections of its alliance partners, the South African Communist Party (SACP) and the Congress of South African Trade Unions (COSATU). SACP and COSATU members complain that "consultations" over economic policy have amounted to little more than the ANC dictating what the policy will be.[8] COSATU and SACP MPs (who sit in Parliament as ANC members) have chafed under the traditions of collective cabinet decisions and "democratic centralism." These simmering internal differences finally exploded in August 2001 when union leaders, cabinet ministers, and the president publicly exchanged insults, and massive strikes were called in an effort to embarrass the government during the United Nations antiracism conference in Durban.

## Problems of Governance

Beyond its handling of its own internal affairs, the manner in which the ANC has treated the institutions of governance is also a cause for concern. The governing party has failed to heed the 1996 Constitution's call that it pass legislation to enable Parliament to amend spending bills. (Currently, MPs only have the choice between accepting a bill or rejecting it altogether.) Additionally, the ANC has recently introduced two pieces of legislation containing seven separate amendments to the Constitution. The most important would reorder the relationship between the Appellate Court and Constitutional Court, scrap constitutional limits on the tenure of Constitutional Court justices, put their tenure in the hands of Parliament, enable the president to appoint two deputy ministers who are not MPs, allow national government intervention in municipal governments that do not comply with financial management standards, and broaden the finance minister's monopoly on introducing financial legislation. Not only does this rapid and far-reaching change have grave implications for the integrity of the Constitution, it is being attempted without giving other parties the opportunity to take positions on each provision separately.[9]

On several occasions, the ANC has invoked party loyalty to prevent Parliament from conducting effective oversight of executive action. In 1996, party leaders reportedly ordered members of the Portfolio Committee on Health to refrain from any tough questioning of the health minister during hearings on the unauthorized expenditure of R14 million for a dubious HIV/AIDS education musical called *Sarafina 11*.[10] And just recently, President Mbeki reportedly blocked internal party demands that Majority Whip Tony Yengeni appear before Parliament's Ethics Committee to explain why he received—but did not report—a discounted luxury truck from a European defense company that was bidding for an arms subcontract.

The most profound crisis in executive-legislative relations, however, originated in the R29.9 billion arms deal of 1999. In the second half of 2000, Parliament's Standing Committee on Public Accounts (SCOPA) began receiving allegations of nepotism, cronyism, and conflict of interest having to do with the negotiation of the deal. After an auditor general's report questioned the government's decision to select one of the more expensive sets of available options and highlighted deviations from accepted procurement practices, SCOPA (which traditionally operates on nonpartisan lines and is headed by an opposition party MP) launched its own inquiry, which included a high-profile anticorruption agency called the Special Investigating Unit (SIU). Although Parliament unanimously adopted a resolution in support of the inquiry, President Mbeki and other ANC leaders quickly attacked the process due to the inclusion of the SIU. The leader of the ANC delegation on SCOPA was replaced. Under pressure from party leaders, SCOPA's ANC members distanced themselves from the inclusion of the SIU, broke off communication with other investigators, and blocked efforts to obtain further information from the army and the government. The significance of this episode is hard to overstate. Parliament may continue to play an active role in developing and amending legislation in areas of no great interest to the executive, but when there is a difference of opinion on matters that are important to the executive, it will always prevail.

Perhaps no event better illustrates the troubling direction that South African politics has taken than what is now simply known as "the plot." When intra-ANC tensions began to surface in 2001, Minister of Safety and Security Steve Tshwete apparently took seriously charges that senior ANC officials were enlisting other party members and journalists in an anti-Mbeki campaign and (improbably) were spreading rumors implicating Mbeki in the 1992 murder of SACP leader Chris Hani. Operating on the strange assumption that the president's life would be endangered if these rumors were widely believed, Tshwete launched a police investigation into the matter and the possible involvement of former premiers Mathwes Phosa and Tokyo Sexwale, as well as Cyril Ramaphosa, the father of the 1993 and 1996 constitutions. Moreover, Tshwete went on national television to name the three as the subject of an official police investigation into a "plot" against Mbeki.

In short, a faction of the ruling party was using the police to deter what appeared to be legitimate canvassing, revealing that those in the highest positions of power are capable of conflating internal lobbying and caucusing with a treasonous "plot." On the positive side, however, both Mbeki and Tshwete quickly drew the wrath of COSATU, the SACP, and other key voices in civil society and the media. Mbeki did eventually say that Tshwete was "wrong" to publicly name the three, yet he chose not to fire the minister and went so far as to say that Tshwete was only doing his duty.[11]

Another worrying aspect of South Africa's institutional development is the gap between the government's aspirations and the state's capacity. While the government has demonstrated an impressive ability to use parastatal agencies to deliver water, electricity, and telephones, and to create government subsidies to allow people to purchase homes, the picture is not nearly so impressive in other areas. The most obvious is crime. Not only have most kinds of crime—especially violent crime—increased substantially since 1994, but the number of prosecutions launched and convictions attained has *declined*.[12] Law enforcement is so hard-pressed to fight ordinary crime that the national police commissioner recently refused the minister of health's request to commit personnel to enforce newly passed antismoking legislation. He also said that there were no resources available to enforce new legislation on domestic violence or on banning the use of cell phones by drivers.

One final problem of democratic governance in South Africa has less to do with political institutions than with the personality of President Thabo Mbeki and his stance on HIV/AIDS. In the face of one of the highest HIV infection rates in the world, Mbeki has consistently chosen to fritter away the considerable symbolic authority of his office by questioning the causal link between HIV and AIDS, investing time and resources in a presidential commission evenly divided between mainstream and "dissident" scientists. The government has stalled, if not blocked, funding for affordable anti-retroviral drugs and the distribution of available drugs that would drastically reduce the rates of mother-to-child transmission of HIV. Most recently, the government has moved to discredit and suppress a report by the country's Medical Research Council that directly contradicts Mbeki's attempts to minimize the impact of AIDS.[13]

## Trends in Public Opinion

A country's political culture does not develop in a vacuum. Rather, it is against a background of economic and political trends and developments that public opinion about a democratic regime, a political system, and citizenship must be assessed and understood. A review of a range of public opinion indicators collected by the Institute for Democracy in South Africa (Idasa) since 1995 demonstrates that South African political culture is not yet mature enough to consolidate democratic practices.[14]

South Africans' support for democracy is lukewarm and has not grown in any substantial way over the past five years. With increasingly tenuous connections between the voters and their government and increasing policy disaffection, trust in government and satisfaction with economic and political performance are declining sharply. Perhaps most importantly, the web of organizations and the impressive tradition of popular participation that emerged to challenge the apartheid system have withered. Indeed, across almost all the key indicators of democratic political culture, South Africans compare quite poorly to their neighbors throughout southern Africa and elsewhere on the continent.

*National identity.* One area of political culture that does not appear to pose a major threat to democracy in South Africa, though it is often thought to do so, is the so-called "national question." The common view holds that, in deeply divided societies such as South Africa, people identify primarily with this or that component part—often their own racial, ethnic, or religious group—rather than with the multiethnic or multinational state. President Mbeki has entered this debate with his "two nations" thesis, which states that South Africa comprises "two nations," one relatively wealthy and largely white and the other relatively poor and overwhelmingly black. Although Mbeki's economic prognosis may still be largely correct, there is no evidence that the word "nation" ought to be applied to these economic divisions.

In fact, surveys since 1995 have revealed widespread popular consensus on the existence of a South African political community that transcends racial and economic divisions. Nationally, 90 percent or more are proud of being called South African, say it is a key part of how they see themselves, and want their children to think of themselves as South African. It is important to note, however, that there are some cracks in this consensus, as the proportions of white and Indian respondents agreeing with some of these items fell an average of 10 percent between 1995 and 2000.

To be sure, these high levels of self-identification with the nation exist alongside strong ties to subnational self-defined identity groups. Yet this may not be so much a contradiction as an indication that members of historically competing groups feel sufficiently comfortable to identify with a larger national community only when they have a strong sense of communal identity. And just as it is mistaken to assume that economic divisions necessarily translate into different visions of nationhood, it is also mistaken to assume that a strong sense of national community necessarily brings about domestic tranquility. Indeed, high levels of national identity coexist with significant levels of in-group chauvinism, out-group rejection, racism, and intolerance.[15]

Yet few South Africans cite racism or discrimination as a problem requiring government intervention. In 1994, six months after the first election, one in five respondents spontaneously cited problems of discrimination and the removal of apartheid as one of the three "most important problems facing this country that government ought to address." Since then, however, no more than 5 percent have mentioned this issue. A recent survey by the South African Institute of Race Relations found that racism was rated ninth on a list of "unresolved problems," with just 8 percent listing it as a priority matter. In fact, 48 percent of the total sample (and 49 percent of black respondents) said that race relations had improved in recent years, while 25 percent said they had deteriorated.[16]

*Support for democracy.* As of July—August 2000, 60 percent of South Africans said that democracy "is preferable to any other kind of government," and 55 percent said that democracy is always the best form of government "even if things are not working." Yet just 30 percent said they were "unwilling" to live under a nonelected government that was also able to "impose law and order, and deliver houses and jobs." On none of these items is there any evidence of increased support for democracy since 1995.

Yet South Africans are likely to reject authoritarian alternatives to liberal democracy when they are mentioned. Three-fourths would disapprove of abandoning multiparty elections for military rule, 66 percent would disapprove of a return to apartheid, but just 56 percent would disapprove of one-party rule. Moreover, only 40 percent reject all four alternatives.[17] South Africans' support for democracy and rejection of authoritarian rule are consistently lower than in most of the eight southern African countries where Afrobarometer surveys have been conducted (generally ahead only of Lesotho and sometimes Namibia); on those items that have been asked in 12 countries across the continent, South Africa ranks as one of the lowest.[18]

Many more South Africans give positive evaluations to the present political system (58 percent) than to the apartheid regime (25 percent). These figures, however, show a significant increase since 1995 in "nostalgia" for the way the country is perceived to have been governed under apartheid, especially among white, "colored," and Indian respondents. And while South Africans widely prefer their present form of government to what they had before, their optimism about how they will be governed in the future has declined noticeably.

An important aspect of South Africans' attitudes toward democracy is their highly economic and substantive understanding of the concept. When unprompted, South Africans spontaneously see democracy as the realization of individual rights and civil liberties. When provided with a list of constitutive elements of democracy, however, an average of 60 percent say that socioeconomic goods are "essential" for a country to be called democratic, while an average of just 35 percent say the same about procedural components like regular elections, multiparty competition, and freedom of speech. This 25-point "gap" between substantive and procedural understandings of democracy is by far the largest in southern Africa.

*Evaluations of democratic performance.* Although many international analysts place South Africa at the forefront of democratic development in Africa,[19] the country's own citizens are not so sanguine. In 2000, one year after the second successful democratic national election, nearly three-quarters thought the 1999 election had been either "completely free and fair" (42 percent) or "free and fair with some minor problems" (31 percent). Yet the citizens of Namibia (78 percent) and Botswana (83 percent) were even more optimistic when evaluating their recent elections. And when asked to assess the extent of democracy in their country, 60 percent of South Africans said the country was either "completely democratic" (26 percent) or "democratic with some minor exceptions" (34 percent). This figure placed South Africans parallel to Zambians and Malawians (62 percent), but behind Namibians (71 percent) and citizens of Botswana (83 percent), the region's oldest democracy. Finally, 52 percent are satisfied with "the way democracy works in South Africa," which is higher than the 41 percent registered in 1995 but down from the 63 percent of November 1998. It is also lower than the figure recorded in Botswana (75 percent), Namibia (64 percent), Zambia (59 percent), or Malawi (57 percent).

*Views of political institutions.* When assessing their political institutions, South Africans are becoming increasingly pessimistic. As of July—August 2000, trust in elected institutions, approval ratings of elected officials' job performances, and the extent to which people saw them as responsive to public opinion were all at the lowest levels yet measured under the new political system. Only 41 percent of respondents said they trusted President Mbeki, and 34 percent said they could trust Parliament. For such state institutions as the army, the courts, the police, and the criminal justice system, trust ranged from 35 to 44 percent. Fifty percent of South Africans approved of Mbeki's performance over the preceding 12 months, and 45 percent approved of Parliament.

A large part of this trend can be attributed to a general economic downturn and the accumulating political problems confronting the Mbeki government. For example, job creation has consistently been seen as the country's "most important problem," cited as such by 76 percent of all respondents in 2000. Yet just 10 percent approved of the government's efforts to create jobs. Sixty percent cited crime and security as a priority concern, yet just 18 percent approved of the way government has handled the problem. Indeed, surveys conducted by the Human Sciences Research Council showed that the proportion who said they felt "safe" or "very safe on most days" fell dramatically from 73 percent in 1994 to 44 percent in 1999.[20]

In addition, while public perceptions of corruption leveled off in 2000, they remain very high. Thus, even before the investigation of the arms deal, 50 percent of all South Africans felt that most or all government officials were involved in corruption. Two-thirds felt that the new government was at least as corrupt as the apartheid regime. How the ANC confronts the growing accusations of influence-buying and conflict of interest in the arms deal will tell us a great deal about the future course of public opinion.

Declining trust in government must also be attributed to the aforementioned flaws in South Africa's representative system. By 2000, only 54 percent of blacks and 46 percent of all respondents felt that the president was interested in their opinions; 48 percent and 42 percent, respectively, felt similarly toward Parliament; and only 33 and 31 percent said so about their local governments.

*Economic evaluations.* Individual evaluations of the economy have paralleled the country's macroeconomic trends. As recently as April 1999, more than half of all South Africans were optimistic about the country's economic future. By July—August 2000, however, just over one-quarter expected the economy to improve in the next year (the figure went from 63 to 35 percent among black respondents). Perceptions of relative deprivation have also increased sharply. Even in 1995, despite one of the highest rates of income inequality in the world, only 32 percent of South Africans said they were worse off than others. This was largely due to the fact that black South Africans tended to compare themselves to other blacks rather than to whites. By mid-2000, however, this figure had increased sharply to 50 percent. In the same survey, 31 percent of blacks said their lives were worse now than under apartheid, up sharply from 13 percent in 1997.

*Citizenship and participation.* The most troubling of the survey results are probably the data on citizen participation and interaction with government. South Africa now has one of the most passive citizenries in southern Africa. As of mid-2000, only 11 percent of South Africans said they "frequently" engaged in political discussion and 12 percent said they paid attention to government and public affairs "always" or "most of the time." Both figures were the lowest yet measured since 1995, and also the lowest out of seven southern African countries. South Africans are less likely to participate in community-level organizations (such as church or self-help groups) or political actions (such as attending election rallies or working for a party) than Zimbabweans, Zambians, Malawians, or Namibians.

Of even greater concern are South Africans' extremely low levels of actual contact with government leaders or other influential community leaders. Just 6 percent said they had contacted a government or party official in the previous year to give them their views, and only 10 percent had contacted any other community leader. Both figures are the lowest in southern Africa. Perhaps the most damning finding of the entire 2000 survey was that just 0.2 percent—that is, only four of the 2,200 respondents—said they had made contact with a sitting member of Parliament in 1999-2000. Absolutely no one in the sample said he had attended any hearing or meeting organized by Parliament or by an MP. This passivity cannot be traced to a lack of information, since South Africans actually have the highest rates of radio, television, and newspaper coverage in the region. Neither can it be traced to poverty, since South Africa's much poorer neighbors tend to have far higher rates of contact.

## Fostering Citizenship

Although the public opinion data reviewed here are worrisome, they do not suggest a deeply held "culture" of norms, values, beliefs, or predispositions inhospitable to democracy. Rather, it would be more accurate to see the current contours of public opinion as *consequences* of, or even *reactions* to, the problems facing South Africa's economic and institutional development. South Africans' support for democracy is modest, in part, because they understand democracy to mean the delivery of a range of socioeconomic goods, and progress toward this goal had been slow.

Surveys show that, compared to other countries in the region, South Africans have had one of the highest rates of participation in protest action in the past and are among the most likely to resort to protest again, given the reason and the opportunity. This rules out any notion of an inherent "culture" of apathy or passivity. South Africans participate at low rates between elections because the system offers them few incentives to do so. They do not contact parliamentarians or attend parliamentary "outreach" hearings at least in part because they do not know who their parliamentarians are and because MPs have no incentive to reach out to people.

Afrobarometer results from southern Africa underscore the strong impact of constitutional design, especially the electoral system, on the degree of citizen-MP contact. In Namibia and South Africa, the two countries with proportional representation, the rate of contact with an MP or attendance at a parliamentary meeting or hearing is 1 percent and 0.2 percent, respectively. Among the five countries with first-past-the-post systems, contact rates are 7 percent in Zimbabwe and Zambia and 5 percent in Malawi and Lesotho. (Botswana is the "outlier" with a contact rate of 2 percent.) While all these figures may sound low, there is a huge difference between one out of every 10 or 20 people in each community having had contact with their elected national representatives and one out of every 100 or 200.

While South Africa is admired internationally for the negotiating skills and processes it has developed since 1990, as well as for its state-of-the-art Constitution, its citizens have been left behind by the past decade's preoccupation with elite bargaining and institutional design.

South Africans need to shift the focus onto problems of citizenship, representation, and participation. In the next decade, they need to put as much emphasis on building a grassroots culture of citizenship as they have already put on building a culture of elite accommodation. This requires renewed emphasis on civic education by schools and civil society organizations, in order to teach citizens the intrinsic value of democracy and equip them with the resources necessary to participate more fully in the political process.

Furthermore, this requires institutions that encourage meaningful participation. South African constitutional designers need to rethink their assumptions about how institutions interact with ordinary people, and they must abandon the view (implicit in the present constitution) that citizen participation emanates from a sense of duty rather than from incentives and self-interest. Therefore, public participation in democratic government should be encouraged not through special processes or forums but by giving citizens reasons to engage with their elected representatives nationally, provincially, and locally. This requires legislators and councilors who can listen to identifiable constituencies and be persuaded by them, and who can in turn act according to the wishes of the voters. This goal can be accomplished by a system of strong separation of powers with weak party discipline, but it can also be accomplished in a parliamentary system, as long as party caucuses are democratic and autonomous from the executive. Either way, more effective constituency representation is a necessary, though not sufficient, condition to bring about greater contact between citizens and representatives.

Indeed, the window for electoral reform in South Africa is now open, if only because existing electoral legislation has lapsed and the ANC has begun the process of amending related legislation in order to cooperate with the NNP. But simply creating single-member or multi-member districts will not be enough. Representatives must also be required to live in their districts, since if parties can "parachute" members into "safe districts" or "helicopter" them out when they face defeat, it will remove any incentive for MPs to anticipate voter reactions. Finally, lifting the ban on floor-crossing, as the ANC recently proposed, is misguided. Changing parties midterm is an undemocratic violation of the implicit contract under which a candidate stands for election, and it also disturbs the proportionality created by the voters. It would be better to amend the Constitution so that MPs have to give up their seats only if they *choose* to leave their political party, not if they are forced out. Mavericks who want to challenge party discipline will be less likely to be intimidated by party bosses if they know they can still keep their parliamentary seats if they are expelled from the party.

Together, these reforms should give legislators greater incentives to reach out to voters and to represent them, and give citizens and interest groups more reason to contact their representatives and interact with legislative bodies. In addition, they could help representatives more effectively oversee and check the actions of mayors, premiers, and presidents. Without such reforms, it is difficult to imagine the consolidation of South African democracy.

## Notes

1. Andrew Whiteford and Dirk San Deventer, *Winners and Losers: South Africa's Changing Income Distribution in the 1990s* (Johannesburg: WEFA, 1999), 25–26.
2. Reg Rumney, "A Question of Perceptions," *Mail and Guardian* (Johannesburg), 3–9 August 2001, 15; Howard Barrell, "Back to the Future: Renaissance and South African Domestic Policy," *African Security Review* 9 (2000): 87; "Housing: A Good News Story," *RDP Monitor* 7 (May 2001): 2; "Electricity: Seeing Clearly Now," *RDP Monitor* 6 (July 2000): 2; and Josey Ballenger, "Troubled School Feeding Plan Is Still Essential," *Reconstruct*, 11 October 1998, 1.
3. John Daniel, "Discussion Paper on Socio-Economic Issues," presented to U. S. Department of State, Bureau of Intelligence and Research seminar on "South Africa: Future of Democratization" (Washington, D. C.: Meridian International Center, 5 April 2001); Jonathan Katzenellenbogen, "Jobless Figures Remain Over 25%," *Business Day* (Johannesburg), 27 January 2001, 3.
4. Andrew Whiteford and Dirk San Deventer, *Winners and Losers*, 11–19; Debbie Budlender, "Earnings Inequality in South Africa, 1995–1998," *Measuring Poverty In South Africa* (Pretoria: Statistics South Africa, 2000).
5. Robert Mattes and Jessica Piombo, "Opposition Parties and the Voters in South Africa's 1999 General Election," *Democratization* 8 (Autumn 2001): 101–28.
6. Cited in Tom Lodge, "Romantic Aspiration," *Mail and Guardian* (Johannesburg), 10–16 August 2001, 17.
7. "Loss or Retention of Membership of National and Provincial Legislatures Bill," (Republic of South Africa) Draft Document: 12 November 2001; and Wyndham Hartley, "President in Driving Seat for Defections," *Business Day* (Johannesburg), 13 November 2001, 1.
8. See the interview with COSATU president Willie Mdasha in Howard Barrell and Sipho Seephe, *Mail and Guardian* (Johannesburg), 31 August–6 September 2001.
9. Patrick Laurence, "Debate These Changes One at a Time," *Focus* 23 (September 2001): 13–15.
10. Richard Calland, ed., *The First Five Years: A Review of South Africa's Democratic Parliament* (Cape Town: Idasa, 1999), 36.
11. Barry Streek, "Tshwete Was 'Wrong' to Name Plotters, Says Mbeki," *Mail and Guardian* (Johannesburg), 1–7 June 2001, 1.
12. David Bruce, "Suspect Crime Statistics Cannot Obscure rim Truth," *Sunday Independent* (Johannesburg), 10 June 2001, 9; Michael Dynes, "South Africa's Huge Steps on Long Walk to Prosperity," *Sunday Independent* (Johannesburg), 26 August 2001, 4; S. Pedrag, "Crime out of Control in South Africa," *MSNBC News*, 29 May 2000, available at *www.msnbc.com*; *Economist*, 24 February 2001, cited in John Daniel, "Discussion Paper on Socio-Economic Issues."
13. Nicoli Nattrass, *Ethics, Economics and AIDS Policy in South Africa*, CSSR Working Paper No. 1 (Cape Town: Centre for Social Science Research, University of Cape Town, August 2001); Howard Barrell and Jaspreet Kandra, "Shocking Aids Report Leaked," *Mail and Guardian* (Johannesburg), 5–11 October 2001, 2. For a detailed review of Mbeki's statements on the disease, see Drew For-

rest, "Behind the Smokescreen," *Weekly Mail & Guardian* (Johannesburg), 26 October to 1 November 2001, 25.

14. For the most comprehensive summary of these findings, see Robert Mattes, Yul Derek Davids, and Cherrel Africa, "Views of Democracy in South Africa and the Region: Trends and Comparisons," *Afrobarometer Working Papers Series*, No. 8 (Cape Town, Accra, and East Lansing: Afrobarometer, 2000); available at *www.afrobarometer.org*.

15. Robert Mattes, Donald Taylor, and Abigail Poore, "The Role of National Identity in Building a Democratic Culture in South Africa," paper presented at the Conference of the International Sociological Association's Research Group on Ethnic, Race and Minority Relations on "Multicultural Citizenship in the New South Africa" (Cape Town: Idasa Cape Town Democracy Centre, 15–17 December 1997).

16. "Racism 9th on Country's List of Problems," *Cape Times* (Cape Town), 24 August 2001, 5.

17. Michael Bratton, "Wide but Shallow: Measuring Popular Support for Democracy in Africa," paper presented at a workshop on "Democracy in Africa in Comparative Perspective," Stanford University, 27 April 2001.

18. The eight southern African states are Botswana, Lesotho, Malawi, Namibia, South Africa, Tanzania, Zambia, and Zimbabwe; the four not in southern Africa are Ghana, Mali, Nigeria, and Uganda.

19. Freedom House, for example, awards South Africa the highest score in southern Africa for 2000–2001 in terms of political rights. Larry Diamond has named it one of the four "liberal democracies" in the region (along with only Botswana, Namibia, and Malawi). See Larry Diamond, "Introduction," in Larry Diamond and Marc F. Plattner, eds., *Democratization in Africa* (Baltimore: Johns Hopkins University Press, 1999), ix-xxvi.

20. Nedbank/ISSS, "Criminal Justice Monitor," *Crime Index* 4 (January–February 2000).

*Robert Mattes* is associate professor in the department of political studies and director of the Democracy in Africa Research Unit in the Centre for Social Studies at the University of Cape Town. He is also an associate with the Institute for Democracy in South Africa (Idasa), and a co-founder and co-director of the Afrobarometer, a regular 12-country survey of Africans' attitudes toward democracy, markets, and civil society.

# Africa's Contradiction:
## *Nigeria on the Path to Democracy*

THOMAS TSAI

Associate Editor, *Harvard International Review*

Since Nigeria gained independence from Great Britain in 1960, democracy has had a difficult time taking root. The country's first post-colonial government was overthrown in January 1966 in a coup led by Major General Johnson Agiuyi Ironsi, who was later killed in a counter-coup in July of the same year by officers loyal to General Yakubu Gowon. More coups followed in July 1975 and February 1976 and the brief interlude of democracy between 1979 and 1986 was ended by another coup. In the 1990s, democracy finally seemed to be emerging during the presidency of Moshood Abiola only to be reversed by the despotic rule of General Sani Abacha.

With the death of Abacha in 1998, Nigeria finally seemed to be heading toward peace. Garnering 62 percent of the vote in February 1999, current president Olusegun Obasanjo has pledged to enact economic and political reforms. With over 120 million people and a position of leadership in African affairs, Nigeria has become Africa's contradiction. It offers the best opportunity for democracy in Africa, yet it is beset by several internal problems that, if not addressed, will make it one of Africa's greatest failures.

## *Ethnic Tensions*

Nigeria's most daunting challenge lies in overcoming the severe divisions among its competing religious and ethnic groups. In January 2002, clashes between the Hausa and Yoruba ethnic groups killed over 300 civilians in the chaotic aftermath of a deadly explosion at the Ikeja military barracks in Lagos. In recent months the Tiv and the Jukun tribal groups of central Nigeria have engaged in genocidal tribal raids. Since the restoration of civilian rule in May 1999, a total of over 10,000 Nigerians have died in civil strife.

These ethnic flare-ups revolving around the Tiv tribal group further highlight the flaws in Nigeria's government. On October 22, 2001, Nigerian soldiers drove into villages in the central Nigerian state of Benue, looting homes and murdering civilians. In that single episode more than 300 people

were killed. Among the more prominent victims were relatives of a former army chief of staff, Victor Malu, whose house was also looted. The army attack was motivated by revenge; Tiv tribesmen had earlier ambushed and killed 19 soldiers. Instead of finding the murderers, the army launched indiscriminate reprisals, and underlying the army's actions was a strong undercurrent of ethnic tension. While Malu is a Tiv, many of the soldiers involved in the attack and the defense minister who dismissed Malu are Junkuns.

Perhaps due to Nigeria's history of coups, Obasanjo has remained silent regarding the abuses of the military. As shown by its involvement in the Tiv-Junkun massacres, the military is still very much motivated by ethnic loyalties, something that the government cannot erase by fiat alone. Many obstacles remain in the quest to construct a unified national identity.

## *Unstable Federalism*

Further undermining national unity, Christian-Muslim antagonism runs deep in Nigeria, where the North is dominated by Muslims. The state of Zamfara in northwestern Nigeria overwhelmingly approved legislation extending the fundamentalist Islamic law code, Shari'a, to criminal cases. The Zamfara government established new Islamic courts and codes and justified the extension of Shari'a by pointing to section 277 of the 1999 constitution, which allows state level Shari'a courts to "exercise jurisdiction in civil proceedings involving questions of Islamic personal law." Christians and other critics in the South have argued that the extension was not legitimate because the constitution forbids a state religion. Although condemned by the federal government in Lagos, other northern states including Bauchi, Borno, Jigawa, Niger, Kano, Katsina, Sokoto, and Yobe have followed Zamfara's example.

The Islamization of the northern states highlights important failures of Nigeria's democracy. Until the constitution itself is revitalized, many Nigerian states will continue to

interpret the law as they wish. Although mandated by the constitution to hold elections in April 2002, numerous members of Nigeria's local government councils have decided not to relinquish their seats until 2003 due to confusion over the electoral laws. Moreover, the Senate's new legislation requires elections to proceed downward in the order of executive, senate, house, state, and local offices, raising the ire of Nigeria's 36 governors. The question of the sequence of elections is of little intrinsic importance, but the debate over the electoral act will have profound implications for legalism in Nigeria's burgeoning democracy.

Obasanjo, who faces re-election in 2003, is currently embroiled in a controversy regarding his own electoral prospects. In early April, scores of his supporters, including high officials in state and national politics, presented an official letter of support for Obasanjo's candidacy in next year's elections. This clarion call for Obasanjo's re-election may not seem egregious, but to many Nigerians it is too reminiscent of the Abacha past. Former Minister of Industry and current Senator Iyorchia Ayu remarked, "The president, if he truly wants to recontest, should come out and then we will assess him critically. If we decide to vote for him, it would be on the basis that we believe in him, not because some people are instigating politicians to come and beg him to run. It is wrong; he should not take the Sani Abacha road." The recent actions of Nigeria's politicians raise the specter of Abacha's reign, during which regional leaders would formally declare their support of Abacha, essentially eliminating the populace from the electoral process.

The challenge of uniting the country still remains to be surmounted. In an episode indicative of the nation's polarized politics, northern governors have alleged that the western states of Oyo and Ogun alone have enjoyed federal projects worth US$250 million while the 19 states of the North have yet to benefit from federal patronage. The northern governors have already rescinded their support for Obasanjo's re-election bid in 2003. Although the autonomy of state and local leaders is a vital component of federalism, Nigeria's harshly divisive regional politics still remains a major stumbling block on the road to democracy.

## Economic Woes

Many had hoped that democratization in Nigeria would bring about an economic renaissance after the corrupt regime of Abacha, who reportedly took US$43 billion from the nation's treasury. Despite Obasanjo's democratic credentials, he has not been immune to the grasp of corruption. Out of 91 nations surveyed by Transparency International's Global Corruption Report last year, Nigeria emerged second on its list of the most corrupt countries. Recurrent among the charges is Obasanjo's nepotism in elevating members of his ethnic group to high office.

Nigerian Senator Tokunbo Afikuyomi remarked last year that the "promises and prospects which the democratic experiment once held in view for most have given away to depression and despair. Some are even tempted to conclude that it would have been better for us to have remained in the Egypt of militarism than the wilderness of democratization without dividends." After three years of democracy, Nigeria's economy is still faltering despite its status as the world's sixth-largest exporter of petroleum, producing 1.9 million barrels a day, or 4.5 percent of the world's total production.

The government's handling of the economy has also been strongly criticized by the International Monetary Fund. Although Obasanjo stated that a tougher import inspection policy had raised customs revenue and limited fraud, the largest item in the 2002 budget is still expected to be military spending, with the defense budget amounting to US$430 million. In this poverty-stricken country of more than 120 million people, the military has for years accounted for the largest share of government spending. According to most military analysts, the military has little to show for the funds it receives because much of the money is siphoned off into private pockets.

Some limited economic reforms have been made. According to Rotimi Subero, a senior lecturer at Nigeria's University of Ibadan, Obasanjo has ambitiously embarked upon exchange rate reform, the privatization of a few public enterprises, an increase in public wages, and the improvement of Nigeria's gross currency reserves. Nevertheless, Nigeria's external debt continues to be a manacle on the nation's economy. In 2002, Nigeria will spend US$3.4 billion servicing its external debt of US$28.6 billion.

Undermining these reforms is the lack of a coherent program and the continuing corruption of Nigeria's politicians, most noticeably in the National Assembly. In 1999 the president of the Senate and the speaker of the House of Representatives were removed from their positions for forgery and perjury.

## Promising Trends

Despite Obasanjo's lack of resolve in his first three years in office, Nigeria remains one of Africa's great hopes. With the adoption of careful reforms, Nigeria can take on a vital role in the leadership of Africa. Last March, Obasanjo called on the presidents and diplomats of 19 African countries to decide on a unified code of conduct for African nations needing Western aid. The assistance plan, dubbed the New Partnership for African Development (NEPAD), calls for the establishment of an African peer-review mechanism and a "Council of the Wise" comprised of respected African figures who would monitor abuses of human rights and democracy. NEPAD has already been embraced by the international community; the inaugural meeting on April 15, 2002, in Dakar was attended by over 1,000 participants, including 20 African presidents and prime ministers, corporate leaders, and UN officials. As a primary architect of NEPAD along with Senegalese President Abdoulaye Wade, Algerian President Abdelaziz Bouteflika, and South African President Thabo Mbeki, Obasanjo has shown that regional cooperation can reap great economic and political dividends.

Another much lauded policy of Obasanjo is his recent commitment to initiate a program for comprehensive HIV testing of all Nigerians. By approving the budgetary establishment of over 300 primary health centers, Obasanjo has taken concrete steps toward stemming the AIDS epidemic in sub-Saharan Africa. Already, approximately 100 primary health care centers, vital additions to Nigeria's growing health care infrastructure, are ready for commissioning.

Professor Ibironke Akinsete, Nigeria's chairman of the National Action Committee on HIV/AIDS, has stated that "any country which aspires to lead Africa must take urgent and practical steps to reverse its... burden of HIV/AIDS." Nigeria has responded to the AIDS crisis by enacting vital measures to ensure the health of its people. In contrast to Mbeki's ignorance of the AIDS epidemic, Obasanjo and his administration have shown that Nigeria can become a leader in the struggle against AIDS in Africa.

## Fresh Opportunities

If actually implemented and coupled with stable government, initiatives such as NE-PAD would be a step toward achieving greater transparency and legitimacy for Nigeria. Echoing the general hope for the success of NEPAD, prominent Nigerian businessman Yemi Akeju declared, "With 700 million people, Africa is significantly a sector of the world that cannot be ignored... But what we are now looking out for are the investors. Investors worldwide are looking for a place where they will have fresh opportunity to do business. With the new climate created in Africa by the NEPAD initiative, one would say there are fresh opportunities here."

Nigeria can provide the leadership that Africa needs to effectively address the issues of globalization and democracy, yet its own democracy is still threatened by corruption and ethnic strife. Nigeria has also shown that it can make changes to ameliorate the legacy of decades of military rule. Although ethnic tension still divides Nigerian society, Obasanjo has the opportunity to mend the divisions by strengthening a legitimate Nigerian democracy.

Among one of the most daunting challenges remaining to be addressed is the relationship between the police and military in Nigeria. Alhaji Ibrahim Coomasie, former inspector general of police, recently noted the Nigerian police "has been torn between the civil populace and the military, so much so that its civil traditions were almost lost to military authoritarianism." In contrast, the current inspector general has embraced the military as a partner in fighting crime, adding uncertainty to the future role of Nigeria's military. Despite the marriage of the police and military, non-governmental organizations such as the Centre for Law Enforcement Education have fostered greater cooperation and trust between civilians and police through police-community partnerships. In order to ensure that the military does not become an agent of illegitimate power, it needs to be completely separated from the civilian police force. Increasing the size of the civilian police force from 180,000 to 577,000 officers, as Obasanjo has recently directed the inspector general to do, is no panacea. Nigeria must increase the transparency of its military and police forces to overcome the legacy of its military past.

Two futures for Africa are possible—one with a democratic and stable Nigeria, and one with a Nigeria stricken by autocratic rule, corruption, and intermittent coups. An entire continent awaits the result of the Nigerian experiment with democracy. Nigeria has the resources and can provide leadership to foster greater regional and international cooperation, leadership that many of Nigeria's neighbors need. A successful Nigerian democracy would provide hope for many of Africa's other burgeoning democracies.

# Article 35

**Special report** Politics in China

# Intimations of mortality

**As China's Communist Party celebrates its 80th birthday,
the country is changing too fast for its rulers to keep up**

BEIJING AND XINGTAI

THE industrial city of Xingtai, in the parched North China Plain, is the kind of place where you would expect to hear complaints about the way the Communist Party is running the country. Many of its state-owned factories are bankrupt. Unemployment is rising. Corruption and crime are rampant. Last year a deputy mayor and more than 30 other officials were arrested for their alleged roles in a multi-million-dollar bribery case. Early this year the authorities announced the arrest of 18 members of a gang of unemployed youths allegedly responsible for more than 130 incidents of mugging and highway robbery in and around the city over the past couple of years.

On the edge of town, one of Xingtai's biggest state-owned enterprises, the Jingniu Group, believes it has found a cure for this economic and moral decay: Mao Zedong Thought. In a country where Maoism is now rarely mentioned and most public images of the late chairman have long since been removed, Jingniu's approach is unusual, to say the least. Three years ago the company erected a statue of Mao in front of its window-pane factory in the suburbs. Then, late last year, it decided to spread the word more widely by setting up a Mao Zedong Thought website (http://www.mzdthought.com/). The company's manager, Wang Changlin, who is also its Communist Party chief, says the website received 400,000 hits in its first five months. "During this process of globalisation, Mao Zedong Thought will become even more important," says Mr Wang.

If only the answer were that simple. As it prepares to celebrate its 80th birthday on July 1st, the Chinese Communist Party is suffering crises of faith, identity and legitimacy. A few members, like Mr Wang, clutch at the past, more out of nostalgia for the supposed clean-living and hard-working spirit of the Maoist era than from any desire for a return to totalitarianism. Not even the party sounds very convinced by communism any more. At the last party congress, in 1997, delegates approved a declaration that achieving communism might take

several tens of generations—in non-Chinese-speak, hundreds of years.

Two forthcoming events are concentrating minds. The first is next year's 16th Communist Party Congress, at which sweeping leadership changes will be unveiled. To consolidate their power, the country's new rulers will need fresh ideas for coping with systemic corruption. They will need to tackle fast-growing crime and social unrest fuelled by economic dislocation and the growth of a disenfranchised underclass. In particular, they will need to satisfy the aspirations of a burgeoning class of people in private business—the "exploiters", whom the party once ruthlessly suppressed. In 1991 China had about 107,000 private businesses (defined as those with more than eight workers), employing 1.8m people. Today more than 24m people work in such businesses, and perhaps another 30m run smaller, or individual, concerns. Yet private businessmen are still officially barred from joining the party, even if their money-making is now given more encouragement.

The other event is China's accession to the World Trade Organisation (WTO), which could happen before the end of the year. This will exacerbate unemployment in some parts of the country. It will also bind China to international rules that will further diminish the role of government in the economy. As that role weakens, so too does the party's ability to intimidate and control ordinary citizens. Workers are leaving state-owned enterprises, with their once all-powerful party branches, in droves. Increasingly, it is market forces and personal skills, rather than party cells, that decide who gets jobs, who gets promoted and who gets the best housing. More optimistic Chinese intellectuals believe that economic globalisation will, over time, transform China politically as well.

## What's Chinese for "reform"?

In order to cope with these challenges, the party urgently needs to undertake political reform. But there are huge divisions, both within the party and outside it, over how best to allow the people to take part in politics without causing China to collapse as the Soviet Union did. Whichever way it turns, the party sees trouble ahead.

At the end of last year, China's Academy of Social Sciences conducted a survey of mid-ranking officials attending the Central Party School, the training centre for China's ruling elite. It found that political reform had displaced reform of state enterprises as their foremost concern. By "political reform", many Chinese officials mean little more than streamlining the bureaucracy. But the academy's report said the interest shown in this subject reflected "new contradictions and problems" in Chinese society—the euphemism for corruption, unemployment and unrest. "If there are no channels for letting off steam, the repressed discontent of individuals could well up into large-scale social instability," concluded a report published in May by the party's Organisation Department.

What is the party doing about this? So far, very little. President Jiang Zemin has at least sent a hint that he perceives a problem. Early last year he rolled out a new theory called the "Three Representatives". According to this, the party stands for "advanced productive forces, advanced Chinese culture and the fundamental interests of the majority." In Chinese terms, this is a breakthrough: Mr Jiang appeared to be redefining the party as everyone's best friend, not just the proletariat's. It could be the best friend of the private sector, too.

Despite the objections of a few diehard Maoists, the "three representatives" idea will probably be written into the party charter at next year's congress. But the party still cannot decide whether to let private businessmen join the ranks of its 65m members (about 5% of the total population). In fact, nearly a fifth of the more than 1.5m owners of private companies are party members anyway, reflecting the massive flow of party and other officials into business as well as lax vetting of new members, especially in the countryside. But formal recognition of these ideologically suspect people is another matter.

## A rural experiment

When foreigners ask about political reform, party officials point proudly to changes in the countryside. Since the late 1980s they have gradually introduced a system whereby villagers choose their leaders without party interference, by secret ballot. Western governments and non-governmental organisations have poured money and expertise into helping China to perfect the new system, hoping that this germ of democracy might one day spread more widely into the body politic. The results have not been encouraging.

The party's main motive in allowing these elections was to strengthen its control over the countryside. It was acutely aware that village party officials often do not have much public support. Many lack the expertise to make important economic decisions and are seen as agents of hated policies, such as China's birth-control programme. If villagers could take control of bread-and-butter issues, they might support the party in other areas.

But it is clear that peasants do not feel more empowered. The Organisation Department's report said confrontations between villagers and officials were becoming bigger and more violent.

These, it said, could cause "chain reactions" leading to social disorder across wider areas. There are several causes of this mounting discontent, ranging from stagnating incomes to the illegal fees exacted from villagers by local officials. But one large cause is the election system itself, which has created rival centres of power in many villages.

Not surprisingly, elected village chiefs often felt they had more authority to represent their communities than village party secretaries, who are chosen by party organs at a higher level. The party, fearful of losing its grip entirely, decided to back its village representatives. Cheng Tongshun, a political scientist at Nankai University in Tianjin, said in a book published last year that most villages were still led by party secretaries who took on most, if not all, of the duties which the elected chiefs are supposed to carry out.

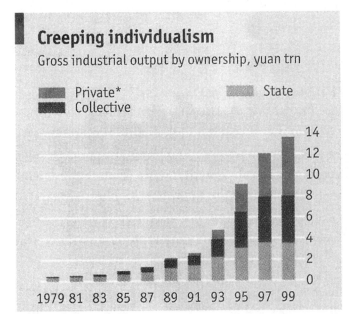

**Creeping individualism**
Gross industrial output by ownership, yuan trn

■ Private*
■ Collective
□ State

1979 81 83 85 87 89 91 93 95 97 99

Source: J.P. Morgan Chase          *Includes foreign ownership

China's experience of rural elections has demonstrated the difficulty of introducing even a modicum of democracy without also allowing the formation of non-party political groups. Thanks to the party's jealously guarded monopoly of power, the only other forces now capable of exerting their interests collectively are generally undesirable: criminal gangs, clans and the self-interested rich. Mr Cheng writes that vote-buying and-selling, stuffing ballot boxes and violence have had a "considerable impact" on rural elections. The Chinese media also speak of frequent, sometimes successful, attempts by wealthy businessmen to buy official positions or seats in local legislatures.

Despite these setbacks, some reformers would like to see the village democracy system extended. But one cautious attempt to do so has faltered. In 1998 Buyun township in Sichuan province caused a stir by conducting, without the central leadership's permission, China's first-ever direct elections to the post of township chief. The party turned a blind eye, but in December this year when fresh elections are due to be held, it is expected that Buyun will end the experiment. This time it will allow voters to choose the candidates, but the winner will be picked by the (party-dominated) township people's congress. Even at this level, the party still considers direct elections too threatening to its power. Not surprisingly, a suggestion made three years ago by Zhu Rongji, the prime minister, that direct elections might one day be considered for China's top leadership posts has gone nowhere at all.

## The ghosts of other parties

Only a few people, most of them little known and ineffectual dissidents, call for the overthrow of the Communist Party and the rapid introduction of a western-style democracy. The experience of post-communist societies in Eastern Europe and the former Soviet Union—as well as the violent suppression of China's anti-government protests in 1989—has been a sobering one for many of China's intellectuals. The mainstream view is that change should be gradual and confined within current political structures. The more corrupt and socially turbulent China becomes, the more this view is reinforced.

But this sense of caution does not mean there is anything like a consensus on how China should proceed. Liberals vie with old-guard Maoists. Neo-leftists contend with free-market capitalists. Each camp uses journals or Internet websites to wage these theoretical battles. There may have been little progress with political reform, but at least the party's grip on the publishing industry has been weakened by market forces. Books and magazines air a far wider range of opinion than would have been possible a decade ago, though praising multi-party democracy is still banned, as is the formation of any organised political group. Activists who three years ago formed the China Democracy Party—the country's first nationwide opposition organisation—remain in jail.

One of the more radical advocates of political reform is Cao Siyuan, who runs a consultancy in Beijing offering advice on bankruptcy and mergers. Mr Cao enjoys a certain stature in China, since he helped to draft the country's bankruptcy law in the 1980s. In the May issue of an influential journal published by the State Statistics Bureau, *China's National Conditions and Strength*, Mr Cao argued that there should be competitive elections for party posts. And he added a provocative thought: "A precondition for competitiveness within a party is that a country allows political parties to compete with each other."

Mr Cao did not go as far as suggesting that the ban on opposition parties should be lifted. But he said that China's eight authorised "democratic parties"—the cowed remnants of pro-communist organisations formed before the communist victory in 1949—should be encouraged to become more independent of the Communist Party. The Soviet Communist Party, he pointed out, collapsed because it failed to allow internal competition.

In an essay in March, this time for a restricted-circulation journal published by a Beijing think-tank, Mr Cao made an even bolder suggestion. The party should change its name to the Socialist Party, thereby making itself more alluring to the private sector and allowing it to cast off the baggage of the past, such as the Cultural Revolution. He diplomatically avoided mentioning the party's biggest historical burden, the suppression of the 1989 unrest in Tiananmen Square, which also landed him in jail for a year.

A change of name is inconceivable for the present—and for the foreseeable future, too. Mr Jiang's designated successor, Hu Jintao, who is likely to take over as party chief next year and as president in 2003, was born only seven years before the Communist takeover. During his tenure, the ranks of middling officials will swell with those who have spent most of their lives in post-Mao China. But few expect Mr Hu to take the steps that Mr Cao suggests. Little is known about him except that, because he suffers from altitude sickness, he (ruthlessly) carried out his job as party secretary for Tibet from a suburb of Beijing. Besides, Mr Jiang himself will probably remain the arbiter of party and state affairs well into the decade.

Why not just keep political reform on the back-burner as Mr Jiang has done? After all, the economy is growing at a strong 7–8% a year. Unrest may be increasing, but the police and paramilitary forces have proved themselves capable of suppressing demonstrations. In case they cannot, there is always the army. Yet China's ability to control unrest depends, precariously now, on efficient decision-making and political unity. Luckily for China's leaders, no major dispute has arisen over the handling of protests since Tiananmen (although the demonstrations by members of the Falun Gong sect in 1999 suggested the security forces cannot always be relied on). But there is still a risk of the kind of policymaking paralysis that nearly shattered the party 12 years ago.

## Diversifying discontents

Educated Chinese have much more freedom now to shape their own careers, go abroad or pursue their research without party interference. But there are far more people now with grievances—especially the unemployed, farmers and victims of official misconduct. The Organisation Department's report said that in Sichuan province, for example, the increasing mobility of the population was making it more difficult for officials to sense potential trouble. It said protests were becoming "conspicuously better organised" and were increasingly tending to break out in different places at the same time, "making it even more difficult to deal with them."

The report laid most of the blame for this unrest on official corruption and abuse of power. Some of this has been occasionally exposed by the party. In the past three years it has sentenced one Politburo member to 16 years in prison and executed two other top officials. A vice-minister is awaiting trial for allegedly accepting bribes from smugglers. But the party is unwilling to set up truly independent anti-corruption commissions, for fear they would cut swathes through the upper echelons of the party. The leadership's handling of a colossal smuggling case in the port city of Xiamen, involving hundreds of local officials, clearly illustrates the party's dilemma. While it looks determined to stamp out corruption, it will not follow trails that lead to the top of the hierarchy. Mr Zhu suggested last month that the multi-storey vice-den in Xiamen where many of the officials used to entertain lavishly and cavort with prostitutes should be turned into an anti-corruption museum. That would satisfy public curiosity, but do little to deal with the problem.

The party could try to reinforce its legitimacy by waving the banner of nationalism more vigorously. But the current leadership is anxious, not least for economic reasons, to preserve stable relations with America, Taiwan and Japan—the top three abominations in the eyes of ultra-nationalists. A growing body of intellectuals who call themselves "neo-leftists" (as opposed to "liberals" like Mr Cao) would like to see the party reverting to its role as the champion of the working class. But this would involve slowing down privatisation and staying out of the WTO, unless the terms of accession were drastically revised. Again, party leaders believe that this would cause economic damage.

As the 16th Congress approaches, debate about political reform will intensify. The "fourth generation" of leaders who will take over at the congress will encourage the think-tanks close to them to explore new ideas. Liberals, neo-leftists, gradual reformists and Maoists will jockey for attention. But do not expect the increasingly feeble and disoriented 80-year-old party to be rejuvenated. The world around it is changing too fast for it to get in step.

---

# Era of deep changes for China's Communists

## Under Jiang, party remade itself into ruling corporation

**By John Pomfret**
*The Washington Post*

**BEIJING:** Thirteen years ago, China's leaders had smashed the biggest freedom movement since they took power and installed an owlish engineer at the pinnacle of Communist power. Mindful of the disintegrating Soviet Union, many experts, including some in China, predicted then that neither the party nor the engineer would last.

But Jiang Zemin, who took over at that fateful moment, defied the odds, as did the Community Party he leads. Starting Friday, Jiang will preside in triumph over the party's 16th Congress, a weeklong gathering of 2,120 delegates held every five years that will anoint a new generation of leaders for the world's largest remaining Communist organization.

China's state-run media have portrayed the gathering as a defining moment for the party, the first such meeting of the 21st century, which many Chinese hope will belong to their country. The congress will set the tone for the next five years of the party's rule, fixing important directions for relations with the United States, economic reforms and the dream of uniting with Taiwan.

Jiang, the 76-year-old president, will step down from his post as general secretary of the party. His successor, Vice President Hu Jintao, will also assume Jiang's title as president in March during China's annual legislative session. But while it appears Jiang is leaving the scene, he is expected to emerge as the victor.

Chinese sources say he has stacked the seven-member, all-powerful Standing Committee of the Politburo with four allies, ensuring his continued influence. In addition, the congress will focus much of its attention on eulogizing Jiang's 13-year rule, seeking to cement his legacy in the line set by Mao Zedong and Deng Xiaoping.

The Jiang period was one of subtle but profound political, economic and social transformation in China. It is that transformation that has allowed the Communist Party to survive, defy a wave of democratization that swept through the old Warsaw Pact countries and the

"Little Tigers" of East Asia and maintain a 9.3 percent annual growth rate.

It is unclear whether this transformation will keep China's Communists in power over the years to come. The party remains above the law, so corruption among Communist officials runs rampant. It is hard to balance political dictatorship with increasing economic freedom. And the bad loans held by Chinese banks could one day make Japan's decade-long crisis look mild.

But during Jiang's rule, the party has done three things it had never done before, thereby strengthening its hand. It kept to a minimum the political infighting that brought the party to the brink of collapse in 1989. It stepped out of people's lives. And it abandoned the downtrodden, siding with those who have emerged as winners in the economic reforms.

As a result, China today acts like a massive corporation with the Communist Party as its board of directors. Under Mao, the party believed it had to control 100 percent of the country's stock—all organizations, religions, businesses, farms, factories, schools and even people's thoughts—to control the country.

But Jiang and his lieutenants have understood something capitalists have known for years: Even if they control less than 50 percent of the stock, as long as they are the biggest shareholder and have the right shares—such as the media, the security services and ways to tax the best companies—they can control China.

Over the past 13 years, the government has withdrawn from the private lives of most Chinese people and opened large sectors of the economy to private or foreign companies. Chinese are now generally free to do business, find work and live almost anywhere they please.

While civil rights guarantees fall short of Western standards, people nonetheless enjoy freedoms that, for them, are unprecedented under their communism.

Without announcements, China has evolved from a totalitarian state, in which the party dominated public and private space, to an authoritarian state, which has allowed unparalleled freedom in the economy and people's private lives but maintains a stranglehold on public life.

# 'There is a pretty stable alliance between the political, economic and intellectual elites. The elite won't challenge the government.'

The party has also divested itself of its former base constituency of workers and farmers. In 13 years, without changing its name, China's Communist Party has become the party of the economic, intellectual and political elite. This shift, from a revolutionary party to a ruling party, is a key reason why the Communists remain in power.

"There is a pretty stable alliance between the political, economic and intellectual elites of China," a sociologist, Kang Xiaoguang, wrote this spring. "The main consequence is that the elite won't challenge the government."

The party's new base will be formally recognized during the congress with new rules welcoming businessmen into the fold and enshrining the "Three Represents" doctrine into the party constitution. That doctrine, attributed to Jiang, states that the party now represents the most advanced productive and cultural forces in society, buzzwords for the elite.

Despite the changes, many urban Chinese say the party does not matter to them, and some have taken this as a sign of the party's irrelevance. "Is this the 11th Party Congress?" asked a cultural maven from Shanghai. A Beijing software executive wondered, "Do they hold these things every four years or five?"

But the reality is that the party matters, and matters a lot.

"To really make it in China, you have to have the party's blessing," a venture capitalist in Beijing said. "Call it a corporation, a mafia, a protection racket, whatever. But they run the show."

The party, Kang wrote recently, keeps the country's people like "a pan of scattered sand," somewhat free as individuals but unable to unite. Any challenges to the party as an organization are met with a ferocious and bloody response. The two-year-old crackdown on the Falun Gong spiritual movement, which has left hundreds dead and thousands jailed, is an example.

"You can say whatever you want in China today," said Liu Xiaobo, a literary critic who spent years in jail after the 1989 crackdown, "as long as you do it alone."

The party has also seemed to weather the fact that it stands for nothing anymore but power. The death of ideology is something that seems to bother foreigners more than Chinese these days, possibly because the Chinese were here when the party stood for something and life was a lot worse.

In any case, Chinese now join the party for the same reason people join a big company in a company town: self-interest.

Lu Guanqiu, a former blacksmith who sits at the helm of a company that manufacturers car parts and is worth $480 million, said he joined the party for a simple reason. "When I first led this company, I was not a party member and business was tough because China is led by the Communist Party," he said. "So I became a party member and things became easier."

Lu was twice a delegate to the party congress.

The party has also been adept at rising to the political challenges posed by new technology.

When the Internet exploded in China in the late 1990s, many predicted it would bring with it a social and political revolution. But Beijing, with 30,000 "Internet police," has acted swiftly to clamp down on dissent through the ethers.

Western companies such as Yahoo and America Online have signed pledges agreeing to cooperate with government censorship regulations. The most recent regulation, which bans Web sites from "producing, posting or disseminating pernicious information that may jeopardize state security and disrupt social stability," took effect Aug. 1.

In the mid-1990s, Western scholars pointed to the explosion of social organizations as signs of the birth of a civil society in China. But again, the party has moved to limit their growth and co-opt or frighten organizers. Since 1999, when the party issued new regulations for nongovernmental organizations, the number of such organizations fell significantly, according to statistics from the Civil Affairs Ministry.

Successes in these areas—intellectuals, the rich, technology and the media—have convinced many in the party leadership that fundamental political reform is unnecessary. In many ways, the Communist leadership today is less pro-democratic than were the men who ran the country in 1989.

Gone is talk about splitting the functions of the party and the government, which reformers had pushed as a way to make the party more answerable to the law. In 1988, not one provincial party secretary simultaneously headed a provincial legislature. Today, 12 of the 32 party secretaries also run legislatures. That number is expected to rise as the leadership in Beijing seeks to ensure that no political experiments grow out of control in the provinces.

In his essay, Kang reasoned that the main source of future political instability would combine a nationwide crisis with unrest among the downtrodden in the cities and countryside. Among those sectors, Kang said, "the reforms in the 1990s have brought mostly pain." Rural incomes, for instance, have fallen since 1996, and more than 30 million people in the cities have been laid off by tottering state-owned companies since 1997.

Democratic deficit

# China stumbles toward a crisis

*By* Gordon G. Chang

## HONG KONG

This time no one is being killed, imprisoned or tortured, and that represents progress, of course. China's Communist Party is choosing a new leader peacefully, and sinologists are hailing the achievement. Hu Jintao will be named general secretary of the party, the most powerful position in the world's most populous nation.

Professor Andrew Nathan, a China expert at Columbia University who is no friend of the regime in Beijing, says that China is "institutionalizing" its politics. Nathan is correct—the party is learning to transfer power "smoothly," to borrow one of its favorite terms. Yet it is important to remember what Nathan and others say: China must also democratize.

The transfer of power at the congress will be as undemocratic as it can possibly be. After the suppression of the pro-democracy protests centered on Tiananmen Square in 1989, Deng Xiaoping chose Jiang Zemin to be his successor and then selected Hu to succeed Jiang. Before he died, Deng wanted to make sure that his successors would be obedient and that the transfers of power would be orderly. It appears that he succeeded on both counts.

The political system, too, remains basically unchanged and inflexible. China may look modern, but its government isn't. As a result, the transition may look peaceful, but it might not be.

There have been two prior transfers of power in China since 1949: from Mao Zedong to Deng and from him to Jiang. Neither transition went according to the script. Mao's chosen successor, Hua Guofeng, was upended by Deng two years after taking over. Deng picked, and later discarded, two successors, Hu Yaobang and Zhao Ziyang, before finally settling on Jiang.

Jiang has been reluctant to give up power. He now seeks to emulate Deng, who remained China's strongman long after giving up his formal positions. Jiang has been packing the key standing committee of the politburo and other senior party posts with his allies in the hope that he can remain "the core of the Third Generation leadership."

If Jiang can retain his leading position in the party—and it now appears that he will succeed—he will create troubles for Hu in the years ahead. Jiang will undoubtedly try to help his key protégé, Zeng Qinghong, take over the post of general secretary from Hu. It may be years before the new leaders, whoever they may be, are able to get settled and set their own course. Until then governance will be on hold.

In the meantime, the regime faces many challenges, some of them unprecedented. China's high rates of economic growth are essentially the product of massive fiscal stimulus, which is draining the central treasury. In the next few years the worst effects of accession to the World Trade Organization will be felt. China's banking system may be the weakest in the world.

There are hundreds of demonstrations each day in the Chinese countryside and cities. Some are small; others involve thousands of people. The rising tide of corruption threatens to engulf Beijing's leaders. When the challenges to China are greatest, the regime will be at its weakest. Instead of tackling the tough issues, party leaders will be fighting among themselves over power.

In reality, the only thing that can reignite the stalled reform process and save China is real reform of the political system. Junior members of the Communist Party now talk about change. Village elections are being held and there is something called "inner Party democracy"—small reforms in the way the party makes internal decisions.

Yes, there is change, but progress is very slow and the party insists that it remain in control. Can reforms be meaningful if they cannot result in ousting the Communist Party and choosing a new government? Younger cadres may talk of political change, but the party's leaders seem interested only in window dressing.

Of course, the transfer of power in China should be peaceful. Yet a smooth transition is not an end in itself. The goal must be a system in which the Chinese people themselves can choose their leaders.

*Gordon G. Chang, author of "The Coming Collapse of China," contributed this comment to the International Herald Tribune.*

Kang identified two possible sparks: a banking failure or an economic slowdown. The number of nonperforming loans in China's banking system, for example, is estimated at 37 percent of the gross domestic product. China's robust growth rate of 7 percent relies on a fiscal stimulus package and deficit spending that cannot go on forever.

But China's leaders still possess enormous resources that could be sold to keep the state afloat. Land has yet to be privatized, and such a sale could generate billions. Telephone companies, oil companies and power plants also could be sold off.

Barring an economic collapse, most observers say, the party will be able to face down challenges from the poor. The increasing number of disturbances, riots, petition drives and strikes by China's dispossessed remain local in nature and the government has the ability—and, so far, the will—to crush them.

From *International Herald Tribune*, November 8, 2002, p. 1, 10. © 2002 by the International Herald Tribune.

# POLITICS AND REFORM:
# The middle class waits in the wings

**The party's mission of serving the proletariat has been shifted**

by James Kynge

Many events in China's modern history appear momentous only in retrospect. The dramatic economic transformation of the past two decades began with a few little-noticed reforms in a single rural county.

The boom of the mid-1990s was touched off by a couple of pithy remarks from former leader Deng Xiaoping during a tour of southern China in 1992.

It is difficult, at this stage, to tell whether posterity will bathe last month's 16th congress of the Chinese Communist party in a similar sepia-tinted glow. But the meeting did mark a watershed in the party's evolution and set forth several important reform initiatives for the next five years.

Most fundamentally, the congress re-oriented the party away from its sworn mission to serve the proletariat and instead emphasised the importance of the middle class.

The "three represents", an awkwardly named new philosophy that enshrines this shift, was written into the party constitution at the congress.

The philosophy, credited to Jiang Zemin, the outgoing party chief who is expected to retain considerable influence in the new government, says that the party will henceforth represent not just workers and peasants but the "advanced productive forces, advanced culture and the broad masses of the people".

---

**'The 16th party congress jettisoned the fundamental purpose of communism'**

---

In other words, private entrepreneurs, stock market investors, real estate speculators, artists and other bourgeois types are as welcome—in theory, at least—into the communist pantheon as the working class.

"The 16th party congress jettisoned the fundamental purpose of communism, that is to enforce public ownership and suppress private ownership," says Cao Siyuan, a leading social commentator who runs his own merger and acquisition consultancy.

Mr Jiang's speech to the congress, a policy blueprint for the next five years, repeatedly reinforced this basic point. He called for the expansion of a market in rural land rights use, a reform that is likely to create a smaller number of farmers controlling bigger lots.

He emphasised the importance of the private sector in creating jobs and called for the legal protection of private property and income. Private businessmen were welcomed to join the party, and a few attended the congress for the first time as delegates.

One capitalist entrepreneur, Zhang Ruimin, head of Haier, a consumer electronics maker, was made an alternate member of the party's central committee.

Mr Jiang also called for a continuation in the reform of state-owned enterprises to create greater efficiency and reduce the direct role of the government in management. Reforms to the banking sector are to be deepened, with interest rates being gradually deregulated—a move that should facilitate financing to private companies and boost consumer credit.

The middle class, Mr Jiang indicated, should be expanded as a means to create consumer demand for a cornucopia of Chinese manufactured products, most of which are in oversupply.

# Changing of the guard: a new generation takes power

## HU JINTAO

Elevated unexpectedly by Deng Xiaoping to the leadership group in 1992, Hu, 59, has fulfilled all expectations by taking the party's top job. But he has largely risen without a trace, leaving his personal imprint on no policy area. All signs point to Hu maintaining Jiang's slow-but-steady economic liberalisation, with some experiments in administrative and political reform, two areas he has authorised for study at the central party school.

## WU BANGGUO

Wu, 60, is a Jiang loyalist from the "Shanghai Gang" with a lacklustre policy record. This is especially so in the area of state-owned enterprise restructuring, which he took over in 1999, when Zhu Rongji temporarily lost credibility as a manager of reform. Wu has gained a reputation as an advocate of stability rather than rapid reform.

## HUANG JU

Huang, 63, is an unpopular figure who will be tagged as just another Jiang crony. But he wins credit for his seven-year stewardship as Shanghai party secretary, during which the city has been transformed into a showcase for the rest of the country and the world. The Singapore-style balance that Huang has managed in Shanghai—of prosperity, with tight control of politics and the media—is a model leaders would like to replicate throughout China.

## WEN JIABAO

Wen, 60, will be the top economic policy maker, he has big shoes to fill with the departure of Zhu Rongji. He is already an accomplished survivor, having maintained his job despite close ties to top officials purged after the 1989 Beijing crackdown. The low-key Wen is considered to have the integrity, policy and bureaucratic skills to do the job, but may lack the toughness that characterised his predecessor.

## WU GUANZHENG

Wu, 63, a tough-nut who has won one of the toughest and most sensitive jobs as head of the Central Discipline Inspection Committee, the party's anti-corruption watchdog. Jiang will be happy to have an ally in a position, the neutrality of which has always been overshadowed by factional power plays. Wu won his spurs overseeing the suppression of followers of the Falun Gong movement when he was party secretary of Shandong province.

## JIA QINGLIN

Jia, 62, is a controversial choice, angering many Chinese who think he should have taken responsibility for a corruption scandal under his watch in Fujian in the mid-nineties. Trained as an engineer, like all nine members of the standing committee, Jia has two things going for him—a ruthless reputation and a close friendship with Jiang going back to when they worked together four decades ago.

## LI CHANGCHU

Li, 58, is another Jiang man, rewarded for returning a modicum of central government control over Guangdong, China's wealthiest province, and an unruly region distant from Beijing and wary of its directives. Before that, he served in senior positions in Henan and Liaoning, two troubled, poor and corruption-plagued provinces which do not appear to have damaged his career.

## ZENG QINGHONG

Zeng, 62, long typecast as little more than Jiang's political fixer, is a serious rival to Hu and also the leader with the most genuine interest in political reform. With an impeccable party pedigree, his parents were revolutionary heroes, Zeng has the most secure power base on the standing committee. Not only has he inherited Jiang's top-level networks and the one he has built for himself, he has displayed the political skills to make full use of them.

## LUO GAN

Luo, 66, is the oldest member of the standing committee, and also the lowest-ranked. Hu joked when introducing him yesterday that he was the committee's "big brother", but his lowly ranking is not a good result for his patron, Li Peng, formerly ranked number two in the Politburo. Li's family members and supporters may feel exposed after this fall from grace. Luo played an important role in Beijing in 1989 in implementing Li's order to crackdown on protestors.

*Text by Richard McGregor*

The men charged with engineering such changes are a "fourth generation" of leaders led by the nine members of the politburo's new standing committee. First among them is Hu Jintao, Mr Jiang's replacement as party general-secretary, who is also expected to take over the post of president at the National People's Congress next March.

From a personnel perspective, the party congress delivered the first orderly transition of leaders since the communist revolution in 1949.

Of the politburo's nine members, all are new apart from Mr Hu. Of 356 members of the central committee, the body from which all senior officials are selected, some 180 were new faces.

In policy terms, the "fourth generation" of leaders are not expected to veer far from the course charted by their predecessors.

This is partly because the new politburo is dominated by officials loyal to Mr Jiang and because, in many instances, it is the march of objective reality rather than the will of individuals that drive China's development.

Mr Jiang, who at 76 is well beyond the retirement age of 70, will retain the powerful post of head of the party's Central Military Commission, just as Mr Deng did before him.

On the politburo, his interests will be upheld primarily by Zeng Qinghong, his trusted confidant, who will also hold the first post in the party's secretariat—giving him oversight for party affairs.

In practice, official sources say, Mr Zeng could prove more powerful than Mr Hu, while Mr Jiang plays the role of an elder statesman who intervenes in policymaking at critical junctures.

Although Mr Zeng, 63, ranks only fifth in the nine-man politburo, his power springs from several sources.

First is his association with Mr Jiang, whom he has served since 1985.

Second is the melding of his own power base and that of his father, Zeng Shan, a revolutionary hero and former senior official.

Third are the jobs in Communist party groups, such as on foreign policy, Taiwan, propaganda and others, that he is expected to hold, official sources say.

Mr Zeng, who made his career in the shadows as Mr Jiang's hatchet man, has a reputation as a back-room manipulator who may struggle in the limelight. But many observers say this characterisation is vastly misplaced.

In fact, Mr Zeng is a lively participant in forums, according to people who have heard him talk. He is interested in pushing forward limited political reform after more than 10 years of stasis.

In foreign affairs, too, he is not quite the neophyte that many take him for.

In 2000 and 2001, Mr Zeng visited Japan, Australia, New Zealand, North Korea and Singapore, and in 1997 he accompanied Mr Jiang to his US meeting with President Bill Clinton.

He was instrumental in building dialogue with the US National Security Council in the aftermath of the 1989 Tiananmen Square massacre, when US-China relations were at their most tense.

In addition, he held secret dialogues with representatives of Lee Teng-hui, the Taiwanese president lambasted by Beijing.

Mr Hu, by comparison, appears staid and conservative. Most observers believe that he will have little choice but to acquiesce to whatever policies the Zeng-Jiang camp push forward.

In the same way, Wen Jiabao, the third-ranking member of the politburo, who is expected to replace Zhu Rongji as premier in March, will also have to do the bidding of Mr Zeng's camp. Many observers believe that Mr Wen lacks the drive and decisiveness of Premier Zhu, and may therefore preside over a slowing in the pace of reform.

Such concerns, however, may be overblown. Pushed by a liberalisation timetable legislated by China's membership in the World Trade Organisation, and faced with the imperative to propel economic growth, no Chinese leader can afford to postpone reforms for too long.

# In March Toward Capitalism, China Has Avoided Russia's Path

**Asia:** Unlike its onetime idol, Beijing has used a gradual approach to developing a market-oriented economy.

By HENRY CHU
TIMES STAFF WRITER

BEIJING—If the Soviet Union always seemed like the terrifying embodiment of Big Brother to the West, then for years it was something of a big brother to China toward the south.

Inspired by the same Marxist-Leninist ideals that first took root in Russia, Beijing alternately held up Moscow as its role model and, in times of disillusionment, its nemesis.

But since the Soviet Union's collapse, China has come to regard Russia as one thing only: its worst nightmare—a country with a political system in disarray; a society in sometimes violent flux; and, now, an economy in free fall.

In attempting to remake itself from a Communist behemoth into a capitalist beacon, China has studiously tried to avoid the path of its onetime idol, preferring a more gradual approach to change. Over the last 20 years, the result has been shaky but mostly upward progress: steady economic growth, an emerging middle class, a new breed of entrepreneurs.

As world leaders and economists reassess the wisdom of free markets amid today's global turmoil, the China model—from the perspective of Russia's collapse and the pain in lesser Asian countries that wholeheartedly embraced capitalism—looks wise enough.

Yet even as Beijing silently congratulates itself on the wisdom of its go-slow approach, analysts say that historical conditions here have been nearly as big

a contributor to China's improvement as current policy.

And as in Russia, major domestic reforms—especially China's latest efforts to shed its money-losing state enterprises and streamline its bloated bureaucracy—have brought about a whole new set of problems, making the final outcome of one of the most ambitious economic transitions in history far from certain.

"It is too soon to say whether China's reforms will succeed," Nicholas Lardy, an economist with the Brookings Institution in Washington, wrote recently.

Like Russia, China has struggled to redesign a planned economy into a market-oriented one. But even though both were Communist in name, the two countries launched their modernization drives at very different stages in their development.

"The Communist revolution in the former Soviet Union was over 70 years old; the Communist revolution in China was 30," said Harry Harding, a Sinologist at George Washington University. "The former Soviet Union was more industrialized; China was still an agricultural, rural society."

China embarked on its transformation when Deng Xiaoping, the nation's late "paramount leader," officially ended Beijing's isolation in 1978 with a series of measures designed to open up and liberalize the world's most populous country.

The enormous rural communes set up by Mao Tse-tung were dismantled. Peasant farmers were permitted to sell food on the private market. Two years later, the doors to foreign investment were thrown open in specially designated zones along the southern coast.

## Setting the Stage

Radical Maoism was dead, discredited after the 1966–76 Cultural Revolution, one of China's darkest periods, during which hundreds of thousands of citizens were killed.

Ironically, however, many scholars now argue that some of Mao's wrongheaded policies actually fostered the political climate and infrastructure necessary for the success of China's long march toward capitalism—or, in Deng's wordplay, "socialism with Chinese characteristics." Fanaticism was replaced by pragmatism and a thirst for a new national direction.

"The Cultural Revolution deinstitutionalized the political system and de-legitimized the Communist Party in ways that made reform both necessary and more possible," Harding said.

Under Mao, much of China's economic decision-making and planning had already devolved to local authorities. After Deng's reforms began, local officials used their knowledge and the fledgling industrial development across China to push for rapid industrialization of the countryside through a combination of tax breaks and enterprising schemes.

Labor was cheap—and plentiful. Three of every four Chinese toiled in the fields and could be redirected into industrial jobs and big, capital-intensive projects. In the Soviet Union, by contrast, industrialization was largely complete when the Soviet empire collapsed, leaving 75% of workers scrambling for hard-to-find jobs in new sectors of the economy.

Chinese cities such as Shenzhen, the first of the special economic zones, mushroomed with activity.

Shiny new skyscrapers now rise from a robust manufacturing base. Millions of Barbie dolls roll off assembly lines into the eager hands of children worldwide. The population of Shenzhen, a onetime fishing village with 30,000 inhabitants across from the Hong Kong border, sky-rocketed a hundredfold to 3 million.

Traders work the Shenzhen stock market. This year, foreign investment through July totaled an impressive $1.6 billion.

Much of the investment in Shenzhen and throughout the rest of China comes from a natural resource that Russia does not have: the ethnic Chinese around the world who still feel strong ties with "the motherland" and who have become one of China's primary engines for growth.

Whereas the Soviet Union splintered along nationalist and ethnic lines after its breakup, overseas Chinese, about 55 million in all, have remained remarkably unified through their common cultural heritage across boundaries of state and time.

"Hong Kong, Taiwan, Singapore and the Chinese diaspora in South [and] East Asia and North America are filled with ethnic Chinese entrepreneurs who have proved to be valuable sources of knowledge and investment and who have served as important bridges to the world economy," Andrew G. Walder, sociologist and specialist in China market reforms at Stanford University, observed in the China Quarterly magazine.

Amazingly, between 75% and 80% of all foreign investment in China (including money from Hong Kong) comes out of the pockets of ethnic Chinese across the globe, whose ranks boasted three dozen billionaires in East Asia in 1994.

Although the regional financial crisis has pinched some of the capital flow from the outside, economists say that money keeps pouring in at a fast clip.

In addition to abundant foreign investment, a comparatively low foreign debt—thanks to Mao's insistence on national self-sufficiency—has been crucial to China's revival as one of the world's major economies.

In stark contrast to Russia, China has not had to resort to crushing bailout packages by the International Monetary Fund to shore up its economy. While the government is struggling to keep expenditures in check as central tax revenue dwindles, Beijing does not need to devote huge resources to servicing short-term foreign debt; 80% of its debt is long-term, according to Hu Biliang, a senior economist with a French securities firm here.

Moscow, meanwhile, has buckled under the weight of $31.2 billion in IMF cash since 1992. And those loans have invariably come with political strings attached, reflecting one of the widest and most important divergences between China and Russia on the way to the free market: their different political systems.

For Russia, economic reform has gone hand in hand with political restructuring. At about the same time that Moscow relinquished its stranglehold on the economy, the Russian people also flung off the totalitarian Communist regime in one violent shudder.

Since then, prescriptions for a free market have been intertwined with efforts to build a free society. Economic shock treatment and the massive unloading of nationalized industries in Russia are bound up with ending the political monopoly of the Communist Party and building a raucous, but functional democracy.

Beijing, on the other hand, represents the last great bastion of Communist control, a one-party dictatorship that oversees one-fifth of humanity. Its authoritarian rule has greatly loosened over the last two decades—some detect the signs of a civil society emerging—but the one-party Communist regime remains China's government.

As such, China's leaders can still rule by fiat, pushing through relatively unpopular measures when necessary, although the regime is careful not to push too hard lest it provoke a popular uprising such as the 1989 Tiananmen Square demonstrations. Even the ensuing massacre that year put only a temporary crimp in the economy, which flagged until Deng launched a "southern tour" of China in 1992 to jump-start greater economic liberalization.

Now many Chinese appear content to ignore the government so long as it allows some personal freedom, such as easier internal movement within China, and the liberty to pursue a higher living standard.

Beijing knows its legitimacy increasingly rests on its handling of the economy, and it has tried to help its citizens discover the truth of Deng's famous maxim: "To get rich is glorious." China's leaders are hoping that an economic overhaul is enough, without knitting it together with a political one, as happened in the former Soviet bloc.

"Where in Eastern Europe [economic] shock therapy and mass privatization are designed in part to dismantle communism and strip former Communists of power and privilege," Walder wrote, "in China gradual reform is intended to allow the party to survive as an instrument of economic development."

As a multi-party state, Russia is now full of vested interests jockeying for position. Politicians, elected by popular vote, must cater to them to stay in power.

The result has been a crony capitalism and democracy stage-managed by a handful of "oligarchs" behind the scenes, who have gobbled up the wealth and used it to wrest favors from Moscow.

So far, China has stayed largely immune to such stresses. But it has spawned a crony capitalism of its own that threatens the stability that the government is obsessed with maintaining.

Among those who have enriched themselves the most from Beijing's market reforms are not the laobaixing, or common people, but the families of high officials, who have used their connections to gain control of some of the most lucrative businesses in China.

Indeed, such corruption was one of the main grievances that drove the laobaixing to Tiananmen Square in 1989, marching for an end to Communist Party privilege and nepotism.

## Fighting Corruption

The issue still ranks as China's No. 1 public beef. Frustrated locals and foreigners alike complain that preferential treatment for party "princelings" or through money passed under the table kills competition and undermines their ability to do honest business.

The Asian financial crisis has put enormous pressure on the government as exports have slowed and the economy tightens. Production surpluses in industries such as steel sit untouched in huge stockpiles. Devastating flooding across China has made government promises of an 8% economic growth rate this year ring hollow.

Unemployment, officially at 3.5% but probably higher, is rising as local authorities eagerly shed their small and medium-sized state-owned enterprises at a speed the government was evidently not prepared for. In some cases, the enterprises were sold for pennies on the dollar to friends and relatives of local officials, though not on the scale of the "false" privatization in Russia that concentrated assets in just a few hands, analysts say.

"There are as yet no media moguls like [Boris] Berezovsky or energy czars like [Viktor] Chernomyrdin, but localities are seething with resentment against those who appropriated local collective enterprises over the past five to 10 years," said Douglas Paal, president of the Asia Pacific Policy Center in Washington and former National Security Council senior staffer under Presidents Reagan and Bush.

Last month, in a sign of growing alarm, the Communist regime issued an official editorial calling for a halt to "blind selling of state-owned firms."

"Leaders in some localities have simplified these serious and complicated reforms, and have taken them to mean merely selling such enterprises," the New China News Agency said. Local authorities should "carefully study" the proper guidelines regulating such sales, it added.

With joblessness on the rise, Beijing has backed off from ambitious plans to make residents buy their own homes and to slash China's bureaucracy in half, a potential loss of 4 million jobs.

Worker protests have already broken out, from Sichuan province in central China to Heilongjiang in the northeast, but are not reported in the official media.

These days, no one is willing to write off China as a potential economic success story, but pessimism hangs in the air among economists and some citizens here over the current state of China's gradual, multi-pronged reform program. It seems clear, however, that the Russian strategy is not an alternative.

"There probably are no panaceas in this world," said Harding. "Neither the Russian model nor the Chinese model is perfect. Or, as the cynic once said, 'The grass is brown on both sides of the fence.'"

# NEW DIMENSIONS OF INDIAN DEMOCRACY

## South Asia Faces the Future

*Susanne Hoeber Rudolph and Lloyd I. Rudolph*

Conventional wisdom has it that India is the world's largest democracy, but few have recognized that it is so against the odds. The Indian experience runs against the widely held view that rich societies are much more likely to be democratic than poor ones, and that societies with large minority populations are prone to ethnic cleansing and civil war. Democracy in India, a poor and notoriously diverse country, has succeeded for more than half the twentieth century and seems likely to succeed as well in the twenty-first. India's democracy has proved substantial as well as durable. Electoral participation has been higher than in the United States, elections have been free and fair, governments have alternated at the center and in the states, and free speech and association are constitutionally protected and widely practiced. But democracy is subject to challenge and change. This essay examines why and how democracy in India during the 1990s responded to a variety of challenges. These may be summarized under seven headings:

*1) A more prominent role for federal states in India's political system.* The states are making themselves heard and felt politically and economically more than they ever have in the half-century since India gained its independence from Britain.

*2) The transformation of the party system.* The era of dominance by the Indian National Congress has ended. Congress remains a major party, but it now must operate within a multiparty system that includes not only the nationally influential Bharatiya Janata Party (BJP) but a host of significant regional and state-based parties as well.

*3) Coalition government.* Stable central governments based on parliamentary majorities have given way to coalition governments that must depend on constellations of regional parties. India has become in this regard like Italy or Israel, both places where small parties can make or break governments and thereby affect the whole nation.

*4) A federal market economy.* Economic liberalization has been marked by a decline in public investment and a rise in private investment, the displacement of the federal Planning Commission by the market, and the emergence of the states as critical actors in economic reform and growth. The result has contributed to a transformation of India's federal system.

*5) The central government as regulator.* Despite what the foregoing might suggest, India's central government is not fading away. The center is holding, but its role has changed. The center had acted as an intervenor. Now it acts as a regulator. In the economic realm, it monitors the initiatives of the several states. It tries (albeit mostly without success) to enforce fiscal discipline. In the political realm, the center acts—through regulatory institutions such as the Supreme Court, the presidency, and the Election Commission—to ensure fairness and accountability. Since the emergence of the first coalition government in 1989, this role as "policeman" or honest broker has grown, while the interventionist institutions, the cabinet and parliament, have waned in significance.

*6) A social revolution.* In most states, and to a significant extent at the center as well, there has been a net flow of power from the upper to the lower castes. Indian politics has experienced a sociopolitical revolution that, in *varna* terms, has meant a move from a Brahman (priests, intellectuals) toward a Shudra (toilers) raj.

*7) Centrism has held against extremism.* The imperatives of centrist politics have checked the momentum of Hindu fundamentalism. India's diverse and pluralist society, the rise of coalition politics, and the need to gain the support of the median voter have transformed the Hindu-nationalist BJP from an extremist to a centrist party.

*1) The rise of the states.* In recent years, the 28 states of India's federal system have played a more prominent role in India's public life. Not least has been their contribution to helping India live peacefully with difference. In a world where armed strife has increasingly taken the form of civil war and ethnic cleansing—of the 96 recorded conflicts between 1989 and 1996, only five were between sovereign states—India's federal system has helped to keep cultural and ethnic differences within relatively peaceful bounds.

---

*Forty years ago, there seemed good reason to fear that India's "fissiparous tendencies" would soon lead to Balkanization or dictatorship. Today such worries seem unpersuasive.*

---

In thinking about something with which to compare India's federalism, the multilingual European Union seems more appropriate than does the United States. Much like the English and the Indians, the Hindi speakers of Bihar state in the shadow of the Himalayas and the Tamil speakers of Tamil Nadu at the subcontinent's southern tip speak quite distinct languages. They share little history and few points of contact. Their traditional rulers, legends, and folk cultures are distinct from one another. Their socioeconomic profiles are as different as those of Sweden and Portugal. Bihar is poor and mostly illiterate. Tamil Nadu is prosperous and advanced. No contrast between any two of the 50 U.S. states comes anywhere close. Forty years ago, there seemed good reason to fear that Selig Harrison was right to warn that India's "fissiparous tendencies," particularly its linguistic differences, would soon lead to Balkanization or dictatorship. Today such worries seem unpersuasive. The federal system has helped India to live peacefully with its marked difference.

How anomalous is a multinational federal state? India reminds us that the nation-state as we know it is a relative historical newcomer, with roots in the post-Revolutionary, post-Napoleonic Europe of the nineteenth century. The nation-state reached its apogee after the two world wars. Before 1914, the numbers of people and extent of territory ruled by nation-states were dwarfed by those which lay under the sway of multinational entities such as the Habsburg, Ottoman, and Romanov empires, or the maritime dominions of Britain and other European colonial powers. After 1945, the working out of Woodrow Wilson's doctrine of self-determination had seemingly conferred sovereignty on enough aspiring "nations" to bring the era of the multinational state to a decisive end. The nation-state, said many scholars, stood revealed as the natural end toward which the history of state formation had been tending.

This claim was soon belied, however, by the formation of the European Community and its successor, the European Union. On 1 May 2001, the *New York Times* reported the proposal by German chancellor Gerhard Schroeder's Social Democratic Party of "a far-reaching plan… to turn the European Union into a more centralized federal system." The EU was becoming more like the sovereignty-sharing Holy Roman Empire than the warring nation-states of the First World War. Had the Holy Roman Empire become the dominant polity in the twelfth century, the process of state formation in Europe would have conformed more closely to the world norm. The path that marks the rise of India's federal, multinational state since 1947 also tracks the emergence of an alternative to the increasingly outmoded nation-state.

By promoting peace among their constituent parts, both the EU and the vast federal republic that is India are saving the world from a great deal of trouble and strife. If it has done nothing else, the EU, the creation of a Europe bloodied, exhausted, and chastened by two gigantic and terrible wars, has radically reduced the prospect of conflict among its member states. Something similar is true of India. Each of its 28 federal states could well be a nation-state unto itself. The largest, Uttar Pradesh, has more people than Germany and France combined, and is nearly as populous as Russia. If Uttar Pradesh and its neighbors were sovereign nation-states, there would be that many more countries living in the Hobbesian world of anarchy and self-help. Instead of ending in domestic arbitration, the dispute between Tamil Nadu and Karnataka over Krishna River water rights could have led to war. The internal conflicts within Punjab and Assam, like the civil wars that roiled Congo-Kinshasa during the 1990s, could have been made worse by outside forces seeking strategic gain. As it is, the international community has quite enough to occupy it as a result of the longstanding dispute between India and Pakistan over the fate of Kashmir, India's northernmost and only Muslim-majority state.

The story of India's state formation since independence has included a story of rising influence on the part of the federal states. At independence in 1947, India inherited the British-brokered constitution of 1935. It embodied two possibilities, a centralized authoritarian "vice-regal" state and a decentralized, or federal, parliamentary state. Mohammad Ali Jinnah, the "great leader" of Pakistan, chose the former option, in effect acting as the successor to Lord Louis Mountbatten, the British raj's last viceroy and governor-general of India. Jawaharlal Nehru, despite his personal penchant for centralized rationalization, selected the latter course and became the prime minister of a parliamentary government in a federal system.

Each choice was a fateful one. Pakistan has known parliamentary democracy for barely half of its five decades as an independent country. The rest of the time, it has been run by generals and authoritarian bureaucrats. Its civilian political landscape has been profoundly troubled, and its unsteady constitutional mixture of unitary and federal features contributed to the violent secession of East Pakistan (present-day Bangladesh) and a related war with India in 1971. India reinforced the federal character of its constitution in 1956 by implementing a sweeping "states reorganization" that redrew state boundaries on the basis of language. Mohandas K. Gandhi had set the stage for this as early as 1920, when he reformed the Indian National Congress by creating 20 Provincial Congress Committees (PCCs) based on regional languages. Arguably, Gandhi's far-seeing decision to provide a form of political expression for ethnocultural identities such as Hindustani, Tamil, and Bengali opened the way for greater popular participation under conditions of democratic pluralism.

Gandhi's linguistic reforms, like his strong support of Muslim causes, flowed from his inclusive understanding of what Indian nationalism should mean. Inclusive nationalism is reflected in the opening years of the twenty-first century by Indians' capacity to live with dual and overlapping national identities, regional and transregional. As one Tamil writer has put it, "Tamil is my mother, India is my father," a gendered metaphor that captures how the linguistic-cultural "home space" fosters a "subjective" sense of care and affection while the national "civil space" promotes a due respect for the "objective" virtues of security, discipline, and the rule of law. In an era of ethnic cleansing and civil war, this kind of federalism has powerfully enhanced a diverse India's capacity to live with difference.

*2) The party system transformed.* The dominant-party system of the Nehru-Gandhi era that led to the formation of Congress majority governments was replaced after the ninth parliamentary election in 1989 by a regionalized multiparty system and coalition governments. The 1989 elections resulted in India's first hung parliament. V.P. Singh's Janata Party, which held the largest bloc of seats in the 545-member Lok Sabha, became the nucleus of India's first coalition government. Each of the four national elections since the watershed has led to a coalition government in which parties based in single states have been key. Today, for instance, the coalition government that came out of the 1999 elections is led by Prime Minister Atul Behari Vajpayee of the BJP, but includes in its 300-seat majority fully 120 members from single-state parties.

According to the Election Commission's classification of parties (national, state, registered, and independents) and its declared election results, the four national ballotings held from 1991 to 1999 saw national-level parties' vote share drop from 77 to 67 percent, while the proportion of seats they controlled slid from 78 to 68 percent. By contrast, parties based in single states went from 17 percent of the votes and 16 percent of the seats to 27 and 29 percent, respectively.

The shift from dominant-party to multiparty politics and the rise of state parties at the expense of national parties have undone the centralizing thrust of the 1950 Constitution. One telling sign of this is the reduced use of Article 356, the "president's rule" clause which was used—some would say misused—by majority-party governments at the center to remove irksome state governments. With state-based parties now holding the balance of power in New Delhi, freewheeling invocations of Article 356 are a thing of the past.

*3) Coalition government.* The third major feature of contemporary Indian democracy, the rise of coalition government, is implicit in what we have said about the transformation of the party system from a dominant to a multiparty system. Strong central governments based on sturdy one-party majorities in the Lok Sabha have given way to precarious coalitions that must cater to state parties in order to survive. Since the era of coalition government began in 1989, coalitions have differed in their ideological make-up and caste composition, but all have depended on subnational parties, particularly those form the southern states of Tamil Nadu and Andhra Pradesh. Following Indian politics since 1989 has become rather like following Italian or Israeli politics, where smaller parties can and do hold national governments hostage in order to advance narrow partisan agendas.

In the 32 years from 1947 to 1989, India had a total of five prime ministers. There have already been six in the 12 years since coalition government began. But perhaps the suggestion of instability carried by these numbers is deceptive. The Narasimha Rao government lasted five years (1991–96), longer than a U.S. presidential term. Until a corruption scandal threatened to trip it up in March 2001, the second government under A.B. Vajpayee seemed likely to complete its five-year term. And at the time of this writing in November 2001, it is still carrying on. Even the combined burden of scandal, Vajpayee's poor health, and dissension in the ranks could not overcome the absence of any viable alternative to him as a national leader.

Now that coalition governments are the order of the day, how are we to judge them? If we think of India as analogous to a potential EU federal government, composed of 15 former nation-states, each with its own identity and interests, we might appreciate the fact that coalition governments can give federal units weight and voice. Coalitions can soften extremism. The BJP, for instance, began as a predominantly north Indian party dedicated to Hindutva (Hindu nationalism), but has had to shelve that agenda in order to accommodate key coalition partners, especially secular state parties from south India that care little for anti-Muslim "communalism."

But this happy outcome is not the only possible result of coalition politics. The unedifying tale of Jayalalitha Jayaram, the corrupt and vindictive chief minister of the ruling AIADMK party in Tamil Nadu, seems to provide a lesson in how coalitions can be hijacked. For years, she shamelessly used the threat of bringing down the Rao and Vajpayee governments to shield herself from the legal consequences of the abuses that she committed while chief minister of Tamil Nadu between 1991 and 1996. Re-elected to that post in May 2001 and sworn in by a faint-hearted governor after she brushed aside the Election Commission's ruling that her criminal convictions disqualified her from office, she was turned out only after the Indian Supreme Court upheld the Commission in a landmark September 2001 ruling.

While the final deposition of the Jayalalitha case may have reduced the danger that state parties will blackmail coalition governments, there are other exigencies that can undermine or threaten coalition governments. One is the bloated, ineffective cabinets that are the byproduct of efforts to cobble together ruling coalitions by handing out ministerial appointments. Another is legislative gridlock as coalition partners and their constituencies jockey for advantage and block ministerial initiatives. The Vajpayee government's difficulties in keeping economic liberalization moving owe something to this effect. The cabinet is committed to privatizing more public-sector undertakings, to enacting an exit policy for labor, and to promoting new initiatives in energy, telecommunications, and transport-infrastructure policy, but political conflicts among ministers have stymied its efforts.

It is clear that coalition government based on a region-favoring multiparty system is a mixed blessing. It has made it possible to avoid ethnic cleansing, civil war, and extremist politics by facilitating the country's capacity to live with difference and to support centrist politics. At the same time, however, coalition government has weakened the country's ability to pursue economic liberalization or achieve vigorous economic growth.

*4) A federal market economy.*   When you opened your daily copy of the *Times of India* back in the 1950s or 1960s, you could read all about the big dams, steel mills, and other megaprojects that master planner P.C. Mahalanobis and his colleagues were launching at the national Planning Commission. The celebrities of the command economy and the "permit-license raj" were the bureaucrats, administrators, economists, and other experts who were helping Prime Minister Nehru build a modern industrial economy of which government held the commanding heights. Today, a decade after the turn toward economic liberalization, newspapers and magazines feature stories about state chief ministers such as Chandrababu Naidu of Andhra, A.M. Krishna of Karnataka, and surprisingly, Jyoti Basu, who until recently headed the Communist government of Bengal state. These stories describe how the chief ministers of various Indian states are traveling the world to meet with business leaders, woo investors, and persuade the likes of Bill Clinton or Bill Gates to endorse the idea of investing in the future of Kerala, Karnataka, or Tamil Nadu.

Economic liberalization, the dismantling of the permit-license raj, and an increasing reliance on markets have fostered the emergence of the "federal market economy." But economic liberalization is only part of the story.

Equally important has been the marked decline in centrally directed public investment, which has reduced the central government's financial leverage and opened up new fields of initiative for enterprising state governments.

In the 1990s, India's deficit-ridden central government found that it could no longer afford planned investment. The center's gross assistance to states' capital formation declined from 27 percent of the center's revenue expenditure in 1990–91 to 12 percent in 1998–99. The more alert state governments have moved in to fill the gap by securing private investment and multilateral assistance. The decline of central public investment and the growth of private investment have given the federal states a greatly expanded role in economic liberalization and in promoting investment and economic growth.

Our use of the term "federal market economy" is meant to draw attention not only to the decentralization of the market and the shift to a region- and state-based multiparty system but also to new patterns of shared sovereignty between the states and the center for economic and financial decision making. This increased sharing shifts India's federal system well beyond the economic provisions of its formal Constitution. Over the past decade, it has become ever more clear that if economic liberalization is to prevail, state governments and their chief ministers must break through the barriers that are holding back economic growth.

*5) The central government as regulator.*   Despite the fading of Nehru's vision of a strongly centralized, development-guiding state, the center is holding. But it is holding in a different way. Regulation is replacing direct intervention as the center's preferred mode of affecting both the polity and the economy. Since 1991, economic liberalization has meant the abandonment of the permit-license raj and central planning. But federal regulatory agencies remain active in monitoring markets for goods, services, and capital to ensure that they perform competitively and effectively. Politically, the shift form one-party dominance to fragile coalition governments has changed the balance among institutions at the center. The cabinet and parliament, the traditional initiators of intervention, have ceded pride of place to regulatory institutions such as the presidency, the Supreme Court, and the Election Commission—enforcers of rules that safeguard the democratic legitimacy of the political system.

The role of regulatory institutions is more procedural than substantive, more about enforcing rules than making law and policies. Regulatory institutions are needed not only to create, sustain, and perfect markets but also to ensure procedural fairness in elections, in the operation of a multiparty system, and in the formation of coalition governments. The travails that many countries around the world are now experiencing as they strive to establish democracy and markets show how vital the rule of law and a viable state are to both. Russia and some other post-Soviet and East European states suffer from what Max

Weber called "political capitalism," meaning the accumulation of wealth through political power (often wielded deceitfully and coercively) rather than economic enterprise and open competition. Transitions to a market economy and to democracy require more than privatization and liberty. They require fair regulatory mechanisms.

---

*The Supreme Court, the presidency, and the Election Commission became more visible and effective in the 1990s as the reputations and authority of ministers, cabinets, and legislatures suffered.*

---

Although India's case is far less dramatic, a similar logic applies. In the economic arena, the role of the center as regulator has been to monitor the states in the name of fiscal discipline. For a few years after 1991 the center backed state-level economic initiatives with sovereign guarantees, but it is now reluctant to do so. Under Article 293 of the Constitution, the center must approve all foreign loans contracted by the states, and has de facto veto power over all domestic borrowing as well. In the spirit of "Do as I say, not as I do," the center tries to make the states accept fiscal discipline by imposing conditions that look suspiciously like those which the International Monetary Fund demands of faltering national economies—and enforces them with a similarly wide latitude of discretion.

The political front has seen a parallel decline of interventionist institutions and an enhancement of regulatory ones. The Supreme Court, the presidency, and the Election Commission became more visible and effective in the 1990s as the reputations and authority of ministers, cabinets, and legislatures suffered. During the Congress party's heyday, executives and legislatures had benefited from association with the Congress-dominated party system, the (declining) political capital left over form the independence struggle, and the authority and resources made available to politicians by the existence of a command economy.

Today, all this has changed. The complexity and fragility of the coalition governments, their rapid turnover, and their dependence on region- and state-based parties have sapped the executive capacity of governments. As ministerial executives and legislatures have receded, they have made room for judges, presidents, and election commissioners to act in ways that highlight their constitutional roles as regulators who make democratic politics possible by ensuring that the game is not rigged.

Structural conditions alone do not tell the whole story of this shift. National prime ministers, state chief ministers, legislators, and civil servants have discredited themselves in the eyes of India's growing, well-educated, and increasingly influential middle classes. As taxpayers, investors, producers, consumers, and citizens, middle-class Indians care a great deal about the reliability and security than cannot be had apart from good governance and the rule of law. In the mid-1980s, they responded to Rajiv Gandhi's promises to provide clean government and a high-tech, environmentally friendly economy that could carry India into the twenty-first century. Rajiv disappointed them, leaving office under a cloud in 1989 after a scandal involving an arms deal with the Swedish Bofors company. The early 1990s saw an unprecedented number of state and national ministers indicted for taking bribes, and the BJP's carefully cultivated reputation for probity will not recover quickly from the Tehelka scandal of March 2001, which was blown wide open by hidden-camera videotapes showing top figure sin that party taking bribes. Amid this atmosphere of public disillusionment and hunger for integrity, the symbolic and practical words and deeds of the Supreme Court, the president, and the Election Commission have taken on a new significance. These institutions, despite weaknesses of their own, are now the repositories of middle-class hopes and aspirations for steady, transparent, and honest government.

The Supreme Court's judicial activism marks a particularly novel turn for a body that spent the first four decades after independence mostly defending the rights of property owners against land redistribution. The Court's decision in the 1980s to begin taking a stand against rights abuses against the poor and powerless and to hear cases based on public-interest legislation—the Indian equivalent of the U.S. class-action lawsuit—paved the way for the judicial activism of the 1990s. With executive power slipping and wobbly coalition governments the order of the day, the Court's activism emphasizes lawfulness and predictability, often in the face of state abuses. Despite overloaded dockets and an often-glacial pace of adjudication, the Court has had some success in protecting citizens' rights, limiting police brutality and inhuman treatment in jails, and safeguarding environmental and other public goods.

In the mid-1990s, coincident with a marked increase in ministerial-level corruption, the Supreme Court moved to assert the independence of the Central Bureau of Investigation (CBI), the Union government's principal investigative agency. That such a proceeding should have achieved even partial success highlights the relative shift in the balance between the executive and regulatory functions of the central government. The CBI had been barred from investigating a department or its minister without prior consultation with and the concurrence of the secretary-to-government of the ministry concerned. "Prior consultation" and "government concurrence" meant that prime ministers, who also controlled CBI appointments, promotions, and transfers, dominated CBI initiatives and actions. In a landmark judgment, the Court removed the requirement of government concurrence that governed CBI investigations and gave the CBI director a minimum two-year term of office. These actions left the CBI somewhat freer to investigate on its own cognizance ministerial cases.

India does not lack environmental legislation, but neither does it lack powerful interests ready to block the enforcement of such laws. In the late 1980s and early 1990s, the Supreme Court—prompted in some cases by assertive NGOs—began to redress the balance by acting to protect such public goods as clean air and water and safe blood supplies. At stake in some of these cases were two of India's greatest assets, the Taj Mahal and the Ganges River. To protect the sixteenth-century mausoleum from further damage by air pollution, the Court had by 1992 closed 212 nearby businesses for chronic violations of environmental regulations. Almost two hundred polluters along the banks of the Ganges found themselves similarly shuttered by Court order. In 1996 and 1997, the Court began beefing up enforcement of clean air and water laws in the heavily polluted Delhi area. By early 2000, the Court had ordered polluting buses and cars off the roads and shut down enterprises that were emitting pollutants into the Yamuna River. When the environmental minister and industry minister of the National Capital Territory defied the Court by trying to keep the outlets open, the Court countered by threatening to jail noncomplying local officials for contempt.

The transformation of the party system and the rise of coalition government have also opened the way for the president to play a regulatory role. In the era of Congress party majorities, presidents had little to do beyond the pro forma duty of asking Congress's leader to form a government. Since 1989, however, the exercise of presidential discretion has become crucial in determining the make-up of governments. Presidents in turn have leveraged this newfound influence into a bigger regulatory role for their office.

Although Article 53 vests the "executive power of the Union" in the president, the president, like modern British monarchs, is expected to act at the behest of the cabinet rather than as a principal. As a constitutional head of state indirectly elected through a weighted voting system in which all federal and state-level elected legislators participate, the president retains a separate and potentially highly prestigious identity as a steward of the nation's interests. He stands apart from and above mere partisan or bureaucratic politics. In the 1990s, presidents Shankar Dayal Sharma and K.R. Narayanan acted in ways that stressed the autonomy of their office. This was most striking when each resisted political pressure to invoke Article 356, the "president's rule" clause, as part of a plan to unseat a state government for partisan advantage. President Narayanan also delivered a remarkable address on the fiftieth anniversary of independence (27 January 2000), in which he questioned the BJP-led government's efforts to change the Constitution by replacing an executive responsible to parliament with a directly elected president

and protecting parliament against dissolution by fixing its term.

Unlike in other national contexts where presidential powers have been used to undermine or destroy democratic institutions, in India recent presidents have exercised their powers on behalf of democratic transparency and accountability.

Starting in 1991 with the tenure of T.N. Sheshan as its chief, the Election Commission joined the Supreme Court and the president in strengthening constitutional government and democratic participation. The Commission is a constitutionally mandated central body whose fixed terms make it independent of the political executive. While the Commission had been a bulwark of free and fair elections in India before 1991, its task became more difficult in the 1990s as India's sprawling electoral process came under well-publicized threats from terrorists and criminal gangs bent on using force to impede or distort the expression of the people's will. The Election Commission gained national fame as a restorer and defender of free and fair voting. Polls indicate that the public trusts it more than any other political institution. When the Supreme Court backed the Commission by removing Jayalalitha from office in September 2001, it enhanced the Commission's role as the guardian par excellence of the democratic process in India. Like the Court and the presidency, the Commission draws enthusiastic support from the educated, urban middle classes, who are eager for solutions to the problem of official corruption and lawlessness. It is not too much to say that the Commission, the Court, and the presidency are the three vital pillars of the new regulatory state in India.

*6) A social revolution.* Since 1947, Indian society has experienced a social revolution with massive political consequences. Political power in the states, and to a significant extent at the center, has moved from the hands of the so-called twice-born upper castes into the hands of lower-caste groups, known in Indian parlance as the "other backward castes" (OBC) and the *dalits* (former "untouchables").

In early postindependence elections, social prestige translated readily into political power. Upper-caste patrons—coming from a social stratum that contained about a fifth of the populace—could tell their lower-caste dependents how to vote, and elections produced state and national cabinets dominated by officials from upper-caste backgrounds. In the 54 years since independence, the OBCs and *dalits*—together about two-thirds of the population—have displaced the upper castes in the seats of power in many state cabinets. At the turn of the twenty-first century, lower-caste chief ministers are no longer rare, and at least one national cabinet—the one that headed the National and Left Front governments of Deve Gowda and I.K. Gujral in the mid-1990s—had almost no upper-caste members. The logic of "one person, one vote" in free and fair elections has put power in the hands of the more numerous lower castes.

Analysts of developing countries often stress the importance of economic growth for political stability and legitimacy. What they notice less often is the contribution that social mobility can make to political stability and legitimacy. Status as well as income matter for both. In India, the "status growth" enjoyed by members of the once-reviled lower castes has been rapid, and this seems to have palliated much discontent with the relatively slow pace of economic growth.

7) *The center holds.*  In the early 1990s, the BJP and its Hindu nationalism appeared to be on the march. Today, centrist structural constraints, coalition politics, and the ideological moderation imposed by the need to attract the median voter have forced the BJP gradually to abandon communalist extremism in favor of a position much nearer the middle of the spectrum.

In 1992, such an outcome seemed unlikely. Two years earlier, BJP leader L.K. Advani had completed an all-India *yatra* or pilgrimage featuring an image of a martial but caged Lord Ram, the site of whose birthplace at Ayodhya in Uttar Pradesh was said to have been usurped by a sixteenth-century Muslim mosque known as the Babri Masjid. Everywhere it went Advani's *yatra* had drawn large crowds, seemingly galvanizing Hindu militants and swelling the BJP's electorate: BJP support jumped from a mere 9 percent of the vote and 2 seats in the 1984 general election to 11 percent and 86 seats five years later, and then to 20 percent and 117 seats—more than a fifth of the Lok Sabha—in 1991. On 6 December 1992, young Hindu extremists acting in the presence of BJP leaders and before the eyes of a global television audience stormed the Babri Masjid and tore it down stone by stone. Hindu-versus-Muslim communal violence exploded across northern and western India. Observers split over the likely impact of this episode, with some claiming that this assault on a prominent Muslim place of worship would fuel the rise of Hindu nationalist politics and others maintaining that it would discredit them. The future was more complex than either group expected.

In retrospect, it appears that the destruction of the Babri Masjid, instead of being the harbinger of a new BJP surge, was the crest of a wave. The violence of the assault and its wanton indifference to life and property shocked many of the moderate Hindus who had been providing the BJP with the bulk of its support. In the 1993 state assembly elections, the BJP lost heavily in four states, especially in its core state of Uttar Pradesh—India's largest state and the heart of the populous "Hindi Belt" across the north-central part of the subcontinent.

Yet the BJP did not collapse, and even gained ground. In the 1996 election it took 20 percent of the vote and 161 seats, though it could not form a government because no other party would join it. In 1998, the BJP garnered 25 percent of the vote and 182 seats—its best showing ever. (In the 1999 balloting, the party held on to its seat share but saw its voter support drop slightly to 24 percent.) Having absorbed the lesson of 1996, the party turned decisively toward moderation two years later. Led by the avuncular and moderate A.B. Vajpayee, it managed to put together a governing coalition, known as the National Democratic Alliance (NDA), by working mostly with regional parties. Conspicuously absent from the NDA's preelection program were such divisive Hindu-nationalist agenda items as calls for stripping Kashmir of its special constitutional status, demands that a Hindu temple be raised on the site of the Babri Masjid, and promises to override Muslim personal law via a uniform civil code.

In recent years the BJP's upper-class leadership has realized that electoral success depends on lower-caste support and living with difference. This explains the party's about-face on the Mandal Report, a government white paper that recommends set-asides for OBCs in school admissions and civil-service employment. The BJP, it would seem, is now seeking to exploit the very social revolution it once bitterly criticized. Whatever maneuvering the leadership may be doing, however, it would be going too far to suggest that the center of gravity of the entire BJP now lies stably in the middle of the Indian political spectrum, or that Indian voters now believe it does. Important organizations affiliated with the party such as the Hindu-extremist Vishva Hindu Parishad (Universal Hindu Organization) are showing signs of serious alienation from what they see as the BJP's excessive centrism. The Swadeshi Jagran Manch (Homemade-Products Promotion Council) continues to challenge economic liberalization. Vajpayee is still shutting the extremists out of the central advisory positions they crave, but his health is failing. The Tehelka tapes have taken a terrible toll on the BJP's good name. State assembly elections as well as by-elections for the Lok Sabha have lately gone badly for both the BJP and its coalition partners. The successful efforts by the BJP family of "saffron" organizations to infiltrate India's cultural organizations and activities and to rewrite the history texts used in schools in order to paint Muslims as invaders and foreigners have produced a backlash. Hindu extremists have turned from seemingly politically counterproductive and more dangerous Muslim targets to the softer targets of India's far smaller Sikh and Christian minorities.

## After Vajpayee?

What can we say about the prospects for democracy in India? We take as given the prior consolidations of democracy—for example, the realization of free and fair elections; alternating governments; freedoms of speech, press, and association; and the more or less successful transition from an interventionist to a regulatory state.

Our story of new dimensions suggests that democracy in India has proved resilient and adaptable. Absent an exogenous shock, centrist politics and coalition govern-ments seem capable of providing stable if not always effective government. With the BJP vote share peaking at 24 percent, upper-caste Hindu extremist politics seems to have slowed. To remain viable as a contender for national office, the BJP will have to continue to reach out to lower castes and minorities and be able to form coalitions with secularist state parties. Judging by its wins and perfor-mance at the state level, the Congress seems to be regain-ing its capacity to practice centrist, inclusivist politics.

The problem for the future is that A.B. Vajpayee has become physically weak and psychologically weary and there is no comparable alternative to him. Congress leader Sonia Gandhi's dynastic legitimacy does not com-pensate adequately for her political inexperience and for-eign provenance, but to date, no one can challenge her.

Business as usual may not be good enough; the coun-try needs to gain, not lose, momentum. A viable regula-tory state may have displaced a failing interventionist state, but if India is to prove its mettle, the country's po-litical and economic life needs to be revitalized.

---

Susanne Hoeber Rudolph is professor of political science at the University of Chicago. Lloyd I. Rudolph is profes-sor of political science at the University of Chicago. Their numerous published works on South Asia and India in-clude In Pursuit of Lakshmi: The Political Economy of the Indian State (1987) and Reversing the Gaze: The Amar Singh Diary—A Colonial Subject's Narrative of Imperial India (2002).

From *Journal of Democracy*, January 2002, pp. 52-66. © by the National Endowment for Democracy and The Johns Hopkins University Press. Reprinted with permission of The Johns Hopkins Univeristy Press.

# Islam Takes a Democratic Turn

By SOLI OZEL

ISTANBUL

**A**n electoral earthquake shook Turkey's politics to its foundations on Sunday and all but eliminated its complacent and exhausted ruling elites. The Justice and Development Party—the third and least Islamist in a sequence of Islamist political parties—led with a third of the votes. Yet these elections were not about Islam or whether Turkey would turn its back on modernization and secularism. These elections were about realigning Turkey's politics; they were the eruption of popular wrath against established parties. The Democratic Left Party of Prime Minister Bulent Ecevit, for instance, received a pitiful 1.3 percent of the vote.

From this perspective, the Justice and Development Party has spoken for the angry, downtrodden, impoverished and excluded masses that have borne the burden of the economic crisis and Turkey's integration with global markets. But the results also indicate the emergence of a new coalition of the provincial middle class, conservative urban professionals and intellectuals.

These constituencies have conflicting interests that will be hard to balance. Doing so may prove to be the Justice and Development Party's great challenge. Should it succeed, it will have claimed the center of the political spectrum with a communitarian-liberal synthesis and established itself as Turkey's predominant party.

Turkey's electoral system allows representation in Parliament only when a party receives 10 percent of the vote. Only two parties passed this threshold on Sunday. Therefore the Justice and Development Party, despite winning only one-third of the vote, has secured a two-thirds majority in Parliament. The other party that made the cutoff is the venerable Republican People's Party, which will take the remaining third of the Parliamentary seats.

Having repudiated early on its own Islamist political tradition, the Justice and Development Party ran on a platform of integrating Turkey with the European Union, advancing democratization and liberalizing the political system. Notwithstanding some comments by party leaders that suggested tinkering with Turkey's economic stabilization program, which is backed by the International Monetary Fund, the party went out of its way to quell the fears and doubts of markets, both at home and abroad.

The party's leader, Recep Tayyip Erdogan—a former mayor of Istanbul and perhaps the country's most popular politician—has been banned from running for office since 1998, when he was given a prison sentence for reading a poem that a court said incited religious hatred. He will, therefore, not be able to assume the post of prime minister.

Mr. Erdogan, 48, who has had a stormy relation with Turkey's secular establishment, was most conciliatory and reassuring in the numerous press conferences he held the night of his victory. His carefully chosen messages were aimed at reassuring both domestic and international audiences of his party's commitment to secularism, the rule of law and Turkey's well-established Western orientation.

At this point, there are no grounds to doubt the sincerity of the party's loyalty to its platform. There also does not seem to be any reason to expect rising tensions with the military—which was instrumental in ousting an Islamist party from power five years ago. The Justice and Development Party fielded respected diplomats and bureaucrats as candidates and was careful not to offend the military during the campaign. The military, in turn, did not appear inclined to look for an early confrontation. There is no reason to expect the party to either challenge the prerogatives of the military or attempt to change Turkey's customary foreign-policy priorities.

The rival Republican People's Party received a great boost to its popularity when Kemal Dervis, the architect of Turkey's economic stabilization program, joined the party. Yet it came in a distant second. This social-democratic party and its leader, Deniz Baykal, arguably wasted a golden opportunity in failing to appeal to the Turkish center. They appeared unable to abandon their elitist, state-centered and bureaucratic traditions. The party was expected to make a powerful case for its own compassionate vision, the social-liberal synthesis that the times demanded and Mr. Dervis's accession briefly promised. But the party was unable to seize the moment even as voters were abandoning the traditional center-right in disgust.

In the post-Sept. 11 environment, when the compatibility of Islam and democracy has been questioned, the current Turkish experiment is of utmost importance. If successful, Turkey will have shown that secularism can indeed be liberal and tolerant—and that democracy can function properly in a Muslim environment. Most of the responsibility to make the experiment succeed lies with Turkey and depends on the ability of both Justice and Development and the secular elites to accommodate one another.

Part of the responsibility, however, lies with the European Union, whose members have been achingly, at times insultingly slow in accepting Turkey's bid for membership. Some of the European animus may be explained by a reluctance to have a member state whose population is mostly Muslim. It appears to be one of modern history's ironies that the Turkish party most willing and able to enter the European Union on Europe's terms, as stated in the party's platform, would be an Islamist one. But this should be seen as an immense opportunity for Europe. The extension of an invitation to Turkey, led by Justice and Development, to start negotiations will consolidate the liberal political changes that have gained such momentum in Turkey. It would also begin reducing the so-called civilizational barriers between Muslim countries and the West. Here is a challenge for us all.

*Soli Ozel is a professor at Istanbul Bilgi University and editor of the Turkish edition of* Foreign Policy.

# Iran: Doubting Reform?

"September 11 and subsequent developments have put to rest any idea that reforms will occur quickly in Iran or that relations will be restored with the United States."

BAHMAN BAKTIARI AND HALEH VAZIRI

Iranian officials and citizens alike have felt the unintended consequences of Al Qaeda's attacks against the United States. September 11 exposed contradictions in the Islamic Republic's politics as Iranian students, just days later, spontaneously organized candlelight vigils for the American victims, catching the ruling clerics—especially conservatives—by surprise. Some reformist Iranian officials expressed their condolences directly, with Tehran Mayor Morteza Alviri and Municipal Council Chief Mohammad Atrianfar sending a letter to New York City Mayor Rudy Giuliani in which they proclaimed that "Tehran's citizens express their deep hatred of this ominous and inhuman move, strongly condemn the culprits, and express their sympathy with the New Yorkers." And, once the Taliban was toppled, the Iranian government aided in Afghanistan's reconstruction.

But the Bush administration suspected Tehran's motives, ultimately identifying the Islamic Republic as a member of the "axis of evil," along with Iraq and North Korea. President George W. Bush's rhetoric angered Iranian officials—including the reformists, who initially closed ranks with the conservatives to deny American accusations of involvement in terrorism and a quest for weapons of mass destruction. Meanwhile, Iranians in general have wondered why the United States has turned its ire against them when they had nothing to do with the September 11 attacks.

Conservatives have found in Washington's stance a new reason to suppress intellectuals, publications, students, and other segments of Iran's nascent civil society whose ideas can be labeled "pro-Western." With repression escalating, President Mohammad Khatami, the leading official advocate of reform, once again seems to have little alternative but to rail against his conservative rivals. Indeed, September 11 and subsequent developments have put to rest any idea that reforms will occur quickly in Iran or that relations will be restored with the United States.

## ONE STEP FORWARD...

Khatami's second electoral victory in June 2001 was expected to give him a mandate for the reforms promised since 1997: government accountability to the citizenry, consistent rule of law, and relaxation of Islamic social codes. In the contest to define the nature of sovereignty in the Islamic Republic, the proponents of popular rights had defeated the advocates of divine rule, at least for that moment. Less than two years later, however, Iranians have become disillusioned with reformist officials.

Prominent proreform personalities have urged Khatami to change his strategy toward the conservatives, demanding that the president become more assertive or resign. Perhaps the most significant protest against Khatami's passivity was Ayatollah Jalaleddin Taheri's resignation in July 2002 from his post as Friday prayer leader in the city of Isfahan. The ayatollah lamented watching the "flowers of virtue being crushed, and values and spirituality on the decline" among Iranians. In a scathing resignation letter, Taheri condemned the ruling clerics' corruption and greed.

Reformist officials had hoped that Taheri's resignation would spark sustained demonstrations by reformist sympathizers. Yet after two days of rioting in Isfahan, the judiciary forbade the press from reporting any news about Taheri's letter or the unrest. When *Norouz* printed the cleric's letter in full, the daily was shut down. Khatami's quiet during this controversy prompted the newspaper *Etemad* to ask, "Where is Khatami? We are all amazed at Khatami's absence... from the [political] scene. Clearly, a silent Khatami is a Khatami who serves the conservatives' interests."

Emboldened by Taheri's resignation, Iran's main proreform party threatened to quit the Islamic Republic unless the conservatives stopped undermining the elected administration. Mohammad-Reza Khatami, the president's younger brother and head of the Islamic Iran Participation Party, warned: "We want to work toward agreement.… But if [the conservatives] do not heed the people's demands… then we can only withdraw the reformist presence—that is to say the legitimate elected representation—from the regime."

As clerical factionalism intensified, President Khatami proposed two controversial pieces of legislation in September that directly challenge the conservatives' power. One bill would enhance the president's ability to deal with officials who violate the Islamic Republic's constitution, and the other would curb the Council of Guardians' role in vetting candidates for elections. With a reformist majority in parliament, these bills will probably become law soon, increasing Khatami's prerogatives, at least on paper.

Conservative officials are likely to pay only lip service to the laws. More than the reformists, conservatives enjoy control over the coercive arm of the state—the judiciary and various security forces—and are willing to resort to force when they perceive their interests are at stake. Khatami is a lame duck whose presidency will end with the 2005 election. His legislative proposals will benefit his successor, but Khatami may have to live with the pattern of one step toward reform and two steps back as conservatives persist in thwarting any moves in the direction of pluralism.

## … AND TWO STEPS BACK

During Khatami's second term in office, conservative officials have wasted no time flexing their muscle. Despite momentary unanimity in the face of American rhetoric about the "axis of evil," the president's second term has seen more frequent episodes of repression. In fact, the Bush administration's position on the Islamic Republic has breathed new life into the conservatives' cause. Anyone daring to dispute the clergy's supremacy, as personified by the *faqih* or supreme leader, Ayatollah Ali Khamenei, risks being accused of conspiring with the United States and other "enemies of the Islamic Republic."

Although rarely commenting publicly on factional disagreements, in August 2002 the Revolutionary Guards denounced the reformists for "working to turn Iran into a secular state and build[ing] ties with Washington." Claiming that the Islamic Republic's opponents had infiltrated the regime, the guards blamed the reformists for "exceed[ing] all bounds by openly supporting subversion on the streets." The guards declared that they would not stand by idly to witness the achievements of the Islamic revolution undermined.

The judiciary and security forces have backed the Revolutionary Guards' warnings to reformist officials with yet another crackdown against their sympathizers, particularly intellectuals and student activists. Perhaps most noteworthy are the arrest warrant issued for proreform strategist Abbas Abdi and the death sentence pronounced against academician Hashem Aghajari in early November. Abdi's "crime" was to contend that reformists in the executive branch and parliament could erode the power of conservative institutions by refusing to cooperate with them—naming his strategy simply "leaving the government" or *"khuruj az hakemiyat."*

Aghajari's words were even more stinging to conservatives ears. During a speech last June in Hamedan, he asserted the ability and rights of the pious to understand their faith without the clergy's intercession, comparing the relationship between Shia Muslims and leading ayatollahs to the "mimicry" practiced by "monkeys." A provincial court tried Aghajari in secret and issued the verdict of death.

The death sentence against Aghajari has provoked national furor. Some 5,000 students poured into the streets of Tehran to protest, inspiring demonstrations in other university cities. The fourth anniversary of the assassination of nationalists Dariush and Parvaneh Foruhar by agents of the Ministry of Information and Intelligence on November 21 strengthened the demonstrators' resolve. Students stayed in city streets during much of November, dispersing only when security forces appeared but then returning to demonstrate again.

Recognizing the students' tenacity, Ayatollah Khamenei threatened that if elected government officials could not quell dissent, he would call on the "forces of the people" to do so—a not-so-thinly veiled reference to *hezbollahi* thugs whose vigilantism conservative clerics sanction. The supreme leader has since softened his tone, ordering a judicial review of Aghajari's sentence, and the students' protests have diminished.

As during the larger student rebellion in July 1999, consistent repression eventually discouraged the protesters—at least for now, until another government decision or policy rouses proreform sympathizers. More significantly perhaps, intellectuals and students, along with other reformist constituencies, such as the press and women's rights activists, have not yet coalesced into a full-fledged movement ready to defy the government or at least conservatives within it. Rather, these constituencies have pursued disparate goals despite their overall support for Khatami and reformist parliamentarians. For their part, reformist officials have walked a tightrope between cultivating these constituencies' support and preserving political stability. When confronted with the choice between accelerating the pace of liberalization or maintaining the system's stability, reformist officials have so far chosen the latter.

## NEITHER EAST NOR WEST— NEITHER THIS NOR THAT?

Like the Islamic Republic's domestic politics, the ruling clerics' policies toward the outside world are marked by factional disagreements. Thus, analysis of Iran's foreign policy since September 11 requires an understanding of the interaction of internal and external factors that shape decision making by the clergy.

Khatami and the proreform Ministry of Foreign Affairs have argued that the implementation of foreign policy should benefit from public debate. Such debate would not only be consistent with the spirit of internal reform but would also enable the Islamic Republic to reenter fully the international community. Reformist officials suspect that Iranians are weary from years of war and regional adventurism, preferring instead that the Islamic Republic engage the world in dialogue and commerce.

Conservative officials, by contrast, have reserved the right to make decisions affecting national security outside the public arena. Moreover, they have not abandoned the posture of the Islamic Republic's first decade, despite numerous setbacks in their attempts to export the revolution. While realizing the importance of dialogue with like-minded international actors and not denying the need for trade and foreign investment, conservatives still believe that the ideology of Islamic universalism should guide Iran's conduct in the world.

Complicating factional disagreements over Iranian foreign policy is the inescapable reality of geography. At the crossroads of Central Asia and the Middle East, surrounded by the waters of the Caspian Sea and Persian Gulf, and rich with natural gas and oil, Iran's strategic value is obvious. The events of September 11 and the Bush administration's declaration of war against terrorism have only increased Iran's strategic value—and its foreign policy dilemmas.

The ruling clerics have maintained their stance "Neither East nor West, Only the Islamic Republic!" Yet reformists have shown a willingness to cooperate in a limited fashion with the United States and its allies in the war against terrorism, although the clerics diverge from Washington on many matters—most notably, on Iran's military buildup, its role in the Persian Gulf, and its stance toward the Arab–Israeli conflict. Khatami and Foreign Affairs Minister Kamal Kharrazi have not resisted the pull of Iran's geography, recognizing that the Islamic Republic could play a constructive role in creating a peaceful and stable Afghanistan free from the Taliban.

As Washington prepared to launch military hostilities against the Taliban in October 2001, Khatami insisted that the Islamic Republic and the United States had established "no secret contacts," despite rumors to the contrary. In the weeks before the American bombing campaign, however, Iran's president twice hosted Britain's Foreign Secretary Jack Straw, who, according the September 25, 2002 *Financial Times,* served "essentially as an intermediary" between Tehran and Washington "in order for both sides to reach some kind of understanding." With war's outbreak, the ruling clerics stepped up their assistance to Iran-based Afghan rebels fighting to wrest control of Herat and reportedly offered to help rescue downed American pilots. Iran's aid was crucial in driving the Taliban out of Afghanistan's northwest, setting off a chain reaction of military defeats elsewhere in the country.

Meanwhile, the anti-Taliban Northern Alliance in Afghanistan sought to persuade its new friends in the Bush administration to work with Iran's leadership in planning Afghanistan's reconstruction. Both American and Iranian officials understood the obstacles to cooperating openly. Yet once out of the limelight, the United Nations and Germany, hosting the Bonn Conference in December 2001, pushed the United States and Iran to acknowledge and further their shared interests. The collaboration of American and Iranian diplomats was vital in establishing the present Afghan government.

Consequently, when President Bush delivered his State of the Union address on January 29, 2002, devoting much of his speech to explaining why Iran, Iraq, and North Korea constitute an "axis of evil," the ruling clerics and other Iranians were shocked, especially the reformists. Iranians of all political stripes united in frustration at Bush's statements. A week later, during celebrations for the Islamic Republic's twenty-third anniversary, almost 100,000 marched in Tehran, carrying placards exclaiming that "Bush is Dracula!" and burning effigies of the American president and Israeli Prime Minister Ariel Sharon. In sermon after sermon, Iranian officials—reformists and conservatives—deplored the Bush administration's belligerence.

Washington's reinvigoration of hostility toward the Islamic Republic reflected suspicions that Iran had tried to undermine the new Afghan government, continuing to arm some warlords, including Ismail Khan in Herat and Rashid Dostum in Mazari-Sharif. American officials failed to reconcile their suspicions with the Islamic Republic's pledge to provide more financial aid to the new Afghan government than any other country, a move winning praise from the United Nations.

The Bush administration, however, pointed to Israel's seizure in January of a ship loaded with arms bound for the Palestinian Authority and thought to have originated in Iran. Although Tehran rejected Israeli accusations, the discovery of the *Karine-A* in the Red Sea aggravated American concerns that Tehran was increasing its support for militant Islamists throughout the Middle East. Interestingly, Iran's conservative officials have done little since the "axis of evil" speech to dissuade American decision makers, particularly hawks within the Department of Defense and National Security Council, not to distrust the Islamic Republic's regional intentions.

Realizing the weakness of their reformist rivals, the conservatives have continued to aid militant Islamist groups in Lebanon and the West Bank and Gaza, to seek Russian and Chinese assistance in developing nuclear power, and to reject any contact with the United States. With the American troops in Afghanistan, Georgia, Kyrgyzstan, and Uzbekistan, conservatives have argued that the Islamic Republic is surrounded. As the Bush administration plans for war against Iraq, Khatami and the Foreign Ministry seem on the defensive in the debate over foreign policy.

When a polling organization, the Ayandeh Research Institute, revealed that more than three-quarters of the Tehran residents it had surveyed last September favored a rapprochement with the United States, conservatives arrested the pollsters, who are now awaiting trial. The Islamic Republic's press court has charged the institute with taking money from the Washington-based Gallup Organization to fabricate the survey results. All national research institutes have since come under the judiciary's microscope, despite parliamentarians' letter of protest to Khatami in November.

In this context, reformist and conservative officials have begun debating how they should respond to a United States attack against Iraq. Tehran has reportedly sent signals to Washington through third parties that it could help American forces by sharing intelligence. And Iranian leaders have not objected to cooperation between their client in the Iraqi opposition, the Supreme Council of the Islamic Revolution in Iraq, and American-funded groups. Yet Tehran will likely adopt a wait-and-see approach until international weapons inspectors complete their job in Iraq. As the impasse between reformist and conservative clerics persists, the Islamic Republic's foreign policy position "Neither East nor West" is actually neither this nor that.

## REPRESSION, REFORM, OR REVOLUTION?

Iran today is at a turning point in both its domestic and foreign policies, but factional gridlock within the ruling clergy shows little sign of ending any time soon. For now, the Islamic Republic's leaders have calculated that stalemate is less costly than a decisive victory by one faction over the other. Khatami's camp cannot afford to quicken the pace of reform, and the conservatives want to avoid resorting to repression on a massive scale that may incite civil war. Popular dissatisfaction with the clerics is growing as Iranians from every walk of life vent their frustrations through the ballot box, in the press, and with political jokes.

Yet proreform constituencies have not managed to capitalize on this widespread disenchantment. These constituencies are insufficiently organized and, with the exception of a few major thinkers close to the ruling clergy, have not articulated a clear ideological alternative to the Islamic Republic. Thinkers such as Abdolkarim Soroush and Mohsen Kadivar have contended that reforms are not feasible without distinguishing between religion and the state. Although these intellectuals have endured the conservatives' brutality, they are still "khodi," or from within the revolution's ranks. The reformist discourse is a relatively elitist phenomenon, engaging a number of Iranians, but certainly not all who have grievances against the government.

Indeed, most Iranians are distracted by the exigencies of daily life and by the prospect of instability along their country's borders. The options Iranians have are few and poor: resigning themselves to the repressive status quo, pushing harder for reforms through the system, or revolting against the Islamic Republic. For now, the ruling clerics are the beneficiaries of a perverse form of luck, a resentful but risk-averse society coupled with a looming foreign threat.

---

BAHMAN BAKTIARI *is the director of the international affairs program and associate professor of political science at the University of Maine.* HALEH VAZIRI *is the regional research manager for Central Asia, the Middle East, and North Africa at the Inter-Media Survey Institute in Washington, D.C. The views expressed in this article are those of the authors.*

# Bin Laden, the Arab "Street," and the Middle East's Democracy Deficit

"Bin Laden speaks in the vivid language of popular Islamic preachers, and builds on a deep and widespread resentment against the West and local ruling elites identified with it. The lack of formal outlets to express opinion on public concerns has created [a] democracy deficit in much of the Arab world, and this makes it easier for terrorists such as bin Laden, asserting that they act in the name of religion, to hijack the Arab street."

## DALE F. EICKELMAN

In the years ahead, the role of public diplomacy and open communications will play an increasingly significant role in countering the image that the Al Qaeda terrorist network and Osama bin Laden assert for themselves as guardians of Islamic values. In the fight against terrorism for which bin Laden is the photogenic icon, the first step is to recognize that he is as thoroughly a part of the modern world as was Cambodia's French-educated Pol Pot. Bin Laden's videotaped presentation of self intends to convey a traditional Islamic warrior brought up-to-date, but this sense of the past is a completely invented one. The language and content of his videotaped appeals convey more of his participation in the modern world than his camouflage jacket, Kalashnikov, and Timex watch.

Take the two-hour Al Qaeda recruitment videotape in Arabic that has made its way to many Middle Eastern video shops and Western news media.[1] It is a skillful production, as fast paced and gripping as any Hindu fundamentalist video justifying the destruction in 1992 of the Ayodhya mosque in India, or the political attack videos so heavily used in American presidential campaigning. The 1988 "Willie Horton" campaign video of Republican presidential candidate George H. W. Bush—in which an off-screen announcer portrayed Democratic presidential candidate Michael Dukakis as "soft" on crime while showing a mug shot of a convicted African-American rapist who had committed a second rape during a weekend furlough from a Massachusetts prison—was a propaganda masterpiece that combined an explicit although conventional message with a menacing, underlying one intended to motivate undecided voters. The Al Qaeda video, directed at a different audience—presumably alienated Arab youth, unemployed and often living in desperate conditions—shows an equal mastery of modern propaganda.

The Al Qaeda producers could have graduated from one of the best film schools in the United States or Europe. The fast-moving recruitment video begins with the bombing of the USS *Cole* in Yemen, but then shows a montage implying a seemingly coordinated worldwide aggression against Muslims in Palestine, Jerusalem, Lebanon, Chechnya, Kashmir, and Indonesia (but not Muslim violence against Christians and Chinese in the last). It also shows United States generals received by Saudi princes, intimating the collusion of local regimes with the West and challenging the legitimacy of many regimes, including Saudi Arabia. The sufferings of the Iraqi people are attributed to American brutality against Muslims, but Saddam Hussein is assimilated to the category of infidel ruler.

*Osama bin Laden… is thoroughly imbued with the values of the modern world, even if only to reject them.*

Many of the images are taken from the daily staple of Western video news—the BBC and CNN logos add to the videos' authenticity, just as Qatar's al-Jazeera satellite television logo rebroadcast by CNN and the BBC has added authenticity to Western coverage of Osama bin Laden.

Alternating with these scenes of devastation and oppression of Muslims are images of Osama bin Laden: posing in front of bookshelves or seated on the ground like a religious scholar, holding the Koran in his hand. Bin Laden radiates charismatic authority and control as he narrates the Prophet Mohammed's flight from Mecca to Medina, when the early Islamic movement was threatened by the idolaters, but returning to conquer them. Bin Laden also stresses the need for jihad, or struggle for the cause of Islam, against the "crusaders" and "Zionists." Later images show military training in Afghanistan (including target practice at a poster of Bill Clinton), and a final sequence—the word "solution" flashes across the screen—captures an Israeli soldier in full riot gear retreating from a Palestinian boy throwing stones, and a reading of the Koran.

# THE THOROUGHLY MODERN ISLAMIST

Osama bin Laden, like many of his associates, is imbued with the values of the modern world, even if only to reject them. A 1971 photograph shows him on family holiday in Oxford at the age of 14, posing with two of his half-brothers and Spanish girls their own age. English was their common language of communication. Bin Laden studied English at a private school in Jidda, and English was also useful for his civil engineering courses at Jidda's King Abdul Aziz University. Unlike many of his estranged half-brothers, educated in Saudi Arabia, Europe, and the United States, Osama's education was only in Saudi Arabia, but he was also familiar with Arab and European society.

The organizational skills he learned in Saudi Arabia came in to play when he joined the mujahideen (guerrilla) struggle against the 1979 Soviet invasion of Afghanistan. He may not have directly met United States intelligence officers in the field, but they, like their Saudi and Pakistani counterparts, were delighted to have him participate in their fight against Soviet troops and recruit willing Arab fighters. Likewise, his many business enterprises flourished under highly adverse conditions. Bin Laden skillfully sustained a flexible multinational organization in the face of enemies, especially state authorities, moving cash, people, and supplies almost undetected across international frontiers.

The organizational skills of bin Laden and his associates were never underestimated. Neither should be their skills in conveying a message that appeals to some Muslims. Bin Laden lacks the credentials of an established Islamic scholar, but this does not diminish his appeal. As Sudan's Sorbonne-educated Hasan al-Turabi, the leader of his country's Muslim Brotherhood and its former attorney general and speaker of parliament, explained two decades ago, "Because all knowledge is divine and religious, a chemist, an engineer, an economist, or a jurist" are all men of learning.[2] Civil engineer bin Laden exemplifies Turabi's point. His audience judges him not by his ability to cite authoritative texts, but by his apparent skill in applying generally accepted religious tenets to current political and social issues.

# THE MESSAGE ON THE ARAB "STREET"

Bin Laden's lectures circulate in book form in the Arab world, but video is the main vehicle of communication. The use of CNN-like "zippers"—the ribbons of words that stream beneath the images in many newscasts and documentaries—shows that Al Qaeda takes the Arab world's rising levels of education for granted. Increasingly, this audience is also saturated with both conventional media and new media, such as the Internet.[3] The Middle East has entered an era of mass education and this also implies an Arabic lingua franca. In Morocco in the early 1970s, rural people sometimes asked me to "translate" newscasts from the standard transnational Arabic of the state radio into colloquial Arabic. Today this is no longer required. Mass education and new communications technologies enable large numbers of Arabs to hear—and see—Al Qaeda's message directly.

Bin Laden's message does not depend on religious themes alone. Like the Ayatollah Ruhollah Khomeini, his message contains many secular elements. Khomeini often alluded to the "wretched of the earth." At least for a time, his language appealed equally to Iran's religiously minded and to the secular left. For bin Laden, the equivalent themes are the oppression and corruption of many Arab governments, and he lays the blame for the violence and oppression in Palestine, Kashmir, Chechnya, and elsewhere at the door of the West. One need not be religious to rally to some of these themes. A poll taken in Morocco in late September 2001 showed that a majority of Moroccans condemned the September 11 bombings, but 41 percent sympathized with bin Laden's message. A British poll taken at about the same time showed similar results.

Osama bin Laden and the Al Qaeda terrorist movement are thus reaching at least part of the Arab "street." Earlier this year, before the September terrorist attacks, United States policymakers considered this "street" a "new phenomenon of public accountability, which we have seldom had to factor into our projections of Arab behavior in the past. The information revolution, and particularly the daily dose of uncensored television coming out of local TV stations like al-Jazeera and international coverage by CNN and others, is shaping public opinion, which, in turn, is pushing Arab governments to respond. We don't know, and the leaders themselves don't know, how that pressure will impact on Arab policy in the future."[4]

Director of Central Intelligence George J. Tenet was even more cautionary on the nature of the "Arab street." In testimony before the Senate Select Committee on Intelligence in February 2001, he explained that the "right catalyst—such as the outbreak of Israeli-Palestinian violence—can move people to act. Through access to the Internet and other means of communication, a restive public is increasingly capable of taking action without any identifiable leadership or organizational structure."

Because many governments in the Middle East are deeply suspicious of an open press, nongovernmental organizations, and open expression, it is no surprise that the "restive" public, increasingly educated and influenced by hard-to-censor new media, can take action "without any identifiable leadership or organized structure." The Middle East in general has a democracy deficit, in which "unauthorized" leaders or critics, such as Egyptian academic Saad Eddin Ibrahim—founder and director of the Ibn Khaldun Center for Development Studies, a nongovernmental organization that promotes democracy in Egypt—suffer harassment or prison terms.

One consequence of this democracy deficit is to magnify the power of the street in the Arab world. Bin Laden speaks in the vivid language of popular Islamic preachers, and builds on a deep and widespread resentment against the West and local ruling elites identified with it. The lack of formal outlets to express opinion on public concerns has created the democracy deficit in much of the Arab world, and this makes it easier for terrorists such as bin Ladin, asserting that they act in the name of religion, to hijack the Arab street.

The immediate response is to learn to speak directly to this street. This task has already begun. Obscure to all except specialists until September 11, Qatar's al-Jazeera satellite television is a premier source in the Arab world for uncensored news and opinion. It is more, however, than the Arab equivalent of CNN. Uncensored news and opinions increasingly shape "public opinion"—a term without the pejorative overtones of "the street"—even in places like Damascus and Algiers. This public opinion in turn pushes Arab governments to be more responsive to their citizens, or at least to say that they are.

Rather than seek to censor al-Jazeera or limit Al Qaeda's access to the Western media—an unfortunate first response of the United States government after the September terror attacks—we should avoid censorship. Al Qaeda statements should be treated with the same caution as any other news source. Replacing Sinn Fein leader Gerry Adams' voice and image in the British media in the 1980s with an Irish-accented actor appearing in silhouette only highlighted what he had to say, and it is unlikely that the British public would tolerate the same restrictions on the media today.

Ironically, at almost the same time that national security adviser Condoleezza Rice asked the American television networks not to air Al Qaeda videos unedited, a former senior CIA officer, Graham Fuller, was explaining in Arabic on al-Jazeera how United States policymaking works. His appearance on al-Jazeera made a significant impact, as did Secretary of State Colin Powell's presence on a later al-Jazeera program and former United States Ambassador Christopher Ross, who speaks fluent Arabic. Likewise, the timing and content of British Prime Minister Tony Blair's response to an earlier bin Laden tape suggests how to take the emerging Arab public seriously. The day after al-Jazeera broadcast the bin Laden tape, Blair asked for and received an opportunity to respond. In his reply, Blair—in a first for a Western leader—directly addressed the Arab public through the Arab media, explaining coalition goals in attacking Al Qaeda and the Taliban and challenging bin Laden's claim to speak in the name of Islam.

## PUTTING PUBLIC DIPLOMACY TO WORK

Such appearances enhance the West's ability to communicate a primary message: that the war against terrorism is not that of one civilization against another, but against terrorism and fanaticism in all societies. Western policies and actions are subject to public scrutiny and will often be misunderstood. Public diplomacy can significantly diminish this misapprehension. It may, however, involve some uncomfortable policy decisions. For instance, America may be forced to exert more diplomatic pressure on Israel to alter its methods of dealing with Palestinians.

Western public diplomacy in the Middle East also involves uncharted waters. As Oxford University social linguist Clive Holes has noted, the linguistic genius who thought up the first name for the campaign to oust the Taliban, "Operation Infinite Justice," did a major disservice to the Western goal. The expression was literally and accurately translated into Arabic as *adala ghayr mutanahiya,* implying that an earthly power arrogated to itself the task of divine retribution. Likewise, President George W. Bush's inadvertent and unscripted use of the word "crusade" gave Al Qaeda spokesmen an opportunity to attack Bush and Western intentions.

Mistakes will be made, but information and arguments that reach the Arab street, including on al-Jazeera, will eventually have an impact. Some Westerners might condemn al-Jazeera as biased, and it may well be in terms of making assumptions about its audience. However, it has broken a taboo by regularly inviting official Israeli spokespersons to comment live on current issues. Muslim religious scholars, both in the Middle East and in the West, have already spoken out against Al Qaeda's claim to act in the name of Islam. Other courageous voices, such as Egyptian playwright Ali Salem, have even employed humor for the same purpose.[5]

We must recognize that the best way to mitigate the continuing threat of terrorism is to encourage Middle Eastern states to be more responsive to participatory demands, and to aid local nongovernmental organizations working toward this goal. As with the case of Egypt's Saad Eddin Ibrahim, some countries may see such activities as subversive. Whether Arab states like it or not, increasing levels of education, greater ease of travel, and the rise of new communications media are turning the Arab street into a public sphere in which greater numbers of people, and not just a political and economic elite, will have a say in governance and public issues.

## NOTES

1. It is now available on-line with explanatory notes in English. See <http://www.ciaonet.org/cbr/cbr00/video/excerpts_index.html>.

2. Hasan al-Turabi, "The Islamic State," in *Voices of Resurgent Islam,* John L. Esposito, ed. (New York: Oxford University Press, 1983), p. 245.

3. On the importance of rising levels of education and the new media, see Dale F. Eickelman, "The Coming Transformation in the Muslim World," *Current History,* January 2000.

4. Edward S. Walker, "The New US Administration's Middle East Policy Speech," *Middle East Economic Survey,* vol. 44, no. 26 (June 25, 2001). Available at <http://www.mees.com/news/a44n26d01.htm>.

5. See his article in Arabic, "I Want to Start a Kindergarten for Extremism," *Al-Hayat* (London), November 5, 2001. This is translated into English by the Middle East Media Research Institute as Special Dispatch no. 298, Jihad and Terrorism Studies, November 8, 2001, at <http://www.memri.org>.

---

DALE F. EICKELMAN *is Ralph and Richard Lazarus Professor of Anthropology and Human Relations at Dartmouth College. His most recent book is* The Middle East and Central Asia: An Anthropological Approach, *4th ed. (Englewood Cliffs, N. J.: Prentice Hall, 2002). An earlier version of this article appeared as "The West Should Speak to the Arab in the Street,"* Daily Telegraph *(London), October 27, 2001.*

Reprinted from *Current History,* January 2002, pp. 36–39. © 2002 by Current History, Inc. Reprinted by permission.

# UNIT 5

# Comparative Politics: Some Major Trends, Issues, and Prospects

## Unit Selections

43. **The Global State of Democracy**, Larry Diamond
44. **Serial Utopia**, Christian Tyler
45. **Capitalism and Democracy**, Gabriel A. Almond
46. **Cultural Explanations: The Man in the Baghdad Café**, *The Economist*
47. **Jihad vs. McWorld**, Benjamin R. Barber

## Key Points to Consider

- What is meant by the first, second, and third waves of democratization? Discuss the reversals that followed the first two.

- Where are most of the countries affected by the third wave located? What factors appear to have contributed to their democratization? What are the signs that the third wave may be over?

- What are some main problems and dilemmas of old and new democracies, according to Larry Diamond?

- In what ways can market capitalism and liberal democracy be said to be mutually supportive? How can they undermine each other? What is the implication of the argument that in economics, one model or "size" is unlikely to "fit all"?

- What does Benjamin Barber mean when he warns that democracy is threatened by globalism and tribalism?

 **Links: www.dushkin.com/online/**
These sites are annotated in the World Wide Web pages.

**Commission on Global Governance**
*http://www.sovereignty.net/p/gov/gganalysis.htm*

**IISDnet**
*http://www.iisd.org/default.asp*

**ISN International Relations and Security Network**
*http://www.isn.ethz.ch*

**United Nations Environment Program**
*http://www.unep.ch/*

**Virtual Seminar in Global Political Economy/Global Cities & Social Movements**
*http://csf.colorado.edu/gpe/gpe95b/resources.html*

The articles in this unit deal with three major political trends or patterns of development that can be observed in much of the contemporary world. It is important at the outset to stress that, with the possible exception of Benjamin Barber, none of the authors predict some form of global convergence in which all political systems would become alike in major respects. On closer examination, even Barber turns out to argue that a strong tendency toward global homogenization is offset by a concurrent tendency toward intensified group differentiation and fragmentation.

Thus the trends or patterns discussed here are neither unidirectional nor universal. They are situationally defined, and therefore come in a great variety. They may well turn out to be temporary and partly reversible. Moreover, they do not always reinforce one another, but show considerable mutual tension. Indeed, their different forms of development are the very stuff of comparative politics, which seeks an informed understanding of the political dimension of social life by making careful comparisons across time and space.

After such cautionary preliminaries, we can proceed to identify three recent developments that singly and together have had a very important role in changing the political world in which we live. One is the *democratic revolution,* which has been sweeping much of the world. This refers to a widespread trend toward some form of *popular government* that often, but not always, takes the form of a search for representative, pluralist democracy in countries that were previously ruled by some form of authoritarian oligarchy or dictatorship.

Another trend, sometimes labeled the *capitalist revolution,* is the even more widespread shift toward some form of *market economy.* It includes a greater reliance on private enterprise and the profit motive, and involves a concurrent move away from strong regulation, central planning, and state ownership. The "social market economy," found in much of Western Europe, remains a form of capitalism, but one which includes a major role for the state in providing services, redistributing income, and setting overall societal goals. In some of the Asian Communist-ruled countries, above all China, we have become used to seeing self-proclaimed revolutionary socialists introduce a considerable degree of capitalist practices into their formerly planned economies.

The third major trend could be called the *revival of ethnic or cultural politics.* This refers to a growing emphasis on some form of an *exclusive group identity* as the primary basis for political expression. In modern times, it has been common for a group to identify itself by its special ethnic, religious, linguistic, or other cultural traits and to make this identity the basis for a claim to rule by and for itself.

The article that makes up the first section covers democratization as the first of these trends, that is, the startling growth in the number of representative governments in recent years. Even if this development is often fragile and likely to be reversed in some countries, we need to remember how remarkable it has been in the first place. Using very different criteria and data, skeptics on both right and left for a long time doubted whether representative government was sufficiently efficient, attractive or legitimate to spread or even survive in the modern world.

Samuel Huntington's widely discussed thesis concerning a recent wave of democratization is usefully summarized and carried further by Larry Diamond. Huntington is one of the best-known observers of democratization, who in the past emphasized the existence of cultural, social, economic, and political obstacles to representative government in most of the world. Even before the collapse of the communist regimes in Europe, however, he had begun to identify a broad pattern of democratization that had started in the mid-1970s, when three dictatorships in southern Europe came to an end (in Greece, Portugal, and Spain). In the following decade, democratization spread to most of Latin America. Central and Eastern Europe then followed, and the trend has also reached some states in East and South Asia like Taiwan or South Korea as well as some parts of Africa, above all South Africa and now, tentatively, Nigeria. The recent transfer of political power in Mexico, after more than seven decades of one-party hegemony, can also be seen in this context.

In a widely adopted phrase, Huntington identified this widespread trend as the "third wave" of democratization in modern history. The "first wave" had been both slow and long in its reach. During two decades, the number of democracies fell from 29 to 12, as many became victims of dictatorial takeovers or subsequent military conquests.

A "second wave" of democratization started with the Allied victory in World War II and continued during the early postwar years of decolonization. This wave lasted until the early 1960s. Then, in the mid-1970s, the important "third wave" of democratization got its start.

At the beginning of the 1990s, Huntington counted about 60 democracies in the world, which roughly amounted to a doubling of their number in less than two decades—an impressive change—but Huntington also pointed out that the process is likely to be reversed once again in a number of the new and unstable democracies. Both Huntington and Diamond's findings lend support to the conclusion that democracy's advance has been at best a "two steps forward, one step back" kind of process.

What are the general conditions that inhibit or encourage the spread and stabilization of democracy? Huntington and other scholars have identified some specific historical factors that appear to have contributed to the third wave. One important factor is the loss of legitimacy by both right- and left-wing authoritarian regimes, as they have become discredited by failures. Another factor is the expansion in some developing countries of an urban middle class, with a strong interest in representative government and constitutional rule. In Latin America, especially, the influence of a recently more liberal Catholic Church has been important. There have also been various forms of external influence by the United States and the European Community, as they have tried, however tentatively, to promote a human rights agenda. Finally, there is the "snowballing" or demonstration effect with the successful early transitions to democracy in countries like Spain or Poland, which served as models for other countries in similar circumstances.

Huntington's rule of thumb is that a democratic form of government can be considered to have become stable when a country has had at least two successive peaceful turnovers of power. Like most other observers, he sees extreme poverty as a principal obstacle to successful democratization.

The second section of this unit covers the trend toward capitalism or, better, market economics. Here Gabriel Almond explores the connections between capitalism and democracy in an article that draws upon both theory and empirical studies. His systematic discussion shows that there are ways in which capitalism and democracy support each other, and ways in which they tend to undermine each other. Is it possible to have the best of both? Almond answers at length that there is a nonutopian manner in which capitalism and democracy can be reconciled, namely in democratic welfare capitalism.

Almond's discussion can be linked to a theme emphasized by some contemporary political economists. They point out that the economic competition between capitalism and socialism, at least in the latter's traditional meaning of state ownership and centralized planning, has become a largely closed chapter in contemporary history. The central question now is which form of capitalism or market economy will be more successful. A similar argument has been made by the French theorist, Michel Albert, who also distinguishes between the British-American and the continental "Rhineland" models of capitalism. The former is more individualistic, antigovernmental, and characterized by such traits as high employee turnovers and short-term profit-maximizing. It differs considerably from what the Germans themselves like to call their "social market economy." The latter is more team-oriented, emphasizes cooperation between management and organized labor, and leaves a considerable role for government in the setting of general economic strategy, the training of an educated labor force, and the provision of social welfare services.

These different conceptions of capitalism can be linked to different histories. Both Britain and the United States experienced a head start in their industrial revolutions and felt no great need for deliberate government efforts to encourage growth. By contrast, Germany and Japan both played the role of latecomers, who looked to government protection in their attempts to catch up. To be sure, governments were also swayed by military considerations to promote German and Japanese industrialization. But the emergence of a kind of "social capitalism" in other continental countries of Europe suggests that cultural and institutional rather than military factors played a major role in this development. A crucial question is whether the relative prosperity and social security associated with this kind of mixed economy can be maintained in a time of technological breakthroughs and global competition. One possible answer will come from the policies and strategies adopted by the new "red-green" government in Germany. Because it seems unlikely that one economic model or size will fit all, as Christian Tyler emphasizes, we should continue to expect differently mixed economies.

The third section deals with the revival of the ethnic and cultural dimension in politics. Until recently, relatively few observers foresaw that this element would play such a divisive role in the contemporary world. There were forewarnings, such as the ethnonationalist stirrings in the late 1960s and early 1970s in peripheral areas of such countries as Britain, Canada, or Spain. It also lay behind many of the conflicts in the newly independent countries of the developing world. But most Western observers seem to have been poorly prepared for the task of anticipating or understanding the resurgence of politicized religious, ethnic, or other cultural forces. Many non-Westerners were taken by surprise as well. Mikhail Gorbachev, for example, grossly underestimated the centrifugal force of the nationality question in his own country.

The politicization of religion in many parts of the world falls into this development of a "politics of identity." In recent years, religious groups in parts of Latin America, Asia, the Middle East, sub-Saharan Africa, Asia, and southern Europe have variously set out on the political road in the name of their faith. As Max Weber warned in a classic lecture shortly before his death, it can be dangerous to seek "the salvation of souls" along the path of politics. The coexistence of people of divergent faiths is possible only because religious conviction need not fully determine or direct a person's or a group's politics. Where absolute and fervent convictions take over, they make it difficult to compromise pragmatically and live harmoniously with people who believe differently. Pluralist democracy requires an element of tolerance, which for many takes the form of a casual "live and let live" attitude.

There is an important debate among political scientists concerning the sources and scope of politics based on ethnic, religious, and cultural differences. Samuel Huntington argues forcefully that our most important and dangerous future conflicts will be based on clashes of civilizations. In his view, they will be far more difficult to resolve than those rooted in socioeconomic or even ideological differences. His critics, including the German Josef Joffe, argue that Huntington distorts the differences *among* civilizations and trivializes the differences *within* civilizations as sources of political conflict. Chandra Muzaffar, a Malaysian commentator, goes further by contending that Huntington's thesis provides a rationalization for a Western policy goal of dominating the developing world. Others have pointed out that ethnic conflicts are in fact often the result of political choices made by elites. This can turn out to be a hopeful thesis because it would logically follow that such conflicts are avoidable if other political choices were made.

In a widely discussed article, Benjamin Barber brings a broad perspective to the discussion of identity politics in the contemporary world. He sees two major tendencies that threaten democracy. One is the force of globalism, brought about by modern technology, communications, and commerce. Its logical end station is what he calls a "McWorld," in which human diversity, individuality, and meaningful identity are erased. The second tendency works in the opposite direction. It is the force of tribalism, which drives human beings to exacerbate their group differences and engage in holy wars or "jihads" against each other. Barber argues that globalism is at best indifferent to liberal democracy, while militant tribalism is deeply antithetical to it. He argues in favor of seeking a confederal solution, based on democratic civil societies, which could provide human beings with a nonmilitant, parochial communitarianism as well as a framework that suits the global market economy fairly well.

# The Global State of Democracy

**"The progress of democracy in the world over the last quarter-century has been nothing less than remarkable.... But if the reach of democracy is greater than ever, it is also thinner and more vulnerable."**

LARRY DIAMOND

Historians and philosophers already see the twentieth century as the bloodiest and the most destructive and brutal century in human history. But a parallel fact is less often noted: the twentieth century witnessed a profound transformation in the way societies are governed. As Freedom House pointed out in its January 2000 annual survey of freedom in the world, not a single country in 1900 would qualify as a democracy by today's standards.[1] By 1950, only 22 of the 80 sovereign political systems in the world (about 28 percent) were democratic. When the most recent wave of global democratization began in 1974, 39 countries were governed by democracies, but the percentage of democracies in the world was about the same, only 27 percent.

By January 2000, Freedom House counted 120 democracies, the highest number and the greatest percentage (62.5) in world history. This represents a dramatic change even from 1990, when less than half the world's independent states were democracies. Freedom House's assessment of the number of "free" states—those that "maintain a high degree of political and economic freedom and respect basic civil liberties"—also is near a recent historic high, with 85 states (44 percent) "free" at the end of 1999.

Since the fall of the Berlin Wall and the collapse of Soviet communism, democracy has been the dominant form of government. It is not difficult to infer from this dramatic expansion a nearly universal legitimacy for democracy—a global hegemony. Indeed, in its most recent Country Reports on Human Rights Practices, the United States Department of State went so far as to identify democracy and human rights as a third "universal language" (after money and the Internet).[2] The State Department's report envisions the emerging transnational network of human rights actors (both public and private) becoming an "international civil society... that will support democracy worldwide and promote the standards embodied in the Universal Declaration of Human Rights."

The globalization of democracy is indeed one of the most historic and profound global changes of the past several decades. In its duration and scope, this third global wave of democratization also stands in sharp contrast to the "second wave" of democratization that began at the end of World War II and expired in less than 20 years. That movement gave way to a "second reverse wave" in which democracy broke down in more than 20 developing countries and military rulers and civilian autocrats brutalized human rights and the rule of law.[3]

Remarkably, a quarter-century after the inception of democratization's third wave in 1974, the world still has not yet entered a "third reverse wave." Not only do more democracies exist than ever before, but very few high-profile democratic reversals have occurred. In fact, during the third wave's first 25 years, only three blatant reversals of democracy took place in countries with more than 20 million people: the military coup in Nigeria at the end of 1983, the 1989 military coup in Sudan, and the 1991 military coup in Thailand. The former two coups occurred in Africa before the third wave of democratization reached the continent in 1991. The Thai coup was a major setback for democracy in Southeast Asia, but it did not last. In little more than a year, the country's military leaders felt compelled to convene national elections to legitimize their rule, and their insistence on installing a nonelected army commander as prime minister triggered massive demonstrations that brought down the authoritarian project. Just 17 months after the February 1991 coup, democracy was restored to Thailand with the election of the first nonmilitary prime minister since the mid-1970s.

If we understand that the military coups in Nigeria and Sudan (and in Ghana in 1981) came before the third wave reached Africa, then, prior to October 1999, democratic reversals during the third wave had been of only three types. First were democratic breakdowns during the 1990s in small, relatively marginal states such as the Republic of Congo (Brazzaville), Gambia, Lesotho, Niger, and Sierra Leone. Second, democratic transitions or possibilities for democratic transitions were reversed or aborted in countries such as Cambodia, Lebanon, Kenya, Nigeria, and several post-Soviet states. And finally, democracy was mangled by elected presidents in Peru and Zambia, but in ways that preserved the framework of competitive, multiparty politics and thus at least some possibility of displacing the autocratic presidents in a future election.

The October 1999 military coup in Pakistan, however, may portend a more ominous trend; Pakistan is a truly strategic country, a regional power with nuclear weapons and a long-running, precarious conflict with India over the disputed territory of Kashmir. The principal causes of democratic breakdown in

Pakistan—the abuse of executive power, human rights, and the rule of law; growing ethnic and religious sectarian violence; and profound economic failure and injustice stemming from structural distortions and administrative incapacity—are not unique to Pakistan. Increasingly, these problems afflict many other large, strategic, emerging democracies in the world, such as Russia, Brazil, Turkey, Nigeria, and the Philippines.

## THE VARIED STATES OF DEMOCRACY

If we look only at the aggregate picture of democracy in the world, we can be cheered. More democracies exist than ever before, and the average level of freedom is also the highest ever recorded in the Freedom House annual survey of political rights and civil liberties. To comprehend the true state of democracy worldwide, however, we must analyze global trends.

Democracies—in the minimal sense, "electoral" democracies—share at least one broad essential requirement. The principal positions of political power in the country are filled through regular, free, and fair elections between competing parties, and an incumbent government can be defeated in those elections. The standard for electoral democracy—what constitutes "free and fair"—is more ambiguous than is often appreciated. As a result of the dubious conduct of recent national elections, such prominent multiparty states as Russia, Ukraine, Nigeria, and Indonesia fall into a gray area that is neither clearly democratic nor clearly undemocratic, even in the minimal electoral sense. Indeed, there is growing evidence of outright fraud in the March 2000 election that confirmed Vladimir Putin in the presidency of Russia.[4] Even short of fraud, Putin had such massive advantages of incumbency and support from crony capitalists that opposition parties virtually conceded his election in advance.

Russia is not unique. Freedom House laudably resists classifying as democracies such countries as Malaysia, Singapore, Peru, and Kenya, where electoral competition has been blatantly tilted in favor of the ruling party or president. But some of Freedom House's "democracies," such as Nigeria, Liberia, Indonesia, and the Kyrgyz Republic, suffer such widespread electoral fraud or systematic unfairness as to render the outcomes dubiously democratic at best. In fact, five of the states classified by Freedom House as democracies in 1999 (Djibouti, the Kyrgyz Republic, Liberia, Niger, and Sierra Leone) suffer from too much fraud, intimidation, or abridgment of free electoral choice to justify that classification. Yet even if we move these states, along with Russia, Ukraine, Nigeria, and Indonesia, out of the category of electoral democracy—while recognizing that Mexico and Senegal became electoral democracies in 2000 as a result of reforms in electoral administration that allowed the opposition finally to capture the presidency—we still find that almost 60 percent of the world's states are democracies. In the long sweep of world history, this is an extraordinary proportion.

However we judge them, elections are only one dimension of democracy. The quality of democracy also depends on its levels of freedom, pluralism, justice, and accountability. The deeper level of liberal democracy requires these conditions:

- Freedom of belief, expression, organization, demonstration, and other civil liberties, including protection from political terror and unjustified imprisonment;
- A rule of law under which all citizens are treated equally and due process is secure;
- Political independence and neutrality of the judiciary and of other institutions of "horizontal accountability" that check the abuse of power, such as electoral administration, audits, and a central bank;
- An open, pluralistic civil society, including not only associational life but the mass media as well;
- Civilian control of the military.[5]

These various dimensions of democratic quality constitute a continuum, and determining exactly when a regime has sufficient freedom, pluralism, lawfulness, accountability, and institutional strength to be considered a liberal democracy is difficult. For some years, I took as a rough indicator the Freedom House designation of a country as "free." Generally, these are countries that receive an average rating of between 1 and 2.5 on the two scales of political rights and civil liberties. (Each scale ranges from 1 to 7, with 1 being "most free" and 7 "least free.") However, countries with average scores of 2.5 have civil liberties scores of 3 on the 7-point scale, indicating serious deficiencies in the rule of law and the protection for individual rights. Typically in such countries (for example, the Philippines, El Salvador, and recently India), the judiciary is weak and ineffectual, if not politically compromised; corruption is widespread; and police and other security forces abuse citizens' rights with impunity. Therefore, we should only consider as minimally "liberal" those countries with an average score of 2.0 or better (that is, lower) on the Freedom House combined scale of political rights and civil liberties. By this standard, only 37 percent of the world's states were liberal democracies at the beginning of 2000.

We also need to consider the stability and rootedness of democracies. For political scientists, democracies are "consolidated" when all significant political elites, parties, and organizations, as well as an overwhelming majority of the public, are firmly committed to the democratic constitutional system and regularly comply with its rules and constraints. Strikingly, the third wave of democratization that began in 1974 has progressed only slowly toward consolidation. Except for the new democracies of southern Europe (Spain, Portugal, and Greece) and a few scattered others, the third-wave democracies have not taken firm root, although they are progressing more rapidly in Central and Eastern Europe.

Global assessments of the state of democracy and freedom in the world mask large differences among groups of countries. This is clearly true with respect to the level of development. The 30 "core" countries of Western Europe, along with the United States, Canada, Australia, New Zealand, Japan, and Israel, are all liberal, consolidated democracies. In fact, these core states account for the clear majority of all liberal democracies with populations over one million. Size also matters in the following respect. "Microstates" (those with populations under 1 million) are overwhelmingly democratic and liberal; and aside from the 30 core countries (eight

**Democracy, Liberal Democracy, and "Free" States by Region (and Cultural Grouping), 1999–2000**

| Region | Number of Countries | Number of Democracies (percent of total) | "Free" States (percent of total) | Liberal Democracies (percent of total) |
|---|---|---|---|---|
| Western Europe and Anglophone states | 28 | 28 (100%) | 28 (100%) | 28 (100%) |
| Latin America and Caribbean | 33 | 29 (88%) | 20 (70%) | 16 (48%) |
| South America | 12 | 11 (92%) | 6 (50%) | 4 (33%) |
| East Central Europe and Baltic States | 15 | 14 (93%) | 10 (67%) | 9 (60%) |
| Former Soviet Union (less Baltics) | 12 | 5 (42%)<br>4 (33%)* | 0 | 0 |
| Asia (East, SE, South) | 26 | 12 (46%) | 8 (31%) | 3 (12%) |
| Pacific Island | 11 | 10 (91%) | 9 (82%) | 9 (82%) |
| Africa (Sub-Sahara) | 48 | 20 (42%)<br>16 (33%)* | 8 (17%) | 5 (10%) |
| Middle East-North Africa | 19 | 2 (11%) | 1 (5%) | 1 (5%) |
| Total | 192 | 120 (63%)<br>115 (69%)* | 85 (44%) | 71 (37%) |
| Arab Countries | 16 | 0 | 0 | 0 |
| Predominantly Muslim Countries | 41 | 8 (20%)<br>5 (12%)* | 1 (2%) | 0 |

*Source*: The 1999 Freedom House Survey; *Journal of Democracy*, January 2000, pp. 187-200.

*Indicates a regime classification of the author that differs from that of Freedom House (FH). Freedom House rates Djibouti, the Kyrgyz Republic, Liberia, Niger, and Sierra Leone as electoral democracies, but all five have levels of coercion and fraud that make the electoral process less than free and fair. Other countries rated as electoral democracies have only dubiously democratic elections, including Russia, Nigeria, and Indonesia.

of which are microstates), no other group of countries in the world has so much political and civil freedom on average. Of the 41 countries with populations under 1 million, two-thirds are liberal democracies and almost four-fifths are democracies. However, these microstates have little scope to influence the direction of many other countries. (Indeed, two-thirds are island states, and hence share no land border with any country.)

As can be seen in the table above, electoral democracy stretches into nearly every major world region, although it is much more prevalent in some areas than in others. Liberal democracy is another story. The fragility and limited reach of liberal democracy is indicated by the fact that 54 of the 71 liberal democracies are either the 30 core countries or other states with populations of less than 1 million. If we set aside the 30 core countries and the other 33 microstates, we have 129 states. Only 13 percent of these 129 states in Asia, Africa, Latin America, the Middle East, and postcommunist Europe are liberal democracies.

Also striking are the differences in the distributions of regimes within regions. The 15 postcommunist states of Central and Eastern Europe (including the Baltic states) are moving to-

ward the liberal democratic West in their levels of freedom; the majority of these states are now liberal democracies, and many are progressing toward democratic consolidation. Of the remaining 12 states of the former Soviet Union, none is a liberal democracy, and less than half are democracies.

Just under half of the 26 states of Asia (East, Southeast, and South) are democracies, and only three are liberal democracies, but we see the effect of size when we compare this group with the 11 Pacific Island states, which are mainly liberal democracies. Similarly, while half the states of Latin America and the Caribbean are liberal democracies, these are mainly clustered in the Caribbean region. Only a third of the 12 South American states are liberal democracies. Liberal democracy is scarcely present (10 percent) among the 48 states of sub-Saharan Africa (the liberal democracies of Africa are again disproportionately microstates), but at least a third of these 48 states are now electoral democracies, a much greater figure than just a decade ago.

In contrast, not a single Arab democracy or majority Muslim country is a liberal democracy; indeed, only slightly more than

10 percent of the states with predominantly Muslim populations are even electoral democracies.

## VARIED PROGRESS TOWARD CONSOLIDATION

If we set aside the core states and the microstates, surprisingly few other democracies in the world are clearly "consolidated" (a democracy is consolidated when all politically significant elites and organizations, as well as the overwhelming majority of the mass public, believe that democracy is the best form of government and comply with its rules and restraints). Among the long-standing democracies in the developing world, India (with all its troubles), Costa Rica, Mauritius, and Botswana could be seen as consolidated. Venezuela and Colombia were considered consolidated democracies in the 1970s and 1980s but have become destabilized and seriously threatened in the past decade by economic mismanagement, corruption, and state decay as established parties and politicians grew complacent and distant from popular concerns. Indeed, the entire Andean region of South America now suffers a deep crisis of governance, sharply eroding the authority and capacity of the state and public confidence in democratic institutions. Like Colombia, Sri Lanka's long-established democracy has also sunk into illiberal and unstable status as a result of protracted internal violence, in this case an ethnic civil war. In Latin America, only Uruguay shows the levels of both elite and popular commitment to democracy that mark consolidation, although the recent presidential elections in Argentina and Chile (as well as the growing readiness of Chile to confront the crimes of the authoritarian past) indicate progress toward consolidation.

Significantly, the region where the most rapid, visible, and frequent strides toward democratic consolidation are being made is Central and Eastern Europe. In that area (including the Baltic states but not much of the Balkans), former communist countries are entrenching democratic practices and norms. Electoral returns, elite behavior, and mass attitudes and values (as revealed in public opinion surveys) show a deepening commitment to democracy in the Czech Republic, Poland, Hungary, Slovenia, Estonia, Latvia, and Lithuania, and progress as well in Slovakia, Bulgaria, and Romania. Popular commitment to democracy is particularly strong among younger people; hence the political culture and party system will become more democratic as voters who have come of age in the postcommunist era become more numerous. Within a decade or two, almost all of Europe from the Atlantic to the former Soviet border will likely consist of consolidated liberal democracies as integration into the expanding architectures of the European Union and the North Atlantic Treaty Organization helps lock the new democracies into place.

It is difficult for people living amid a profound but slow-moving transformation to recognize its historical significance. But the creation of a new, enlarged, unified, and entirely democratic Europe will be seen by historians a few decades hence as one of the truly great and lasting changes in the political character of the world.

Levels of freedom, democratic quality, and mass support for democracy are all considerably weaker in the non-Baltic former Soviet countries. In 1998, for example, Richard Rose of the University of Strathclyde in Glasgow found that 41 percent of Russians and 51 percent of Ukrainians favored the restoration of Communist rule (and only slightly lower percentages said they would approve suspending parliament and having strong single-leader rule). By contrast, only one in five respondents from Central and Eastern Europe supported either alternative. In Russia and Ukraine, as well as in other post-Soviet electoral "democracies," power is wielded much more roughly, elections are less fair, the rule of law is much more tenuous, and thus people are much more cynical about their politics and government.

The key question for the European community of democracies is whether this postcommunist divide can be overcome. In particular, will the new Europe include Russia? Will Russia gravitate, economically and politically, to the democratic West, or will it fall back on some version of its authoritarian and imperial tradition? As former national security adviser Zbigniew Brzezinski argued in the Fall 2000 *National Interest*, the United States and its European allies, in their ongoing engagement with Russia, should hold open the option of a "truly democratic Russia" becoming closely associated with both the European Union and NATO. At the same time, however, they should move forward vigorously with expanding both organizations to include ultimately all the former communist states of Central Europe. Such a strategy would cement the construction of an enlarged and democratically unified Europe while creating the context for a truly post-Soviet generation of Russian leaders to realize "that in order to recover Russia must opt for the West."

## THE FUTURE OF THE "SWING" STATES

The future of democracy in the world will be heavily determined by the political trajectory of the most powerful and the most populous states outside the wealthy, liberal democratic core. Depending on where the line is drawn (a population of 100 million or 50 million, or a GNP of $100 billion or $50 billion), 20 or 30 such states can be identified. Because of their political, economic, and demographic weight, these states will have a disproportionate influence on the democratic prospects of their regions. Among the most influential, troubled, and changeable are China, India, Russia, Brazil, Colombia, Mexico, Turkey, Pakistan, the Philippines, Iran, Nigeria, South Africa, and Indonesia. Because few of these states have stable consolidated regimes (whether democratic or authoritarian), they are "strategic swing states."[6] Only a few of this group of 30 influential states—South Korea, Taiwan, Chile, Poland, and the Czech Republic—might be considered liberal and in some respects consolidated democracies, and even some of these states have flawed democratic functioning. India's democracy is consolidated, but it faces serious problems with respect to entrenching good government and the rule of law.

Most of the 30 strategic swing states are much more deeply troubled and unstable than India. Their instability stems from three interrelated crises of governance, all of which were dramatically manifested in Pakistan as its democracy reeled toward collapse in the 1990s. First, they suffer a pervasive lack of accountability and a weak rule of law that permits endemic corruption, smuggling, violence, personalization of power, and abuse of human rights. Second, they have not been able to find workable, credible institutional formulas and civic codes to manage regional and ethnic divisions peacefully and give all citizens an inclusive stake in the political system. Third, they have faced economic crisis, stagnation, or instability because they have not sufficiently liberalized their economies, reduced state ownership and control, or rationalized and strengthened their corrupt, swollen state bureaucracies.

These crises of governance are not unique to large strategic states of the developing and postcommunist worlds. They afflict the smaller states as well. They represent the core problems that inhibit sustainable democratic progress and that threaten either the complete breakdown of democracy, as in Pakistan, or the kind of progressive erosion that has been occurring for a decade in Colombia and Venezuela.

None of the governance challenges confronting the swing states is more serious and pervasive than controlling corruption. Probably not a single threatened and vulnerable democracy in the world today has dilemmas that do not stem from rampant political corruption, rent-seeking behavior, and, more broadly, the weakness of the rule of law. In the next decade the prospects for sustainable democratic progress in the world will be heavily shaped by one question: Will emerging democracies and transitional regimes adopt the institutional reforms to control corruption and ensure a predictable, fair, credible, accessible, and efficient administration of justice?

To a great extent, we now know what must be done. Judiciaries must be modernized and professionalized, and their independence must be rigorously protected through reforms that insulate the appointment, remuneration, administration, and supervision of judges and prosecutors from partisan political influence. A wide range of other independent institutions of horizontal accountability must not only be established but given similar constitutional autonomy, substantial resources, and capable, dedicated leadership. These include:

- A countercorruption commission for receiving and monitoring the declared assets of public officials and for investigating corruption charges;

- A human rights commission to receive and investigate citizen complaints about violations of constitutional rights, and to educate people about their rights and obligations as democratic citizens;

- An independent, supreme auditing agency to audit the accounts of any state agency on a regular basis and on suspicion of specific wrongdoing;

- An ombudsman's office to provide citizens an outlet for grievances about unfair treatment and abuse of power by government agencies; and

- A truly independent electoral commission, which would ensure that abusive and corrupt elected officials can be removed from office in free and fair elections, and that all parties and officials can be disciplined in advance of elections.

The progress of democracy in the world over the last quarter-century has been nothing less than remarkable. No period in world history has seen a wider expansion of the democratic form of government and of the ability of citizens, armed with universal suffrage, to change their political leaders in relatively free and fair elections. But if the reach of democracy is greater than ever, it is also thinner and more vulnerable. The great challenge of the next decade is to deepen, stabilize, and consolidate the many emerging and struggling democracies outside the core. To do that, most will have to address seriously the triple crisis of governance outlined here. Most important, if they are to win the permanent and unconditional support of their citizens, these troubled democracies must make dramatic progress in controlling corruption and strengthening the rule of law.

It is too often forgotten that the challenge of building democracy heavily overlaps that of establishing the authority and capacity of a viable but restrained state. Whether this broad challenge can be effectively addressed, especially through legal, institutional, and economic reforms of the state's structure and role, will determine whether democracy continues to prosper in the world or gives way to a third "reverse wave" of democratic breakdowns.

## NOTES

1. Freedom House is an independent nongovernmental organization based in New York that advocates for democracy and human rights worldwide. Its annual survey of freedom in the world, which it has conducted for the past 30 years, is available on its website, www.freedomhouse.org.

2. *1999 Country Reports on Human Rights Practices* (Washington, D.C.: United States Department of State, Bureau of Democracy, Human Rights, and Labor, February 25, 2000).

3. Samuel P. Huntington, *The Third Wave: Democratization in the Late Twentieth Century* (Norman: University of Oklahoma Press, 1991).

4. For extensive documentation of fraud in Russia's March 2000 presidential election—sufficient to question its legitimacy—see the special report in *The Moscow Times*, September 11, 2000 (www.themoscowtimes.com).

5. For a fuller description, see Larry Diamond, *Developing Democracy: Toward Consolidation* (Baltimore: Johns Hopkins University Press, 1999), 10–12.

6. Larry Diamond, "Is Pakistan the (Reverse) Wave of the Future?" *Journal of Democracy*, July 2000.

---

LARRY DIAMOND *is a senior research fellow at the Hoover Institution, coeditor of the* Journal of Democracy, *and codirector of the National Endowment for Democracy's International Forum for Democratic Studies.*

---

# Serial Utopia

Economic models, like their fashion equivalents, come and go. But will one size ever fit all, asks **Christian Tyler**

Like any fashion model, today's ideal economy is supposed to be slim to the point of anorexic. In a post-collective, minimal-welfare age, the model must carry no fat. She must be long in the leg but light on her feet, not top-heavy nor too comfortable, but flexible, wiry—and competitive.

She should have the racing lines of, let us say, Irma Pantaeva, the six-foot supermodel from Siberia who wears an (American) dress size six. Pantaeva left her home on the shores of Lake Baikal in Russia after the collapse of communism—and found her way to New York where her doll-like Eskimo looks have landed her a part in a Woody Allen film.

Miss Pantaeva knew where she was going. Many economic theorists, especially American ones, regard the US as the ultimate model for an era famously described by Francis Fukuyama as "the end of history."

Others disagree, even violently. Too slim a line, they protest, is bad for the public health.

Starve your social structure too much, rely too much on material palliatives (sport, sex, shopping) for assuaging people's insecurity and spiritual hunger, and you are in danger of falling right off the catwalk. If not the US, who is the millennial supermodel?

The tiger-cub economies of Asia—especially Thailand, Malaysia, and Indonesia—are out of the contest for the moment. They have been put back in their cages, tails between their legs, punished by the markets for practising a fat-cat capitalism in which the banking system was allowed to become the plaything of the rich and powerful.

## Germany lacks the will to break up a labour hierarchy which goes back to the Middle Ages

We must look elsewhere in a world ever more locked together by trade and technology.

Utopias have always been with us. But they are not always places we would choose to live in. For even the most zealous economic libertarian prizes his quality of life, his slippers warming by a thermally inefficient hearth.

Sir Thomas More, Chancellor under Henry VIII, was mockingly ambivalent about his *Utopia*, according to Peter Ackroyd's new biography. More appeared to praise its Platonic *dirigisme*. Yet he called his narrator Hythlodaeus, which means "babbler" in Greek, the island's capital Amaurotum ("gloomy") and its principal river Anydrus ("waterless").

The poet Coleridge could find no subscribers for his "Pantisocracy", an egalitarian commune in the New World. And no doubt Samuel Butler would have run a mile rather than live in his *Erewhon* ("Nowhere").

And how many will sign up for the latest Utopian project: a 1,400-metre, 2.7m-tonne, 30-storey ship called "Freedom" designed to carry 65,000 rich residents in tax-exempt bliss round the globe in "the world's first ideal community"?

Many "ideal communities" have been held up for admiration this century. Even the Siberian supermodel's homeland, now in the grip of gangster capitalism, had its moment of glory.

According to the historian Eric Hobsbawin, Soviet central planning was an influential precedent for political leaders in the west anxious to forge a social contract—full employment and a welfare state—that would prevent a recurrence of economic slump, political extremism and war.

From the rubble of wartime Germany a powerful new model emerged, even as Britain began to understand the reality of its own post-imperial decline. Envious eyes were cast on this virtuous example of a high-wage, high-output economy where everyone, from baker's boy to finance director, had to serve his apprenticeship; where wage negotiations took account of the size of the national cake and rarely ended in strikes; where workers had seats on big company boards.

What was "concerted action" to Germany was "corporatism" to Thatcher's Britain. Today, Germany, having paid the bill to absorb its bankrupt eastern half after the fall of the Berlin wall, is considered too fat to prosper in the lean regime demanded by global competition. Even its most loyal supporters suspect it lacks the will to break up a labour hierarchy which goes back (as it did in the UK) to the guilds of the Middle Ages.

Among other social market economies, Austria has its adherents, but none attracts such devotion as the glamorous Swedish model. Exotically high taxes supported generous public services, and each year better-off white-collar workers conceded a "solidarity" wage transfer to their poorer comrades. Sweden was glamorous, but lacked stamina. In 1990, under a coalition government, the model repented of its public expenditure excesses.

In the 25 years of post second world war prosperity which Hobsbawin has described as a golden age, France attracted supporters for its modernising *élan*. Railways, airports and nuclear power plants were built, homes were computer-linked, and cultural monuments were erected by a ruling elite which moved effortlessly between civil service, government and industry. They wrote books, talked philosophy—and never cut short their lunch.

Italy had its 15 minutes of fame. In spite of a corrupt and chaotic political system, a ludicrous bureaucracy and massive national debt, it managed to pull ahead, briefly, of the UK.

The *sorpasso* of 1987 may have been statistical sleight-of-hand, but it left thrifty north Europeans musing about the strengths of a family-based, moonlighting economy.

There was even a small vogue—among trade union visionaries—for the Yugoslav model. After breaking with Stalin in 1948, Tito became the west's Good Communist, challenged for the title only by the "maverick", as he was so often described, Nicolae Ceausescu of Romania.

Tito liberalised the economy, devolved power to the regions, eased up a bit on political dissent, and gave his vizier Edvard Kardelj the unenviable job of reconciling "self-management"—workers chose their bosses and paid themselves wages—with the leading and guiding role of the party.

By the 1970s, of course, the world was being dazzled by the rising sun of Japan. Craftily borrowing western production ideas without at the same time compromising their culture, the Japanese had the audacity to make them work better than the west could.

At first, competitors laughed at the company songs, the lifetime employment, the pitifully few holidays, the stay-at-work strikes. Soon they were trembling for their jobs.

By fair means or foul (including strange excuses for low import penetration—that Japanese snow was "the wrong kind" for American skis, for instance) Japan inundated the world with its exports of cars and electronics.

Then suddenly, in 1990, following a stock market blowout, Japan hit the buffers. Today, kids wear baseball caps, and cars are imported; and there has been a surge in youth crime, along with a credit crunch, bankruptcies and rising unemployment.

The Asian tigers were on Japan's heels. South Korea, now also in crisis, was the industrial powerhouse but western pundits were more fascinated by the island states. Hong Kong, hitherto derided for making cheap plastic toys, began building textile factories in Switzerland. Taiwan gave the west an ideologically useful stick with which to beat communist China, then itself beginning to open.

As for Singapore, the streets were cleared of litter and riff-raff, miscreants were given a sound thrashing, and opposition politics became the riskiest choice of career. It was, the writer William Gibson observed, that rare place where residents went to a neighbouring Moslem country for their hanky-panky. Yet law-and-order capitalism appeared to work. Perhaps there was something in these "Asian values" after all.

The current blizzard in Asia has confirmed Fukuyama in his belief that economies will converge round a western (if not specifically US) model.

"Of all the alternatives, only a kind of paternalist Asian one looked remotely plausible," he said this week, speaking from George Mason University, Virginia. "Now that has been shown not to be viable."

What about China's version of a market economy? "I would be extremely surprised if the Communist party stays in power," he declared. Others are beginning to wonder if this conventional wisdom is correct, as they observe Beijing's increasingly pragmatic management of its economic revolution.

If another "third way" is emerging, the fashion show is not over yet. Indeed, the world could see a proliferation of capitalisms, says Professor John Gray, of the London School of Economics. In a new polemic, *False Dawn*, Gray warns that US efforts to impose a free-market, free-trade diet on the rest of the world will be rejected.

A defector from the radical right, Gray thinks the US has neither the power, nor the will, to enforce what he calls just another form of social engineering. Americans may tolerate the consequences—ghettoes, gross income inequalities and a huge prison population; but exported to other cultures, this brand of capitalism is doomed to self-destruction.

So who now takes the crown?

"If you are talking about efficiency," says Nicholas Crafts, professor of economic history at the LSE, "then I still think the US has got it more nearly right than most. But the model is deeply unattractive to many people, including me. My judgment is that Americans care too little about redistribution."

Asked to pick the supermodel for the millennium, Fukuyama nominated Canada, as a free-market country, socially liberal, with its own cultural accessories.

Gray nominated the Netherlands for its combination of reformed welfare state, freed-up labour market and social tolerance. Sweden still has her fans, as do Austria and Denmark.

In any beauty contest, jurors cannot conceal their local bias. But it is not just for that reason that Blair's "cool Britannia", which lost the crown early this century, is getting votes these days from its native judges. Britain, they say, could be the model for Europe. At the least, it is looking like a plausible model for itself.

And this is the conclusion pundits seem to like best. Countries may pinch one another's clothes, but they should not dress up in gear that doesn't suit the body they were born into. "There is no One Size Fits All," says Roderick Nye of the Social Market Foundation, a London think-tank.

Geoff Mulgan, another tankie now working at Tony Blair's policy unit, puts it well: "The fashion for using other countries is waning, and that's a healthy thing. It's bound to end in mistaken borrowings, and it's bound to end in tears."

# Capitalism and Democracy*

**Gabriel A. Almond**

Joseph Schumpeter, a great economist and social scientist of the last generation, whose career was almost equally divided between Central European and American universities, and who lived close to the crises of the 1930s and '40s, published a book in 1942 under the title, *Capitalism, Socialism, and Democracy*. The book has had great influence, and can be read today with profit. It was written in the aftergloom of the great depression, during the early triumphs of Fascism and Nazism in 1940 and 1941, when the future of capitalism, socialism, and democracy all were in doubt. Schumpeter projected a future of declining capitalism, and rising socialism. He thought that democracy under socialism might be no more impaired and problematic than it was under capitalism.

He wrote a concluding chapter in the second edition which appeared in 1946, and which took into account the political-economic situation at the end of the war, with the Soviet Union then astride a devastated Europe. In this last chapter he argues that we should not identify the future of socialism with that of the Soviet Union, that what we had observed and were observing in the first three decades of Soviet existence was not a necessary expression of socialism. There was a lot of Czarist Russia in the mix. If Schumpeter were writing today, I don't believe he would argue that socialism has a brighter future than capitalism. The relationship between the two has turned out to be a good deal more complex and intertwined than Schumpeter anticipated. But I am sure that he would still urge us to separate the future of socialism from

that of Soviet and Eastern European Communism.

Unlike Schumpeter I do not include Socialism in my title, since its future as a distinct ideology and program of action is unclear at best. Western Marxism and the moderate socialist movements seem to have settled for social democratic solutions, for adaptations of both capitalism and democracy producing acceptable mixes of market competition, political pluralism, participation, and welfare. I deal with these modifications of capitalism, as a consequence of the impact of democracy on capitalism in the last half century.

At the time that Adam Smith wrote *The Wealth of Nations*, the world of government, politics and the state that he knew—pre-Reform Act England, the French government of Louis XV and XVI—was riddled with special privileges, monopolies, interferences with trade. With my tongue only half way in my check I believe the discipline of economics may have been traumatized by this condition of political life at its birth. Typically, economists speak of the state and government instrumentally, as a kind of secondary service mechanism.

I do not believe that politics can be treated in this purely instrumental and reductive way without losing our analytic grip on the social and historical process. The economy and the polity are the main problem solving mechanisms of human society. They each have their distinctive means, and they each have their "goods" or ends. They necessarily interact with each other, and transform each other in the process. Democracy in particular generates goals and programs. You cannot give people the suffrage,

and let them form organizations, run for office, and the like, without their developing all kinds of ideas as to how to improve things. And sometimes some of these ideas are adopted, implemented and are productive, and improve our lives, although many economists are reluctant to concede this much to the state.

My lecture deals with this interaction of politics and economics in the Western World in the course of the last couple of centuries, in the era during which capitalism and democracy emerged as the dominant problem solving institutions of modern civilization. I am going to discuss some of the theoretical and empirical literature dealing with the themes of the positive and negative interaction between capitalism and democracy. There are those who say that capitalism supports democracy, and those who say that capitalism subverts democracy. And there are those who say that democracy subverts capitalism, and those who say that it supports it.

The relation between capitalism and democracy dominates the political theory of the last two centuries. All the logically possible points of view are represented in a rich literature. It is this ambivalence and dialectic, this tension between the two major problem solving sectors of modern society—the political and the economic —that is the topic of my lecture.

## Capitalism Supports Democracy

Let me begin with the argument that capitalism is positively linked with democracy, shares its values and culture, and facilitates its development. This case has been made in historical, logical, and statistical terms.

Albert Hirschman in his *Rival Views of Market Society* (1986) examines the values, manners and morals of capitalism, and their effects on the larger society and culture as these have been described by the philosophers of the 17th, 18th, and 19th centuries. He shows how the interpretation of the impact of capitalism has changed from the enlightenment view of Montesquieu, Condorcet, Adam Smith and others, who stressed the *douceur* of commerce, its "gentling," civilizing effect on behavior and interpersonal relations, to that of the 19th and 20th century conservative and radical writers who described the culture of capitalism as crassly materialistic, destructively competitive, corrosive of morality, and hence self-destructive. This sharp almost 180-degree shift in point of view among political theorists is partly explained by the transformation from the commerce and small-scale industry of early capitalism, to the smoke blackened industrial districts, the demonic and exploitive entrepreneurs, and exploited laboring classes of the second half of the nineteenth century. Unfortunately for our purposes, Hirschman doesn't deal explicitly with the capitalism–democracy connection, but rather with culture and with manners. His argument, however, implies an early positive connection and a later negative one.

Joseph Schumpeter in *Capitalism, Socialism, and Democracy* (1942) states flatly, "History clearly confirms... [that]... modern democracy rose along with capitalism, and in causal connection with it... modern democracy is a product of the capitalist process." He has a whole chapter entitled "The Civilization of Capitalism," democracy being a part of that civilization. Schumpeter also makes the point that democracy was historically supportive of capitalism. He states, "... the bourgeoisie reshaped, and from its own point of view rationalized, the social and political structure that preceded its ascendancy..." (that is to say, feudalism). "The democratic method

was the political tool of that reconstruction." According to Schumpeter capitalism and democracy were mutually causal historically, mutually supportive parts of a rising modern civilization, although as we shall show below, he also recognized their antagonisms.

Barrington Moore's historical investigation (1966) with its long title, *The Social Origins of Dictatorship and Democracy; Lord and Peasant in the Making of the Modern World*, argues that there have been three historical routes to industrial modernization. The first of these followed by Britain, France, and the United States, involved the subordination and transformation of the agricultural sector by the rising commercial bourgeoisie, producing the democratic capitalism of the 19th and 20th centuries. The second route followed by Germany and Japan, where the landed aristocracy was able to contain and dominate the rising commercial classes, produced an authoritarian and fascist version of industrial modernization, a system of capitalism encased in a feudal authoritarian framework, dominated by a military aristocracy, and an authoritarian monarchy. The third route, followed in Russia where the commercial bourgeoisie was too weak to give content and direction to the modernizing process, took the form of a revolutionary process drawing on the frustration and resources of the peasantry, and created a mobilized authoritarian Communist regime along with a state-controlled industrialized economy. Successful capitalism dominating and transforming the rural agricultural sector, according to Barrington Moore, is the creator and sustainer of the emerging democracies of the nineteenth century.

Robert A. Dahl, the leading American democratic theorist, in the new edition of his book (1990) *After the Revolution? Authority in a Good Society*, has included a new chapter entitled "Democracy and Markets." In the opening paragraph of that chapter, he says:

It is an historical fact that modern democratic institutions... have existed only in countries with predominantly privately owned, market-oriented economies, or

capitalism if you prefer that name. It is also a fact that all "socialist" countries with predominantly state-owned centrally directed economic orders—command economies—have not enjoyed democratic governments, but have in fact been ruled by authoritarian dictatorships. It is also an historical fact that some "capitalist" countries have also been, and are, ruled by authoritarian dictatorships.

To put it more formally, it looks to be the case that market-oriented economies are necessary (in the logical sense) to democratic institutions, though they are certainly not sufficient. And it looks to be the case that state-owned centrally directed economic orders are strictly associated with authoritarian regimes, though authoritarianism definitely does not require them. We have something very much like an historical experiment, so it would appear, that leaves these conclusions in no great doubt. (Dahl 1990)

Peter Berger in his book *The Capitalist Revolution* (1986) presents four propositions on the relation between capitalism and democracy:

Capitalism is a necessary but not sufficient condition of democracy under modern conditions.

If a capitalist economy is subjected to increasing degrees of state control, a point (not precisely specifiable at this time) will be reached at which democratic governance becomes impossible.

If a socialist economy is opened up to increasing degrees of market forces, a point (not precisely specifiable at this time) will be reached at which democratic governance becomes a possibility.

If capitalist development is successful in generating economic growth from which a sizable proportion of the population benefits, pressures toward democracy are likely to appear.

This positive relationship between capitalism and democracy has also been sustained by statistical studies. The "Social Mobilization" theorists of the 1950s and 1960s which included

Daniel Lerner (1958), Karl Deutsch (1961), S. M. Lipset (1959) among others, demonstrated a strong statistical association between GNP per capita and democratic political institutions. This is more than simple statistical association. There is a logic in the relation between level of economic development and democratic institutions. Level of economic development has been shown to be associated with education and literacy, exposure to mass media, and democratic psychological propensities such as subjective efficacy, participatory aspirations and skills. In a major investigation of the social psychology of industrialization and modernization, a research team led by the sociologist Alex Inkeles (1974) interviewed several thousand workers in the modern industrial and the traditional economic sectors of six countries of differing culture. Inkeles found empathetic, efficacious, participatory and activist propensities much more frequently among the modern industrial workers, and to a much lesser extent in the traditional sector in each one of these countries regardless of cultural differences.

The historical, the logical, and the statistical evidence for this positive relation between capitalism and democracy is quite persuasive.

## Capitalism Subverts Democracy

But the opposite case is also made, that capitalism subverts or undermines democracy. Already in John Stuart Mill (1848) we encounter a view of existing systems of private property as unjust, and of the free market as destructively competitive—aesthetically and morally repugnant. The case he was making was a normative rather than a political one. He wanted a less competitive society, ultimately socialist, which would still respect individuality. He advocated limitations on the inheritance of property and the improvement of the property system so that everyone shared in its benefits, the limitation of population growth, and the improvement of the quality of the labor force through the provision of high quality education for all by the state. On the eve of the emergence of the modern democratic capi-

talist order John Staurt Mill wanted to control the excesses of both the market economy and the majoritarian polity, by the education of consumers and producers, citizens and politicians, in the interest of producing morally improved free market and democratic orders. But in contrast to Marx, he did not thoroughly discount the possibilities of improving the capitalist and democratic order.

Marx argued that as long as capitalism and private property existed there could be no genuine democracy, that democracy under capitalism was bourgeois democracy, which is to say not democracy at all. While it would be in the interest of the working classes to enter a coalition with the bourgeoisie in supporting this form of democracy in order to eliminate feudalism, this would be a tactical maneuver. Capitalist democracy could only result in the increasing exploitation of the working classes. Only the elimination of capitalism and private property could result in the emancipation of the working classes and the attainment of true democracy. Once socialism was attained the basic political problems of humanity would have been solved through the elimination of classes. Under socialism there would be no distinctive democratic organization, no need for institutions to resolve conflicts, since there would be no conflicts. There is not much democratic or political theory to be found in Marx's writings. The basic reality is the mode of economic production and the consequent class structure from which other institutions follow.

For the followers of Marx up to the present day there continues to be a negative tension between capitalism, however reformed, and democracy. But the integral Marxist and Leninist rejection of the possibility of an autonomous, bourgeois democratic state has been left behind for most Western Marxists. In the thinking of Poulantzas, Offe, Bobbio, Habermas and others, the bourgeois democratic state is now viewed as a class struggle state, rather than an unambiguously bourgeois state. The working class has access to it; it can struggle for its interests, and can attain partial benefits from it. The state is now viewed as autonomous, or as relatively autonomous, and it can be re-

formed in a progressive direction by working class and other popular movements. The bourgeois democratic state can be moved in the direction of a socialist state by political action short of violence and institutional destruction.

Schumpeter (1942) appreciated the tension between capitalism and democracy. While he saw a causal connection between competition in the economic and the political order, he points out "... that there are some deviations from the principle of democracy which link up with the presence of organized capitalist interests.... [T]he statement is true both from the standpoint of the classical and from the standpoint of our own theory of democracy. From the first standpoint, the result reads that the means at the disposal of private interests are often used in order to thwart the will of the people. From the second standpoint, the result reads that those private means are often used in order to interfere with the working of the mechanism of competitive leadership." He refers to some countries and situations in which "... political life all but resolved itself into a struggle of pressure groups and in many cases practices that failed to conform to the spirit of the democratic method." But he rejects the notion that there cannot be political democracy in a capitalist society. For Schumpeter full democracy in the sense of the informed participation of all adults in the selection of political leaders and consequently the making of public policy, was an impossibility because of the number and complexity of the issues confronting modern electorates. The democracy which was realistically possible was one in which people could choose among competing leaders, and consequently exercise some direction over political decisions. This kind of democracy was possible in a capitalist society, though some of its propensities impaired its performance. Writing in the early years of World War II, when the future of democracy and of capitalism were uncertain, he leaves unresolved the questions of "... Whether or not democracy is one of those products of capitalism which are to die out with it..." or "... how well or ill capitalist society qualifies for the task of working the democratic method it evolved."

Non-Marxist political theorists have contributed to this questioning of the reconcilability of capitalism and democracy. Robert A. Dahl, who makes the point that capitalism historically has been a necessary precondition of democracy, views contemporary democracy in the United States as seriously compromised, impaired by the inequality in resources among the citizens. But Dahl stresses the variety in distributive patterns, and in politico-economic relations among contemporary democracies. "The category of capitalist democracies" he writes, "includes an extraordinary variety... from nineteenth century, laissez faire, early industrial systems to twentieth century, highly regulated, social welfare, late or postindustrial systems. Even late twentieth century 'welfare state' orders vary all the way from the Scandinavian systems, which are redistributive, heavily taxed, comprehensive in their social security, and neocorporatist in their collective bargaining arrangements to the faintly redistributive, moderately taxed, limited social security, weak collective bargaining systems of the United States and Japan" (1989).

In *Democracy and Its Critics* (1989) Dahl argues that the normative growth of democracy to what he calls its "third transformation" (the first being the direct city-state democracy of classic times, and the second, the indirect, representative inegalitarian democracy of the contemporary world) will require democratization of the economic order. In other words, modern corporate capitalism needs to be transformed. Since government control and/or ownership of the economy would be destructive of the pluralism which is an essential requirement of democracy, his preferred solution to the problem of the mega-corporation is employee control of corporate industry. An economy so organized, according to Dahl, would improve the distribution of political resources without at the same time destroying the pluralism which democratic competition requires. To those who question the realism of Dahl's solution to the

problem of inequality, he replies that history is full of surprises.

Charles E. Lindblom in his book, *Politics and Markets* (1977), concludes his comparative analysis of the political economy of modern capitalism and socialism, with an essentially pessimistic conclusion about contemporary market-oriented democracy. He says

We therefore come back to the corporation. It is possible that the rise of the corporation has offset or more than offset the decline of class as an instrument of indoctrination.... That it creates a new core of wealth and power for a newly constructed upper class, as well as an overpowering loud voice, is also reasonably clear. The executive of the large corporation is, on many counts, the contemporary counterpart to the landed gentry of an earlier era, his voice amplified by the technology of mass communication.... [T]he major institutional barrier to fuller democracy may therefore be the autonomy of the private corporation.

Lindblom concludes, "The large private corporation fits oddly into democratic theory and vision. Indeed it does not fit."

There is then a widely shared agreement, from the Marxists and neo-Marxists, to Schumpeter, Dahl, Lindblom, and other liberal political theorists, that modern capitalism with the dominance of the large corporation, produces a defective or an impaired form of democracy.

## Democracy Subverts Capitalism

If we change our perspective now and look at the way democracy is said to affect capitalism, one of the dominant traditions of economics from Adam Smith until the present day stresses the importance for productivity and welfare of an economy that is relatively free of intervention by the state. In this doctrine of minimal government there is still a place for a framework of rules and services essential to the productive and efficient performance of the economy. In part the government has to protect the market from itself. Left to their

own devices, according to Smith, businessmen were prone to corner the market in order to exact the highest possible price. And according to Smith businessmen were prone to bribe public officials in order to gain special privileges, and legal monopolies. For Smith good capitalism was competitive capitalism, and good government provided just those goods and services which the market needed to flourish, could not itself provide, or would not provide. A good government according to Adam Smith was a minimal government, providing for the national defense, and domestic order. Particularly important for the economy were the rules pertaining to commercial life such as the regulation of weights and measures, setting and enforcing building standards, providing for the protection of persons and property, and the like.

For Milton Friedman (1961, 1981), the leading contemporary advocate of the free market and free government, and of the interdependence of the two, the principal threat to the survival of capitalism and democracy is the assumption of the responsibility for welfare on the part of the modern democratic state. He lays down a set of functions appropriate to government in the positive interplay between economy and polity, and then enumerates many of the ways in which the modern welfare, regulatory state has deviated from these criteria.

A good Friedmanesque, democratic government would be one "... which maintained law and order, defended property rights, served as a means whereby we could modify property rights and other rules of the economic game, adjudicated disputes about the interpretation of the rules, enforced contracts, promoted competition, provided a monetary framework, engaged in activities to counter technical monopolies and to overcome neighborhood effects widely regarded as sufficiently important to justify government intervention, and which supplemented private charity and the private family in protecting the irresponsible, whether madman or child ...."
Against this list of proper activities for a free government, Friedman pinpointed more than a dozen activities

of contemporary democratic governments which might better be performed through the private sector, or not at all. These included setting and maintaining price supports, tariffs, import and export quotas and controls, rents, interest rates, wage rates, and the like, regulating industries and banking, radio and television, licensing professions and occupations, providing social security and medical care programs, providing public housing, national parks, guaranteeing mortgages, and much else.

Friedman concludes that this steady encroachment on the private sector has been slowly but surely converting our free government and market system into a collective monster, compromising both freedom and productivity in the outcome. The tax and expenditure revolts and regulatory rebellions of the 1980s have temporarily stemmed this trend, but the threat continues. "It is the internal threat coming from men of good intentions and good will who wish to reform us. Impatient with the slowness of persuasion and example to achieve the great social changes they envision, they are anxious to use the power of the state to achieve their ends, and confident of their own ability to do so." The threat to political and economic freedom, according to Milton Friedman and others who argue the same position, arises out of democratic politics. It may only be defeated by political action.

In the last decades a school, or rather several schools, of economists and political scientists have turned the theoretical models of economics to use in analyzing political processes. Variously called public choice theorists, rational choice theorists, or positive political theorists, and employing such models as market exchange and bargaining, rational self interest, game theory, and the like, these theorists have produced a substantial literature throwing new and often controversial light on democratic political phenomena such as elections, decisions of political party leaders, interest group behavior, legislative and committee decisions, bureaucratic, and judicial behavior, lobbying activity, and substantive public policy areas such as constitutional arrangements, health and environment policy, regulatory policy, national security and foreign policy, and the like. Hardly a field of politics and public policy has been left untouched by this inventive and productive group of scholars.

The institutions and names with which this movement is associated in the United States include Virginia State University, the University of Virginia, the George Mason University, the University of Rochester, the University of Chicago, the California Institute of Technology, the Carnegie Mellon University, among others. And the most prominent names are those of the leaders of the two principal schools: James Buchanan, the Nobel Laureate leader of the Virginia "Public Choice" school, and William Riker, the leader of the Rochester "Positive Theory" school. Other prominent scholars associated with this work are Gary Becker of the University of Chicago, Kenneth Shepsle and Morris Fiorina of Harvard, John Ferejohn of Stanford, Charles Plott of the California Institute of Technology, and many others.

One writer summarizing the ideological bent of much of this work, but by no means all of it (William Mitchell of the University of Washington), describes it as fiscally conservative, sharing a conviction that the "... private economy is far more robust, efficient, and perhaps, equitable than other economies, and much more successful than political processes in efficiently allocating resources...." Much of what has been produced "... by James Buchanan and the leaders of this school can best be described as contributions to a theory of the failure of political processes." These failures of political performance are said to be inherent properties of the democratic political process. "Inequity, inefficiency, and coercion are the most general results of democratic policy formation." In a democracy the demand for publicly provided services seems to be insatiable. It ultimately turns into a special interest, "rent seeking" society. Their remedies take the form of proposed constitutional limits on spending power and checks and balances to limit legislative majorities.

One of the most visible products of this pessimistic economic analysis of democratic politics is the book by Mancur Olson, *The Rise and Decline of Nations* (1982). He makes a strong argument for the negative democracy–capitalism connection. His thesis is that the behavior of individuals and firms in stable societies inevitably leads to the formation of dense networks of collusive, cartelistic, and lobbying organizations that make economies less efficient and dynamic and polities less governable. "The longer a society goes without an upheaval, the more powerful such organizations become and the more they slow down economic expansion. Societies in which these narrow interest groups have been destroyed, by war or revolution, for example, enjoy the greatest gains in growth." His prize cases are Britain on the one hand and Germany and Japan on the other.

The logic of the argument implies that countries that have had democratic freedom of organization without upheaval or invasion the longest will suffer the most from growth-repressing organizations and combinations. This helps explain why Great Britain, the major nation with the longest immunity from dictatorship, invasion, and revolution, has had in this century a lower rate of growth than other large, developed democracies. Britain has precisely the powerful network of special interest organization that the argument developed here would lead us to expect in a country with its record of military security and democratic stability. The number and power of its trade unions need no description. The venerability and power of its professional associations is also striking.... In short, with age British society has acquired so many strong organizations and collusions that it suffers from an institutional sclerosis that slows its adaptation to changing circumstances and technologies. (Olson 1982)

By contrast, post-World War II Germany and Japan started organizationally from scratch. The organizations that led them to defeat were all dissolved, and under the occupation inclusive organizations like the general trade union movement and general organizations of the industrial and commercial community were first formed. These inclusive organizations had more regard for the general national interest and exercised some discipline on the narrower interest organizations. And both countries in the post-war decades experienced "miracles" of economic growth under democratic conditions.

The Olson theory of the subversion of capitalism through the propensities of democratic societies to foster special interest groups has not gone without challenge. There can be little question that there is logic in his argument. But empirical research testing this pressure group hypothesis thus far has produced mixed findings. Olson has hopes that a public educated to the harmful consequences of special interests to economic growth, full employment, coherent government, equal opportunity, and social mobility will resist special interest behavior, and enact legislation imposing anti-trust, and anti-monopoly controls to mitigate and contain these threats. It is somewhat of an irony that the solution to this special interest disease of democracy, according to Olson, is a democratic state with sufficient regulatory authority to control the growth of special interest organizations.

## Democracy Fosters Capitalism

My fourth theme, democracy as fostering and sustaining capitalism, is not as straightforward as the first three. Historically there can be little doubt that as the suffrage was extended in the last century, and as mass political parties developed, democratic development impinged significantly on capitalist institutions and practices. Since successful capitalism requires risk-taking entrepreneurs with access to investment capital, the democratic propensity for redistributive and regulative policy tends to reduce the incentives and the resources available for risk-taking and creativity. Thus it can be argued that propensities inevitably resulting from democratic politics, as Friedman, Olson and many

others argue, tend to reduce productivity, and hence welfare.

But precisely the opposite argument can be made on the basis of the historical experience of literally all of the advanced capitalist democracies in existence. All of them without exception are now welfare states with some form and degree of social insurance, health and welfare nets, and regulatory frameworks designed to mitigate the harmful impacts and shortfalls of capitalism. Indeed, the welfare state is accepted all across the political spectrum. Controversy takes place around the edges. One might make the argument that had capitalism not been modified in this welfare direction, it is doubtful that it would have survived.

This history of the interplay between democracy and capitalism is clearly laid out in a major study involving European and American scholars, entitled *The Development of Welfare States in Western Europe and America* (Flora and Heidenheimer 1981). The book lays out the relationship between the development and spread of capitalist industry, democratization in the sense of an expanding suffrage and the emergence of trade unions and left-wing political parties, and the gradual introduction of the institutions and practices of the welfare state. The early adoption of the institutions of the welfare state in Bismarck Germany, Sweden, and Great Britain were all associated with the rise of trade unions and socialist parties in those countries. The decisions made by the upper and middle class leaders and political movements to introduce welfare measures such as accident, old age, and unemployment insurance, were strategic decisions. They were increasingly confronted by trade union movements with the capacity of bringing industrial production to a halt, and by political parties with growing parliamentary representation favoring fundamental modifications in, or the abolition of capitalism. As the calculations of the upper and middle class leaders led them to conclude that the costs of suppression exceeded the costs of concession, the various parts of the welfare state began to be put in place—accident, sickness, unemployment insurance, old age insurance,

and the like. The problem of maintaining the loyalty of the working classes through two world wars resulted in additional concessions to working class demands: the filling out of the social security system, free public education to higher levels, family allowances, housing benefits, and the like.

Social conditions, historical factors, political processes and decisions produced different versions of the welfare state. In the United States, manhood suffrage came quite early, the later bargaining process emphasized free land and free education to the secondary level, an equality of opportunity version of the welfare state. The Disraeli bargain in Britain resulted in relatively early manhood suffrage and the full attainment of parliamentary government, while the Lloyd George bargain on the eve of World War I brought the beginnings of a welfare system to Britain. The Bismarck bargain in Germany produced an early welfare state, a postponement of electoral equality and parliamentary government. While there were all of these differences in historical encounters with democratization and "welfarization," the important outcome was that little more than a century after the process began all of the advanced capitalist democracies had similar versions of the welfare state, smaller in scale in the case of the United States and Japan, more substantial in Britain and the continental European countries.

We can consequently make out a strong case for the argument that democracy has been supportive of capitalism in this strategic sense. Without this welfare adaptation it is doubtful that capitalism would have survived, or rather, its survival, "unwelfarized," would have required a substantial repressive apparatus. The choice then would seem to have been between democratic welfare capitalism, and repressive undemocratic capitalism. I am inclined to believe that capitalism as such thrives more with the democratic welfare adaptation than with the repressive one. It is in that sense that we can argue that there is a clear positive impact of democracy on capitalism.

We have to recognize, in conclusion, that democracy and capitalism are both positively and negatively related, that they both support and subvert each other. My colleague, Moses Abramovitz, described this dialectic more surely than most in his presidential address to the American Economic Association in 1980, on the eve of the "Reagan Revolution." Noting the decline in productivity in the American economy during the latter 1960s and '70s, and recognizing that this decline might in part be attributable to the "tax, transfer, and regulatory" tendencies of the welfare state, he observes,

> The rationale supporting the development of our mixed economy sees it as a pragmatic compromise between the competing virtues and defects of decentralized market capitalism and encompassing socialism. Its goal is to obtain a measure of distributive justice, security, and social guidance of economic life without losing too much of the allocative efficiency and dynamism of private enterprise and market organization. And it is a pragmatic compromise in another sense. It seeks to retain for most people that measure of personal protection from the state which private property and a private job market confer, while obtaining for the disadvantaged minority of people through the state that measure of support without which their lack of property or personal endowment would amount to a denial of individual freedom and capacity to function as full members of the community. (Abramovitz 1981)

Democratic welfare capitalism produces that reconciliation of opposing and complementary elements which makes possible the survival, even enhancement of both of these sets of institutions. It is not a static accommodation, but rather one which fluctuates over time, with capitalism being compromised by the tax-transfer-regulatory action of the state at one point, and then correcting in the direction of the reduction of the intervention of the state at another point, and with a learning process over time that may reduce the amplitude of the curves.

The case for this resolution of the capitalism-democracy quandary is made quite movingly by Jacob Viner who is quoted in the concluding paragraph of Abramovitz's paper, "… If… I nevertheless conclude that I believe that the welfare state, like old Siwash, is really worth fighting for and even dying for as compared to any rival system, it is because, despite its imperfection in theory and practice, in the aggregate it provides more promise of preserving and enlarging human freedoms, temporal prosperity, the extinction of mass misery, and the dignity of man and his moral improvement than any other social system which has previously prevailed, which prevails elsewhere today or which outside Utopia, the mind of man has been able to provide a blueprint for" (Abramovitz 1981).

## References

Abramovitz, Moses. 1981. "Welfare Quandaries and Productivity Concerns." *American Economic Review*, March.

Berger, Peter. 1986. *The Capitalist Revolution*. New York: Basic Books.

Dahl, Robert A. 1989. *Democracy and Its Critics*. New Haven: Yale University Press.

____. 1990. *After the Revolution: Authority in a Good Society*. New Haven: Yale University Press.

Deutsch, Karl. 1961. "Social Mobilization and Political Development." *American Political Science Review*, 55 (Sept.).

Flora, Peter, and Arnold Heidenheimer. 1981. *The Development of Welfare States in Western Europe and America*. New Brunswick, NJ: Transaction Press.

Friedman, Milton. 1981. *Capitalism and Freedom*. Chicago: University of Chicago Press.

Hirschman, Albert. 1986. *Rival Views of Market Society*. New York: Viking.

Inkeles, Alex, and David Smith. 1974. *Becoming Modern: Individual Change in Six Developing Countries*. Cambridge, MA: Harvard University Press.

Lerner, Daniel. 1958. *The Passing of Traditional Society*. New York: Free Press.

Lindblom, Charles E. 1977. *Politics and Markets*. New York: Basic Books.

Lipset, Seymour M. 1959. "Some Social Requisites of Democracy." *American Political Science Review*, 53 (September).

Mill, John Stuart. 1848, 1965. *Principles of Political Economy*, 2 vols. Toronto: University of Toronto Press.

Mitchell, William. 1988. "Virginia, Rochester, and Bloomington: Twenty-Five Years of Public Choice and Political Science." *Public Choice*, 56: 101–119.

Moore, Barrington. 1966. *The Social Origins of Dictatorship and Democracy*. New York: Beacon Press.

Olson, Mancur. 1982. *The Rise and Decline of Nations*. New Haven: Yale University Press.

Schumpeter, Joseph. 1946. *Capitalism, Socialism, and Democracy*. New York: Harper.

---

*Lecture presented at Seminar on the Market, sponsored by the Ford Foundation and the Research Institute on International Change of Columbia University, Moscow, October 29—November 2.

---

Gabriel A. Almond, professor of political science emeritus at Stanford University, is a former president of the American Political Science Association.

# CULTURAL EXPLANATIONS

## The man in the Baghdad café

### Which "civilisation" you belong to matters less than you might think

GOERING, it was said, growled that every time he heard the word culture he reached for his revolver. His hand would ache today. Since the end of the cold war, "culture" has been everywhere—not the opera-house or gallery kind, but the sort that claims to be the basic driving force behind human behaviour. All over the world, scholars and politicians seek to explain economics, politics and diplomacy in terms of "culture-areas" rather than, say, policies or ideas, economic interests, personalities or plain cock-ups.

Perhaps the best-known example is the notion that "Asian values" explain the success of the tiger economies of South-East Asia. Other accounts have it that international conflict is—or will be—caused by a clash of civilisations; or that different sorts of business organisation can be explained by how much people in different countries trust one [an]other. These four pages review the varying types of cultural explanation. They conclude that culture is so imprecise and changeable a phenomenon that it explains less than most people realise.

To see how complex the issue is, begin by considering the telling image with which Bernard Lewis opens his history of the Middle East. A man sits at a table in a coffee house in some Middle Eastern city, "drinking a cup of coffee or tea, perhaps smoking a cigarette, reading a newspaper, playing a board game, and listening with half an ear to whatever is coming out of the radio or the television installed in the corner." Undoubtedly Arab, almost certainly

Muslim, the man would clearly identify himself as a member of these cultural groups. He would also, if asked, be likely to say that "western culture" was alien, even hostile to them.

Look closer, though, and the cultural contrasts blur. This coffee-house man probably wears western-style clothes—sneakers, jeans, a T-shirt. The chair and table at which he sits, the coffee he drinks, the tobacco he smokes, the newspaper he reads, all are western imports. The radio and television are western inventions. If our relaxing friend is a member of his nation's army, he probably operates western or Soviet weapons and trains according to western standards; if he belongs to the government, both his bureaucratic surroundings and the constitutional trappings of his regime may owe their origins to western influence.

The upshot, for Mr Lewis, is clear enough. "In modern times," he writes, "the dominating factor in the consciousness of most Middle Easterners has been the impact of Europe, later of the West more generally, and the transformation—some would say dislocation—which it has brought." Mr Lewis has put his finger on the most important and least studied aspect of cultural identity: how it changes. It would be wise to keep that in mind during the upsurge of debate about culture that is likely to follow the publication of Samuel Huntington's new book, "The Clash of Civilisations and the Remaking of World Order".

### The clash of civilisations

A professor of international politics at Harvard and the chairman of Harvard's Institute for Strategic Planning, Mr Huntington published in 1993, in *Foreign Affairs*, an essay which that quarterly's editors said generated more discussion than any since George Kennan's article (under the by-line "x") which argued in July 1947 for the need to contain the Soviet threat. Henry Kissinger, a former secretary of state, called Mr Huntington's book-length version of the article "one of the most important books... since the end of the cold war."

The article, "The Clash of Civilisation?", belied the question-mark in its title by predicting wars of culture. "It is my hypothesis", Mr Huntington wrote, "that the fundamental source of conflict in this new world will not be primarily ideological or primarily economic. The great division among humankind and the dominating source of conflict will be cultural."

After the cold war, ideology seemed less important as an organising principle of foreign policy. Culture seemed a plausible candidate to fill the gap. So future wars, Mr Huntington claimed, would occur "between nations and groups of different civilisations"—western, Confucian, Japanese, Islamic, Hindu, Orthodox and Latin American, perhaps African and Buddhist. Their disputes would "dominate global politics" and the battle-lines of the future would follow the fault-lines between these cultures.

No mincing words there, and equally few in his new book:

> Culture and cultural identities… are shaping the patterns of cohesion, disintegration and conflict in the post-cold war world… Global politics is being reconfigured along cultural lines.

Mr Huntington is only one of an increasing number of writers placing stress on the importance of cultural values and institutions in the confusion left in the wake of the cold war. He looked at the influence of culture on international conflict. Three other schools of thought find cultural influences at work in different ways.

• **Culture and the economy**. Perhaps the oldest school holds that cultural values and norms equip people—and, by extension, countries—either poorly or well for economic success. The archetypal modern pronouncement of this view was Max Weber's investigation of the Protestant work ethic. This, he claimed, was the reason why the Protestant parts of Germany and Switzerland were more successful economically than the Catholic areas. In the recent upsurge of interest in issues cultural, a handful of writers have returned to the theme.

It is "values and attitudes—culture", claims Lawrence Harrison, that are "mainly responsible for such phenomena as Latin America's persistent instability and inequity, Taiwan's and Korea's economic 'miracles', and the achievements of the Japanese." Thomas Sowell offers other examples in "Race and Culture: A World View". "A disdain for commerce and industry", he argues, "has… been common for centuries among the Hispanic elite, both in Spain and in Latin America." Academics, though, have played a relatively small part in this debate: the best-known exponent of the thesis that "Asian values"—a kind of Confucian work ethic—aid economic development has been Singapore's former prime minister, Lee Kuan Yew.

• **Culture as social blueprint**. A second group of analysts has looked at the connections between cultural factors and political systems. Robert Putnam, another Harvard professor, traced Italy's social and political institutions to its "civic culture", or lack thereof. He claimed that, even today, the parts of Italy where democratic institutions are most fully developed are similar to the areas which first began to generate these institutions in the 14th century. His conclusion is that democracy is not something

that can be put on like a coat; it is part of a country's social fabric and takes decades, even centuries, to develop.

Francis Fukuyama, of George Mason University, takes a slightly different approach. In a recent book which is not about the end of history, he focuses on one particular social trait, "trust". "A nation's well-being, as well as its ability to compete, is conditioned by a single, pervasive cultural characteristic: the level of trust inherent in the society," he says. Mr Fukuyama argues that "low-trust" societies such as China, France and Italy—where close relations between people do not extend much beyond the family—are poor at generating large, complex social institutions like multinational corporations; so they are at a competitive disadvantage compared with "high-trust" nations such as Germany, Japan and the United States.

• **Culture and decision-making**. The final group of scholars has looked at the way in which cultural assumptions act like blinkers. Politicians from different countries see the same issue in different ways because of their differing cultural backgrounds. Their electorates or nations do, too. As a result, they claim, culture acts as an international barrier. As Ole Elgstrom puts it: "When a Japanese prime minister says that he will 'do his best' to implement a certain policy," Americans applaud a victory but "what the prime minister really meant was 'no'." There are dozens of examples of misperception in international relations, ranging from Japanese-American trade disputes to the misreading of Saddam Hussein's intentions in the weeks before he attacked Kuwait.

## What are they talking about?

All of this is intriguing, and much of it is provocative. It has certainly provoked a host of arguments. For example, is Mr Huntington right to lump together all European countries into one culture, though they speak different languages, while separating Spain and Mexico, which speak the same one? Is the Catholic Philippines western or Asian? Or: if it is true (as Mr Fukuyama claims) that the ability to produce multinational firms is vital to economic success, why has "low-trust" China, which has few such companies, grown so fast? And why has yet-more successful "low-trust" South Korea been able to create big firms?

This is nit-picking, of course. But such questions of detail matter because behind

them lurks the first of two fundamental doubts that plague all these cultural explanations: how do you define what a culture is?

In their attempts to define what cultures are (and hence what they are talking about), most "culture" writers rely partly on self definition: cultures are what people think of themselves as part of. In Mr Huntington's words, civilisation "is the broadest level of identification with which [a person] intensely identifies."

The trouble is that relatively few people identify "intensely" with broad cultural groups. They tend to identify with something narrower: nations or ethnic groups. Europe is a case in point. A poll done last year for the European Commission found that half the people of Britain, Portugal and Greece thought of themselves in purely national terms; so did a third of the Germans, Spaniards and Dutch. And this was in a part of the world where there is an institution—the EU itself—explicitly devoted to the encouragement of "Europeanness".

The same poll found that in every EU country, 70% or more thought of themselves either purely in national terms, or primarily as part of a nation and only secondly as Europeans. Clearly, national loyalty can coexist with wider cultural identification. But, even then, the narrower loyalty can blunt the wider one because national characteristics often are—or at least are often thought to be—peculiar or unique. Seymour Martin Lipset, a sociologist who recently published a book about national characteristics in the United States, called it "American Exceptionalism". David Willetts, a British Conservative member of Parliament, recently claimed that the policies espoused by the opposition Labour Party would go against the grain of "English exceptionalism". And these are the two components of western culture supposedly most like one another.

In Islamic countries, the balance between cultural and national identification may be tilted towards the culture. But even here the sense of, say, Egyptian or Iraqi or Palestinian nationhood remains strong. (Consider the competing national feelings unleashed during the Iran-Iraq war.) In other cultures, national loyalty seems pre-eminent: in Mr Huntington's classification, Thailand, Tibet and Mongolia all count as "Buddhist". It is hard to imagine that a Thai, a Tibetan and a Mongolian really have that much in common.

So the test of subjective identification is hard to apply. That apart, the writers define

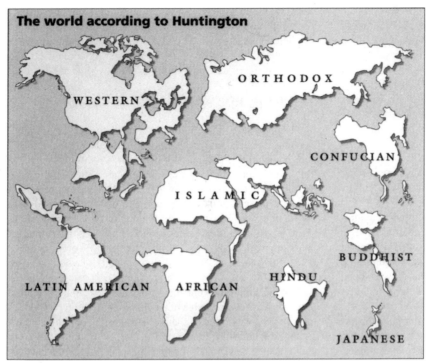

**The world according to Huntington**

WESTERN

ORTHODOX

CONFUCIAN

ISLAMIC

BUDDHIST

LATIN AMERICAN  AFRICAN  HINDU

JAPANESE

Source: Adapted by The Economist from "The Clash of Civilisations and the Remaking of World Order" by Samuel Huntington

a culture in the usual terms: language, religion, history, customs and institutions and so on. Such multiple definitions ring true. As Bernard Lewis's man in the Levantine café suggests, cultures are not singular things: they are bundles of characteristics.

The trouble is that such characteristics are highly ambiguous. Some push one way, some another.

## Culture as muddle

Islamic values, for instance, are routinely assumed to be the antithesis of modernising western ones. In Islam, tradition is good; departure from tradition is presumed to be bad until proven otherwise. Yet, at the same time, Islam is also a monotheistic religion which encourages rationalism and science. Some historians have plausibly argued that it was the Islamic universities of medieval Spain that kept science and rationalism alive during Europe's Dark Ages, and that Islam was a vital medieval link between the ancient world of Greece and Rome and the Renaissance. The scientific-rationalist aspect of Islam could well come to the fore again.

If you doubt it, consider the case of China and the "Confucian tradition" (a sort of proxy for Asian values). China has been

at various times the world's most prosperous country and also one of its poorest. It has had periods of great scientific innovation and times of technological backwardness and isolation. Accounts of the Confucian tradition have tracked this path. Nowadays, what seems important about the tradition is its encouragement of hard work, savings and investment for the future, plus its emphasis on co-operation towards a single end. All these features have been adduced to explain why the tradition has helped Asian growth.

To Max Weber, however, the same tradition seemed entirely different. He argued that the Confucian insistence on obedience to parental authority discouraged competition and innovation and hence inhibited economic success. And China is not the only country to have been systematically misdiagnosed in this way. In countries as varied as Japan, India, Ghana and South Korea, notions of cultural determination of economic performance have been proved routinely wrong (in 1945, India and Ghana were expected to do best of the four—partly because of their supposed cultural inheritance).

If you take an extreme position, you could argue from this that cultures are so complicated that they can never be used to explain behaviour accurately. Even if you

do not go that far, the lesson must be that the same culture embraces such conflicting features that it can produce wholly different effects at different times.

That is hard enough for the schools of culture to get to grips with. But there is worse to come. For cultures never operate in isolation. When affecting how people behave, they are always part of a wider mix. That mix includes government policies, personal leadership, technological or economic change and so on. For any one effect, there are always multiple causes. Which raises the second fundamental doubt about cultural explanations: how do you know whether it is culture—and not something else—that has caused some effect? You cannot. The problem of causation seems insoluble. The best you can do is work out whether, within the mix, culture is becoming more or less important.

## Culture as passenger

Of the many alternative explanations for events, three stand out: the influence of ideas, of government and what might be called the "knowledge era" (shorthand for globalisation, the growth of service-based industries and so forth). Of these, the influence of ideas as a giant organising principle is clearly not what it was when the cold war divided the world between communists and capitalists. We are all capitalists now. To that extent, it is fair to say that the ideological part of the mix has become somewhat less important—though not, as a few people have suggested, insignificant.

As for the government, it is a central thesis of the cultural writers that its influence is falling while that of culture is rising: cultures are in some ways replacing states. To quote Mr Huntington again "peoples and countries with similar cultures are coming together. Peoples and countries with different cultures are coming apart."

In several respects, that is counter-intuitive. Governments still control what is usually the single most powerful force in any country, the army. And, in all but the poorest places, governments tax and spend a large chunk of GDP—indeed, a larger chunk, in most places, than 50 years ago.

Hardly surprising, then, that governments influence cultures as much as the other way around. To take a couple of examples. Why does South Korea (a low-trust culture, remember) have so many internationally competitive large firms? The answer is that the government decided that it should. Or another case: since 1945 German politicians of every stripe have been insisting that they want to "save Germany from itself"—an attempt to assert political control over cultural identity.

South Korea and Germany are examples of governments acting positively to create something new. But governments can act upon cultures negatively: ie, they can destroy a culture when they collapse. Robert Kaplan, of an American magazine *Atlantic Monthly*, begins his book, "The Ends of the Earth", in Sierra Leone: "I had assumed that the random crime and social chaos of West Africa were the result of an already-fragile cultural base." Yet by the time he reaches Cambodia at the end of what he calls "a journey at the dawn of the 21st century" he is forced to reconsider that assumption:

> Here I was… in a land where the written script was one thousand two hundred years old, and every surrounding country was in some stage of impressive economic growth. Yet Cambodia was eerily similar to Sierra Leone: with random crime, mosquito-borne disease, a government army that was more like a mob and a countryside that was ungovernable.

His conclusion is that "The effect of culture was more a mystery to me near the end of my planetary journey than at its beginning." He might have gone further: the collapse of governments causes cultural turbulence just as much as cultural turbulence causes the collapse of governments.

## Culture as processed data

Then there is the "knowledge era". Here is a powerful and growing phenomenon. The culture writers do not claim anything different. Like the Industrial Revolution before it, the knowledge era—in which the creation, storage and use of knowledge becomes the basic economic activity—is generating huge change. Emphasising as it does rapid, even chaotic, transformation, it is anti-traditional and anti-authoritarian.

Yet the cultural exponents still claim that, even in the knowledge era, culture remains a primary engine of change. They do so for two quite different reasons. Some claim that the new era has the makings of a world culture. There is a universal language, English. There are the beginnings of an international professional class that cuts across cultural and national boundaries: increasingly, bankers, computer programmers, executives, even military officers are said to have as much in common with their opposite numbers in other countries as with their next-door neighbors. As Mr Fukuyama wrote in his more famous book: the "unfolding of modern natural science… guarantees an increasing homogenisation of all human societies." Others doubt that technology and the rest of it are producing a genuinely new world order. To them, all this is just modern western culture.

Either way, the notion that modernity is set on a collision course with culture lies near the heart of several of the culture writers' books. Summing them up is the title of Benjamin Barber's "Jihad versus McWorld". In other words, he argues that the main conflicts now and in future will be between tribal, local "cultural" values (Jihad) and a McWorld of technology and democracy.

It would be pointless to deny that globalisation is causing large changes in every society. It is also clear that such influences act on different cultures differently, enforcing a kind of natural selection between those cultures which rise to the challenge and those which do not.

But it is more doubtful that these powerful forces are primarily cultural or even western. Of course, they have a cultural component: the artefacts of American culture are usually the first things to come along in the wake of a new road, or new television networks. But the disruptive force itself is primarily economic and has been adopted as enthusiastically in Japan, Singapore and China as in America. The world market is not a cultural concept.

Moreover, to suggest that trade, globalisation and the rest of it tend to cause conflict, and then leave the argument there, is not enough. When you boil the argument down, much of its seems to be saying that the more countries trade with each other, the more likely they are to go to war. That seems implausible. Trade—indeed, any sort of link—is just as likely to reduce the potential for violent conflict as to increase it. The same goes for the spread of democracy, another feature which is supposed to encourage civilisations to clash with each other. This might well cause ructions within countries. It might well provoke complaints from dictators about "outside interference". But serious international conflict is a different matter. And if democracy really did spread round the world, it might tend to reduce violence; wealthy democracies, at any rate, are usually reluctant to go to war (though poor or angrily nationalist ones may, as history has shown, be much less reluctant).

In short, the "knowledge era" is spreading economic ideas. And these ideas have three cultural effects, not one. They make cultures rub against each other, causing international friction. They also tie different cultures closer together, which offsets the first effect. And they may well increase tensions within a culture-area as some groups accommodate themselves to the new world while others turn their back on it. And all this can be true at the same time because cultures are so varied and ambiguous that they are capable of virtually any transformation.

The conclusion must be that while culture will continue to exercise an important influence on both countries and individuals, it has not suddenly become more important than, say, governments or impersonal economic forces. Nor does it play the all-embracing defining role that ideology played during the cold war. Much of its influence is secondary, ie, it comes about partly as a reaction to the "knowledge era". And within the overall mix of what influences people's behaviour, culture's role may well be declining, rather than rising, squeezed between the greedy expansion of the government on one side, and globalisation on the other.

**The books mentioned in this article are:**

Benjamin Barber. Jihad versus McWorld (Random House; 1995; 400 pages; $12.95).

Francis Fukuyama. The End of History and the Last Man (Free Press; 1992; 419 pages; $24.95. Hamish Hamilton; £20.) and Trust: The Social Virtues and the Creation of Prosperity (Free Press; 1995; 480 pages; $25. Hamish Hamilton; £25).

Lawrence E. Harrison. Who Prospers? How Cultural Values Shape Economic and Political Success (Basic Books; 1992; 288 pages; $14).

Samuel Huntington. The Clash of Civilisations? *Foreign Affairs* Vol. 72 (Summer 1993) and The Clash of Civilisations and the Remaking of World Order (Simon & Schuster; 1996; 367 pages; $26).

Robert Kaplan. The Ends of the Earth (Random House; 1996; 475 pages; $27.50. Papermac; £10).

Bernard Lewis. The Middle East (Wiedenfeld & Nicolson; 1995; 433 pages; £20. Simon & Schuster; $29.50).

Seymour Martin Lipset. American Exceptionalism (Norton; 1996; 352 pages; $27.50 and £19.95).

Robert Putnam. Making Democracy Work: Civic Traditions in Modern Italy (Princeton; 1993; 288 pages; $24.95 and £18.95).

Thomas Sowell. Race and Culture: A World View (Basic Books; 1994; 331 pages; $14).

# Jihad vs. McWorld

*The two axial principles of our age—tribalism and globalism—clash at every point except one: they may both be threatening to democracy*

## Benjamin R. Barber

Just beyond the horizon of current events lie two possible political figures—both bleak, neither democratic. The first is a retribalization of large swaths of humankind by war and bloodshed: a threatened Lebanonization of national states in which culture is pitted against culture, people against people, tribe against tribe—a Jihad in the name of a hundred narrowly conceived faiths against every kind of interdependence, every kind of artificial social cooperation and civic mutuality. The second is being borne in on us by the onrush of economic and ecological forces that demand integration and uniformity and that mesmerize the world with fast music, fast computers, and fast food—with MTV, Macintosh, and McDonald's, pressing nations into one commercially homogenous global network: one McWorld tied together by technology, ecology, communications, and commerce. The planet is falling precipitantly apart and coming reluctantly together at the very same moment.

These two tendencies are sometimes visible in the same countries at the same instant: thus Yugoslavia, clamoring just recently to join the New Europe, is exploding into fragments; India is trying to live up to its reputation as the world's largest integral democracy while powerful new fundamentalist parties like the Hindu nationalist Bharatiya Janta Party, along with nationalist assassins, are imperiling its hard-won unity. States are breaking up or joining up: the Soviet Union has disap-

peared almost overnight, its parts forming new unions with one another or with like-minded nationalities in neighboring states. The old interwar national state based on territory and political sovereignty looks to be a mere transitional development.

The tendencies of what I am here calling the forces of Jihad and the forces of McWorld operate with equal strength in opposite directions, the one driven by parochial hatreds, the other by universalizing markets, the one re-creating ancient subnational and ethnic borders from within, the other making national borders porous from without. They have one thing in common: neither offers much hope to citizens looking for practical ways to govern themselves democratically. If the global future is to pit Jihad's centrifugal whirlwind against McWorld's centripetal black hole, the outcome is unlikely to be democratic—or so I will argue.

### McWORLD, OR THE GLOBALIZATION OF POLITICS

Four imperatives make up the dynamic of McWorld: a market imperative, a resource imperative, an information-technology imperative, and an ecological imperative. By shrinking the world and diminishing the salience of national borders, these imperatives have in combination achieved a considerable victory over factiousness and

particularism, and not least of all over their most virulent traditional form—nationalism. It is the realists who are now Europeans, the utopians who dream nostalgically of a resurgent England or Germany, perhaps even a resurgent Wales or Saxony. Yesterday's wishful cry for one world has yielded to the reality of McWorld.

*The market imperative.* Marxist and Leninist theories of imperialism assumed that the quest for ever-expanding markets would in time compel nation-based capitalist economies to push against national boundaries in search of an international economic imperium. Whatever else has happened to the scientist predictions of Marxism, in this domain they have proved farsighted. All national economies are now vulnerable to the inroads of larger, transnational markets within which trade is free, currencies are convertible, access to banking is open, and contracts are enforceable under law. In Europe, Asia, Africa, the South Pacific, and the Americas such markets are eroding national sovereignty and giving rise to entities—international banks, trade associations, transnational lobbies like OPEC and Greenpeace, world news services like CNN and the BBC, and multinational corporations that increasingly lack a meaningful national identity—that neither reflect nor respect nationhood as an organizing or regulative principle.

The market imperative has also reinforced the quest for international peace and stability, requisites of an efficient international economy. Markets are enemies of parochialism, isolation, fractiousness, war. Market psychology attenuates the psychology of ideological and religious cleavages and assumes a concord among producers and consumers—categories that ill fit narrowly conceived national or religious cultures. Shopping has little tolerance for blue laws, whether dictated by pub-closing British paternalism, Sabbath-observing Jewish Orthodox fundamentalism, or no-Sunday-liquor-sales Massachusetts puritanism. In the context of common markets, international law ceases to be a vision of justice and becomes a workaday framework for getting things done—enforcing contracts, ensuring that governments abide by deals, regulating trade and currency relations, and so forth.

Common markets demand a common language, as well as a common currency, and they produce common behaviors of the kind bred by cosmopolitan city life everywhere. Commercial pilots, computer programmers, international bankers, media specialists, oil riggers, entertainment celebrities, ecology experts, demographers, accountants, professors, athletes—these compose a new breed of men and women for whom religion, culture, and nationality can seem only marginal elements in a working identity. Although sociologists of everyday life will no doubt continue to distinguish a Japanese from an American mode, shopping has a common signature throughout the world. Cynics might even say that some of the recent revolutions in Eastern Europe have had as their true goal not liberty and the right to vote but well-paying jobs and the right to shop (although the vote is proving easier to acquire than consumer goods). The market imperative is, then, plenty powerful; but, notwithstanding some of the claims made for "democratic capitalism," it is not identical with the democratic imperative.

*The resource imperative.* Democrats once dreamed of societies whose political autonomy rested firmly on economic independence. The Athenians idealized what they called autarky, and tried for a while to create a way of life simple and austere enough to make the polis genuinely self-sufficient. To be free meant to be independent of any other community or polis. Not even the Athenians were able to achieve autarky, however: human nature, it turns out, is dependency. By the time of Pericles, Athenian politics was inextricably bound up with a flowering empire held together by naval power and commerce—an empire that, even as it appeared to enhance Athenian might, ate away at Athenian independence and autarky. Master and slave, it turned out, were bound together by mutual insufficiency.

The dream of autarky briefly engrossed nineteenth-century America as well, for the underpopulated, endlessly bountiful land, the cornucopia of natural resources, and the natural barriers of a continent walled in by two great seas led many to believe that America could be a world unto itself. Given this past, it has been harder for Americans than for most to accept the inevitability of interdependence. But the rapid depletion of resources even in a country like ours, where they once seemed inexhaustible, and the maldistribution of arable soil and mineral resources on the planet, leave even the wealthiest societies ever more resource-dependent and many other nations in permanently desperate straits.

Every nation, it turns out, needs something another nation has; some nations have almost nothing they need.

*The information-technology imperative.* Enlightenment science and the technologies derived from it are inherently universalizing. They entail a quest for descriptive principles of general application, a search for universal solutions to particular problems, and an unswerving embrace of objectivity and impartiality.

Scientific progress embodies and depends on open communication, a common discourse rooted in rationality, collaboration, and an easy and regular flow and exchange of information. Such ideals can be hypocritical covers for power-mongering by elites, and they may be shown to be wanting in many other ways, but they are entailed by the very idea of science and they make science and globalization practical allies.

Business, banking, and commerce all depend on information flow and are facilitated by new communication technologies. The hardware of these technologies tends to be systemic and integrated—computer, television, cable, satellite, laser, fiber-optic, and microchip technologies combining to create a vast interactive communications and information network that can potentially give every person on earth access to every other person, and make every datum, every byte, available to every set of eyes. If the automobile was, as George Ball once said (when he gave his blessing to a Fiat factory in the Soviet Union during the Cold War), "an ideology on four wheels," then electronic telecommunication and information systems are an ideology at 186,000 miles per second—which makes for a very small planet in a very big hurry. Individual cultures speak particular languages; commerce and science increasingly speak English; the whole world speaks logarithms and binary mathematics.

Moreover, the pursuit of science and technology asks for, even compels, open societies. Satellite footprints do not respect national borders; telephone wires penetrate the most closed societies. With photocopying and then fax machines having infiltrated Soviet universities and *samizdat* literary circles in the eighties, and computer modems having multiplied like rabbits in communism's bureaucratic warrens thereafter, *glasnost* could not be far behind. In their social requisites, secrecy and science are enemies.

The new technology's software is perhaps even more globalizing than its hardware. The information arm of international commerce's sprawling body reaches out and touches distinct nations and parochial cultures, and gives them a common face chiseled in Hollywood, on Madison Avenue, and in Silicon Valley. Throughout the 1980s one of the most-watched television programs in South Africa was *The Cosby Show*. The demise of apartheid was already in production. Exhibitors at the 1991 Cannes film festival expressed growing anxiety over the "homogenization" and "Americanization" of the global film industry when, for the third year running, American films dominated the awards ceremonies. America has dominated the world's popular culture for much longer, and much more decisively. In November of 1991 Switzerland's once insular culture boasted best-seller lists featuring *Terminator 2* as the No. 1 movie, *Scarlett* as the No. 1 book, and Prince's *Diamonds and Pearls* as the No. 1 record album. No wonder the Japanese are buying Hollywood film studios even faster than Americans are buying Japanese television sets. This kind of software supremacy may in the long term be far more important than hardware superiority, because culture has become more potent than armaments. What is the power of the Pentagon compared with Disneyland? Can the Sixth Fleet keep up with CNN? McDonald's in Moscow and Coke in China will do more to create a global culture than military colonization ever could. It is less the goods than the brand names that do the work, for they convey life-style images that alter perception and challenge behavior. They make up the seductive software of McWorld's common (at times much too common) soul.

Yet in all this high-tech commercial world there is nothing that looks particularly democratic. It lends itself to surveillance as well as liberty, to new forms of manipulation and covert control as well as new kinds of participation, to skewed, unjust market outcomes as well as greater productivity. The consumer society and the open society are not quite synonymous. Capitalism and democracy have a relationship, but it is something less than a marriage. An efficient free market after all requires that consumers be free to vote their dollars on competing goods, not that citizens be free to vote their values and beliefs on competing political candidates and programs. The free market flourished in junta-run Chile, in military-governed Taiwan and Korea, and, earlier, in a variety of autocratic European empires as well as their colonial possessions.

*The ecological imperative.* The impact of globalization on ecology is a cliché even to world leaders who ignore it. We know well enough that the German forests can be destroyed by Swiss and Italians driving gas-guzzlers fueled by leaded gas. We also know that the planet can be asphyxiated by greenhouse gases because Brazilian farmers want to be part of the twentieth century and are burning down tropical rain forests to clear a little land to plough, and because Indonesians make a living out of converting their lush jungle into toothpicks for fastidious Japanese diners, upsetting the delicate oxygen balance and in effect puncturing our global lungs. Yet this ecological consciousness has meant not only greater awareness but also greater inequality, as modernized nations try to slam the door behind them, saying to developing nations, "The world cannot afford your modernization; ours has wrung it dry!"

Each of the four imperatives just cited is transnational, transideological, and transcultural. Each applies impartially to Catholics, Jews, Muslims, Hindus, and Buddhists; to democrats and totalitarians; to capitalists and socialists. The Enlightenment dream of a universal rational society has to a remarkable degree been realized—but in a form that is commercialized, homogenized, depoliticized, bureaucratized, and, of course, radically incomplete, for the movement toward McWorld is in competition with forces of global breakdown, national dissolution, and centrifugal corruption. These forces, working in the opposite direction, are the essence of what I call Jihad.

# JIHAD, OR THE LEBANONIZATION OF THE WORLD

OPEC, the World Bank, the United Nations, the International Red Cross, the multinational corporation… there are scores of institutions that reflect globalization. But they often appear as ineffective reactors to the world's real actors: national states and, to an ever greater degree, subnational factions in permanent rebellion against uniformity and integration—even the kind represented by universal law and justice. The headlines feature these players regularly: they are cultures, not countries; parts, not wholes; sects, not religions; rebellious factions and dissenting minorities at war not just with globalism but with the traditional nation-state. Kurds, Basques, Puerto Ricans, Ossetians, East Timoreans, Quebecois, the Catholics of Northern Ireland, Abkhasians, Kurile Islander Japanese, the Zulus of Inkatha, Catalonians, Tamils, and, of course, Palestinians—people without countries, inhabiting nations not their own, seeking smaller worlds within borders that will seal them off from modernity.

A powerful irony is at work here. Nationalism was once a force of integration and unification, a movement aimed at bringing together disparate clans, tribes, and cultural fragments under new, assimilationist flags. But as Ortega y Gasset noted more than sixty years ago, having won its victories, nationalism changed its strategy. In the 1920s, and again today, it is more often a reactionary and divisive force, pulverizing the very nations it once helped cement together. The force that creates nations is "inclusive," Ortega wrote in *The Revolt of the Masses*. "In periods of consolidation, nationalism has a positive value, and is a lofty standard. But in Europe everything is more than consolidated, and nationalism is nothing but a mania.…"

This mania has left the post-Cold War world smothering with hot wars; the international scene is little more unified than it was at the end of the Great War, in Ortega's own time. There were more than thirty wars in progress last year, most of them ethnic, racial, tribal, or religious in character, and the list of unsafe regions doesn't seem to be getting any shorter. Some new world order!

The aim of many of these small-scale wars is to redraw boundaries, to implode states and resecure parochial identities: to escape McWorld's dully insistent impera-

tives. The mood is that of Jihad: war not as an instrument of policy but as an emblem of identity, an expression of community, an end in itself. Even where there is no shooting war, there is fractiousness, secession, and the quest for ever smaller communities. Add to the list of dangerous countries those at risk: In Switzerland and Spain, Jurassian and Basque separatists still argue the virtues of ancient identities, sometimes in the language of bombs. Hyperdisintegration in the former Soviet Union may well continue unabated—not just a Ukraine independent from the Soviet Union but a Bessarabian Ukraine independent from the Ukrainian republic; not just Russia severed from the defunct union but Tatarstan severed from Russia. Yugoslavia makes even the disunited, ex-Soviet, nonsocialist republics that were once the Soviet Union look integrated, its sectarian fatherlands springing up within factional motherlands like weeds within weeds within weeds. Kurdish independence would threaten the territorial integrity of four Middle Eastern nations. Well before the current cataclysm Soviet Georgia made a claim for autonomy from the Soviet Union, only to be faced with its Ossetians (164,000 in a republic of 5.5 million) demanding their own self-determination within Georgia. The Abkhasian minority in Georgia has followed suit. Even the good will established by Canada's once promising Meech Lake protocols is in danger, with Francophone Quebec again threatening the dissolution of the federation. In South Africa the emergence from apartheid was hardly achieved when friction between Inkatha's Zulus and the African National Congress's tribally identified members threatened to replace Europeans' racism with an indigenous tribal war. After thirty years of attempted integration using the colonial language (English) as a unifier, Nigeria is now playing with the idea of linguistic multiculturalism—which could mean the cultural breakup of the nation into hundreds of tribal fragments. Even Saddam Hussein has benefited from the threat of internal Jihad, having used renewed tribal and religious warfare to turn last season's mortal enemies into reluctant allies of an Iraqi nationhood that he nearly destroyed.

The passing of communism has torn away the thin veneer of internationalism (workers of the world unite!) to reveal ethnic prejudices that are not only ugly and deep-seated but increasingly murderous. Europe's old scourge, anti-Semitism, is back with a vengeance, but it is only one of many antagonisms. It appears all too easy to throw the historical gears into reverse and pass from a Communist dictatorship back into a tribal state.

Among the tribes, religion is also a battlefield. ("Jihad" is a rich world whose generic meaning is "struggle"—usually the struggle of the soul to avert evil. Strictly applied to religious war, it is used only in reference to battles where the faith is under assault, or battles against a government that denies the practice of Islam. My use here is rhetorical, but does follow both journalistic practice and history.) Remember the Thirty Years War? Whatever forms of Enlightenment universalism might once have come to grace such historically related forms of monotheism as Judaism, Christianity, and Islam, in many of their modern incarnations they are parochial rather than cosmopolitan, angry rather than loving, proselytizing rather than ecumenical, zealous rather than rationalist, sectarian rather than deistic, ethnocentric rather than universalizing. As a result, like the new forms of hypernationalism, the new expressions of religious fundamentalism are fractious and pulverizing, never integrating. This is religion as the Crusaders knew it: a battle to the death for souls that if not saved will be forever lost.

The atmospherics of Jihad have resulted in a breakdown of civility in the name of identity, of comity in the name of community. International relations have sometimes taken on the aspect of gang war—cultural turf battles featuring tribal factions that were supposed to be sublimated as integral parts of large national, economic, postcolonial, and constitutional entities.

## THE DARKENING FUTURE OF DEMOCRACY

These rather melodramatic tableaux vivants do not tell the whole story, however. For all their defects, Jihad and McWorld have their attractions. Yet, to repeat and insist, the attractions are unrelated to democracy. Neither McWorld nor Jihad is remotely democratic in impulse. Neither needs democracy; neither promotes democracy.

McWorld does manage to look pretty seductive in a world obsessed with Jihad. It delivers peace, prosperity, and relative unity—if at the cost of independence, community, and identity (which is generally based on difference). The primary political values required by the global market are

order and tranquility, and freedom—as in the phrases "free trade," "free press," and "free love." Human rights are needed to a degree, but not citizenship or participation—and no more social justice and equality than are necessary to promote efficient economic production and consumption. Multinational corporations sometimes seem to prefer doing business with local oligarchs, inasmuch as they can take confidence from dealing with the boss on all crucial matters. Despots who slaughter their own populations are no problem, so long as they leave markets in place and refrain from making war on their neighbors (Saddam Hussein's fatal mistake). In trading partners, predictability is of more value than justice.

The Eastern European revolutions that seemed to arise out of concern for global democratic values quickly deteriorated into a stampede in the general direction of free markets and their ubiquitous, television-promoted shopping malls. East Germany's Neues Forum, that courageous gathering of intellectuals, students, and workers which overturned the Stalinist regime in Berlin in 1989, lasted only six months in Germany's mini-version of McWorld. Then it gave way to money and markets and monopolies from the West. By the time of the first all-German elections, it could scarcely manage to secure three percent of the vote. Elsewhere there is growing evidence that *glasnost* will go and *perestroika*—defined as privatization and an opening of markets to Western bidders—will stay. So understandably anxious are the new rulers of Eastern Europe and whatever entities are forged from the residues of the Soviet Union to gain access to credit and markets and technology—McWorld's flourishing new currencies—that they have shown themselves willing to trade away democratic prospects in pursuit of them: not just old totalitarian ideologies and command-economy production models but some possible indigenous experiments with a third way between capitalism and socialism, such as economic cooperatives and employee stock-ownership plans, both of which have their ardent supporters in the East.

Jihad delivers a different set of virtues: a vibrant local identity, a sense of community, solidarity among kinsmen, neighbors, and countrymen, narrowly conceived. But it also guarantees parochialism and is grounded in exclusion. Solidarity is secured through war against outsiders. And solidarity often means obedience to a hierarchy in governance, fanaticism in beliefs,

and the obliteration of individual selves in the name of the group. Deference to leaders and intolerance toward outsiders (and toward "enemies within") are hallmarks of tribalism—hardly the attitudes required for the cultivation of new democratic women and men capable of governing themselves. Where new democratic experiments have been conducted in retribalizing societies, in both Europe and the Third World, the result has often been anarchy, repression, persecution, and the coming of new, non-communist forms of very old kinds of despotism. During the past year, Havel's velvet revolution in Czechoslovakia was imperiled by partisans of "Czechland" and of Slovakia as independent entities. India seemed little less rent by Sikh, Hindu, Muslim, and Tamil infighting than it was immediately after the British pulled out, more than forty years ago.

To the extent that either McWorld or Jihad has a *natural* politics, it has turned out to be more of an antipolitics. For McWorld, it is the antipolitics of globalism: bureaucratic, technocratic, and meritocratic, focused (as Marx predicted it would be) on the administration of things—with people, however, among the chief things to be administered. In its politico-economic imperatives McWorld has been guided by laissez-faire market principles that privilege efficiency, productivity, and beneficence at the expense of civic liberty and self-government.

For Jihad, the antipolitics of tribalization has been explicitly antidemocratic: one-party dictatorship, government by military junta, theocratic fundamentalism—often associated with a version of the *Führerprinzip* that empowers an individual to rule on behalf of a people. Even the government of India, struggling for decades to model democracy for a people who will soon number a billion, longs for great leaders; and for every Mahatma Gandhi, Indira Gandhi, or Rajiv Gandhi taken from them by zealous assassins, the Indians appear to seek a replacement who will deliver them from the lengthy travail of their freedom.

## THE CONFEDERAL OPTION

How can democracy be secured and spread in a world whose primary tendencies are at best indifferent to it (McWorld) and at worst deeply antithetical to it (Jihad)? My guess is that globalization will eventually vanquish retribalization. The ethos of material "civilization" has not yet encountered an obstacle it has been unable to thrust aside. Ortega may have grasped in the 1920s a clue to our own future in the coming millennium.

Everyone sees the need of a new principle of life. But as always happens in similar crises—some people attempt to save the situation by an artificial intensification of the very principle which has led to decay. This is the meaning of the "nationalist" outburst of recent years… things have always gone that way. The last flare, the longest; the last sigh, the deepest. On the very eve of their disappearance there is an intensification of frontiers—military and economic.

Jihad may be a last deep sigh before the eternal yawn of McWorld. On the other hand, Ortega was not exactly prescient; his prophecy of peace and internationalism came just before blitzkrieg, world war, and the Holocaust tore the old order to bits. Yet democracy is how we remonstrate with reality, the rebuke our aspirations offer to history. And if retribalization is inhospitable to democracy, there is nonetheless a form of democratic government that can accommodate parochialism and communitarianism, one that can even save them from their defects and make them more tolerant and participatory: decentralized participatory democracy. And if McWorld is indifferent to democracy, there is nonetheless a form of democratic government that suits global markets passably well—representative government in its federal or, better still, confederal variation.

With its concern for accountability, the protection of minorities, and the universal rule of law, a confederalized representative system would serve the political needs of McWorld as well as oligarchic bureaucratism or meritocratic elitism is currently doing. As we are already beginning to see, many nations may survive in the long term only as confederations that afford local regions smaller than "nations" extensive jurisdiction. Recommended reading for democrats of the twenty-first century is not the U.S. Constitution or the French Declaration of Rights of Man and Citizen but the Articles of Confederation, that suddenly pertinent document that stitched together the thirteen American colonies into what then seemed a too loose confederation of independent states but now appears a new form of political realism, as veterans of

Yeltsin's new Russia and the new Europe created at Maastricht will attest.

By the same token, the participatory and direct form of democracy that engages citizens in civic activity and civic judgment and goes well beyond just voting and accountability—the system I have called "strong democracy"—suits the political needs of decentralized communities as well as theocratic and nationalist party dictatorships have done. Local neighborhoods need not be democratic, but they can be. Real democracy has flourished in diminutive settings: the spirit of liberty, Tocqueville said, is local. Participatory democracy, if not naturally apposite to tribalism, has an undeniable attractiveness under conditions of parochialism.

Democracy in any of these variations will, however, continue to be obstructed by the undemocratic and antidemocratic trends toward uniformitarian globalism and intolerant retribalization which I have portrayed here. For democracy to persist in our brave new McWorld, we will have to commit acts of conscious political will—a possibility, but hardly a probability, under these conditions. Political will requires much more than the quick fix of the transfer of institutions. Like technology transfer, institution transfer rests on foolish assumptions about a uniform world of the kind that once fired the imagination of colonial administrators. Spread English justice to the colonies by exporting wigs. Let an East Indian trading company act as the vanguard to Britain's free parliamentary institutions. Today's well-intentioned quick-fixers in the National Endowment for Democracy and the Kennedy School of Government, in the unions and foundations and universities zealously nurturing contacts in Eastern Europe and the Third World, are hoping to democratize by long distance. Post Bulgaria a parliament by first-class mail. Fed Ex the Bill of Rights to Sri Lanka. Cable Cambodia some common law.

Yet Eastern Europe has already demonstrated that importing free political parties, parliaments, and presses cannot establish a democratic civil society; imposing a free market may even have the opposite effect. Democracy grows from the bottom up and cannot be imposed from the top down. Civil society has to be built from the inside out. The institutional superstructure comes last. Poland may become democratic, but

then again it may heed the Pope, and prefer to found its politics on its Catholicism, with uncertain consequences for democracy. Bulgaria may become democratic, but it may prefer tribal war. The former Soviet Union may become a democratic confederation, or it may just grow into an anarchic and weak conglomeration of markets for other nations' goods and services.

Democrats need to seek out indigenous democratic impulses. There is always a desire for self-government, always some expression of participation, accountability, consent, and representation, even in traditional hierarchical societies. These need to be identified, tapped, modified, and incorporated into new democratic practices with an indigenous flavor. The tortoises among the democratizers may ultimately outlive or outpace the hares, for they will have the time and patience to explore conditions along the way, and to adapt their gait to changing circumstances. Tragically, democracy in a hurry often looks something like France in 1794 or China in 1989.

It certainly seems possible that the most attractive democratic ideal in the face of the brutal realities of Jihad and the dull realities of McWorld will be a confederal union of semi-autonomous communities smaller than nation-states, tied together into regional economic associations and markets larger than nation-states—participatory and self-determining in local matters at the bottom, representative and accountable at the top. The nation-state would play a diminished role, and sovereignty would lose some of its political potency. The Green movement adage "Think globally, act locally" would actually come to describe the conduct of politics.

This vision reflects only an ideal, however—one that is not terribly likely to be realized. Freedom, Jean-Jacques Rousseau once wrote, is a food easy to eat but hard to digest. Still, democracy has always played itself out against the odds. And democracy remains both a form of coherence as binding as McWorld and a secular faith potentially as inspiring as Jihad.

---

*Benjamin R. Barber is the Whitman Professor of Political Science at Rutgers University. Barber's most recent books are* Strong Democracy *(1984),* The Conquest of Politics *(1988), and* An Aristocracy of Everyone.

From *The Atlantic Monthly*, March 1992, pp. 53–55, 58–63. © 1992 by Benjamin R. Barber. Reprinted by permission.

# Index

# Index

# Test Your Knowledge Form

We encourage you to photocopy and use this page as a tool to assess how the articles in *Annual Editions* expand on the information in your textbook. By reflecting on the articles you will gain enhanced text information. You can also access this useful form on a product's book support Web site at *http://www.dushkin.com/online/*.

NAME: _____ DATE: _____

TITLE AND NUMBER OF ARTICLE: _____

BRIEFLY STATE THE MAIN IDEA OF THIS ARTICLE:

_____

LIST THREE IMPORTANT FACTS THAT THE AUTHOR USES TO SUPPORT THE MAIN IDEA:

_____

WHAT INFORMATION OR IDEAS DISCUSSED IN THIS ARTICLE ARE ALSO DISCUSSED IN YOUR TEXTBOOK OR OTHER READINGS THAT YOU HAVE DONE? LIST THE TEXTBOOK CHAPTERS AND PAGE NUMBERS:

_____

LIST ANY EXAMPLES OF BIAS OR FAULTY REASONING THAT YOU FOUND IN THE ARTICLE:

_____

LIST ANY NEW TERMS/CONCEPTS THAT WERE DISCUSSED IN THE ARTICLE, AND WRITE A SHORT DEFINITION:

# We Want Your Advice

ANNUAL EDITIONS revisions depend on two major opinion sources: one is our Advisory Board, listed in the front of this volume, which works with us in scanning the thousands of articles published in the public press each year; the other is you—the person actually using the book. Please help us and the users of the next edition by completing the prepaid article rating form on this page and returning it to us. Thank you for your help!

## ANNUAL EDITIONS: Comparative Politics 03/04

### ARTICLE RATING FORM

Here is an opportunity for you to have direct input into the next revision of this volume.
We would like you to rate each of the articles listed below, using the following scale:

1. **Excellent: should definitely be retained**
2. **Above average: should probably be retained**
3. **Below average: should probably be deleted**
4. **Poor: should definitely be deleted**

Your ratings will play a vital part in the next revision.
Please mail this prepaid form to us as soon as possible.
Thanks for your help!

| RATING | ARTICLE | RATING | ARTICLE |
|---|---|---|---|
| _____ | 1. A Constitutional Revolution in Britain? | _____ | 32. Fox's Mexico: Same as It Ever Was? |
| _____ | 2. The Second Term: Tony's Big Ambitions | _____ | 33. South Africa: Democracy Without the People? |
| _____ | 3. Laborites Meet and Blair Takes a Beating | _____ | 34. Africa's Contradiction: Nigeria on the Path to Democracy |
| _____ | 4. Scandals and Squabbles Weigh Down Britain's Sinking Tories | _____ | 35. Intimations of Mortality |
| _____ | 5. Second Place Up for Grabs, Kennedy Believes | _____ | 36. Era of Deep Changes for China's Communists |
| _____ | 6. France? It's Like 1970s America | _____ | 37. Politics and Reform: The Middle Class Waits in the Wings |
| _____ | 7. A Divided Self | _____ | 38. In March Toward Capitalism, China Has Avoided Russia's Path |
| _____ | 8. How Germany Was Suffocated | _____ | 39. New Dimensions of Indian Democracy |
| _____ | 9. Gerhard Schröder Clings On | _____ | 40. Islam Takes a Democratic Turn |
| _____ | 10. Germany Adrift: The New Germany | _____ | 41. Iran: Doubting Reform? |
| _____ | 11. Radical Reverts to the Old Pattern | _____ | 42. Bin Laden, the Arab "Street," and the Middle East's Democracy Deficit |
| _____ | 12. Setting Sun? Japan Anxiously Looks Ahead | _____ | 43. The Global State of Democracy |
| _____ | 13. Public Opinion: Is There a Crisis? | _____ | 44. Serial Utopia |
| _____ | 14. Political Parties: Empty Vessels? | _____ | 45. Capitalism and Democracy |
| _____ | 15. Interest Groups: Ex Uno, Plures | _____ | 46. Cultural Explanations: The Man in the Baghdad Café |
| _____ | 16. Women in National Parliaments | _____ | 47. Jihad vs. McWorld |
| _____ | 17. Europe Crawls Ahead … | | |
| _____ | 18. Campaign and Party Finance: What Americans Might Learn From Abroad | | |
| _____ | 19. What Democracy Is … and Is Not | | |
| _____ | 20. Congress and the House of Commons: Legislative Behavior and Legislative Roles in Two Democracies | | |
| _____ | 21. The Gavel and the Robe | | |
| _____ | 22. The People's Voice | | |
| _____ | 23. Can These Bones Live? | | |
| _____ | 24. A Constitution for Europe: The Latest Battle for the Continent's New Shape | | |
| _____ | 25. From Talking Shop to Crucible of High Politics: Europe's Convention Is Evolving Into a Historic Undertaking | | |
| _____ | 26. In Search of Europe's Borders: The Politics of Migration in the European Union | | |
| _____ | 27. Letter From Poland | | |
| _____ | 28. Ten Myths About Russia: Understanding and Dealing With Russia's Complexity and Ambiguity | | |
| _____ | 29. Deepening Russian Democracy | | |
| _____ | 30. Globalization's Double Edge | | |
| _____ | 31. Why Outsiders Are In in Latin America | | |

*(Continued on next page)*

**NO POSTAGE
NECESSARY
IF MAILED
IN THE
UNITED STATES**

## BUSINESS REPLY MAIL
FIRST-CLASS MAIL   PERMIT NO. 84   GUILFORD CT

POSTAGE WILL BE PAID BY ADDRESSEE

**McGraw-Hill/Dushkin
530 Old Whitfield Street
Guilford, Ct 06437-9989**

Ill.....ll...l...l..ll.l...ll.l..l.l..l..l.l..l.l.l.l

## ABOUT YOU

Name                                                                Date

_____

Are you a teacher?  ❏    A student?  ❏
Your school's name

_____

Department

_____

Address                          City                          State          Zip

_____

School telephone #

_____

## YOUR COMMENTS ARE IMPORTANT TO US!

Please fill in the following information:
For which course did you use this book?

_____

Did you use a text with this ANNUAL EDITION?  ❏  yes  ❏  no
What was the title of the text?

_____

What are your general reactions to the *Annual Editions* concept?

_____

Have you read any pertinent  articles recently that you think should be included in the next edition? Explain.

_____

Are there any articles that  you feel should be replaced in the next edition? Why?

_____

Are there any World Wide Web sites that you feel should be included in the next edition? Please annotate.

_____

May we contact you for editorial input?  ❏  yes  ❏  no
May we quote your comments?  ❏  yes  ❏  no